Volume I:
From Colonial Americ
to the Age of the Civil W

American
History

Other titles in the Perspectives on History series include:

Volume 1:
From Colonial America to the Age of the Civil War

American History

Original and Secondary Source Readings

Michael S. Mayer, Book Editor
University of Montana

Daniel Leone, President
Bonnie Szumski, Publisher
Scott Barbour, Managing Editor

Perspectives
on History

GREENHAVEN
PRESS ®

THOMSON
GALE ™

San Diego • Detroit • New York • San Francisco • Cleveland • New Haven, Conn. • Waterville, Maine • London • Munich

LIBRARY OF CONGRESS CATALOGING-IN-PUBLICATION DATA

Mayer, Michael S., 1952–
  American history / by Michael S. Mayer.
    p. cm. — (Perspectives on history)
Includes bibliographical references and indexes.
  ISBN 0-7377-0708-9 (v. 1: lib.: alk. paper) — ISBN 0-7377-0707-0
(v. 1: pbk.: alk. paper) — ISBN 0-7377-0710-0 (v. 2: lib.: alk. paper)
— ISBN 0-7377-0709-7 (v. 2: pbk.: alk. paper)
  1. United States—History. I. Title. II. Series.
E178.1 .M454 2003
973—dc21

                                                          2002007923

Printed in the United States of America

Contents

UNIT 1
Colonial America

UNIT 2
The Age of the American Revolution

Benjamin Franklin Speaks in Favor of the Constitution
Thomas Jefferson Considers the New Constitution
The Federalist, No. 10

UNIT 3
Antebellum America

UNIT 4
The Age of the Civil War

Acknowledgments

It is a cliché to observe that no one undertakes a project such as this one alone, but clichés are often true. Over the long course of completing these volumes, I have accumulated a series of debts that require acknowledgment. First, I would like to thank Steve Schonebaum, then of Greenhaven Press, who recruited me to the project. I would also like to thank Jim Miller, who designed the series of which these volumes are a part. Bonnie Szumski edited the work, tried to keep me on task, and constantly reminded me of my audience. Ari Field, the production editor, and Jessica Knott, the production manager, caught errors and saw the volumes through to their final form. Karin Barnes supervised production.

I also would like to thank colleagues and students whom I accosted with requests to read parts of the manuscript. Of those, Linda Frey deserves special mention. I also owe a debt of gratitude to the Ambrose-Tubbs Fund administered by the history department at the University of Montana, which provided much-needed research assistance. That assistance was provided ably by two graduate students, Rob Lynn and Erica Stukel. Susan Mayer put up with the hours the project consumed and the sometimes foul moods of the editor. Finally, I owe a special debt to Stewart Justman, who read parts of the manuscript and who listened while countless other parts were read over the phone to check for clarity, expression, and coherence. Of course, any remaining errors or infelicities are not the responsibility of these good people.

To the Instructor

This collection of primary and secondary readings is designed to supplement textbooks used in introductory survey courses in U.S. history. Volume I begins with contact between Europeans and Native Americans, and the units continue chronologically through the Civil War. Volume II starts with Reconstruction and continues through the present. Obviously, no book of this length can be comprehensive. Thus, the volumes focus on key problems in American history. Each unit covers a fairly broad chronological span, and each chapter focuses on a specific issue within that time period. Further, each unit attempts to cover a wide variety of topics, including political, social, cultural, and intellectual history. Particular attention is paid to the history of minorities and women.

The secondary readings include excerpts from some of the finest historians past and present. All contribute to understanding not only history but also how historians approach their subject. For example, chapter 5 includes an excerpt from Perry Miller's enduring study of Jonathan Edwards as well as one from Lyle Koehler's more recent work on Anne Hutchinson and antinomianism. Koehler's analysis brings issues of gender to bear on a well-known episode and challenges traditional interpretations of that incident. Taken together, the two essays provide insight into the broader topic of religion in colonial America.

The primary sources enrich students' understanding of the theme of the chapter. Sometimes they focus on a particular aspect of the chapter. For instance, the primary documents in chapter 20 all come from diaries kept by Southern women during the Civil War. All of the women are young, but one comes from a large plantation in rural western Virginia. Another lives in Baton Rouge, Louisiana, and is the daughter of a lawyer and judge who opposed secession. The third comes from a Jewish merchant family in the South's largest city, New Orleans. The differences and commonalities of these women provide insight into the experience of Southern women during the war.

The introductions to each unit and to each chapter contain sets of questions intended to guide students through the main themes of the chapter and unit. In addition, each reading contains a more specific set of questions. The questions are not designed simply to get students to identify material in the reading. They are intended to prompt students to think about the essay or document, to encourage them to think of the reading in the context of the chapter, or to place the reading in the context of what they may have read in a textbook. Above all, the documents provide students with a chance to engage in the work of creating history.

In short, this collection is designed to supplement the textbooks and lectures in an introductory course. It provides a wide selection of topics for discussion. Beyond that, however, it is intended to take students beyond the "facts," to get them to understand the past, and to consider how historians go about their business.

Michael S. Mayer
University of Montana

To the Student

Introductory courses in American history usher students into the vast sweep of the topic. History consists of more than dates, names, and places. It comprises politics, wars, presidents, and generals, but it also includes how ordinary people lived their lives; how they earned a living; how they courted, married, and had children; what they thought and read; what music they listened to; and what religion they followed. American history includes all of the diverse people who made up the population of the land that would become the United States.

This collection of readings is designed to supplement one of the many textbooks instructors normally assign in introductory courses in American history. The textbook provides a narrative of American history. Therefore, this collection is not a comprehensive history of the United States; that is the role of the textbook. Rather, these essays and documents are intended to enrich and expand a student's understanding of the information one finds in the textbook.

The selections in this book include two kinds of readings. The first two selections of each chapter are secondary readings. They are written by historians and introduce students to how historians analyze and interpret the past. The work of historians is not so much to learn what happened as it is to understand what happened, and that is also the work of students in any history class. Students must ultimately determine for themselves how best to understand the past. Still, in order to have any validity, conclusions must be based on evidence and sound reasoning.

The next three readings in each chapter consist of primary documents. These allow people of the past to speak for themselves. Some are excerpts from letters or diaries; others are government documents or newspaper accounts. Primary documents serve as grist for the historian's mill. Students can use them to gain insight into how the past looked to the people of a given time. This, in turn, will help students arrive at their own understanding of the past.

One of the most important lessons people can learn from the study of history is that people in the past, even our own ancestors, did not necessarily see the world as we do. They approached it with different assumptions; they arrived at different understandings. In that sense, history is an exercise in humility. Students of history must not assume that the way they think is the only way to think or the only right way to think. Historians must be open to understanding how people, even people we may not like, saw and understood the world in which they lived. Always keep in mind, for example, that the people of the 1920s had no idea that the stock market would crash in 1929 and that a prolonged and severe economic depression would follow.

No matter how different people of the past may have been, they were people nonetheless and therefore had much in common with people of our time. Whatever else they did, Americans of earlier times loved, laughed, cried, thought, quarreled, and fell ill, much as people do today.

The introductions to each unit and to each chapter, along with the headnotes to each reading, provide necessary background to working with the primary sources and secondary readings. The questions that follow the introduction to each unit and chapter will guide students through the main themes of the unit and chapter. The questions after each document will help students probe the document and consider it in the context of other readings in the chapter or unit.

In the final analysis, history is never simple because people are not simple. History is never black and white; it is written in shades of gray. The study of history can challenge cherished assumptions and beliefs. As students examine the trends and events of the past, they come to a greater understanding of their own society and of themselves. This collection of readings is designed to help students embark on that adventure.

Michael S. Mayer
University of Montana

Timeline:
From Colonial America to the Age of the Civil War

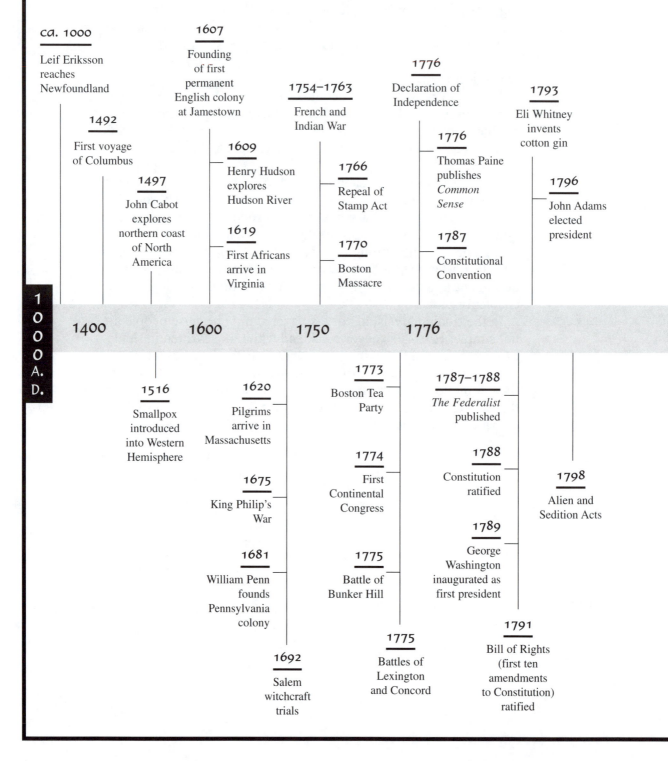

ca. 1000
Leif Eriksson reaches Newfoundland

1492
First voyage of Columbus

1497
John Cabot explores northern coast of North America

1607
Founding of first permanent English colony at Jamestown

1609
Henry Hudson explores Hudson River

1619
First Africans arrive in Virginia

1754–1763
French and Indian War

1766
Repeal of Stamp Act

1770
Boston Massacre

1776
Declaration of Independence

1776
Thomas Paine publishes *Common Sense*

1787
Constitutional Convention

1793
Eli Whitney invents cotton gin

1796
John Adams elected president

1000 A.D.

1400   **1600**   **1750**   **1776**

1516
Smallpox introduced into Western Hemisphere

1620
Pilgrims arrive in Massachusetts

1675
King Philip's War

1681
William Penn founds Pennsylvania colony

1692
Salem witchcraft trials

1773
Boston Tea Party

1774
First Continental Congress

1775
Battle of Bunker Hill

1775
Battles of Lexington and Concord

1787–1788
The Federalist published

1788
Constitution ratified

1789
George Washington inaugurated as first president

1791
Bill of Rights (first ten amendments to Constitution) ratified

1798
Alien and Sedition Acts

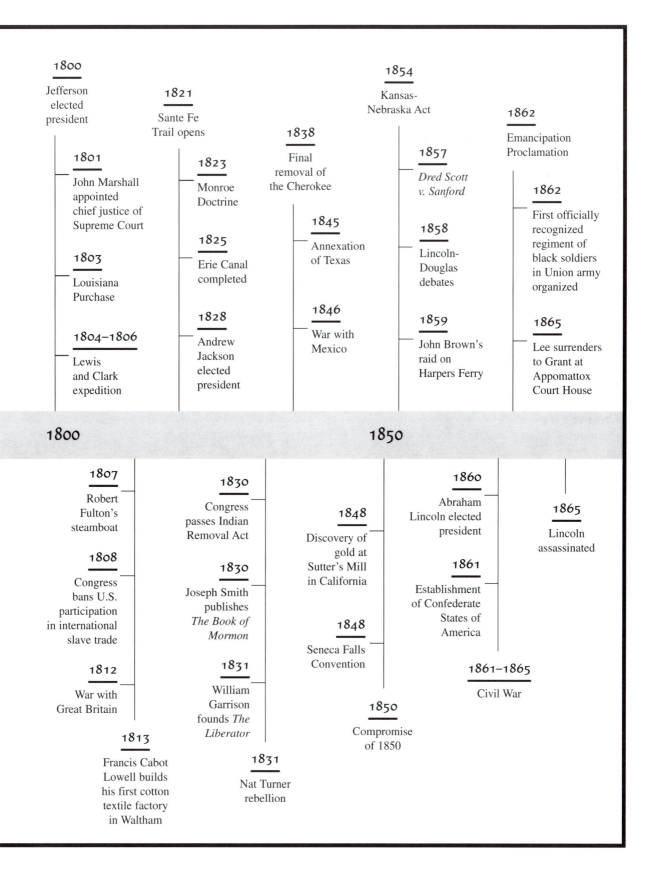

1800
Jefferson elected president

1801
John Marshall appointed chief justice of Supreme Court

1803
Louisiana Purchase

1804–1806
Lewis and Clark expedition

1821
Sante Fe Trail opens

1823
Monroe Doctrine

1825
Erie Canal completed

1828
Andrew Jackson elected president

1838
Final removal of the Cherokee

1845
Annexation of Texas

1846
War with Mexico

1854
Kansas-Nebraska Act

1857
Dred Scott v. Sanford

1858
Lincoln-Douglas debates

1859
John Brown's raid on Harpers Ferry

1862
Emancipation Proclamation

1862
First officially recognized regiment of black soldiers in Union army organized

1865
Lee surrenders to Grant at Appomattox Court House

1800

1850

1807
Robert Fulton's steamboat

1808
Congress bans U.S. participation in international slave trade

1812
War with Great Britain

1813
Francis Cabot Lowell builds his first cotton textile factory in Waltham

1830
Congress passes Indian Removal Act

1830
Joseph Smith publishes *The Book of Mormon*

1831
William Garrison founds *The Liberator*

1831
Nat Turner rebellion

1848
Discovery of gold at Sutter's Mill in California

1848
Seneca Falls Convention

1850
Compromise of 1850

1860
Abraham Lincoln elected president

1861
Establishment of Confederate States of America

1861–1865
Civil War

1865
Lincoln assassinated

Unit 1

Colonial America

Contents

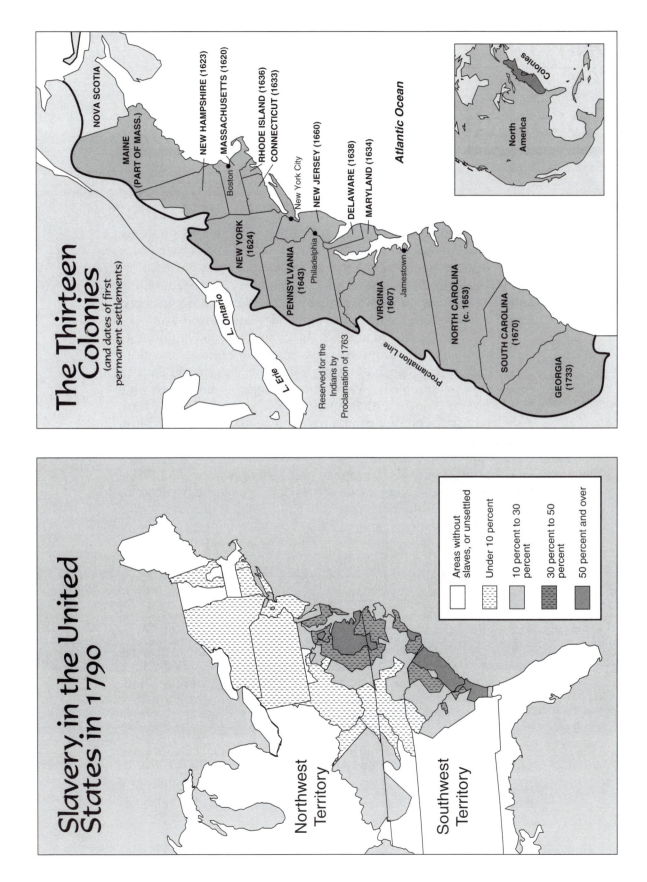

The Thirteen Colonies
(and dates of first permanent settlements)

NOVA SCOTIA

MAINE (PART OF MASS.)

NEW HAMPSHIRE (1623)
MASSACHUSETTS (1620)
RHODE ISLAND (1636)
CONNECTICUT (1633)

Boston

New York City

NEW JERSEY (1660)
DELAWARE (1638)
MARYLAND (1634)

Atlantic Ocean

North America

Colonies

L. Ontario

L. Erie

NEW YORK (1624)

PENNSYLVANIA (1643)

Philadelphia

Reserved for the Indians by Proclamation of 1763

VIRGINIA (1607)

Jamestown

Proclamation Line

NORTH CAROLINA (c. 1653)

SOUTH CAROLINA (1670)

GEORGIA (1733)

Slavery in the United States in 1790

Northwest Territory

Southwest Territory

Areas without slaves, or unsettled

Under 10 percent

10 percent to 30 percent

30 percent to 50 percent

50 percent and over

UNIT 1

Colonial America

American history did not begin with the voyages of Columbus. The Native American communities he encountered had been living in the Western Hemisphere for thousands of years. A great variety of Indian civilizations, whose social structures ranged from fairly simple to extremely complex, inhabited the Western Hemisphere. These cultures traded, engaged in diplomacy, and waged war.

Though Europeans did not introduce conquest and empire into the hemisphere, the religious, economic, and political developments in Europe which led to European expansion shaped the attitudes and institutions that Europeans brought with them to what would become known as the Americas. Events in the Middle East, Asia, and Africa contributed to developments in Europe and consequently in the Americas. Thus, the history of the United States is at once relatively new and very old.

The contact between European and Native American civilizations had profound consequences for both. The biological and cultural exchange profoundly altered both societies. Each civilization encountered new crops, animals, diseases, technologies, religions, and institutions. Interaction between Europeans and Indians ranged from cooperation to exploitation and conflict. Perhaps the most striking aspect of the contact between civilizations was how little basis there was for understanding on either side.

The story of the Americas was not, however, a biracial one. Throughout the Western Hemisphere, Europeans turned to African slaves for labor. Slavery had a devastating impact on those enslaved. It also played a formative role in the emerging new societies in the Americas. African crops, cooking techniques, languages, and religions contributed to the development not just of African American culture and society but of European American society and culture as well.

Settlement in a new environment inevitably changed European institutions. As Europeans established communities in the Americas, traditions, ideas, and practices were adapted to the realities of a new and different world. Contact with other cultures also helped to

18

reshape the way of life Europeans had intended to reproduce in their new homes. Church, religion, courtship, marriage, and family life all evolved (sometimes consciously and deliberately, other times not).

After reading this unit, consider these questions:

1. What was the impact of a new environment on European customs, traditions, and institutions?

2. How did Indian and African cultures contribute to the new society emerging in North America?

3. To what extent are ideas shaped by the social context in which they form or to which they are transplanted?

4. In what respect is human behavior consistent? In what respects is it formed by a specific social, economic, and cultural environment?

CHAPTER 1

Contact

Long before Europeans "discovered" North America, native peoples occupied the land, established civilizations, and altered the environment. Indian societies evolved to occupy a wide variety of ecological niches; they farmed, hunted, and fished. The original inhabitants of the continent developed diverse languages, religions, political systems, art forms, and styles of architecture. These various societies engaged in trade, diplomacy, and warfare.

Thus, the first Europeans who explored North America contacted diverse Indian peoples. While Indian societies had never been static, contact with Europeans produced rapid and profound changes in both societies. The biological and cultural interaction altered both worlds forever. Europeans brought new animals and plants to the Western Hemisphere and found animals and plants that did not exist in Europe, Africa, or Asia. Among the most profound consequences of this exchange was the introduction of European diseases to the hemisphere. Smallpox, influenza, measles, and tuberculosis, previously unknown in the Americas, had a devastating impact on Indian populations that lacked resistance to those diseases. Unchecked epidemics wrought traumatic transformations on Indian societies.

The coming of Europeans brought other disruptions to Indian cultures and social structures. Europeans introduced Indians to goods such as woolen clothing, metal items, alcohol, and firearms. Trade among Indians introduced some groups to European goods and diseases long before they ever encountered a European. Not only did the use of new products alter Indian practices, but patterns of life changed as the focus of activities became acquiring new material goods. Seeking items to trade, Indian hunters catered to the preferences of European traders rather than to the needs of their communities. Commercial hunting also led to overhunting and to conflicts over hunting grounds. Moreover, the introduction of metal weapons and guns disrupted the balance of power among Indian tribes.

European attitudes toward land use and ownership differed from those of Native Americans, and Europeans lacked the intellectual basis on which to develop a respect for the very different values of Indian peoples. In addition, many European settlers came from

England, Holland, or France, where land was scarce. Thus, Europeans developed rationalizations for taking "vacant" land or for taking land from native inhabitants. Encroachments on Indian lands led to tensions and often to warfare.

Conflict with Europeans served to undermine the authority of traditional Indian leaders. As tensions grew, so did the influence of younger war chiefs, who had formerly exercised only limited and temporary authority. Europeans sought Indian allies against other Indians and against European rivals; consequently, imperial conflicts entangled Indians in a century of warfare. For some Indians, war became a way of life, and this, too, disrupted their traditional communities.

European technology enabled the new inhabitants to have a greater impact on the environment than did the Indians. Domesticated animals from Europe had even more immediate and substantial ecological consequences. Europeans introduced horses, cattle, pigs, chickens, sheep, and goats to the Americas, species whose introduction led to the extinction of some native animals and plants. Further, the transformation of the environment by European farming practices, technology, crops, and animals made it more difficult for Indians to make a living through traditional methods.

In addition to technology and new plants and animals, Europeans brought Christianity to the Americas. Some Indians became converts; others grafted Christian beliefs and practices onto existing religions and rituals. Still others looked to Christianity as a means of adaptation and survival. Finally, some remained skeptical of Christianity.

The interchange between cultures was not one-directional. European colonies in North America developed in close, constant contact with Native Americans. Influences from Native Americans shaped the emerging civilization European colonists were building in the Americas. Europeans adopted Indian crops and farming techniques. Native crops, such as maize, manioc, pumpkins, beans, potatoes, cocoa, paprika, sassafras, and tobacco transformed European diets and habits not only in the Americas but in Europe as well. European settlers copied Indian clothing, methods of hunting, and modes of travel. Intermarriage created still another form of cultural interaction and created a whole new people.

The arrival of Europeans devastated the world of the Indians. Individuals and tribes reacted in different ways. Some Indians fought European encroachment; others did not. In either case, Indians did not disappear after being defeated by the Europeans. Cultural interaction continued, shaping both European and Indian civilizations for generations to come.

After reading this chapter, consider these questions:

1. In what ways did the interaction of European and Indian cultures change both?

2. What factors shaped the way members of each civilization viewed each other?

3. What issues led to friction between native and immigrant cultures? What cultural and political factors made resolution of differences more difficult? What contributed to resolution of difficulties?

SELECTION 1:

Europeans Introduce Devastating Disease

lfred W. Crosby Jr.'s influential book The Columbian Exchange *discusses the numerous forms of biological exchange resulting from contact between Europeans and the native peoples of the Western Hemisphere. Crosby, a professor of American studies at the University of Texas at Austin, explains that Europeans encountered new food crops (such as maize, sweet potatoes, potatoes, and manioc), tobacco, and other plants as well as products from plants (such as rubber). On the other hand, Europeans introduced horses, cattle, pigs, chickens, sheep, and goats to the Americas. As Crosby notes, perhaps the most profound immediate impact of the Columbian interaction on human populations was the exchange of diseases.*

After the Spanish conquest an Indian of Yucatan wrote of his people in the happier days before the advent of the European:

> There was then no sickness; they had no aching bones; they had then no high fever; they had then no smallpox; they had then no burning chest; they had then no abdominal pain; they had then no consumption; they had then no headache. At that time the course of humanity was orderly. The foreigners made it otherwise when they arrived here.

It would be easy to attribute this statement to the nostalgia that the conquered always feel for the time before the conqueror appeared, but the statement is probably in part true. During the millennia before the European brought together the compass and the three-masted vessel to revolutionize world history, men moved slowly, seldom over long distances and rarely across the great oceans. Men lived in the same continents where their great-grandfathers had lived and seldom caused violent and rapid changes in the del-

Excerpted from *The Columbian Exchange,* by Alfred W. Crosby Jr. (Westport, CT: Greenwood Press, 1972). Copyright © 1972 by Alfred W. Crosby Jr. Reprinted by permission of the publisher.

icate balance between themselves and their environments. Diseases tended to be endemic rather than epidemic. It is true that man did not achieve perfect accommodation with his microscopic parasites. Mutation, ecological changes, and migration brought the Black Death to Europe, and few men lived to the proverbial age of three-score years and ten without knowing epidemic disease. Yet ecological stability did tend to create a crude kind of mutual toleration between human host and parasite. Most Europeans, for instance, survived measles and tuberculosis, and most West Africans survived yellow fever and malaria.

Migration of man and his maladies is the chief cause of epidemics. And when migration takes place, those creatures who have been longest in isolation suffer most, for their genetic material has been least tempered by the variety of world diseases. Among the major divisions of the species homo sapiens, with the possible exception of the Australian aborigine, the American Indian probably had the dangerous privilege of longest isolation from the rest of mankind. Medical historians guess that few of the first rank killers among the diseases are native to the Americas.

These killers came to the New World with the explorers and the conquistadors. The fatal diseases of the Old World killed more effectively in the New, and the comparatively benign diseases of the Old World turned killer in the New. There is little exaggeration in the statement of a German missionary in 1699 that "the Indians die so easily that the bare look and smell of a Spaniard causes them to give up the ghost."

The most spectacular period of mortality among the American Indians occurred during the first hundred years of contact with the Europeans and Africans. Almost all the contemporary historians of the early settlements, from Bartolomé de las Casas to William Bradford of Plymouth Plantation, were awed by the ravages of epidemic disease among the native populations of America. In Mexico and Peru, where there were more Europeans and Africans—and, therefore, more contact with the Old World—and a more careful chronicle of events kept than in most other areas of America, the record shows something like fourteen epidemics in the former and perhaps as many as seventeen in the latter between 1520 and 1600.

The annals of the early Spanish empire are filled with complaints about the catastrophic decline in the number of native American subjects. When Antonio de Herrera wrote his multivolume history of that empire at the beginning of the seventeenth century, he noted as one of the main differences between the Old and New Worlds the extreme susceptibility of the natives of the latter to diseases, especially smallpox. . . .

It has often been suggested that the high mortality rates of these post-Columbian epidemics were due more to the brutal treatment of the Indians by the Europeans than to the Indians' lack of resistance to imported maladies. But the early chroniclers reported that the first epidemics following the arrival of Old World peoples in a given area of the New World were the worst, or at least among the worst. European exploitation had not yet had time to destroy the Indians' health.

The record shows that several generations of Indian contact with Europeans and Africans seemed to lead not to the total destruction of the Indians, but only to a sharp diminution of numbers, which was then followed by renewed population growth among the aborigines. The relationships between these phenomena are too complex to be explained by any one theory. However, their sequence is perfectly compatible with the theory that the Indians had little or no resistance to many diseases brought from the Old World, and so first died in great numbers upon first contact with immigrants from Europe and Africa; and when those Indians with the weakest resistance to those maladies had died, interbreeding among the hardy survivors and, to some unmeasured extent, with the immigrants, led to the beginning of population recovery. . . .

The New World gave much in return for what it received from the Old World. In the writings of Desiderius Erasmus, one can find mention of nearly every significant figure, event, crusade, fad, folly, and misery of the decades around 1500. Of all the miseries visited upon Europe in his lifetime, Erasmus judged few more horrible than the French disease, or syphilis. He reckoned no malady more contagious, more terrible for its victims, or more difficult to cure . . . or more fashionable! "It's a most presumptuous pox," exclaims one of the characters in the *Colloquies*. "In a showdown, it wouldn't yield to leprosy, elephantiasis, ringworm, gout, or sycosis."

The men and women of Erasmus's generation were the first Europeans to know syphilis, or so they said, at least. The pox, as the English called it, had struck like a thunderbolt in the very last years of the fifteenth century. But unlike most diseases that appear with such abruptness, it did not fill up the graveyards and then go away, to come again some other day or perhaps never. Syphilis settled down and became a permanent factor in human existence.

Syphilis has a special fascination for the historian because, of all mankind's most important maladies, it is the most uniquely "historical." The beginnings of most diseases lie beyond man's earliest rememberings. Syphilis, on the other hand, has a beginning. Many men, since the last decade of the fifteenth century, have insisted that they knew almost exactly when syphilis appeared on the world stage, and even where it came from. "In the yere of Chryst 1493 or there aboute," wrote Ulrich von Hutten, one of Erasmus's correspondents, "this most foule and most grevous dysease beganne to sprede amonge the people." Another contemporary, Ruy Díaz de Isla, agreed that 1493 was the year and went on to say that "the disease had its origin and birth from always in the island which is now named Española." Columbus had brought it back, along with samples of maize and other American curiosities. . . .

Europeans drew the world together by means of ocean voyages. Their great travelers were sailors. The epidemiology of syphilis has a special characteristic: it is usually transmitted by sexual contact and spreads when a society's or a group's allegiance to marital fidelity fails. Sailors, by the nature of their profession, are men without women, and therefore, men of many women. If we may assume that the nature of sailors in the sixteenth century was not radically different than in the twentieth, then we can imagine no group of the former century more perfectly suited for guaranteeing that venereal syphilis would have worldwide distribution. Whether Columbus's sailors or his Indians brought it across the Atlantic makes little difference. European sailors carried it to every continent but Antarctica and Australia before Columbus was in his grave.

After reading this selection, consider these questions:

1. On what does Crosby base his conclusion that syphilis originated in the Western Hemisphere and that Columbus's voyages brought it back to Europe?

2. How does Crosby account for the decline of Indian populations after the arrival of Europeans?

SELECTION 2:

European Views of Indians

In the following excerpt, James Axtell, a professor of history at William and Mary College in Virginia, discusses the cultural context in which European attitudes toward Native Americans evolved.

The invasion of North America by European men, machines, and microbes was primarily an aggressive attempt to subdue the newfound land and its inhabitants, and to turn them to European profit. Because it was not totally unlike that of Europe, the land itself could be brought to terms by the increasingly effective methods of Western technology and capitalist economy. The American natives, however, posed a more serious problem. While they shared certain characteristics with the rest of mankind known to Europe, their cultures were so strange, so numerous, and so diverse that the invaders found it impossible to predict their behavior. If the Europeans hoped to harness, or at least neutralize, the numerically superior natives, they could ill afford to tolerate behavior that was as unpredictable as it was potentially dangerous. . . .

European traders quickly discovered that the Indians were no strangers to an economy of barter and exchange. Even without the medium of mutually intelligible languages, Europeans exchanged Indian furs, skins, and food for manufactured goods with the aid of elemental sign languages or trade jargons. Where language was lacking, the familiar behavior of trade communicated the Indians' intentions and terms. Military officers who sought native allies against less receptive natives—or who were sought as allies by native factions—recognized with equal ease the normative behavior of military allies. If their Indian partners seldom conducted war with the martial discipline of Europe, they at least shared a common enemy and a common understanding of strategic alliance.

But traders and soldiers were soon greatly outnumbered, especially in the English colonies, by invaders whose goals were much less compatible with the life-styles of the eastern woodland Indians. When European farmers and townsmen arrived in the New World, they brought no interest in any aspect of Indian culture or behavior. To these colonists—who quickly established the distinctive character of the European invasion—the native possessors of the soil stood as living impediments to agricultural "civilization," little different from stony mountains, unfordable rivers, and implacable swamps. Since it was highly unlikely that the Indians would vanish into thin air or exile themselves to some arid corner of the continent, the best these invaders could hope for was their pacification and resettlement away from the plowed paths of prosperity. In any event, they had to be rendered predictable to make America safe for Europeans.

As if heaven-sent, a small but determined cadre of invaders offered the ultimate answer to the settlers' prayers. Christian missionaries, who had come to America in the earliest phases of invasion, espoused a set of spiritual goals which colored but ultimately lent themselves to the more material ends of their countrymen. From the birth of European interest in the New World, religious men had ensured that the public goals of exploration and colonization included a prominent place for the conversion of the natives to Christianity. But the Christianity envisioned was not a disembodied spiritual construct but a distinct cultural product of Western Europe. Conversion was tantamount to a complete transformation of cultural identity. To convert the Indians of America was to replace their native characters with European personae, to transmogrify their behavior by substituting predictable European modes of thinking and feeling for unpredictable native modes. By seeking to control the Indians' thoughts and motives, the missionaries sought to control—or at least anticipate—their actions, which could at any time spell life or death for the proliferating but scattered settlements on the farming frontier. Unwittingly or not, they lent powerful support to the European assault upon America by launching their own subversive invasion within. . . .

From the European perspective, the Indians were deficient in three essential qualities: Order, Industry, and Manners. This meant in essence that they were non-Europeans, the polar opposite of what they should be and should want to be. So with characteristic confidence the missionaries proceeded in the heady decades after settlement

Excerpted from *The European and the Indian,* by James Axtell (New York: Oxford University Press, 1981). Copyright © 1981 by James Axtell. Reprinted by permission of the publisher.

to prescribe a veritable pharmacopoeia of remedies for their savage condition. . . .

The immediate concern of the Europeans was to remove the Indians from their "disordered riotous rowtes and companies, to a wel governed common wealth," from what they took to be civil anarchy to the rule of European law. For of all "humane Artes," the missionaries knew, "Political government is the chiefest." To men accustomed to kings and queens, administrative bureaucracies, standing armies, police, courts, and all the punitive technology of justice known to "civilized" states, the Indians seemed to suffer from unbenign neglect. If they were acknowledged to have any government at all, it was usually the capricious tyranny of an absolute theocrat, such as Powhatan in Virginia or Uncas in Connecticut. More prevalent was the view that the "common rules of order in the administration of justice"—the rules followed in Parliament or the Estates General—were not observed in Indian society. Indeed, so subtle and covert were the workings of Indian justice that the colonists were "astonished to find that such societies can remain united" at all. Cast in such a light, these "wild people" obviously needed the Europeans to "bring them to Political life, both in Ecclesiastical society and in Civil, for which," the missionaries assured themselves, "they earnestly long and enquire."

Another disturbing symptom of native disorder was their "scattered and wild course of life." "Towns they have none," wrote an English visitor with England in mind, "being always removing from one place to another for conveniency of food." The predominantly hunting tribes of Canada and Maine were the least fixed because survival depended on following the non-herding big game animals in small family groups and living off the stingy land. Even their more sedentary southern neighbors spent only five or six months congregated around their corn fields in villages ranging in size from a few families to a thousand inhabitants. And then they too broke up and moved more than once in search of fish, shellfish, berries, nuts, game, maple sap, "warme and thicke woodie bottomes" to escape the winter winds, more wood for their fires, or simply relief from the fearless fleas of summer.

It was obviously disconcerting to Europeans accustomed to finding towns in the same place year after year to discover a village of a hundred wigwams gone "within a day or two" for parts and reasons unknown. Not only were such a people physically uncontrollable but, perhaps worse, they were unpredictable, and surprise was the last thing the invaders wanted in the New World. Equally upsetting was the discovery that the natives, in all their basest "savagery," dared to break God-graven class lines by usurping the privileges of the European aristocracy. Forever tweaking the nose of authority, Thomas Morton of Merrymount all but visibly rubbed his hands over his observation that when the Indians "are minded to remoove," they "remoove for their pleasures . . . after the manner of the gentry of Civilized nations." . . .

To have viewed the Indians as America's noblemen, commuting conspicuously between winter "castle" and summer cottage-by-the-sea, would clearly not have served. Better that their movements be seen as the vagrant shiftings of dissolute barbarians. For then, in the name of European civility and the Christian religion, such flagrant "disorder" and "chaos" could be . . . brought under control.

The natives were considered deficient not only in civil order but in industry as well. In one of his first meetings with the Massachusetts John Eliot told them that they and the English were already "all one save in two things," the first being that the English were Christians and they were not. The second difference was somewhat less obvious but to English minds nearly as important: "we labour and work in building, planting, clothing our selves, &c. and they doe not." The key word in Eliot's comparison was "labour." To the idealistic missionaries, many of whom had pursued the life of learning because their constitutions were "unsuited to labour," it did not mean simply to "work" (as Eliot's additional use of that word implies), for even the Indians could be said to "work" by expending energy and thought upon various tasks. Rather it meant to work *laboriously* in the sense of severe, painful, or compulsory *toil,* the kind that a plowman knows as he walks behind a pair of huge oxen in the late-spring heat. In that sense, of course, the Indians had never known work, a deficiency exacerbated by what all Europeans diagnosed as a congenital "national vice"—idleness.

In the midst of their back-breaking efforts to hew villages and farms from the American forests, the first settlers were struck by the contrast with their native neighbors. . . . So tempting was the native way of life that many Indian converts apostatized because, as the English admitted, they can live with less labour, and more pleasure and plenty, as Indians, than they can with us." In fact, one of the reasons given by colonists who either ran away to the Indians or refused to return from captivity was that amongst the Indians they enjoyed the "most perfect freedom, the ease of living, [and] the absence of those cares and corroding solicitudes which so often prevail with us."

When the colonists found idleness endemic to Indian culture, the cultural norm by which they judged applied to only half the native population—the male half. For upon closer examination it appeared to European observers, almost all of whom were male, that, while Indian men were indeed epitomes of slothful indulgence, the work done by Indian women came respectably, even pitiably, close to the missionaries' ideal of "labour." Since such behavior ran counter to their civilized expectations, there was double cause for raised eyebrows. . . .

Bred like all people to an ethnocentric worldview, the European invaders saw what they expected to see in Indian life. Initially jarred by the half-correct observation that native men were not responsible for the agricultural livelihood of their society, the colonists never recovered their visual focus enough to notice that what was normal behavior in Europe did not always obtain in America, that Indian men played a role in their economy every bit as important as European farmers did in theirs, and that Indian women did not view their social position in the light cast by the male observers from another culture. . . .

A southern gentleman put his finger on the true cause of English concern when he noted, after an extensive survey of the Indian country between Virginia and North Carolina, that native men "are quite idle, or at most employ'd only in *Gentlemanly* Diversions of Hunting and Fishing." By this William Byrd II, the English-bred scion of one of the wealthiest families in Virginia, indicated that the Indians' greatest offense was the usurpation of aristocratic privilege, the disorderly jumping of class lines. For in England the only people who hunted were members of the upper classes, who did not kill to eat, or poachers who did and risked their ears—or necks—in the attempt. Forests were not public property but belonged to the nobility who regarded them as private game preserves. Guns were expensive and their ownership was generally forbidden by law.

These were the assumptions that the colonists carried to America, where the forests seemed to belong to no man, where guns became a household fixture, where hunting was often a necessity, and where English class lines failed to replicate themselves. In spite of all the social and environmental changes that should have engendered a different outlook toward hunting (and in some instances did toward their own), the colonists who did not rely on Indian hunters for marketable furs and skins continued to view the economic activities of Indian men with Old World eyes. Regarded as the social inferiors of all Englishmen, the Indians were harshly judged by semi-feudal standards that simply made no sense in the New World, much less in an alien culture.

After reading this selection, consider these questions:

1. In what ways did their English backgrounds shape the colonists' attitudes toward Indian settlements?

2. How well did Europeans understand Native American life and society? What contributed to understanding? What contributed to misunderstanding?

SELECTION 3:

Powhatan's Speech to Captain John Smith

Powhatan led the powerful Powhatan Confederacy that dominated what today is the coast of Virginia. Powhatan's confederacy more closely resembled an empire based on conquest. Relations between these Indians and European settlers developed amid a complex set of circumstances. Because the Virginia Company, which sponsored the settlement of Jamestown, failed to provide adequate provisions and recruited unwisely, "gentleman adventurers" proved unskilled at growing crops or founding a self-sustaining settlement. In her essay, "Indian Cultural Adjustment to European Civilization," anthropologist Nancy Lurie contended that Powhatan decided to help the vulnerable settlement at least in part because he saw them as potential allies against the tribes of the Piedmont region to the west. Keep in mind also that John Smith was a soldier of fortune who had once been enslaved by the Turks, and that he commanded a settlement organized along military lines. Perhaps because of his personal experience, or perhaps because he understood his weak military position, Smith seemed to prefer raiding Indian settlements for necessary supplies of food rather than relying on Powhatan's largesse. During the winter of 1608, the English again desperately needed provisions, and their raids led to confrontations with Powhatan. This was the context for the following address by Powhatan to Smith in 1609.

Captaine Smith, you may understand that I having seene the death of all my people thrice, and not any one living of these three generations but my selfe; I know the difference of Peace and Warre better than any in my Country. But now I am old and ere long must die, my brethren, namely Opitchapam, Opechancanough, and Kekataugh, my two sisters, and their two daughters, are distinctly each others successors. I wish their experience no lesse then mine, and your love to them no lesse then mine to you. But this bruit [noise] from Nandsamund, that you are come to destroy my Country, so much affrighteth all my people as they dare not visit you. What will it availe you to take that by force you may quickly have by love, or to destroy them that provide you food. What can you get by warre, when we can hide our provisions and fly to the woods? whereby you must famish by wronging us your friends. And why are you thus jealous of our loves seeing us unarmed, and both doe, and are willing still to feede you, with that you cannot get but by our labours? Thinke you I am so simple, not to know it is better to eate good meate, lye well, and sleepe quietly with my women and chil-

Excerpted from *The Complete Works of Captain John Smith*, edited by Philip L. Barbour (Chapel Hill: University of North Carolina Press, 1986).

dren, laugh and be merry with you, have copper, hatchets, or what I want being your friend: then be forced to flie from all, to lie cold in the woods, feede upon Acornes, rootes, and such trash, and be so hunted by you, that I can neither rest, eate, nor sleepe; but my tyred men must watch, and if a twig but breake, every one cryeth there commeth Captaine Smith: then must I fly I know not whether: and thus with miserable feare, end my miserable life, leaving my pleasures to such youths as you, which through your rash unadvisednesse may quickly as miserably end, for want of that, you never know where to finde. Let this therefore assure you of our loves, and every yeare our friendly trade shall furnish you with Corne; and now also, if you would come in friendly manner to see us, and not thus with your guns and swords as to invade your foes.

After reading this selection, consider these questions:

1. This version of Powhatan's speech was recorded by Captain John Smith. How might Smith's biases have influenced his translation of Powhatan's actual words? Do you think it accurately captures the general sense of Powhatan's speech?

2. If one were to reject Smith's account as a source, how else would one go about finding out what Powhatan said?

3. What did Powhatan hope to achieve by making this speech? How likely were the English to be persuaded by it?

SELECTION 4:

Governor Bradford's Account of the Pequot War

In the following excerpt from his book, Of Plymouth Plantation, *William Bradford, governor of the Plymouth colony, describes the Pequot War of 1637. As the Puritans migrated into the Connecticut valley, they clashed with the Pequot, the tribe that had controlled the area. Raids by both sides escalated, and the Pequot attacked the town of Wethersfield in April, killing nine and capturing two English settlers. The English made common cause with the Narragansett, traditional enemies of the Pequot. An allied force of English and Narragansett attacked the main Pequot village and killed most of its residents, including women and children. The ferocity of the attack shocked even the Narragansett allies of the English.*

Excerpted from *History Of Plymouth Plantation 1620–1647,* by William Bradford (Boston: The Massachusetts Historical Society, 1912).

In the fore part of this year, the Pequots fell openly upon the English at Connecticut, in the lower parts of the river, and slew sundry of them as they were at work in the fields, both men and women, to the great terrour of the rest, and went away in great pride and triumph, with many high threats. They also assaulted a fort at the river's mouth, though strong and well defended; and though they did not there prevail, yet it struck them with much fear and astonishment to see their bold attempts in the face of danger. Which made them in all places to stand upon their guard and to prepare for resistance, and earnestly to solicit their friends and confederates in the Bay of Massachusetts to send them speedy aid, for they looked for more forcible assaults. . . .

In the meantime, the Pequots, especially in the winter before, sought to make peace with the Narragansetts, and used very pernicious arguments to move them thereunto: as that the English were strangers and began to overspread their country, and would deprive them thereof in time, if they were suffered to grow and increase. And if the Narragansetts did assist the English to subdue them, they did but make way for their own overthrow, for if they were rooted out, the English would soon take occasion to subjugate them. And if they would hearken to them they should not need to fear the strength of the English, for they would not come to open battle with them but fire their houses, kill their cattle, and lie in ambush for them as they went abroad upon their occasions; and all this they might easily do without any or little danger to themselves. The which course being held, they well saw the English could not long subsist but they would either be starved with hunger or be forced to forsake the country. With many the like things; insomuch that the Narragansetts were once wavering and were half minded to have made peace with them, and joined against the English. But again, when they considered how much wrong they had received from the Pequots, and what an opportunity they now had by the help of the English to right themselves; revenge was so sweet unto them as it prevailed above all the rest, so as they resolved to join with the English against them, and did.

The Court [the General Court (a legislative, as well as judicial, body) of Massachusetts Bay] here agreed forthwith to send fifty men at their own charge; and with as much speed as possibly

they could, got them armed and had made them ready under sufficient leaders, and provided a bark to carry them provisions and tend upon them for all occasions. But when they were ready to march, with a supply from the Bay, they had word to stay; for the enemy was as good as vanquished and there would be no need.

I shall not take upon me exactly to describe their proceedings in these things, because I expect it will be fully done by themselves who best know the carriage and circumstances of things. I shall therefore but touch them in general. From Connecticut, who were most sensible of the hurt sustained and the present danger, they set out a party of men, and another party met them from the Bay, at Narragansetts', who were to join with them. The Narragansetts were earnest to be gone before the English were well rested and refreshed, especially some of them which came last. It should seem their desire was to come upon the enemy suddenly and undiscovered. There was a bark of this place, newly put in there, which was come from Connecticut, who did encourage them to lay hold of the Indians' forwardness, and to show as great forwardness as they, for it would encourage them, and expedition might prove to their great advantage. So they went on, and so ordered their march as the Indians brought them to a fort of the enemy's (in which most of their chief men were) before day. They approached the same with great silence and surrounded it both with English and Indians, that they might not break out; and so assaulted them with great courage, shooting amongst them, and entered the fort with all speed. And those that first entered found sharp resistance from the enemy who both shot at and grappled with them; others ran into their houses and brought out fire and set them on fire, which soon took in their mat; and standing close together, with the wind all was quickly on a flame, and thereby more were burnt to death than was otherwise slain; It burnt their bowstrings and made them unserviceable; those that scaped the fire were slain with the sword, some hewed to pieces, others run through with their rapiers, so as they were quickly dispatched and very few escaped. It was conceived they thus destroyed about 400 at this time. It was a fearful sight to see them thus frying in the fire and the streams of blood quenching the same, and horrible was the stink and scent thereof; but the victory seemed a sweet sacrifice, and they gave the praise thereof to God, who had wrought so wonderfully for them, thus to enclose their enemies in their hands and give them so speedy a victory over so proud and insulting an enemy.

The Narragansett Indians all this while stood round about, but aloof from all danger and left the whole execution to the English, except it were the stopping of any that broke away.

After reading this selection, consider these questions:

1. How might Bradford have known about the efforts of the Pequot to enlist the Narragansett? How reliable would his information have been? What factors might have slanted the version Bradford received?

2. What does Bradford say about the Narragansett role in the attack on the village? What might have colored his view? Suggest another explanation for the actions of the Narragansett warriors.

3. The Pequot proved correct in their assessment of the danger posed by the English settlers. Why did the Narragansett side with the English?

SELECTION 5:

A French Priest Observes the Indians

The Jesuits (members of the Society of Jesus of the Roman Catholic Church) attempted to convert Indians virtually from the beginning of Spanish, Portuguese, and French colonization. Jesuit missionaries arrived in New France in the first part of the seventeenth century. In contrast to some other sects, Jesuits lived with the Indians, learned their languages, and endured their hardships. Jesuits in Canada regularly reported on their mission; the following document is from one such report, written by Paul Le Jeune in Quebec in 1634. Born in France in 1591, Le Jeune became a Jesuit in 1613 and came to French North America in 1632. He returned to France in 1649. Although Le Jeune admired certain aspects of Indian life and culture, he retained an intense commitment to his Catholic faith, believing that faith to be the true Word of God and rejecting other belief systems as wrong or, at the very least, inferior. Thus, Le Jeune's ability to accept, and even to understand, Indian life was limited.

Excerpted from *The Jesuit Relations and Allied Documents: Travels and Explorations of the Jesuit Missionaries in New France, 1610–1791*, edited by Reuben Gold Thwaites (Cleveland: The Burrows Brothers Company, 1897).

I have already reported that the Savages believe that a certain one named Atachocam had created the world, and that one named Messou had restored it. I have questioned upon this subject the famous Sorcerer and the old man with whom I passed the Winter; they answered that they did not know who was the first Author of the world,—that it was perhaps Atahocham, but that was not certain; that they only spoke of Atahocam as one speaks of a thing so far distant that nothing sure can be known about it; . . .

As to the Messou, they hold that he restored the world, which was destroyed in the flood; whence it appears that they have some tradition of that great universal deluge which happened in the time of Noë. . . .

They also say that all animals, of every species, have an elder brother, who is, as it were, the source and origin of all individuals, and this elder brother is wonderfully great and powerful. . . . Now these elders of all the animals are the juniors of the Messou. Behold him well related, this worthy restorer of the Universe, he is elder brother to all beasts. If any one, when asleep, sees the elder or progenitor of some animals, he will have a fortunate chase; if he sees the elder of the Beavers, he will take Beavers; if he sees the elder of the Elks, he will take Elks, possessing the juniors through the favor of their senior whom he has seen in the dream. . . .

Their Religion, or rather their superstition, consists besides in praying; but O, my God, what prayers they make! In the morning, when the little children come out from their Cabins, they shout, *Cacouakhi Pakhais Amiscouakhi, Pakhais Mousouakhi, Pakhais,* "Come, Porcupines; come, Beavers; come, Elk;" and this is all of their prayers.

When the Savages sneeze, and sometimes even at other times, during the Winter, they cry out in a loud voice, *Etouctaian miraouinam an Mirouscamikhi,* "I shall be very glad to see the Spring."

At other times, I have heard them pray for the Spring, or for deliverance from evils and other similar things; and they express all these things in the form of desires, crying out as loudly as they can, "I would be very glad if this day would continue, if the wind would change," etc. I could not say to whom these wishes are addressed, for they themselves do not know, at least those whom I have asked have not been able to enlighten me. . . .

These are some of their superstitions. How much dust there is in their eyes, and how much trouble there will be to remove it that they may see the beautiful light of truth! I believe, nevertheless, that any one who knew their language perfectly, in order to give them good reasons promptly, would soon make them laugh at their own stupidity; for sometimes I have made them ashamed and confused, although I speak almost entirely by my hands, I mean by signs. . . .

If we begin with physical advantages, I will say that they possess these in abundance. They are tall, erect, strong, well proportioned, agile; and there is nothing effeminate in their appearance. Those little Fops that are seen elsewhere are only caricatures of men, compared with our Savages. I almost believed, heretofore, that the Pictures of the Roman Emperors represented the ideal of the painters rather than men who had ever existed, so strong and powerful are their heads; but I see here upon the shoulders of these people the heads of Julius Caesar, of Pompey, of Augustus, of Otho, and of others, that I have seen in France, drawn upon paper, or in relief on medallions.

As to the mind of the Savage, it is of good quality. I believe that souls are all made from the same stock, and that they do not materially differ; hence, these barbarians having well formed bodies, and organs well regulated and well arranged, their minds ought to work with ease. Education and instruction alone are lacking. Their soul is a soil which is naturally good, but loaded down with all the evils that a land abandoned since the birth of the world can produce. I naturally compare our Savages with certain villagers, because both are usually without education, though our Peasants are superior in this regard; and yet I have not seen any one thus far, of those who have come to this country, who does not confess and frankly admit that the Savages are more intelligent than our ordinary peasants.

Moreover, if it is a great blessing to be free from a great evil, our Savages are happy; for the two tyrants who provide hell and torture for many of our Europeans, do not reign in their great forests,—I mean ambition and avarice. As they have neither political organization, nor offices, nor dignities, nor any authority, for they only obey their Chief through good will toward him, therefore they never kill each other to acquire these honors. Also, as they are contented with a mere living, not one of them gives himself to the Devil to acquire wealth.

They make a pretence of never getting angry, not because of the beauty of this virtue, for which they have not even a name, but for their own contentment and happiness, I mean, to avoid the bitterness caused by anger. . . .

They are very much attached to each other, and agree admirably. You do not see any disputes, quarrels, enmities, or reproaches among them. Men leave the arrangement of the household to the women, without interfering with them. . . .

The Savages, being filled with errors, are also haughty and proud. Humility is born of truth, vanity of error and falsehood. They are void of the knowledge of truth, and are in consequence, mainly occupied with thought of themselves. They imagine that they ought by right of birth, to enjoy the liberty of Wild ass colts, rendering no homage to any one whomsoever, except when they like. They have reproached me a hundred times because we fear our Captains, while they laugh at and make sport of theirs. All the authority of their chief is in his tongue's end; for he is powerful in so far as he is eloquent; and, even if he kills himself talking and haranguing, he will not be obeyed unless he pleases the Savages. . . .

I have shown in my former letters how vindictive the Savages are toward their enemies, with what fury and cruelty they treat them, eating them after they have made them suffer all that an incarnate fiend could invent. This fury is common to the women as well as to the men, and they even surpass the latter in this respect. I have said that they eat the lice they find upon themselves, not that they like the taste of them, but because they want to bite those that bite them.

These people are very little moved by compassion. When any one is sick in their Cabins, they ordinarily do not cease to cry and storm, and make as much noise as if everybody were in good health. They do not know what it is to take care of a poor invalid, and to give him the food which is good for him; if he asks for something to drink, it is given to him, if he asks for something to eat, it is given to him, but otherwise he is neglected; to coax him with love and gentleness, is a language which they do not understand. As long as a patient can eat, they will carry or drag him with them; if he stops eating, they believe that it is all over with him and kill him, as much to free him from the sufferings that he is enduring, as to relieve themselves of the trouble of taking him with them when they go to some other place. I have both admired and pitied the patience of the invalids whom I have seen among them. . . .

Lying is as natural to Savages as talking, not among themselves, but to strangers. Hence it can be said that fear and hope, in one word, interest, is the measure of their fidelity. I would not be willing to trust them, except as they would fear to be punished if they failed in their duty, or hoped to be rewarded if they were faithful to it. They do not know what it is to keep a secret, to keep their word, and to love with constancy,— especially those who are not of their nation, for they are harmonious among themselves, and their slanders and raillery do not disturb their peace and friendly intercourse.

After reading this selection, consider these questions:

1. Le Jeune maintains that the Indians had "neither political organization, nor offices, nor dignities, nor any authority." Is he correct? What might have led him to such a conclusion?

2. What faults does Le Jeune observe in the Indians? Which observations might be attributed to cultural differences? Which can be generalized as human failings?

3. Le Jeune dismisses Indian religious practices as "superstition," yet he took the trouble to document such practices. What might be missing from his account of Indian religion? What other sources could one consult to learn about the Indian religions Le Jeune documented?

CHAPTER 2

Colonial Slavery

The English colonies in North America developed in constant contact not only with Native Americans but also with African populations. From their earliest settlement in North America, English colonists faced a critical shortage of labor. Enslavement of Indians proved unsatisfactory for a variety of reasons, as did various forms of temporary servitude such as indenture. By the end of the seventeenth century, the English colonists had turned to African slaves to remedy the labor shortage. Slavery as an institution had existed throughout human history. What distinguished slavery in North America was its inextricable association with race. By the dawn of the eighteenth century, English colonists functioned on the assumption that Africans and their descendants were slaves.

Historians have explored the process by which slavery became the normal condition of blacks in English North America. Racial slavery was not established immediately upon English settlement in North America. No model of slavery existed in England; and, from the early days of settlement, some blacks were free. Nevertheless, by the end of the first century of English colonization, racial slavery had become fully institutionalized. In attempting to understand the evolution of racial slavery, historians have debated whether slavery caused racial prejudice or racial prejudice caused slavery. At present, the paucity of evidence and the complexity of the question precludes final resolution of that debate.

In recent years, historians have expanded their interest beyond the institution of slavery and turned their attention to the experience of Africans and their descendants in North America. Instead of limiting their inquiries to the causes of slavery or whether and how the institution changed over time, historians have investigated daily life under slavery. They have explored the culture, food, language, and religion of enslaved black communities. New questions have emerged, including the extent of African influence on African American (and American) culture, the relationship between slavery and gender, and the response of individual slaves to the experience of enslavement.

After reading this chapter, consider these questions:

1. What led the English colonists to resort to slavery? What other options were available?

2. Compare the relative roles of culture and economics in the development of slavery.

3. How did slavery shape the family lives of slaves?

4. What role did gender play in shaping slavery? What role did slavery play in defining gender roles?

5. What impact did enslavement and slavery have on individuals held in bondage?

SELECTION 1:

Gullah: A Creole Language

One of the most creative and powerful attempts to understand slave culture is Charles Joyner's book, Down by the Riverside, *which won the National University Press Book Award in 1984. Joyner, a professor of history at Coastal Carolina University who holds doctorates in both history and folklore, draws on a variety of disciplines (including history, folklore, and anthropology) to explore the nature and development of a slave community in the South Carolina low country. According to linguists, a creole language combines two or more languages to form a third, distinct language. In the following selection, Joyner applies the linguistic model of creolization to analyze Gullah (the language of the black community in coastal South Carolina). Elsewhere in his book, Joyner applies the theory of creolization to a wide variety of cultural manifestations. He demonstrates how the huts slaves constructed, the quilts they made, the religion they practiced, the way they worked, and the food they prepared combined elements of African and European traditions to form a new and distinct tradition. In addition to its clever incorporation of other disciplines, Joyner's book also demonstrates how historians have used careful, detailed studies of small places to answer larger questions about American history.*

Excerpted from *Down by the Riverside: A South Carolina Slave Community,* by Charles Joyner (Chicago: University of Illinois Press, 1984). Copyright © 1984 by the Board of Trustees of the University of Illinois. Reprinted with permission.

Perhaps the most striking aspect of slave folklife to visitors on the rice plantations of the Waccamaw was the strangeness of the slaves' speech. One reason for that strangeness lay in the fact that numerous Africans inhabited All Saints Parish as late as the mid-nineteenth century . . . Many of them continued to count and pray in their native African languages and to call objects by their African names. These aging Africans were the last of the thousands who had personally experienced the shock of enslavement and the outrage of the middle passage, the last who still viewed the world through an African lens, and the last who could still speak their unadulterated African tongues. But the speech of American-born slaves was also alien to northern and European ears. Whether they described it as gibberish or jabbering, whether they were able to "overhear some of the words" or required translation from plantation whites, travelers repeatedly confessed their inability to understand the speech of the slaves. . . .

When one speaks of language among a people so imperfectly understood by visitors, one speaks with inevitable imprecision; but one might at least say that the slaves of All Saints Parish belonged to a distinctive speech community. One who would attempt to understand their folklife must attempt to understand Gullah—the common language that the slaves forged out of diverse traditions and uncertain circumstances—for it was through Gullah that Africans from various backgrounds not only communicated with and entertained one another but also linked themselves into a community, gave shape to a common culture, and handed down that culture to their posterity. And it was through Gullah that the symbolic group identity that the slaves created for themselves was impressed most powerfully upon the generations to come. Thus the study of Gullah is the study of the central element in slave culture. As a moving force in the creation of Afro-American culture in the crucible of slavery, the development of Gullah was comparable to the development of English, German, or French in the creation of these respective national cultures.

It is now impossible to say with any certainty what Gullah sounded like as spoken by the slaves. The Gullah speech of present-day All Saints Parish is probably no more than a pale reflection of antebellum slave speech. Such

sources as Genevieve Willcox Chandler's interviews with ex-slaves who had learned to speak the language in the mid-nineteenth century offer tantalizing glimpses of its vocabulary and its pronunciation and an opportunity to discover its grammatical rules.

As a language Gullah did not behave like English; it formed plurals and indicated possession and negation differently; it used a somewhat simpler system of pronouns and a somewhat more complex system of verbs than did English. Certain of the most distinctive features of the language merit brief consideration here. To concentrate on Gullah as spoken by the last generation of slaves in All Saints Parish, in the context of slave folklife, is not to imply that their speech was unrelated to black speech elsewhere and at other times—any more than studies of contemporary black speech in comparative linguistics imply that speech exists in isolation from other aspects of culture.

Gullah pronouns in All Saints Parish made no distinction between men and women. In this behavior Gullah retained a structure common to a number of African languages, such as Ibo, Ga, and Yoruba. The initial all-purpose Gullah pronoun was *e*, as in "After de war '*e* come back and took into big drinking and was' 'em till '*e* fall tru" (After the war he came back and took into big drinking and wasted it [his money] until it fell through [i.e., he lost it]). *E* served as the masculine, feminine, and neuter pronoun. Later, under the influence of English, *he* became the all-purpose Gullah pronoun, although *e* was not completely replaced during slavery, when the last generation of slaves was learning to speak the language. The Gullah pronoun *he* was not the same, however, as the English pronoun *he,* but served for masculine, feminine, and neuter gender. Interchangeable with *e, he* could serve as a subject or to indicate possession, as in *"He* broke *he* whiskey jug" (He broke his whiskey jug), or "Sam *he* husband name" (Sam was her husband's name). The Gullah pronoun for objects in All Saints Parish was *em,* which served for masculine, feminine, and neuter gender, whether singular or plural, as in "See '*em* the one time" ([I] saw him once); "Grandfather took old Miss Sally on he back to hid '*em* in the wood where Maussa"

(Grandfather took old Miss Sally on his back to hide her in the woods where the master [was hiding]); "He couldn't believe *'em*" (He couldn't believe it); and "Flat *'em* all up to Marlboro" ([They] took them all on flatboats up to Marlboro [District]).

Gullah pronouns of the slavery period were more complex than English pronouns in one respect, however: Gullah included a form for second person plural, which English lacks. Standard English pronouns cannot distinguish between singular and plural in second person. Writers variously represent the Gullah pronoun for second person plural as *yinnah* or *unna*. Like other Gullah pronouns, the same form was used as a subject or to indicate possession, as in "*Yinnah* talk big storm hang people up on tree?" (Are you [all] talking about the big storm that hung people up in the trees?) or "if *unna* kyant behave *unna* self, I'll tek yu straight home!" (If you can't behave yourselves, I'll take you straight home).

Two other features of the Gullah nominal system that distinguished it from English should be mentioned. One was that Gullah speakers marked possession by juxtaposition rather than by word forms, as in "*He* people wuz always free" (His people were always free) or "Joshuaway been *Cindy* pa" (Joshua was Cindy's father). The other distinctive feature of the Gullah nominal system was the practice of non-redundant plurals. If pluralization were otherwise indicated in a Gullah sentence, it was not also indicated by the noun, as in "Dan'l and Summer two both my *uncle*" (Both Daniel and Summer were my uncles). This practice was in sharp contrast to English, which required agreement in number between determiners and the nouns they modify.

The prepositions of slave speech in All Saints Parish, unlike English prepositions, did not use different forms to indicate whether one was approaching some location or one was already there. The same form was used for approach prepositions—"Old people used to go *to* Richmond Hill, Laurel Hill, and Wachesaw and have those prayer-meeting"—or for static-locative prepositions—"One stop *to* Sandy Island, Montarena landing" (One [Yankee gun boat] stopped at Sandy Island, Mt. Arena landing).

The verbal system of Gullah was considerably more complex than that of English. First, equating verbs occurred in past tense, as in "When my mother *been* young woman, work in rice" (When my mother was a young woman, she worked in rice); but they were usually omitted in present tense, as in "Dem Yankee wicked kind a people, drive me from me home" (Those Yankees are a wicked kind of people to drive me from my home). The omission of an equating verb is called zero copula. Gullah sentences used zero copula for verbal adjectives, as in "I *glad* for freedom till I *fool*" (I was so glad for freedom that I appeared foolish). In this regard, Gullah retains the verbal adjective construction of several West African languages, including Ewe, Fante, Kikongo, and Yoruba, but contrasts strongly with English.

Another All Saints Gullah construction that retained West African linguistic forms was the combination of verbs both to take an object and to serve as a connective. The most common verbs used in this construction were *say* and *go* (usually in the form *gone*). The following are examples: "One gentman at de gate *tell me say* he Messus broder, is Messus dare in?" (A gentleman at the gate told me he is the Mistress's brother; is the Mistress therein?) and "They didn't do a God thing but *gone and put* a beating on you, darling" (They didn't do a God's thing but put a beating on you, darling). In this usage the slaves retained both the form and the function of the same construction in Ibo and Twi.

Perhaps the most unique feature of the Gullah verbal system was its distinction between continuing and momentary actions (aspect) rather than specifying the relative time of the action (tense). In their emphasis on aspect over time, Gullah speakers in All Saints Parish retained the grammatical rules of such West African languages as Ewe, Kimbundu, Mandinka, and Yoruba. Unlike English, Gullah rarely distinguished between present and past tenses in the verbal system. When the slaves did mark past tense in Gullah, they used the verb form *been:* "When the Yankee come I *been* on the loom" (When the Yankees came I was on the loom). In the preceding sentence, ex-slave Ellen Godfrey used both marked and unmarked verb forms for simple past tense (*been* and *come,* respectively). If the slaves only occasionally marked past tense, they often marked aspect, whether ongoing, completed, or habitual. They indicated continuing actions by using the old creole form *duh* preceding the verb or the newer form *-ing* following the verb: "Yuh can't rest, bubber, w'en hag *duh* ride yuh" (You can't rest, brother, when a hag is riding you [i.e., when you have nightmares]), or "You *getting* this beating not for you task—for you flesh!" (You are getting this beating not for [failing to finish] your task—[but] for your flesh!). *Duh* and *-ing* were interchangeable but were not used together. Waccamaw slaves marked continuing actions in the past with *been* plus the action verb, as in "Aunt Ellen *been looking* for you all day" (Aunt Ellen has been looking for you all day). The slaves indicated habitual actions, past or present, by using *be* plus the action verb, as for example, "You orter *be* carry money with you" (You should [habitually] carry money with you). . . .

Three final distinctive features of slave speech should be discussed. One is that certain verbs that normally take complements in English did not necessarily take complements in Gullah. Margaret Bryant's lament, "Missus, I *ain't wuth.* I *ain't wuth!*" (I am not worth [anything, i.e., I am not feeling very good]), requires a complement in English, but not in Gullah. Second, Gullah speakers expressed passive voice in a construction that would indicate active voice in English, as, for example, "How come you *wanter bury* Watsaw?" (Why do you want to be buried at Wachesaw?) or "A crow *kin eat*" (A crow can be eaten [i.e., is edible]). A similar construction is prominent in Afro-American speech in Jamaica. Third, the slaves transformed declarations into yes/no questions by adding the word *enty* at the end of statements, as in "Chillun, ain't find duh plum, enty?" (Children, you didn't find the plums [did you]?) *Enty* has been variously translated as *n'est ce pas* and *ain't it.*

The last generation of slaves in All Saints Parish thus spoke a language that differed from English in several fundamental features. . . . While house servants may have spoken nearly standard English, many Gullah speakers in the Waccamaw rice fields were quite consistent in their use of these features. Whatever else might be said of the relationships between black and white speech in America, Gullah—as spoken by the last generation of slaves—followed a different set of grammatical rules than did English. Those white commentators who considered Gullah an imperfect result of "a savage and primitive people's endeavor to acquire for themselves the highly organized language of a very highly civilized race" were not only racist, but linguistically ignorant. However much Gullah and English may have shared the same vocabulary, Gullah and English were not the same language.

Gullah did not, of course, spring forth full-grown in the mid-nineteenth century. . . . In retrospect it seems clear that the speech of the slaves on Waccamaw rice plantations resulted from the convergence of a number of African languages with English. The resulting speech, Gullah, exemplified a creole language, which in turn developed from an earlier pidgin. The terms *pidgin* and *creole,* although frequently misunderstood, are technical linguistic terms and imply no value judgments, derogatory or otherwise. A pidgin is by definition a second language: it has no native speakers. Pidgins are developed as a means of communication among speakers of various languages. The linguistic elements in a pidgin are simplified within a context of restricted use—usually for trade. Pidgins are neither broken languages nor distortions of the grammatical structure of the source languages. On the contrary, pidgins are quite regular in grammatical structure as the result of the simplification process, although their specific grammatical patterns may not be the same as those of any single source language. Whenever a pidgin is passed on to succeeding generations as a native tongue, it is said to be a creole language. Since creole languages must serve all the functions of a language, not just the limited linguistic interactions for which pidgins are devised, creole languages expand rapidly in complexity in succeeding generations. This intricate process in which a language based upon the convergence of other languages undergoes expansion in both use and form is called creolization.

To gain some perspective on the creolization process in Gullah, it may be helpful to move back in time from All Saints Parish in the mid-nineteenth century to West Africa in the age of the slave trade, simply to note the varieties and structural similarities of West African languages. West Africa was a region of several hundred mutually unintelligible languages. With a constant need for communication with neighboring peoples who spoke diverse tongues, linguistic skills became highly developed among West Africans. Many in the Senegal-Gambia region, for instance, were bilingual, fluent in both Wolof and Mandingo, the two most widespread languages of the region. Bilingualism at some level was a necessity in polyglot West Africa. Despite their mutual unintelligibility, however, there were several similar linguistic patterns that African languages shared and that set them apart from other languages of the world. In particular, the two great West African language families, Bantu and Sudanese, shared strong structural similarities.

Thus the process of pidginization began in Africa out of the need for speakers of disparate languages to communicate with one another, and the process was helped along by structural similarities among otherwise different tongues. Perhaps the most unusual catalyst for pidginization, and certainly the most ironic, was the slave trade. In the slave baracoons of the West African coast and in the wretched shipholds of the Middle Passage, enslaved Africans from various regions, speakers of distinct tongues with centuries of tradition behind them, were forced to seek similarities in their languages and to develop whatever means of communication they could. Wolof speakers from Senegambia may have served as interpreters among the enslaved Africans and between the slaves and their captors, lending a strong Wolof cast to the emerging pidgin.

Pidginization became widespread among Africans in the New World. Those linguistic patterns among the mutually unintelligible languages most familiar to the largest number of Africans had the best chance of surviving in the new pidgin. Much of the vocabulary was supplied by the alien languages of the masters. Thus there developed an Afro-Dutch pidgin in the Virgin Islands; Afro-Portuguese pidgins in Brazil and Curaçao; Afro-Spanish pidgins in Cuba, Puerto Rico, and Colombia; Afro-French pidgins in Louisiana, French Guiana (influenced by Portuguese), Haiti, Guadeloupe, Grenada, and the other Antilles. There were both Afro-French and Afro-English pidgins in Trinidad and Tobago. Afro-English pidgins developed in Barbados, Antigua, Guyana, Jamaica, and South Carolina. The Dutch colony of Surinam was a special case. It developed an Afro-English pidgin as well as an Afro-Portuguese pidgin with strong English lexical influences, rather than an Afro-Dutch pidgin. Many of these pidgins were adopted by succeeding generations and became creoles.

The first generation of slaves in South Carolina came mostly from the Caribbean, where they had already learned an Afro-English pidgin. Because they constituted only a small proportion of Carolina's small population, and because in their generation contacts between enslaved Africans and their English-speaking masters were of necessity close and personal, their speech may have been nearer to standard English than that of later generations who came directly from Africa. But the great expansion of rice culture in the early eighteenth century brought about an enormous increase in the young colony's slave trade. The expansion in both rice and slaves was caused in part by the opening up of the rich rice lands north of the Santee, including those along the Waccamaw. The importation of thousands of slaves annually from West Africa fostered intercultural contact on a scale unprecedented in South Carolina, not only between Africans and Europeans, but among diverse groups of Africans. With a higher ratio of Africans to Europeans than anywhere else on the North American mainland, Georgetown District became the mainland equivalent of a Caribbean colony in the eighteenth and nineteenth centuries. . . .

[M]ost Africans coming into the Waccamaw region in the eighteenth century spoke little if any English. When confronted with the harsh dilemmas of their new environment—as slaves of alien, white-skinned people whose shouted commands they could not understand—their response must have been to lapse into silence, struggling to find meaning in the words yelled at them, straining to isolate some familiar sound in the stream of gibberish. Where once they had lived among family and friends whose languages and folkways they shared, now they found themselves among strangers who had also fallen victim to the slave trade, strangers who could understand neither one another nor their white masters. Two overwhelming needs—to comprehend the masters and to comprehend one another—had profound and complex, and sometimes contradictory, effects on the linguistic response of the Africans to their enslavement. If there were forces at work on the plantations to discourage retention of their native languages, there were also circumstances that had an opposite effect. While the social dominance of the masters served as a strong incentive to learn English, the numerical dominance of the blacks facilitated their retention of African patterns of speech. While they lacked a common linguistic heritage, through trial and error in their efforts to communicate with one another Africans increasingly became aware of common elements in their diverse tongues. More and more they found other speakers of their own or similar African languages. Out of these opposing tendencies—to learn English and to retain African speech patterns —they created a new language: Gullah.

This new language took root to such an extent among enslaved Africans that it was passed on to succeeding generations on the Waccamaw and elsewhere in the lowcountry. To African-born slaves Gullah would have remained a pidgin, a second language, but to the American-born generations it was a creole, a native tongue. Once Gullah acquired native speakers and assumed all the functions of a language, it expanded rapidly in complexity. From then on, incoming Africans learned Gullah neither through trial-and-error nor from the plantation whites, but from American-born blacks. . . .

The culture contact of transplanted Africans and transplanted Europeans in All Saints Parish fostered processes of creolization by which African pronunciations, meanings, and grammatical patterns converged with English vocabulary and some English pronunciations and meanings. Gullah, originating as a pidgin, became the native tongue of the black speech community. In the course of creolization Gullah passed from pidgin to creole to the beginnings of decreolization in the direction of the regional standard.

After reading this selection, consider these questions:

1. Apply the model of creolization to different cultural manifestations, such as the building of houses or the preparation of food.

2. What accounts for the development of a creole language (Gullah) in coastal South Carolina and not elsewhere in the South?

SELECTION 2:

The Double Bonds of Race and Sex

In this essay, Joan Rezner Gundersen explores similarities and differences in the lives of black and white women in eighteenth-century

Virginia. Gundersen uses church records, including tithe lists and the parish register, to develop quantitative information regarding life in colonial King William Parish.

Phillis, a black slave, and Elizabeth Chastain LeSueur, her mistress, worked and raised families together for over thirty-two years in King William Parish, Virginia. In their small world, about thirty miles west of Richmond, shared ties of gender created a community of women but not a community of equals. The bonds of race and slavery provided constraints that divided the experience of Phillis from that of Elizabeth. Like most women of their day, they left but a faint trail through the records. Elizabeth Chastain LeSueur was probably the older, born about 1707, while all that is certain about Phillis is that she was born before 1728. Both women died sometime after David LeSueur's estate went through probate in early 1773. Both bore and raised children, worked at the many domestic tasks assigned to women in the colonies, and experienced the growth of slavery in their region. The similarities and differences between their lives (and the lives of the other women of the parish) reveal much about the ways gender and race interacted in the lives of colonial women.

The lives of black women such as Phillis have yet to be explored in depth by the new social historians. We have, however, learned something about the lives of women like her mistress, Elizabeth Chastain LeSueur. In recent years historians have examined the life expectancy of seventeenth-century blacks, the effects of demographics and demand upon the introduction of slavery in the Chesapeake, the impact of a black majority upon South Carolina development, the patterns of slave resistance in eighteenth-century Virginia, and the structure of eighteenth-century slave families. In all of this the black woman appears as a cipher, notable in the seventeenth century and first part

of the eighteenth by her absence and by her lack of overt resistance to slavery; she seems essential only to the study of fertility. But just as the experience of white women such as Elizabeth Chastain LeSueur differed from that of white males in the colonies, the black female's experience in slavery differed from the male's, and to ignore that difference would be to misunderstand the nature of slavery. Gender not only separated female slaves from males, it also forged bonds with white women. After all, black women lived among whites, and in order fully to understand their lives, it is necessary to compare their experiences with those of white women. Only then can we begin to understand what it meant to be black and female in colonial Virginia.

This essay looks at slavery from a comparative female perspective in King William Parish during the eighteenth century. The findings suggest that the bonds of a female slave were twofold, linking her both to an interracial community of women and setting her apart as a slave in ways that make evident the special burden of being black and female in a white, patriarchal society. . . .

The slave women who arrived at King William Parish in the early eighteenth century did not make a simple transfer from an African past to an English colonial present (even with intermediary stops). Rather, they came to a community itself in transformation from a French Protestant refugee culture to an English colonial one. The Virginia House of Burgesses created King William Parish for Huguenot refugees who settled at Manakin Town in 1700. Changing county boundaries placed the settlement at various times in Henrico, Goochland, Cumberland, and Chesterfield counties before 1777. The tiny handful of slaves present before 1720 belonged to a community in which French was the dominant language. The decade of the 1720s, during which the first expansion of the slave population occurred, is also the period in which the Huguenot community leadership and property passed into the

Excerpted from "The Double Bonds of Race and Sex: Black and White Women in a Colonial Virginia Parish," by Joan Rezner Gundersen, *The Journal of Southern History,* August 1986. Copyright © 1986 by the Southern Historical Association. Reprinted with permission.

hands of those who, like Elizabeth Chastain LeSueur, either had arrived in Virginia as infants or had been born there. An epidemic in 1717–1718 greatly disrupted the community and its institutions, speeding the transfer of leadership to a new generation.

The economy of King William Parish, based on wheat and other grains, was also in transition, and the adoption of slavery was a reflection of this change. The first black women thus had to adapt to both a culture and an economy in transition. In the 1720s some land passed into English hands, and tobacco became a secondary crop. Slavery and tobacco together grew in importance in the parish over time. English interlopers did not introduce either slavery or tobacco, but they did provide a bridge to the agricultural patterns of the rest of the colony. The first slaveholding families in the community, including Elizabeth LeSueur's family, were French, and the purchase of slaves signified their claim to be members of the gentry. . . .

Overall, from 1710 to 1776, the parish's adult sex ratio for blacks was 6:5, or nearly even. This is very close to the ratio that the whites of the parish had achieved by 1714. . . .

[W]hites outnumbered blacks until after 1750. By the late 1730s black men and women comprised half of the tithables of King William Parish. Since white women were excluded from the count of tithables, and since there were many more white children than black, . . . blacks were still part of a minority in the community, but among a majority of those who worked the fields. . . . Phillis lived in a community almost evenly divided between whites and blacks and between men and women, but belonging to a numerical majority did not loosen either the bonds of slavery or gender.

Ironically, black women had an opportunity for a more normal family life than did black men because they were less desirable purchases. Because black women were outnumbered by men in King William Parish, it was easier for women to form families. Even so, the evidence suggests that black women took their time. Several factors complicated a black woman's search for a partner. The dispersed patterns of ownership meant few black women lived in a slave quarter or with other blacks. Initially blacks, and especially black women, were scattered singly or in small groups among those families who owned slaves. Over one-third of the families owned some slaves or rented them. No family before 1744 paid taxes on more than six blacks over age sixteen. Before 1744 only two or three families owned enough slaves to have both adult males and females. Thus black women had to search for mates on nearby farms. Furthermore, many black women lived relatively short times in Manakin, disappearing from the tithe records after only a few years. . . . Such transience delayed the process of forming a family. In the early years this experience did not necessarily set black women apart from whites; immigrants of whatever race tended to marry later. As the community aged, however, the black woman's delay in starting a family did set her apart, for native-born white women began families earlier than their immigrant sisters, black or white. . . .

[B]lack and white women were subjected to the same gender-imposed cultural restraints in naming. Of course, only white males had the security of a stable surname, but putting that issue aside, naming patterns reveal a subtle power structure in which gender played as important a role as did race. It is fitting that the first black woman resident in King William Parish was called Bety, because Bett (Beti, Bety, Betty) would prove to be one of the most common names for slave women in the parish. Of the 737 blacks studied, the 336 women bore only 71 names. Nine of these names were used seventeen times or more and account for over half of all the women. Conversely, the 401 men bore 117 names, only 5 of which were used seventeen times or more, representing only one-quarter of all male names. Thus the men bore more individualistic names. The men's names included those with more recognizable African roots such as Ebo, Manoc, and Morocco. The women's names were more Anglicized. The most common female names among slaves were western names that closely resembled African ones, such as Betty and Jude. Hence the names represent a compromise of cultures. It is possible that the lack of recognizable African roots reflected the insistence by owners that black women fit the cultural norms for women while accepting the idea that black men might be "outlandish."

Slave naming patterns may have been affected by the French community. Manakin whites bear frustratingly few names, especially among women. Nine women's names account for over 90 percent of the more than 600 white women associated with the Manakin community before 1776. While both black and white women drew their names from a much smaller pool than did men, the pool of black names had a diversity to begin with only eventually matched by white families who added new names through intermarriage. That black women shared the same names more frequently than black men parallels the pattern of the white community. But there was a further commonality among women's names that cut across racial lines. Slave names were often the diminutives of white names, for example, Betty for Elizabeth and Will for William. White women also were known by diminutives such as Sally, Patsy, and Nancy. They appear this way even in formal documents such as wills. Nicknames and diminutives are not used for adult white males. Hence diminutives were shared by women, both black and white, but not by all groups of men. White women shared in unaltered form several common names with black women, including Sarah, Hannah, and Janne. Male slaves did not bear the same names as white males, although a white youth might be called by a nickname such as Tom, which was also a common slave name. On legal documents and at adulthood, however, white men claimed the distinction granted by the formal versions of their names. Slaveowners apparently found it more necessary to distinguish between white and black males than to distinguish between white and black females by changing the form of their names or choosing names for slaves not used by whites. Such distinctions in naming patterns helped to reinforce the status and power of white men. . . .

[T]he gender constraints of Virginia meant that women of both races shared a naming experience that offered them fewer choices, accorded them less individuality, and reinforced a dependent status.

Childbirth is an experience shared by women of all races, but in King William Parish the patterns of childbearing reveal another way in which black women lived within a community of women and yet encountered a separate experience. Next to the ordinary rhythms of work, childbirth may have been the most common experience for women. Pregnancy, childbirth, and nursing provided a steady background beat to the lives of women in the colonies. Recent research has shown that colonial white women made childbirth a community event, infused with rituals of support by other women, and that these rituals of lying-in were shared with black women. The evidence from Manakin, however, suggests that the risks of childbirth were greater for black women than for white. Although they may have participated in the rituals surrounding childbirth, black women were the center of attention less frequently because they had fewer children; moreover, participation in this women's culture required them to abandon some of their African traditions. Truly, childbirth was a bittersweet experience for black women.

The fragmentary King William Parish Register includes the records of births of slaves among forty-eight owners for the years from 1724 to 1744. . . . The average birth interval was about 28 months, but was often less than two years. . . . In general, for the black women of Manakin, the most frequent interval was 20 months. Fifty-six percent of the birth intervals were between 15 and 34 months. However, another quarter of the intervals fell into a block running 36 to 47 months. The interval between births, however, was much more ragged than these figures suggest. Many women had long gaps in their childbearing histories. Other women had few or no children. . . .

While the average and median for childbirth intervals were similar for black and white women in the parish, there were also major differences. The black woman was much more likely to have an intermittent history of childbirth with long gaps, ending much sooner than it did for the whites of Manakin. Birth intervals for whites were more tightly clustered around 24 months than black births. Seventy-four percent of the white births fell in the interval between 15 and 34 months. Elizabeth Chastain LeSueur, for example, bore children every two to three years with almost clockwork regularity from 1728 to 1753, while her slave Phillis had two children 30 months apart and then had no more children for at least seven years.

The child-spacing patterns for black and white women of King William Parish provide important clues to the adaptation of black women to American slavery and their participation in a community culture surrounding childbirth. African customs of nursing were different from those of Europeans. In Africa women often nursed children for more than three years, abstaining from sexual relations during that period. Black women continued these patterns in the Caribbean slave communities, as did seventeenth-century blacks in the Chesapeake. The secondary cluster of birth intervals of three to four years suggests that a number of immigrant black women, including Phillis, continued that tradition in the Manakin area. European women, however, nursed for a shorter time and had resultingly closer birth intervals of about two years. . . . [A] number of . . . black women in the parish adopted the shorter European traditions of nursing. Whether this adoption of European custom came at the urging of owners or as part of a cultural accommodation by black women, the result was that [black women] had one more bond with white women.

In another way, however, the birth intervals explain how childbirth set black and white women apart, for black women had many fewer children per mother than the white women did. . . . The difference may be a result of fewer black births, owners more frequently forgetting to register black births, or a combination of the two. All of the possibilities suggest a different experience for black women. Other evidence, such as estate inventories, suggests that fewer births account for most of the difference. . . .

That most black women were immigrants and most whites were native-born accounts for some of the difference in numbers of children, for immigrant women often delayed starting families while searching for mates or found their marriages disrupted. Others reached menopause before they had been in the Manakin area twenty years. The gaps in the middle of black women's childbearing years, however, are at least as signif-

icant as any shortening of the years at risk by late starts. Those mid-life gaps in childbearing were due in part to black life expectancy. Africans and other immigrants to the South had high death rates, even in the more healthful eighteenth century. Disruptions caused by the death of a partner could inhibit the total number of children a woman bore, especially while the black community was small, for finding a new partner might take years. Although white women also lost partners, by 1730 the population of King William Parish was colonial-born and more resistant to the endemic fevers. Thus their marriages were more stable. The slave population, however, continued to be heavily immigrant and thus continued to have a higher rate of marriage disruption. Transfers of ownership and removal to other areas increased the possibility of separation from partners and hence lowered the number of children born. . . .

The white women of Manakin expected their children to survive to adulthood. A black woman could not. . . . Only 44 out of 151 of the slave children whose births were recorded in the parish register appear in any other legal and church record, and for some that second appearance was as a child. Death explains many of the disappearances. For example, Beti, slave of Gideon Chambon, bore children Jean (John) in 1727 and Marye in 1733. When Chambon's estate inventory was filed in 1739 neither child appeared on the list. Given Chambon's age and economic condition, the most likely explanation is that the children died, not that he sold or gave them away. . . . Owners registered two and three children by the same name over the years. . . . Apparently they were doing what many families also did following the death of a white child, that is, replacing it by another of the same name.

The work patterns of black women fostered the high death rate among their children by exhausting mothers and making infant care difficult. . . .

[W]hile the Manakin families might not have been rich enough to provide the elaborate lying-ins for black women that Mary Beth Norton has described, the birth experience was not left entirely to the black community. Since we also know that black women helped at the births of white children, the physical act of giving birth may have been one of the most significant ways in which black and white women served each other in a single community.

As with the other aspects of their lives, work both separated and brought black women together with whites. . . . [B]lack women were considered a basic part of the agricultural labor force in a way that white women were not. Undoubtedly, Phillis had spent part of her time working in the LeSueur fields. When the LeSueurs purchased her they had no children old enough to help with farm work, and David and Elizabeth LeSueur were planting without any regular help. Phillis's arrival assured Elizabeth that she could withdraw from occasional help in the fields to her many household duties and garden.

While white women seldom worked away from home, black women sometimes did. Slave rentals kept the labor supply flexible, cut costs for care by owners, and provided an income for widows and orphans. Two major sources for rental slaves were estates managed to provide an income for widows and orphans, and wealthy farmers who hired out their surplus women and children slaves. Women slaves were hired out more frequently than men. Thus black women might be separated from family and friends in order to secure the income that allowed a white woman to remain on the family farm. . . .

The rental of female slaves thus seems to have been an integral part of the Manakin labor system, allowing aspiring farmers to add to their small labor forces while providing income for widows and orphans. Once again the community's perception of black women primarily as field hands set black and white women apart.

Phillis might have spent much of her time in the fields, but she also worked with Elizabeth LeSueur on the many tasks associated with women's work. Domestic work was not a single occupation but a variety of highly skilled tasks shared by women on the plantation. For example, clothmaking occupied both white and black women in the Manakin area. When David LeSueur died in 1772, the family owned working farms in both Buckingham and Cumberland counties. Only the home plantation in Cumberland, however, had cotton, wool and cotton cards, a wool wheel, two spindles, four flax wheels, and parts for two looms. Elizabeth obviously oversaw and worked with Phillis and Phillis's two grown daughters in the making of a variety of cloth. The LeSueurs were not unusual, for inventories throughout the Manakin region mention several crops including flax, the tools necessary to produce linen thread, and, somewhat less frequently, looms for weaving. . . . The usefulness of women in the tasks of cloth production may have encouraged owners to purchase women slaves. From its beginning the colony at Manakin provided Virginia cloth, used to clothe slaves and the poor. Black women worked with white women in this production on the small farm, thus providing another way in which a community of women cut across racial lines.

The smallness of slaveholdings and the relatively short life expectancies of owners created major instabilities in the lives of black women that exceeded the uncertainties of life for their white mistresses. Although owners recognized that black families existed, and while there is convincing evidence that kinship ties were strong among blacks, the value of slaves as property meant that black family stability was tied to the life cycle of their owners. Short life expectancies and parental willingness to establish adult children on farms of their own as soon as possible accelerated the cycle in the Manakin area. Life patterns in the late seventeenth and early eighteenth centuries were such that most Chesapeake parents expected to die before all their children came of age. One result of this expectation was the willingness of parents to give adult children their shares of the estate when they came of age or married. . . . Thus even a long-lived owner was no guarantee of stability in a slave family.

Most blacks in the Manakin area changed hands upon the death of an owner or the coming of age of a child of the owner. Because slaves were valuable legacies to children, they were often divided among several heirs. Daughters, especially, received slaves as their share of the estate, either as dowries or legacies. With slaveholdings small, black families were divided at each period of change within the white family. Most bequests in the Manakin area (except for life interests to widows) were of one or two slaves. David LeSueur, for example, granted each of his eight surviving children one slave. Phillis, her two oldest children, and another male (probably husband to her daughter) stayed with their mistress, Elizabeth Chastain LeSueur, but all of Phillis's younger children and grandchildren were scattered. Owners when possible left very small children with slave mothers or bequeathed the slave mother to a married son or daughter and the slave's children to the children of the son or daughter. Thus black women received some recognition of bonds with children not accorded to men. . . .

Black women might wait for years before the pain of such divisions became real. While the marriage of older children of the owners caused some separation among black families, the major estate divisions came when the owner died. Many estates remained intact for years awaiting the coming of age of minor children or the remarriage or death of a widow. Thus the fate of black women (and men) depended on the fate of their white mistresses. . . . The black woman on a larger estate had a better chance of remaining with kin following the death of an owner. The few large estates included in the study divided slaves on the basis of where they lived, often giving a particular farm and its slaves to an heir. . . .

Life for black women in the Manakin area was filled with insecurity. Some risks, such as childbirth, were shared with white women, but others were not. As part of a double minority black women enjoyed a favorable marriage market, but dispersion of holdings threatened the families formed by black women with separation. . . . Slave rentals, which affected women more than men, added another dimension of instability to that ensured by the short life spans of spouses and owners. The decisions made by widows to remarry, farm, or hire out slaves for income not only determined whether white families would remain intact, but whether black ones would too. Most black women in the Manakin area lived on small farms or quarters where their field work was supplemented by sharing in the household tasks of the white women on the farm. The "bonds of womanhood" surrounded her life as much as the bonds of slavery, beginning with the very choice of a name. Childbearing was especially frustrating for the black woman, filled with the pain of frequent infant death, heavy workloads when pregnant, and separation from children. But childbirth also meant sharing in a woman's network that stretched across racial lines. The life of a black woman was thus constantly subjected to the cross-pressures of belonging to a woman's subculture without full membership.

After reading this selection, consider these questions:

1. In what ways were the "bonds of womanhood" greater than the divisions of race? In what ways did the divisions of race and status (free versus slave) surmount the "bonds of womanhood?"

2. How does Gundersen use quantitative evidence to answer qualitative issues of life?

3. How did the life patterns of slave-owning white families (marriages, deaths, changes in fortune) influence the lives of their slaves?

4. To what extent did issues of gender shape the development of slavery?

SELECTION 3:

The Stono Rebellion

By the beginning of the eighteenth century, blacks constituted a majority of the population in South Carolina. In September 1739, a group of slaves attempted to escape to Spanish Florida, where the government had offered sanctuary to slaves escaping from the English colonies to the north. The slaves began by attacking a store at Stono, a settlement south of Charleston. After killing the owner and another man, they armed themselves and attacked nearby houses, killing as many as thirty whites. Along the way, the rebels attracted new recruits, and their number grew to nearly one hundred. The militia caught them near the Edisto River and killed many of the rebels. Reprisals against blacks continued for weeks after the main body of rebels had been killed or captured. The system of slavery withstood the challenge, but the white minority's anxiety regarding slave rebellions became even more acute. The following document, from The Colonial Records of the State of Georgia, *is a white account of the uprising.*

Sometime since there was a Proclamation published at Augustine, in which the King of Spain (then at Peace with Great Britain) promised Protection and Freedom to all Negroes [*sic*] Slaves that would resort thither. Certain Negroes belonging to Captain Davis escaped to Augustine, and were received there. They were demanded by General Oglethorpe who sent Lieutenant Demere to Augustine, and the Governour assured the General of his sincere Friendship, but at the same time showed his Orders from the Court of Spain, by which he was to receive all Run away Negroes. Of this other Negroes having notice, as it is believed, from the Spanish Emissaries, four or five who were Cattel-Hunters, and knew the Woods, some of whom belonged to Captain Macpherson, ran away with His Horses, wounded his Son and killed another Man. These marched f [*sic*] for Georgia, and were pursued, but the Rangers

being then newly reduced [*sic*] the Countrey people could not overtake them, though they were discovered by the Saltzburghers, as they passed by Ebenezer. They reached Augustine, one only being killed and another wounded by the Indians in their flight. They were received there with great honours, one of them had a Commission given to him, and a Coat faced with Velvet. Amongst the Negroe Slaves there are a people brought from the Kingdom of Angola in Africa, many of these speak Portugueze [which Language is as near Spanish as Scotch is to English,] by reason that the Portugueze have considerable Settlement, and the Jesuits have a Mission and School in that Kingdom and many Thousands of the Negroes there profess the Roman Catholic Religion. Several Spaniards upon diverse Pretences have for some time past been strolling about Carolina, two of them, who will give no account of themselves have been taken up and committed to Jayl in Georgia. The good reception of the Negroes at Augustine was spread about, Several attempted to escape to the Spaniards, & were taken, one

---

Excerpted from *The Colonial Records of the State of Georgia,* edited by Allen D. Candler (London: Public Record Office, 1913).

of them was hanged at Charles Town. In the latter end of July last Don Pedro, Colonel of the Spanish Horse, went in a Launch to Charles Town under pretence of a message to General Oglethorpe and the Lieutenant Governour.

On the 9th day of September last being Sunday which is the day the Planters allow them to work for themselves, Some Angola Negroes assembled, to the number of Twenty; and one who was called Jemmy was their Captain, they suprized a Warehouse belonging to Mr. Hutchenson at a place called Stonehow [Stono]; they there killed Mr. Robert Bathurst, and Mr. Gibbs, plundered the House and took a pretty many small Arms and Powder, which were there for Sale. Next they plundered and burnt Mr. Godfrey's house, and killed him, his Daughter and Son. They then turned back and marched Southward along Pons Pons, which is the Road through Georgia to Augustine, they passed Mr. Wallace's Tavern towards day break, and said they would not hurt him, for he was a good Man and kind to his Slaves, but they broke open and plundered Mr. Lemy's House, and killed him, his wife and Child. They marched on towards Mr. Rose's resolving to kill him; but he was saved by a Negroe, who having hid him went out and pacified the others. Several Negroes joyned them, they calling out Liberty, marched on with Colours displayed, and two Drums beating, pursuing all the white People they met with, and killing Man Woman and Child when they could come up to them. Collonel Bull, Lieutenant Governour of South Carolina, who was then riding along the Road, discovered them, was pursued, and with much difficulty escaped & raised the Countrey. They burnt Colonel Hext's house and killed his Overseer and his Wife. They then burnt Mr. Sprye's house, then Mr. Sacheverell's, and then Mr. Nash's house, all lying upon the Pons Pons Road, and killed all the white People they found in them. Mr. Bullock got off, but they burnt his House, by this time many of them were drunk with the Rum they had taken in the Houses. They increased every minute by new Negroes coming to them, so that they were above Sixty, some say a hundred, on which they halted in a field, and set to dancing, Singing and beating Drums, to draw more Negroes to them, thinking they were now victorious over the whole Province, having marched ten miles & burnt all before them without Opposition, but the Militia being raised, the Planters with great briskness pursued them and when they came up, dismounting; charged them on foot. The Negroes were soon routed, though they behaved boldly, several being killed on the Spot, many ran back to their Plantations thinking they had not been missed, but they were there taken and Shot. Such as were taken in the field also, were, after being examined, shot on the Spot. And this is to be said to the honour of the Carolina Planters, that notwithstanding the Provocation they had received from so many Murders, they did not torture one Negroe, but only put them to an easy death. All that proved to be forced & were not concerned in the Murders & Burnings were pardoned, And this sudden Courage in the field, & the Humanity afterwards hath had so good an Effect that there hath been no farther Attempt, and the very Spirit of Revolt seems over. About 30 escaped from the fight, of which ten marched about 30 miles Southward, and being overtaken by the Planters on horseback, fought stoutly for some time and were all killed on the Spot. The rest are yet untaken. In the whole action about 40 Negroes and 20 whites were killed. The Lieutenant Governour sent an account of this to General Oglethorpe, who met the advices on his return from the Indian Nation. He immediately ordered a Troop of Rangers to be ranged, to patrole through Georgia, placed some Men in the Garrison at Palichocolas, which was before abandoned, and near which the Negroes formerly passed, being the only place where Horses can come to swim over the River Savannah for near 100 miles, ordered out the Indians in pursuit, and a Detachment of the Garrison at Port Royal to assist the Planters on any Occasion, and published a Proclamation ordering all the Constables &ca. of Georgia to pursue and seize all Negroes, with a Reward for any that should be taken. It is hoped these measures will prevent any Negroes from getting down to the Spaniards.

After reading this selection, consider these questions:

1. The author of the document asserts that "to the honour of the Carolina Planters" the rebellious slaves were shot on the spot and not one was tortured. In fact, the rounding up of rebels and suspected rebels continued for some time, and some were hanged. What should one make of the document's assertion?

2. Why would the government of Spanish Florida offer asylum to runaway slaves from the English colonies?

3. The document indicates that the rebels killed two men at Hutchenson's storehouse. It does not mention that both were beheaded and their heads left on the front steps. Why might this fact have been omitted from the account?

SELECTION 4:

North Carolina Statutes

Slavery presented particular problems for English colonists. Slavery did not exist under the common law; that is, the accepted legal system did not recognize any such entity as a slave or any such property as a slave. Further, slaves constituted a peculiar form of property, for which common law did not provide adequate protection. Moreover, unlike chairs, tables, or even mules or dogs, slaves had a conscience and human volition. This raised difficult issues under the law. Could slaves be held responsible for their criminal acts? Under the law, was killing a slave the same as killing a free person? Examining one of these issues provides a sense of the complexity as well as changing attitudes toward the issue. In a series of laws passed throughout the eighteenth century, North Carolina established and revised penalties for the killing of a slave.

Act of 1741

44. *And be it further enacted by the authority aforesaid,* That if in the dispersing any unlawful assemblies of rebel slaves or conspirators, or seizing the arms and ammunition of such as prohibited by this act to keep the same, or in apprehending runaways, or in correction by order of the county court, any slave shall happen to be killed or destroyed, the court of the county where such slave shall be killed, upon application of the owner of such slave, and due proof thereof made, shall put a valuation, in proclamation money, upon such slave so killed, and certify such valuation to the next session of assembly; that the said assembly may make suitable allowance thereupon, to the master or owner of such slave.

45. *Provided always, and be it further enacted,* That nothing herein contained, shall be so construed, deemed, or taken, to defeat or bar the action of any person or persons, whose slave or slaves shall happen to be killed by any other person whosoever, contrary to the directions and true intent and meaning of this act; but that all

Excerpted from *North Carolina State Law,* Act of 1741.

and every owner or owners of such slave or slaves, shall and may bring his, her, or their action, for recovery of damages for such slave or slaves so killed.

Act of 1774

XXVI. § 3. If the slave so willfully and maliciously killed, shall be the property of another and not of the offender, he shall, on the first conviction thereof, pay the owner thereof such sum as shall be the value of the said slave, to be assessed by the inferior court of the county where such slave was killed, and shall stand committed to the jail of the district where such conviction shall happen, until he shall satisfy and pay the said sum so assessed.

Act of 1791

3. And whereas by another act of Assembly passed in the year 1774, the killing a slave, however wanton, cruel and deliberate, is only punishable in the first instance by imprisonment and paying the value thereof to the owner; which distinction of criminality between the murder of a white person and of one who is equally an human creature, but merely of a different complexion, is disgraceful to humanity and degrading in the highest degree to the laws and principles of a free, christian and enlightened country: *Be it enacted by the authority aforesaid,* That if any person shall hereafter be guilty of wilfully and maliciously killing a slave, such offender shall upon the first conviction thereof be adjudged guilty of murder, and shall suffer the same punishment as if he had killed a free man: (a) any

law, usage or custom to the contrary notwithstanding. *Provided always,* That this act shall not extend to any person killing a slave outlawed by virtue of any act of Assembly of this state, or to any slave in the act of resistance to his lawful owner or master, or to any slave dying under moderate correction.

After reading this selection, consider these questions:

1. With what situation does section 44 of the Act of 1741 attempt to deal? Is the owner assured of compensation for the loss of a slave?

2. Under section 45 of the Act of 1741, killing a slave is not a crime (an act against the Crown and punishable by the state); rather, it is a civil matter (a matter between two private parties). What does this indicate about the status of slaves?

3. Under the Act of 1774, is killing a slave a crime or a civil trespass? Under what conditions does this law provide for the state to become involved?

4. The Act of 1791 makes killing a slave a criminal act. What does this indicate? Does anything in the law bar a master from seeking compensation under civil law if someone kills his or her slave? What might one conclude from this?

5. What influences might have persuaded North Carolina's legislature to enact the Act of 1791 at the time it did?

SELECTION 5:

Olaudah Equiano's Enslavement

By his own account, the veracity of which has recently been questioned by historians, Olaudah Equiano (also known as Gustavus Vassa, the name given to him by a European master) was born into the Ibo tribe in 1745 and kidnapped from his home in West Africa by other Africans when he was eleven. After being sold several times to other Africans, he was sold to a British slaver. The ship on which he came to the Americas landed first in Barbados; when no one purchased him there, he was sent to Virginia, where he briefly worked on a tobacco plantation. His master then sold him to an officer in the British navy. In his new capacity, Equiano served his master and the navy during the Seven Years' War. He also learned to read and write as well as to become a skilled sailor. After the war, he was sold to a Quaker merchant, who allowed him to buy and sell goods on his own. Eventually, he earned enough money to buy his freedom. After retiring from the sea, Equiano became involved in the antislavery movement. In 1789, as part of a campaign against the slave trade, he published an autobiography (The Interesting Narrative of the Life of Olaudah Equiano, or Gustavus Vassa, the African). *His narrative is full of exciting and dramatic tales of the sea; the following excerpt describes the trauma of capture and depicts in shocking detail the horror of the so-called Middle Passage, the transatlantic voyage.*

I hope the reader will not think I have trespassed on his patience in introducing myself to him with some account of the manners and customs of my country. They had been implanted in me with great care, and made an impression on my mind, which time could not erase, and which all the adversity and variety of fortune I have since experienced, served only to rivet and record: for, whether the love of one's country be real or imaginary, or a lesson of reason, or an instinct of nature, I still look back with pleasure on the first scenes of my life, though that pleasure has been for the most part mingled with sorrow.

I have already acquainted the reader with the time and place of my birth. My father, besides many slaves, had a numerous family, of which seven lived to grow up, including myself and sister, who was the only daughter. As I was the youngest of the sons, I became, of course, the greatest favorite with my mother, and was always with her; and she used to take particular pains to form my mind. I was trained up from my earliest years in the art of war: my daily exercise was shooting and throwing javelins, and my mother adorned me with emblems, after the manner of our

Excerpted from *The Interesting Narrative of the Life of Olaudah Equiano*, by Olaudah Equiano (London: Olaudah Equiano, 1789).

greatest warriors. In this way I grew up till I had turned the age of eleven, when an end was put to my happiness in the following manner: Generally, when the grown people in the neighborhood were gone far in the fields to labor, the children assembled together in some of the neighboring premises to play; and commonly some of us used to get up a tree to look out for any assailant, or kidnapper, that might come upon us—for they sometimes took those opportunities of our parents' absence, to attack and carry off as many as they could seize. One day as I was watching at the top of a tree in our yard, I saw one of those people come into the yard of our next neighbor but one, to kidnap, there being many stout young people in it. Immediately on this I gave the alarm of the rogue, and he was surrounded by the stoutest of them, who entangled him with cords, so that he could not escape, till some of the grown people came and secured him. But, alas! ere long it was my fate to be thus attacked, and to be carried off, when none of the grown people were nigh.

One day, when all our people were gone out to their works as usual, and only I and my dear sister were left to mind the house, two men and a woman got over our walls, and in a moment seized us both, and, without giving us time to cry out, or make resistance, they stopped our mouths, and ran off with us into the nearest wood. Here they tied our hands, and continued to carry us as far as they could, till night came on, when we reached a small house, where the robbers halted for refreshment, and spent the night. We were then unbound, but were unable to take any food; and, being quite overpowered by fatigue and grief, our only relief was some sleep, which allayed our misfortune for a short time. The next morning we left the house, and continued travelling all the day. For a long time we had kept the woods, but at last we came into a road which I believed I knew. I had now some hopes of being delivered; for we had advanced but a little way before I discovered some people at a distance, on which I began to cry out for their assistance; but my cries had no other effect than to make them tie me faster and stop my mouth, and then they put me into a large sack. They also stopped my sister's mouth, and tied her hands; and in this

manner we proceeded till we were out of sight of these people. When we went to rest the following night, they offered us some victuals, but we refused it; and the only comfort we had was in being in one another's arms all that night, and bathing each other with our tears. But alas! we were soon deprived of even the small comfort of weeping together.

The next day proved a day of greater sorrow than I had yet experienced; for my sister and I were then separated, while we lay clasped in each other's arms. It was in vain that we besought them not to part us; she was torn from me, and immediately carried away, while I was left in a state of distraction not to be described. I cried and grieved continually; and for several days did not eat anything but what they forced into my mouth. At length, after many days' travelling, during which I had often changed masters, I got into the hands of a chieftain, in a very pleasant country. This man had two wives and some children, and they all used me extremely well, and did all they could do to comfort me; particularly the first wife, who was something like my mother. Although I was a great many days' journey from my father's house, yet these people spoke exactly the same language with us. This first master of mine, as I may call him, was a smith, and my principal employment was working his bellows, which were the same kind as I had seen in my vicinity. . . . I believe it was gold he worked, for it was of a lovely bright yellow color, and was worn by the women on their wrists and ankles.

I was there I suppose about a month, and they at last used to trust me some little distance from the house. This liberty I used in embracing every opportunity to inquire the way to my own home; and I also sometimes, for the same purpose, went with the maidens, in the cool of the evenings, to bring pitchers of water from the springs for the use of the house. I had also remarked where the sun rose in the morning, and set in the evening, as I had travelled along; and I had observed that my father's house was towards the rising of the sun. I therefore determined to seize the first opportunity of making my escape, and to shape my course for that quarter; for I was quite oppressed and weighed down by grief after my mother and friends; and my love of liberty, ever great, was strengthened by the mortifying circumstance of not daring to eat with the free-born children, although I was mostly their companion.

While I was projecting my escape, one day an unlucky event happened, which quite disconcerted my plan, and put an end to my hopes. I used to be sometimes employed in assisting an elderly slave to cook and take care of the poultry; and one morning, while I was feeding some chickens, I happened to toss a small pebble at one of them, which hit it on the middle, and directly killed it. The old slave, having soon after missed the chicken, inquired after it; and on my relating the accident (for I told her the truth, for my mother would never suffer me to tell a lie), she flew into a violent passion, and threatened that I should suffer for it; and, my master being out, she immediately went and told her mistress what I had done. This alarmed me very much, and I expected an instant flogging, which to me was uncommonly dreadful, for I had seldom been beaten at home. I therefore resolved to fly; and accordingly I ran into a thicket that was hard by, and hid myself in the bushes. Soon afterwards my mistress and the slave returned, and, not seeing me, they searched all the house, but not finding me, and I not making answer when they called to me, they thought I had run away, and the whole neighborhood was raised in the pursuit of me.

In that part of the country, as in ours, the houses and villages were skirted with woods, or shrubberies, and the bushes were so thick that a man could readily conceal himself in them, so as to elude the strictest search. The neighbors continued the whole day looking for me, and several times many of them came within a few yards of the place where I lay hid. I expected every moment, when I heard a rustling among the trees, to be found out, and punished by my master; but they never discovered me, though they were often so near that I even heard their conjectures as they were looking about for me; and I now learned from them that any attempts to return home would be hopeless. Most of them supposed I had fled towards home; but the distance was so great, and the way so intricate, that they thought I could never reach it, and that I should be lost in the woods. When I heard this I was seized with a violent panic, and abandoned myself to despair. Night, too, began to approach, and aggravated all my fears. I had before entertained hopes of getting home, and had determined when it should be dark to make the attempt; but I was now convinced it was fruitless, and began to consider that, if possibly I could escape all other animals, I could not those of the human kind; and that, not knowing the way, I must perish in the woods. . . .

I heard frequent rustlings among the leaves, and being pretty sure they were snakes, I expected every instant to be stung by them. This increased my anguish, and the horror of my situation became now quite insupportable. I at length quitted the thicket, very faint and hungry, for I had not eaten or drank anything all the day, and crept to my master's kitchen, from whence I set out at first, which was an open shed, and laid myself down in the ashes with an anxious wish for death, to relieve me from all my pains. I was scarcely awake in the morning, when the old woman slave, who was the first up, came to light the fire, and saw me in the fireplace. She was very much surprised to see me, and could scarcely believe her own eyes. She now promised to intercede for me, and went for her master, who soon after came, and, having slightly reprimanded me, ordered me to be taken care of, and not ill treated.

Soon after this, my master's only daughter, and child by his first wife, sickened and died, which affected him so much that for sometime he was almost frantic, and really would have killed himself, had he not been watched and prevented. However, in a short time afterwards he recovered, and I was again sold. . . .

From the time I left my own nation, I always found somebody that understood me till I came to the sea coast. The languages of different nations did not totally differ, nor were they so copious as those of the Europeans, particularly the English. They were therefore easily learned; and, while I was journeying thus through Africa, I acquired two or three different tongues. . . .

I was again sold, and carried through a number of places, till after travelling a considerable time, I came to a town called Tinmah, in the most beautiful country I had yet seen in Africa. It was extremely rich, and there were many rivulets which flowed through it, and supplied a large pond in the centre of the town, where the people washed. Here I saw for the first time cocoanuts, which I thought superior to any nuts I had ever tasted before; and the trees, which were loaded, were also interspersed among the houses, which had commodious shades adjoining, and were in the same manner as ours, the insides being neatly plastered and whitewashed. Here I also saw and tasted for the first time, sugar-cane. Their money consisted of little white shells, the size of the finger nail. I was sold here for one hundred and seventy-two of them, by a merchant who lived and brought me there.

I had been about two or three days at his house, when a wealthy widow, a neighbor of his, came there one evening, and brought with her an only son, a young gentleman about my own age and size. Here they saw me; and, having taken a fancy to me, I was bought of the merchant, and went home with them. Her house and premises were situated close to one of those rivulets I have mentioned, and were the finest I ever saw in Africa: they were very extensive, and she had a number of slaves to attend her.

The next day I was washed and perfumed, and when meal time came, I was led into the presence of my mistress, and ate and drank before her with her son. This filled me with astonishment; and I could scarce help expressing my surprise that the young gentleman should suffer me, who was bound, to eat with him who was free; and not only so, but that he would not at any time either eat or drink till I had taken first, because I was the eldest, which was agreeable to our custom. Indeed, every thing here, and all their treatment of me, made me forget that I was a slave. The language of these people resembled ours so nearly, that we understood each other perfectly. They had also the very same customs as we. There were likewise slaves daily to attend us, while my young master and I, with other boys, sported with our darts and bows and arrows, as I had been used to do at home. In this resemblance to my former happy state, I passed about two months;

and I now began to think I was to be adopted into the family, and was beginning to be reconciled to my situation, and to forget by degrees my misfortunes, when all at once the delusion vanished; for, without the least previous knowledge, one morning early, while my dear master and companion was still asleep, I was awakened out of my reverie to fresh sorrow, and hurried away even amongst the uncircumcised. . . .

All the nations and people I had hitherto passed through, resembled our own in their manners, customs, and language; but I came at length to a country, the inhabitants of which differed from us in all those particulars. I was very much struck with this difference, especially when I came among a people who did not circumcise, and ate without washing their hands. They cooked also in iron pots, and had European cutlasses and cross bows, which were unknown to us, and fought with their fists among themselves. Their women were not so modest as ours, for they ate, and drank, and slept with their men. But above all, I was amazed to see no sacrifices or offerings among them. In some of those places the people ornamented themselves with scars, and likewise filed their teeth very sharp. They wanted sometimes to ornament me in the same manner, but I would not suffer them; hoping that I might some time be among a people who did not thus disfigure themselves, as I thought they did. At last I came to the banks of a large river which was covered with canoes, in which the people appeared to live with their household utensils, and provisions of all kinds. I was beyond measure astonished at this, as I had never before seen any water larger than a pond or a rivulet; and my surprise was mingled with no small fear when I was put into one of these canoes, and we began to paddle and move along the river. We continued going on thus till night, and when we came to land, and made fires on the banks, each family by themselves; some dragged their canoes on shore, others stayed and cooked in theirs, and laid in them all night. Those on the land had mats, of which they made tents, some in the shape of little houses; in these we slept; and after the morning meal, we embarked again and proceeded as before. I was often very much astonished to see some of the women, as well as the men, jump into the water, dive to the bottom, come up again, and swim about.

Thus I continued to travel, sometimes by land, sometimes by water, through different countries and various nations, till, at the end of six or seven months after I had been kidnapped, I arrived at the sea coast. . . .

The first object which saluted my eyes when I arrived on the coast, was the sea, and a slave ship, which was then riding at anchor, and waiting for its cargo. These filled me with astonishment, which was soon converted into terror, when I was carried on board. I was immediately handled, and tossed up to see if I were sound, by some of the crew; and I was now persuaded that I had gotten into a world of bad spirits, and that they were going to kill me. Their complexions, too, differing so much from ours, their long hair, and the language they spoke (which was very different from any I had ever heard), united to confirm me in this belief. Indeed, such were the horrors of my views and fears at the moment, that, if ten thousand worlds had been my own, I would have freely parted with them all to have exchanged my condition with that of the meanest slave in my own country. When I looked round the ship too, and saw a large furnance of copper boiling, and a multitude of black people of every description chained together, every one of their countenances expressing dejection and sorrow, I no longer doubted of my fate; and, quite overpowered with horror and anguish, I fell motionless on the deck and fainted. When I recovered a little, I found some black people about me, who I believed were some of those who had brought me on board, and had been receiving their pay; they talked to me in order to cheer me, but all in vain. I asked them if we were not to be eaten by those white men with horrible looks, red faces, and long hair. They told me I was not, and one of the crew brought me a small portion of spirituous liquor in a wine glass; but being afraid of him, I would not take it out of his hand. One of the blacks therefore took it from him and gave it to me, and I took a little down my palate, which, instead of reviving me, as they thought it would, threw me into the greatest consternation at the strange feeling it produced, having never tasted any such liquor before. Soon after this, the blacks who brought me on board went off, and left me abandoned to despair.

I now saw myself deprived of all chance of returning to my native country, or even the least glimpse of hope of gaining the shore, which I now considered as friendly; and I even wished for my former slavery in preference to my present situation, which was filled with horrors of every kind, still heightened by my ignorance of what I was to undergo.

After reading this selection, consider these questions:

1. Equiano's father owned slaves, but among the Ibo, people became slaves through warfare or as punishment for a crime. How would this have shaped Equiano's reaction to his enslavement? What expectations might he have had?

2. What was Equiano's reaction on first seeing Europeans?

3. In what ways was Equiano's narrative calculated to stir antislavery sentiment?

4. Who first enslaved Equiano? How did he come into the hands of Europeans?

CHAPTER 3
Family

Settlement in a new environment strained European institutions and eventually reshaped them. Church, family, marriage, and notions of community all evolved in contact with realities of the North American continent. The institution of the family was central to the social organization of all European settlers. It served as the main source of recreation, an economic unit, and the means of educating children. Puritan settlers in New England also regarded the family as the central unit of society. Puritan families included relationships not only between husbands and wives, parents and children, and brothers and sisters, but also between masters and servants (free, bonded, and slave) as well as dependent relatives. Puritans regarded the family as both the central building block in the regenerated community they hoped to achieve and a bulwark against conditions they feared would reduce them to savagery. So central was the family that magistrates in early New England required all single persons to live within a family; individuals living alone, they believed, would be unable to resist impulses to sin and barbarism.

In addition to the social importance of the family, other factors shaped colonial attitudes toward the institution. English settlement of North America occurred at a time when ideas about the family were undergoing significant changes in Europe. For example, harsher approaches were giving way to more gentle treatment of children. Further, greater emphasis was placed on developing children as individual personalities and as members of the family and the larger community. In many respects, child rearing in North America, whether Puritan, Anglican, or Catholic, had much in common with English and European practices. Thus, despite some particularities, child-rearing practices were more similar than different in European settlements in North America, whether the colony was English, French, or Dutch.

Family structure in different settlements in North America also was strikingly uniform, and similar to structures in England and Europe. The family was patriarchal; the husband represented the household in public realms, such as politics. A father commanded his wife's property and the wages earned by his children. In Puritan New

England, both law and church doctrine commanded wives, children, and servants to submit to the authority of the father. This does not mean that a wide diversity of family circumstances did not exist; gender roles and expectations for children differed depending on social and economic class. Demographic factors distinguished family life in New England from that in the Chesapeake. It should be noted, however, that the most distinctive aspects of life in English North America involved governmental institutions, not the family.

After reading this chapter, consider these questions:

1. What in the colonial experience shaped family structures?

2. How did marriage and family function as social institutions?

SELECTION 1:

The Puritan Family

In this selection, Steven Mintz, an associate professor of history at the University of Houston, and anthropologist Susan Kellogg discuss the Puritan family as a social institution.

In 1629, eight years after the Pilgrims arrived in Plymouth, an advance guard of four hundred English Puritans set up a self-governing commonwealth in Salem, Massachusetts. They undertook this "errand into the wilderness" in order to create a pure and godly commonwealth, "a Modell of Christian Charity," which would serve as an example for the reformation of England. In New England—a barren wilderness without such relics of Catholicism as bishops, ecclesiastical courts, priestly vestments, and elaborate rituals—they hoped to create a new and undefiled social

Excerpted from *Domestic Revolutions: A Social History of American Family Life,* by Steven Mintz and Susan Kellogg (New York: The Free Press, 1988). Copyright © 1988 by The Free Press, a division of Simon and Schuster. Reprinted with permission.

order that conformed strictly to the teachings of the Bible. . . .

The roughly twenty thousand Puritan men, women, and children who sailed to Massachusetts between 1629 and 1640 carried with them ideas about the family utterly foreign to Americans today. The Puritans never thought of the family as purely a private unit, rigorously separated from the surrounding community. To them it was an integral part of the larger political and social world; it was "the Mother Hive, out of which both those swarms of State and Church, issued forth." Its boundaries were elastic and inclusive, and it assumed responsibilities that have since been assigned to public institutions.

Although most Puritan families were nuclear in structure, a significant proportion of the population spent part of their lives in other families' homes, serving as apprentices, hired laborers, or servants. At any one time, as many as a third of all Puritan households took in servants. Convicts, the children of the poor, single men and women, and recent immigrants were compelled by select-men to live within existing "well Governed families" so that "disorders may bee prevented and ill weeds nipt."

For the Puritans, family ties and community ties tended to blur. In many communities, individual family members were related by birth or marriage to a large number of their neighbors. . . . The small size of the seventeenth-century communities, combined with high rates of marriage and remarriage, created kinship networks of astonishing complexity. In-laws and other distant kin were generally referred to as brothers, sisters, aunts, uncles, mothers, fathers, and cousins.

Today spousal ties are emphasized, and obligations to kin are voluntary and selective. Three centuries ago the kin group was of great importance to the social, economic, and political life of the community. Kinship ties played a critical role in the development of commercial trading networks and the capitalizing of large-scale investments. In the absence of secure methods of communication and reliable safeguards against dishonesty, prominent New England families, such as the Hutchinsons and Winthrops, relied on relatives in England and the West Indies to achieve success in commerce. Partnerships among family members also played an important role in the ownership of oceangoing vessels. Among merchant and artisan families, apprenticeships were often given exclusively to their own sons or nephews, keeping craft skills within the kinship group.

Intermarriage was also used to cement local political alliances and economic partnerships. Marriages between first cousins or between sets of brothers and sisters helped to bond elite, politically active and powerful families together. Among the families of artisans, marriages between a son and an uncle's daughter reinforced kinship ties.

In political affairs the importance of the kin group persisted until the American Revolution. By the early eighteenth century, small groups of interrelated families dominated the clerical, economic, military, and political leadership of New England. . . .

Unlike the contemporary American family, which is distinguished by its isolation from the world of work and the surrounding society, the Puritan family was deeply embedded in public life. The household—not the individual—was the fundamental unit of society. The political order was not an agglomeration of detached individuals; it was an organic unity composed of families. This was the reason that Puritan households received only a single vote in town meetings. Customarily it was the father, as head of the household, who represented his family at the polls. But if he was absent, his wife assumed his prerogative to vote. The Puritans also took it for granted that the church was composed of families and not of isolated individuals. Family membership—not an individual's abilities or attainments—determined a person's position in society. Where one sat in church or in the local meetinghouse or even one's rank at Harvard College was determined not by one's accomplishments but by one's family identity.

The Puritan family was the main unit of production in the economic system. Each family member was expected to be economically useful. Older children were unquestionably economic assets; they worked at family industries, tended gardens, herded animals, spun wool, and cared for younger brothers and sisters. Wives not only raised children and cared for the home but also cut clothes, supervised servants and apprentices, kept financial accounts, cultivated crops, and marketed surplus goods.

In addition to performing a host of productive functions, the Puritan family was a primary educational and religious unit. A 1642 Massachusetts statute required heads of households to lead their households in prayers and scriptural readings; to teach their children, servants, and apprentices to read; and to catechize household members in the principles of religion and law. The family was also an agency for vocational training, assigned the duty of instructing servants and apprentices in methods of farming, housekeeping, and craft skills. And finally the Puritan family was a welfare institution that carried primary responsibility for the care of orphans, the infirm, or the elderly. . . .

For both Puritan women and men, marriage stood out as one of the central events in life. Despite their reputation as sexually repressed, pleasure-hating bigots, the Puritans did not believe that celibacy was a condition morally superior to marriage. The only thing that Saint Paul might have said in favor of marriage was that it is "better to marry than to burn," but the Puritans extolled marriage as a sacrament and a social duty. . . .

For the Puritans love was not a prerequisite for marriage. They believed that the choice of a marriage partner should be guided by rational considerations of property, religious piety, and family interest, not by physical attraction, personal feelings, or romantic love. Affection, in their view, would develop after marriage. This attitude reflected a recognition of the essential economic functions of the colonial family. Marriage was a partnership to which both bride and groom were expected to bring skills and resources. A prospective bride was expected to contribute a dowry (usually in the form of money or household goods) worth half of what the bridegroom brought to the marriage. Artisans tended to choose wives from families that practiced the same trade precisely because these women would be best able to assist them in their work. In New England the overwhelming majority of men and women married— and many remarried rapidly after the death of a spouse—because it was physically and economically difficult to live alone.

According to Puritan doctrine, a wife was to be her husband's helpmate, not his equal. Her role was "to guid the house &c. not guid the Husband." The Puritans believed that a wife should be submissive to her husband's commands and should exhibit toward him attitude of "reverence.". . .

Of all the differences that distinguish the seventeenth-century family from its present-day counterpart, perhaps the most striking involves the social experience of children. Three centuries ago, childhood was a much less secure and shorter stage of life than it is today. In recent years it has become fashionable to complain about the "disappearance of childhood," but historical perspective reminds us that—despite high divorce rates—childhood is more stable than it was during the colonial era. For a child to die during infancy was a common occurrence in colonial New England; more deaths occurred among young children than in any other age group. . . . It cannot be emphasized too strongly that high infant death rates did not necessarily make parents indifferent toward their young children. . . .

Not only were children more likely to die in infancy or to be orphaned than today, they were raised quite differently. In certain respects young children were treated, by our standards, in a casual way. Child rearing was not the family's main function; the care and nurture of children were subordinate to other family interests. In colonial New England newborn infants of well-to-do families were sometimes "put out" to wet nurses who were responsible for breast-feeding, freeing mothers to devote their time to their household duties. As in Europe, new babies were sometimes named for recently deceased infants. In contrast to Europeans, however, New Englanders did not wrap infants in tightly confining swaddling clothes, and carelessly supervised children sometimes crawled into fires or fell into wells.

The moral upbringing of Puritan children was never treated casually. The Puritan religion taught that even newborn infants were embodiments of guilt and sin (traceable to Adam's transgression in Eden), who, unless saved by God, were doomed to writhe in Satan's clutches for eternity. This belief in infant depravity and original sin exerted a powerful influence on methods of child rearing. In their view the primary task of child rearing was to break down a child's sinful will and internalize respect for divinely instituted authority through weekly catechisms, repeated admonitions, physical beatings, and intense psychological pressure. "Better whipt, than damned," was Cotton Mather's advice to parents.

Although Calvinists could be indulgent with very small children, among many parents their religious faith led to an insistence that, after the age of two, any assertion of a child's will be broken. . . . A child's willfulness could be suppressed through fierce physical beatings, exhibition of corpses, and tales of castration and abandonment—techniques designed to drive out "the old Adam" and produce traits of tractableness and peaceableness highly valued by Calvinists. . . .

Without a doubt the most striking difference between seventeenth-century child rearing and practices today was the widespread custom of sending children to live with another family at the age of fourteen or earlier, so that a child would receive the proper discipline its natural parents could not be expected to administer. Children of all social classes and both sexes were frequently fostered out for long periods in order to learn a trade, to work as servants, or to attend a school. Since the family was a place of work and its labor needs and its financial resources often failed to match its size and composition, servants or apprentices might temporarily be taken in or children bound out. . . .

For New Englanders, migration across the Atlantic gave the family a significance and strength it had lacked in the mother country. In the healthful environment of New England, family ties grew tighter than they had ever been in the Old World. The first settlers lived much longer than their contemporaries in England and were much more likely to live to see their grandchildren. Marriages lasted far longer than they did in contemporary England, and infant mortality rates quickly declined to levels far below those in the old country. Migration to the New World did not weaken paternal authority; it strengthened it by increasing paternal control over land and property. . . .

Contrary to an older view that the New World environment dissolved extended family ties, it now seems clear that the family in early-seventeenth-century New England was a more stable, disciplined, and cohesive unit than its English counterpart in the Old World.

After reading this selection, consider these questions:

1. What role did the family play in the social structure of Puritan New England?

2. How did Puritan families differ from modern American families? In what ways were they similar?

3. What impact did migration across the Atlantic have on family structure?

SELECTION 2:

White Women in Seventeenth-Century Maryland

In the following essay, Lois Green Carr, a professor of history at the University of Maryland, and Lorena S. Walsh, a historian who works for the St. Mary's City (Maryland) Commission, use historical demography (the study of human populations) to reconstruct the life experiences of white women in seventeenth-century Maryland. Relying heavily on statistical data, they explore questions such as how demographic factors affected family life.

Four facts were basic to all human experience in seventeenth-century Maryland. First, for most of the period the great majority of inhabitants had been born in what we now call Britain. Population increase in Maryland did not result primarily from births in the colony before the late 1680s and did not produce a predominantly native population of adults before the first decade of the eighteenth century. Second, immigrant men could not expect to live beyond age forty-three, and 70 percent would die before age fifty. Women may have had even shorter lives. Third, perhaps 85 percent of the immigrants, and practically all the unmarried immigrant women, arrived as indentured servants and consequently married late. Family groups were never predominant in the immigration to Maryland and were a significant part for only a brief time at mid-century. Fourth, many more men than women immigrated during the whole period. These facts—immigrant predominance, early death, late marriage, and sexual imbalance—created circumstances of social and demographic disruption that deeply affected family and community life. . . .

There were degrading aspects of servitude, although these probably did not characterize the lot of most women; there were fewer restraints on social conduct, especially in courtship, than in England; women were less protected but also more powerful than those who remained at home; and at least some of these changes survived the appearance in Maryland of New World creole communities. . . .

Whatever their status, one fact about immigrant women is certain: many fewer came than men. . . .

Why did not more women come? Presumably, fewer wished to leave family and community to venture into a wilderness. But perhaps more important, women were not as desirable as men to merchants and planters who were making fortunes raising and marketing tobacco, a crop that requires large amounts of labor. The gradual im-provement in the sex ratio among servants toward the end of the century may have been the result of a change in recruiting the needed labor. In the late 1660s the supply of young men willing to emigrate stopped increasing sufficiently to meet the labor demands of a growing Chesapeake population. Merchants who recruited servants for planters turned to other sources, and among these sources were women. . . .

To ask the question another way, why did women come? Doubtless, most came to get a husband, an objective virtually certain of success in a land where women were so far outnumbered. The promotional literature, furthermore, painted bright pictures of the life that awaited men and women once out of their time; and various studies suggest that for a while, at least, the promoters were not being entirely fanciful. Until the 1660s, and to a less degree the 1680s, the expanding economy of Maryland and Virginia offered opportunities well beyond those available in England to men without capital and to the women who became their wives.

Nevertheless, the hazards were also great, and the greatest was untimely death. Newcomers promptly became ill, probably with malaria, and many died. What proportion survived is unclear; so far no one has devised a way of measuring it. Recurrent malaria made the woman who survived seasoning less able to withstand other diseases, especially dysentery and influenza. She was especially vulnerable when pregnant. Expectation of life for everyone was low in the Chesapeake, but especially so for women. A woman who had immigrated to Maryland took an extra risk, though perhaps a risk not greater than she might have suffered by moving from her village to London instead.

The majority of women who survived seasoning paid their transportation costs by working for a four- or five-year term of service. The kind of work depended on the status of the family they served. . . .

An additional risk for the woman who came as a servant was the possibility of bearing a bastard. At least 20 percent of the female servants who came to Charles County between 1658 and 1705 were presented to the county court for this cause. A servant woman could not marry unless

Excerpted from "The Planter's Wife: The Experience of White Women in Seventeenth-Century Maryland," by Lois Green Carr and Lorena S. Walsh, *William and Mary Quarterly,* October 1977. Copyright © 1977 by Lois Green Carr. Reprinted with permission.

someone was willing to pay her master for the term she had left to serve. If a man made her pregnant, she could not marry him unless he could buy her time. Once a woman became free, however, marriage was clearly the usual solution. Only a handful of free women were presented in Charles County for bastardy between 1658 and 1705. Since few free women remained either single or widowed for long, not many were subject to the risk. The hazard of bearing a bastard was a hazard of being a servant.

This high rate of illegitimate pregnancies among servants raises lurid questions. Did men import women for sexual exploitation? Does John Barth's Whore of Dorset have a basis outside his fertile imagination? In our opinion, the answers are clearly No. Servants were economic investments on the part of planters who needed labor. A female servant in a household where there were unmarried men must have both provided and faced temptation, for the pressures were great in a society in which men outnumbered women by three to one. Nevertheless, the servant woman was in the household to work—to help feed and clothe the family and make tobacco. She was not primarily a concubine. . . .

Some masters surely did exploit their female servants sexually. Nevertheless, masters were infrequently accused of fathering their servants' bastards, and those found guilty were punished as severely as were other men. Community mores did not sanction their misconduct.

A female servant paid dearly for the fault of unmarried pregnancy. She was heavily fined, and if no one would pay her fine, she was whipped. Furthermore, she served an extra twelve to twenty-four months to repay her master for the "trouble of his house" and labor lost, and the fathers often did not share in this payment of damages. On top of all, she might lose the child after weaning unless by then she had become free, for the courts bound out bastard children at very early ages.

Some women escaped all or part of their servitude because prospective husbands purchased the remainder of their time. . . .

Were women sold for wives against their wills? No record says so, but nothing restricted a man from selling his servant to whomever he wished. Perhaps some women were forced into such marriages or accepted them as the least evil. But the man who could afford to purchase a wife—especially a new arrival—was usually already an established landowner. Probably most servant women saw an opportunity in such a marriage. In addition, the shortage of labor gave women some bargaining power. Many masters must have been ready to refuse to sell a woman who was unwilling to marry a would-be purchaser.

If a woman's time was not purchased by a prospective husband, she was virtually certain to find a husband once she was free. . . .

The woman who immigrated to Maryland, survived seasoning and service, and gained her freedom became a planter's wife. She had considerable liberty in making her choice. There were men aplenty, and no fathers or brothers were hovering to monitor her behavior or disapprove her preference. This is the modern way of looking at her situation, of course. Perhaps she missed the protection of a father, a guardian, or kinfolk, and the participation in her decision of a community to which she felt ties. There is some evidence that the absence of kin and the pressures of the sex ratio created conditions of sexual freedom in courtship that were not customary in England. A register of marriages and births for seventeenth-century Somerset County shows that about one-third of the immigrant women whose marriages are recorded were pregnant at the time of the ceremony—nearly twice the rate in English parishes. There is no indication of community objection to this freedom so long as marriage took place. No presentments for bridal pregnancy were made in any of the Maryland courts. . . .

Because of the age at which an immigrant woman married, the number of children she would bear her husband was small. She had lost up to ten years of her childbearing life—the possibility of perhaps four or five children, given the usual rhythm of childbearing. At the same time, high mortality would reduce both the number of children she would bear over the rest of her life and the number who would live. One partner to a marriage was likely to die within seven years, and the chances were only one in three that a marriage would last ten years. In these circumstances, most women would not bear more than three or four children—not counting those stillborn—to any one husband, plus a posthumous child were she the survivor. The best estimates suggest that nearly a quarter, perhaps more, of the children born alive died during their first year and that 40 to 55 percent would not live to see age twenty. Consequently, one of her children would probably die in infancy, and another one or two would fail to reach adulthood. . . .

For the immigrant woman, then, one of the major facts of life was that although she might bear a child about every two years, nearly half would not reach maturity. The social implications of this fact are far-reaching. Because she married late in her childbearing years and because so many of her children would die young, the number who would reach marriageable age might not replace, or might only barely replace, her and her husband or husbands as child-producing members of the society. Consequently, so long as immigrants were heavily predominant in the adult female population, Maryland could not grow much by natural increase. It remained a land of newcomers. . . .

A hazard of marriage for seventeenth-century women everywhere was death in childbirth, but this hazard may have been greater than usual in the Chesapeake. Whereas in most societies women tend to outlive men, in this malaria-ridden area it is probable that men outlived women. Hazards of childbirth provide the likely reason that Chesapeake women died so young. Once a woman in the Chesapeake reached forty-five, she tended to outlive men who reached the same age. . . .

This argument, however, suggests that immigrant women may have lived longer than their native-born daughters, although among men the opposite was true. Life tables created for men in Maryland show that those native born who survived to age twenty could expect a life span three to ten years longer than that of immigrants, depending upon the region where they lived. The reason for the improvement was doubtless immunities to local diseases developed in childhood. A native woman developed these immunities, but, as we shall see, she also married earlier than immigrant women usually could and hence had more children.

Thus she was more exposed to the hazards of childbirth and may have died a little sooner. . . .

However long they lived, immigrant women in Maryland tended to outlive their husbands—in Charles County, for example, by a ratio of two to one. This was possible, despite the fact that women were younger than men at death, because women were also younger than men at marriage. Some women were widowed with no living children, but most were left responsible for two or three. These were often tiny, and nearly always not yet sixteen.

This fact had drastic consequences, given the physical circumstances of life. People lived at a distance from one another, not even in villages, much less towns. The widow had left her kin 3,000 miles across an ocean, and her husband's family was also there. She would have to feed her children and make her own tobacco crop. Though neighbors might help, heavy labor would be required of her if she had no servants, until—what admittedly was usually not difficult—she acquired a new husband. . . .

Remarriage was the usual and often the immediate solution for a woman who had lost her husband. The shortage of women made any woman eligible to marry again, and the difficulties of raising a family while running a plantation must have made remarriage necessary for widows who had no son old enough to make tobacco. . . .

One result of remarriage was the development of complex family structures. Men found themselves responsible for stepchildren as well as their own offspring, and children acquired half-sisters and half-brothers. Sometimes a woman married a second husband who himself had been previously married, and both brought children of former spouses to the new marriage. They then produced children of their own. The possibilities for conflict over the upbringing of children are evident, and crowded living conditions, found even in the households of the wealthy, must have added to family tensions. Luckily, the children of the family very often had the same mother. In Charles County, at least, widows took new husbands three times more often than widowers took new wives. . . .

Early death in this immigrant population thus had broad effects on Maryland society in the seventeenth century. It produced what we might call a pattern of serial polyandry, which enabled more men to marry and to father families than the sex ratios otherwise would have permitted. It produced thousands of orphaned children who had no kin to maintain them or preserve their property, and thus gave rise to an institution almost unknown in England, the orphans' court, which was charged with their protection. And early death, by creating families in which the mother was the unifying element, may have increased her authority within the household. . . .

So far we have considered primarily the experience of immigrant women. What of their daughters? How were their lives affected by the demographic stresses of Chesapeake society?

One of the most important points in which the experience of daughters differed from that of their mothers was the age at which they married. In this woman-short world, the mothers had married as soon as they were eligible, but they had not usually become eligible until they were mature women in their middle twenties. Their daughters were much younger at marriage. . . .

Were some of these girls actually child brides? It seems unlikely that girls were married before they had become capable of bearing children. Culturally, such a practice would fly in the face of English, indeed Western European, precedent, nobility excepted. Nevertheless, the number of girls who married before age sixteen, the legal age of inheritance for girls, is astonishing. . . .

Not only did native girls marry early, but many of them were pregnant before the ceremony. Bridal pregnancy among native-born women was not as common as among immigrants. Nevertheless, in seventeenth-century Somerset County 20 percent of native brides bore children within eight and one half months of marriage. This was a somewhat higher percentage than has been reported from seventeenth-century English parishes.

These facts suggest considerable freedom for girls in selecting a husband. Almost any girl must have had more than one suitor, and evidently many had freedom to spend time with a suitor in a fashion that allowed her to become pregnant. We might suppose that such pregnancies were not incurred until after the couple had become betrothed, and that they were consequently an allowable part of courtship, were it not that girls whose fathers were living were usually not the culprits. In Somerset, at least, only 10 percent of the brides with fathers living were pregnant, in contrast to 30 percent of those who were orphans. . . .

Native girls married young and bore children young; hence they had more children than immigrant women. This fact ultimately changed the composition of the Maryland population. Native-born females began to have enough children to enable couples to replace themselves. These children, furthermore, were divided about evenly between males and females. By the mid-1680s, in all probability, the population thus began to grow through reproductive increase, and sexual imbalance began to decline.

After reading this selection, consider these questions:

1. How do Carr and Walsh use quantitative data to answer qualitative questions?

2. Discuss the role of mothers in the complex families of early colonial Maryland.

3. Compare the families that Carr and Walsh studied in Maryland with those Mintz and Kellogg studied in New England.

SELECTION 3:

Laws of the New Haven Colony, 1656

Distance from England gave settlers an opportunity to develop their own structures of self-government and codes of law. Typically, New Haven not only established rules of government but set forth rules for the family relationships they considered essential for a well-ordered community.

Capitall Laws

. . . If any man or woman, shall lye with any beast, or bruite creature by carnall copulation, he, or she, shall surely be put to death, and the beast shall be slaine, buried, and not eaten. . . .

If any man lyeth with mankinde, as a man lyeth with a woman, both of them have committed abomination, they both shall surely be put to death. . . . And if any woman change the naturall use, into that which is against nature, . . . she shall be liable to the same sentence, and punishment, or if any person, or persons, shall commit any other kinde of unnaturall and shamefull filthinesse, called in Scripture the going after strange flesh, or other flesh then God alloweth, by carnall knowledge of another vessel then God in nature hath appointed to become one flesh, whether it be by abusing the contrary part of a grown woman, or child of either sex, or unripe vessel of a girle, wherein the naturall use of the woman is left, which God hath ordained for the propagation of posterity, and Sodomiticall filthinesse (tending to the destruction of the race of mankind) is committed by a kind of rape, nature being forced, though the will were inticed, every such person shall be put to death. Or if any man shall act upon himself, and in the sight of others

spill his owne seed, by example, or counsel, or both, corrupting or tempting others to doe the like, which tends to the sin of Sodomy, if it be not one kind of it; or shall defile, or corrupt himself and others, by any other kind of sinfull filthinesse, he shall be punished according to the nature of the offence; or if the case considered with the aggravating circumstances, shall according to the mind of God revealed in his word require it, he shall be put to death, as the court of magistrates shall determine. Provided that if in any of the former cases, one of the parties were forced, and so abused against his or her will, the innocent person (crying out, or in due season complaining) shall not be punished, or if any of the offending parties were under fourteen year old, when the sin was committed, such person shall onely be severely corrected, as the court of magistrates considering the age, and other circumstances, shall judge meet.

If any man married, or single, commit adultery with a marryed or espoused wife, the adulterer and adulteresse shall surely be put to death. . . .

If any child, or children, above sixteen year old, and of competent understanding, shall curse, or smite, his, her, or their naturall father, or mother, each such child shall be put to death . . . unless it be proved, that the parents have been very unchristianly negligent in the education of such child, or children, or so provoked them by extream and cruell correction, or usage, that they

Excerpted from *Blue Laws of Connecticut,* by John Trumbull (Hartford, CT: John Trumbull, 1878).

have been urged or forced thereunto, to preserve themselves from death or maiming.

If any man have a stubborn rebellious son, of sufficient age and understanding, namely sixteen year old, or upward, which will not obey the voyce of his father, or the voyce of his mother; and that when they have chastned him, will not hearken unto them, then shall his father and his mother (being his naturall parents) lay hold on him, and bring him to the magistrates assembled in court, and testifie unto them, that their son is stubborn and rebellious, and will not obey their voyce and chastisement, but lives in sundry notorious crimes; such a son shall be put to death. . . .

Children's Education

Whereas too many parents and masters, either through an over tender respect to their own occasions, and businesse, or not duly considering the good of their children, and apprentices, have too much neglected duty in their education, while they are young, and capable of learning, it is ordered, That the deputies for the particular court, in each plantation within this jurisdiction for the time being; or where there are no such deputies, the constable, or other officer, or officers in publick trust, shall from time to time, have a vigilant eye over their brethren, and neighbours, within the limits of the said plantation, that all parents and masters, doe duly endeavour, either by their own ability and labour, or by improving such schoolmaster, or other helps and means, as the plantation doth afford, or the family may conveniently provide, that all their children, and apprentices as they grow capable, may through God's blessing, attain at least so much, as to be able duly to read the Scriptures, and other good and profitable printed books in the English tongue, being their native language, and in some competent measure, to understand the main grounds and principles of Christian Religion necessary to salvation. . . .

Divorce, or a Marriage Declared a Nullity, Desertion, &c.

If any marryed person proved an adulterer, or an adulteresse, shall by flight, or otherwise, so withdraw or keep out of the jurisdiction, that the course of justice (according to the mind and law of God here established) cannot proceed to due execution, upon complaint, proof, and prosecution, made by the party concerned, and interessed, a separation or divorce, shall by sentence of the court of magistrates be granted and published, and the innocent party shall in such case have liberty to marry again. . . .

And if any man marrying a woman fit to bear children, or needing and requiring conjugall duty, and due benevolence from her husband, it be found (after convenient forbearance and due tryall) and satisfyingly proved, that the husband, neither at the time of marriage, nor since, hath been, is, nor by the use of any lawfull means, is like to be able to perform or afford the same, upon the wive's due prosecution, every such marriage shall by the court of magistrates, be declared voyd, and a nullity, the woman freed from all conjugall relation to that man, and shall have liberty in due season, if she see cause, to marry another; but if in any such case, deceipt be charged and proved, that the man before marriage knew himself unfit for that relation, and duty, and yet proceeded, sinfully to abuse an ordinance of God, and in so high a measure to wrong the woman, such satisfaction shall be made to the injuried woman, out of the estate of the offendor, and such fine paid to the jurisdiction, as the court of magistrates shall judge meet. But if any husband after marriage, and marriage duty performed, shall by any providence of God be disabled, he falls not under this law, nor any penalty therein. And it is further declared, that if any husband shall without consent, or just cause shewn, willfully desert his wife, or the wife her husband, actually and peremptorily refusing all matrimoniall society, and shall obstinately persist therein, after due means have been used to convince and reclaim, the husband or wife so deserted, may justly seek and expect help and relief. . . .

Marriage

For the preventing of much inconvenience which may grow by clandestine and unlawful marriages: It is ordered, That no persons shal be either contracted, or joyned in marriage before the intention of the parties proceeding therein, hath been three times published, at some time of publick lecture, or town meeting in the town, or towns where the parties, or either of them dwel, or do ordinarily reside; or be set up in writing upon some post of their meeting house door, in publick view, there to stand so as it may be easily read by the space of fovrteen daies; and that no man unless he be a magistrate in this jurisdiction, or expressly allowed by the general court shall marry any persons, and that in a publick place, if they be able to go forth under the penalty of five pounds fine for every such miscarriage.

And the court considering that much sin hath been committed against God, and much inconvenience hath growen to some members of this jurisdiction by the irregular and disorderly carriage of young persons of both sexes, upon purpose or pretence of marriage, did and do order, that whosoever within this jurisdiction shal attempt, or indeavor to inveagle, or draw the affections of any maide, or maide-servant, whether daughter, kinswoman, or in other relation, for himself, or for any other person, without the consent of father, master, guardian, governor, or such other, who hath the present interest, or charge, or (in the absence of such) of the nearest magistrate, whether it be by speech, writing, message, company-keeping, unnecessary familiarity, disorderly night meetings, sinful dalliance, gifts, or any other way, directly or indirectly, every such person (beside all damages which the parent, governor or person intrusted or interested, may sustain by such unlawful proceedings) shall pay to the plantation forty shillings for the first offence; and for the second offence towards the same party four pounds; and for the third offence he shal be further fined, imprisoned, or corporally punished. . . .

And whereas some persons men or women do live, or may come to settle within this colony, whose wives, or husbands are in England or elsewhere, by means whereof they are exposed to great temptations, and some of them live under suspition of uncleanesse, if they do not fal into lewd and sinful courses: It is therefore ordered, That all such persons living within this jurisdiction, shal by the first opportunity, repair to their said relations, (unless such cause be shewen to the satisfaction of the plantation court, that further respite and liberty be given) under the penalty of paying twenty pounds fine, for contempt, or neglect herein. Provided that this order do not extend to such as are, or shal come over to make way for their families, or are in a transient way for traffick, merchandise, or other just occasions for some smal time. . . .

Single Persons

To prevent, or suppress inconvenience, and disorder in the course and carriage of sundry single persons, who live not in service, nor in any family relation, answering the mind of God in the fift commandement: It is ordered, That no single person of either sex, do henceforward board, diet, sojourn, or be permitted so to do, or to have lodging; or house room within any of the plantations of this jurisdiction, but either in some allowed relation, or in some approved family licensed thereunto, by the court, or by a magistrate, or some officer, or officers in that plantation, appointed thereunto, where there is no magistrate; the governor of which family, so licensed, shal as he may conveniently, duly observe the course, carriage, and behaviour, of every such single person, whether he, or she walk diligently in a constant lawful imployment, attending both family duties, and the publick worship of God, and keeping good order day and night, or otherwise.

After reading this selection, consider these questions:

1. What various social interests dictate the education of children?

2. What accounts for the requirement that single people live in families? What does the law say about people living away from their spouses (particularly spouses in England)? In what ways are the two issues similar from the perspective of the New Haven colonists?

SELECTION 4:

A Marriage Contract, 1654

In chapter 4, John C. Miller's essay stresses the economic aspects of courtship and marriage. Keep such issues in mind as you read the following marriage contract, made in Hartford, Connecticut, in 1654.

Whereas I, Joseph Mygatt, of Hartford upon the River and in the jurisdiction of Connecticut in New England, have in the behalf of my son Jacob and at his request made a motion to Mrs. Susanna Fitch, in reference to her daughter Sarah Whiting, that my said son Jacob might with her good liking have free liberty to endeavor the gaining of her said daughter Sarah's affection towards himself in a way of marriage: now this present writing showeth that the said Mrs. Susanna Fitch having consented thereunto, I do hereby promise and engage that if God, in the wide disposition of His providence, shall so order it that my son Jacob and her daughter Sarah shall be contracted together in reference to marriage, I will pay thereupon unto my said son as his marriage portion the full sum of two hundred pounds sterling, upon a just valuation in such pay as shall be to the reasonable satisfaction of the said Mrs. Fitch, and so much more as shall fully equalize the estate or portion belonging to her said daughter Sarah. And do further engage for the present to build a comfortable dwelling house for my said son and her daughter to live in by themselves, as shall upon a true account cost me fifty pounds sterling. And [I] will also give them therewith near the said house one acre of ground planted with apple trees and other fruit trees, which said house, land, and trees shall be and remain to my said son as an addition to his marriage portion,

before mentioned, and to his heirs forever. And I do also further promise and engage that at the day of my death I shall and will leave unto him my said son and his heirs so much estate besides the dwelling house, ground, and trees, before given and engaged, as shall make the two hundred pounds, before engaged and to be paid [at] present, more than double the portion of the said Sarah Whiting. And for the true and sure performance hereof I do hereby engage and bind over my dwelling house and all my lands and buildings in Hartford, with whatsoever estate in any kind is therein and thereupon. And I do further engage that my daughter Mary's portion of one hundred pounds being first paid to her, I will leave to my said son and his heirs forever my whole estate at the day of my death, whatsoever it shall amount unto, and in what way, kind, or place soever it lies, he paying to my wife during her natural life twelve pounds a year, and allowing to her a dwelling entire to herself in the two upper rooms and cellar belonging to my now dwelling house, with the going of half the poultry and a pig for her comfort in each year during her said life; also allowing her the use of half the household stuff during her life, which she shall have power to dispose of to Jacob or Mary at her death, as she shall see cause. And I do further engage that the portion my said son shall have with her daughter Sarah shall (with the good liking of the said Mrs. Susanna Fitch and such friends as she shall advise with) be laid out wholly upon a farm for the sole use and benefit of my said son, her daughter, and their heirs forever. And upon the contraction in reference to marriage I do en-

Excerpted from "Marriage Settlement of Jacob Mygatt, of Hartford, Connecticut," *Collections of the Connecticut Historical Society*, 1912.

gage to jointure her said daughter Sarah in the whole estate or portion my son hath with her, laid out or to be laid out in a farm as aforesaid or otherwise, and in the thirds of his whole estate otherwise, to be to her sole and proper use and benefit during her life and after her death to their heirs forever. And lastly I do engage that the sole benefit of the Indian trade shall be to the sole advantage of my son Jacob, and do promise that I will during my life be [an] assistant and helpful to my said son in the best ways I can, both in his trading with the Indians, his stilling, and otherwise, for his comfort and advantage which I will never bring to any account with him; only I do explain myself and engage that in case my son Jacob shall depart this life before her daughter Sarah, and leave no issue of their bodies, then her said daughter Sarah shall have the full value of her portion left to her, not only for her life as before, but to her as her property to dispose of at her death as she shall see cause, and her thirds in all his other estate for her life, as is before expressed. It being also agreed and consented to that my wife after my decease and during her natural life shall have the use of two milch cows which my son Jacob shall provide for her, she paying the charge of their wintering and summering out of her annuity of twelve pounds a year. In witness whereunto, and to every particular on this and the other side, I have subscribed my name, this 27th of November, 1654.

Witnesses hereunto
John Webster
John Cullick

The mark of J M

John Tallcott

Joseph Mygatt

After reading this selection, consider these questions:

1. How did Joseph Mygatt provide for his wife in the event of his death? How did he provide for the possibility of his son's wife becoming a widow? What conclusions can one draw from these provisions about the social function of the family?

2. What aspirations did Joseph Mygatt and Susanna Fitch hope to achieve through the union of their children?

SELECTION 5:

Solomon Williams's Advice to His Daughters

The Reverend Solomon Williams of Lebanon, Connecticut, jotted down some "advice to my daughters" around 1740. Williams's advice reflected many prevalent ideas about the role of women in marriage and the relationship of women, through their marriages, to the larger community.

Excerpted from *Remarkable Providences,* edited by John Demos (Boston: Northeastern University Press, 1972).

The care of a married woman is to please. And let it be your first and daily care to please God by a conscientious endeavor in all things to obey him, acting for his glory, with a strict eye to his laws and careful observance of all his admonitions, in public, in the family, and in secret. . . .

The next care is to please your husbands, in order to which be inviolably faithful to your conjugal banns. And with strict modesty avoid everything that carries any suspicion of disaffection to him or lightness. Don't affect finery but always neatness. Let your persons be ever neat, and your house and the affairs of it cleanly. Be always pleasant, good-humored, and agreeable in your carriages. Maintain as far as you can the humor of your husbands. Be blind to their failings. If anything falls out disagreeable to you, show not anger or resentment. Bear it with patience, and take the most seasonable opportunity, when you can do it without offence, to intimate your desires in such a way as will make him esteem your prudence and value more your love and tenderness. Never let him think you suspect his judgement or think your own superior, but [rather] that his mistakes spring from want of more time for thought or the common infirmities of mortal man. Be careful to retain his affection. Don't depend on it that because he has sworn to love you he has and will continue to do so, however you behave. But remember the flame of love is to be kept alive by love, the practice of virtue, and your patience, fidelity, neatness, and care to please. When a woman once loses the affection of her husband, or lets him think she has no concern about it, 'tis hard to recover it; and their state will be very indifferent, if not very unhappy.

Treat your husband's friends and such as he values with a frankness and kindness that may discover you are pleased with what pleases him (supposing they be persons of virtue). For if he should be so unhappy as to have other friends, it will [be necessary] for his and your heart to endeavor the best measures and [illegible words] to disengage him from them.

In the economy of your house, never be covetous but always thrifty and prudent. 'Tis not expected that a woman can increase the estate by her labor so much as by her prudent and sensible economy.

If you have children, receive them as God's gift. Love them more for God's sake than your own. And remember your business is to nurse and bring them up for God. Take prudent care for the health of their bodies, that [they] may be sound and robust and employed in such business and exercise as is suitable for them. But take more care of their minds, that they may be formed from their infancy to virtue, religion, and usefulness in the world. Their pride, passions, and wills must be early and always kept under prudent, steady government and restraint. Never let your fondness for them indulge sin, pride, or self-will in them. You will find the best method to effect them will be by careful instruction, diligent employment, a calm, affectionate, dispassionate, steady exercise of your just authority and worthy example. Commit them to God in your daily prayers. If you have servants, treat them justly and kindly. . . . Expect no more of them than is reasonable. Their infirmities and lesser faults 'tis best not to see. Their obstinacy, willfulness, and wickedness fail not to correct and restrain. If from these they will not be reformed, endeavor that they may not dwell in your house. Be courteous to your neighbors. And to your ability be kind to the poor. Be just to all you are concerned with; be forgiving to your enemies, good to your friends, and let the law of kindness be in your heart and lips. By modesty, virtue, . . . piety maintain the dignity of your place. Live in a constant hatred and contempt of the idols of the world and lust of the flesh, lust of the eye, and the pride of life, i.e. sensuality, covetousness, and ambition. Love one another. Love your brethren. And love and thank God in all. . . .

I commend these hints to you, hoping by the blessing [that] they be of use to you. . . . I am your affectionate father, Solomon Williams.

After reading this selection, consider these questions:

1. Discuss Williams's ideas about child rearing.

2. What broader social obligations are inherent in the role of a wife?

3. In *Paradise Lost*, John Milton, the great Puritan poet, described the marriage relationship as "He for God only, she for God in him." How closely does Williams echo Milton's vision?

CHAPTER 4

Men and Women

Most people in colonial America believed that marriage should be governed by social and economic considerations, and that families on both sides should have a major say in forming a union. Puritans, for example, expected the couple to learn to love one another as they conceived and raised children, functioned as a household, and fulfilled their responsibilities in the community. The previous chapter considered marriage as a social institution; however, marriage was, inevitably, far more than that. Whether in Puritan New England or in the southern colonies, marriage was not exclusively a social institution; it was a private relationship between two individuals. Successful marriages seem most often to have involved love; they always involved complex interactions between individuals.

The relationship between husband and wife of course involved sexual intimacy, and procreation was only part of that relationship. Like people in all places and all times, colonists felt sexual desire, and marriage was considered the proper place to express that desire. Despite their reputation as "puritanical," Puritans believed that sexual relations constituted a duty each spouse owed the other and that sex enhanced the marriage. Indeed, impotence constituted grounds for a wife to divorce her husband. Puritans did not condemn or attempt to eliminate sexual expression; rather, they tried to channel it into socially acceptable forms.

Whatever the efforts to control sexuality, human beings remained human beings, and deviance from socially prescribed forms of sexual expression persisted. Although Puritans made adultery a capital crime in New England, capital punishment was rarely imposed. Society dealt more harshly with women who engaged in premarital or extramarital sex than it did with men who committed the same offenses. Nothing, however, could eliminate adultery or sexual deviance entirely. Colonial laws against bestiality and occasional prosecutions of violators testified to the historical continuity of human sexual urges and forms of deviance.

Children learned about sex not only from moral instruction but from observation in small living quarters and in the barnyard. In the home, sex did not have what Laurel Thatcher Ulrich has described as "the ceremonial sanctity of a separate setting." Separate bedrooms were rare in seventeenth-century New England. Typically, family members slept in the same room, though the parents' bed might be partitioned by a curtain. In addition, the practice of sharing beds (for warmth or simply for lack of more than one bed) provided some children with their first exposure to adult sexuality.

As children grew to adulthood they sought out partners for marriage. Church and various social functions, such as barbeques and dances, provided opportunities for young people to meet. As they formed attachments, young men called on young women at their homes. Bundling, a practice that allowed a young man and woman to share a bed (usually fully clothed), provided an opportunity for some degree of sexual experimentation within a confined environment.

Married couples kept house, engaged in sex, had children, and quarreled. Sometimes disagreements escalated, and court records tell of incidents of domestic violence, separation, desertion, and divorce. In all, relations between men and women were no less vexing and no less rewarding than those of today.

After reading this chapter, consider these questions:

1. How did relations between men and women differ in colonial North America from those of today? What accounts for those differences?

2. How did the status of women affect relations between the sexes?

SELECTION 1:

Courtship in Colonial America

In the following excerpt, John C. Miller, a professor of history at Stanford University, describes both the social context in which courtship occurred and the practices of courtship. The British soldier's reaction to bundling testifies to the evolution of different practices and attitudes in different cultures.

Excerpted from *The First Frontier: Life in Colonial America,* edited by John C. Miller (New York: Bantam Dell Publishing Group, 1966).

In colonial America, most parents considered marriage too serious a matter to be left to the young people directly concerned. Because of its financial and social consequences, the choice of a life partner was often made by parents for their offspring—a choice that the young men and women were expected to ratify dutifully. Law and custom required that a suitor make application to the parents for permission to court the young lady. If permission were not forthcoming, the young man proceeded at his peril, for the law was prepared to deal with pertinacious swain who would not take no—from the girl's father rather than from the girl herself—for an answer. Of course, when a dowry was at issue, fathers could discourage unwanted suitors by letting it be known that they intended to withhold financial assistance if their daughters married without parental consent. . . .

To account the world well lost for love was a maxim seldom acted upon by upper-class Americans or those who aspired to enter the upper class. Rather, the principal objectives of marriage were wealth, social position and love—usually in that order. Laced as they were with dowries and jointures, marriages resembled business arrangements more than plighted troths.

The manner in which negotiations were carried on is shown in the following exchange of letters between John Walker and Bernard Moore of Virginia:

May 27, 1764.
Dear Sir: My son, Mr. John Walker, having informed me of his intention of paying his addresses to your daughter Elizabeth, if he should be agreeable to yourself, lady, and daughter, it may not be amiss to inform you what I think myself able to afford for their support in case of an union. My affairs are in an uncertain state; but I will promise one thousand pounds, to be paid in the year 1765, and one thousand pounds to be paid in the year 1766; and the further sum of two thousand pounds I promise to give him, but the uncertainty of my present affairs prevents my fixing on a time of payment. The above sums are all to be in money or lands and other effects at the option of my said son, John Walker.

I am, Sir, your humble servant.
John Walker.

To: Col. Bernard Moore, Esq. in King William.
May 28, 1764.
Dear Sir: Your son, Mr. John Walker, applied to me for leave to make his addresses to my daughter Elizabeth. I gave him leave, and told him at the same time that my affairs were in such a state that it was not in my power to pay him all the money this year that I intended to give my daughter, provided he succeeded; but would give him five hundred pounds next spring, and five hundred pounds more as soon as I could raise or get the money; which sums, you may depend, I will most punctually pay to him. I am, sir, your obedient servant,

Bernard Moore

. . . The long winters and the small and inadequately heated houses of New England and New York created a serious problem for unmarried young men and women. Where could the rites of courtship be performed? The family fireside, around which the entire family usually congregated, was too public for the kind of intimacy the circumstances demanded, yet to remove any distance from its benign glow was apt to chill the ardor of even the most hot-blooded lover. A solution was found in the ancient and parentally approved custom of bundling. A young man and woman, fully clothed, lay down together in bed, crawled under the blankets and exchanged confidences and, insofar as possible, endearments. Bundling was governed by a rigorous code that even the most amorous were expected to observe: "Thus far and no farther" was a motto that might appropriately have been hung at the head of a bed reserved for bundling.

Lieutenant Francis Anbury, a British officer who served in America during the War of Independence, described bundling as he knew it from personal experience:

The night before we came to this town [Williamstown, Mass.] being quartered at a small log hut, I was convinced in how innocent a view the Americans look upon that indelicate custom they call *bundling*. Though they have remarkable good feather beds, and are extremely neat and clean, still I preferred my hard mattress, as being accustomed to it; this evening, however, owing to the badness of the roads, and the weakness of my mare, my servant had not arrived with my baggage at the time for retiring to rest. There being only two beds in the house, I inquired which I was to sleep in, when the old woman replied, "Mr. Ensign," here I should observe to you, that the New England people are very inquisitive as to the rank you have in the army; "Mr. Ensign," says she, "our Jonathan and I will sleep in this, and our Jemima and you shall sleep in that." I was much astonished at such a proposal, and offered to sit up all night, when Jonathan immediately replied, "Oh la! Mr. Ensign, you won't be the first man our Jemima has bundled with, will it Jemima?" when little Jemima, who, by the bye, was a very pretty, black-eyed girl, of about sixteen or seventeen, archly replied, "No, father, not by many, but it will be with the first Britisher" (The name they give to Englishmen). In this dilemma, what could I do? The smiling invitation of pretty Jemima— the eye, the lip, the—Lord ha' mercy, where am I going to? But wherever I may be going now, I did not go to bundle with her—in the same room with her father and mother, my kind *host* and *hostess* too! I thought of that—I thought of more besides—to struggle with the passions of nature; to clasp Jemima in my arms—to—do what? you'll ask—why, to do—nothing! for if amid all these temptations, the lovely Jemima had melted into kindness, she had been outcast from the world—treated with contempt, abused by violence, and left perhaps to perish! No, Jemima; I could have endured all this to have been blest with you, but it was too vast a sacrifice, when you were to be the victim! Suppose how great the test of virtue must, or how cold the American constitution, when this unaccountable custom is in hospitable repute, and perpetual practice.

Bundling began to go out of fashion about the time of the French and Indian War—perhaps because the British soldiers quartered in the colonies did not abide by the rules of the game. Clergymen began to take disapproving note of the practice in their sermons; what had once been regarded as a harmless and comfortable way of courting was stigmatized as a sin. Moreover, the construction of larger and better-heated houses

in New England weakened the case for bundling. And so, after over a century of popularity, the custom was loaded with obloquy and banished from the land. Not until the advent of the automobile did young Americans recover one of the freedoms they had lost in the colonial period.

After bundling fell into disrepute, the Yankees and the Dutch each claimed that they had learned the practice from the other but the young people of both sections were more disposed to praise than to blame the originators. New Englanders also charged that the Dutch used bundling as a cover for sexual irregularities. Certainly the penalties meted out to transgressors against the code of bundling were more severe in New England than in New Netherlands. Among the Puritans, couples who had children a suspiciously short time after marriage were often compelled to confess publicly in church that they had indulged in premarital relations. More easygoing in such matters, the Dutch permitted men and women to live together after they had published the marriage bans.

Death provided almost as much occasion for remarriage as divorce does today. It sometimes happened that a man or woman remarried so soon after the death of his or her partner that they were consoled upon the death of the late lamented and congratulated upon the choice of a successor at the same time. The first marriage celebrated in Plymouth was that between Edward Winslow, a widower of seven weeks standing, and Susanna White, who had lost her husband less than twelve weeks previously. The governor of New Hampshire married a widow ten days after she buried her husband. Before he was forty-seven years old, Samuel Washington, George's brother, had been married five times. Although colonial Americans did not quite attain the multiplicity of wives enjoyed by the patriarchs in Biblical times, they were not far behind their illustrious predecessors in that regard, even though their wives did come in sequence. . . .

Instead of getting on in the world by hard work, thrift and frugality, many young Americans preferred to make their fortune in an easier way—by marrying a rich widow. The high mortality rate ensured a plentiful supply of widows and, since they inherited at least one-third of their deceased husband's estate, many were accounted wealthy by the standards of the time. When a widow remarried, her property passed into the legal possession of her new husband. In consequence, an enterprising young man, provided he did not fear comparison with his predecessor, could set himself up for life by marrying a widow blessed with a sizeable jointure.

For the same reason that an unmarried woman was looked upon as a sad quirk of nature, so confirmed bachelors were thought to shirk their duty to God, the community and womankind. In some colonies, a special tax was levied upon bachelors in order to drive home the lesson that two could live more cheaply than one. Thus American men were presented with a hard choice, between accepting the certain penalties of the law or risking the uncertain penalties of the married state.

So brisk was the demand for widows that some Americans marveled that the maidens ever found husbands. And, indeed, the girls had reason to complain that the widows got the cream of the crop. For example, Thomas Jefferson married a wealthy widow who brought him property worth over $100,000 dollars, including 135 slaves; by this advantageous marriage, Jefferson doubled his estate. In Martha Custis, whom he married seven months after the death of Daniel Custis, Washington landed a rich prize. All of Martha's property was vested in her new husband and he was free to dispose of it as he pleased.

In the pursuit of rich widows, bachelors were given hot competition by widowers. For, by the same token that there were many widows, there were also many widowers; indeed, death, aided by excessive childbearing, tended to cut down in their prime more women than men. Particularly when they were left with the care of small children, widowers were inclined to assume that they had prior claims upon the favors, fortunes and services of widows.

Even so, few girls went unmarried, and most were wives and mothers before they were out of their teens. William Byrd observed that matrimony throve so well in Virginia that "an Old Maid or an Old Bachelor are as scarce among us and reckoned as ominous as a Blazing Star." When his eldest daughter at the age of twenty-three had not found a husband, he was inclined to write her off as an "antique Virgin." He worried lest she become "the most calamitous creature in nature"—an old maid. On the other hand, Byrd might well have rejoiced that his daughter was still alive: his sister, Ursula, married at sixteen, had died in childbirth a year later.

After reading this selection, consider these questions:

1. How does Miller explain the custom of bundling? What evidence does he offer?

2. What made widows attractive as prospective spouses? What drawbacks might there have been to marrying a widow?

3. Modern "blended" families are most often the product of divorce; but given the frequency of the death of one spouse and the remarriage of the surviving spouse, blended families were not uncommon in colonial America. What strains might have resulted from blended families? How would those strains have been similar to those experienced by modern families? How would they have been different?

SELECTION 2:

An Incident in Newbury

In the following passage, Laurel Thatcher Ulrich, a professor of history at Harvard University, narrates an incident that occurred in 1663 and suggests ways to comprehend it. In reading this account, keep in mind that the property rights represented by a woman's chastity were vested not in the woman, but in her parents or her husband. Thus, Henry Greenland's attentions to Mary Rolfe amounted to a trespass on the property rights of John Rolfe. Indeed, soon after his return from the sea, John Rolfe successfully sued Greenland for damages.

It might have been a Restoration comedy. In the spring of 1663 John Rolfe, a Newbury fisherman, went off to Nantucket, leaving behind a comely and "merily disposed" young wife named Mary. Being "a verie loving husband," Rolfe arranged for Mary to "live Cherfully as he thought and want for nothing" in his absence. Betty Webster, a single woman in the neighborhood, agreed to stay with Mary. Betty's stepfather, Goodman John Emery, promised to be a father to both. But Rolfe's careful arrangements proved a snare. No sooner had he sailed out of Newbury harbor than two strangers from old England sailed in. Henry Greenland and John Cordin, physicians and gentlemen, came to lodge at the Emery house.

Mary confided to Betty Webster that "Mr Cording was as pretty a Carriadg man as Ever shee saw in hir life." But Greenland proved more interesting still. He was uninhibited by the pious manners of the Newbury folk. At supper, before Goodman Emery could half finish prayer, "Mr Grenland put on his hatt and spread his napkin and stored the sampe [hominy] and said Com Landlord light supper short grace." Mary was both enticed and troubled by his attentions. When he pulled her toward him by her apron strings, she resisted at first, only giving way, as she said, "to save my apron." One minute she rebuked him for acting "an uncivell part." The next she was laughing and eating samp with him out of one dish and with one spoon.

Late one night Betty was in bed with Mary, who was nursing her baby, when Henry Greenland knocked on the window. Frightened, the women made no answer, "Bettye, Bettye," Greenland called. "Will you let me stand here and starve with the cold?" Betty answered that they were already in bed, that they would not let him in, that they were afraid of him. When he continued to plead, protesting that he "would doe them noe hirt, but desired to smoke a pipe of tobacco," Betty let him in. Still in bed, Mary told her to rake up the fire to give Mr. Greenland some light. While the maid bent over the hearth, Greenland pulled off his clothes and climbed into bed with Mary, who fainted.

"Sir," cried Betty, "what have you done? You have put the woman into a fitt."

"The Devell has such fitts," said Greenland, scrambling out of bed. "It is nothing but a mad fitt."

"What offence have I given that you should speke such words?" Mary exclaimed. Seeing that his conquest was conscious, Greenland jumped back into bed. "Lord help me," she cried.

Excerpted from *Good Wives: Image and Reality in the Lives of Women in Northern New England, 1650–1750,* by Laurel Thatcher Ulrich (New York: Alfred A. Knopf, 1982). Copyright © 1982 by Laurel Thatcher Ulrich. Reprinted by permission of the publisher.

At that moment Henry Lessenby, a neighbor's servant, just happened to walk by. He had earlier observed Greenland's attentions to Goody Rolfe. Hearing the cry, he ran to the Rolfe door and knocked loudly. "Lye still," whispered Greenland, "for now there are two witnesses, we shall be tried for our lives." But Lessenby was not to be discouraged by silence. He climbed through the window, stumbled into the room in the dark, and felt his way to the bedside. In the dim light from the fireplace he discerned a gentleman's clothes on a box by the bed. Reaching for the pillow, he felt a beard. Just as he suspected, it was Greenland.

Lessenby might have raised a commotion, but he chose instead to act the part of the stage servant who, loving a secret, is drawn through vanity or cupidity into the intrigues of his betters. As he later reported it, "The woman and I went adore [outdoors] to Consider what was best to be done so we thought becas he was a stranger and a great man it was not best to make an up Rore but to let him go way in a private manner."

Here the plot calls for deeper entanglements, for pacts between the gentleman and the maid, half-kept promises whispered on the doorstep in the dark, and finally the return of the cuckolded husband. But this little drama was not enacted on the London stage but in a Massachusetts village. In this case the young wife was rescued by an old wife, the husband was avenged, and the denouement was played in the county court. Goody Rolfe had a pious mother and an observant sister. At meeting on Sunday, Sarah Bishop saw that Mary had been crying and alerted their mother.

Goody Bishop visited the Rolfe house the next morning. As she approached, she met a boy rushing out with a glass—to get liquor for Dr. Greenland, he said. For two hours she sat in the house, watching and observing and waiting for Greenland to leave. Finally she had a chance to question Mary, who seemed to fear telling her mother all that had happened. Mary admitted that the gentleman had "with many Arguments inticed her to the act of uncleanness," but she insisted that "God had hitherto helped her resist him."

"Will you venture to lay under these temptations & concealed wickedness?" exclaimed the mother. "You may Provoak God to Leave you & then you will come under Great Blame."

"I know not what to doe," Mary sighed. "Hee is in Creditt in the Towne, some take him to be godly & say hee hath grace in his face, he have an honest loke, he have such a carrige that he deceive many: It is saide the Governer sent him a letter Counting it a mercy such an Instrument was in the Country, and what shall such a pore young woman as I doe in such a case, my husband being not at home?"

Goody Bishop was troubled. "These things are not to bee kept private," she insisted. "Goodman Emery beeing grand Jury-man must present them." But when confronted, Goodman Emery proved unwilling to act the part of moral guardian. (Had he seen too much "merriness" on Mary's part?) He promised to keep closer watch on Greenland, to lock up the hard drink, and to see that the Doctor stayed home when half drunk, but he felt matters were best kept quiet for the moment. He could see no harm done.

Goody Bishop was not to be soothed by promises. On her way home she encountered *Goody* Emery and explained to her all that had happened. The wife proved more sympathetic than the husband. Together the two women returned to the Rolfe house, pressed Mary and Betty further, and concluded that Greenland's actions had been "more gross" than they had first believed.

"I dare not keep such things as these private upon my owne head," said Mary's mother as the two women parted.

"Doe wisely," answered her friend.

That night, having asked for God's direction, Goody Bishop revealed all that she knew to a "wise man" in the town, asking for his advice. He directed her to the magistrates. Henry Greenland was tried by jury at his own request, perhaps counting on his good reputation in the town, but was convicted of attempted adultery and fined the whopping sum of £30. The citizens of Newbury supported the pious mother against the dazzling stranger. John Rolfe returned from Nantucket avenged.

To understand this village morality play, we must determine the historical meaning of the characters. That they do not represent the classical stage triangle—husband, wife, and lover—is in itself significant. What can we make of a plot which casts a mother as moral guardian, a dashing Englishman as assailant, and a pretty young bride as victim?

One obvious interpretation would make Puritanism the real protagonist. Surely Goody Bishop represents the community surveillance characteristic of the rule of the saints. As Mary Rolfe's mother, she upheld a morality thundered from the pulpit and enforced by the court. As for Henry Greenland, the libertine Englishman, he was a Thomas Morton (or Tom Jones) caught in a society he did not understand, incriminated as much by his attitude as by his acts. How many of his reported boasts—that it didn't matter that he had a wife in England, that Mary need not worry about consequences, that he could afford two wives—were in jest? He insisted that he meant no harm, but in Newbury his carefree words condemned him. In this view, Mary Rolfe hardly matters. The real conflict was between two cultures—Puritan Massachusetts and Merry England.

Yet a close examination of the case suggests that the most serious division was not between the town and the stranger but within the community itself—and perhaps in the mind of Mary Rolfe. Dragged into court by outraged neighbors, John Emery angrily reported that before the fateful night someone had put "fig dust" (tobacco shavings) and pebbles in Greenland's bed. Had Mary Rolfe surreptitiously invited the pretty gentleman to rap on her window and ask for a light? Had Betty Webster or someone else in Emery's family been playing tricks on them both?

Since the 1930s, discussion of sexual behavior in New England has focused on the relationship between religion and repression. Despite the efforts of Edmund S. Morgan to dispel the stereotype of the "sad and sour" saints, historians continue to ask, "How 'Puritan' were the Puritans?" Michael Zuckerman insists they were hostile to the flesh. Philip Greven says that some of them were. For our purposes, the question is badly put. To understand the historical drama in Newbury, one must give less attention to ideology than to gender, taking the characters pretty much at their surface value. Goody Bishop was an old woman. Mary Rolfe was a young woman. Henry Greenland was an aggressive male. The really crucial issues are exposed in the action itself, with all its confusion and apparent inconsistency. Mary Rolfe was obviously attracted to Greenland. She was also afraid of him. She openly flirted with him. At the same time, she was troubled by her own feelings and by the potential consequences of her behavior.

Her dilemma was created by the coexistence in one rural village of a hierarchal social order (by no means limited to New England), a conservative religious tradition (not exclusively Puritan), and sex-linked patterns of sociability (rooted in English folkways). All three elements determined her behavior. Accustomed to deference—to her mother, to her husband, to the selectman next door—she was easily dazzled by the genteel appearance and apparent good name of Greenland. What right had she to question his behavior? Though taught to fear God, she had not yet acquired the kind of confidence in her own sense of right which propelled her mother to challenge both a popular gentleman and a respected neighbor by bringing the case to court. Finally, in her easy compliance with Greenland's initial advances, Mary Rolfe was responding to a lifetime of instruction in femininity. Massachusetts girls, like ordinary Englishwomen everywhere, knew how to light pipes for strangers. . . .

As might be expected, the vocabulary describing the sexual misbehavior of women was richer and more direct than that for men. Even the epithets *cuckold* and *pimp* turn on female rather than on male promiscuity. The opposite of *whore* was rogue, a term which mixed sexual and more general meanings. For a woman, sexual reputation was everything; for a man, it was part of a larger pattern of responsibility. A *whore* bestowed her favors indiscriminately, denying any man exclusive right to her body. A *rogue* tricked or forced a woman into submission with no regard for consequences. The words mirror traditional gender relationships. A woman gave; a man took. Because the female role was in its nature more ambiguous, less clearly active without quite being passive, a woman could lose her reputation simply in being attacked. . . .

So Mary Rolfe smiled when Henry Greenland pulled on her apron strings. She ate out of his dish and laughed at his jokes, and perhaps enjoyed the game of conquest and resistance. When the plot grew more serious, she found herself confused. To call for help would be an admission of complicity. Who would believe her story against a man in credit in the town, especially when everyone knew she was young, pretty, and "often merrily disposed"? Her only recourse was to petition the court and confess herself "a poor young woman and in an aflicted Condition." The same vulnerability which led to her trouble might save her from it.

If the role of Mary Rolfe was clear, so was that of Goody Bishop. She had earned her position through experience. In New England, ultimate authority to police sexual behavior was given to men—to justices, juries, ministers, and elders. In reality, primary responsibility for controlling female sexuality was in the hands of women. The formal role of midwives in fornication cases grew out of a larger and more pervasive system of informal justice. Just as Goody Bishop instinctively turned to Goody Emery in determining her course in response to Henry Greenland, so older women throughout New England acted as advisers, counselors, and ultimately as judges, though sometimes their visible role was intentionally muted. . . .

A hierarchal social structure which made female chastity the property of men, a religious tradition which demanded morality from both sexes, and patterns of feminine behavior rooted in traditional fatalism and in the rhythms of village life—against this backdrop men and women in northern New England played out an old drama of conquest and seduction.

After reading this selection, consider these questions:

1. What does Ulrich mean when she writes that "primary responsibility for controlling female sexuality was in the hands of women"? How does this story bear out her observations?

2. Does this story support or contradict the idea that Puritanism was sexually repressive?

3. Once Mary Rolfe began to flirt with Henry Greenland, what options did she have when he sought to escalate the flirtation?

SELECTION 3:

A Puritan Prescription for a Good Marriage

Benjamin Wadsworth, a minister and one-time president of Harvard, wrote The Well-Ordered Family, or, Relative Duties in 1712, long after the community of saints intended by the Massachusetts Bay Colony had begun to break down. Wadsworth's book deals with social and economic obligations as well, but in the following excerpt, he discusses the personal relationship between husband and wife.

*T*he Duties of Husband and Wives. Concerning the Duties of this Relation, we may assert a few things; and then draw some inferences therefrom. Concerning *Husband and Wife* we may therefore assert.

Tis their duty to cohabit or dwell together with one another. By God's own Ordinances Husband and Wife are brought into the nearest Union and Relation to each other; God's Word calls them one *flesh. . . . A man shall leave his Father and his Mother, and shall cleave to his Wife; and they shall be one flesh. . . . They twain shall be one flesh.* Being thus nearly *United,* surely they should *dwell together. . . .* The Greek word signifies, to *dwell in an house together,* or keep house together. If one house can't hold them, surely they're not affected to each other as they should be. Indeed men's necessary Occasions often call them abroad, and sometimes (Seamen especially) to be absent for many weeks or months together; and when necessity requires such an absence of Husbands from their Wives, there ought to be a willing compliance with the call of Providence. But they should not separate nor live apart, out of disgust, dislike, or out of choice; but should *dwell together* as constantly, as their necessary affairs will permit. . . . The Duties of Husband and Wife one to another, oblige them to dwell together as much as may be: *To avoid fornication, let every man have his own wife; and let every woman have her own husband. Let the Husband render unto the Wife due benevolence, and likewise also the Wife to the Husband. The Wife hath not power of her own body, but the Husband; and likewise also the Husband hath not power of his own Body, but the Wife: Defraud not one the other, that Satan tempt you not for your incontinency.* Thus tis plain from Scripture, that Husband and Wife ought to dwell together; if therefore they quarrel and so live separate from each other, then they sin very greatly, they act quite contrary to God's plain commands. If any have thus done, they ought heartily to repent of it, and fly to the Blood of Jesus for pardon.

Excerpted from *The Well-Ordered Family, or, Relative Duties,* by Benjamin Wadsworth (Boston: Benjamin Wadsworth, 1712).

They should have a very great and tender love and affection to one another. This is plainly commanded by God. *Husbands love your wives, even as Christ also loved the Church.* That is, with a great, steady, constant, operative love. . . . This duty of love is mutual; it should be perform'd by each, to each of them. They should endeavour to have their affections really, cordially and closely knit, to each other. If therefore the *Husband is bitter against his Wife,* beating or striking of her (as some vile wretches do) or in any unkind carriage, ill language, hard words, morose, peevish, surly behavior; nay, if he is not kind, loving, tender in his words and carriage to her, he then shames his profession of Christianity, he breaks the Divine Law, he dishonours God and himself too, by this ill behaviour. The same is true of the *Wife* too. If she strikes her Husband (as some shameless, impudent wretches will), if she's unkind in her carriage, give ill language, is sullen, pouty, so cross that she'l scarce eat or speak sometimes; nay if she neglects to manifest real love and kindness, in her words or carriage either; she's then a shame to her profession of Christianity, she dishonours and provokes the glorious God, tramples his Authority under her feet; she not only affronts her Husband, but also God her Maker, Lawgiver and Judge, by this her wicked behaviour. The indisputable Authority, the plain Command of the Great God, requires Husbands and Wives, to have and manifest very great affection, love and kindness to one another. They should (out of Conscience to God) study and strive to render each others life, easy, quiet and comfortable; to please, gratifie and oblige one another, as far as lawfully they can. When therefore they contend, quarrel, disagree, then they do the Devils work, he's pleas'd at it, glad of it. But such contention provokes God, it dishonours him; it's a *vile example* before Inferiours in the Family; it tends to prevent *Family Prayer. . . .* Though they should *love* one another as has been said, yet let this caution be minded, that they dont love inordinately, because death will soon part them.

They should be chaste, and faithful to one another. The Seventh Commandment requires this. *Thou shalt not commit Adultery.* So the Apostle tells us, the man must have *his own wife,* and the

Woman *her own Husband*. They must have nothing to do with any but their *own*. *Rejoyce with the wife of thy youth, . . . let her Breasts satisfie thee at all times, and be thou ravish'd always with her love. And why wilt thou my Son, be ravish'd with a strange woman, and imbrace the bosome of a stranger? This is the will of God, even your Sanctification, that ye should abstain from fornication; that every one of you, should know how to possess his vessel in sanctification and honour.* As for Christians, their Bodies as well as Souls belong to Christ, and that by special dedication. Tis therefore a most vile aggravated wickedness in those that call themselves Christians (tis bad in any, but worse in them) to commit *fornication* or *adultery. Know ye not that your bodies are the members of Christ? Shall I then take the members of Christ, and make them the members of an harlot? God forbid.* There's a solemn Covenant between *Husband & Wife,* God is witness of it, and observes when any treacherously break it. And he himself will avenge such wickedness.

The Husband and Wife *should be helpful to each other*. The Lord said, it is not good that the man should be alone, I will make *an help meet for him*. The Wife should be a meet help to her Husband; he also should do what he can, to help forward her good and comfort. They should do one another all the good they can.

After reading this selection, consider these questions:

1. Why might Wadsworth have written this book when he did? Is the publication of this manual a sign of religious dominance or of concern about changing behavior and attitudes?

2. Aside from any social arrangement, what (at least according to Wadsworth) constituted a Puritan marriage?

3. Does Wadsworth's prescription for a good marriage bear out Morgan's thesis about Puritans and sex?

SELECTION 4:

The Unhappy Marriage of a Puritan Minister

The diary of the Reverend Jacob Eliot of Lebanon, Connecticut, tells the story of an unhappy marriage. Divorce was neither common nor readily obtainable, and incompatibility was not considered sufficient grounds for divorce. Thus, the Eliots remained together for years. The following excerpt is from 1763.

Excerpted from *Remarkable Providences,* edited by John Demos (Boston: Northeastern University Press, 1972).

Nov. 24. Another quarrel, after having plagued my heart out all the morning, in directing and dictating about all my affairs, charging me with, and often twitting me for, being too honest, neglecting my business much, trusting too much to other folks, not overseeing my own business, nor foreseeing things, events, and dangers as I might and ought, and reflecting as if [I were] incapable of it, etc., till I could bear no longer. I showed some heat and anger (God forgive me) and earnestly begged of her to forbear and not insist upon them things anymore, for it was more than flesh and blood could bear. Or, if she did not, I would complain to her friends and expose her—upon which she flew into the utmost rage and fury again, calling me a cursed Devil, kicked at me, and struck me with her fist again, and took up a powder horn to strike me over the head with. But, defending myself, I warded off the blows, etc. But she protested she would expose me to all the parish, have nothing more to do with me, nor hear me again, as long as she lived, etc. But after a while, on my tamely submitting to hear all the bad stories about first wife, Betty Higley etc., and crying with her, and not carrying to her as before, ever since I saw her etc., and bearing the greatest insults from her, her passion at last subsided.

Decem. 3. Another venged quarrel for nothing but jesting with her about getting her a calico gown in spring, in a cheerly manner suggesting it was a good while to spring, and hadn't she calico gowns enough etc. She took me in earnest and flew into a violent passion and protested [that] she would never ask me for anything again, but would get what she wanted without being beholden to me, that my first wife might have anything she asked for, or my mistress Mrs. Robinson, Betty Higley, or the widow Kellogg. [She] would not go to breakfast with me. (When courted, and the sugar pot offered to take sugar for coffee, [she] refused, saying no, I set it away from her as far as I could at other times, she had long observed, and therefore she would not touch it now.) And when I offered to put sugar in her dish (declaring I was only in jest before, and crying out shame upon her) she said she would not drink any of it if I did, and, further, that if it was from a young man she could take a jest, but not from such a covetous old man as I. And she knew I was in earnest, and that soon after we were married, when she asked me for a few yards of ferret for binding for her riding hood, I refused to let her have it and said she might stay till she had

earned it first etc., which was made out of the whole cloth and as D—h a lie as ever told with tongue, unless I was asleep, or drunk and knew not what I said. At last [she] seemed to get over her passion, but remained muggy a good while.

Decem. 19. Another most V. Q., after long preaching to me upon the old score about doing nothing about settling with Jacob and 1000 bugbears raised about her and Josie being left destitute etc. etc. till I could bear no longer (and it is marvelous I have borne so much). I with some zeal earnestly begged and entreated her to forbear and not trouble me and herself with those things—I intended to take care about them as soon as I could conveniently etc.—on which she flew into her usual, most violent, and uncurbed passion, and with utmost rage and fury and malice cried out "God damn you, leave your devilling, begone out of the house or I will." Upon which I said, "you may go, and you will for I shan't." This she took in a great dudgeon, flung the child into my arms, and went quick out of the room. Patty went after her, but could not find her for a while [and] at last found her in the study closet. Then she came in again, and after Jacob and Patty were gone to bed, protested she would never lie with me again as long as she lived. (Though before they went off, [she] asked Patty for the key of the little chamber, to lie there; I said she should not have it.) Then [we] had a long parley, whether she or I should lie up-chamber. I said I would not and she should not, but earnestly advised her out of compassion to herself and the child, if she had none for me, to go to bed in the study, and I offered to warm it for her, or she might warm it herself, but she refused. And so we sat debating the case for an hour or two, except [for a] great part of the time she, as sullen and surly as a mad bull, would say nothing at all. At last she said that if I would give her my word that I would not come to bed at all to her, she would go to bed (for if I did she would get out again, for she would never have anything more to do with me, for I was no husband to her etc.), to which I (like a fool, for peace sake) consented and submitted, and accordingly warmed the bed for her, and she went to bed in state with the child. And poor Pill Garlick was forced to sit by the fire and expected to do it all night to watch her (tho' were it not for fear she would do herself, or the child, mischief, I would have sent her to Jericho before I would have done it). However, I tamely yielded and built up a good fire for that end. After I sat a while, she bid me go and sit in the kitchen. I told her I hoped she would allow me the liberty of my own fire and not be so cruel to the poor old man as to make him sit in the kitchen such a cold night (and as cold as almost ever known) without fire (for that was raked up), and I would not disturb her. After we had then sat silent a while, she with sovereign authority said, "I command you to go and lie up-chamber." At which I laughed and replied that she had expressly inverted the sacred text now and read it (as the woman did to her blind husband), "Husbands obey your wives." After profound silence again for a while, I at last very lovingly said, "My dear, if you will make up so far as to admit me to bed with you tonight, then if we can't make up matters between ourselves, and you think it worthwhile, we'll refer the case between us to any one indifferent person whom you please on the morrow," to which she faintly consented. Then I raked up the fire and went to bed. She was muggy a while and said she meant I should go to bed up-chamber. [She] advised me to turn my back and not my face to her, but at last partially made up the matter, and we lay peaceably till the morning when we wholly finished the matter and got pretty well reconciled. (Though she had before said she never would be reconciled again, but [would] expose me to the whole parish and go home, and after [being] abed got up twice in her smock to look after me, going into the closet and into the kitchen.) And so the controversy ended for that time.

After reading this selection, consider these questions:

1. What seems to be the most common cause for argument between the Eliots?

2. No one ever lost an argument in his or her own diary. How might the account differ if we had Mrs. Eliot's version?

3. What was the point of Eliot and his wife each threatening to expose the other to the community?

SELECTION 5:

The Married Life of a Virginia Gentleman

By the beginning of the eighteenth century, Virginia had developed a class of landed gentry. Even as they assumed the position of a colonial elite, members of this gentry remained painfully aware of their status as provincials. In many respects, William Byrd II (1674–1744) personified the colonial landed elite. Byrd's father, one of Virginia's wealthiest planters, inherited substantial holdings, married well, and had a good head for business and politics. After spending much of his youth in England, William Byrd II returned to Virginia in 1705 after the death of his father. He married Lucy Parke in 1706. The marriage ended with Lucy's death in 1716. The following document is from the diary Byrd began in 1709.

April 7, 1709

I rose before 6 o'clock and read two chapters in Hebrew and 250 verses in Homer's *Odyssey* and made an end of it. I said my prayers devoutly. I ate milk for breakfast. I danced my dance. The men began to work this day to dig for brick. I settled my accounts and read Italian. I reproached my wife with ordering the old beef to be kept and the fresh beef used first contrary to good management, on which she was pleased to be very angry and this put me out of humor. I ate nothing but boiled beef for dinner. I went away presently after dinner to look after my people. When I returned I read more Italian and then my wife came and begged my pardon and we were friends again. I read in Dr. Lister again very late. I said my prayers. I had good health, good thoughts, and bad humor, unlike a philosopher. . . .

April 9, 1709

I rose at 5 o'clock and read a chapter in Hebrew and 150 verses in Homer. I said my prayers devoutly and ate milk for breakfast. My wife and I had another scold about mending my shoes but it was soon over by her submission. I settled my accounts and read Dutch. I ate nothing but cold roast beef and asparagus for dinner. In the afternoon Mr. Custis complained of a pain in his side for which he took a sweat of snakeroot. I read more Dutch and took a little nap. In the evening we took a walk about the plantation. My people made an end of planting the corn field. I had an account from Rappahannock that the same distemper began to rage there that had been so fatal on the Eastern Shore. I had good health, good thoughts and good humor, thanks be to God Almighty. I said my prayers. . . .

November 2, 1709

I rose at 6 o'clock and read a chapter in Hebrew and some Greek in Lucian. I said my prayers and ate milk for breakfast, and settled some accounts, and then went to court where we made an end of the business. We went to dinner about 4 o'clock and I ate boiled beef again. In the evening I went to Dr. [Barret's] where my wife came this afternoon. Here I found Mrs. Chiswell, my sister Custis, and other ladies. We sat and talked till about 11 o'clock and then retired to our chambers. I played at [r-m] with Mrs. Chiswell and kissed her on the bed till she was angry and my wife also was uneasy about it, and cried as soon as the company was gone. I neglected to say my prayers, which I should not have done, because I ought to beg pardon for the lust I had for another man's wife. However I had good health, good thoughts, and good humor, thanks be to God Almighty. . . .

July 30, 1710

I rose at 5 o'clock and wrote a letter to Major Burwell about his boat which Captain Broadwater's people had brought round and sent Tom with it. I read two chapters in Hebrew and some Greek in Thucydides. I said my prayers and ate boiled milk for breakfast. I danced my dance. I read a sermon in Dr. Tillotson and then took a little [nap]. I ate fish for dinner. In the afternoon my wife and I had a little quarrel which I reconciled with a flourish. Then she read a sermon in Dr. Tillotson to me. It is to be observed that the flourish was performed on the billiard table. I read a little Latin. In the evening we took a walk about the plantation. I neglected to say my prayers but had good health, good thoughts, and good humor, thanks be to God. . . .

February 5, 1711

I rose about 8 o'clock and found my cold still worse. I said my prayers and ate milk and potatoes for breakfast. My wife and I quarreled about her pulling her brows. She threatened she would not go to Williamsburg if she might not pull them; I refused, however, and got the better of her, and maintained my authority. About 10 o'clock we went over the river and got to Colonel Duke's about 11. There I ate some toast and canary. Then we proceeded to Queen's Creek, where we all found all well, thank God. We ate roast goose for supper. The women prepared to go to the Governor's the next day and my brother and I talked of old stories. My cold grew exceedingly bad so that I thought I should be sick. My sister gave me some sage tea and leaves of [s-m-n-k] which made me mad all night so that I could not sleep but was much disordered by it. I neglected to say my prayers in form but had good thoughts, good humor, and indifferent health, thank God Almighty. . . .

April 30, 1711

I rose at 5 o'clock and said a short prayer and then drank two dishes of chocolate. Then I took my leave about 6 o'clock and found it very cold. I met with nothing extraordinary in my journey and got home about 11 o'clock and found all well, only my wife was melancholy. We took a walk in the garden and pasture. We discovered that by the contrivance of Nurse and Anaka Prue got in at the cellar window and stole some strong beer and cider and wine. I turned Nurse away upon it and punished Anaka. I ate some fish for dinner. In the afternoon I caused Jack and John to be whipped for drinking at John [Cross] all last Sunday. In the evening I took a walk about the plantation and found things in good order. At night I ate some bread and butter. I said my prayers and had good health, good thoughts, and good humor, thank God Almighty. The weather was very cold for the season. I gave my wife a powerful flourish and gave her great ecstasy and refreshment. . . .

December 31, 1711

I rose about 7 o'clock and read a chapter in Hebrew and six leaves in Lucian. I said my prayers and ate boiled milk for breakfast. The weather continued warm and clear. I settled my accounts and wrote several things till dinner. I danced my dance. I ate some turkey and chine for dinner. In the afternoon I weighed some money and then read some Latin in Terence and then Mr. Mumford came and told me my man Tony had been very sick but he was recovered again, thank God. . . . Then he and I took a walk about the plantation. When I returned I was out of humor to find the negroes all at work in our chambers. At night I ate some broiled turkey with Mr. Mumford and we talked and were merry all the evening. I said my prayers and had good health, good thoughts, and good humor, thank God Almighty. My wife and I had a terrible quarrel about whipping Eugene while Mr. Mumford was there but she had a mind

to show her authority before company but I would not suffer it, which she took very ill; however for peace sake I made the first advance towards a reconciliation which I obtained with some difficulty and after abundance of crying. However it spoiled the mirth of the evening, but I was not conscious that I was to blame in that quarrel.

January 1, 1712

I lay abed till 9 o'clock this morning to bring my wife into temper again and rogered her by way of reconciliation. I read nothing because Mr. Mumford was here, nor did I say my prayers, for the same reason. However I ate boiled milk for breakfast, and after my wife tempted me to eat some pancakes with her. Mr. Mumford and I went to shoot with our bows and arrows but shot nothing, and afterwards we played at billiards till dinner, and when we came we found Ben Harrison there, who dined with us. I ate some partridge for dinner. In the afternoon we played at billiards again and I won two bits. I had a letter from Colonel Duke by H-l the bricklayer who came to offer his services to work for me. Mr. Mumford went away in the evening and John Bannister with him to see his mother. I took a walk about the plantation and at night we drank some mead of my wife's making which was very good. I gave the people some cider and a dram to the negroes. I read some Latin in Terence and had good health, good thoughts, and good humor, thank God Almighty. I said my prayers.

After reading this selection, consider these questions:

1. On February 5, 1711, Byrd and his wife quarreled about her "pulling her brows." Why was this so important? Byrd noted that he "got the better of her and maintained my authority." What was Byrd's concern?

2. After an argument on December 31, 1711, Byrd and his wife engaged in "make-up sex" on the following morning. Although he was always conscious of maintaining his status as a gentleman, Byrd wrote that he "rogered" his wife. Gentlemen did not refer to marital relations in such terms. Why might he have used such coarse language in this context?

CHAPTER 5

Religion

In the first part of the twentieth century, historians such as Vernon Louis Parrington and James Truslow Adams called into question religious belief as a motivator of colonial behavior. Thus, they rejected earlier interpretations that focused on religion and explained the history of colonial New England in economic terms. Beginning in the 1930s, Samuel Eliot Morison, a historian at Harvard, and Perry Miller, who taught English at Harvard, challenged that interpretation. Morison and Miller focused attention once again on the theological and intellectual aspects of Puritanism. In recent years, historians have turned their attention to different issues, such as family structure, community, relations with Native Americans, as well as other elements of life in Puritan New England. In all of these areas, however, ideas, and specifically religious ideas, played an important role.

After Henry VIII broke with the Catholic Church, most people in England practiced a religion not appreciably different from Catholicism. English followers of John Calvin, however, wanted a more Protestant religion. Known as Puritans because they wanted to "purify" the English church, this group became both increasingly dissatisfied and more influential in the last years of the reign of Elizabeth I. The Puritans wanted to abolish what they considered unnecessary ceremony, ritual, and hierarchy—things they associated with Roman Catholicism. Another, smaller, group of religious dissenters known as Separatists believed that the English church was so corrupt that they needed to establish their own, separate congregations.

Elizabeth's successor, James I, disliked Puritans and moved away from Elizabeth's policy of religious tolerance. His son and successor, Charles I, moved still more aggressively against Puritanism. Against this background, a group of Separatists established the first English colony in New England, which they called Plymouth. Subsequent migrations of nonseparatist Puritans settled in the Massachusetts Bay Colony.

Although they left England to find freedom to practice their own version of Christianity, the Puritans, whether Separatist or not, had little tolerance for religious beliefs or practices different from their own. Indeed, disagreements among Puritan settlers resulted in the founding of new colonies. For example, after being banished from the Massachusetts Bay Colony for his religious views, Roger Williams and his followers established the town of Providence. Another outspoken religious dissenter, Anne Hutchinson, was banished as well, but not until her spectacular trial shook the colony. She and her followers relocated in the settlement established by Williams, where they set up a separate community at Portsmouth.

Religion was no less significant in the colonies to the south. The colony of Maryland began as a land grant to the Calverts, a Catholic family who hoped to establish a colony of their coreligionists. Although Catholics did go to Maryland, the colony had a large Protestant majority from its earliest days. This situation led Cecilius Calvert, Lord Baltimore, to agree to a Toleration Act that guaranteed religious freedom to all "professing to believe in Jesus Christ." William Penn, a Quaker, founded a colony as a "Holy Experiement." The Quaker belief in the "inner light" led to a greater degree of religious toleration than in Maryland. Even in Virginia, founded for economic reasons, the Anglican Church and religion played a significant role in the colony's development.

During the 1730s and 1740s, an evangelical revivalist movement known as the Great Awakening swept first through the middle colonies and then spread to the other colonies. In highly emotional sermons, revivalist preachers emphasized salvation through faith and the conversion experience. The Great Awakening had not only profound religious but social consequences as well.

After reading this chapter, consider these questions:

1. How did religion influence social and political developments?

2. To what extent did social and political factors shape religious beliefs and practices?

3. In what ways were marriage and relations with Native Americans, discussed in earlier chapters, influenced by religious ideas?

SELECTION 1:

Anne Hutchinson and Antinomianism

Both in England and in America, Puritans agonized over the path to salvation. John Calvin had taught that at the beginning of time an infinitely powerful God had selected certain individuals for salvation. This presented problems, however, for a society based on Calvin's teachings. If some people had already been elected, they did not need to follow laws made by church or state in order to assure their salvation. Moreover, since most people were damned to hell, they had no reason to behave well. Puritans responded by teaching that, although only a few were saved, all had a responsibility to prepare themselves for God's grace. Besides, they reasoned, though God might not reward all who led virtuous lives, he would surely punish sinners. Some went so far as to argue that God offered his grace to all who would receive it. This went too far for John Cotton, a Puritan minister who emphasized that God's grace was free and absolute. He taught that those who were saved would do good works, but their actions derived from the spirit of God that resided in them. Some thought that Cotton's ideas freed individuals from the duty to adhere to temporal law. The belief that good works could not influence whether one was chosen to be saved and that those chosen for salvation need not be bound by laws of church and state was called Antinomianism and had long been deemed a heresy. One of Cotton's followers, Anne Hutchinson, expressed dissatisfaction with the teaching of local ministers, maintaining that they placed too much emphasis on the role of works in achieving salvation. In doing so, she challenged not only the theology of Boston's established clergy but the role of women in Puritan society as well. The belief that good works alone could win admission to heaven, known as Arminianism, was one of the beliefs associated with the Church of England that Puritans rejected. After a sensational trial, Anne Hutchinson and some of her followers were exiled from the colony. In the following excerpt, Lyle Koehler, a historian affiliated with the University of Cincinnati, focuses on the relationship between Antinomianism and Hutchinson's challenge to male authority.

Excerpted from "The Case of the American Jezebels: Anne Hutchinson and Female Agitation during the Years of Antinomian Turmoil, 1636–1640," by Lyle Koehler, *William and Mary Quarterly,* January 1974. Copyright © 1974 by Lyle Koehler. Reprinted with permission.

That Anne Hutchinson and many other Puritan women should at stressful times rebel, either by explicit statement or by implicit example, against the role they were expected to fulfill in society is readily understandable, since that role, in both old and New England, was extremely limiting. The model English woman was weak, submissive, charitable, virtuous, and modest. Her mental and physical activity was limited to keeping the home in order, cooking, and bearing and rearing children, although she might occasionally serve the community as a nurse or midwife. She was urged to avoid books and intellectual exercise, for such activity might overtax her weak mind, and to serve her husband willingly, since she was by nature his inferior. In accordance with the Apostle Paul's doctrine, she was to hold her tongue in church and be careful not "to teach, nor to usurp authority over the man, but to be in silence." . . .

The female role definition that the Massachusetts ministers and magistrates perpetuated severely limited the assertiveness, the accomplishment, the independence, and the intellectual activity of Puritan women. Bay Colony women who might resent such a role definition before 1636 had no ideological rationale around which they could organize the expression of their frustration —whatever their consciousness of the causes of that frustration. With the marked increase of Antinomian sentiment in Boston and Anne Hutchinson's powerful example of resistance, the distressed females were able—as this article will attempt to demonstrate—to channel their frustration into a viable theological form and to rebel openly against the perpetuators of the spiritual and secular status quo. Paradoxically enough, the values that Antinomians embraced minimized the importance of individual action, for they believed that salvation could be demonstrated only by the individual feeling God's grace within.

The process of salvation and the role of the individual in that process was, for the Puritan divines, a matter less well defined. The question of the relative importance of good works (i.e., individual effort) and grace (i.e., God's effort) in preparing man for salvation and concerned English Puritans from their earliest origins, and clergymen of old and New England attempted to walk a broad, although unsure, middle ground between the extremes of Antinomianism and Arminianism. But in 1636 Anne Hutchinson's former mentor and the new teacher of the Boston church, John Cotton, disrupted the fragile theological balance and led the young colony into controversy when he "warned his listeners away from the specious comfort of preparation and re-emphasized the covenant of grace as something in which God acted alone and unassisted." Cotton further explained that a person could become conscious of the dwelling of the Holy Spirit within his soul and directed the Boston congregation "not to be afraid of the word *Revelation*." The church elders, fearing that Cotton's "Revelation" might be dangerously construed to invalidate biblical law, requested a clarification of his position.

While the elders debated with Cotton the religious issues arising out of his pronouncements, members of Cotton's congregation responded more practically and enthusiastically to the notion of personal revelation by ardently soliciting converts to an emerging, loosely-knit ideology which the divines called pejoratively Antinomianism, Opinionism, or Familism. According to Thomas Weld, fledgling Antinomians visited new migrants to Boston, "especially, men of note, worth, and activity, fit instruments to advance their designe." Antinomian principles were defended at military trainings, in town meetings, and before the court judges. [Governor John] Winthrop charged the Opinionists with causing great disturbance in the church, the state, and the family, and wailed, "All things are turned upside down among us."

The individual hungry for power could, as long as he perceived his deep inner feeling of God's grace to be authentic, use that feeling to consecrate his personal rebellion against the contemporary authorities. Some Boston merchants used it to attack the accretion of political power in the hands of a rural-dominated General Court based on land instead of capital. Some "ignorant and unlettered" men used it to express contempt for the arrogance of "black-coates that have been at the Ninneversity." Some women, as we will see, used it to castigate the authority of the magistrates as guardians of the state, the ministers as guardians of the church, and their husbands as guardians of the home. As the most outspoken of these women, Anne Hutchinson diffused her opinions among all social classes by means of contacts made in the course of her profession of midwifery and in the biweekly teaching sessions she held at her home. Weld believed that Ms. Hutchinson's lectures were responsible for distributing "the venome of these [Antinomian] opinions into the very veines and vitalls of the People in the Country."

Many women identified with Ms. Hutchinson's rebellious intellectual stance and her aggressive spirit. Edward Johnson wrote that "the weaker Sex" set her up as "a Priest" and "thronged" after her. . . . Winthrop blamed Anne for causing "divisions between husband and wife . . . till the weaker give place to the stronger, otherwise it turnes to open contention," and Weld charged the Antinomians with using the yielding, flexible, and tender women as "an Eve, to catch their husbands also." . . .

From late 1636 through early 1637 female resistance in the Boston church reached its highest pitch. At one point, when pastor John Wilson rose to preach, Ms. Hutchinson left the congregation and many women followed her out of the meetinghouse. These women "pretended many excuses for their going out," an action which made it impossible for the authorities to convict them of contempt for Wilson. Other rebels did, however, challenge Wilson's words as he spoke them, causing Weld to comment, "Now the faithfull Ministers of Christ must have dung cast on their faces, and be no better than Legall Preachers, Baals Priests, Popish Factors, Scribes, Pharisees, and Opposers of Christ himselfe."

Included among these church rebels were two particularly active women, Jane (Mrs. Richard) Hawkins and milliner William Dyer's wife Mary, both of whom Winthrop found obnoxious. The governor considered the youthful Ms. Dyer to be "of a very proud spirit," "much addicted to revelations," and "notoriously infected with Mrs. Hutchinson's errors." Ms. Dyer weathered Winthrop's wrath and followed Anne to Rhode Island, but her "addictions" were not without serious consequence. Twenty-two years later she would return to Boston and be hanged as a Quaker. The other of Hutchinson's close female associates, Jane Hawkins, dispensed fertility potions to barren women and occasionally fell into

a trance-like state in which she spoke Latin. Winthrop therefore denounced her as "notorious for familiarity with the devill," and the General Court, sharing his apprehension, on March 12, 1638, forbade her to question "matters of religion" or "to meddle" in "surgery, or phisick, drinks, plaisters, or oyles." Ms. Hawkins apparently disobeyed this order, for three years later the Court banished her from the colony under the penalty of a severe whipping or such other punishment as the judges thought fit.

Other women, both rich and poor, involved themselves in the Antinomian struggle. William Coddington's spouse, like her merchant husband, was "taken with the familistical opinions." Mary Dummer, the wife of wealthy landowner and Assistant Richard Dummer, convinced her husband to move from Newbury to Boston so that she might be closer to Ms. Hutchinson. Mary Oliver, a poor Salem calenderer's wife, reportedly exceeded Anne "for ability of speech, and appearance of zeal and devotion" and, according to Winthrop, might "have done hurt, but that she was poor and had little acquaintance [with theology]." Ms. Oliver held the "dangerous" opinions that the church was managed by the "heads of the people, both magistrates and ministers, met together," instead of the people themselves, and that anyone professing faith in Christ ought to be admitted to the church and the sacraments. Between 1638 and 1650 she appeared before the magistrates six times for remarks contemptuous of ministerial and magisterial authority and experienced the stocks, the lash, the placement of a cleft stick on her tongue, and imprisonment. One of the Salem magistrates became so frustrated with Ms. Oliver's refusal to respect his authority that he seized her and put her in the stocks without a trial. She sued him for false arrest and collected a minimal ten shillings in damages. Her victory was short-lived, however, and before she left Massachusetts in 1650 she had managed to secure herself some reputation as a witch.

Mary Oliver and the other female rebels could easily identify with the Antinomian ideology because its theological emphasis on the inability of the individual to achieve salvation echoed the inability of women to achieve recognition on a sociopolitical level. As the woman realized that she could receive wealth, power, and status only through the man, her father or her husband, so the Antinomian realized that he or she could receive grace only through God's beneficence. Thus, women could have found it appealing that in Antinomianism *both* men and women were relegated vis-á-vis God to the status that women occupied in Puritan society vis-á-vis men, that is, to the status of malleable inferiors in the hands of a higher being. All power, then, emanated from God, raw and pure, respecting no sex, rather than from male authority figures striving to interpret the Divine Word. Fortified by a consciousness of the Holy Spirit's inward dwelling, the Antinomians could rest secure and self-confident in the belief that they were mystic participants in the transcendent power of the Almighty, a power far beyond anything mere magistrates and ministers might muster. Antinomianism could not secure for women such practical earthly powers as sizable estates, professional success, and participation in the church and civil government, but it provided compensation by reducing the significance of these powers for the men. Viewed from this perspective, Antinomianism extended the feminine experience of humility to both sexes, which in turn paradoxically created the possibility of feminine pride, as Anne Hutchinson's dynamic example in her examinations and trials amply demonstrated. . . .

Neither Anne's rebellion nor the rebellion of her female followers was directed self-consciously against their collective female situation or toward its improvement. Specific feminist campaigns for the franchise, divorce reform, female property ownership after marriage, and the like would be developments of a much later era. For Anne Hutchinson and her female associates Antinomianism was simply an ideology through which the resentments they intuitively felt could be focused and actively expressed.

After reading this selection, consider these questions:

1. According to Koehler, what is the connection between Antinomian beliefs and women's dissatisfaction with their status in colonial New England?

2. Some historians have criticized Koehler's analysis for attempting to impose a twentieth-century perspective on seventeenth-century women and issues. Does Koehler seem to do so in this section? If so, is this an appropriate means of comprehending Anne Hutchinson and her followers? If so, why? If not, why not?

SELECTION 2:

Jonathan Edwards and the Great Awakening

Perry Miller, professor of English at Harvard University, wrote extensively about Puritans and Puritanism from the 1930s into the 1950s. The following essay, written in 1952, reflects not only Miller's extensive research and thought about the Puritan experience, but also the concerns of his own day. The Red Scare and the rise of anticommunist senator Joseph McCarthy left Miller, like many intellectuals of the 1950s, suspicious of mass movements. To some extent, the experience of his own time colored his view of the Great Awakening.

Although in the year 1740 some fairly flagrant scenes of emotional religion were being enacted in Boston, it was mainly in the Connecticut Valley that the frenzy raged and whence it spread like a pestilence to the civilized East. The Harvard faculty of that time would indeed have considered the Great Awakening a "crisis," because to them it threatened everything they meant by culture or religion or just common decency. It was a horrible business that should be suppressed and altogether forgotten. . . .

As far as they could see, it was nothing but an orgy of the emotions. They called it—in the lexicon of the Harvard faculty this word conveyed the utmost contempt—"enthusiasm." It was not a religious persuasion: it was an excitement of overstimulated passions that understandably slopped over into activities other than the ecclesiastical and increased the number of bastards in the Valley, where already there were too many. And above all, in the Valley lived their archenemy [Jonathan Edwards], the deliberate instigator of this crime, who not only fomented the frenzy but was so lost to shame that he brazenly defended it as a positive advance in American culture. To add insult to injury, he justified the Awakening by employing a science and a psychological conception with which nothing they had learned at Harvard had prepared them to cope.

It was certainly a weird performance. Edwards delivered his revival sermons—for example the goriest, the one at Enfield that goes by the title "Sinners in the Hands of an Angry God" and is all that most people nowadays associate with his name—to small audiences in country churches. In these rude structures (few towns had yet prospered enough to afford the Georgian churches of the later eighteenth century which are now the charm of the landscape) the people yelled and shrieked, they rolled in the aisles, they crowded up to the pulpit and begged him to stop, they cried for mercy. . . .

Of course, in a short time the opinion of the Harvard faculty appeared to be vindicated. In 1740 Edwards had writhing in the churches not only his own people but every congregation he spoke to, and he dominated the entire region. Ten years later he was exiled, thrown out of his church and town after a vicious squabble (the fight against him being instigated by certain of the first citizens, some of them his cousins, who by adroit propaganda mobilized "the people" against him), and no pulpit in New England would invite this terrifying figure. He had no choice but to escape to the frontier, as did so many misfits in American history. He went to Stockbridge, where he eked out his last years as a missionary to a lot of moth-eaten Indians. Because of the works he produced under these— shall we call them untoward?—circumstances, and because he was still the acknowledged leader of the revival movement, he was invited in 1758 to become president of the College of New Jersey (the present-day Princeton), but he died a few weeks after his inauguration, so that his life really belongs to the Connecticut Valley.

One may well ask what makes such a chronicle of frenzy and defeat a crisis in American history. From the point of view of the social historian and still more from that of the sociologist it was a phenomenon of mass behavior, of which poor Mr. Edwards was the deluded victim. No sociologically trained historian will for a moment accept it on Edwards's terms—which were, simply, that it was an outpouring of the Spirit of God upon the land. And so why should we, today, mark it as a turning-point in our history, especially since thereafter religious revivals became a part of the American social pattern, while our intellectual life developed, on the whole, apart from these vulgar eruptions? The answer is that this first occurrence did actually involve all the interests of the community, and the definitions that arose out of it were profoundly decisive and meaningful. In that perspective Jonathan Edwards, being the most acute definer of the terms on which the revival was conducted and the issues on which it went astray, should be regarded—even by the social historian—as a formulator of propositions that the American society, having been shaken by this experience, was henceforth consciously to observe. . . .

I mean specifically what it did to the conception of the relation of the ruler— political or ecclesiastical—to the body politic. However, before we can pin down this somewhat illusive development, we are confronted with the problem of whether the Great Awakening is properly to be viewed as a peculiarly American phenomenon at all. It would be possible to write about it—as has been done—as merely one variant of a universal occurrence in Western culture. Between about 1730 and 1760 practically all of Western Europe was swept by some kind of religious emotionalism. . . .

Once this international viewpoint is assumed, the American outburst becomes merely one among many—a colonial one at that—and one hesitates to speak about it as a crisis in a history specifically American. What was at work throughout the Western world is fairly obvious: the upper or the educated classes were tired of the religious squabbling of the seventeenth century, and turned to the more pleasing and not at all contentious generalities of eighteenth-century rationalism; the spiritual hungers of the lower classes or of what, for shorthand purposes, we may call "ordinary" folk were not satisfied by Newtonian demonstrations that design in the universe proved the existence of God. Their aspirations finally found vent in the revivals, and in each country we may date the end of a Calvinist or scholastic or, in short, a theological era by the appearance of these movements, and thereupon mark what is by now called the era of Pietism or Evangelicalism.

In this frame of reference, the Great Awakening was only incidentally American. It is only necessary to translate the European language into the local terminology to have an adequate account. In this phraseology, the Great Awakening in New England was an uprising of the common people who declared that what Harvard and Yale graduates were teaching was too academic. This sort of rebellion has subsequently proved so continuous that one can hardly speak of it as a crisis. It is rather a chronic state of affairs. And in this view of it, the uprising of 1740 belongs to the history of the eighteenth century rather than to any account of forces at work only on this continent.

Told in this way, the story will be perfectly true. Because we talk so much today of the unity of Western European culture, maybe we ought to tell it in these terms, and then stop. But on the other hand there is a curiously double aspect to the business. If we forget about Germany and Holland and even England—if we examine in detail the local history of Virginia, Pennsylvania, and New England—we will find that a coherent narrative can be constructed out of the cultural developments in each particular area. The Awakening can be seen as the culmination of factors long at work in each society, and as constituting, in that sense, a veritable crisis in the indigenous civilization.

The church polity established in New England was what today we call Congregational. This meant, to put it crudely, that a church was conceived as being composed of people who could certify before other people that they had a religious experience, that they were qualified to become what the founders called "visible saints." The founders were never so foolish as to suppose that everybody who pretended to be a saint *was* a saint, but they believed that a rough approximation of the membership to the Covenant of Grace could be worked out. A church was composed of the congregation, but these were only the professing Christians. The rest of the community were to be rigorously excluded; the civil magistrate would, of course, compel them to come to the church and listen to the sermon, collect from them a tax to support the preacher, but they could not be actual members. Those who qualified were supposed to have had something happen to them that made them capable—as the reprobate was not—of swearing to the covenant of the church. They were able, as the others were not, *physically* to perform the act.

The basic contention of the founders was that a church is based upon the covenant. Isolated individuals might be Christians in their heart of hearts, but a corporate body could not come into being unless there was this preliminary clasping of hands, this taking of the official oath in the open and before all the community, saying, in effect: "We abide by this faith, by this covenant." In scholastic language, the congregation were the "matter" but the covenant was the "form" of the church. They objected above all things to the practice in England, whereby churches were made by geography; that a lot of people, merely because they resided in Little Willingdon, should make the church of Little Willingdon, seemed to them blasphemy. That principle was mechanical and unreal; there was no spiritual participation in it —no covenant.

That was why they (or at any rate the leaders and the theorists) came to New England. . . .

The essence of their conception was the covenant. As soon as they were disembarked, as soon as they could collect in one spot enough people to examine each other and acknowledge that each seemed visibly capable of taking the oath, they incorporated churches—in Boston, Charlestown, and Watertown, and, even in the first decade, in the Connecticut Valley. But we must always remember that even in those first days, when conviction was at its height, and among so highly selected and dedicated numbers as made up the Great Migration, only about one fifth of the population were found able, or could find themselves able, to take the covenant. The rest of them—with astonishingly few exceptions—accepted their exclusion from the churches, knowing that they were not "enabled" and praying for the grace that might yet empower them.

From that point on, the story may seem somewhat peculiar, but after a little scrutiny it becomes an old and a familiar one: it is what happens to a successful revolution. The New Englanders did not have to fight on the barricades or at Marston Moor; by the act of migrating, they *had* their revolution. Obeying the Biblical command to increase and multiply, they had children—hordes of them. Despite the high rate of infant mortality, these children grew up in New England knowing nothing, except by hearsay and rumor, of the struggles in Europe, never having lived amid the tensions of England. This second generation were, for the most part, good people; but they simply did not have—they could not have—the kind of emotional experience that made them ready to stand up before the whole community and say: "On Friday the 19th, I was smitten while plowing Deacon Jones's meadow; I fell to the earth, and I knew that the grace of God was upon me." . . .

In 1662, the churches of New England convoked a synod and announced that the children of the primitive church members were included in the covenant by the promise of God to Abraham. This solution was called at the time the Halfway Covenant, and the very phrase itself is an instructive demonstration of the New Englanders' awareness that their revolution was no longer revolutionary. These children, they decided, must be treated as members of the church, although they had not had the kind of experience that qualified their fathers. They must be subject to discipline and censures, because the body of the saints must be preserved. But just in case the authorities might be mistaken, they compromised by giving to these children only a "halfway" status, which made them members but did not admit them to the Lord's Supper.

This provision can easily be described as a pathetic, where it is not a ridiculous, device. It becomes more comprehensible when we realize that it was an accommodation to the successful revolution. Second and third generations grow up inheritors of a revolution, but are not themselves revolutionaries.

For the moment, in the 1660's and 1670's, the compromise worked, but the situation got worse. For one thing, New England suffered in King Philip's War, when the male population was decimated. Then, in 1684, the charter of Massachusetts was revoked, and after 1691 the colony had to adjust itself to the notion that its governor was imposed by the royal whim, not by the election of the saints. Furthermore, after 1715 all the colonies were prospering economically; inevitably they became more and more concerned with earthly things—rum, land, furs. On the whole they remained a pious people. . . . Nevertheless, everybody was convinced that the cause of religion had declined. Something had to be done.

As early as the 1670's the ministers had found something they could do: they could work upon the halfway members. They could say to these hesitants: "You were baptized in this church, and if you will now come before the body and 'own' the covenant, then your children can in turn be baptized." Gradually a whole segment of doctrine was formulated that was not in the original theory—which made it possible to address these citizens who were neither outside the pale nor yet snugly inside, which told them that however dubious they might be as saints, visible or invisible, they yet had sufficient will power to perform the public act of "owning the covenant."

With the increasing pressures of the late seventeenth and early eighteenth centuries, the practice of owning the covenant gradually became a communal rite. It was not enough that the minister labored separately with John or Elizabeth to make an acknowledgement the next Sunday: a day was appointed when all the Johns and Elizabeths would come to church and do it in unison, the whole town looking on. It is not difficult to trace through the increasing reenactments of this ceremony a mounting crescendo of communal action that was, to say the least, wholly foreign to the original Puritanism. The theology of the founders conceived of man as single and alone, apart in a corner or in an empty field, wrestling with his sins; only after he had survived this experience in solitude could he walk into the church and by telling about it prove his right to the covenant. But this communal confession—with everybody doing it together, under the urgencies of an organized moment—this was something new, emerging so imperceptibly that nobody recognized it as an innovation (or rather I should say that some did, but they were shouted down) that by the turn of the century was rapidly becoming the focus for the ordering of the spiritual life of the town.

The grandfather of Jonathan Edwards, Solomon Stoddard of Northampton, was the first man who openly extended the practice of renewal of covenant to those who had never been in it at all. In short, when these occasions arose, or when he could precipitate them, he simply took into the church and up to the Lord's Supper everyone who would or could come. He called the periods when the community responded *en masse* his "harvests," of which he had five: 1679, 1683, 1696, 1712, 1718. The Mathers attacked him for so completely letting down the bars, but in the Connecticut Valley his success was envied and imitated.

The Great Awakening of 1740, seen in the light of this development, was nothing more than the culmination of the process. It was the point at which the method of owning the covenant became most widely and exultingly extended, in which the momentum of the appeal got out of hand, and the ministers, led by Jonathan Edwards, were forced by the logic of evolution not only to admit all those who would come, but to excite and to drive as many as possible, by such rhetorical stimulations as "Sinners in the Hands of an Angry God," into demanding entrance.

All of this, traced historically, seems natural enough. What 1740 did was present a number of leading citizens, like the Harvard faculty, with the results of a process that had been going on for decades but of which they were utterly ignorant until the explosion. Then they found themselves trying to control it or censure it by standards that had in fact been out of date for a century, although they had all that while professed them in filial piety. In this sense—which I regret to state has generally eluded the social historian—the Great Awakening was a crisis in the New England society.

Professional patriots, especially those of New England descent, are fond of celebrating the Puritans as the founders of the American tradition of rugged individualism, freedom of conscience, popular education, and democracy. The Puritans were not rugged individualists; they did indeed believe in education of a sort, but not in the "progressive" sense; they abhorred freedom of conscience; and they did not believe at all in democracy. They advertised again and again that their church polity was not democratic. The fact that a church was founded on a covenant and that the minister happened to be elected by the mass of the church—this emphatically did not constitute a democracy. . . . [E]ven though the people did select the person, the office was prescribed; they did not define its functions, nor was it responsible to the will or the whim of the electors. . . .

In other words, the theory of early New England was basically medieval. Behind it lay the conception of an authoritative scheme of things, in which basic principles are set down once and for all, entirely before, and utterly without regard for, political experience. The formulation of social wisdom had nothing to do with the specific problems of any one society. It was not devised by a committee on ways and means. Policy was not to be arrived at by a discussion of strategy—for example (in modern terms), shouldn't we use the atomic bomb now? This sort of argument was unavailing, because the function of government was to maintain by authority that which was inherently—and definably—the true, just, and honest. . . .

What actually came about, through the device of renewing the covenant, was something that in fact completely contradicted the theory. (We must remember that the church was, during this century, not merely something "spiritual," but the institutional center of the organized life.) Instead of the minister standing in his pulpit, saying: "I speak; you keep quiet," he found himself, bit by bit, assuming the posture of pleading with the people: "Come, and speak up." He did not know what was happening. He began to find out only in the Great Awakening, when the people at last and multitudinously spoke up.

The greatness of Jonathan Edwards is that he understood what had happened. But note this carefully. He was not Thomas Jefferson; he did not preach democracy, and he had no interest whatsoever in any social revolution. He was the child of this aristocratic, medieval system; he was born to the purple, to ecclesiastical authority. But he was the man who hammered it home to the people that they *had* to speak up, or else they were lost.

Edwards was a Puritan and a Calvinist. He believed in predestination and original sin . . . Edwards did not submit these doctrines to majority vote, and he did not put his theology to the test of utility. But none of this was, in his existing situation, an issue. Granting all that, the question he had to decide was: What does a man do who leads the people? Does he, in 1740, say with the Winthrop of 1645 that they submit to what he as an ontologist tells them is good, just, and honest?

What he realized (lesser leaders of the Awakening, like Gilbert Tennent, also grasped the point, but none with the fine precision of Edwards) was that a leader could no longer stand before the people giving them mathematically or logically impregnable postulates of the eternally good, just, and honest. . . . By 1740 the leader had to get down amongst them, and bring them by actual participation into an experience that was no longer private and privileged, but social and communal.

After reading this selection, consider these questions:

1. How does Miller's exposition of Puritan governance shed light on the threat that Anne Hutchinson posed?

2. What is Miller's attitude toward religious revivalism?

3. What in Miller's essay reveals his distrust of mass or popular movements? Is Miller any more or less guilty of injecting contemporary political concerns into his historical analysis than Koehler?

4. What connection does Miller make between the Great Awakening and the emergence of political democracy?

SELECTION 3:

The Trial of Anne Hutchinson

Lyle Koehler focuses on the threat Anne Hutchinson posed to male authority. However, Antinomian beliefs challenged the authority of ministers and the civil government as well. If salvation came only as a free gift of God, good works could not win salvation. Further, those elected for salvation were virtually freed from the constraints of church or civil law. Adding to an already highly charged religious dispute, Antinomians accused several ministers of preaching the so-called covenant of works (the belief that good works could win salvation). The accused ministers resented such allegations and denied that they were teaching salvation through good works; rather, they advocated good behavior only as preparation for God's grace. Anne Hutchinson, the wife of a prosperous businessman, arrived in Massachusetts Bay in 1634. Before long, she began to hold religious discussions in her home. In November 1637, the leaders of the Massachusetts Bay Colony banished John Wheelwright, Anne's brother-in-law and a minister whose views were similar to those of John Cotton. The same month, Anne was tried before the General Court. The following is an excerpt from the transcript of her trial.

November 1637. The Examination of Mrs. Ann Hutchinson at the court at Newtown.

Mr. Winthrop governor. Mrs. Hutchinson, you are called here as one of those that have troubled the peace of the commonwealth and the churches here; you are known to be a woman that hath had a great share in the promoting and divulging of those opinions that are causes of this trouble, and to be nearly joined not only in affinity and affection with some of those the court had taken notice of and passed censure upon, but you have spoken divers things as we have been informed very prejudicial to the honour of the churches and ministers thereof, and you have maintained a meeting and an assembly in your house that hath been condemned by the general assembly as a thing not tolerable nor comely in the sight of God nor fitting for your sex, and notwithstanding that was cried down you have continued the same, therefore we have thought good to send for you to understand how things are, that if you be in an erroneous way we may reduce you that so you may become a profitable member here among us, otherwise if you be obstinate in your course that then the court may take such course that you may trouble us no further, therefore I would intreat you to express whether you do not assent and hold in practice to those opinions and factions that have been handled in court already, that is to say, whether you do not justify Mr. Wheelwright's sermon and the petition.

Mrs. Hutchinson. I am called here to answer before you but I hear no things laid to my charge.

Gov. I have told you some already and more I can tell you.

Mrs. H. Name one Sir.

Gov. Have I not named some already?

Mrs. H. What have I said or done?

Excerpted from *The History of the Colony and Province of Massachusetts-Bay,* by Thomas Hutchinson (Cambridge, MA: Harvard University Press, 1936). Copyright © 1936 by the president and fellows of Harvard College. Reprinted with permission.

Gov. Why for your doings, this you did harbour and countenance those that are parties in this faction that you have heard of.

Mrs. H. That's matter of conscience, Sir.

Gov. Your conscience you must keep or it must be kept for you.

Mrs. H. Must not I then entertain the saints because I must keep my conscience.

Gov. Say that one brother should commit felony or treason and come to his brother's house, if he knows him guilty and conceals him he is guilty of the same. It is his conscience to entertain him, but if his conscience comes into act in giving countenance and entertainment to him that hath broken the law he is guilty too. So if you do countenance those that are transgressors of the law you are in the same fact.

Mrs. H. What law do they transgress?

Gov. The law of God and of the state.

Mrs. H. In what particular?

Gov. Why in this among the rest, whereas the Lord doth say honour thy father and thy mother.

Mrs. H. Ey Sir in the Lord.

Gov. This honour you have broke in giving countenance to them.

Mrs. H. In entertaining those did I entertain them against any act (for there is the thing) or what God hath appointed?

Gov. You knew that Mr. Wheelwright did preach this sermon and those that countenance him in this do break a law.

Mrs. H. What law have I broken?

Gov. Why the fifth commandment.

Mrs. H. I deny that for he saith in the Lord.

Gov. You have joined with them in the faction.

Mrs. H. In what faction have I joined with them?

Gov. In presenting the petition.

Mrs. H. Suppose I had set my hand to the petition what then?

Gov. You saw that case tried before.

Mrs. H. But I had not my hand to the petition.

Gov. You have councelled them.

Mrs. H. Wherein?

Gov. Why in entertaining them.

Mrs. H. What breach of law is that Sir?

Gov. Why dishonouring of parents.

Mrs. H. But put the case Sir that I do fear the Lord and my parents, may not I entertain them that fear the Lord because my parents will not give me leave?

Gov. If they be the fathers of the commonwealth, and they of another religion, if you entertain them then you dishonour your parents and are justly punishable.

Mrs. H. If I entertain them, as they have dishonoured their parents I do.

Gov. No but you by countenancing them above others put honor upon them.

Mrs. H. I may put honor upon them as the children of God and as they do honor the Lord.

Gov. We do not mean to discourse with those of your sex but only this; you do adhere unto them and do endeavor to set forward this faction and so you do dishonour us.

Mrs. H. I do acknowledge no such thing neither do I think that I ever put any dishonour upon you.

Gov. Why do you keep such a meeting at your house as you do every week upon a set day?

Mrs. H. It is lawful for me so to do, as it is all your practices and can you find a warrant for yourself and condemn me for the same thing? . . .

Gov. . . . . If your meeting had answered to the former it had not been offensive, but I will say that there was no meeting of women alone, but your meeting is of another sort for there are sometimes men among you.

Mrs. H. There was never any man with us.

Gov. Well, admit there was no man at your meeting and that you was sorry for it, there is no warrant for your doings, and by what warrant do you continue such a course?

Mrs. H. I conceive there lyes a clear rule in Titus, that the elder women should instruct the younger and then I must have a time wherein I must do it.

Gov. All this I grant you, I grant you a time for it, but what is this to the purpose that you Mrs. Hutchinson must call a company together from their callings to come to be taught of you?

Mrs. H. Will it please you to answer me this and to give me a rule for them I will willingly submit to any truth. If any come to my house to be instructed in the ways of God what rule have I to put them away?

Gov. But suppose that a hundred men come unto you to be instructed will you forbear to instruct them?

Mrs. H. As far as I conceive I cross a rule in it.

Gov. Very well and do you not so here?

Mrs. H. No Sir for my ground is they are men.

Gov. Men and women all is one for that, but suppose that a man should come and say Mrs. Hutchinson I hear that you are a woman that God hath given his grace unto and you have knowledge in the word of God I pray instruct me a little, ought you not to instruct this man?

Mrs. H. I think I may. Do you think it not lawful for me to teach women and why do you call me to teach the court?

Gov. We do not call you to teach the court but to lay open yourself.

Mrs. H. I desire you that you would then set me down a rule by which I may put them away that come unto me and so have peace in so doing.

Gov. You must shew your rule to receive them.

Mrs. H. I have done it.

Gov. I deny it because I have brought more arguments than you have. . . .

Dep. Gov. [Thomas Dudley] I would go a little higher with Mrs. Hutchinson. About three years ago we were all in peace. Mrs. Hutchinson from that time she came hath made a disturbance, and some that came over with her in the ship did inform me what she was as soon as she was landed. I being then in place dealt with the pastor and teacher of Boston and desired them to enquire of her, and then I was satisfied that she held nothing different from us, but within half a year after, she had vented divers of her strange opinions and had made parties in the country, and at length it comes that Mr. Cotton and Mr. [Henry] Vane [an ally of the Antinomians, who was elected governor in 1636 and lost to Winthrop the following year] were of her judgment, but Mr. Cotton hath cleared himself that he was not of that mind, but now it appears by this woman's meeting that Mrs. Hutchinson hath so forestalled the minds of many by their resort to her meeting that now she hath a potent party in the country. Now if all these things have endangered us as from that foundation and if she in particular hath disparaged all our ministers in the land that they have preached a covenant of works, and only Mr. Cotton a covenant of grace, why this is not to be suffered, and therefore being driven to the foundation and it being found that Mrs. Hutchinson is she that hath depraved all the ministers and hath been the cause of what is fallen out, why we must take away the foundation and the building will fall.

Mrs. H. I pray Sir prove it that I said they preached nothing but a covenant of works.

Dep. Gov. Nothing but a covenant of works, why a Jesuit may preach truth sometimes.

Mrs. H. Did I ever say they preached a covenant of works then?

Dep. Gov. If they do not preach a covenant of grace clearly, then they preach a covenant of works.

Mrs. H. No Sir, one may preach a covenant of grace more clearly than another, so I said.

D. Gov. We are not upon that now but upon position.

Mrs. H. Prove this then Sir that you say I said.

D. Gov. When they do preach a covenant of works do they preach truth?

Mrs. H. Yes Sir, but when they preach a covenant of works for salvation, that is not truth.

D. Gov. I do but ask you this, when the ministers do preach a covenant of works do they preach a way of salvation?

Mrs. H. I did not come hither to answer to questions of that sort.

D. Gov. Because you will deny the thing.

Mrs. H. Ey, but that is to be proved first.

D. Gov. I will make it plain that you did say that the ministers did preach a covenant of works.

Mrs. H. I deny that.

D. Gov. And that you said they were not able ministers of the new testament, but Mr. Cotton only.

Mrs. H. If ever I spake that I proved it by God's word.

After reading this selection, consider these questions:

1. What did Anne Hutchinson do or say that posed such a threat to the Massachusetts Bay Colony?

2. What, if any, law did Hutchinson break?

3. Does anything in Hutchinson's testimony support Lyle Koehler's thesis that she was rejecting male authority?

SELECTION 4:

Justification by Faith Alone

Jonathan Edwards was perhaps the most powerful preacher of the Great Awakening and certainly one of the most original theologians of his time. He attacked the growing materialism of the community and new doctrines of easy salvation for all. His sermons stressed the absolute sovereignty of God, the necessity of experiencing a sense of election (Puritans believed that God informed those who had been chosen to be saved), and salvation by God's grace alone. Beginning in the mid-1730s, he led a religious revival that focused on the younger members of his congregation in Northampton, Massachusetts. The following sermon, from the mid-1730s, argues his case for the absolute sovereignty of God and salvation by God's grace alone.

The Scripture treats of this doctrine, as a doctrine of very great importance. That there is a certain doctrine of justification by faith, in opposition to justification by the works of the law, that the Apostle Paul insists upon as of the greatest importance, none will deny; because there is nothing in the Bible more apparent. . . .

The adverse scheme lays another foundation of man's salvation than God hath laid. I do not now speak of that ineffectual redemption that they suppose to be universal, and what all mankind are equally the subjects of; but I say, it lays entirely another foundation of man's actual, discriminating salvation, or that salvation, wherein true Christians differ from wicked men. We suppose the foundation of this to be Christ's worthiness and righteousness: on the contrary, that scheme supposes it to be men's own virtue; even so, that this is the ground of a saving interest in Christ itself. It takes away Christ out of the place of the bottom stone, and puts in men's own virtue in the room of him: so that Christ himself in the affair of distinguishing, actual salvation, is laid upon this foundation. And the foundation being so different, I leave it to every one to judge whether the difference between the two schemes consists only in punctilios of small consequence. The foundations being contrary, makes the whole scheme exceeding diverse and opposite: the one is a gospel scheme, the other a legal one.

It is in this doctrine that the most essential difference lies between the covenant of grace and the first covenant. The adverse scheme of justification supposes that we are justified by our works. . . .

I am sensible the divines of that entirely disclaim the Popish doctrine of merit; and are free to speak of our utter unworthiness, and the great imperfection of all our services: but after all, it is our virtue, imperfect as it is, that recommends men to God, by which good men come to have a saving interest in Christ, and God's favor, rather than others; and these things are bestowed in testimony of God's respect to their goodness. So that whether they will allow the term *merit* or no, yet they hold, that we are accepted by our own merit . . .

It is no gospel at all; it is law: it is no covenant of grace, but of works: it is not an evangelical, but a legal doctrine. . . .

Excerpted from *The Works of President Edwards,* by Jonathan Edwards (New York: Jonathan Edwards, 1844).

This is the main thing that fallen men stood in need of divine revelation for, to teach us how we that have sinned may come to be again accepted of God; or, which is the same thing, how the sinner may be justified. Something beyond the light of nature is necessary to salvation chiefly on this account. Mere natural reason afforded no means by which we could come to the knowledge of this, it depending on the sovereign pleasure of the Being that we had offended by sin. . . .

The contrary scheme of justification derogates much from the honor of God and the Mediator. I have already shown how it diminishes the glory of the Mediator, in ascribing that to man's virtue and goodness, which belongs alone to his worthiness and righteousness.

By the apostle's sense of the matter it renders Christ needless: Gal. v. 4, "Christ is become of no effect to you, whosoever of you are justified by the law." If that scheme of justification be followed in its consequences, it utterly overthrows the glory of all the great things that have been contrived, and done, and suffered in the work of redemption. Gal. ii. 21, "If righteousness come by the law, Christ is dead in vain." It has also been already shown how it diminishes the glory of divine grace (which is the attribute God hath especially set himself to glorify in the work of redemption); and so that it greatly diminishes the obligation to gratitude in the sinner that is saved: yea, that in the sense of the apostle, it makes void the distinguishing grace of the gospel. Gal. v. 4, "Whosoever of you are justified by the law, ye are fallen from grace." It diminishes the glory of the grace of God and the Redeemer, and proportionably magnifies man: it makes him something before God, when indeed he is nothing: it makes the goodness and excellency of fallen man to be something, which I have shown are nothing. I have also already shown, that it is contrary to the truth of God in the threatening of his holy law, to justify the sinner for his virtue. And whether it were contrary to God's truth or no, it is a scheme of things very unworthy of God, that supposes that God, when about to lift up a poor, forlorn malefactor, condemned to eternal misery for sinning against his Majesty, out of his misery, and to make him unspeakably and eternally happy, by bestowing his Son and himself upon him, as it

were, sets all this to sale, for the price of his virtue and excellency. I know that those we oppose do acknowledge, that the price is very disproportionate to the benefit bestowed; and say, that God's grace is wonderfully manifested in accepting so little virtue, and bestowing so glorious a reward for such imperfect righteousness. But seeing we are such infinitely sinful and abominable creatures in God's sight, and by our infinite guilt have brought ourselves into such wretched and deplorable circumstances, and all our righteousnesses are nothing, and ten thousand times worse than nothing (if God looks upon them as they be in themselves), is it not immensely more worthy of the infinite majesty and glory of God, to deliver and make happy such poor, filthy worms, such wretched vagabonds and captives, without any money or price of theirs, or any manner of expectation of any excellency or virtue in them, in any wise to recommend them? Will it not betray a foolish, exalting opinion of ourselves, and a mean one of God, to have a thought of offering any thing of ours, to recommend us to the favor of being brought from wallowing, like filthy swine, in the mire of our sins, and from the enmity and misery of devils in the lowest hell, to the state of God's dear children, in the everlasting arms of his love, in heavenly glory; or to imagine that that is the constitution of God, that we should bring our filthy rags, and offer them to him as the price of this?

The opposite scheme does most directly tend to lead men to trust in their own righteousness for justification, which is a thing fatal to the soul. . . .

But this scheme does directly teach men to trust in their own righteousness for justification; in that it teaches them that this is indeed what they must be justified by, being the way of justification that God himself has appointed. So that if a man had naturally no disposition to trust in his own righteousness, yet if he embraced this scheme, and acted consistent with it, it would lead him to it.

After reading this selection, consider these questions:

1. How does Edwards support his contention that the covenant of works limits the power of God and "renders Christ needless"?

2. What in Edwards's message might appeal to younger members of the community, particularly those facing limited economic opportunities?

3. After the religious fervor died down, the leading families of Northampton voted to remove Edwards from the pulpit. What in his preaching led to his ouster?

SELECTION 5:

Benjamin Franklin Recalls a Sermon by George Whitfield

In his autobiography, Benjamin Franklin recalls hearing a sermon by the great revivalist preacher George Whitfield. Although he heard Whitfield preaching in 1739, Franklin did not begin writing his autobiography until 1771, and it took almost two decades to complete. By his own account, Franklin did not share Whitfield's religious views, but Franklin's detached, ironic account nevertheless bears witness to Whitfield's power as a preacher.

In 1739 arrived among us from England the Rev. Mr. Whitfield, who had made himself remarkable there as an itinerant preacher. He was at first permitted to preach in some of our churches; but the clergy, taking a dislike to him, soon refused him their pulpits, and he was obliged to preach in the fields. The multitudes of all sects and denominations that attended his sermons were enormous, and it was matter of speculation to me, who was one of the number, to observe the extraordinary influence of his oratory on his hearers and how much they admired and respected him, notwith-

standing his common abuse of them, by assuring them they were naturally "half beasts and half devils." It was wonderful to see the change soon made in the manners of our inhabitants; from being thoughtless or indifferent about religion, it seemed as if all the world were growing religious, so that one could not walk thro' the town in an evening without hearing psalms sung in different families of every street. And it being found inconvenient to assemble in the open air subject to its inclemencies, the building of a house to meet in was no sooner proposed and persons appointed to receive contributions, but sufficient sums were soon received to procure the ground and erect the building which was one hundred feet long and seventy broad, about the size of Westminster Hall; and the work was carried on

Excerpted from *Benjamin Franklin: The Autobiography and Other Writings,* edited by L. Jesse Lemisch (New York: New American Library, 1961).

with such spirit as to be finished in a much shorter time than could have been expected. Both house and ground were vested in trustees expressly for the use of any preacher of any religious persuasion who might desire to say something to the people of Philadelphia, the design in building not being to accommodate any particular sect but the inhabitants in general, so that even if the Mufti of Constantinople were to send a missionary to preach Mahometanism to us, he would find a pulpit at his service.

Mr. Whitfield, in leaving us, went preaching all the way thro' the Colonies to Georgia. The settlement of that province had lately been begun; but instead of being made with hardy, industrious husbandmen accustomed to labour, the only people fit for such an enterprise, it was with families of broken shopkeepers and other insolvent debtors, many of indolent and idle habits, taken out of the gaols—who, being set down in the woods, unqualified for clearing land and unable to endure the hardships of a new settlement, perished in numbers, leaving many helpless children unprovided for. The sight of their miserable situation inspired the benevolent heart of Mr. Whitfield with the idea of building an orphan house there in which they might be supported and educated. Returning northward he preached up this charity and made large collections; for his eloquence had a wonderful power over the hearts and purses of his hearers, of which I myself was an instance. I did not disapprove of the design, but as Georgia was then destitute of materials and workmen and it was proposed to send them from Philadelphia at a great expence, I thought it would have been better to have built the house here and brought the children to it. This I advised, but he was resolute in his first project and rejected my counsel, and I thereupon refused to contribute. I happened soon after to attend one of his sermons, in the course of which I perceived he intended to finish with a collection, and I silently resolved he should get nothing from me. I had in my pocket a handful of copper money, three or four silver dollars, and five pistoles in gold. As he proceeded, I began to soften and concluded to give the coppers. Another stroke of his oratory made me ashamed of that and determined me to give the silver; and he finished so admirably that I emptied my pocket wholly into the collector's dish, gold and all. At this sermon there was also one of our club, who being of my sentiments respecting the building in Georgia and suspecting a collection might be intended, had by precaution emptied his pockets before he came from home; towards the conclusion of the discourse, however, he felt a strong desire to give and applied to a neighbour who stood near him to borrow some money for the purpose.

After reading this selection, consider these questions:

1. Franklin recorded this account several decades after the actual event. What impact might this lapse in time have had on his account?

2. What is Franklin's attitude toward revivalists and revivalism?

3. In what ways does Franklin's account indicate that the Great Awakening served as an early unifying experience for the American colonists?

UNIT 2

The Age of the American Revolution

CONTENTS

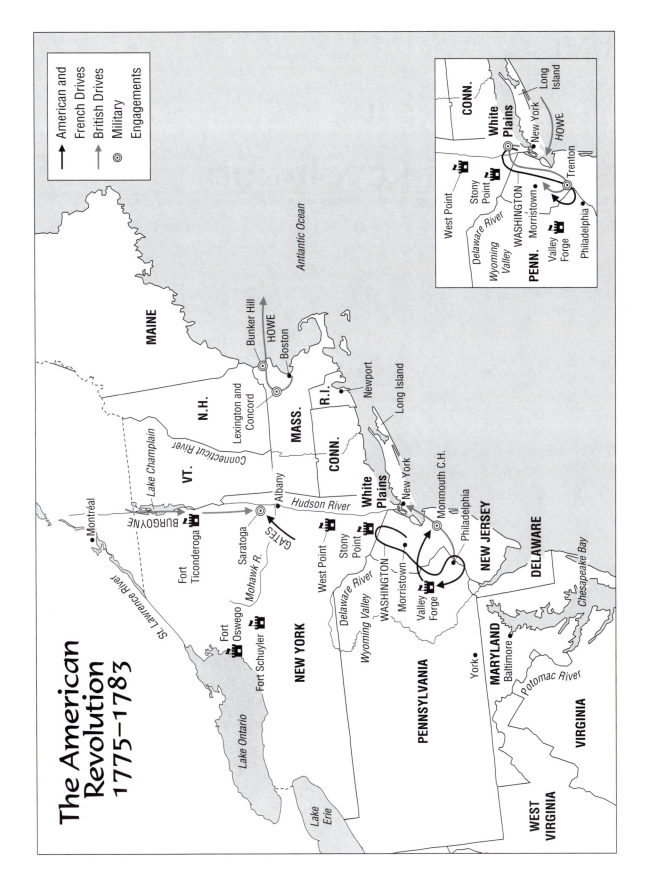

The American Revolution 1775–1783

Legend:
- American and French Drives
- British Drives
- ◎ Military Engagements

Unit 2

The Age of the American Revolution

A series of colonial wars in the mid–eighteenth century expanded and solidified English control of large areas of North America and substantially eliminated threats from Spain and France. These wars and the expanded territorial holdings that resulted from them necessitated a reorganization of the British Empire, which, in turn, led to friction between England and its colonies in North America. The colonies had become accustomed to a large degree of autonomy, and many in the colonies had come to regard that autonomy as a right. Thus, England's efforts to raise revenue from the colonies to help provide for the maintenance of the empire generated growing opposition in America.

The assorted grievances against Great Britain coalesced into a revolutionary ideology that argued for the elimination of monarchy and hereditary titles as well as independence from Britain. Leaders, not to mention followers, of the revolutionary movement concluded that the basis of government should be the consent of the governed. Although the founders of the American republic drew on a variety of sources, including classical republicanism and their own self-interests, the ideology of the Whig opposition in Great Britain provided a basis for the emergence of a powerful revolutionary ideology.

The American Revolution both resulted from and gave impetus to larger social changes underway in the colonies. Thanks to abundant land and a scarcity of labor, the hierarchical British social system had never really taken root in America. Some of the same factors led to the diminishment of paternal authority in the second half of the eighteenth century. Increasing secularization of society and the revolutionary movement combined to alter the decisions young adults made about careers. Service in the Revolution produced a more egalitarian attitude in many common soldiers. The dislocations of the war and dissatisfaction with government policies gave rise to popular discontent, which alarmed many leaders

106

of the movement for independence. This, in turn, led to calls for a more powerful national government.

For women, the American Revolution opened doors. Although traditional roles remained in force, women did take on new responsibilities. Women took up the cause of independence, and, when war came, they managed farms and businesses while husbands or fathers fought in the army. Women also spoke out more on political topics. With the establishment of the new republic, women's education became a higher priority, and some courts took a more sympathetic view of women's property rights. Basically, however, women gained little in the way of economic or political rights during the Revolutionary and early national eras.

For African Americans and Native Americans, the Revolution had different implications. Although African Americans supported and fought for American independence, most slaves, particularly those living south of New England, sided with Great Britain. British promises of freedom to slaves who ran away and fought for the king attracted thousands. At the same time, however, egalitarian Revolutionary rhetoric caused many whites to reconsider the institution of slavery. Even though the Constitution accorded recognition to the institution of slavery, Northern states either abolished or provided for the gradual abolition of the institution.

Native Americans sided with the British in most instances. Some tribes had been allies of Great Britain during the colonial wars of midcentury, and Great Britain provided a check on American westward expansion. With American victory in the war for independence, an armed new nation cast its eyes westward. Moreover, since most tribes had sided with the British, Americans tended to regard them as enemies. Even those tribes who supported American independence, however, were not immune to the territorial demands of the new nation. Indian tribes and leaders adopted different approaches to deal with the threat to their lands and ways of life.

For all of the social consequences of the American Revolution, the most striking result was the creation of a new nation and the founding of the first modern republic. After a brief and unsatisfactory experience with the Articles of Confederation, leaders from twelve states gathered in Philadelphia to revamp the national government. The Constitution they drafted established the American federal system, a marvel of checks and balances. It reflected the influences of American Revolutionary ideology, the Revolutionary experience, the experiment with the Articles of Confederation, and the interests of the framers. In his closing speech to the Constitutional Convention, Benjamin Franklin concluded, "Thus I consent, Sir, to the Constitution, because I expect no better, and because I am not sure that it is not the best."

The Constitution met and surpassed Franklin's expectations. The genius and flexibility of that document is revealed by its status today as the oldest instrument of government still in use.

After reading this unit, consider these questions:

1. How did the American colonial experience give rise to an ideology capable of initiating and sustaining a revolution?

2. In what ways did social developments in the colonies lead to a drive for independence?

3. What was the impact of the American Revolution on gender roles?

4. How did the Revolution affect African Americans and Native Americans?

CHAPTER 6

Ideology

Great Britain emerged from the Great War for Empire (referred to in its American theater as the French and Indian War and in its European theater as the Seven Years' War) with a significantly expanded and more secure empire in the Western Hemisphere. Victory, however, had its costs. The new, larger dominion would cost more to protect and to administer. Moreover, the English government had spent an enormous amount on the war, much of which it had borrowed. The cost of servicing and retiring the debt, combined with the expense of maintaining the expanded empire, exceeded what British taxpayers could reasonably be expected to bear. Britain thus turned to the colonies to help pay for the costs of maintaining the empire.

Up to this point, Great Britain had granted the American colonies a considerable amount of freedom to determine their own affairs, something many in the colonies had come to regard as a right. Thus, British attempts to tighten imperial controls and to raise money in America to help pay for the cost of maintaining the empire inevitably generated resentment among Americans. The Sugar Act of 1764 led to an outcry in America. A number of pamphlets published in the North American colonies argued that Parliament had no right to tax Americans because the colonists had no direct representation in Parliament. The Stamp Act of 1775 further inflamed opinion in America and led many in the colonies to conclude that their rights as English citizens had been violated.

Americans then, as now, did not like paying taxes, and high taxes only added to the misery caused by the depression after the Seven Years' War. What transformed a particular set of grievances into revolutionary movement was a set of assumptions and beliefs shared by many leaders in the colonies. Americans believed that they possessed the rights of Englishmen, including the protection of the English constitution and common law. The unwritten English constitution consisted of a set of traditions that included the principle of shared power. According to those traditions, the power to tax lay exclusively with the representatives of the people. Thus, although many leaders in America conceded the right of Parliament to regulate trade, some held that only the colonial assemblies had the power to levy domestic taxes on the colonies.

What emerged as a powerful revolutionary ideology derived from many sources. In England, radical Whigs had long warned that the distribution of power established by the English constitution was being subverted by kings and ministers who sought to expand royal authority. The radical Whigs had only a limited appeal in England, but they found a receptive audience in the American colonies, where their works were widely available. The religious ideas of the Puritans and the political experience of the various colonies also contributed to the outlook of American revolutionaries. However, it was the ideas of the radical Whigs that gave potentially revolutionary beliefs and notions coherence and a larger meaning.

Thus, events combined with an evolving set of ideas to form a powerful ideology, one that would shape a set of grievances into a basis for revolution.

After reading this chapter, consider these questions:

1. What tensions within the British Empire led to the split between the colonies and England?

2. What role did ideology play in the coming of the American Revolution?

3. How important was the colonists' sense of themselves as Englishmen in moving them from resistance to rebellion?

SELECTION 1:

Anglicization and the Colonial Bar

In the following excerpt, John M. Murrin, a professor of history at Princeton University, argues that the American colonies became increasingly and more self-consciously English from the middle of the eighteenth century, a process he describes as "Anglicization." He further maintains that this process of Anglicization helped bring about and then shaped the American Revolution. Murrin focuses his attention on the legal profession in Massachusetts. The Puritan founders of the colony had no use for lawyers and actually prohibited pleading for hire. However, the complexity of imperial trade created a demand for skilled lawyers. Further, as it became evident that a career in the law could provide a means to obtain imperial offices, the number of lawyers began to increase, and men of higher social standing began to enter the profession. The bar became more professionalized, and professionalized lawyers banded together in an effort to maintain standards and limit access to the profession. This highly professionalized and Anglicized bar provided a striking number of leaders for the Revolutionary movement.

Between 1686 and 1702 the court system of Massachusetts was altered drastically. The Dominion of New England imposed unwanted changes on the colony from outside which Massachusetts repudiated during the Glorious Revolution. Yet in a series of legislative enactments between 1692 and 1702, the General Court adopted practically the entire court system of the hated Dominion. Colonial courts designed to implement Puritan or "American" law yielded to a simplified and rationalized structure of English common law courts. Trial by jury, which Puritan magistrates had all but eliminated in criminal cases involving non-capital offenses, revived under steady royal pressure during the first generation under the new charter. . . .

This transformation of the courts within a fifteen-year period was a momentous event in New England history. . . . The legal revolution of the eighteenth century had to go much farther before it could mean much at all. It had to touch the lives and minds and hearts of the men pleading before the courts and passing judgment within them. This task was as difficult as it was fundamental. Unlike the court system, it could not be enacted by statute, and it would take much longer than fifteen years to achieve. But it too was done. By the eve of the Revolution, the judges and lawyers of Massachusetts were more self-consciously English than they had ever been before.

The Puritans never allowed their reverence for law to betray them into respect for lawyers, men who profited by the distress of others and who found occupational reasons for encouraging disputes, and hence litigation, within the community. Article 26 of the Body of Liberties of 1641 prohibited anyone from accepting a fee to assist another in court. . . . [T]he legislature omitted this restriction from the Code of 1648, but in 1663 it again displayed its old suspicion by barring from a seat in the legislature any person "who is an usual and Common Attorney in any Inferior Court.". . .

The major break with tradition came during the brief rule of . . . [Sir Edmund] Andros. In 1686 the new Superior Court or governor's council conceded to attorneys, not just the right to exist, but even a kind of professional status as officers of the court when it initiated the practice of licensing them. Soon a qualified professional arrived from New York only to remind the province how pleasant things had been without him. . . .

[T]his change became permanent under the new charter. The various acts establishing courts between 1692 and 1699 grudgingly yielded a place for lawyers within the judicial system. When these laws were disallowed, the General Court finally responded in 1701 with a statute devoted exclusively to attorneys. While one clause permitted plaintiff or defendant either to plead his own cause or to accept "the assistance of such other person as he shall procure," another revealed through the low fees it established the province's continuing distrust of . . . [lawyers]. In Massachusetts, so long as the General Court would have its way, attorneys would exist for the welfare of their clients, not clients for the enrichment of their attorneys. . . .

Prejudice against lawyers was powerful in England too, but there the legal corps was sufficiently

Excerpted from *Colonial America: Essays in Politics and Social Development*, by Stanley N. Katz and John M. Murrin (New York: Alfred A. Knopf, 1983). Copyright © 1983 by John M. Murrin. Reprinted with permission.

entrenched within the social system to thrive despite these obstacles.

This was not so in Massachusetts. An old profession can survive community prejudice far more readily than a new profession can establish itself against the same obstacle. Yet in 1708 the General Court reluctantly acknowledged the importance of an attorney to his client when it forbade anyone to employ more than two attorneys in one case, "that the adverse party may have liberty to retain others of them to assist him, upon his tender of the establish'd fee, which," the legislators added sourly, "they may not refuse."

Not surprisingly the provincial bar grew slowly under these accumulated discouragements. Before 1706 three sons of Massachusetts did journey to the Inns of Court to study law, but when they returned to the province they all sought the prestige of the bench rather than the strife of the bar. . . .

For a generation after the Glorious Revolution, the best trained lawyers in Massachusetts earned their livings primarily from other sources than the actual practice of law. . . .

Consequently the regular practice of law fell to a host of "pettifoggers" whose conduct easily confirmed the province's direst fears that life for the lawyers would mean death for the law. In Hampshire County, an ex-tailor, Cornelius Jones, outraged the court with his unmatched talent for postponing the execution of justice. . . .

Lack of numbers among the skilled and lack of skill among the numbers who practiced law left a vacuum which gentlemen amateurs often filled in individual cases, perhaps most often as favors for their friends. A few ministers accepted occasional cases for members of their congregations. . . . Only in the Boston area did standards noticeably improve during the first generation under the new charter, doubtless because the expanding commercial life of the capital created a genuine need for specialized legal talents. One newcomer under Andros, Thomas Newton, had apparently read law in an attorney's office in England.

When Boston overthrew Andros, Newton fled to New York where he became crown prosecutor in the notorious Leisler-Milborne trial of 1691. When Phips and the new charter reached Boston

the following spring, Newton hastened back to Massachusetts just in time to display similar talents as prosecutor in the still more notorious witch trials in Salem, arguing successfully for the admission of spectral evidence. Probably realizing that he had no important competition in Boston, he decided to stay, even when his zeal for the Navigation Acts cost him the office of attorney general, which he failed to regain despite persistent efforts.

Newton, in short, became the first professional lawyer in Massachusetts simply by default. . . . Only [John] Valentine joined Newton as a full-time lawyer and even this situation lasted only until Newton once again became a part-time attorney when he finally obtained the comptrollership of the customs. . . .

Significantly, every talented attorney in this period . . . at one time or another held appointive office under the crown. Just as the crown was the primary engine for transforming the court system of New England, so too would it elevate the bench and bar.

If Newton and Valentine improved the standards of their profession in Boston, both were dead by 1724, and they had trained no successors. At most they had created a demand for competent attorneys, a demand which still had to be filled from outside. But already another transformation had occurred, a development which was considerably more important for both bench and bar. For only after the training of judges had improved could the standards of the bar rise accordingly. And by 1720 the governors, through a series of intelligent appointments, had transformed the character of the Superior Court. . . .

A standard of apprenticeship was slowly emerging. The ideal, typified by Paul Dudley, was a college graduate with years of legal experience, in his case as attorney general rather than as county judge. . . . The quality of associate justices, and also of Inferior Court judges, improved markedly during the same period. . . .

Any body of trained judges will make exacting demands upon the bar. In the case of provincial Massachusetts, this response followed quickly. John Read, an ex-clergyman who had already built a considerable practice in Connecticut, moved to Boston around 1720 where he soon stood preeminent in the profession, after the deaths of Newton (1721) and Valentine (1724). Three other newcomers arrived from Britain between 1716 and 1730. Two possessed thorough legal training, Robert Auchmuty at the Middle Temple and William Shirley at the Inner Temple. Auchmuty . . . apparently inaugurated the practice of accepting understudies in his office, for within a decade he had trained another British immigrant, William Bollan, who built a considerable practice for himself before Shirley's arrival in 1730. Between them, these four engrossed most of the province's legal business in the Superior Court by the early 1730's.

Together the three Britons conclusively demonstrated that a man could open a spectacular career for himself through the practice of law despite the low fees established by the General Court. Auchmuty became judge of vice-admiralty in 1733. Shirley rose to governor within eleven years of his arrival, and Bollan later retired to a profitable mercantile career in England where he served as provincial agent under his father-in-law, Governor Shirley. . . .

As Shirley, Auchmuty, and Bollan dramatically proved, the conscientious practice of law was now a highway to royal favor and patronage.

Accordingly, Massachusetts men began reaching for the opportunities which the new profession offered. . . .

By 1750 the nucleus of a bar existed in every county in the province, except on the islands of Nantucket and Martha's Vineyard. . . .

By the 1740's a college education and several years of apprenticeship in the office of an established attorney, if not yet mandatory requirements, were rapidly becoming normal procedure for the practice of law. . . .

If this achievement was impressive, the steady advance of the next twenty years was phenomenal. . . . Just before the collapse of royal government in 1774, perhaps eighty to ninety lawyers were practicing in Massachusetts. At the same date, the province had about four hundred Congregational clergymen. In other words, the legal profession had grown to a fifth the size of the established ministry, whereas even a generation earlier any comparison between the two would

have been ludicrous. Right down to independence and beyond, English law continued to erode the New England Way. The men who practiced it for a living rejected the ministry and flirted with Anglicanism, or worse still, with deism and skepticism.

Yet size alone barely illustrates the remarkable growth which the bar experienced in the generation before independence. Perhaps even more important were its expanding prestige and its increasing solidarity.

No longer did leading families spurn the profession. . . . There were other signs of creeping respectability. Before 1730, many gentlemen felt qualified to practice law on the side without bothering to study it. A generation later, gentlemen were beginning to study it with no intention of practicing it. . . .

Th[e] movement of lawyers into politics was a significant event in itself, and it occurred within a remarkably short period, roughly the ten years after 1754. . . . In other words, the domination of local politics by lawyers had its beginnings, at least in Massachusetts, less than a generation before the Revolution, which lawyers would largely shape and define. . . .

One acute observer, a young Harvard graduate, brought together all the contradictory tensions, anxieties and aspirations which for a whole generation had been propelling men into the law. . . .

[The] agonizing rejection of New England churches in favor of English law did not drive this man towards a royal governorship or even towards Toryism. Instead it vaulted John Adams towards the presidency of the United States. He too had to become painfully more English before he could help to create a new American nation.

Even if the growing respectability of the law attracted an increasing number of men from the provincial elite, the profession still remained an avenue of upward mobility for less exalted individuals. Adams craved fame, integrity and respectability, and he won more than he ever sought. He was not alone. Thanks to the Revolution, others such as John Lowell, Timothy Pickering, Theodore Sedgwick and Theophilus Parsons could soar to the top, not simply of a small province within an enormous Empire, but of an entire new nation which needed their specialized talents and which gladly paid them the social respect for which they all yearned. Ironically, without the assistance of English courts and English law, they would never have been equipped for their role.

Soon the bar demonstrated that its growing self-consciousness would keep pace with its heightened prestige. With no difficulty at all, it found two targets against which to uncoil the taut spring of its adolescent pride. First it challenged the bench itself. Then it assaulted the amorphous band of "pettifoggers" or semi-professionals who in earlier days had swarmed into the void created by the lack of trained attorneys. . . .

[In 1761, when the new royal governor appointed Lt. Governor Thomas Hutchinson chief justice of the Superior Court, a young lawyer, James Otis Jr., organized a fierce opposition against both of them, partly because he believed his father had been promised the first vacancy on the court.]

Thus began the famous "opening round of the Revolution"—a demand, not to get out of the Empire, but to get into one of its highest offices. The fight over the chief justiceship seriously divided bench and bar. Hutchinson badly needed some issue which would reunite both groups under his own leadership. He soon found an appropriate victim in the pettifoggers still loitering on the fringes of the legal profession.

Until mid-century, many persons with no college education or formal apprenticeship had sought legal careers. Some . . . had won their positions early enough to escape the coming wrath of the professionals. After 1750 such success was extremely rare. It might come to a talented person willing to build his practice in an obscure corner of the province. . . . Or it might flow to someone of incredible dexterity, like Captain Ebenezer Thayer of Braintree. John Adams ransacked his vocabulary in vain search of appellations sufficiently dishonorable to epitomize his townsman, Thayer. Bankruptcy had rewarded the other three Braintree residents who had foully sought to better themselves through pettifoggery, noted Adams with glee, and he lamented that no similar fate would overtake Thayer, who had as-

sured himself of ample routine business from people who could supply it.

Had the pettifoggers encountered no enemy more dangerous than the spleen of Adams, they might have continued to thrive. Not Adams, but Chief Justice Hutchinson decreed otherwise, for he desperately needed the support of the bar. In 1762 Hutchinson decided to cloak the entire profession in exterior dignity by requiring distinct gowns for judges, barristers and attorneys. He also decided to give substance to these different ranks by importing their English prototypes. The lawyers enthusiastically joined the campaign. Even in the 1750's, the county bar had assumed the right to recommend new attorneys to the court. Now in each county the lawyers organized a formal bar association which promptly accepted the English ranking system by establishing minimum requirements for attorneys and barristers.

According to the new standards, a man needed a liberal arts education or its equivalent and three years' apprenticeship with a recognized barrister before he could ask the bar to recommend him to the county court as an attorney. Even then he could practice only in the Inferior Court for the next two years, after which, again subject to the recommendation of the bar, he could be promoted to attorney in the Superior Court. Finally after two more years he could be raised to barrister, the only rank entitled to plead before the Superior Court.

These accumulated developments consciously and effectively shaped the bar along English lines. At the top of the profession stood the judges, corresponding to their English counterparts but lacking the additional title of "sergeant-at-law." Next came the barristers and then the attorneys, two ranks directly imported from the mother country with one significant difference. In Britain these titles denoted permanent ranks within the profession. A man might be either attorney or barrister through his entire career. By contrast the rank of attorney in Massachusetts was a normal first step to the higher rank of barrister, though a permanent corps of attorneys might have been arising by the 1770's. In any case the presumption of mobility still distinguished the province from Great Britain.

A second difference was really a corollary of the first. By the eighteenth century, England had evolved separate methods for training attorneys and barristers. An attorney learned his profession through apprenticeship and was admitted to practice by the courts, but a barrister, who alone could plead in court, studied for three years at one of the Inns and was admitted to practice by the Inn itself. Attorneys were always officers of the courts, but barristers remained members of their Inns.

To some extent, the use of the term "barrister" in Massachusetts reflected a provincial inflation of titles. If Massachusetts barristers copied the function of their English models, they did not undergo the same training. By this standard they were simply attorneys with seven years of apprenticeship instead of three. . . . But by the time the young republic began to establish law schools in the 1790's, the Revolution had already undercut the ideal of England's privileged, hierarchical bar. Consequently these schools produced, not barristers, but American "lawyers."

Similarly, colonial barristers remained officers of the courts, like English attorneys, again because no Inns existed to which they could belong instead. Ultimately the bar association and the bar examination would provide American substitutes for the English Inns. But even before the Revolution, Massachusetts arranged an institutional compromise—a typical New World amalgam of several Old World originals. Through this arrangement the court appointed barristers only upon the recommendation of the bar. Had Massachusetts established a law school before independence, the gap between attorneys and barristers would have widened enormously. But because law schools came only after the Revolution and shared its ideological condemnation of privilege, the effect was just the reverse. Even so, right up to 1776 the trend in Massachusetts was clearly towards increased differentiation between barristers and attorneys.

No longer officially recognized as part of the profession were the remaining pettifoggers, struggling to keep alive beneath the vast superstructure erected by Hutchinson and the bar. By the 1760's these men could not plead in court on either the county or province level. They were reduced to the lowly function of drafting legal documents and scraping up business for established lawyers. . . .

Between 1760 and 1775, the Massachusetts bar consciously restructured itself along English lines. Significantly, a revolutionary movement which was defined and largely dominated by lawyers exploded, not while the profession groped towards something uniquely American, but precisely when it was more belligerently English than it had ever been before.

The relationship between the rise of the bar and the Revolution is one of the strangest paradoxes of early American history. On the one hand most lawyers were Tories. On the other hand, those who were Patriots won control of the movement and gave it consistent intellectual goals. In 1765 the professional lawyer was the intellectual mainstay of the Patriot opposition of the Stamp Act. A decade later he was indispensable to both sides. The greatest Whig-Tory debate in New England did not pit a lawyer against a layman. It matched two lawyers against each other, John Adams and Daniel Leonard.

In 1774 forty-seven barristers were practicing law in Massachusetts, among whom the politics of all but one are ascertainable. Of the forty-six, only fifteen were confirmed Patriots and four were "reluctant Patriots." Nineteen were avowed Tories, of whom seventeen became refugees during the Revolutionary War. Eight others were Tory sympathizers. . . .

A significant correlation appears between a barrister's age and his political leanings. Those who finished college before 1740 divided evenly between Whigs and Tories. No graduate before 1742 became a Tory refugee, probably because the thought of beginning a new career elsewhere was unbearable to an older man. Most Loyalists finished college during the "Tory" administrations of Governors [William] Shirley and [Francis] Bernard. Most Whigs graduated either before Shirley or under Thomas Pownall, the "Patriot" governor. Until 1765, younger men showed pronounced Tory leanings, a clear reflection of the growing power and attraction of the crown between 1741 and 1765.

After 1765 this trend reversed. If one counts both attorneys and barristers of known political leanings, Tories outnumbered Whigs thirteen to seven in the college classes from 1761 to 1765. But among those graduating between 1766 and 1772, Patriots outstripped Loyalists eleven to five. Quite possibly the pronounced Toryism of most young lawyers was a major reason for the sharp decline in new recruits to the profession after the Stamp Act crisis. Certainly the Stamp Act itself is the key to the remarkable shift towards Whiggery among the young men who did venture into the profession after 1765. . . .

In other words, lawyers over fifty-five years of age in 1774 were likely to choose either side. Most of those under thirty became Patriots. But the crown won and held the loyalties of most lawyers between those age limits, which accounted for the vast majority of the lawyers in the province. The[se] lawyers owed their growing prestige to the support of the crown. Without this encouragement, their prestige might wane or even vanish.

The universal unpopularity of the Stamp Act changed everything. Throughout the colonies its major opponents were nearly all lawyers . . . Hence after 1765 new lawyers imitated, not the youthful Tory majority of the profession, but the confident and articulate though small Patriot minority, which became enormously powerful in the next ten years.

This escalation in the importance of the lawyer was by no means peculiar to Massachusetts. It was general throughout the thirteen colonies. Twenty-five of fifty-six signers of the Declaration of Independence were lawyers. So were thirty-one of the fifty-five delegates to the Constitutional Convention. A thorough knowledge of the English constitution and English law provided the colonists with an intellectual basis for unity until they could manufacture their own nationalism to take its place. Without the common heritage of English law, the Carolinians, Virginians, Pennsylvanians, New Yorkers and Yankees who assembled in continental congresses after 1774 would have found embarrassingly little in common to talk about, much less agree upon. They might have revolted; they would hardly have united. Until independence generated its own revolutionary substitute, England remained the only common denominator among Americans[.]

After reading this selection, consider these questions:

1. How did the growing Anglicization of the bar lead to support for rebellion against English rule?

2. How does Murrin explain the fact that lawyers led both the Revolutionary movement and the opposition to it?

SELECTION 2:

The Ideological Origins of the American Revolution

Bernard Bailyn, a professor of history at Harvard University, has been one of the most influential scholars in interpreting the American Revolu-

tion. He has maintained that the Revolution "was above all else an ideological, constitutional, political struggle, and not primarily a controversy between social groups undertaken to force changes in the organization of the society or the economy." In order for the events of the mid–eighteenth century to acquire a meaning that led to resistance against Great Britain, people of that time had to view them in a larger context. Bailyn contends that such a context was provided by an ideology derived in large part from ideas of the British opposition, known variously as radical Whigs, "Commonwealthmen," or "the Country party." In the following selection, Bailyn describes how the ideas of the British government and those of the leaders of the American colonies led to conflict and eventually to revolution.

The colonists had been groping toward this denial of Parliament's power from the beginning of the controversy. For a decade they had been engaged in a remarkable constitutional debate with the British over the nature of the empire. This debate exposed for the first time just how divergent America's previous political experience had been from that of the mother country. By the 1770s the colonists had arrived at a very different understanding of the empire from most Englishmen.

Virtual versus actual representation. With the passage of the Stamp Act, Parliament's first unmistakable tax levy on Americans, American intellectual resistance was immediately raised to the highest plane of principle. "It is inseparably essential to the freedom of a people, and the undoubted rights of Englishmen," the Stamp Act Congress declared in 1765, "that no taxes should be imposed on them, but with their own consent, given personally, or by their representatives." And since "the people of these colonies are not, and from their local circumstances, cannot be represented in the House of Commons in Great Britain," the colonists would be represented and taxed only by persons who were known and chosen by themselves and who served in their respective legislatures. This statement defined the American position at the outset of the controversy, and despite subsequent confusion and stumbling the colonists never abandoned this essential point.

Once the British ministry sensed a stirring of colonial opposition to the Stamp Act, a number of English government pamphleteers set out to explain and justify Parliament's taxation of the colonies. Although the arguments of these writers differed, they all eventually agreed that Americans, like Englishmen everywhere, were subject to acts of Parliament through a system of "virtual" representation. These writers argued that it was this concept of virtual representation, as distinct from actual representation, that gave Parliament its supreme authority—its sovereignty. One government pamphleteer wrote that even though the colonists, like "nine-tenths of the people of Britain," did not in fact choose any representative to the House of Commons, they were undoubtedly "a part, and an important part of the Commons of Great Britain: they are represented in Parliament in the same manner as those inhabitants of Britain are who have not voices in elections."

During the eighteenth century the British electorate made up only a tiny proportion of the nation; probably only one in six British adult males had the right to vote, compared with two out of three in America. In addition Britain's electoral districts were a confusing mixture of sizes and shapes left over from past centuries. Some of the constituencies were large, with thousands of voters, but others were virtually in the pocket of a single great landowner. Many of the electoral districts had few voters, and some so-called rotten boroughs had no inhabitants at all. . . . At the same time, some of England's largest cities, such as Manchester and Birmingham, which had grown suddenly in the mid–eighteenth century, sent no representatives to Parliament. Although radical reformers, among them John Wilkes, increasingly criticized this political structure, parliamentary reform was slow in coming and would not begin until 1832. Many Englishmen justified this hodgepodge of representation by claiming that each member of Parliament represented the whole British nation, and not just the particular locality he came from. . . . According to this view, virtual representation in England was proper and effective not because of the process of election, which was incidental, but rather because of the mutual interests that members of Parliament were presumed to share with all Englishmen for whom they spoke—including those, like the colonists, who did not actually vote for them.

The Americans immediately and strongly rejected these British claims that they were "virtually" represented in the same way that the non-voters of cities like Manchester and Birmingham were. In the most notable colonial pamphlet written in opposition to the Stamp Act, *Considerations on the Propriety of Imposing Taxes* (1765), Daniel Dulany of Maryland admitted the relevance in England of virtual representation, but he denied its applicability to America. For America, he wrote, was a distinct community from England and thus could hardly be represented by members of Parliament with whom it had no common interests. Others pushed beyond Dulany's argument, however, and challenged the very idea of virtual representation. If the people were to be properly represented in a legislature, many colonists said, they not only had to vote directly for the members of the legislature but had to be represented by members whose numbers were proportionate to the size of the population they spoke for. . . .

In the New World, electoral districts were not the products of history that stretched back centuries, but rather were recent and regular creations that were related to changes in population and the formation of new towns and counties. As a consequence many Americans had come to believe in a very different kind of representation from that of the English. Their belief in "actual" representation made election not secondary but central to representation. Actual representation stressed the closest possible connection between the local electors and their representatives. For Americans it was only proper that representatives be residents of the localities they spoke for and that people of the locality have the right to instruct their representatives. Americans thought it only fair that localities be represented in proportion to their population. In short the American belief in actual representation pointed toward the fullest and most equal participation of the people in the process of government that the modern world had ever seen.

The problem of sovereignty. Yet while Americans were denying Parliament's right to tax them because they were not represented in the House of Commons, they knew that Parliament had exercised some authority over their affairs during the previous century. They therefore tried to explain what that authority should be. What was the "due subordination" that the Stamp Act Congress admitted Americans owed Parliament? Could the colonists accept parliamentary legislation but not taxation—"external" customs duties for the purpose of regulating trade, but not "internal" stamp taxes for the purpose of raising revenue? In his famous *Letters from a Farmer in Pennsylvania,* John Dickinson rejected the idea that Parliament could rightly impose "external" or "internal" taxes and made clear that the colonists opposed *all* forms of parliamentary taxation. Dickinson recognized nevertheless that the empire required some sort of central regulatory authority, particularly for commerce, and conceded Parliament's supervisory legislative power so far as it preserved "the connection between the several parts of the British empire." The empire, it seemed to many colonists, was a unified body for some affairs but not for others.

To counter all of these halting and fumbling efforts by the colonists to divide parliamentary authority, the British offered a simple but powerful argument. Since they could not conceive of the empire as anything but a single, unified community, they found absurd and meaningless all these American distinctions between trade regulations and taxation, between "external" and "internal" taxes, and between separate spheres of authority. . . .

What made this British argument so powerful was its basis in the widely accepted doctrine of sovereignty—the belief that in every state there could be only one final, indivisible, and uncontestable supreme authority. This was the most important concept of eighteenth-century English political theory, and it became the issue over which the empire was finally broken.

This idea that, in the end, every state had to have one single supreme undivided authority had been the basis of the British position from the beginning. The British expressed this concept of sovereignty officially in the Declaratory Act of 1766, which, following the repeal of the Stamp Act, affirmed Parliament's authority to make laws binding the colonists "in all cases whatsoever." . . .

By 1773 many Americans despaired of trying to divide what royal officials told them could not be divided. . . . If, as [Massachusetts] Governor [Thomas] Hutchinson had said, there was no middle ground between the supreme authority of Parliament and the total independence of the colonies from Parliament, the House members felt that there could be no doubt that "we were thus independent." The logic of sovereignty therefore forced a fundamental shift in the American position. By 1774 the leading colonists, including Thomas Jefferson and John Adams, were arguing that only the separate American legislatures were sovereign in America. According to this argument Parliament had no final authority over America, and the colonies were connected to the empire only through the king. The most the colonists would concede was that Parliament had the right to regulate their external commerce—"from the necessity of the case, and a regard to the mutual interest of both countries," as the Declarations and Resolves of the First Continental Congress put it. But the British government remained committed to the principle of the Declaratory Act, which no leader of the Revolution could any longer take seriously.

It was now only a matter of time before these irreconcilable positions would be brought to the point of conflict.

After reading this selection, consider these questions:

1. Discuss the relationship between ideas, interests, and events in the coming of the American Revolution.

2. Does Bailyn's emphasis on ideology explain why the Revolution could not have occurred earlier or later?

3. Were the positions of the British government and the American colonists "irreconcilable," according to Bailyn?

SELECTION 3:

Instructions of the Town of Braintree to Their Representative

News of the Stamp Act reached the colonies in April 1765. Even before the law went into effect on November 1, protests against the act sprang up all over the colonies. Opposition was particularly strong in Massachusetts. On October 14 John Adams wrote these instructions for the town of Braintree's representative to the Massachusetts General Assembly. The town meeting adopted them unanimously and without amendment. Adams argued that the Stamp Act was contrary to the English constitution and violated the rights of English citizens.

We hear from Braintree that the freeholders and other inhabitants of that town, legally assembled on Tuesday, the twenty-fourth of September last, unanimously voted that instructions should be given their representative for his conduct in General Assembly on this great occasion. The substance of these instructions is as follows:

TO EBENEZER THAYER, ESQ.

Sir: In all the calamities which have ever befallen this country, we have never felt so great a concern or such alarming apprehensions as on this occasion. Such is our loyalty to the King, our veneration for both houses of Parliament, and our affection for all our fellow subjects in Britain that measures which discover any unkindness in that country towards us are the more sensibly and intimately felt. And we can no longer forbear complaining that many of the measures of the late ministry and some of the late acts of Parliament have a tendency, in our apprehension, to divest us of our most essential rights and liberties. We shall confine ourselves, however, chiefly to the act of Parliament commonly called the Stamp Act by which a very burthensome and, in our opinion, unconstitutional tax is to be laid upon us all, and we subjected to numerous and enormous penalties, to be prosecuted, sued for, and recovered at the option of an informer in a court of admiralty without a jury.

We have called this a burthensome tax because the duties are so numerous and so high and the embarrassments to business in this infant, sparsely-settled country so great that it would be totally impossible for the people to subsist under

it if we had no controversy at all about the right and authority of imposing it. Considering the present scarcity of money, we have reason to think the execution of that act for a short space of time would drain the country of its cash, strip multitudes of all their property, and reduce them to absolute beggary. And what the consequence would be to the peace of the province from so sudden a shock and such a convulsive change in the whole course of our business and subsistence we tremble to consider. We further apprehend this tax to be unconstitutional. We have always understood it to be a grand and fundamental principle of the constitution that no freeman should be subject to any tax to which he has not given his own consent, in person or by proxy. And the maxims of the law, as we have constantly received them, are to the same effect, that no freeman can be separated from his property but by his own act or fault. We take it clearly, therefore, to be inconsistent with the spirit of the common law and of the essential fundamental principles of the British constitution that we should be subject to any tax imposed by the British Parliament, because we are not represented in that assembly in any sense, unless it be by a fiction of law, as insensible in theory as it would be injurious in practice if such a taxation should be grounded on it.

But the most grievous innovation of all is the alarming extension of the power of courts of admiralty. In these courts one judge presides alone! No juries have any concern there! The law and the fact are both to be decided by the same single judge, whose commission is only during pleasure, and with whom, as we are told, the most mischievous of all customs has become established, that of taking commissions on all condemnations, so that he is under a pecuniary temptation always against the subject. Now, if the wisdom of the mother country has thought the independence of

Excerpted from *The Political Writings of John Adams: Representative Selections,* edited by George A. Peek Jr. (Indianapolis: Bobbs-Merrill Company, 1954).

the judges so essential to an impartial administration of justice as to render them independent of every power on earth—independent of the King, the Lords, the Commons, the people, nay, independent in hope and expectation of the heir-apparent, by continuing their commissions after a demise of the crown, what justice and impartiality are we at three thousand miles distance from the fountain to expect from such a judge of admiralty? . . . We cannot help asserting, therefore, that this part of the act will make an essential change in the constitution of juries, and it is directly repugnant to the Great Charter itself; for by that charter, "no amerciament shall be assessed but by the oath of honest and lawful men of the vicinage;" and, "no freeman shall be taken, or imprisoned, or disseized of his freehold, or liberties of free customs, nor passed upon, nor condemned, but by lawful judgment of his peers, or by the law of the land." So that this act will "make such a distinction and create such a difference between" the subjects in Great Britain and those in America as we could not have expected from the guardians of liberty in "both."

As these, sir, are our sentiments of this act, we, the freeholders and other inhabitants, legally assembled for this purpose, must enjoin it upon you to comply with no measures or proposals for countenancing the same or assisting in the execution of it, but by all lawful means, consistent with our allegiance to the King and relation to Great Britain, to oppose the execution of it till we can hear the success of the cries and petitions of America for relief.

We further recommend the most clear and explicit assertion and vindication of our rights and liberties to be entered on the public records, that the world may know in the present and all future generations that we have a clear knowledge and a just sense of them, and, with submission to Divine Providence, that we never can be slaves.

After reading this selection, consider these questions:

1. What specific rights under the English constitution does Adams claim are violated by the Stamp Act?

2. How does Adams's argument relate to the ideological conflict discussed in Bernard Bailyn's selection?

3. In what ways does Adams's statement support John M. Murrin's thesis?

SELECTION 4:

Thomas Jefferson on Independence

By August 25, 1775, when Thomas Jefferson wrote this letter to John Randolph, the king's attorney general in Virginia and a Loyalist who had decided to depart for England, shots had already been exchanged at Lexington, Concord, and Bunker Hill.

Excerpted from *The Portable Thomas Jefferson,* edited by Merrill D. Peterson (New York: Penguin Press, 1983).

I am sorry the situation of our country should render it not eligible to you to remain longer in it. I hope the returning wisdom of Great Britain will e'er long put an end to this unnatural contest. There may be people to whose tempers and dispositions contention may be pleasing, and who may therefore wish a continuance of confusion. But to me it is of all states, but one, the most horrid. My first wish is a restoration of our just rights; my second a return of the happy period when, consistently with duty, I may withdraw myself totally from the public stage and pass the rest of my days in domestic ease and tranquillity, banishing every desire of afterwards even hearing what passes in the world. Perhaps ardour for the latter may add considerably to the warmth of the former wish. Looking with fondness towards a reconciliation with Great Britain, I cannot help hoping you may be able to contribute towards expediting this good work. I think it must be evident to yourself that the ministry have been deceived by their officers on this side the water, who (for what purposes I cannot tell) have constantly represented the American opposition as that of a small faction, in which the body of the people took little part. This you can inform them of your own knolege to be untrue. They have taken it into their heads too that we are cowards and shall surrender at discretion to an armed force. The past and future operations of the war must confirm or undeceive them on that head. I wish they were thoroughly and minutely acquainted with every circumstance relative to America as it exists in truth. I am persuaded this would go far towards disposing them to reconciliation. Even those in parliament who are called friends to America seem to know nothing of our real determinations. I observe they pronounced in the last parliament that the Congress of 1774 did not mean to insist rigorously on the terms they held out, but kept something in reserve to give up; and in fact that they would give up everything but the article of taxation. Now the truth is far from this, as I can affirm, and put my honor to the assertion; and their continuance in this error may perhaps have very ill consequences. The Congress stated the lowest terms they thought possible to be accepted in order to convince the world they were not unreasonable. They gave up the monopoly and regulation of trade, and all the acts of parliament prior to 1764, leaving to British generosity to render these at some future time as easy to America as the interest of Britain would admit. But this was before blood was spilt. I cannot affirm, but have reason to think, these terms would not now be accepted. I wish no false sense of honor, no ignorance of our real intentions, no vain hope that partial concessions of right will be accepted may induce the ministry to trifle with accomodation till it shall be put even out of our own power ever to accomodate. If indeed Great Britain, disjoined from her colonies, be a match for the most potent nations of Europe with the colonies thrown into their scale, they may go on securely. But if they are not assured of this, it would certainly be unwise, by trying the event of another campaign, to risque our accepting a foreign aid which perhaps may not be obtainable but on a condition of everlasting avulsion from Great Britain. This would be thought a hard condition to those who still wish for reunion with their parent country. I am sincerely one of those, and would rather be in dependance on Great Britain, properly limited, than on any nation upon earth, or than on no nation. But I am one of those too who rather than submit to the right of legislating for us assumed by the British parliament and which late experience has shewn they will so cruelly exercise, would lend my hand to sink the whole island in the ocean.

If undeceiving the minister as to matters of fact may change his dispositions, it will perhaps be in your power by assisting to do this, to render service to the whole empire, at the most critical time certainly that it has ever seen. Whether Britain shall continue the head of the greatest empire on earth, or shall return to her original station in the political scale of Europe depends perhaps on the resolutions of the succeeding winter. God send they may be wise and salutary for us all!

I shall be glad to hear from you as often as you may be disposed to think of things here. You may be at liberty I expect to communicate some things consistently with your honor and the duties you will owe to a protecting nation. Such a communication among individuals may be mutually beneficial to the contending parties. On this or any future occasion if I affirm to you any facts, your knolege of me will enable you to decide on their credibility; if I hazard opinions on the dispositions of men, or other speculative points, you can only know they are my opinions. My best wishes for your felicity attend you wherever you go, and beleive me to be assuredly Your friend & servt.

After reading this selection, consider these questions:

1. What is Jefferson's position on independence at this point?

2. In what ways are Jefferson's positions similar to those of John Adams?

3. How does Jefferson assess the power relationship between Great Britain and the American colonies?

SELECTION 5:

Common Sense

Even after the shooting began at Lexington, Concord, and Bunker Hill, most Americans professed to be fighting for their rights as English citizens, not for separation from Great Britain. A forty-seven-page pamphlet by Thomas Paine helped change that. Published in January 1776, Common Sense sold an estimated 120,000 copies in only three months. A far greater number of people undoubtedly read the pamphlet. Paine, who had failed to find success as a corset maker, a customs inspector, and a schoolmaster, had arrived from England only a year before publication of his great pamphlet.

I draw my idea of the form of government from a principle in nature, which no art can overturn, viz. that the more simple any thing is, the less liable it is to be disordered, and the easier repaired when disordered; and with this maxim in view, I offer a few remarks on the so much boasted constitution of England. That it was noble for the dark and slavish times in which it was erected is granted. When the world was over-run with tyranny the least remove therefrom was a glorious rescue. But that it is imperfect, subject to convulsions, and incapable of producing what it seems to promise, is easily demonstrated.

Excerpted from *Common Sense,* edited by Isaac Kramnick (New York: Penguin Press, 1984).

Absolute governments (tho' the disgrace of human nature) have this advantage with them, that they are simple; if the people suffer, they know the head from which their suffering springs, know likewise the remedy, and are not bewildered by a variety of causes and cures. But the constitution of England is so exceedingly complex, that the nation may suffer for years together without being able to discover in which part the fault lies, some will say in one and some in another, and every political physician will advise a different medicine.

I know it is difficult to get over local or long standing prejudices, yet if we will suffer ourselves to examine the component parts of the English constitution, we shall find them to be the base remains of two ancient tyrannies, compounded with some new republican materials.

First.—The remains of monarchical tyranny in the person of the king.

Secondly.—The remains of aristocratical tyranny in the persons of the peers.

Thirdly.—The new republican materials, in the persons of the commons, on whose virtue depends the freedom of England.

The two first, by being hereditary, are independent of the people; wherefore in a *constitutional sense* they contribute nothing towards the freedom of the state.

To say that the constitution of England is a *union* of three powers reciprocally *checking* each other, is farcical, either the words have no meaning, or they are flat contradictions.

To say that the commons is a check upon the king, presupposes two things.

First.—That the king is not to be trusted without being looked after, or in other words, that a thirst for absolute power is the natural disease of monarchy.

Secondly.—That the commons, by being appointed for that purpose, are either wiser or more worthy of confidence than the crown.

But as the same constitution which gives the commons a power to check the king by withholding the supplies, gives afterwards the king a power to check the commons, by empowering him to reject their other bills; it again supposes that the king is wiser than those whom it has already supposed to be wiser than him. A mere absurdity! . . .

Some writers have explained the English constitution thus; the king, say they, is one, the people another; the peers are an house in behalf of the king; the commons in behalf of the people; but this hath all the distinctions of an house divided against itself; and though the expressions be pleasantly arranged, yet when examined they appear idle and ambiguous; and it will always happen, that the nicest construction that words are capable of, when applied to the description of some thing which either cannot exist, or is too incomprehensible to be within the compass of description, will be words of sound only, and though they may amuse the ear, they cannot inform the mind, for this explanation includes a previous question, viz. *How came the king by a power which the people are afraid to trust, and always obliged to check?*

Such a power could not be the gift of a wise people, neither can any power, *which needs checking,* be from God; yet the provision, which the constitution makes, supposes such a power to exist. . . .

That the crown is this overbearing part in the English constitution needs not be mentioned, and that it derives its whole consequence merely from being the giver of places and pensions is self-evident, wherefore, though we have been wise enough to shut and lock a door against absolute monarchy, we at the same time have been foolish enough to put the crown in possession of the key.

The prejudice of Englishmen, in favour of their own government by king, lords, and commons, arises as much or more from national pride than reason. Individuals are undoubtedly safer in England than in some other countries, but the *will* of the king is as much the *law* of the land in Britain as in France, with this difference, that instead of proceeding directly from his mouth, it is handed to the people under the most formidable shape of an act of parliament. For the fate of Charles the First, hath only made kings more subtle—not more just.

Wherefore, laying aside all national pride and prejudice in favour of modes and forms, the plain truth is, that *it is wholly owing to the constitution of the people, and not to the constitution of the government* that the crown is not as oppressive in England as in Turkey.

An inquiry into the *constitutional errors* in the English form of government is at this time highly necessary; for as we are never in a proper condition of doing justice to others, while we continue under the influence of some leading partiality, so neither are we capable of doing it to ourselves while we remain fettered by any obstinate prejudice. And as a man, who is attached to a prostitute, is unfitted to choose or judge of a wife, so any prepossession in favour of a rotten constitution of government will disable us from discerning a good one. . . .

Volumes have been written on the subject of the struggle between England and America. Men of all ranks have embarked in the controversy, from different motives, and with various designs; but all have been ineffectual, and the period of debate is closed. Arms, as the last resource, decide the contest; the appeal was the choice of the king, and the continent hath accepted the challenge. . . .

By referring the matter from argument to arms, a new era for politics is struck; a new method of thinking hath arisen. All plans, proposals, &c. prior to the nineteenth of April, *i.e.* to the commencement of hostilities, are like the almanacks of the last year; which, though proper then, are superceded and useless now. Whatever was advanced by the advocates on either side of the question then, terminated in one and the same point, viz. a union with Great Britain; the only difference between the parties was the method of effecting it; the one proposing force, the other friendship; but it hath so far happened that the first hath failed, and the second hath withdrawn her influence. . . .

I have heard it asserted by some, that as America hath flourished under her former connexion with Great Britain that the same connexion is necessary towards her future happiness, and will always have the same effect. Nothing can be more fallacious than this kind of argument. We may as well assert, that because a child has thrived upon milk, that it is never to have meat; or that the first twenty years of our lives is to become a precedent for the next twenty. But even this is admitting more than is true, for I answer roundly, that America would have flourished as much, and probably much more, had no European power had any thing to do with her. The commerce by which she hath enriched herself are the necessaries of life, and will always have a market while eating is the custom of Europe.

But she has protected us, say some. That she hath engrossed us is true, and defended the continent at our expence as well as her own is admitted, and she would have defended Turkey from the same motive, viz. the sake of trade and dominion.

Alas, we have been long led away by ancient prejudices, and made large sacrifices to superstition. We have boasted the protection of Great Britain, without considering, that her motive was *interest* not *attachment;* that she did not protect us from *our enemies* on *our account,* but from *her enemies* on *her own account,* from those who had no quarrel with us on any *other account,* and who will always be our enemies on the *same account.* Let Britain wave her pretensions to the continent, or the continent throw off the dependance, and we should be at peace with France and Spain were they at war with Britain. The miseries of Hanover last war ought to warn us against connexions. . . .

But Britain is the parent country, say some. Then the more shame upon her conduct. Even brutes do not devour their young, nor savages make war upon their families; wherefore the assertion, if true, turns to her reproach; but it happens not to be true, or only partly so, and the phrase *parent* or *mother country* hath been jesuitically adopted by the [king] and his parasites, with a low papistical design of gaining an unfair bias on the credulous weakness of our minds. Europe, and not England, is the parent country of America. This new world hath been the asylum for the persecuted lovers of civil and religious liberty from *every part* of Europe. Hither have they fled, not from the tender embraces of the mother, but from the cruelty of the monster; and it is so far true of England, that the same tyranny which drove the first emigrants from home, pursues their descendants still.

In this extensive quarter of the globe, we forget the narrow limits of three hundred and sixty miles (the extent of England) and carry our friendship on a larger scale; we claim brotherhood with [every] European christian, and triumph in the generosity of the sentiment. . . .

But admitting that we were all of English descent, what does it amount to? Nothing. Britain, being now an open enemy, extinguishes every other name and title: And to say that reconciliation is our duty, is truly farcical. The first king of England, of the present line (William the Conqueror) was a Frenchman, and half the peers of England are descendants from the same country; wherefore by the same method of reasoning, England ought to be governed by France. . . .

I challenge the warmest advocate for reconciliation, to shew, a single advantage that this continent can reap, by being connected with Great Britain. I repeat the challenge, not a single advantage is derived. Our corn will fetch its price in any market in Europe, and our imported goods must be paid for buy them where we will.

But the injuries and disadvantages we sustain by that connexion, are without number; and our duty to mankind at large, as well as to ourselves, instruct us to renounce the alliance: Because, any submission to, or dependance on Great Britain, tends directly to involve this continent in European wars and quarrels; and sets us at variance with nations, who would otherwise seek our friendship, and against whom, we have neither anger nor complaint. As Europe is our market for trade, we ought to form no partial connexion with any part of it. It is the true interest of America to steer clear of European contentions, which she never can do, while by her dependance on Britain, she is made the make-weight in the scale of British politics.

Europe is too thickly planted with kingdoms to be long at peace, and whenever a war breaks out between England and any foreign power, the trade of America goes to ruin, *because of her connexion with Britain.* . . . Every thing that is right or natural pleads for separation. The blood of the slain, the weeping voice of nature cries, 'TIS TIME TO PART. Even the distance at which the Almighty hath placed England and America, is a strong and natural proof, that the authority of the one, over the other, was never the design of Heaven. . . .

It is repugnant to reason, to the universal order of things, to all examples from the former ages, to suppose, that this continent can longer remain subject to any external power. The most sanguine in Britain does not think so.

After reading this selection, consider these questions:

1. What, if anything, in Paine's discussion of the English constitution seems to support Bernard Bailyn's argument? Does anything in it support John M. Murrin's thesis?

2. To what extent does Paine's criticism of the English constitution extend beyond that of the oppositionists in Britain?

3. In what ways does Paine's argument differ from that of John Adams? What might account for the differences?

CHAPTER 7

Social Change

The American Revolution was not simply a matter of a change in government. Historians have long debated the extent to which the Revolution altered society. The colonial elite remained in control of government, and there was no redistribution of land or wealth. Yet social conflict within the colonies shaped the Revolution, and the Revolution itself set in motion powerful forces that threatened existing social arrangements. For the colonial elite, the challenge to British rule brought with it considerable risk. Would they be able to maintain their standing, command deference, or even hold on to their property in the absence of British authority? In addition, local matters often influenced the course of events.

The Revolutionary era was a time of social upheaval. Artisans mobilized to resist Britain in the mid-1760s and demanded greater power. Tenant farmers protested against their landlords, and debtors protested against their creditors. The American Revolution itself unleashed egalitarian forces, as the experience of George Robert Twelves Hewes, discussed in the selection by Alfred Young in this chapter demonstrates.

A religious fault line further divided Americans. Evangelical revivals swept through the colonies in the first half of the eighteenth century, and the impact of the religious enthusiasm continued well after the Great Awakening had faded. In many instances, class as well as theology divided evangelicals from followers of established churches. The Revolution ultimately led to the disestablishment of the Anglican Church and a greater degree of religious toleration. Rhys Isaac's selection attempts to relate the social divisions generated by the evangelical movement to the coming of the American Revolution.

Economic change played an important role during this era as well. Economic tensions within the British Empire contributed to Revolutionary discontent. The growth of the American population resulted in a declining dependence on immigrant indentured servants, although labor remained a valuable commodity. After the Revolution, the decline of British trade and exclusion from the British Empire created a new market economy in the American republic. These changes generated new paths for young people to enter the working world and new choices for graduates of America's early colleges.

Just as Revolutionary ideology had to balance the preservation of property and order with the demands of a democratic republic, the same tensions were reflected in the attempt to reconstitute a social structure. No longer would connection with the imperial government constitute the basis of social authority. Moreover, the Revolutionary experience led some to question the deference to which the colonial elite had become accustomed. Even the most elemental relationships, such as that between parents and children, came under pressure.

The working out of these issues shaped the contours of the new republic.

After reading this chapter, consider these questions:

1. In what ways did the American Revolution foster social change?

2. To what extent did social ferment in the colonies contribute to the coming of the Revolution? To what extent did social ferment in the colonies shape the Revolution?

SELECTION 1:

Evangelical Revolt, the Gentry, and the Making of a Revolution

R*hys Isaac, the author of the following essay, teaches history at La Trobe University in Australia. Drawing on insights from anthropology, Isaac examines the impact of evangelical revivalism on the political culture of Virginia. He maintains that Virginia was dominated by a gentry culture characterized by individual self-assertion, gregariousness, and display. The gentry exhibited these traits on court days, in churches, and at horse races. During the mid–eighteenth century, an opposition culture based on religious revivalism emerged. In direct opposition to the values* *of gentry culture, the alternative culture stressed sobriety, self-discipline, continence, and egalitarianism. Such a value system challenged the basis of the dominance of the gentry. As the gentry came to recognize the threat this oppositional culture posed to the social order, they responded, in some instances violently.*

Isaac presents his ideas at length in his prize-winning book The Transformation of Virginia, 1740–1790 *(1983). A decade earlier, he sketched out his argument in the following essay. While one might imagine that the conflict between cultures would have made unified opposition to Great Britain unlikely, Isaac argues the opposite in* The Transformation of Virginia. *Each side had concerns that enabled it to join with the other in common cause against British rule. In particular, the planter elite used the patriot cause to reassert its own leadership.*

The gentry style . . . is best understood in relation to the concept of honor—the proving of prowess. A formality of manners barely concealed adversary relationships; the essence of social exchange was overt self-assertion.

Display and bearing were important aspects of this system. We can best get a sense of the self-images that underlay it from the symbolic importance of horses. . . . It was noted repeatedly in the eighteenth century that Virginians would "go five miles to catch a horse, to ride only one mile upon afterwards." This apparent absurdity had its logic in the necessity of being mounted when making an entrance on the social scene. The role of the steed as a valuable part of proud self-presentation is suggested by the intimate identification of the gentry with their horses. . . .

Where did the essential display and self-assertion take place? There were few towns in Virginia; the outstanding characteristic of settlement was its diffuseness. Population was rather thinly scattered in very small groupings throughout a forested, river-dissected landscape. If there is to be larger community in such circumstances, there must be centers of action and communication. Insofar as cohesion is important in such an agrarian society, considerable significance must attach to the occasions when, coming together for certain purposes, the community realizes itself. The principal public centers in traditional Virginia were the parish churches and the county courthouses, with lesser foci established in a scatter of inns or "ordinaries." The principal general gatherings apart from these centers were for gala events such as horse race meetings and cockfights. Although lacking a specifically community character, the great estate house was also undoubtedly a very significant locus of action. By the operation of mimetic process and by the reinforcement of expectations concerning conduct and relationships, such centers and occasions were integral parts of the system of social control.

The most frequently held public gatherings at generally distributed centers were those for Sunday worship in the Anglican churches and chapels. An ideal identification of parish and community had been expressed in the law making persistent absence from church punishable. The continuance of this ideal is indicated by the fact that prosecutions under the law occurred right up to the time of the Revolution.

Philip Fithian has left us a number of vivid sketches of the typical Sunday scene at a parish church, sketches that illuminate the social nature and function of this institution. It was an important center of communication, especially among the elite, for it was "a general custom on Sundays here, with Gentlemen to invite one another home to dine, after Church; and to consult about, determine their common business, either before or after

Excerpted from "Evangelical Revolt: The Nature of the Baptists' Challenge to the Traditional Order in Virginia, 1765 to 1775," by Rhys Isaac, *William and Mary Quarterly,* July 1974. Copyright © 1974 by Rhys Isaac. Reprinted with permission.

Service," when they would engage in discussing "the price of Tobacco, Grain etc. and settling either the lineage, Age, or qualities of favourite Horses." The occasion also served to demonstrate to the community, by visual representation, the rank structure of society. Fithian's further description evokes a dramatic image of haughty squires trampling past seated hoi polloi to their pews in the front. He noted that it was "not the Custom for Gentlemen to go into Church til Service is beginning, when they enter in a Body, in the same manner as they come out."

Similarly, vestry records show that fifty miles to the south of Fithian's Westmoreland County the front pews of a King and Queen County church were allocated to the gentry, but the pressure for place and precedence was such that only the greatest dignitaries . . . could be accommodated together with their families; lesser gentlemen represented the honor of their houses in single places while their wives were seated farther back.

The size and composition of the ordinary congregations in the midst of which these representations of social style and status took place is as yet uncertain, but Fithian's description of a high festival is very suggestive on two counts: "This being Easter-Sunday, all the Parish seem'd to meet together High, Low, black, White all come out." We learn both that such general attendance was unusual, and that at least once a year full expression of ritual community was achieved. The whole society was then led to see itself in order.

The county courthouse was a most important center of social action. Monthly court days were attended by great numbers, for these were also the times for markets and fairs. The facts of social dominance were there visibly represented by the bearing of the "gentlemen justices" and the respect they commanded. On court days economic exchange was openly merged with social exchange (both plentifully sealed by the taking of liquor) and also expressed in conventional forms of aggression—in banter, swearing, and fighting.

The ruling gentry, who set the tone in this society, lived scattered across broad counties in the midst of concentrations of slaves that often amounted to black villages. Clearly the great houses that they erected in these settings were

important statements: they expressed a style, they asserted a claim to dominance. The lavish entertainments, often lasting days, which were held in these houses performed equally important social functions in maintaining this claim, and in establishing communication and control within the elite itself. Here the convivial contests that were so essential to traditional Virginia social culture would issue in their most elaborate and stylish performances. . . .

The importance of sporting occasions such as horse racing meets and cockfights for the maintenance of the values of self-assertion, in challenge and response, is strongly suggested by the comments of the marquis de Chastellux concerning cockfighting. His observations, dating from 1782, were that "when the principal promoters of this diversion [who were certainly gentry] propose to [match] their champions, they take great care to announce it to the public; and although there are neither posts, nor regular conveyances, this important news spreads with such facility, that the planters for thirty or forty miles round, attend, some with cocks, but all with money for betting, which is sometimes very considerable." An intensely shared interest of this kind, crossing but not leveling social distinctions, has powerful effects in transmitting style and reinforcing the leadership of the elite that controls proceedings and excels in the displays.

Discussion so far has focused on the gentry, for *there* was established in dominant form the way of life the Baptists appeared to challenge. Yet this way was diffused throughout the society. All the forms of communication and exchange noted already had their popular acceptances with variations appropriate to the context. . . .

The importance of pastime as a channel of communication, and even as a bond, between the ranks of a society such as this can hardly be too much stressed. People were drawn together by occasions such as horse races, cockfights, and dancing as by no other, because here men would become "known" to each other—"known" in the ways which the culture defined as "real." Skill and daring in that violent duel, the "quarter race"; coolness in the "deep play" of the betting that necessarily went with racing, cockfighting, and cards—these were means whereby Virginia males could prove themselves. Conviviality was an essential part of the social exchange, but through its soft coating pressed a harder structure of contest, or "emulation" as the contemporary phrase had it. Even in dancing this was so. Observers noted not only the passion for dancing— "*Virginians* are of genuine Blood—They will dance or die!"—but also the marked preference for the jig—in effect solo performances by partners of each sex, which were closely watched and were evidently competitive. In such activities, in social contexts high or low, enhanced eligibility for marriage was established by young persons who emerged as virtuosos of the dominant style. Situations where so much could happen presented powerful images of the "good life" to traditional Virginians, especially young ones. It was probably true, as alleged, that religious piety was generally considered appropriate only for the aged.

When one turns to the social world of the Baptists, the picture that emerges is so striking a negative of the one that has just been sketched that it must be considered to have been structured to an important extent by processes of reaction to the dominant culture.

Contemporaries were struck by the contrast between the challenging gaiety of traditional Virginia formal exchange and the solemn fellowship of the Baptists, who addressed each other as "Brother" and "Sister" and were perceived as "the most melancholy people in the world"—people who "cannot meet a man upon the road, but they must ram a text of Scripture down his throat." The finery of a gentleman who might ride forth in a gold-laced hat, sporting a gleaming Masonic medal, must be contrasted with the strict dress of the Separate Baptist, his hair "cut off" and such "superfluous forms and Modes of Dressing . . . as cock't hatts" explicitly renounced.

Their appearance was austere, to be sure, but we shall not understand the deep appeal of the evangelical movement, or the nature and full extent of its challenging contrast to the style and vision of the gentry-oriented social world, unless we look into the rich offerings beneath this somber exterior. The converts were proffered some escape from the harsh realities of disease, debt, overindulgence and deprivation, violence and sudden death, which were the common lot of small farmers. They could seek refuge in a close, supportive, orderly community, "a congregation of faithful persons, called out of the world by divine grace, who mutually agree to live together, and execute gospel discipline among them."

Entrance into this community was attained by the relation of a personal experience of profound importance to the candidates, who would certainly be heard with respect, however humble their station. There was a community resonance for deep feelings, since, despite their sober face to the outside world, the Baptists encouraged in their religious practice a sharing of emotion to an extent far beyond that which would elicit crushing ridicule in gentry-oriented society. Personal testimonies of the experiences of simple folk have not come down to us from that time, but the central importance of the ritual of admission and its role in renewing the common experience of ecstatic conversion is powerfully evoked by such recurrent phrases in the church books as "and a dore was opened to experience." This search for deep follow-feeling must be set in contrast to the formal distance and rivalry in the social exchanges of the traditional system.

The warm supportive relationship that fellowship in faith and experience could engender appears to have played an important part in the spread of the movement. . . .

A concomitant of fellowship in deep emotions was comparative equality. Democracy is an ideal, and there are no indications that the pre-Revolutionary Baptists espoused it as such, yet there can be no doubt that these men, calling each other brothers, who believed that the only authority in their church was the meeting of those in fellowship together, conducted their affairs on a footing of equality in sharp contrast to the explicit preoccupation with rank and precedence that characterized the world from which they had been called. Important Baptist church elections generally required unanimity and might be held up by the doubts of a few. The number of preachers who were raised from obscurity to play an epic role in the Virginia of their day is a clear indication of the opportunities for fulfillment that the movement opened up to men who would have found no other avenue for public achievement. There is no reason to doubt the contemporary reputation of the early Virginia Baptist movement as one of the poor and unlearned. Only isolated converts were made among the gentry, but many among the slaves.

The tight cohesive brotherhood of the Baptists must be understood as an explicit rejection of the formalism of traditional community organization. The antithesis is apparent in the contrast between Fithian's account of a parish congregation that dispersed without any act of worship when a storm prevented the attendance of both parson and clerk, and the report of the Baptist David Thomas that "when no minister . . . is expected, our people meet notwithstanding; and spend . . . time in praying, singing, reading, and in religious conversation."

The popular style and appeal of the Baptist Church found its most powerful and visible expression in the richness of its rituals, again a total contrast to the "prayrs read over in haste" of the colonial Church of England, where even congregational singing appears to have been a rarity. The most prominent and moving rite practiced by the sect was adult baptism, in which the candidates were publicly sealed into fellowship. . . .

[The ritual of baptism] was also a vivid enactment of *a* community within and apart from *the* community. We must try to see that closed circle for the laying on of hands through the eyes of those who had been raised in Tidewater or Piedmont Virginia with the expectation that they would always have a monistic parish community encompassing all the inhabitants within its measured liturgical celebrations. The antagonism and violence that the Baptists aroused then also become intelligible. . . .

More intimate, yet evidently important for the close community, were the rites of fellowship. The forms are elusive, but an abundance of ritual is suggested by the simple entry of Morgan Edwards concerning Falls Creek: "In this church are admitted, Evangelists, Ruling Elders, deaconesses, laying on of hands, feasts of charity, anointing the sick, kiss of charity, washing feet, right hand of fellowship, and devoting children."

Far from being mere formal observances, these and other rites, such as the ordaining of "apostles" to "pervade" the churches, were keenly experimented with to determine their efficacy.

Aspects of preaching also ought to be understood as ritual rather than as formal instruction. It was common for persons to come under conviction or to obtain ecstatic release "under preaching," and this established a special relationship between the neophyte and his or her "father in the gospel." Nowhere was the ritual character of the preaching more apparent than in the great meetings of the Virginia Separate Baptist Association. The messengers would preach to the people along the way to the meeting place and back; thousands would gather for the Sunday specially set aside for worship and preaching. There the close independent congregational communities found themselves merged in a great and swelling collective. The varieties of physical manifestations such as crying out and falling down, which were frequently brought on by the ritualized emotionalism of such preaching, are too well known to require description. . . .

As "seriousness" spread, with fear of hell-fire and concern for salvation, it was small wonder that a gentleman of Loudoun County should find to his alarm "that the *Anabaptists* . . . growing very numerous . . . seem to be increasing in affluence [influence?]; and . . . quite destroying pleasure in the Country; for they encourage ardent Pray'r; strong and constant faith, and an intire Banishment of *Gaming, Dancing,* and Sabbath-Day Diversions." That the Baptists were drawing away increasing numbers from the dominant to the insurgent culture was radical enough, but the implications of solemnity, austerity, and stern sobriety were more radical still, for they called into question the validity—indeed the propriety—of the occasions and modes of display and association so important in maintaining the bonds of Virginia's geographically diffuse society. Against the system in which proud men were joined in rivalry and convivial excess was set a reproachful model of an order in which God-humbled men would seek a deep sharing of emotion while repudiating indulgence of the flesh. Yet the Baptist movement, although it must be understood as a revolt against the traditional system, was not primarily negative. Behind it can be discerned an impulse toward a tighter, more effective system of values and of exemplary conduct to be established and maintained within the ranks of the common folk.

In this aspect evangelicalism must be seen as a popular response to mounting social disorder. It would be difficult—perhaps even impossible— to establish an objective scale for measuring disorder in Virginia. What can be established is that during the 1760s and 1770s disorder was perceived by many as increasing. This has been argued for the gentry by [scholars] Jack P. Greene and Gordon S. Wood, and need not be elaborated here. What does need to be reemphasized is that the gentry's growing perception of disorder was focused on those forms of activity which the Baptists denounced and which provided the main arenas for the challenge and response essential to the traditional "good life." It was coming to be felt that horse racing, cockfighting, and card play, with their concomitants of gambling and drinking, rather than serving to maintain the gentry's prowess, were destructive of it and of social order generally. Display might now be negatively perceived as "luxury."

Given the absence of the restraints imposed by tight village community in traditional Virginia, disorder was probably an even more acute problem in the lower than in the upper echelons of society—more acute because it was compounded by the harshness and brutality of everyday life, and most acute in proportion to the social proximity of the lowest stratum, the enslaved. The last named sector of society, lacking sanctioned marriage and legitimated familial authority, was certainly disorderly by English Protestant standards, and must therefore have had a disturbing effect on the consciousness of the whole community.

As the conversion experience was at the heart of the popular evangelical movement, so a sense of a great burden of guilt was at the heart of the conversion experience. . . . The hypothesis here advanced is that the social process was one in which popular perceptions of disorder in society—and hence by individuals in themselves— came to be expressed in the metaphor of "sin.". . .

A further indication of the importance of order-disorder preoccupations for the spread of the new vision with its contrasted life style was the insistence on "works." Conversion could ultimately be validated among church members only by a radical reform of conduct. The Baptist church books reveal the close concern for the disciplinary supervision of such changes. . . .

The recurrent use of the words "order," "orderly," "disorderly" in the Baptist records reveals a preoccupation that lends further support to the hypothesis that concern for the establishment of a securer system of social control was a powerful impulse for the movement. "Is it orderly?" is the usual introduction to the queries concerning right conduct that were frequently brought forward for resolution at monthly meetings. . . .

When the Baptist movement is understood as a rejection of the style of life for which the gentry set the pattern and as a search for more powerful popular models of proper conduct, it can be seen why the ground on which the battle was mainly fought was not the estate or the great house, but the neighborhood, the farmstead, and the slave quarter. This was a contemporary perception, for it was generally charged that the Baptists were "continual fomenters of discord" who "not only divided good neighbours, but slaves and their masters; children and their parents . . . wives and their husbands." . . . The struggle for allegiance in the homesteads between a style of life modeled on that of the leisured gentry and that embodied in evangelicalism was intense. In humbler, more straitened circumstances a popular culture based on the code of honor and almost hedonist values was necessarily less securely established than among the more affluent gentry. Hence the anxious aggressiveness of popular anti–New Light feeling and action.

The Baptists did not make a bid for control of the political system—still less did they seek a leveling or redistribution of worldly wealth. It was clearly a mark of the strength of gentry hegemony and of the rigidities of a social hierarchy with slavery at its base that the evangelical revolt should have been so closely restricted in scope. Yet the Baptists' salvationism and sabbatarianism effectively redefined morality and human relationships; their church leaders and organization established new and more popular foci of authority, and sought to impose a radically different and more inclusive model for the maintenance of order in society. Within the context of the traditional monistic, face-to-face, deferential society such a regrouping necessarily constituted a powerful challenge.

The beginnings of a cultural disjunction between gentry and sections of the lower orders, where hitherto there had been a continuum, posed a serious threat to the traditional leaders of the community; their response was characteristic. The popular emotional style, the encouragement given to men of little learning to "exercise their gifts" in preaching, and the preponderance of humble folk in the movement gave to the proud gentry their readiest defense—contempt and ridicule. The stereotype of the Baptists as "an ignorant . . . set . . . of . . . the contemptible class of the people," a "poor and illiterate sect" which "none of the rich or learned ever join," became generally established. . . .

The class of folk who filled the Baptist churches were a great obstacle to gentry participation. Behind the ridicule and contempt, of course, lay incomprehension, and behind that, fear of this menacing, unintelligible movement. . . .

Fear breeds fantasy. So it was that alarmed observers put a very crude interpretation on the emotional and even physical intimacy of this intrusive new society. Its members were associated with German Anabaptists, and a "historical" account of the erotic indulgences of that sect was published on the front page of the *Virginia Gazette*.

Driven by uneasiness, although toughened by their instinctive contempt, some members of the establishment made direct moves to assert proper social authority and to outface the upstarts. Denunciations from parish pulpits were frequent. . . .

Great popular movements are not quelled, however, by outfacing, nor are they stemmed by the ridicule, scorn, or scurrility of incomprehension. Moreover, they draw into themselves members of all sections of society. Although the social worlds most open to proselytizing by the Baptists were the neighborhoods and the slave quarters, there were converts from the great houses too.

Some of the defectors, such as Samuel Harris, played a leading role in the movement. The squirearchy was disturbed by the realization that the contemptible sect was reaching among themselves. . . . The pride and assurance of the gentry could be engaged by awareness that their own members might withdraw from their ranks and choose the other way. . . .

The intensity of the conflict for allegiance among the people and, increasingly, among the gentry, makes intelligible the growing frequency of violent clashes. . . . The violence was, however, one-sided and self-defeating. The episode of April 1771 in which the parson brutally interfered with the devotions of the preacher, who was then horsewhipped by the sheriff, must have produced a shock of revulsion in many quarters. Those who engaged in such actions were not typical of either the Anglican clergy or the country gentlemen. The extreme responses of some, however, show the anxieties to which all were subject, and the excesses in question could only heighten the tension. . . .

The Revolution ultimately enshrined religious pluralism as a fundamental principle in Virginia. It rendered illegitimate the assumptions concerning the nature of community religious corporateness that underlay aggressive defense against the Baptists. It legitimated new forms of conflict, so that by the end of the century the popular evangelists were able to counterattack and symbolize social revolution in many localities by having the Episcopal Church's lands and even communion plate sold at auction. . . . The diametrical opposition of the swelling Baptist movement to traditional mores shows it to have been indeed a radical social revolt, indicative of real strains within society.

After reading this selection, consider these questions:

1. It seems entirely possible that evangelical behavior was similar in other colonies, and it seems equally likely that those colonies had dominant cultures that differed from that of Virginia. Assuming that both suppositions are true, what would that mean for Isaac's interpretation?

2. Anthropologists observe their subjects firsthand. Isaac and other historians who use anthropological techniques obviously cannot do so and must rely on written records and physical evidence. How might this limitation affect the conclusions Isaac draws?

3. Why did the evangelical culture pose such a threat to the social order of Virginia?

SELECTION 2:

A Boston Shoemaker and the American Revolution

Alfred F. Young is professor emeritus of history at Northern Illinois University. In the following essay on George Robert Twelves Hewes, Young illustrates the emphasis historians have placed in recent years on the experiences of ordinary people. In particular, this selection deals with the role of a common shoemaker in the coming of the American Revolution. Hewes achieved notoriety near the end of his life as one of the last living participants of the Boston Tea Party. He began life in modest circumstances, and his father's death left the family impoverished. Apprenticed at the age of fourteen to a shoemaker (an unpromising occupation), Hewes attempted to enlist in the British army during the colonial wars with France, only to be rejected because he was too short. Hewes eventually became a shoemaker, if an unsuccessful one, and worked in that occupation, with two interruptions, until the Revolution. The interruptions came when, attempting to improve his fortunes, he went to sea with his brother.

Late in 1762 or early in 1763, George Robert Twelves Hewes, a Boston shoemaker in the last year or so of his apprenticeship, repaired a shoe for John Hancock and delivered it to him at his uncle Thomas Hancock's store in Dock Square. Hancock was pleased and invited the young man to "come and see him on New Year's day, and bid him a happy New-Year," according to the custom of the day, a ritual of noblesse oblige on the part of the gentry. We know of the episode through Benjamin Bussey Thatcher, who interviewed Hewes and wrote it up for his *Memoir* of Hewes in 1835. [On New Year's Day, Hewes washed his face and put on his best jacket before heading for Hancock House. On his arrival, Hewes took off his hat and bowed. In Hancock's presence, Hewes was so intimidated that he could barely speak. He managed to rush through a prepared speech, after which Hancock gave him a crown-piece.] . . .

The episode is a demonstration of what the eighteenth century called deference.

Another episode catches the point at which Hewes had arrived a decade and a half later. In

Excerpted from "George Robert Twelves Hewes, 1742–1840: A Boston Shoemaker and the Memory of the American Revolution," by Alfred F. Young, *William and Mary Quarterly*, October 1981. Copyright © 1981 by Alfred F. Young. Reprinted with permission.

1778 or 1779, after one stint in the war on board a privateer and another in the militia, he was ready to ship out again, from Boston. As Thatcher tells the story: "Here he enlisted, or engaged to enlist, on board the Hancock, a twenty-gun ship, but not liking the manners of the Lieutenant very well, who ordered him one day in the streets to take his hat off to him—which he refused to do for any man,—he went aboard the 'Defence,' Captain Smedley, of Fairfield Connecticut." This, with a vengeance, is the casting off of deference.

What had happened in the intervening years? What had turned the young shoemaker tongue-tied in the face of his betters into the defiant person who would not take his hat off for any man? . . .

George Robert Twelves Hewes was born in Boston in 1742 and died in Richfield Springs, New York, in 1840. He participated in several of the principal political events of the American Revolution in Boston, among them the Massacre and the Tea Party, and during the war he served as a privateersman and militiaman. A shoemaker all his life, and intermittently or concurrently a fisherman, sailor, and farmer, he remained a poor man. . . .

In 1756, when Hewes was fourteen, he was apprenticed to a shoemaker. . . . The town's shoemakers were generally poor and their prospects were worsening. . . .

The economic odds were against a Boston shoemaker thriving these years. . . . The patriot boycott would have raised his hopes; the Boston town meeting of 1767 put men's and women's shoes on the list of items Bostonians were encouraged to buy from American craftsmen. But if this meant shoes made in Lynn—the manufacturing town ten miles to the north that produced 80,000 shoes in 1767 alone—it might well have put Hewes at a competitive disadvantage, certainly for the ladies' shoes for which Lynn already had a reputation. And if Hewes was caught up in the system whereby Lynn masters were already "putting out" shoes in Boston, he would have made even less. . . .

Between 1768 and 1775, the shoemaker became a citizen—an active participant in the events that led to the Revolution, an angry, assertive man who won recognition as a patriot. What explains the transformation? We have enough evidence to take stock of Hewes's role in three major events of the decade: the Massacre (1770), the Tea Party (1773), and the tarring and feathering of [customs agent and Royalist] John Malcolm (1774). . . .

The presence of British troops in Boston beginning in the summer of 1768—four thousand soldiers in a town of fewer than sixteen thousand inhabitants—touched Hewes personally. . . . He knew how irritating it was to be challenged by British sentries after curfew (his solution was to offer a swig of rum from the bottle he carried).

More important, he was personally cheated by a soldier. Sergeant Mark Burk ordered shoes allegedly for Captain Thomas Preston, picked them up, but never paid for them. Hewes complained to Preston, who made good and suggested he bring a complaint. A military hearing ensued, at which Hewes testified. The soldier, to Hewes's horror, was sentenced to three hundred fifty lashes. He "remarked to the court that if he had thought the fellow was to be punished so severely for such an offense, bad as he was, he would have said nothing about it." And he saw others victimized by soldiers. . . .

First in time, and vividly recalled by Hewes, was the murder of eleven-year-old Christopher Seider on February 23, ten days before the Massacre. Seider was one of a large crowd of schoolboys and apprentices picketing the shop of Theophilus Lilly, a merchant violating the anti-import resolutions. Ebenezer Richardson, a paid customs informer, shot into the throng and killed Seider. Richardson would have been tarred and feathered, or worse, had not whig leaders intervened to hustle him off to jail. At Seider's funeral, only a week before the Massacre, five hundred boys marched two by two behind the coffin, followed by two thousand or more adults, "the largest [funeral] perhaps ever known in America," [Governor] Thomas Hutchinson thought.

Second, Hewes emphasized the bitter fight two days before the Massacre between soldiers and workers at Gray's ropewalk down the block from Hewes's shop. Off-duty soldiers were allowed to moonlight, taking work from civilians. On Friday, March 3, when one of them asked for work at Gray's, a battle ensued between a few score soldiers and ropewalk workers joined by others in the maritime trades. The soldiers were beaten and sought revenge. Consequently, in Thatcher's words, "quite a number of soldiers, in a word, were determined to have a row on the night of the 5th."

Third, the precipitating events on the night of the Massacre, by Hewes's account, were an attempt by a barber's apprentice to collect an overdue bill from a British officer, the sentry's abuse of the boy, and the subsequent harassment of the sentry by a small band of boys that led to the calling of the guard commanded by Captain Preston. Thatcher found this hard to swallow—"a dun from a greasy barber's boy is rather an extraordinary explanation of the origin, or one of the occasions, of the massacre of the 5th of March" —but at the trial the lawyers did not. They battled over defining "boys" and over the age, size, and degree of aggressiveness of the numerous apprentices on the scene.

Hewes viewed the civilians as essentially defensive. On the evening of the Massacre he appeared early on the scene at King Street, attracted by the clamor over the apprentice. "I was soon on the ground among them," he said, as if it were only natural that he should turn out in defense of fellow townsmen against what was assumed to be the danger of aggressive action by soldiers. He was not part of a conspiracy; neither was he there out of curiosity. He was unarmed, carrying neither club nor stave as some others did. He saw snow, ice, and "missiles" thrown at the soldiers. When the main guard rushed out in support of the sentry, Private Kilroy dealt Hewes a blow on his shoulder with his gun. Preston ordered the townspeople to disperse. Hewes believed they had a legal basis to refuse: "they were in the king's highway, and had as good a right to be there" as Preston.

The five men killed were all workingmen. Hewes claimed to know four: Samuel Gray, a ropewalk worker; Samuel Maverick, age seventeen, an apprentice to an ivory turner; Patrick Carr, an apprentice to a leather breeches worker; and James Caldwell, second mate on a ship—all but Christopher Attucks. Caldwell, "who was shot in the back was standing by the side of Hewes, and the latter caught him in his arms as he fell," helped carry him to Dr. Thomas Young in Prison Lane, then ran to Caldwell's ship captain on Cold Lane.

More than horror was burned into Hewes's memory. He remembered the political confrontation that followed the slaughter, when thousands of angry townspeople faced hundreds of British troops massed with ready rifles. "The people," Hewes recounted, "then immediately chose a committee to report to the governor the result of Captain Preston's conduct, and to demand of him satisfaction." Actually the "people" did not choose a committee "immediately." In the dark hours after the Massacre a self-appointed group of patriot leaders met with officials and forced Hutchinson to commit Preston and the soldiers to jail. Hewes was remembering the town meeting the next day, so huge that it had to adjourn from Fanueil Hall, the traditional meeting place that held only twelve hundred, to Old South Church, which had room for five to six thousand. This meeting approved a committee to wait on the officials and then adjourned, but met again the same day, received and voted down an offer to remove one regiment, then accepted another to remove two. This was one of the meetings at which property bars were let down.

What Hewes did not recount, but what he had promptly put down in a deposition the next day, was how militant he was after the Massacre. At 1:00 A.M., like many other enraged Bostonians, he went home to arm himself. On his way back to the Town House with a cane he had a defiant exchange with Sergeant Chambers of the 29th Regiment and eight or nine soldiers, "all with very large clubs or cutlasses." A soldier, Dobson, "ask'd him how he far'd; he told him very badly to see his townsmen shot in such a manner, and asked him if he did not think it was a dreadful thing." Dobson swore "it was a fine thing" and "you shall see more of it." Chambers "seized and forced" the cane from Hewes, "saying I had no right to carry it. I told him I had as good a right to carry a cane as they had to carry clubs."

The Massacre had stirred Hewes to political action. He was one of ninety-nine Bostonians who gave depositions for the prosecution that were published by the town in a pamphlet. Undoubtedly, he marched in the great funeral procession for the victims that brought the city to a standstill. He attended the tempestuous trial of Ebenezer Richardson, Seider's slayer, which was linked politically with the Massacre. . . . He seems to have attended the trial of the soldiers or Preston or both. . . .

He turned out because of a sense of kinship with "his townsmen" in danger; he stood his ground in defense of his "rights"; he was among the "people" who delegated a committee to act on their behalf; he took part in the legal process by giving a deposition, by attending the trials, and, as he remembered it, by testifying. In sum, he had become a citizen, a political man.

Four years later, at the Tea Party on the night of December 16, 1773, the citizen "volunteered" and became the kind of leader for whom most historians have never found a place. The Tea Party, unlike the Massacre, was organized by the radical whig leaders of Boston. They mapped the strategy, organized the public meetings, appointed the companies to guard the tea ships at Griffin's Wharf (among them Daniel Hewes, George's brother), and planned the official boarding parties. As in 1770, they converted the town meetings into meetings of "the whole body of the people," one of which Hutchinson found "consisted principally of the Lower ranks of the People & even Journeymen Tradesmen were brought in to increase the number & the Rabble were not excluded yet there were divers Gentlemen of Good Fortunes among them."

The boarding parties showed this same combination of "ranks.". . . The recollection of Joshua Wyeth, a journeyman blacksmith, verified Hewes's story in explicit detail: "It was proposed that young men, not much known in town and not liable to be easily recognized should lead in the business." Wyeth believed that "most of the persons selected for the occasion were apprentices and journeymen, as was the case with myself, living with tory masters." Wyeth "had but a few hours warning of what was intended to be done." Those in the officially designated parties, about thirty men better known, appeared in well-prepared Indian disguises. As nobodies, the volunteers—anywhere from fifty to one hundred men—could get away with hastily improvised disguises. Hewes said he got himself up as an Indian and daubed his "face and hands with coal dust in the shop of blacksmith." In the streets "I fell in with many who were dressed, equipped and painted as I was, and who fell in with me and marched in order to the place of our destination."

At Griffin's Wharf the volunteers were orderly, self-disciplined, and ready to accept leadership.

When we arrived at the wharf, there were three of our number who assumed an authority to direct our operations, to which we readily submitted. They divided us into three parties, for the purpose of boarding the three ships which contained the tea at the same time. The name of him who commanded the division to which I was assigned was Leonard Pitt [Lendell Pitts]. The names of the other commanders I never knew. We were immediately ordered by the respective commanders to board all the ships at the same time, which we promptly obeyed.

But for Hewes there was something new: he was singled out of the rank and file and made an officer in the field.

The commander of the division to which I belonged, as soon as we were on board the ship, appointed me boatswain, and ordered me to go to the captain and demand of him the keys to the hatches and a dozen candles. I made the demand accordingly, and the captain promptly replied, and delivered the articles; but requested me at the same time to do no damage to the ship or rigging. We then were ordered by our commander to open the hatches, and take out all the chests of tea and throw them overboard, and we immediately proceeded to execute his orders; first cutting and splitting the chests with our tomahawks, so as thoroughly to expose them to the effects of the water. In about three hours from the time we went on board, we had thus broken and thrown overboard every tea chest to be found in the ship; while those in the other ships were disposing of the tea in the same way, at the same time. We were surrounded by British armed ships, but no attempt was made to resist us.

We then quietly retired to our several places of residence, without having any conversation with each other, or taking any measures to discover who were our associates.

. . . That Hewes was a leader is confirmed by the reminiscence of Thompson Maxwell, a teamster from a neighboring town who was making a delivery to Hancock the day of the event. Hancock asked him to go to Griffin's Wharf. "I went accordingly, joined the band under one Captain Hewes; we mounted the ships and made tea in a trice; this done I took my team and went home as any honest man should." "Captain" Hewes—it was not impossible. . . .

A month later, at the third event for which we have full evidence, Hewes won public recognition for an act of courage that almost cost his life and precipitated the most publicized tarring and feathering of the Revolution. The incident that set it off would have been trivial at any other time. On Tuesday, January 25, 1774, at about two in the afternoon, the shoemaker was making his way back to his shop after his dinner. According to the very full account in the *Massachusetts Gazette,*

Mr. George-Robert-Twelves Hewes was coming along Fore-Street, near Captain Ridgway's, and found the redoubted John Malcolm, standing over a small boy, who was pushing a little sled before him, cursing, damning, threatening and shaking a very large cane with a very heavy ferril on it over his head. The boy at that time was perfectly quiet, notwithstanding which Malcolm continued his threats of striking him, which Mr. Hewes conceiving if he struck him with that weapon he must have killed him out-right, came up to him, and said to him, Mr. Malcolm I hope you are not going to strike this boy with that stick.

Malcolm had already acquired an odious reputation with patriots of the lower sort. A Bostonian, he had been a sea captain, an army officer, and recently an employee of the customs service. He was so strong a supporter of royal authority that he had traveled to North Carolina to fight the Regulators and boasted of having a horse shot out from under him. He had a fiery temper. As a customs informer

he was known to have turned in a vessel to punish sailors for petty smuggling, a custom of the sea. In November 1773, near Portsmouth, New Hampshire, a crowd of thirty sailors had "genteely tarr'd and feather'd" him, as the *Boston Gazette* put it: they did the job over his clothes. Back in Boston he made "frequent complaints" to Hutchinson of "being hooted at in the streets" for this by "tradesmen"; and the lieutenant governor cautioned him, "being a passionate man," not to reply in kind.

The exchange between Malcolm and Hewes resonated with class as well as political differences:

Malcolm returned, you are an impertinent rascal, it is none of your business. Mr. Hewes then asked him, what had the child done to him. Malcolm damned him and asked him if he was going to take his part? Mr. Hewes answered no further than this, that he thought it was a shame for him to strike the child with such a club as that, if he intended to strike him. Malcolm on that damned Mr. Hewes, called him a vagabond, and said he would let him know he should not speak to a gentleman in the street. Mr. Hewes returned to that, he was neither a rascal nor vagabond, and though a poor man was in as good credit in town as he was. Malcolm called him a liar, and said he was not, nor ever would be. Mr. Hewes retorted, be that as it will, I never was tarred nor feathered any how. On this Malcolm struck him, and wounded him deeply on the forehead, so that Mr. Hewes for some time lost his senses. Capt. Godfrey, then present, interposed, and after some altercation, Malcolm went home.

Hewes was rushed to Joseph Warren, the patriot doctor, his distant relative. Malcolm's cane had almost penetrated his skull. . . . Warren dressed the wound, and Hewes was able to make his way to a magistrate to swear out a warrant for Malcolm's arrest "which he carried to a constable named Justice Hale." Malcolm, meanwhile, had retreated to his house, where he responded in white heat to taunts about the half-way tarring and feathering in Portsmouth with "damn you let me see the man that dare do it better."

In the evening a crowd took Malcolm from his house and dragged him on a sled into King Street "amidst the huzzas of thousands." At this point "several gentlemen endeavoured to divert the populace from their intention." The ensuing dialogue laid bare the clash of conceptions of justice between the sailors and laboring people heading the action and Sons of Liberty leaders. The "gentlemen" argued that Malcolm was "open to the laws of the land which would undoubtedly award a reasonable satisfaction to the parties he had abused," that is, the child and Hewes. The answer was political. Malcolm "had been an old impudent and mischievious [sic] offender—he had joined in the murders at North Carolina—he had seized vessels on account of sailors having a bottle or two of gin on board—he had in other words behaved in the most capricious, insulting and daringly abusive manner." He could not be trusted to justice. "When they were told the law would have its course with him, they asked what course had the law taken with Preston or his soldiers, with Capt. Wilson or Richardson? And for their parts they had seen so much partiality to the soldiers and customhouse officers by the present Judges, that while things remained as they were, they would, on all such occasions, take satisfaction their own way, and let them take it off." The references were to Captain Preston who had been tried and found innocent of the Massacre, the soldiers who had been let off with token punishment, Captain John Wilson, who had been indicted for inciting slaves to murder their masters but never tried, and Ebenezer Richardson, who had been tried and found guilty of killing Seider, sentenced, and then pardoned by the crown.

The crowd won and proceeded to a ritualized tarring and feathering, the purpose of which was to punish Malcolm, force a recantation, and ostracize him. . . .

The event was reported in the English newspapers, popularized in three or four satirical prints, and dramatized still further when Malcolm went to England, where he campaigned for a pension and ran for Parliament (without success) against John Wilkes, the leading champion of America. The event confirmed the British ministry in its punitive effort to bring rebellious Boston to heel.

What was lost to the public was that Hewes was at odds with the crowd. He wanted justice from the courts, not a mob; after all, he had sworn out a warrant against Malcolm. And he could not bear to see cruel punishment inflicted on a man, any more than on a boy. . . .

The denouement of the affair was an incident several weeks later. "Malcolm recovered from his wounds and went about as usual. 'How do you do, Mr. Malcolm?' said Hewes, very civilly, the next time he met him. 'Your humble servant, Mr. George Robert Twelves Hewes,' quoth he,—touching his hat genteely as he passed by. 'Thank ye,' thought Hewes, 'and I am glad you have learned better manners at last.'" Hewes's mood was one of triumph. Malcolm had been taught a lesson. The issue was respect for Hewes, a patriot, a poor man, an honest citizen, a decent man standing up for a child against an unspeakably arrogant "gentleman" who was an enemy of his country.

Hewes's role in these three events fits few of the categories that historians have applied to the participation of ordinary men in the Revolution. He was not a member of any organized committee, caucus, or club. He did not attend the expensive public dinners of the Sons of Liberty. He was capable of acting on his own volition without being summoned by any leaders (as in the Massacre). He could volunteer and assume leadership (as in the Tea Party). He was at home on the streets in crowds but he could also reject a crowd (as in the tarring and feathering of Malcolm). He was at home in the other places where ordinary Bostonians turned out to express their convictions: at funeral processions, at meetings of the "whole body of the people," in courtrooms at public trials. He recoiled from violence to persons if not to property. The man who could remember the whippings of his own boyhood did not want to be the source of pain to others, whether Sergeant Burk, who tried to cheat him over a pair of shoes, or John Malcolm, who almost killed him. It is in keeping with his character that he should have come to the aid of a little boy facing a beating.

Nevertheless, Hewes was more of a militant than he conveyed or his biographers recognized in 1833 and 1835. . . .

What moved Hewes to action? It was not the written word; indeed there is no sign he was much of a reader until old age, and then it was the Bible he read. "My whole education," he told Hawkes, "consisted of only a moderate knowledge of reading and writing." He seems to have read one of the most sensational pamphlets of 1773, which he prized enough to hold onto for more than fifty years, but he was certainly not like Harbottle Dorr, the Boston shopkeeper who pored over every issue of every Boston newspaper, annotating Britain's crimes for posterity.

Hewes was moved to act by personal experiences that he shared with large numbers of other plebeian Bostonians. He seems to have been politicized, not by the Stamp Act, but by the coming of the troops after 1768, and then by things that happened to him, that he saw, or that happened to people he knew. Once aroused, he took action with others of his own rank and condition—the laboring classes who formed the bulk of the actors at the Massacre, the Tea Party, and the Malcolm affair— and with other members of his family: his uncle Robert, "known for a staunch Liberty Boy," and his brother Daniel, a guard at the tea ship. Shubael, alone among his brothers, became a tory. These shared experiences were interpreted and focused more likely by the spoken than the written word and as much by his peers at taverns and crowd actions as by leaders in huge public meetings.

As he became active politically he may have had a growing awareness of his worth as a shoemaker. . . . In city after city, "cobblers" were singled out for derision by conservatives for leaving their lasts to engage in the body politic. Hewes could not have been unaware of all this; he was part of it.

He may also have responded to the rising demand among artisans for support of American manufacturers, whether or not it brought him immediate benefit. He most certainly subscribed to the secularized Puritan ethic—self-denial, industry, frugality—that made artisans take to the nonimportation agreement with its crusade against foreign luxury and its vision of American manufactures. . . .

But what ideas did Hewes articulate? He spoke of what he did but very little of what he thought. In the brief statement he offered [James] Hawkes about why he went off to war in 1776, he expressed a commitment to general principles as they had been brought home to him by his experiences. "I was continually reflecting upon the unwarrant-able sufferings inflicted on the citizens of Boston by the usurpation and tyranny of Great Britain, and my mind was excited with an unextinguishable desire to aid in chastising them." When Hawkes expressed a doubt "as to the correctness of his conduct in absenting himself from his family," Hewes "emphatically reiterated" the same phrases, adding to a "desire to aid in chastising them" the phrase "and securing our independence." This was clearly not an afterthought; it probably reflected the way many others moved toward the goal of Independence, not as a matter of original intent, but as a step made necessary when all other resorts failed. Ideology thus did not set George Hewes apart from Samuel Adams or John Hancock. The difference lies in what the Revolution did to him as a person. His experiences transformed him, giving him a sense of citizenship and personal worth. Adams and Hancock began with both; Hewes had to arrive there, and in arriving he cast off the constraints of deference.

After reading this selection, consider these questions:

1. Do you accept Young's premise that Hewes was typical of "the humble classes"? If so, why? If not, why not?

2. The "memoirs" (essentially oral histories) on which Young bases his analysis were recorded in the mid-1830s, nearly fifty years after the American Revolution. What impact might this have had on Hewes's recollection of events? In parts of the article not included above, Young attempts to account for possible distortions or mistakes by verifying names, dates, and places with outside sources. He also compares the two memoirs and considers how subsequent events might have shaped Hewes's recollections. Why would Young rely so heavily on sources that present such problems?

3. In what ways do the forces for social leveling at work in Hewes's experiences correspond to those described by Rhys Isaac in his account of the evangelical revolt in Virginia?

SELECTION 3:

Career Patterns of Harvard and Yale Graduates

Puritans brought with them from England an abiding hostility toward lawyers. The Massachusetts Bay Colony prohibited anyone from taking a fee to represent another person in court. Not until 1683 did the colony formally recognize the right to practice law. By then, the colony had changed in ways that increased the demand for legal services. The founders of the colony had consciously intended to establish a model of a godly community. Disputes, they believed, should be settled face to face with the guidance of the larger community if necessary. The second generation lacked the utopian zeal of their parents. Rather than making a decision to found a godly community, the children of the founders had simply been born into one.

In addition, towns grew increasingly crowded; thus, boundaries dividing one family's land from that of their neighbors, which had once been informal and imprecise, became contested matters. Residents turned to courts for judgments that would resolve definitely who owned what.

By the first half of the eighteenth century, the increasingly complex trade within the British Empire demanded more sophisticated legal instruments and therefore greater legal expertise in drafting them. Law, which had been a lower-class occupation, began to attract sons of the landed gentry. An increasingly professional legal class emerged, and that class provided leadership for the American Revolution (even though a majority of lawyers remained loyal to England).

If lawyers helped shape the Revolution, the Revolution also had a significant impact on the bar. Before the Revolution, elite lawyers in America, particularly in the middle and southern colonies, had depended on training in England. Egalitarian forces unleashed by the Revolution, however, reversed the pre-Revolutionary trend toward increasing standards of education and apprenticeship as requirements for admission to the bar.

In addition, the decline in piety of the second generation of New Englanders influenced whether children of the elite decided to enter the ministry, as did the religious revivalism of the Great Awakening.

Such developments could not help but have an effect on the decisions young college graduates made when choosing a career.

Excerpted from "Professional Distribution of College and University Graduates," by Bailey B. Burritt, *United States Bureau of Education Bulletin*, 1912.

Harvard University: Academic Department—Graduates

Years	Number of graduates	Ministry	Law	Medicine	Education	Commercial pursuits	Public service	Engineering	Agriculture	Literature/Journalism	Unclassified
1642–1645	20	14	–	1	1	–	–	–	1	–	3
1646–1650	25	16	–	2	2	–	–	–	–	–	5
1651–1655	31	20	–	2	1	1	–	–	–	–	7
1656–1660	40	26	1	3	4	1	–	–	–	–	5
1661–1665	39	15	–	5	8	–	3	–	1	–	7
1666–1670	30	17	–	3	3	3	–	–	–	–	4
1671–1675	27	14	1	7	–	–	–	–	–	–	5
1676–1680	22	14	–	1	2	–	1	–	–	–	4
1681–1685	35	21	–	1	5	–	1	–	1	–	6
1686–1690	54	29	5	3	3	3	1	–	–	–	10
1691–1695	59	34	4	4	3	3	3	–	–	–	8
1696–1700	64	42	1	2	3	1	6	–	–	–	9
1701–1705	61	31	5	3	5	1	6	–	1	–	9
1706–1710	56	35	3	1	4	7	1	–	1	–	4
1711–1715	63	31	–	1	5	5	6	–	1	1	13
1716–1720	88	53	3	7	6	6	9	–	–	–	4
1721–1725	196	91	2	14	12	28	11	–	–	–	38
1726–1730	169	67	5	15	11	30	15	–	–	–	26
1731–1735	164	69	14	9	17	26	8	–	1	–	20
1736–1740	148	66	8	17	9	14	9	–	5	–	20
1741–1745	134	50	5	10	8	16	18	1	5	–	21
1746–1750	105	34	8	17	7	14	8	–	2	–	15
1751–1755	126	51	13	14	9	12	14	–	–	–	13
1756–1760	144	53	12	19	13	14	12	–	–	–	21
1761–1765	225	75	29	30	21	26	11	–	3	–	30
1766–1770	197	56	29	39	19	20	3	–	4	–	27
1771–1775	235	41	31	41	13	29	13	–	6	–	61
1776–1780	173	33	36	31	11	25	11	–	2	–	24
1781–1785	168	35	37	19	9	24	13	–	2	–	29
1786–1790	213	48	64	31	5	23	2	–	–	2	38
1791–1795	171	41	44	19	10	32	5	–	2	1	17
1796–1800	228	38	81	28	11	13	4	–	4	–	49
1801–1805	245	45	93	27	14	15	5	–	3	2	41
1806–1810	220	32	82	35	7	16	3	–	3	3	39
1811–1815	279	37	78	55	12	31	7	–	4	5	50
1816–1820	328	55	79	51	28	36	4	–	4	2	69

Yale University: Academic Department—Graduates

Years	Number of graduates	Ministry	Law	Medicine	Education	Commercial pursuits	Public service	Engineering	Agriculture	Literature/Journalism	Unclassified
1702–1705	11	7	1	–	2	–	1	–	–	–	–
1706–1710	22	14	–	1	–	2	1	1	2	–	1
1711–1715	20	13	–	–	1	3	–	–	2	–	1
1716–1720	35	24	1	–	–	2	2	–	1	–	5
1721–1725	60	30	2	3	4	3	4	–	5	–	9
1726–1730	80	34	7	6	3	5	6	–	1	–	18
1731–1735	80	44	6	6	2	7	2	–	2	–	21
1736–1740	89	38	6	6	2	9	3	–	2	–	23
1741–1745	103	56	8	7	2	11	6	–	3	–	10
1746–1750	116	46	9	18	2	8	7	–	4	–	22
1751–1755	92	35	10	12	2	3	3	–	7	–	18
1756–1760	198	71	20	18	4	27	7	–	9	–	42
1761–1765	159	72	28	24	5	19	1	–	13	–	27
1766–1770	135	45	12	17	5	16	3	–	7	–	30
1771–1775	143	47	17	17	8	20	9	–	4	–	21
1776–1780	190	34	50	24	7	24	15	–	5	2	29
1781–1785	217	51	67	16	11	32	7	–	5	–	28
1786–1790	198	60	67	34	1	20	4	–	–	–	12
1791	27	9	12	–	1	4	1	–	–	–	–
1797	37	14	16	3	1	2	–	–	1	–	–
1802	56	17	18	5	1	10	–	–	5	–	–
1813, 1814	152	38	55	21	8	18	–	–	9	3	–
1821, 1822, 1824	214	72	66	43	10	17	–	–	6	–	–

Harvard University: Academic Department—Percentages

Years	Ministry	Law	Medicine	Education	Commercial pursuits	Public service	Engineering	Agriculture	Literature/Journalism	Unclassified
1642–1645	70.0	–	5.0	5.0	–	–	–	5.0	–	15.0
1646–1650	64.0	–	8.0	8.0	–	–	–	–	–	20.0
1651–1655	64.5	–	6.5	3.2	3.2	–	–	–	–	22.6
1656–1660	65.0	2.5	7.5	10.0	2.5	–	–	–	–	12.5
1661–1665	38.5	–	12.8	20.5	–	7.7	–	2.6	–	17.9
1666–1670	56.8	–	10.0	10.0	10.0	–	–	–	–	13.3
1671–1675	51.9	3.7	25.9	–	–	–	–	–	–	18.5
1676–1680	63.6	–	4.5	9.1	–	4.5	–	–	–	18.2
1681–1685	60.0	–	2.9	14.3	–	2.9	–	2.9	–	17.1
1686–1690	53.6	9.3	5.7	5.7	5.7	1.9	–	–	–	18.5
1691–1695	57.6	6.8	6.8	5.9	5.9	5.9	–	–	–	13.6
1696–1700	65.6	1.6	3.1	4.7	1.6	9.4	–	–	–	14.7
1701–1705	50.8	8.2	4.9	8.2	1.6	9.8	–	1.6	–	14.8
1706–1710	62.5	5.4	1.8	7.8	12.5	1.8	–	1.8	–	7.8
1711–1715	49.2	–	1.6	7.9	7.9	9.5	–	1.6	1.6	20.6
1716–1720	60.2	3.4	7.9	6.8	6.8	10.2	–	–	–	4.5
1721–1725	46.4	1.3	7.1	6.1	14.3	5.6	–	–	–	19.4
1726–1730	39.6	2.9	8.9	6.5	17.8	8.9	–	–	–	15.4
1731–1735	42.8	8.5	5.5	10.4	15.9	4.9	–	.6	–	12.2
1736–1740	44.6	5.4	11.5	6.9	9.5	6.9	–	3.4	–	13.5
1741–1745	37.3	3.7	7.5	5.9	11.2	13.4	.7	3.7	–	15.7
1746–1750	32.4	7.6	16.2	6.7	13.3	7.6	–	1.9	–	14.3
1751–1755	40.5	10.3	11.1	7.1	9.5	11.1	–	–	–	10.3
1756–1760	36.8	8.3	13.2	9.3	9.7	8.3	–	–	–	14.6
1761–1765	33.3	12.9	13.3	9.3	11.6	4.9	–	1.3	–	13.3
1766–1770	28.4	14.7	19.8	9.6	10.2	1.5	–	2.4	–	13.7
1771–1775	17.4	13.2	17.4	5.5	12.3	5.5	–	2.6	–	25.9
1776–1780	19.8	20.8	17.9	6.4	14.5	6.4	–	1.2	–	13.9
1781–1785	20.8	22.3	11.3	5.4	14.3	7.7	–	1.2	–	17.2
1786–1790	22.5	30.5	14.6	2.3	10.8	.9	–	–	.9	17.8
1791–1795	23.9	25.7	11.1	5.8	18.7	2.9	–	1.2	.5	9.9
1796–1800	16.7	35.5	12.3	4.8	5.7	1.8	–	1.8	–	21.5
1801–1805	18.4	37.9	11.3	5.7	6.1	2.5	–	1.2	.8	16.7
1806–1810	14.5	37.3	15.9	3.2	7.3	1.4	–	1.4	1.4	17.7
1811–1815	13.3	27.9	19.7	4.3	11.1	2.5	–	1.4	1.8	17.9
1816–1820	16.8	24.9	15.5	8.5	10.9	1.2	–	1.2	.6	21.4

Yale University: Academic Department—Percentages

Years	Ministry	Law	Medicine	Education	Commercial pursuits	Public service	Engineering	Agriculture	Literature/Journalism	Unclassified
1702–1705	63.6	9.1	–	18.2	–	9.1	–	–	–	–
1706–1710	63.6	–	4.5	–	9.1	4.5	4.5	9.1	–	4.5
1711–1715	65.0	–	–	5.0	15.0	–	–	10.0	–	5.0
1716–1720	68.6	2.9	–	–	5.7	5.7	–	2.9	–	14.3
1721–1725	50.0	3.3	5.0	6.7	5.0	6.7	–	8.3	–	15.0
1726–1730	42.5	8.7	7.5	3.7	6.2	7.5	–	1.2	–	22.5
1731–1735	48.9	6.7	6.7	2.2	7.8	2.2	–	2.2	–	23.3
1736–1740	42.7	6.7	6.7	2.2	10.1	3.4	–	2.2	–	25.8
1741–1745	54.4	7.8	6.8	1.9	10.7	5.8	–	2.9	–	9.7
1746–1750	39.7	7.8	15.5	1.7	6.9	6.4	–	3.4	–	18.9
1751–1755	38.5	10.9	13.5	2.2	5.4	3.3	–	7.6	–	19.6
1756–1760	35.9	10.1	9.1	2.3	13.9	3.5	–	4.5	–	21.2
1761–1765	38.1	14.8	12.7	2.6	10.6	0.5	–	6.9	–	14.3
1766–1770	33.3	8.9	12.6	3.7	11.9	2.2	–	5.2	–	22.2
1771–1775	32.9	11.9	11.9	5.6	13.9	6.3	–	2.8	–	14.7
1776–1780	17.9	26.3	12.6	3.7	12.6	7.9	–	2.6	1.6	15.3
1781–1785	23.5	30.9	7.4	5.7	14.7	3.2	–	2.3	–	12.9
1786–1790	30.3	33.6	17.2	0.5	10.1	2.3	–	–	–	6.7
1791	33.3	44.4	–	3.7	14.8	3.7	–	–	–	–
1797	39.0	42.0	8.0	3.0	6.0	–	–	3.0	–	–
1802	30.0	33.0	8.0	2.0	17.0	–	–	9.0	–	–
1813, 1814	25.0	36.0	14.0	5.0	12.0	–	–	6.0	2.0	–
1821, 1822, 1824	34.0	31.0	20.0	5.0	15.0	–	–	5.0	–	–

After reading this selection, consider these questions:

1. What is the overall trend (in numbers and percentages) of Harvard and Yale graduates choosing to enter the ministry? Using a text book to establish a chronology, consider whether the Great Awakening had an impact. Did the Great Awakening have greater impact at Harvard or Yale? What might account for that?

2. What is the overall trend (in numbers and percentages) of Harvard and Yale graduates choosing law as a profession? Did the Great Awakening influence the decision of graduates to enter the law? What impact did the American Revolution have?

3. Trace the number and percentage of graduates entering the medical profession.

4. Relate major social and economic changes to the choices graduates of Harvard and Yale made.

SELECTION 4:

Abigail Adams and Thomas Jefferson on Shays's Rebellion

A *commercial depression in 1785–1786 hit Massachusetts particularly hard. Trade with the West Indies slowed and farm prices fell, which made taxation, already a point of contention, unbearably heavy, especially for many farmers. Foreclosures on property led to widespread hostility against lawyers and courts. In 1786 rebellion broke out in central and western Massachusetts. Led by Captain Daniel Shays, mobs broke up sessions of courts and threatened the armory at Springfield. Eventually a militia raised in eastern Massachusetts put down the rebellion. Shays's Rebellion generated concern that the Articles of Confederation did not provide for a strong enough government. The rebellion therefore generated impetus for the Constitution. The first letter excerpted here, written by Abigail Adams to Thomas Jefferson on January 2, 1787, expresses Adams's concern (one shared by many prominent citizens) that Shays's Rebellion threatened property and order. The second letter partially excerpted here, written by Jefferson to James Madison on January 30, 1787, demonstrates no such alarm. Indeed, the letter contains Jefferson's famous remark that "a little rebellion now and then is a good thing." Shays's Rebellion and the reactions of Adams and Jefferson reflect the concern for balancing democratic forces and order that characterized the Revolutionary era.*

A*bigail Adams to Thomas Jefferson, January 2, 1787.* With regard to the Tumults in my Native state which you inquire about, I wish I could say that report had exagerated them. It is too true Sir that they have been carried to so allarming a Height as to stop the Courts of justice in several Counties. Ignorant, wrestless desperadoes, without conscience or principals, have led a deluded multitude to follow their standard, under pretence of grievances which have no existance but in their immaginations. Some of them were crying out for a paper currency, some for an equal distribution of property, some were for annihilating all debts, others complaning that the Senate was a useless Branch of Government, that the Court of common pleas was unnecessary, and that the sitting of the General Court in Boston was a grievance. By this list you will see the materials which compose this

Excerpted from *Sources of the American Republic: A Documentary History of Politics, Society, and Thought,* by Marvin Meyers, Alexander Kern, and John G. Cawelti (Chicago: Scott, Foresman and Company, 1960). Copyright © 1960 by Scott, Foresman and Company. Reprinted with permission.

rebellion, and the necessity there is of the wisest and most vigorus measures to quell and suppress it. Instead of that laudible spirit which you approve, which makes a people watchfull over their Liberties and alert in the defence of them, these mobish insurgents are for sapping the foundation, and distroying the whole fabrick at once.—But as these people make only a small part of the state, when compared to the more sensible and judicious, and altho they create a just allarm and give much trouble and uneasiness, I cannot help flattering myself that they will prove sallutary to the state at large, by leading to an investigation of the causes which have produced these commotions. Luxery and extravagance both in furniture and dress had pervaded all orders of our Countrymen and women, and was hastning fast to sap their independance by involving every class of citizens in distress, and accumulating debts upon them which they were unable to discharge. Vanity was becoming a more powerfull principal than patriotism. The lower order of the community were prest for taxes, and tho possest of landed property they were unable to answer the demand, whilst those who possest money were fearfull of lending, least the mad cry of the mob should force the Legislature upon a measure very different from the touch of Midas.

By the papers I send you, you will see the beneficial effects already produced. An act of the Legislature laying duties of 15 per cent upon many articles of British manufacture and totally prohibiting others—a number of Vollunteers Lawyers physicians and Merchants from Boston made up a party of Light horse commanded by Col. Hitchbourn, Leit. Col. Jackson and Higgenson, and went out in persuit of the insurgents and were fortunate enough to take 3 of their principal Leaders, Shattucks Parker and Page. Shattucks defended himself and was wounded in his knee with a broadsword. He is in Jail in Boston and will no doubt be made an example of.

Thomas Jefferson to James Madison, January 30, 1787. I am impatient to learn your sentiments on the late troubles in the Eastern states. So far as I have yet seen, they do not appear to threaten serious consequences. Those states have suffered by the stoppage of the channels of their commerce, which have not yet found other issues. This must render money scarce, and make the people uneasy. This uneasiness has produced acts absolutely unjustifiable: but I hope they will provoke no severities from their governments. A consciousness of those in power that their administration of the public affairs has been honest, may perhaps produce too great a degree of indignation: and those characters wherein fear predominates over hope may apprehend too much from these instances of irregularity. They may conclude too hastily that nature has formed man insusceptible of any other government but that of force, a conclusion not founded in truth, nor experience. Societies exist under three forms sufficiently distinguishable. 1. Without government, as among our Indians. 2. Under governments wherein the will of every one has a just influence, as in the case in England in a slight degree, and in our states in a great one. 3. Under governments of force: as in the case in all other monarchies and in most of the other republics. To have an idea of the curse of existence under these last, they must be seen. It is a government of wolves over sheep. It is a problem, not clear in my mind, that the 1st. condition is not the best. But I believe it to be inconsistent with any great degree of population. The second state has a great deal of good in it. The mass of mankind under that enjoys a precious degree of liberty and happiness. It has it's evils too: the principal of which is the turbulence to which it is subject. But weigh this against the oppressions of monarchy, and it becomes nothing. *Malo periculosam libertatem quam quietam servitutem.* [I prefer perilous liberty to quiet servitude.] Even this evil is productive of good. It prevents the degeneracy of government, and nourishes a general attention to the public affairs. I hold it that a little rebellion now and then is a good thing, and as necessary in the political world as storms in the physical. Unsuccessful rebellions indeed generally establish the incroachments on the rights of the people which have produced them. An observation of this truth should render honest republican governors so mild in their punishment of rebellions, as not to discourage them too much. It is a medicine necessary for the sound health of government.

After reading this selection, consider these questions:

1. What specific demands of the rebels does Abigail Adams list? How does she regard these demands? What are her larger concerns?

2. What benefits does Jefferson see coming from the unrest?

3. Jefferson was in France during Shays's Rebellion. How might that have affected his attitude toward the uprising?

SELECTION 5:

Apprenticeship Contracts in Philadelphia, 1771–1772

Apprenticeship gradually replaced the indentured servitude of immigrants as the primary form of bound labor in the eighteenth century. Unlike indentured servants, apprentices were usually native-born children or adolescents. They were sent to live with a master, for whom they worked in exchange for food and shelter as well as training in the master's trade. Parents often paid a sum to the master for training, improved living standards, or better education. Because of these circumstances, apprentices held a higher status than indentured servants and enjoyed greater protections. For example, apprentices could not be sold by their masters.

For women and girls in particular there were disadvantages as well as advantages to the changing pattern of bound labor. Female indentured servants usually sold their labor for four to five years in exchange for passage and maintenance during the period of indenture. These women were typically eighteen to twenty-five years old. Female apprentices, on the other hand, might begin their apprenticeships at eleven or twelve and be bound for as many as ten years.

The following is a sample of apprenticeship contracts entered in the city of Philadelphia's record of "Individuals Bound out as Apprentices, Servants, Etc." during 1771–1772.

Male Apprentices

Excerpted from *Early American Women: A Documentary History, 1600–1900,* edited by Nancy Woloch (Belmont, CA: Wadsworth Publishing Company, 1992).

Oct. 14, 1771
Bell, James
Indenture to Frazier Kinsley, Philadelphia
House carpenter, to be taught the art, trade, and mystery of a house carpenter, have two winters

schooling, and be taught the first five rules in common arithmetic.
5 yrs. [term of service]

Oct. 5, 1771
Desher, Charles
Indenture to Abraham Hasselbery and his assigns, Philadelphia
To be taught the art, trade and mystery of a tin plate worker, and be found meat, drink, washing, and lodging only.
3 yrs., 6 mo.

Oct. 9, 1771
Cauffman, Jacob
Indenture to Thomas Atmore and his assigns, Philadelphia
Apprentice, to be taught the art, trade and mystery of a hatmaker and found in hats, to find him meat, drank, and lodging, the last six years and six months of the term.
7 yrs., 6 mo.

Oct. 21, 1771
Outerbridge, Rumsey White
Indenture to Joseph Dean, Philadelphia
Taught the art and mystery of a merchant and bookkeeping, found meat, drank, washing, lodging, apprentice[ship] free, the mother to provide sufficient apparel.
3 yrs., 6 mo.

Oct. 22, 1771
Brown, William
Indenture to John Duche and his assigns, Southwark
Taught the boatbuilder's trade, have three quarters evening schooling, found meat, drank, lodging, and working apparel, and at expiration have the tools he works with.
3 yrs., 2 mo., 23 d.

Oct. 22, 1771
Row, Jacob
Indenture to Philip Clumperg and his assigns, Philadelphia
Taught the business of a surgeon barber, read in the bible, write a legible hand, & cypher.
6 yrs.

Oct 31, 1771
Hardie, Robert, Jr.
Indenture to Capt. Thomas Edward Wallace, Philadelphia
Taught the art, trade and mystery of a mariner and navigator, found meat, drink, washing, and lodging, his uncle to provide apparel.
5 yrs., 6 mo.

Female Apprentices

Oct. 21, 1771
Lynch, Mary
Indenture to William Faris and wife, Philadelphia
Taught housewifery, sew plain work, read in the Bible, write a legible hand.
9 yrs., 3 mo.

Nov. 4, 1771
Rone, Mary, Jr.
Indenture to Thomas Pugh and his wife, Philadelphia
Apprentice, taught housewifery, sew plain work, have one year schooling. To be found all necessaries and at the expiration have two complete suits of apparel, one whereof is to be new.
8 yrs., 10 mo.

Nov. 12, 1771
Inglis, Sarah
Indenture to John Kelly and his assigns, Philadelphia
Taught to read, write, and cypher, housewifery, and to sew.
10 yrs., 11 mo.

Nov. 14, 1771
Magere, Lydia
Indenture to Ann Paice and her heirs, Philadelphia
Taught housewifery, quilting, to sew and knit, have 9 months day schooling.
9 yrs., 4 mo., 11 d.

Jan. 23, 1772
Davis, Sarah
Indenture to William Logan and his assigns, W. Nantmeal twp., Northampton Co.
Apprentice, taught housewifery, sew, knit, spin, read in Bible, write a legible hand.
11 yrs., 6 mo.

June 23, 1772
Hughes, Jane
Indenture to William Snowden and Ann, his wife, Philadelphia
Apprentice, taught mantua [gown] maker's trade, have three quarters' schooling, in case of her death, the indenture to be void. To be found all necessaries and at expiration have one new suit of apparel, besides the old.
3 yrs., 9 mo., 13 d.

June 25, 1772
Woodward, Nice
Indenture to Joseph Johnson and his assigns, Southwark
Apprentice, taught housewifery, sew, knit and spin, read and write perfectly.
11 yrs.

July 21, 1772
Mannin, Elizabeth
Indenture to John Hilson, Philadelphia
Apprentice, taught housewifery and mantua maker's trade, and make bonnets and cloaks, have one year schooling. To be found all necessaries and at the expiration have freedom dues.
7 yrs., 6 mo., 14 d.

Sept. 29, 1772
Boyle, Mary
Jonathan Fell and wife, Warwick twp, Bucks Co.
Apprentice, taught housewifery, sew, knit, and spin, read in Bible, write a legible hand, and when she arrives at the age of twelve, give her one ewe. To be found all necessaries and at the expiration have two complete suits of apparel, one whereof to be new, and one spinning wheel.
9 yrs., 10 mo., 19 d.

Oct. 5, 1772
Brockington, Mary
Captain Thomas Powell and Wife, Philadelphia
Apprentice, taught housewifery and sew, time to go to school two years, the grandfather paying expense of schooling and the master to give such further schooling as will perfect her in reading and writing. To be found all necessaries and at expiration have freedom dues.
12 yrs., 9 mo.

Oct. 8, 1772
Adams, Abigail
Indenture to James Painter and his assigns, E. Bradford Co.
Apprentice, taught to read in Bible, write a legible hand, cypher as far and through the rule of multiplication, and spin, also housewifery.
14 yrs., 1 mo., 25 d.

Oct. 10, 1772
Anderson, Mary
Indenture to Benjamin Dismant and his assigns, N. Providence, Philadelphia Co.
Apprentice, taught to read in Bible, write a legible hand, sew, knit, spin and housewifery. To be found all necessaries and at the expiration have two complete suits of apparel, one whereof to be new, a new spinning wheel, a cow, or £5 in money in lieu of the cow.
14 yrs.

After reading this selection, consider these questions:

1. What was the average period of apprenticeship for males? What was the average for females? What might account for the difference?

2. What might explain the very different terms of apprenticeship among the various occupations?

3. What proportion of male apprenticeships included provisions for training in reading and arithmetic? What proportion of female apprenticeships did? How might one explain any differences?

CHAPTER 8

Women in the Revolutionary Era

Social and political upheavals like the American Revolution change many aspects of daily life; in other respects, however, daily life goes on unchanged. To the extent major political events do change society, they are more likely to accelerate changes underway than to reverse developing social trends. These observations apply, at least in a general way, to the American Revolution.

The Revolutionary crisis drew women to political activity. Boycotts of British goods in the 1760s disrupted domestic life and inherently involved women. Further, women who produced homespun cloth to replace British textiles played an important role in the developing conflict between Britain and the American colonies. Perhaps as a result, women became more likely to comment on political matters. Moreover, Revolutionary rhetoric that stressed liberty and equality provided a basis for at least some women to question their status in society.

Nevertheless, independence and the creation of the United States did not bring about dramatic changes in the legal or political status of women. The abolition of primogeniture improved the legal status of women; married women, however, had no legal identity of their own, and they could not own property independent of their husbands. In general, women could not vote or otherwise participate in the political process.

If the political and legal status of women changed very little, the imperial crisis and the War for Independence did alter the lives of many women. Some were widowed by the war; some had their homes, farms, or plantations destroyed. In addition, with husbands away at war, women had to run farms, plantations, and businesses. The conflict with England cut off the supply of European consumer goods, leaving a gap that was filled largely by household manufactures, in many cases made by women.

Perhaps even more important, the Revolutionary crisis contributed to changes that had been underway, in some cases throughout the eighteenth century. Particularly in the second half of the century, patriarchal authority had diminished within the family. For example, children claimed a right to choose a spouse. In a related change, marriage came to be considered the result of a loving relationship rather than a partnership that might lead to more tender affections. Finally, education took on a new significance. Once considered a means to personal advancement, education became a means to strengthen the republic. In that context, educational opportunities became more widely available for women.

Above all, the struggle for independence opened a debate about the role of women in a republic. No modern republic existed for a model, so the options were constrained only by existing social relationships and the imagination of the founding generation. Women were clearly not to be full participating citizens in the sense that men were. But what was the role of women in a republic? The answer that evolved established an important, if subordinate, role for women. Women were to be good republican wives, to lead their husbands to virtue. Perhaps most importantly, women were to be good republican mothers and raise sons to be virtuous citizens and leaders of the new republic.

After reading this chapter, consider these questions:

1. What impact did the American Revolution have on the roles of women?

2. In what respects did the Revolution leave women's lives unchanged?

3. How did the founders of the new nation envision the relationship between the institution of marriage and the republic?

SELECTION 1:

The Republican Wife

The notion that the personal is political is far older than the modern women's movement. In the following essay, Jan Lewis, a professor of history at Rutgers University, argues that people in the early American republic envisioned a link between the private partnership of marriage and the public roles the couple would play. Further, marriage itself was seen as a microcosm of social relations in the larger republic.

When the American colonists commenced rebellion against the British government and assumed the separate and equal station to which they believed the laws of God and nature both entitled them, they found in marriage—"that SOCIAL UNION, which the beneficent Creator instituted for the happiness of Man"—a metaphor for their ideal of social and political relationships. In the republic envisioned by American writers, citizens were to be bound together not by patriarchy's duty or liberalism's self-interest, but by affection, and it was, they believed, marriage, more than any other institution, that trained citizens in this virtue. . . . Marriage was the very pattern from which the cloth of republican society was to be cut.

Revolutionary-era writers held up the loving partnership of man and wife in opposition to patriarchal dominion as the republican model for social and political relationships. The essays, stories, poems, and novels that established this model created in republican marriage an ideal that drew upon recent social trends and infused them with political meaning; in so doing, their authors created for women an important new political role, not so much as a mother, . . . but, rather, as a wife. As an indispensable half of the conjugal union that served as the ideal for political as well as familial relationships, the Republican Wife exemplified the strengths and weaknesses of the Revolutionary era's notion of woman's role and, indeed, of republicanism itself; neither can be understood fully except in the context of the other.

Because historians have begun to question whether American political discourse in the period 1775–1815 can be understood in terms of republicanism alone, it is important to note that the adjective "republican" will be used here much as Americans of the period used it—to signify not only classical republicanism but also that fusion of civic humanism and evangelical ardor achieved by Americans at the eve of the Revolu-

Excerpted from "The Republican Wife: Virtue and Seduction in the Early Republic," by Jan Lewis, *William and Mary Quarterly,* October 1987. Copyright © 1987 by Jan Lewis. Reprinted with permission.

tion. The key to republicanism is virtue, the self-sacrificial and disinterested quality that was prized in both sacred and secular traditions. The premium that republican thought placed upon disinterestedness has obscured the revolutionary nature of its views about women. To be sure, republican theorists were unwilling to think of women, or any other group, as having different and perhaps antagonistic interests; hence, they did not address women as a separate group. Republicanism assumed, however, that America's dawning glory would cast its beneficent rays upon the whole of society, a new and different society in which women would be required to play a new and unprecedented role. . . .

Finally, we must note that much of what was read in America had been written in Britain. Popular British novels were brought out in American editions, and American editors, unable to fill their periodicals with original works, borrowed freely from each other and from their British counterparts. Yet what matters is not only the origin and intent of such works but also the lessons Americans might have derived from them. . . .

Indeed, a British work might be edited for the American audience in ways that would make it more applicable to the American situation. In *Clarissa,* the novel of the patriarchal family par excellence, the heroine is . . . "purely a victim caught between two tyrannies," that of the father and that of the seducer. Although [novelist Samuel] Richardson held the disobedient daughter partly responsible for her sad fate, eighteenth-century American editions of the book removed that assessment of the heroine from both the subtitle and the introduction, making Clarissa instead the innocent victim of male arrogance, imperiousness, and design. Yet *Clarissa* was more than a seduction story; it was a political parable with particular lessons for Americans, as a fearful John Adams recognized when he observed that "Democracy is [Robert] Lovelace and the people are Clarissa."

Americans who aimed for the separate station of a viable republic would have to learn better than Clarissa how to resist the tyrannies and seductions that republican theorists were certain they faced. Because eighteenth-century thought placed the family and the state on one continuum, that of "society," and did not yet—as the nineteenth-century would—erect a barrier between the private sphere of the family and the public one of the world, it could dramatize issues of authority in terms of relationships between members of a family. Accordingly, the young woman's quest for a suitable husband and her attempt to navigate between the eighteenth-century's Scylla of overweening power and its Charybdis of seductive liberty was the nation's plot as well. [Refers to the Greek myth, here meaning "between a rock and a hard place."]

Americans, successfully completing a revolution against one sort of tyranny, were bound to conclude that their young men and women also could achieve independence. The anti-patriarchalism of Revolutionary ideology dictated that tyranny presented the most immediate and obvious threat to American happiness, and patriarchal domination the chief obstacle to happy and virtuous marriage. . . .

So resonant was this anti-patriarchal theme that well after the Revolution American magazines published articles excoriating "parents . . . who are daily offering up the honour and happiness of their children at the shrine of interest and ambition," much as the British government had sacrificed its American colonies. Instead, "marriages should be contracted from motives of affection, rather than of interest." Fortunately, such unions were possible in "happy America," where partible inheritance—"provided our conduct does not render us unworthy"—formed "the basis of equality and the incitement to industry and caution." If America's sons and daughters were educated to "virtue and good morality," they would choose to marry for love rather than interest. Being capable of exercising sound judgment, children were not obligated to obey the injunctions of narrow-minded or rapacious parents. . . .

Historians of the family have shown that parental control of marriage declined over the course of the eighteenth century, while children's autonomy increased. That trend had its roots in the Reformation; Protestantism, with its insistence that "mutual comfort" was one of marriage's primary purposes, had licensed the consensual, affectionate union. Although American Puritan ministers still retained for parents, by virtue of their supposedly superior wisdom, a key role in selecting their children's mates, they nonetheless recognized that "marriage is one of the weightiest actions of a person's life, and as the Yoke fellow is suitable or unsuitable, so that condition is like to be very comfortable or uncomfortable." . . . During the eighteenth century, parents grew less willing or able to exert the full range of pressures at their command to shape their children's destinies; the balance tipped in favor of the younger generation's discretion.

Thus rhetoric that implicitly likened late eighteenth-century parents to designing court ministers, bent upon subjecting their dependents, grossly exaggerated the control that parents retained over their children's marriages and, in fact, overstated the power parents had held a century earlier. Nonetheless, the rhetoric of marriage, much like that of politics, served both to expose underlying fears and to legitimate and encourage patterns that had already come to prevail.

Republican theorists endeavored to show how, in a post-patriarchal world, citizens could govern themselves, how they could form a society bound by love rather than fear. Because they deemed marriage the school of affection, authors who wrote about the institution were addressing one of their age's most pressing questions: how to make citizens fit for a republic. For example, if the choice of a mate were, or should be, the individual's, he or she must know how to select wisely. And if the parents no longer did, or should, have control, substitute parents could still give advice, which they did at great length in numerous tracts and essays. Parents did not abdicate; rather, they refashioned themselves into friendly paternalists who exerted influence in their families by more subtle, psychological means and in the wider world by words of friendly counsel. . . .

What sort of man made the ideal husband? He was republican virtue incarnate, moderation personified. He was "devout without superstition, and pious without melancholy, . . . careful without avarice, [manifesting] a kind of unconcernedness without negligence." He should be well educated but not "a pedant." A woman should look for "virtuous conduct, good temper, discretion, regularity and industry," and a "mild and even" disposition. Unlike her European sisters, who supposedly married to raise their status, the American maid aimed at—and hoped to maintain —a happy medium, a domestic version of that steadily improving yet never-changing society identified as the ideal society of republican dreams. . . .

The good husband was like the good citizen; he wed "not by interest but by choice," and "he treats his wife with delicacy as a woman, with tenderness as a friend." He "ever studied the happiness of the woman he loved more than his own." In fact, the ideal husband resembled more than a little the popular portrait of the Revolutionary War officer. . . . The qualities that made a man honorable in public life, then, distinguished him as a potential husband as well.

Men, likewise, were supposed to select republicans as their life partners. As the author of "On the Choice of a Wife" put it, "virtue, wisdom, presence of mind, patience, vigour, capacity, and application, are not *sexual* qualities; they belong to all who have duties to perform and evils to endure." Echoing standard Protestant assumptions, Americans and the British writers they chose to republish argued that the most important considerations in the selection of a wife were her "qualifications as a *companion* and a *helper.*". . .

Men and women both were thus advised to seek for their mates what we can recognize as embodiments of republican ideology. They were warned at even greater length to avoid certain notorious types, those associated with the despicable aspects of European court life: flatterers, deceivers, flirts, fops, coxcombs, coquettes, and all persons lacking in honor and virtue. . . . They promise ruin not only for themselves and their victims but also for the infant nation, for they practice habits that were commonly believed to spell the death of republics. . . .

When courtship and marriage are infused with political meaning, women inevitably and inescapably become political beings. Make no mistake: these first formulations of a feminine political role were not fundamentally feminist. They were not devised by women in particular, nor was their aim primarily to enhance the position of women. The dynamic, rather, was republican and anti-patriarchal: it juxtaposed the virtuous, independent child and the oppressive, corrupting parent, and it found in the union of two virtuous individuals the true end of society and the fit paradigm for political life. Such a conceptualization of the relationship between family and polity represents more a subtle shift than a clean break from earlier models. When Puritans designated the family "a little commonwealth," they meant it to be "a schoole wherein the first principles and grounds of government and subjection are learned: whereby men are fitted to greater matters in Church or commonwealth." In such a family the relationship between parent and child was most important.

When anti-patriarchalists in the eighteenth century substituted marriage for parenthood as the fundamental familial relationship, they did not, however, question the assumption that the family was but the society in miniature. Society still appeared as the family writ large, with the same sorts of relationships deemed appropriate for both the as-yet-undifferentiated spheres of home and world. Yet in shifting interest from the parent-child nexus to the husband-wife bond, eighteenth-century authors necessarily raised women to a new moral and political stature. . . . If the affectionate union between a man and his wife, freely entered into, without tyrannical interference, is the model for all the relationships in the society and the polity, then the wife, as an indispensable half of the marital union, is a political creature.

To the extent that the success of the republican endeavor rested upon the character of citizens, republicanism demanded virtue of women, not because it numbered them as citizens but because it recognized how intimately women, in consensual unions, were connected to men. A virtuous man required a virtuous mate. Moreover, republicanism called upon every means at its disposal to assure male virtue. . . .

"A woman of virtue and prudence is a public good—a public benefactor." She has the power to make "public decency . . . a fashion—and public virtue the only example." And how is woman to accomplish that great end? By her influence over the manners of men. . . .

The height of a woman's influence was reached during the period of "love and courtship," which, "it is universally allowed, invest a lady with more authority than in any other situation that falls to the lot of human beings." . . .

Once she had seduced him into virtue, the married woman's task was to preserve her husband in the exalted state to which her influence had raised him. . . .

Unless we recognize how grandiose American expectations could be and how terrifying was the possibility that they might not be realized, we cannot fully appreciate how central female education was to the republican agenda. While it is true that some reformers advocated educating women so that they, in turn, could teach their children, the more important consideration, always, was to make women into fit companions for republican men and, especially, reliable guarantors of masculine virtue. . . .

That republican marriage was symmetrical does not mean that it was fully egalitarian; rather, men and women were opposite sides of the same coin or, as a popular fable had it, two halves of a being that had once been sundered. . . .

Like republicanism, the doctrine of symmetrical marriage subordinated individual interest to the greater good of the whole. Accordingly, marriages based upon interest were to be loathed; true marriage was the model for disinterested benevolence. . . .

It is tempting to suppose that the ideology of the republican marriage was but the rhetorical manifestation of the newly affectionate conjugal union, and that both rhetoric and reality represented positive and progressive change. Yet we must remember that republicanism . . . looked to the past as well as to the future; it focused more upon the welfare of the society than the well-being of the individual. Thus it had an implicitly anti-individualistic dimension, one that was exposed whenever conflict arose. We can see that tendency in the ideal of marital concord, which could be—and was—used to legitimate both coverture and the exclusion of women from direct participation in politics. Indeed, the rhetoric of harmony seems almost a gloss upon the doctrine of marital unity—the English common law fiction that in marriage the husband and wife are one, and the husband is the one. It has puzzled some historians that American Revolutionaries did not jettison coverture along with other pieces of undemocratic British baggage such as primogeniture and entail. Yet republican theorists prized harmony above all else; they created the ideal of the affectionate marriage not so much to liberate the individual as to assure concord in the family, the building-block of society. . . .

Still, because women figured so prominently in it, we must ask what bearing the literature of republican marriage had for actual republican women. We see embedded in these works many of the themes that historians have already exposed: a growing acceptance of affection as the only proper basis of marriage, increasing respect for feminine virtue, the feminization of religion, the idealization of chastity, and, finally, a growing interest in the possibilities for feminine influence. These themes are all compressed into the person of the Republican Wife: affectionate, virtuous, chaste, and capable of enormous moral authority over her husband. The Republican Wife represented, in the ideology at least, a real and important role. Yet even as an image, she was limited. Indeed, she led to a dead end, for her capability always depended upon masculine susceptibility. She had no more power than man allowed, and even if republican doctrine suggested that men ought to welcome feminine influence, that doctrine held no sway over those who did not subscribe to its credo. That generalization, of course, describes the fundamental weakness in republicanism; it had no power over those who were not or did not want to be virtuous.

In that sense republicanism served women no more poorly than it did men: all were baffled by unalloyed vice. Even though republicanism enhanced woman's status and legitimated improvements in her education as well as her entry into benevolent reform movements, it also placed implicit checks upon her power.

After reading this selection, consider these questions:

1. In what ways does Lewis regard the ideology of the republican wife as expanding the power of women?

2. What limitations does the model of the republican wife impose on women?

3. How does Lewis establish a relationship between the ideology she describes and social reality?

SELECTION 2:

Marital Discord in Pennsylvania, 1730–1830

In the previous essay, Jan Lewis discusses the ideology of marriage in Revolutionary America. By examining cases of marital discord, Merril D. Smith, an adjunct professor of history at Temple University, attempts to analyze the impact of the ideology Lewis describes on individual marriages.

Nearly all adults in early America expected to marry at some point in their lives. Husbands and wives fought and quarreled, loved and hated, and in many ways behaved much as they do today. What marriage—and the roles of husband and wife—meant to the people of early America, however, was much different from today. It was a time when Americans glorified marriage, which joined together husband and wife as a symbol of the bonds that held together the disparate aspects of republican society. Eighteenth- and early nineteenth-century Americans considered marriage a microcosm of a larger world. It was through marriage that men and women could learn to be virtuous citizens as well as to instill virtue in future generations.

But not everyone was happily married, and those who were unhappily married came from all walks of life. It is impossible to know how many people were unhappy in their marriages. Most probably left no traces in legal records or other standard sources. The majority of unhappily married people in early America, in fact, did not divorce. Instead, they found solace in socializing with family members and friends, in alcohol, or through involvement in extramarital affairs. Some vented their anger and frustrations by abusing family members or deserting their spouses and families. For those intent upon breaking free from their spouses, however, desertion probably remained the easiest and most frequent method. . . .

Throughout this time period in Pennsylvania, there was a sometimes bitter and ongoing clash between two opposing sets of marital ideals: the older one emphasized patriarchal authority, wifely obedience, rigidly defined gender roles, and it permitted a double standard of sexuality. The other set stressed love, companionship, a single standard of sexuality, and complementary gender roles. I begin with the following questions: Were married couples affected by these conflicting ideals? To what extent did the idealization of marriage in this period lead to unreasonable expectations in marriage? What subsequent problems arose? How did husbands and wives cope when tensions developed? Did the grounds for divorce change over this period?

I have limited the geographical scope of this study to Pennsylvania, particularly the southeastern region, encompassing Philadelphia and Chester County. . . . Pennsylvania is unique in some interesting ways. The divorce law of 1785, for example, was the first divorce law in the nation to include cruelty as grounds for divorce, though this "divorce" was more of a legal separation than what we know today. . . .

Pennsylvania had no clear procedure for divorce until 1785. Although the Assembly granted a few divorces, Parliament forbade this process in 1772. Thus, Pennsylvania granted no more divorces until after the Revolution. The Pennsylvania divorce act of 1785, influenced by Revolutionary ideas of personal freedom and republican ideals concerning virtuous citizenry, once again provided Pennsylvanians with a legal way to leave their spouse—but the people who took advantage of the law were only a fraction of those involved in unhappy marriages. Most did not divorce. Instead, as they did before the passage of the divorce law, they tried to endure their marriages, or left without the benefit of litigation. Consequently, studying the ways people reacted in troubled marriages when they did not divorce, as well as when they did, gives us a broader and more complete picture of marital discord. . . .

Studying marital discord illuminates much about families and communities. Throughout the period, the support of family and neighbors remained important to those involved in contentious marriages. To a man or woman betrayed or abused by a spouse, they gave comfort and solace; to a man or woman deserted by a spouse, they gave economic support. The testimonies of family members and neighbors indicate, furthermore, the ways in which the community felt the couple upheld or violated its moral standards. In the eye of the law and the community, what constituted a troubled marriage?

. . . My goal has been to explore the expectations of normal marriage, marriages under strain, and those split by desertion or divorce as part of a continuum whose tenuous boundaries often remain ambiguous and vague.

This study analyzes the years before, during, and after the Revolution to search for changes over time in the expectations and experiences of marriage. . . . During this time, patriarchal forms and methods of "self-divorce" coexisted with new expectations about how marriage should work and more frequent legal divorce. Moreover, the changing American culture around them helped men and women to form gender identities that often opposed each other. Families, neighbors, and religious authorities, as well as prescriptive literature and laws, all influenced men and women on how to be husbands and wives, and on what a marriage should be like. Thus, men and women brought a wide range of expectations to marriage, and they reacted to tensions in their marriages in quite different ways. Yet, despite such evolution in marital anticipations, couples faced many of the same problems in the 1830s as in the 1730s. Typically, they quarreled over money, sex, drinking, abusive behavior, and in-laws.

People changed their ideas about marriage in the eighteenth century. Although seventeenth-century Americans expected husbands and wives to feel affection for one another, often this came after the marriage. In choosing a mate, they were supposed to be guided by their parents. Later in the eighteenth century couples expected to choose their own spouses and married primarily for love.

By the time of the Revolution, these new ideas about marriage had strengthened and were expressed in popular literature throughout the colonies. Republican rhetoric stressed partnership and mutual affection between husband and wife. In addition, as [historians] Linda Kerber and Jan Lewis have shown, the roles of wife and mother assumed more importance in the ideology of the new republic—concepts that continued to be stressed into the nineteenth century. Both male and female writers described the ideal wife as a loving friend to her husband. Guided by the concept of republican virtue in the eighteenth century and influenced by the evangelical and reform movements in the nineteenth, she would be pure and virtuous, and able to reform a drunken or unfaithful husband by her good example. She would also be willing to submit to his authority, however. These contradictory ideas frequently led to friction between husbands and wives.

Americans also expected husbands to behave themselves in particular ways. They, too, were supposed to be loving spouses and kind fathers. Nevertheless, both traditional outlooks and the law made them the breadwinners and heads of the household. Yet not every husband could achieve these standards of respectability.

Although marriage, republican style, stressed partnership and mutual affection, it continued to emphasize the differences between men and women. The role of each was supposed to complement the other. The idea was not to regard one another as equals. These differences in roles contributed to separate cultures for men and women, and often led to discontentment between husbands and wives. In addition, the economic control which most husbands possessed gave them considerable power over their wives.

My thesis, simply stated, is that women and men were influenced both by the new ideals about marriage concerning how wives and husbands should behave, and by traditional patriarchal notions about men being the head of the household, especially in terms of earning and controlling the money to support the family. Conflicts arose when couples could not reconcile expectations about marriage with the reality of it, especially when one partner, usually the wife, anticipated a marriage based upon the new ideals and her husband expected a traditional patriarchal one. Both husbands and wives, moreover, often found that they could not live up to the image their society demanded of them. In order to receive help when a marriage failed, however, it was wives who had to prove that they were blameless, pure, and virtuous. The new ideology trapped them just as much as the old patriarchal norms had.

Yet women discovered ways to manipulate the legal system in order to gain some relief from their marital problems. By portraying themselves as virtuous wives and innocent victims, women were often successful in obtaining economic support, if not a final break from their spouses. Changes in the divorce laws also benefited women. Between 1785 and 1815, there were 236 women out of a total of 367 applicants who appealed for divorces from the Pennsylvania Supreme Court. The court granted 114 (48%) of their petitions.

Because Pennsylvania had no clear policy on divorce until 1785, it is impossible to use divorce records exclusively as a gauge of marital expectations in this state. In some ways, the law itself can be seen as a watershed. Before the law, divorces were mostly sought by men. After the law, more women than men petitioned for divorce. The emergence of a divorce law, however, should not be seen as the sole indicator of rising marital discord. There were men and women who found themselves caught in unhappy marriages earlier in the century, and many of them found ways to leave their marriages without a divorce law. At the same time, there were men and women, who for various reasons—lack of money or inclination, inability to travel to the Supreme Court, or entanglement in marital troubles unrecognized by the 1785 divorce law—continued to use alternative methods of leaving their marriages even after the divorce law was enacted.

Conditions in America made desertion a relatively easy way to quit a marriage. Many people left a spouse across the ocean, and remarried in the new world. Others abandoned their husbands or wives in America in order to return to Ireland or France. In a port city, such as Philadelphia, it was relatively simple to take a ship to another colony/state, or farther—if one had the money for passage. As travel became easier, it was less difficult for the unhappily married individual to leave his or her spouse to go to the frontier.

Nevertheless, women often fared worse than men when their marriages collapsed. Being deserted by a husband frequently meant a woman was left without means of support. Many times she was pregnant and/or had young children. She might even have her home and belongings sold to pay an absent husband's debts. The physical act of leaving was probably easier for men, who would not be as conspicuous traveling alone, who would find it easier to obtain work, and who would not have to worry about pregnancy or nursing infants. Yet, despite the risks and difficulties involved, women did leave their husbands. . . .

Besides changes in public perceptions regarding marriage, laws and the public institutions bearing on it in Pennsylvania evolved significantly. They permitted more options for beleaguered couples. Prior to the 1785 divorce statute, divorce was possible in Pennsylvania only through submission of a private bill to the Assembly. Changes in the law were most profound for women—the new legislation permitted divorce on grounds of both desertion and cruelty, which was not possible prior to the law. Moreover, women could receive alimony in cases of cruelty. Thus, the act appears to have been influenced by new beliefs about what marriage should be. Nevertheless, it retained older patriarchal characteristics. These women seeking divorces were still seen as wives—part of the conjugal unit, rather than as distinct adult women who could function on their own. Only later did legislation in the 1830s and 1840s give married women more control over their own money and property.

Changing marital beliefs [had an impact] on the marital expectations of eighteenth- and early nineteenth-century couples in Pennsylvania. . . . The new ideals affected men's and women's ideas about marriage, and the impact these expectations had on the marriages themselves. . . .

As today, sometimes sexual tensions caused marital problems, and sometimes they were the result of problems already existing in a troubled marriage. . . . Far from being "passionless," some women sought sexual encounters as a way of finding the love their society taught them they should find. A double standard remained, however. Although society supposed that both husbands and wives would remain faithful to one another, wives most of all were expected to practice the norms of sexual self-control, and to forgive and reform their husbands when they lapsed.

Violence between husband and wife is . . . not just a modern problem. Early Pennsylvanians, too, had to determine how, and how far, they would interfere between husband and wife when violence arose. Family members and neighbors were crucial in offering both physical intervention to curb conflict and testimony in court depositions, despite claims by many historians that the privacy of the family was beginning to be held sacred. Also within the period studied, laws began to change to help women who were abused by their husbands. . . .

Wives and husbands . . . deserted their spouses. The reasons for and the results of desertion differed according to gender. The term "desertion" actually had a different meaning as applied to men and to women. Women who left their husbands or refused to cohabit with them were often labeled disobedient or immoral. Husbands who abandoned their wives were considered lazy or irresponsible, and they could be forced to provide support for their wives. . . .

If marriage can be compared to a woven fabric, then this work is a study of how that cloth was woven in eighteenth- and early nineteenth-century Pennsylvania and what conditions made it unravel. This examination of marital discord reveals a picture of discontentment caused both by evolving societal expectations and by distinctions between how husbands and wives viewed marriage. Changes in American society between the mid-eighteenth and early nineteenth centuries promoted and spread a view of marriage as "companionate," where husband and wife were loving partners who shared in making important decisions. The older tradition of marriage as a patriarchal institution continued, however, both within the laws and as a part of individual beliefs. The encumbrances of coverture, for instance, kept married women second-class citizens, legally dependent upon their husbands for economic support.

Within troubled marriages, men and women often had disparate beliefs about their roles. When either spouse felt unable to conform to his or her presumed part, it caused problems within the marriage. Similarly, tensions arose when a wife or husband believed that his or her spouse did not meet the accepted norms. Conflicts ensued in some cases when husbands retained their patriarchal viewpoints while their wives embraced newer companionate forms of marriage, and in other instances emerged when husbands failed to take charge as the master of the house. Thus, it was not only the development of new expectations, but also gender distinctions regarding the new ways of looking at marriage that caused marital discord during this time.

After reading this selection, consider these questions:

1. What expectations did changing ideas of marriage arouse in men and women?

2. How did those expectations lead to problems in marriages?

3. What impact did the American Revolution have on marriages?

SELECTION 3:

Correspondence Between John and Abigail Adams, 1776

The following letters were exchanged between John Adams, a member of the Continental Congress (which was meeting in Philadelphia), and his wife, Abigail, in Braintree, Massachusetts. The Adamses' marriage reflected in many respects emerging ideas about marriage described by Jan Lewis and Merril D. Smith. Throughout their married lives, John and Abigail were partners.

The first letter contains Abigail's famous admonition to her husband to "Remember the Ladies." Her tone is jocular, but there is more than a little seriousness behind her message as well. Abigail presents something of a contradiction to modern observers. She vigorously advocated independence, yet once that had been achieved, she denounced all opponents of the new federal government as dangerous and advocated suppression of a free press. In spite of her forceful advocacy of legal rights and educational opportunities for women, she believed that women belonged in the home.

The second letter, John's reply, parries Abigail's thrust by asserting that men had "only the name of masters." The letter also indicates John's concern about the social unrest unleashed by resistance to British rule.

Abigail to John Adams. I wish you would ever write me a Letter half as long as I write you; and tell me if you may where your Fleet are gone?

What sort of Defence Virginia can make against our common Enemy? Whether it is so situated as to make an able Defence? Are not the Gentery Lords and the common people vassals, are they not like the uncivilized Natives Brittain represents us to be? I hope their Riffel Men who have shewen themselves very savage and even Blood thirsty are not a specimen of the Generality of the people.

Excerpted from *America's Families: A Documentary History,* edited by Donald M. Scott and Bernard Wishy (New York: Harper & Row, 1817).

I am willing to allow the Colony great merrit for having produced a [George] Washington but they have been shamefully duped by a [Lord] Dunmore [Virginia's last royal governor].

I have sometimes been ready to think that the passion for Liberty cannot be Eaquelly Strong in the Breasts of those who have been accustomed to deprive their fellow Creatures of theirs. Of this I am certain that it is not founded upon that generous and christian principal of doing to others as we would that others should do unto us.

Do not you want to see Boston: I am fearfull of the small pox, or I should have been in before this time. I got Mr. Crane to go to our House and see what state it was in. I find it has been occupied by one of the Doctors of a Regiment, very dirty, but no other damage has been done to it. The few things which were left in it are all gone. Cranch has the key which he never delivered up. I have wrote to him for it and am determined to get it cleand as soon as possible and shut it up. I look upon it a new acquisition of property, a property which one month ago I did not value at a single Shilling, and could with pleasure have seen it in flames.

The Town in General is left in a better state than we expected, more oweing to a percipitate flight than any Regard to the inhabitants, tho some individuals discovered a sense of honour and justice and have left the rent of the Houses in which they were, for the owners and the furniture unhurt, or if damaged sufficient to make it good.

Others have committed abominable Ravages. . . .

I feel very differently at the approach of spring to what I did a month ago. We knew not then whether we could plant or sow with safety, whether when we had toild we could reap the fruits of our own industery, whether we could rest in our own Cottages, or whether we should not be driven from the sea coasts to seek shelter in the wilderness, but now we feel as if we might sit under our own vine and eat the good of the land. . . .

Tho we felicitate ourselves, we sympathize with those who are trembling least the Lot of Boston should be theirs. But they cannot be in similar circumstances unless pusilanimity and cowardise should take possession of them. They have time and warning given them to see the Evil and shun it.—I long to hear that you have declared an independancy—and by the way in the new Code of Laws which I suppose it will be necessary for you to make I desire you would Remember the Ladies, and be more generous and favourable to them than your ancestors. Do not put such unlimited power into the hands of the Husbands. Remember all Men would be tyrants if they could. If perticuliar care and attention is not paid to the Ladies we are determined to foment a Rebelion, and will not hold ourselves bound by any Laws in which we have no voice, or Representation.

That your Sex are Naturally Tyrannical is a Truth so thoroughly established as to admit of no dispute, but such of you as wish to be happy willingly give up the harsh title of Master for the more tender and endearing one of Friend. Why then, not put it out of the power of the vicious and the Lawless to use us with cruelty and indignity with impunity. Men of Sense in all Ages abhor those customs which treat us only as the vassals of your Sex. Regard us then as Beings placed by providence under your protection and in immitation of the Supreem Being make use of that power only for our happiness.

John Adams to Abigail. You justly complain of my short Letters, but the critical State of Things and the Multiplicity of Avocations must plead my Excuse.—You ask where the Fleet is. The inclosed Papers will inform you. You ask what Sort of Defence Virginia can make. I believe they will make an able Defence. Their Militia and minute Men have been some time employed in training them selves, and they have Nine Battallions of regulars as they call them, maintained among them, under good Officers, at the Continental Expence. They have set up a Number of Manufactories of Fire Arms, which are busily employed. They are tolerably supplied with Powder, and are successfull and assiduous, in making Salt Petre. Their neighbouring Sister or rather Daughter Colony of North Carolina, which is a warlike Colony, and has several Battallions at the Continental Expence, as well as a pretty good Militia, are ready to assist them, and they are in very good Spirits, and seem determined to make a brave Resistance.—The Gentry are very rich, and the common People very poor. This Inequality of Property, gives an Aristocratical Turn to all their Proceedings and occasions a strong Aversion in their Patricians, to Common Sense. But the Spirit of these Barons, is coming down, and it must submit.

You have given me some Pleasure, by your Account of a certain House in Queen Street. I had burned it, long ago, in Imagination. It rises now to my View like a Phoenix.—What shall I say of the Solicitor General? I pity his pretty Children, I pity his Father, and his sisters. I wish I could be clear that it is no moral Evil to pity him and his Lady. Upon Repentance they will certainly have a large Share in the Compassions of many. But let Us take Warning and give it to our Children. Whenever Vanity, and Gaiety, a Love of Pomp and Dress, Furniture, Equipage, Buildings, great Company, expensive Diversions, and elegant Entertainments get the better of the Principles and Judgments of Men or Women there is no knowing where they will stop, nor into what Evils, natural, moral, or political, they will lead us. . . .

As to Declarations of Independency, be patient. Read our Privateering Laws, and our Commercial Laws. What signifies a Word.

As to your extraordinary Code of Laws, I cannot but laugh. We have been told that our Struggle has loosened the bands of Government every where. That Children and Apprentices were disobedient—that schools and Colledges were grown turbulent—that Indians slighted their Guardians and Negroes grew insolent to their Masters. But your Letter was the first Intimation that another Tribe more numerous and powerfull than all the rest were grown discontented.—This

is rather too coarse a Compliment but you are so saucy, I wont blot it out.

Depend upon it, We know better than to repeal our Masculine systems. Altho they are in full Force, you know they are little more than Theory. We dare not exert our Power in its full Latitude. We are obliged to go fair, and softly, and in Practice you know We are the subjects. We have only the Name of Masters, and rather than give up this, which would compleatly subject Us to the Despotism of the Petticoat, I hope General Washington, and all our brave Heroes would fight. I am sure every good Politician would plot, as long as he would against Despotism, Empire, Monarchy, Aristocracy, Oligarchy, or Ochlocracy.—A fine Story indeed. I begin to think the Ministry as deep as they are wicked. After stirring up Tories, Land-jobbers, Trimmers, Bigots, Canadians, Indians, Negroes, Hanoverians, Hessians, Russians, Irish Roman Catholicks, Scotch Renegadoes, at last they have stimulated the [women] to demand new Priviledges and threaten to rebell.

After reading this selection, consider these questions:

1. In what ways did the Adamses' marriage reflect the new norms of marriage described by Jan Lewis and Merril D. Smith?

2. What analogies does Abigail Adams draw between the colonists' demands for independence and women's rights?

3. What is John Adams's concern about the possible consequences of independence from Great Britain?

4. Can you reconcile Abigail Adams's advocacy of education for women with her belief that women belonged in the home?

SELECTION 4:

Letters from Abigail Adams to John Quincy Adams, 1780–1783

Abigail Adams was the wife of one president and the mother of another. The following letters were written to her son, John Quincy Adams. During the American Revolution, John, then a teenager, accompanied his father on a diplomatic mission to Europe. When Abigail wrote the first letter, the younger Adams was a student at the University of Leyden in Holland. At the time of the second letter, written three years later, John Quincy Adams had served as secretary to Francis Dana, the American minister to Russia.

2O March, 1780

My Dear Son,

Your letter, last evening received from Bilboa, relieved me from much anxiety; for, having a day or two before received letters from your papa, Mr. Thaxter [John Adams's private secretary], and brother, in which packet I found none from you, nor any mention made of you, my mind, ever fruitful in conjectures, was instantly alarmed. I feared you were sick, unable to write, and your papa, unwilling to give me uneasiness, had concealed it from me; and this apprehension was confirmed by every person's omitting to say how long they should continue in Bilboa.

Your father's letters came to Salem, yours to Newburyport, and soon gave ease to my anxiety, at the same time that it excited gratitude and thankfulness to Heaven, for the preservation you all experienced in the imminent dangers which threatened you. You express in both your letters a degree of thankfulness. I hope it amounts to more than words, and that you will never be insensible to the particular preservation you have experienced in both your voyages. You have seen how inadequate the aid of man would have been, if the winds and the seas had not been under the particular government of that Being, who "stretched out the heavens as a span," who "holdeth the ocean in the hollow of his hand," and "rideth upon the wings of the wind."

If you have a due sense of your preservation, your next consideration will be, for what purpose you are continued in life. It is not to rove from clime to clime, to gratify an idle curiosity; but every new mercy you receive is a new debt upon you, a new obligation to a diligent discharge of the various relations in which you stand connected; in the first place, to your great Preserver; in the next, to society in general; in particular, to your country, to your parents, and to yourself.

The only sure and permanent foundation of virtue is religion. Let this important truth be engraven upon your heart. And also, that the foundation of religion is the belief of the one only God, and a just sense of his attributes, as a being infinitely wise, just, and good, to whom you owe the highest reverence, gratitude, and adoration; who superintends and governs all nature, even to clothing the lilies of the field, and hearing the young ravens when they cry; but more particularly regards man, whom he created after his own

Excerpted from *Letters of Mrs. Adams, the Wife of John Adams,* edited by Charles Francis Adams (Boston: Wilkens Carter & Company, 1848).

image, and breathed into him an immortal spirit, capable of a happiness beyond the grave; for the attainment of which he is bound to the performance of certain duties, which all tend to the happiness and welfare of society, and are comprised in one short sentence, expressive of universal benevolence, "Thou shalt love thy neighbor as thyself." This is elegantly defined by Mr. [Alexander] Pope, in his "Essay on Man."

> Remember, man, the universal cause
> Acts not by partial, but by general laws,
> And makes what happiness we justly call,
> Subsist not in the good of one, but all.
> There's not a blessing individuals find,
> But some way leans and hearkens to the kind.

Thus has the Supreme Being made the good will of man towards his fellow-creatures an evidence of his regard to Him, and for this purpose has constituted him a dependent being and made his happiness to consist in society. Man early discovered this propensity of his nature, and found

> Eden was tasteless till an Eve was there.

Justice, humanity, and benevolence are the duties you owe to society in general. To your country the same duties are incumbent upon you, with the additional obligation of sacrificing ease, pleasure, wealth, and life itself for its defence and security. To your parents you owe love, reverence, and obedience to all just and equitable commands. To yourself—here, indeed, is a wide field to expatiate upon. To become what you ought to be, and what a fond mother wishes to see you, attend to some precepts and instructions from the pen of one, who can have no motive but your welfare and happiness, and who wishes in this way to supply to you the personal watchfulness and care, which a separation from you deprived you of at a period of life, when habits are easiest acquired and fixed; and though the advice may not be new, yet suffer it to obtain a place in your memory, for occasions may offer, and perhaps some concurring circumstances unite, to give it weight and force.

Suffer me to recommend to you one of the most useful lessons of life, the knowledge and study of yourself. There you run the greatest hazard of being deceived. Self-love and partiality cast a mist

before the eyes, and there is no knowledge so hard to be acquired, nor of more benefit when once thoroughly understood. Ungoverned passions have aptly been compared to the boisterous ocean, which is known to produce the most terrible effects. "Passions are the elements of life," but elements which are subject to the control of reason. Whoever will candidly examine themselves, will find some degree of passion, peevishness, or obstinacy in their natural tempers. You will seldom find these disagreeable ingredients all united in one; but the uncontrolled indulgence of either is sufficient to render the possessor unhappy in himself, and disagreeable to all who are so unhappy as to be witnesses of it, or suffer from its effects.

You, my dear son, are formed with a constitution feelingly alive; your passions are strong and impetuous; and, though I have sometimes seen them hurry you into excesses, yet with pleasure I have observed a frankness and generosity accompany your efforts to govern and subdue them. Few persons are so subject to passion, but that they can command themselves, when they have a motive sufficiently strong; and those who are most apt to transgress will restrain themselves through respect and reverence to superiors, and even, where they wish to recommend themselves, to their equals. The due government of the passions has been considered in all ages as a most valuable acquisition. Hence an inspired writer observes, "He that is slow to anger, is better than the mighty; and he that ruleth his spirit, than he that taketh a city." This passion, coöperating with power, and unrestrained by reason, has produced the subversion of cities, the desolation of countries, the massacre of nations, and filled the world with injustice and oppression. Behold your own country, your native land, suffering from the effects of lawless power and malignant passions, and learn betimes, from your own observation and experience, to govern and control yourself. Having once obtained this self-government, you will find a foundation laid for happiness to yourself and usefulness to mankind. "Virtue alone is happiness below"; and consists in cultivating and improving every good inclination, and in checking and subduing every propensity to evil. I have been particular upon the passion of anger, as it is generally the most predominant passion at your age, the soonest excited, and the least pains are taken to subdue it;

What composes man, can man destroy.

I do not mean, however, to have you insensible to real injuries. He who will not turn when he is trodden upon is deficient in point of spirit; yet, if you can preserve good breeding and decency of manners, you will have an advantage over the aggressor, and will maintain a dignity of character, which will always insure you respect, even from the offender.

I will not overburden your mind at this time. I mean to pursue the subject of self-knowledge in some future letter, and give you my sentiments upon your future conduct in life, when I feel disposed to resume my pen.

In the mean time, be assured, no one is more sincerely interested in your happiness, than your ever affectionate mother,

A.A.

Do not expose my letters. I would copy, but hate it.

Braintree, 26 December, 1783
My Dear Son,
. . . The early age at which you went abroad gave you not an opportunity of becoming acquainted with your own country. Yet the revolution, in which we were engaged, held it up in so striking and important a light, that you could not avoid being in some measure irradiated with the view. The characters with which you were connected, and the conversation you continually heard, must have impressed your mind with a sense of the laws, the liberties, and the glorious privileges, which distinguish the free, sovereign, independent States of America.

Compare them with the vassalage of the Russian government you have described, and say, were this highly favored land barren as the mountains of Switzerland, and covered ten months in the year with snow, would she not have the advantage even of Italy, with her orange groves, her breathing statues, and her melting strains of music? or of Spain, with her treasures from Mexico and Peru? not one of which can boast that first of blessings, the glory of human nature, the inestimable privilege of sitting down under their vines and fig-trees, enjoying in peace and security whatever Heaven has lent them, having none to make them afraid.

Let your observations and comparisons produce in your mind an abhorrence of domination and power, the parent of slavery, ignorance, and barbarism, which places man upon a level with his fellow tenants of the woods;

A day, an hour, of virtuous liberty
Is worth a whole eternity of bondage.

You have seen power in its various forms—a benign deity, when exercised in the suppression of fraud, injustice, and tyranny, but a demon, when united with unbounded ambition—a wide-wasting fury, who has destroyed her thousands. Not an age of the world but has produced characters, to which whole human hecatombs have been sacrificed.

What is the history of mighty kingdoms and nations, but a detail of the ravages and cruelties of the powerful over the weak? Yet it is instructive to trace the various causes, which produced the strength of one nation, and the decline and weakness of another; to learn by what arts one man has been able to subjugate millions of his fellow creatures, the motives which have put him upon action, and the causes of his success; sometimes driven by ambition and a lust of power; at other times swallowed up by religious enthusiasm, blind bigotry, and ignorant zeal; sometimes enervated with luxury and debauched by pleasure, until the most powerful nations have become a prey and been subdued by these Sirens, when neither the number of their enemies nor the prowess of their arms, could conquer them. . . .

The history of your own country and the late revolution are striking and recent instances of the mighty things achieved by a brave, enlightened, and hardy people, determined to be free; the very yeomanry of which, in many instances, have shown themselves superior to corruption, as Britain well knows. . . . Glory, my son, in a country which has given birth to characters, both in the civil and military departments, which may vie with the wisdom and valor of antiquity. As an immediate descendant of one of those characters, may you be led to an imitation of that disinterested patriotism and that noble love of your country, which will teach you to despise wealth, titles, pomp, and equipage, as mere external advantages, which cannot add to the internal excellence of your mind, or compensate for the want of integrity and virtue.

May your mind be thoroughly impressed with the absolute necessity of universal virtue and goodness, as the only sure road to happiness, and may you walk therein with undeviating steps—is the sincere and most affectionate wish of

Your mother,
A. Adams

After reading this selection, consider these questions:

1. In what ways do Abigail Adams's letters reflect her duty as a republican mother?

2. Relate Adams's discussion of tyranny in Russia to the ideas about the role of women expressed in the letter she wrote to her husband seven years earlier. [see selection 3 in this chapter.]

3. What does Adams believe threatens the survival of the republic?

SELECTION 5:

Eliza Wilkinson Reflects on the Revolution

The American Revolution opened some new possibilities for women. Revolutionary ideology could be understood to have implications for women, as Abigail Adams maintained, and the social upheaval of the war created opportunities and placed new demands on women. As a consequence, women became more likely to express political views. One such woman was Eliza Wilkinson, a young widow living on the Sea Islands of South Carolina. During the war she managed one of her parents' plantations. An ardent supporter of the American cause, she wrote the following letter to a friend ("my dear Mary") in 1782, after having encountered some American officers and a group of Tories they had taken prisoner.

After various discourses, the conversation took a turn on the subject of the present war. I was proud to hear my friends express themselves in a manner not unworthy of their country. Maj.

Moore [an American officer] made a comparison, which, as I perfectly remember, I will give you. Your opinion is also required of the same.

"Suppose," said he, "I had a field of wheat, upon these conditions, that out of that field I was to give so much to a certain person yearly; well, I think nothing of it, I give it cheerfully, and am very punctual; it goes on thus for some years; at

Excerpted from *Letters of Eliza Wilkinson,* edited by Caroline Gilman (New York: Samuel Colman, 1839).

length the person sends me word I must let him have so much more, for he wants it; still I comply with cheerfulness. The next year he requires a still larger supply, and tells me he cannot do without it. This startles me! I find him encroaching, by little and little, on my property. I make some difficulty in complying; however, as he says he 'cannot do without it,' I let him have it, though I see it hurts me; but it puts me on my guard. Well, things go on so for some time; at length he begins again, and at last seems to have a design of taking my whole field. Then what am I to do?—Why, if I give it up, I am ruined, I must lie at his mercy. Is not this slavery? For my part," continued he, "I would rather explore unknown regions, blessed with liberty, than remain in my native country if to be cursed with slavery.". . .

I do not love to meddle with political matters; the men say we have no business with them, it is not in our sphere! and Homer (did you ever read Homer, child?) gives us two or three broad hints to mind our domestic concerns, spinning, weaving, &c. and leave affairs of higher nature to the men; but I must beg his pardon—I won't have it thought, that because we are the weaker sex as to *bodily* strength, my dear, we are capable of nothing more than minding the dairy, visiting the poultry-house, and all such domestic concerns; our thoughts can soar aloft, we can form conceptions of things of higher nature; and have as just a sense of honor, glory, and great actions, as these "Lords of the Creation." What cotemptible *earth worms* these authors make us! They won't even allow us the liberty of thought, and that is all I want. I would not wish that we should meddle in what is unbecoming female delicacy, but surely we may have sense enough to give our opinions to commend or discommend such actions as we may approve or disapprove; without being reminded of our spinning and household affairs as the only matters we are capable of thinking or speaking of with justness or propriety. I won't allow it, positively won't. Homer has a deal of morality in his works, which is worthy of imitation; his Odyssey abounds with it. But I will leave Homer to better judges, and proceed in my narration.

While the officers were there discoursing, word was brought that a party of the enemy were at a neighboring plantation, not above two miles off, carrying provisions away. In an instant the men were under arms, formed and marched away to the place. We were dreadfully alarmed at the first information, but, upon seeing with what eagerness our friends marched off, and what high spirits they were in, we were more composed, but again relapsed into our fears when we heard the discharge of firearms; they did not stay out long; but returned with seven prisoners, four whites and three blacks. When they came to the door, we looked out, and saw two of M'Girth's men [Tories] with them, who had used us so ill [the British had invaded the islands in 1780]; my heart relented at sight of them, and I could not forbear looking at them with an eye of pity. Ah! thought I, how fickle is fortune! but two days ago these poor wretches were riding about as if they had nothing to fear, and terrifying the weak and helpless by their appearance; now, what a humbled appearance do *they* make! But, basely as they have acted in taking up arms against their country, they have still some small sense left that they were once Americans, but now no longer so, for all who act as they do, forfeit that name; and by adopting the vices of those they join, become one with them; but these poor creatures seem to have yet remaining some token of what they once were—else why did they, last Thursday, behave so much better to us than the Britons did, when we were equally as much in their power as we were in the others'? I will let them see I have not forgot it. I arose, and went out to them. "I am sorry, my friends (I could not help calling them *friends* when they were in our power), to see you in this situation, you treated us with respect; and I cannot but be sorry to see you in distress." "It is the fortune of war, Madam, and soldiers must expect it." "Well, you need not make yourselves uneasy; I hope Americans won't treat their prisoners ill. Do, my friends (to the soldiers), use these men well—they were friendly to us." "Yes, Madam," said they; "they shall be used well if it was only for that." I asked if they would have any thing to drink. Yes, they would be glad of some water. I had some got, and as their hands were tied, I held the glass to their mouths; they bowed, and were very thankful for it. . . .

In the meanwhile Miss Samuells [a friend] was very busy about a wounded officer who was brought to the house (one of M'Girth's); he had a ball through his arm; we could find no rag to dress his wounds, every thing in the house being thrown into such confusion by the plunderers; but (see the native tenderness of an American!) Miss Samuells took from her neck the only remaining handkerchief the Britons had left her, and with it bound up his arm! Blush, O Britons, and be confounded! . . . No; I cannot think we shall be overcome while we act with justice and mercy—those are the attributes of heaven. If our cause is just, as it certainly appears to be, we need not doubt success; an Almighty arm has visibly supported us; or a raw, undisciplined people, with so many disadvantages too on their side, could never have withstood, for so long a time, an army which has repeatedly fought and conquered, and who are famed for, or rather *were* famed, for their valor and determined bravery; but now their glory is fallen, and, thank heaven, we are their equals, if not their superiors in the field.

After reading this selection, consider these questions:

1. In what respects does this letter reflect an attempt to fashion an appropriate role for women in the new republic?

2. In what ways can one find echoes of Revolutionary rhetoric in Wilkinson's plea for the expression of women's political views?

3. How does this letter manifest greater educational opportunities for women in the late eighteenth century?

CHAPTER 9

African Americans
and Native Americans

The American Revolution meant different things to different groups. The social upheaval accompanying the war and independence inevitably brought changes for African Americans and Native Americans. While the young American nation rejoiced in its victory and proclaimed its liberty, American victory and American liberty had very different meanings and implications for black Americans and for Indians.

In New England some slaves perceived a possibility of gaining freedom by joining the rebels. Most slaves south of New England, however, sided with Great Britain. In 1775 Virginia's last royal governor, Lord Dunmore, promised freedom for slaves who fled from their masters and joined the British as soldiers. Eight hundred slaves did just that. Throughout the war, thousands of slaves took advantage of opportunities to escape. Perhaps as many as 10 percent of all slaves (roughly fifty thousand people) escaped from their owners during the Revolution. Most remained in the United States as free people, but the British did evacuate approximately twenty thousand. Thousands of African Americans also fought for American independence.

To many Americans, fighting a war for liberty while holding slaves seemed to be a stark contradiction. Vermont, Massachusetts, and New Hampshire abolished slavery; Pennsylvania, Connecticut, and Rhode Island adopted plans for gradual emancipation. By 1804, every northern state had either abolished the institution or provided for its gradual abolition. In the upper South, revolutionary idealism combined with a changing economic situation (as many farmers switched from tobacco to cereal grains) to weaken the region's commitment to slavery. A number of slaves were manumitted, or granted freedom. In the lower South, however, where blacks often outnumbered whites and the system of agriculture depended heavily on slave labor, whites demonstrated almost no interest in emancipation or manumission.

Events surrounding the Revolution did create a much larger population of free blacks, particularly in the upper South. This group, although substantially excluded from institutions established for whites, had grown large enough to establish its own schools, churches, and other institutions.

Native Americans had the same stake in the Revolutionary struggle as did the American colonists, namely independence. Despite American commitment to the cause of natural rights, however, Indian tribes did not necessarily regard American victory as in their best interests. The threat of American expansion led the majority of tribes involved to make common cause with the British. For their part, the British actively sought assistance from various tribes and began a policy of arming Indians in 1777. Conflict on the western frontier was often particularly brutal, and both sides committed atrocities. After its military defeat, Great Britain simply abandoned its Indian allies. An armed and organized new nation pressed the tribes formerly allied with Great Britain for concessions. Even those tribes that had thrown in their lot with the Americans were not exempt from the new nation's demands for territory.

After reading this chapter, consider these questions:

1. What led the colonists to turn to African slavery?

2. How did Revolutionary ideology influence attitudes towards African Americans?

3. What role did Native Americans play in the American Revolution?

4. What impact did the Revolution have on Native Americans?

5. How significant was race in the creation of the American republic?

SELECTION 1:

Slavery and Freedom: The American Paradox

Many historians have posited a contradiction between the ideology of the American Revolution, which created the freest society the world had known, and the institution of slavery. How could freedom coexist with slavery? In his presidential address to the Organization of American His-

torians in 1972, Edmund S. Morgan, one of the most distinguished historians of colonial America and now an emeritus professor of history at Yale University, provides a provocative answer to that question. He contends that American freedom depended on slavery.

American historians interested in tracing the rise of liberty, democracy, and the common man have been challenged in the past two decades by other historians, interested in tracing the history of oppression, exploitation, and racism. The challenge has been salutary, because it has made us examine more directly than historians have hitherto been willing to do, the role of slavery in our early history. Colonial historians, in particular, when writing about the origin and development of American institutions have found it possible until recently to deal with slavery as an exception to everything they had to say. I am speaking about myself but also about most of my generation. We owe a debt of gratitude to those who have insisted that slavery was something more than an exception, that one fifth of the American population at the time of the Revolution is too many people to be treated as an exception.

We shall not have met the challenge simply by studying the history of that one fifth, fruitful as such studies may be, urgent as they may be. Nor shall we have met the challenge if we merely execute the familiar maneuver of turning our old interpretations on their heads. The temptation is already apparent to argue that slavery and oppression were the dominant features of American history and that efforts to advance liberty and equality were the exception, indeed no more than a device to divert the masses while their chains were being fastened. To dismiss the rise of liberty and equality in American history as a mere sham is not only to ignore hard facts, it is also to evade the problem presented by those facts. The rise of liberty and equality in this country was accompanied by the rise of slavery. That two such contradictory developments were taking place si-

multaneously over a long period of our history, from the seventeenth century to the nineteenth, is the central paradox of American history.

The challenge, for a colonial historian at least, is to explain how a people could have developed the dedication to human liberty and dignity exhibited by the leaders of the American Revolution and at the same time have developed and maintained a system of labor that denied human liberty and dignity every hour of the day. . . .

Put the challenge another way: how did England, a country priding itself on the liberty of its citizens, produce colonies where most of the inhabitants enjoyed still greater liberty, greater opportunities, greater control over their own lives than most men in the mother country, while the remainder, one fifth of the total, were deprived of virtually all liberty, all opportunities, all control over their own lives? We may admit that the Englishmen who colonized America and their revolutionary descendants were racists, that consciously or unconsciously they believed liberties and rights should be confined to persons of a light complexion. When we have said as much, even when we have probed the depths of racial prejudice, we will not have fully accounted for the paradox. Racism was surely an essential element in it, but I should like to suggest another element, that I believe to have influenced the development of both slavery and freedom as we have known them in the United States.

Let us begin with Jefferson, this slaveholding spokesman of freedom. Could there have been anything in the kind of freedom he cherished that would have made him acquiesce, however reluctantly, in the slavery of so many Americans? The answer, I think, is yes. The freedom that Jefferson spoke for was not a gift to be conferred by governments, which he mistrusted at best. It was a freedom that sprang from the independence of the individual. The man who depended on another for his living could never be truly free. We may seek a clue to Jefferson's enigmatic posture toward slavery in his attitude toward those who enjoyed a seeming freedom without the independence needed to sustain it. For such persons Jefferson harbored a profound distrust, which found expression in two phobias that crop up from time to time in his writings.

The first was a passionate aversion to debt. Although the entire colonial economy of Virginia depended on the willingness of planters to go into debt and of British merchants to extend credit, although Jefferson himself was a debtor all his adult life—or perhaps because he was a debtor—he hated debt and hated anything that made him a debtor. He hated it because it limited his freedom of action. He could not, for example, have freed his slaves so long as he was in debt. Or so at least he told himself. But it was the impediment not simply to their freedom but to his own that bothered him. . . .

Though Jefferson's concern with the perniciousness of debt was almost obsessive, it was nevertheless altogether in keeping with the ideas of republican liberty that he shared with his countrymen. The trouble with debt was that by undermining the independence of the debtor it threatened republican liberty. Whenever debt brought a man under another's power, he lost more than his own freedom of action. He also weakened the capacity of his country to survive as a republic. It was an axiom of current political thought that republican government required a body of free, independent, property-owning citizens. A nation of men, each of whom owned enough property to support his family, could be a republic. It would follow that a nation of debtors, who had lost their property or mortgaged it to creditors, was ripe for tyranny. Jefferson accordingly favored every means of keeping men out of debt and keeping property widely distributed. He insisted on the abolition of primogeniture and entail; he declared that the earth belonged to the living and should not be kept from them by the debts or credits of the dead; he would have given fifty acres of land to every American who did not have it—all because he believed the citizens of a republic must be free from the control of other men and that they could be free only if they were economically free by virtue of owning land on which to support themselves.

If Jefferson felt so passionately about the bondage of the debtor, it is not surprising that he should also have sensed a danger to the republic from another class of men who, like debtors, were nominally free but whose independence was illusory. Jefferson's second phobia was his distrust of the landless urban workman who labored in manufactures. In Jefferson's view, he was a free man in name only. . . . Both [Jefferson's] distrust for artificers and his idealization of small landholders as "the most precious part of a state" rested on his concern for individual independence as the basis of freedom. Farmers made the best citizens because they were "the most vigorous, the most independant, the most virtuous. . . ." Artificers, on the other hand, were dependent on "the casualties and caprice of customers." If work was scarce, they had no land to fall back on for a living. In their dependence lay the danger. . . .

In Jefferson's distrust of artificers we begin to get a glimpse of the limits—and limits not dictated by racism—that defined the republican vision of the eighteenth century. For Jefferson was by no means unique among republicans in his distrust of the landless laborer. Such a distrust was a necessary corollary of the widespread eighteenth-century insistence on the independent, property-holding individual as the only bulwark of liberty. . . .

[Jefferson distrusted] men who were free in name while their empty bellies made them thieves, threatening the property of honest men, or else made them slaves in fact to anyone who would feed them. Jefferson's own solution . . . was given in a famous letter to [James] Madison, prompted by the spectacle Jefferson encountered in France in the 1780s, where a handful of noblemen had engrossed huge tracts of land on which to hunt game, while hordes of the poor went without work and without bread. Jefferson's proposal, characteristically phrased in terms of natural right, was for the poor to appropriate the uncultivated lands of the nobility. And he drew for the United States his usual lesson of the need to keep land widely distributed among the people.

Madison's answer, which is less well known than Jefferson's letter, raised the question whether it was possible to eliminate the idle poor in any country as fully populated as France. . . . "A certain degree of misery," Madison concluded, "seems inseparable from a high degree of populousness.". . .

In a country where population grew by geometric progression, it was not too early to think about a time when there might be vast numbers of landless poor, when there might be those mobs in great cities that Jefferson feared as sores on the body politic. In the United States as Jefferson and Madison knew it, the urban labor force as yet posed no threat, because it was small; and the agricultural labor force was, for the most part, already enslaved. In Revolutionary America, among men who spent their lives working for other men rather than working for themselves, slaves probably constituted a majority. In Virginia they constituted a large majority. If Jefferson and Madison, not to mention [George] Washington, were unhappy about that fact and yet did nothing to alter it, they may have been restrained, in part at least, by thoughts of the role that might be played in the United States by a large mass of free laborers.

When Jefferson contemplated the abolition of slavery, he found it inconceivable that the freed slaves should be allowed to remain in the country. In this attitude he was probably moved by his or his countrymen's racial prejudice. But he may also have had in mind the possibility that when slaves ceased to be slaves, they would become instead a half million idle poor, who would create the same problems for the United States that the idle poor of Europe did for their states. The slave, accustomed to compulsory labor, would not work to support himself when the compulsion was removed. This was a commonplace among Virginia planters before the creation of the republic and long after. . . .

Jefferson's plan for freeing his own slaves (never carried out) included an interim educational period in which they would have been half-taught, half-compelled to support themselves on rented land; for without guidance and preparation for self support, he believed, slaves could not be expected to become fit members of a republican society. . . .

It seems probable that the Revolutionary champions of liberty who acquiesced in the continued slavery of black labor did so not only because of racial prejudice but also because they shared . . . a distrust of the poor that was inherent in eighteenth-century conceptions of republican liberty. Their historical guidebooks had made them fear to enlarge the free labor force.

After reading this selection, consider these questions:

1. How, according to Morgan, was American freedom dependent on slavery?

2. Does Morgan's analysis explain the existence of slavery in the northern colonies?

SELECTION 2:

Images of the Indian During the Revolution

When looking at American Indians, European settlers always saw them through a lens distorted by cultural perceptions brought from Europe and then refined in the Western Hemisphere. Two persistent images dominated European and white American thinking about the Indian. One perceived Native Americans as savages, people who lived without civilization, decency, and social order. The other regarded Indians as benign innocents, reminiscent of the inhabitants of the Garden of Eden. As Bernard W. Sheehan, a professor of history at Indiana University, points out in the following essay, both images played a role in the American Revolution. These images not only influenced relations between the contesting sides and Native Americans, but they also shaped the way the British and Americans saw each other.

It can be argued plausibly that the American Indians played only a minor role in the American Revolution. Early in the war they threatened the southern frontier, and after 1777 they kept the Kentucky and Ohio settlements on edge. But it cannot be said that the activities of the native warriors, as inconvenient and damaging as these might have been, in any appreciable way effected the outcome of the conflict. The war was won on the battlegrounds of the East by an army constructed and trained according to European standards and was not won in the West against the irregular soldiers of the native tribes, who employed a mode of warfare that Europeans had long identified with the "savage" condition. Yet both sides in the conflict eventually sought out the tribes as allies, and the British especially made extensive use of them during the war. It

might be contended that the experience of the imperial wars, waged between 1689 and 1763 and still a vivid memory for both Englishmen and Americans, led easily to the belief that the native tribes might be valued allies in the achievement of victory as they had been assumed to be in the long hostilities between Britain and France in the New World. If so, the conviction was more likely the consequence of habit than conscious decision since the native tribes, for all of their activity in the imperial wars, had not been critical for the outcome.

But if the native people did not play an extensive or vital role in the war itself, they were an important factor in the thinking of Englishmen and Americans about the war. The symbolic Indian was nothing new in the New World experience but seldom in the past had the native carried quite the weight and significance that he was required to bear during the Revolution. From the earliest period of discovery and settlement, Europeans had incorporated the Indians into an intellectual scheme that satisfied the white man's need but bore little resemblance to the actuality of native life.

Although the phrase "noble savage" was not used until John Dryden invented it in 1664, and the term ignoble savage until much later, the word savage was employed from the very beginning. The word associated the Indians with the wilderness. They were assumed to represent the antithesis to civility and its distinguishing social elements. Montaigne formulated the classic definition in the late sixteenth century. According to his view the native people lived without society, government, economy, mental pursuits, and virtually every other characteristic of humanity or social order. . . . Of course it must be stressed that we have here an exercise in the European imagination, or better an expression of a very important mythic formulation. The idea of the "savage" in no way reflects the way any group of human beings live or have lived. All human organisms form societies, have language, govern themselves by some system of law or custom, and engage in economic activity. In European thinking and later in the American conception of native life, the condition of the savage could take either of two forms, though sometimes the images became mixed and the savage figure contained contradictory qualities. The noble savage was a benign, passive figure, utterly innocent, and reminiscent of the inhabitants of the Garden of Eden. The ignoble savage represented the summation of human vice. He was infinitely violent, inconstant, treacherous, and degraded. For Europeans and eighteenth-century Americans the noble savage represented an ideal from which they had fallen and to which they wished to return. Conversely the ignoble savage posed a threat to civil order and human decency.

As this dual figure of mythic proportions, the Indian served the propaganda purposes of both the British and the Americans. Overtly the ignoble savage was much more significant. Both sides interpreted the merits of their own position in contrast to the image of the savage. They both claimed to represent virtue and resorted easily to the accusations that their enemies betrayed the nature of their cause by behaving in a savage manner or allying themselves with savage Indi-

ans. At the same time Americans tended to couch public expressions describing the objects of their Revolution in terms plainly paralleled of the virtues long attributed to the noble savage.

The issue of the Indian arose in virtually the first moments of fighting between the Americans and the British. On April 19, 1775, at the North Bridge in Concord, one of the wounded British soldiers left behind by his retreating comrades was struck over the head with an ax by one of the young men of the town. Soon after, a contingent of British troops that had proceeded beyond the town searching for military supplies recrossed the bridge and sighted the dead soldier. They concluded from the spectacle that the Americans had fallen to scalping the wounded and spread rumors to this effect when they joined their comrades.

The charge that Americans scalped enemies appeared in the reports of the encounter turned in by British officers and in the official account sent by the commanding general, Thomas Gage, to the government in London. . . . A number of popular pamphleteers in England took up the issue, adding to their broader condemnation of the American cause the accusation that "the Americans fought like the savages of the country."

The Americans were no less sensitive than the British about this supposed descent into savagery. Touched by British propaganda the Massachusetts Provincial Congress took depositions, which were duly published, from the two townsmen who had buried the British bodies. There were no signs of scalping. Thomas Gordon, a Roxbury minister, arrived in Concord within days of the battle seeking authentic information. In a short account published soon after and later in his history of the Revolution he told the true story. But the issue went beyond truth or falsity; it concerned the very nature of the Revolutionary conflict. In a contest increasingly ideological, both sides could not but think the worst of the opposition.

On the return march from Concord, the British troops, exhausted from the long hours under arms, severely mauled by farmers who seemed to break all the rules of civilized war, and perhaps provoked by the rumors of American barbarism, made free use of the bayonet and killed many Americans. The Americans reacted to this bloodletting by accusing the British of abandoning all restraint, of behaving like savage Indians who subscribed to none of the limitations that moderated civilized conflict. Thus almost instinctively in this first clash of the revolutionary conflict, both sides invoked the image of the Indian to condemn the behavior of their opponents.

The uniform disrelish of what was assumed to be the Indian mode of war did not inhibit either side from seeking native allies. The experience of the imperial wars made it likely that the Indians would join the fray, but the Americans had good reason to suspect that it would not be on their side. After some initial effort by provincial commanders to recruit the warriors, American policy was devoted to keeping the Indians neutral. Except for the Oneidas and a faction of the Cherokees, the native peoples joined the British cause. For some, indeed, the reason may have resided in their clearheaded conviction that in the long run their interests would be better served by the British than by a newly independent nation of American farmers.

In the past the imperial government had shown an inclination to protect the tribes from the hasty advance of the frontier into the Indian country. And no doubt the Indians could expect little sympathy from an American government beholden to settlers hungry for new land. But the more immediate reason for the success of the British in attracting the loyalty of the tribes was bureaucratic. In the mid-1750s the imperial government had attempted to remove Indian affairs from the jurisdiction of the separate colonies and place them in the hands of two superintendents, one north of the Potomac and one south. The new policy . . . did succeed in establishing an effective Indian department in the colonies. . . . Hence, when the Revolution shattered imperial unity, most of the tribes remained wedded to the network of agents that had for the past twenty years heeded their interests.

British success in gaining Indian allies put them at a decided disadvantage in the propaganda war. They found themselves embattled not only by the Americans but by the political opposition in England. In the Declaration of Independence Jefferson could add a further item to the long indictment of the Crown for making alliance with "merciless Indian Savages, whose known rule of warfare, is an undistinguished destruction of all ages, sexes and conditions." In Parliament the Rockingham Whigs kept up an intermittent barrage of criticism over Britain's native allies, using similar images. Furthermore, there can be little doubt that the British were themselves uneasy about the relationship. . . .

Between the end of the Thirty Years' War in 1648 and the beginnings of the wars of revolution in the 1790s Europeans made a conscious effort to moderate the ferocity of international conflict. War during these decades was carried on by professional forces for limited objects, and civilian populations, where possible, remained unaffected. For the British the exceptions to this trend had been their internecine conflict with the Scots and the interminable hostilities involving the native peoples of America. Wars in these theaters had proved unamenable to the moderating spirit of eighteenth-century humanitarianism. Instead it retained the ferocity and totality long thought to be characteristic of conflict involving savage people. For the British to have purposefully abandoned these canons of civil conflict by employing Indians, struck many Americans as entirely appropriate. Since their intention was the reduction of America under "an obsolute despotism," that is the obliteration of civil society, they had chosen the means necessary to their end. Total war had been characteristic of conflict in America and now the British, it seemed, had adopted it as a positive policy. . . .

[I]n a war of images and propaganda the actual activities of the Indians, the near constant raiding of small bands of warriors with British or loyalist aid, meant less than a number of spectacular incidents seized on by the Americans to make their case against the British. When General John Burgoyne moved south from Canada into New York in the early summer of 1777, he was accompanied not only by an elaborate and cumbersome train of wagons but by a contingent of warriors. Burgoyne needed the Indians to ease his way in the wilderness, a point he knew well enough, but he plainly had misgivings about their mode of war. Burgoyne was a bon vivant, raconteur, and a playwright whose personal style fell easily into bombast. One would find it difficult to conceive of a character less likely to gain insight into Indian culture or less likely to succeed in changing the native way of making war. But these were precisely the ends Burgoyne had in mind. He wished to employ Indians on his own terms, which meant that the warriors were to cease being savages and to fight according to the rules of war honored in Europe. Of course he failed utterly to convince the warriors that they should change their ways. As his army advanced south the Indians played their usual havoc in the surrounding countryside. This aroused the ire of the frontier settlements and helped to gather the American militia who halted Burgoyne's advance and then forced his surrender.

In late July an incident occurred that deepened Burgoyne's dilemma (he needed the warriors but at the same time he found their behavior distasteful) and became the source of much controversy. Jane McCrea, a young woman from a loyalist family whose fiancé served with Burgoyne, had been captured by Indians in the British service and then murdered when the warriors argued over whose prisoner she would be. One Wyandot Panther appeared in camp with the scalp. News spread quickly, and Burgoyne was forced to take action. He found the act appalling, indeed not only was the victim a loyal subject of the Crown but he had given explicit instructions against taking the scalps of noncombatants. Torn between the need to uphold what he saw as the standards of civilized war and the fear of losing the Indians' aid Burgoyne closed the incident by merely reprimanding the warriors responsible.

For the Americans the incident would not be so easily forgotten. Jane McCrea's political affiliation receded behind the overwhelming fact that she had been wantonly murdered by savage Indians in alliance with the British. The American commander, Horatio Gates, chided Burgoyne for responsibility, and the instruments of American propaganda immediately made all they could of the event. Jane McCrea became a symbol of innocence and virtue much like the infant republic, the victim of a brutal and conscienceless murder. In the immediate situation the killing contributed

to Burgoyne's defeat, but more significant Jane McCrea became one of those important images used by white men to explain the meaning of the Indian in relation to the Americans' struggle to preserve their liberty. Later John Vanderlyn's fanciful painting of the affair (two burly Indians, one poised with a tomahawk and the other prepared to take a scalp, stand over the kneeling, terrified Miss McCrea) impressed it on the American imagination and made it legendary. . . .

The American response to the border conflict was twofold. George Rogers Clark attempted to cut off the British attacks at the source by capturing Detroit and neutralizing the western tribes, and Washington dispatched a continental expedition under John Sullivan into the heart of the Iroquois country in the hope of quieting the New York and Pennsylvania frontiers. . . .

Clark never succeeded in taking Detroit, but with the support of Virginia and the Kentucky settlements he did manage for a time to clear the British from the upper Mississippi Valley and to diminish the security of the western tribes. . . .

Whatever Clark's larger strategic intentions, his deepest personal objective was to strike a blow at savagery and at those Britons who promoted savage war. . . .

The native mode could be extraordinarily attractive to white men, especially to Indian fighters like Clark who entered the wilderness with the intention of sweeping aside the native way of life. Clark was not one of those white Indians of the revolutionary period, men like Louis Wetzel, Simon Girty, or even William Wells, who in the popular imagination had become Indians. On the contrary, he remained consciously on the civil side of the border. And yet he argued that the most efficient way to break Indian power was to adopt native methods of warfare. Thus he dressed in the native style and encouraged his followers to do the same. His men gave the war whoop, danced and feasted like Indians, and took Indian scalps, all practices that for white men characterized the native way of life. . . .

One need not overdo the significance of this process of indianization to note that such practices were quite widespread during the Revolution, as they had been before and would continue to be after. Examples can be found in the most unlikely places. Although Washington fought the war according to a European design and was reluctant to jeopardize positions held against the British for a limited success on the frontier, he sanctioned Indian-like behavior. Soon after taking command of the congressional forces before Boston in 1775, he welcomed a contingent of riflemen from Virginia led by Daniel Morgan. These frontier fighters carried long rifles, wore hunting shirts and moccasins, carried scalping knives and tomahawks, and generally disported themselves in ways inimical to the discipline of a European-style army. Washington came to believe them wasteful of ammunition and to question the usefulness in battle of the long rifle, but he found their Indian-like manners a practicable addition to the army's tactics. He hoped in particular to convey a message to his British enemies. American soldiers who dressed like Indians, carried knives and tomahawks the way Indians did, and whooped like savages might also engage in the sort of atrocities that inevitably accompanied war in the wilderness. Perhaps he remembered that great fear that afflicted Braddock's soldiers in 1755 as they marched toward the debacle on the Monongahela. The troops, many of them raw, had become convinced that torture and mutilation awaited them in the forest at the hands of men who would deny them the civilities soldiers could depend on in Europe. Later Washington's tactics were, of course, calculated, but they would not have been possible if Morgan's men and others like them had not resembled Indians.

One might suppose that the incongruence between attitudes and action might have been a source of a great tension during the Revolution. The burden of opinion about the native people was so negative that any obvious process of indianization would have to be unthinking or so patently ironic as to elicit comment. . . . It may be that the British did so badly in the propaganda contest not only because they had been more astute in gaining native allies but because they were more torn than the Americans over uniting the forces of civility with those of savagery. A mind as acute as Jefferson's saw the risk in indianization, but he was far more impressed by the advantages in berating the British for their policy than he was in preventing an American drift into the savage world.

Although the war had shifted the British and American conception of the native people toward the ignoble side of the dichotomy, the noble savage was far from dead in the revolutionary age. Some historians, especially in recent times, have attempted to interpret the Revolution and the later movement toward the establishment of a new government as a conscious attempt to imitate the native way of life. The principal problem with this explanation is that it attributes to native societies a number of traits that are plainly anachronistic—democracy and political unity, the two major characteristics. In fact what this interpretation must assume is that the American Indian was indeed a noble savage . . . One will not find this interpretation in any of the major works devoted directly to the Revolution. Here the sources of the breakup of the empire are located in a wrongheaded ministerial policy, internal social developments in the colonies, or the tradition of British oppositionist thought. The Indian hardly enters into the subject.

But if the Indian was not a noble savage and if the Americans paid little attention to real Indians as they formulated the meaning of their revolution, the symbolic Indian did play an important role. The principal question concerned the problem of self-identity. The Americans could not, after all, make a revolution or even establish their independence until they had managed to distinguish America from Europe. And many of the qualities that tended to set off the American—what Crèvecœur called "this new man"—from the European turned out to be precisely the qualities of noble savagery. The Indian in this sense possessed all the attributes that had been lost or forgotten in Europe. Thus Americans —and Indians—were pristine, simple, rustic, open, unaffected, honest, disciplined, equal, individualistic, and free. Europeans against whom the Americans made their revolution were burdened by the past, effete, devious, corrupt, sunk in luxury, and subjected to despotic authority. As this contrast became more apparent in the development of the revolutionary ideology, it was difficult for American commentators to resist an appeal to the qualities of noble savagery. Hence in the years after the Revolution one finds the increasing presence of the Indian in American public iconography. But it must be stressed that direct reference to the noble savage or explicit references to the need to imitate native societies are few during the Revolution. The image of the ignoble savage predominated during the years of conflict. . . .

And yet it is difficult to conceive of the Revolution without reference to the Indians. During the war they remained an issue of immense significance. Both sides sought self-definition by reference to their conception of the native people. The Americans, in particular, could scarcely have defined the nature of their virtuous republic if they could not have pointed out that the British had fallen from virtue by allying themselves with ignoble savages. Conversely, the American conception of virtue, the meaning and intellectual substance of the Revolution, drew heavily from the noble savage convention. The Indian as symbol proved indispensable in the making of American independence.

After reading this selection, consider these questions:

1. What role did the image of the "noble savage" play in how Americans conceived of themselves?

2. How did Americans use the image of the savage against the British?

SELECTION 3:

Slaves Petition for Freedom, 1773

As the conflict between the colonies and Great Britain developed and the colonists adopted the rhetoric of natural rights, many Americans, both black and white, came to question the morality of slavery. Particularly in northern colonies, where slaves made up less than 5 percent of the population, calls for gradual emancipation and the end of the Atlantic slave trade won considerable support. Slaves in the middle and northern colonies began to petition courts, governors, and legislatures for freedom. Beginning in 1773 and extending throughout the war, the Massachusetts legislature received a number of such petitions, of which the following document is an early example.

Excerpted from *Collections,* by the Massachusetts Historical Society (Boston: Massachusetts Historical Society, 1877).

Boston, April 20th, 1773

Sir, The efforts made by the legislative of this province in their last sessions to free themselves from slavery, gave us, who are in that deplorable state, a high degree of satisfaction. We expect great things from men who have made such a noble stand against the designs of their *fellow-men* to enslave them. We cannot but wish and hope Sir, that you will have the same grand object, we mean civil and religious liberty, in view in your next session. The divine spirit of *freedom,* seems to fire every humane breast on this continent, except such as are bribed to assist in executing the execrable plan.

We are very sensible that it would be highly detrimental to our present masters, if we were allowed to demand all that of *right* belongs to us for past services; this we disclaim. Even the *Spaniards,* who have not those sublime ideas of freedom that English men have, are conscious that they have no right to all the services of their fellowmen, we mean the *Africans,* whom they have purchased with their money; therefore they allow them one day in a week to work for themselves, to enable them to earn money to purchase the residue of their time, which they have a right to demand in such portions as they are able to pay for (a due appraizement of their services being first made, which always stands at the purchase money.) We do not pretend to dictate to you Sir, or to the Honorable Assembly, of which you are a member. We acknowledge our obligations to you for what you have already done, but as the people of this province seem to be actuated by the principles of equity and justice, we cannot but expect your house will again take our deplorable case into serious consideration, and give us that ample relief which, *as men,* we have a natural right to.

But since the wise and righteous governor of the universe, has permitted our fellow men to make us slaves, we bow in submission to him, and determine to behave in such a manner as that we may have reason to expect the divine approbation of, and assistance in, our peaceable and lawful attempts to gain our freedom.

We are willing to submit to such regulations and laws, as may be made relative to us, until we leave the province, which we determine to do as soon as we can, from our joynt labours procure money to transport ourselves to some part of the Coast of *Africa,* where we propose a settlement. We are very desirous that you should have instructions relative to us, from your town, therefore we pray you to communicate this letter to them, and ask this favor for us.

In behalf of our fellow slaves in this province, and by order of their Committee.

Peter Bestes,
Sambo Freeman,
Felix Holbrook,
Chester Joie.

For the Representative of the town of Thompson.

After reading this selection, consider these questions:

1. How do the slaves use the rhetoric of natural rights to support their own claims to freedom?

2. For what do the slaves petition the legislature? Why do you think they did not demand immediate emancipation for themselves and their children?

3. What reasons might the slaves have had for asking to be sent to Africa?

SELECTION 4:

Free Blacks Petition Against the South Carolina Poll Tax

Although some slaves fought for the Revolutionary cause, most determined that their best prospects for freedom lay with the British. Perhaps as many as fifty thousand slaves (approximately 10 percent of the total in the American colonies) fled their masters during the course of the war. The American Revolution freed thousands of slaves, mostly in the South; yet by the end of the century, the institution had expanded and had become more entrenched in that region. Even in the South, however, not all African Americans were slaves. Whether they lived in the North or in the South, free blacks did not receive equal treatment. In 1789 the South Carolina legislature passed a law, effective in 1791, requiring all free blacks to pay a poll tax (not a tax on voting but a per capita tax) of twenty-five cents per year. This tax was in addition to other general taxes that free blacks had to pay. The following undated petition, signed by twenty-three free black men and women from Camden, reached the legislature in December 1793.

To the Honourable David Ramsay Esquire President of the Honourable Senate, and to the others the Honourable the Members of the same—

The Petition of John Morris William Morris and other Inhabitants of Camden District in behalf of themselves and others who come under the description of Free Negroes Mulattoes and Mustizoes—

Humbly Sheweth

That with submission your Petitioners beg leave to observe that they conceive their ancestors merited the Publick confidence and obtained the Title of a Free People by rendering some particular Services to their Country, which the Wisdom & goodness of Government thought just and

right to notice and to reward their Fidelity with Emancipation, & other singular Privileges.

That before the War, and till very lately your Petitioners who were Freeholders or Tradesmen, paid a Tax only for their Lands, trades, and other Taxable property in common with others the Free White Citizens of the State, and in consequence of their paying the same, was Exempted from paying a Pole-Tax for any of their children while under their Jurisdiction.—

That in March 1789, an Ordinance was passed that a Tax of One fourth of a Dollar per head per Annum be Imposed upon all Negroes Mustizoes & Mulattoes: the same to commence in February 1791, and from thence continue for the space of Ten years.—

That by a Subsequent Act, Intitled an Act for raising Supplies for the year of our Lord One thousand seven hundred and ninety two, past the 21st day of December last past, your Petitioners

Excerpted from *A Documentary History of the Negro People in the United States,* edited by Herbert Aptheker (New York: The Citidel Press, 1951).

besides paying a Tax for their Lands & other Taxable property are made liable & have accordingly paid the sum of Two Dollars per head for themselves—the same sum per head for their Wives—and the same sum per head for each of their Children above Sixteen Years of age, who are under their Jurisdiction:

That your Petitioners are generally a Poor needy People; have frequently large Families to maintain; and find it exceeding difficult and distressing to support the same, and answer the large demands of the Publick; which appears to them considerably more than double what was formerly Exacted from them; In consequence of which they conceive their Situation in life but a small remove from Slavery; that they are likely to suffer continued inconvenience & disadvantages; and in the end to be reduced to poverty and want itself.—

In confidence therefore of the high Opinion we entertain of your Honours Veracity, and readiness to redress every Grievance which may appear really such, We do most humbly Pray, That your Honours would condescend to take the distressed Case of your Petitioners into your wise Consideration, and Vouchsafe to Grant them such relief as your Honours in your Wisdom shall see meet.—

And your Petitioners as in duty bound shall ever Pray &c.

After reading this selection, consider these questions:

1. On what grounds do the petitioners object to the imposition of a tax on them?

2. On what basis do they ask that the legislature repeal the tax?

3. Why might the South Carolina legislature have passed the tax?

SELECTION 5:

Letter from Benjamin Banneker to Thomas Jefferson

Benjamin Banneker, a largely self-educated free African American from Maryland, won respect as a scientist and mathematician, and in 1791 he published an astronomical almanac. His work came to the attention of Thomas Jefferson. On Jefferson's recommendation, President George Washington appointed Banneker to serve on the commission that planned the new capital city.

Thomas Jefferson's draft of the Declaration of Independence included a passage condemning King George III for the slave trade: "He has waged cruel war against human nature itself, violating its most sacred rights of life and liberty in the persons of distant people who never offended him, captivating and carrying them into slavery in another hemisphere, or to incur miserable death in their transportation thither." Objections from the representatives of southern colonies prevented the passage's inclusion in the final draft of the declaration.

In spite of such sentiments, Jefferson harbored serious doubts about the abilities of African Americans, which he expounded on in his Notes on the State of Virginia: *"Comparing them by their faculties of memory, reason, and imagination, it appears to me, that in memory they [blacks] are equal to the whites; in reason much inferior." Banneker read* Notes on the State of Virginia *and sent a copy of his almanac to Jefferson with the following letter. Jefferson responded immediately, thanking Banneker for the almanac. "No body," Jefferson wrote, "wishes more than I do to see such proofs as you exhibit, that nature has given to our black brethren, talents equal to those of the other colors of men, and that the appearance of a want of them is owing merely to the degraded condition of their existence." Jefferson forwarded the copy of the almanac to the marquis de Condorcet, secretary of the Academy of Sciences in Paris.*

August 19th, 1791
Thomas Jefferson
Secretary of State
Sir, I am fully sensible of the greatness of that freedom which I take with you on the present occasion; a liberty which Seemed to me Scarcely allowable, when I reflected on that distinguished, and dignifyed station in which you Stand; and the almost general prejudice and prepossession which is so previlent in the world against those of my complexion.

I suppose it is a truth too well attested to you, to need a proof here, that we are a race of Beings who have long laboured under the abuse and censure of the world, that we have been looked upon with an eye of contempt, and that we have long been considered rather as brutish than human, and Scarcely capable of mental endowments.

Sir, I hope I may Safely admit, in consequence of that report which hath reached me, that you are a man far less inflexible in Sentiments of this nature, than many others; that you are measurably friendly and well disposed towards us, and that you are willing and ready to Lend your aid and assistance to our relief from those many distresses and numerous calamaties to which we are reduced.

Now, Sir, if this is founded in truth, I apprehend you will readily embrace every opportunity to eradicate that train of absurd and false ideas and opinions which so generally prevail with respect to us, and that your Sentiments are concurrent with mine, which are that one universal Father hath given being to us all, and that he hath not only made us all of one flesh, but that he hath also without partiality afforded us all the Same Sensations, and endued us all with the same faculties, and that however variable we may be in Society or religion, however diversified in Situation or colour, we are all of the Same Family, and Stand in the Same relation to him. . . .

Sir, I freely and Chearfully acknowledge, that I am of the African race, and, in that colour which is natural to them of the deepest dye; and it is under a Sense of the most profound gratitude to the Supreme Ruler of the universe, that I now confess to you, that I am not under that state of tyrannical thraldom, and inhuman captivity, to which too many of my brethren are doomed; but that I have abundantly tasted of the fruition of those blessings which proceed from that free and unequalled liberty with which you are favoured and which I hope you will willingly allow you have received from the immediate Hand of that Being from whom proceedeth every good and perfect gift.

Sir, Suffer me to recall to your mind that time in which the Arms and tyranny of the British Crown were exerted with every powerful effort, in order to reduce you to a State of Servitude; look back I entreat you on the variety of dangers to which you were exposed, reflect on that time in which every human aid appeared unavailable,

Excerpted from *Sources of the African-American Past,* edited by Roy E. Finkenbine (New York: Longman Press, 1997).

and in which even hope and fortitude wore the aspect of inability to the Conflict, and you cannot but be led to a Serious and grateful Sense of your miraculous and providential preservation; You cannot but acknowledge, that the present freedom and tranquillity which you enjoy you have mercifully received, and that it is the peculiar blessing of Heaven.

This, Sir, was a time in which you clearly saw into the injustice of a State of Slavery, and in which you had just apprehensions of the horrors of its condition, it was now Sir, that your abhorrence was so excited, that you publickly held forth this true and invaluable doctrine, which is worthy to be recorded and remembered in all Succeeding ages. "We hold these truths to be Self evident, that all men are created equal, and that they are endowed by their creator with certain inalienable rights, that amongst these are life, liberty, and the pursuit of happiness."

Here, Sir, was a time in which your tender feelings for yourselves engaged you thus to declare, you were then impressed with proper ideas of the great valuation of liberty, and the free possession of those blessings to which you were entitled by nature; but Sir how pitiable it is to reflect, that altho you were so fully convinced of the benevolence of the Father of mankind, and of his equal and impartial distribution of those rights and privileges which he had conferred upon them, that you should at the Same time counteract his mercies, in detaining by fraud and violence so numerous a part of my brethren under groaning captivity and cruel oppression, that you should at the Same time be found guilty of that most criminal act, which you professedly detested in others, with respect to yourselves. . . .

And now, Sir, altho my Sympathy and affection for my brethren hath caused my enlargement thus far, I ardently hope that your candour and generosity will plead with you in my behalf, when I make known to you, that it was not originally my design; but that having taken up my pen in order to direct to you a present, a copy of an Almanack which I have calculated for the Succeeding year, I was unexpectedly and unavoidably led thereto.

This calculation, Sir, is the production of my arduous study, in this advanced Stage of life; for having long had unbounded desires to become Acquainted with the Secrets of nature, I have had to gratify my curiosity herein thro my own assiduous application to Astronomical Study, in which I need not to recount to you the many difficulties and disadvantages which I have had to encounter . . . .

And now Sir, I Shall conclude and Subscribe my Self with the most profound respect,

Your most Obedient and humble Servant
Benjamin Banneker

After reading this selection, consider these questions:

1. Does Edmund S. Morgan's discussion of slavery and freedom explain the seemingly contradictory sentiments Jefferson expressed in the Declaration of Independence and in his *Notes on the State of Virginia?*

2. How does Banneker use the rhetoric and spirit of the American Revolution to attack slavery?

3. In what ways was Banneker similar to Benjamin Franklin?

CHAPTER 10

Politics

Politics involves far more than winning elections. It consists of the larger way in which people approach issues of governance. Rather than rehearse the specific matters that members of the Continental Congress or the Constitutional Convention debated or the disagreements between Federalists and their Jeffersonian opponents, the essays in this chapter focus on some of the more comprehensive issues involving the relationship of the people to those who govern them.

The American Revolution was more than a simple change in government or independence from Great Britain. It led to the formation of the first modern republic as well as to whole new approaches to governance and to the way people envisioned social relationships. The American rebels knew that they had embarked on something new, something risky. They had undertaken not only to gain independence from Great Britain but also to establish a republic.

The War for Independence influenced the course of the republican experiment. For one thing, it revealed the weakness of Congress. For another, as the composition of the Continental army changed, it inevitably influenced ideas about politics, as evidenced by Alfred Young's essay on George Robert Twelves Hewes in chapter 7. Even after the Articles of Confederation, military victory over the British, and independence, the national government remained weak. It could not pay its debts, defeat the Indians of the Ohio Territory, or force the British to abandon their forts on the Great Lakes. In the minds of many leading Americans, the national government also proved its inadequacy in dealing with social unrest, particularly in the instance of Shays's Rebellion. Consequently, a group of nationalist leaders gathered in Philadelphia during the summer of 1787 and drafted a new constitution that created the American federal system. After much debate, the Constitution won ratification and went into effect in 1789. The leaders of the opposition to British rule had won independence and established a new republic. Beyond that, they had truly created what they claimed on the Great Seal of the United States: novus ordo seclorum, "a new order for the ages."

After reading this chapter, consider these questions:

1. In what ways was the American Revolution a social revolution? In what respects was it not?

2. What did American political thinkers of the eighteenth century mean by "independence"?

3. How did the experience of men who served in the military help to shape the early republic?

4. What arguments did supporters of the Constitution offer? What reservations did opponents (and some supporters) of the Constitution have?

SELECTION 1:

The Republican Revolution

Gordon S. Wood, professor of history at Brown University, is one of the most influential interpreters of American political culture in Revolutionary and postrevolutionary America. In the following essay, he addresses the issue of whether the American Revolution was in fact revolutionary. Was it simply a change in government or did it alter the social structure? In answering that question, Wood asks readers to suspend their modern notions of class and social organization. Instead, he reconstructs the eighteenth-century political and social structure as well as the way people of that time understood it. In that context, he concludes that the Revolution did indeed involve profound social change and that out of it came an entirely different way of understanding social relationships.

Because the American Revolution was not like other revolutions, it is not easily interpreted. Most of us cannot quite believe that we had a real revolution like other nations and peoples have had: where property was destroyed, people were killed, society was disrupted, and everything became different. The American Revolution had no reign of terror, and many of the leaders who began it were in control at its end. It does not appear to have the same kinds of social causes or social character that other revolutions have had. The American colonists were not an oppressed people; they had no crushing imperial chains to throw off. In fact, the colonists knew they were freer, more prosperous, and less burdened with cumber-

Excerpted from *Main Problems in American History,* edited by Howard H. Quint, Milton Cantor, and Dean Albertson (Chicago: The Dorsey Press, 1987). Copyright © 1987 by The Dorsey Press. Reprinted with permission.

some feudal and monarchical restraints than any part of mankind in the eighteenth century. To be sure, there were growing social distinctions in the colonies and increasing poverty in the provincial cities; but in eighteenth-century America, there was nothing remotely comparable to the fabulous wealth of the English nobility or the vile and violent slums of London. Hence, explaining the Revolution in social terms, as a class conflict or as an uprising of the poor against the rich, has been very difficult. The American Revolution does not seem to involve the sorts of social oppression or economic deprivation that lie behind other revolutions.

Consequently, much of our history writing has minimized the radical and social character of the American Revolution. Most often it has been viewed as an intellectual defense of American constitutional rights against British encroachment ("no taxation without representation"), fought not to change the existing social order, but to preserve it. Some historians have even seen the Revolution as nothing but a colonial war for independence. In short, our Revolution as we like to say, was a peculiarly conservative affair, exclusively concerned with politics and with political rights and, in comparison with the social purposes and social character of other revolutions, hardly a revolution at all.

Much of this is true enough; but the conservative, exclusively political interpretation of the Revolution is ultimately misleading. Of course, the American Revolution was different from other revolutions, but it was not less radical and social for being different. It was radical and social, however, in a very special eighteenth-century sense. No doubt much of the concerns and language of the premodern, pre-Marxian eighteenth century were almost entirely political. That was because men in that different, distant world could not conceive of society apart from politics. Social distinctions, social deprivations, and social evils were generally still regarded as rooted in the abuses of government. Titles of social rank, privileges and monopolies, even property and wealth of various sorts, all seemed ultimately to flow from connections to government, in the end, to royal authority. Hence, when

eighteenth-century radicals on both sides of the Atlantic talked in what seem to be only political terms—of protecting liberty from royal power and privilege, purifying a corrupt constitution, and becoming republicans—they nevertheless had a decidedly social message. In our eyes, the American Revolutionaries appear to be absorbed in changing only their governments, not their society. But, in destroying monarchy and establishing republican governments they were changing their society, too, and they knew it. Republicanism implied a new kind of social order.

We cannot appreciate what republicanism meant for the Revolutionaries unless we understand something of the nature of the old society it replaced. Eighteenth-century Anglo-American society, as the English historian Harold Perkin describes it, was still essentially precapitalist, a society of personal influence and dependent relationships that sustained a world totally unlike that of nineteenth-century America or today. This old society was a hierarchy of different levels and ranks that ran from the king at the top to the black slaves on the bottom. In between there were various degrees of dependency, including large numbers of bonded white persons. Even a modest household was likely to have apprentices or indentured servants. In such a society "men were acutely aware of their exact relation to those immediately above and below them, but only vaguely conscious except at the very top of their connections with those of their own level." This society was bound together by vertical lines of interest and connection rather than by the horizontal solidarities of class and occupation that we are more familiar with. Individuals did not think in modern class terms—of society divided into mutually hostile layers each united against the others by a common source of income or common occupation. The only horizontal cleavage of great importance was that between gentlemen and common people, and that was scarcely defined solely in economic terms. Up and down the social chains ran links of vertical connection—two-way relations between patrons and clients based on mutual trust—"a social nexus peculiar to the old society, less formal and inescapable than feudal homage, more personal and comprehensive than the contractual, employment relationships of the capitalist 'Cash Payment.' For those who lived within its embrace," says Perkin, this vertical relationship "was so much an integral part of the texture of life that they had no name for it save 'friendship.'". . .

Such patronage was, of course, most evident in politics. The key to Sir Lewis Namier's great success as a historian in opening up the nature of eighteenth-century politics for us in the twentieth century was his perception of the special character of these vertical relationships, and his understanding of the peculiar behavior of the politicians in whom the vertical chains of patronage and "friendship" converged. Politics in this society was highly personal, dependent on face-to-face relations or on the widespread use of personal correspondence. Such politics . . . involved a great deal of personal contacts, personal maneuvering and manipulation, and put a premium on certain traits of character—on circumspection, caution, prudence, and calculation. It was this personal structure of politics, this prevalence of numerous vertical links and loyalties, and not simply men's abhorrence of division, that explains the absence of organized political parties in the eighteenth century. We now know that it was not really any sort of extensive legal restrictions on the suffrage that kept most colonists from political participation. As yet, only a few members of the society thought of politics as a means by which the problems of their lives could be resolved. Some historians have grasped at the notion of deference to explain the willing acceptance by most eighteenth-century men of elite gentry rule; but "deference" seems too simple a concept to explain the complexity of these innumerable ties of dependency, patronage, and connection. . . .

In the end, for America and for Great Britain, it was the disintegration of this older patronage society of dependent relationships that prepared the way for the emergence of the liberal, modern, capitalistic world of the early nineteenth century. In America, the disintegration had begun early. The reordering of colonial life in the first century and a half of American history had either prohibited or inhibited a duplication of the normal social patterns of the mother country. To the extent that the colonists had already destroyed or had never established this traditional society, to the degree that Americans were splintered by religious and ethnic diversity and were more independent, more resentful and mistrustful of one another—to that extent, eighteenth-century America was already more modern than England.

Not only did colonial society lack a titled nobility, but the American upper level of gentlemen was weak and thin in comparison with the English gentry. The American "aristocracy," such as it was, was far more bourgeois in its nature and far more precariously based in the economy. It consequently had to scramble for its wealth and symbols of distinction far more greedily than the more stable gentry of England. Hence, the American gentlemanly leaders always appeared far more mercenary than did the English squirearchy; they were never able to duplicate the paternalism, the mutual protection and allegiance between superiors and inferiors that made the English aristocracy so relatively secure.

The use of personal influence in religion, in the economy, or in politics was never as deeply entrenched in America as it was in England. Militia officers were often selected by their companies; ministers were hired by their congregations; and many politicians were elected by an extremely broad electorate. Landed tenantry was rare in America, and yeoman farmers, in contrast to England, maintained a remarkable degree of independence. Everywhere multiplying religions and ethnic groups—whether Baptists in New England or Germans in Pennsylvania—sought the support of their own kind, and they often cut through traditional lines of interest and patronage. Mistrust, jealousy, and competition among individuals and groups were always more extensive in America than in England. All sorts of privileges and monopolies, from military contracts to tavern licenses, which made sense in the hierarchical patronage society of the mother country, were continually suspect in the colonies. The recipients of such privileges—those in whom the lines of personal influence were supposed to converge—were never as readily identifiable in America. In fact, the very weakness of the patronage society in the colonies only made the bonds of personal influence that did exist seem more arbitrary and unjust, and hence, more vulnerable to challenge.

By the middle of the eighteenth century, what remained of this older paternalistic world in the colonies was steadily eroding. Not only were new commercial arrangements—like the Scottish factorage system in the Chesapeake—emerging to break apart older personal marketing and credit relationships, but new immigration and the internal movement of tens of thousands of settlers—down the Appalachian valley into the Carolinas, up the Connecticut river into Vermont—shattered traditional communal and kinship ties.

It was in politics, however, where the erosions of the old society were most manifest; and it was in politics where the battle lines were drawn. During the middle decades of the eighteenth century, colonial politics became increasingly popularized as opposition groups in the colonial assemblies resorted to making more and more appeals to the people, as a counterweight to the use of royal authority by the governors. The weakening of older connections, and the further fragmentation of colonial interests, forced Crown officials and other conservatives into strenuous efforts to tighten up the society and to lessen popular participation in politics. Some of them attempted to restrict the expansion of popular representation in the assemblies, to limit the meetings of the assemblies, and to control the laws passed by the assemblies. Others toyed with plans for remodeling the colonial governments, for making the salaries of royal officials independent of the colonial legislatures, and for strengthening the royal councils or upper houses in the legislatures. Some even suggested introducing a titled nobility into America in order to stabilize colonial society. But most royal officials simply tried to use whatever traditional instruments of political patronage and influence they had available to them to curb popular disorder and pressure—relying on intricate maneuvering and personal manipulation of individuals in place of appeals to the people.

In the 1760s, all of these efforts became hopelessly entangled in the British government's attempts to extract revenue from the colonists and to reform the awkwardly structured empire. Everything came together to threaten each American's expanding expectations of liberty and independence. In the emotionally charged atmosphere of the 1760s and 70s, all the British and royal efforts at reform seemed to be an evil extension of what was destroying liberty in England itself. Through the manipulation of puppets or placemen in the House of Commons, the Crown—since 1760 in the hands of a new young Tory king, George III—unhinged the English constitution and sapped the strength of popular representation in Parliament. As events in the 1760s and 70s show, the Crown with the aid of a pliant Parliament was trying to reach across the Atlantic to corrupt Americans in the same way.

Already in some colonies this corruption, this use of patronage and preferments, had created tiny pockets of Crown influence, even among some of the royally commissioned justices of the peace. It had turned much of America into a dumping ground for worthless English place-seekers, and allowed even native Americans, like the clan of Thomas Hutchinson in Massachusetts, to pile up offices to the exclusion of those who, John Adams and James Otis felt, were better men. The prevailing revulsion against this sort of corruption even spilled over to affect those who were unconnected with royal authority, and it explains some of the anger of Virginians, like Thomas Jefferson, James Madison, Patrick Henry, and Richard Henry Lee, against the older clique of tidewater planters who tended to look after one another and to restrain the entry of others into their inner circle. Nothing was worse, Virginia critics of this clique said, than that "dreaded foe to public virtue, warm and private friendship." Although the focus of American thinking in the 1760s and 70s was on politics, such attacks on "friendship" could not be confined to government or even to Crown officials.

In this peculiar eighteenth-century context, one can best understand the Revolutionaries' appeal for independence—not just the independence of the United States, but the independence of different parts of the government from one another (particularly the independence of the legislature from the executive) and, most importantly, the independence of individuals from personal influence and "warm and private friendship."

The republican ideology that American leaders invoked in their struggle with Great Britain was centrally concerned with independence and the elimination of corruption. It drew on a Western tradition stretching back to the classical times of ancient Greece and Rome. As developed and refined by eighteenth-century English radicals, this republican heritage could be used to explain and to justify American resistance and revolution as well as the erection of new independent governments. In the new revolutionary constitutions of 1776, nearly all the states struck out at corruption in government and forbade members of the executive from simultaneously holding seats in the legislatures (which forever prohibited the development of parliamentary cabinet government in America). Everywhere, Americans sought to reduce the artificial influence of government over the shape of their society.

By invoking republicanism and by attacking corruption, however, Americans were not simply expressing their resentment toward particular political practices that had denied some of them the highest offices of government. They were actually tearing at the bonds holding the traditional society together. Their assault was therefore as much social as it was political. But the social meaning was not one of class conflict; it grew out of that distinctive eighteenth-century society. The great social antagonists of the pre-Revolutionary period were not the poor versus the rich, or even democrats versus aristocrats, but rather patriots versus courtiers. Courtiers were persons whose position or rank came artificially from above—from personal connections and influence that ultimately flowed from the Crown or court. Patriots, though, were those who not only loved their country but were free of independent connections and influence; their position or rank came naturally from their talent, from below, and from recognition by the people.

A society of patriots was in effect a republic. Hence, the Americans' eventual resort to republicanism in 1776 flowed naturally from their goals and possessed immense social significance—a significance that for the eighteenth century was as radical as Marxism to the nineteenth century. Republicanism presumed, as the Virginia Declaration of Rights stated in 1776, that men would be "equally free and independent." Citizens in a republic would relate to each other and to the state voluntarily and equally. Unlike monarchies, whose corrupting influence and numerous dependent ranks maintained public order, even over a large and diverse populace, republics had to be held together by the people's willingly offered service, from patriotism or, as the eighteenth century called it, from "virtue."

From this belief, heightened by the knowledge of what had happened to the republics of antiquity, it is not surprising that Americans would become obsessed with their own morality.

This morality or virtue demanded independent individuals. For, as Jefferson said, "dependence begets subservience and venality, suffocates the germ of virtue, and prepares fit tools for the designs of ambition." Hence, the sturdy independent yeomen, Jefferson's "chosen people of God," were regarded as the most incorruptible and therefore the best citizens for a republic. The celebration of the farmer in the years following the Revolution was not a literary conceit but a scientifically based imperative of republican government.

In such a world of free independent men, slavery, which had existed for over a century without substantial criticism, suddenly became an excruciating anomaly. Since the seventeenth century, most colonists had taken slavery for granted as simply the most base and dependent status in a hierarchy of different dependent ranks. But republican equality now compelled Americans to confront the aberration of slavery in their midst as they never had to before, and if they were to retain it, to defend and justify it as a "peculiar institution."

Despite republicanism's stress on equality, the Revolutionaries did not intend to level their society. Jefferson still envisioned social and economic distinctions; only now these distinctions would be based, not on private connections or governmental influence, but on merit. Republicanism was opposed to all legal privileges and unequal and artifically created inheritance patterns; but equality did not mean a redistribution of property. Although excessive wealth might be dangerous in a republic, the individual possession of property was central to a republic. For property, particularly landed property, guaranteed a man's independence. Jefferson feared the rabble of the cities precisely because they were propertyless and dependent. All dependents, such as women and young men, could be denied the vote, because, as a convention of Essex County, Massachusetts, declared in 1778, they were "so situated as to have no wills of their own." Jefferson was so keen on this equation of property with citizenship that he proposed in 1776 that the new state of Virginia grant fifty acres of land to every man who did not have as much.

Of course, the Revolution in the end went farther than most American leaders in 1776 intended. Indeed, republicanism created a society, in some respects, the exact opposite of what was hoped for. The republican stress on equality was expanded and was soon used to question the natural distinctions the Revolutionary leaders had taken for granted. Even as early as the 1780s, the claim that one man was as good as any other seemed to breed licentiousness in the states and to require a restrengthening of governmental and executive authority. Independent patriots were not supposed to become selfish, moneymaking individualists; but the permissiveness of republicanism made it difficult to restrain individualistic and capitalistic pressures. By freeing persons from older social connections and dependencies, and by making them the independent shapers of their destinies, republicanism helped to create the nineteenth-century acquisitive society of scrambling self-made men. . . . Yet, for all of its unanticipated consequences, republicanism summed up the meaning of the American Revolution. It identified us as a people and defined most of our noblest ideals and values. It gave us our sense, that we were in the vanguard of history, pointing the way toward a society different from what men had ever known—where people were freer, more independent, more equal, and more able to achieve their aspirations.

After reading this selection, consider these questions:

1. Describe the social structure of eighteenth-century Britain and its North American colonies.

2. What forces in America undermined what Wood describes as the vertical organization of society even before the Revolutionary crisis?

3. In what ways did American revolutionaries incorporate a social critique within their political discourse?

4. How does Gordon S. Wood's discussion of the concept of independence compare with that of Edmund S. Morgan (chapter 9)?

SELECTION 2:

Protest and Defiance in the Continental Army

J*ames Kirby Martin is a distinguished university professor of history at the University of Houston and an authority on the social history of the Continental army. Martin maintains that the Continental army of*

1775–1776 consisted of citizens "who had respectable amounts of property and who were defending hearth and home." They joined for what they believed would be a short war in which their "virtue and moral commitment" would triumph over British regulars fighting for nothing more than salaries. As the prospect of a long and difficult struggle became apparent, however, many such men of property and standing began to purchase substitutes or to pay fines (often nominal) for failing to serve. Thus, after 1777, the substantial majority of the Continental army came from the lower social and economic levels of American society. The poor farmers, laborers, indentured servants, slaves, and freedmen of color who made up the bulk of the army fought less for noble ideals of liberty or against British "corruption," as described by Gordon S. Wood, and more for promises of free land and, in the case of bound servants, freedom. As the army changed, the reaction to unfulfilled promises by state legislatures and the Continental Congress evolved from individual to collective forms of protest.

A sequence of events inconceivable to Americans raised on patriotic myths about the Revolution occurred in New Jersey during the spring of 1779. For months the officers of the Jersey brigade had been complaining loudly about everything from lack of decent food and clothing to pay arrearages and late payments in rapidly depreciating currency. They had petitioned their assembly earlier, but nothing had happened. They petitioned again in mid-April 1779, acting on the belief that the legislature should "be informed that our pay is now only *minimal,* not *real,* that four months' pay of a private will not procure his wretched wife and children a single bushel of wheat." Using "the most plain and unambiguous terms," they stressed that "unless a speedy and ample remedy be provided, the total dissolution of your troops is inevitable." The Jersey assembly responded to this plea in its usual fashion—it forwarded the petition to the Continental Congress without comment. After all, the officers, although from New Jersey, were a part of the Continental military establishment.

The assembly's behavior only further angered the officers, and some of them decided to demonstrate their resolve. On May 6 the brigade received orders to join John Sullivan's expedition against the Six Nations [the Iroquois confederacy]. That same day, officers in the First Regiment sent forth yet another petition. They again admonished the assembly about pay and supply issues. While they stated that they would prepare the regiment for the upcoming campaign, they themselves would resign as a group unless the legislators addressed their demands. Complaints had now turned into something more than gentlemanly protest. Protest was on the verge of becoming nothing less than open defiance of civil authority, and the Jersey officers were deadly serious. They had resorted to their threatened resignations to insure that the assembly would give serious attention to their demands—for a change.

When George Washington learned about the situation, he was appalled. . . . What would happen, he asked rhetorically, "if their example should be followed and become general?" The result would be the "ruin" and "disgrace" of the rebel cause, all because these officers had *"reasoned wrong about the means of obtaining a good end."*

So developed a little known but highly revealing confrontation. Washington told Congress that he would have acted very aggressively toward

Excerpted from *Arms and Independence: The Military Character of the American Revolution,* edited by Ronald Hoffman and Peter J. Albert (Charlottesville: University of Virginia Press, 1984). Copyright © 1984 by the University of Virginia Press. Reprinted with permission.

the recalcitrant officers, except that "the causes of discontent are too great and too general and the ties that bind the officers to the service too feeble" to force the issue. What he did promise was that he would not countenance any aid that came "in [such] a manner extorted." On the other hand, the officers had been asking the assembly for relief since January 1778, but to no avail. They, too, were not about to be moved.

The New Jersey legislature was the political institution with the ability to break the deadlock. Some of the legislators preferred disbanding the brigade. The majority argued that other officers and common soldiers might follow the First Regiment's lead and warned that the war effort could hardly succeed without a Continental military establishment. The moment was now ripe for compromise. The assemblymen agreed to provide the officers with whatever immediate relief could be mustered in return for the latter calling back their petitions. That way civil authorities would not be succumbing to intimidation by representatives of the military establishment, and the principle of subordination of military to civil authority would remain inviolate. The assembly thus provided an immediate payment of £200 to each officer and $40 to each soldier. Accepting the compromise settlement as better than nothing, the brigade moved out of its Jersey encampment on May 11 and marched toward Sullivan's bivouac at Easton, Pennsylvania. Seemingly, all now had returned to normal.

The confrontation between the New Jersey officers and the state assembly serves to illuminate some key points about protest and defiance in the Continental ranks during the years 1776–83. Most important here, it underscores the mounting anger felt by Washington's regulars as a result of their perceived (and no doubt very real) lack of material and psychological support from the society that had spawned the Continental army. It is common knowledge that Washington's regulars suffered from serious supply and pay shortages throughout the war. Increasingly, historians are coming to realize that officers and common soldiers alike received very little moral support from the general populace. As yet, however, scholars have not taken a systematic look at

one product of this paradigm of neglect, specifically, protest and defiance. The purpose of this essay is to present preliminary findings that will facilitate that task.

Given that there was a noticeable relationship between lack of material and psychological support from the civilian sector and mounting protest and defiance in the ranks, it is also important to make clear that patterns of protest were very complex. A second purpose of this essay is to outline those basic patterns and to indicate why protest and defiance did not result in serious internal upheaval between army and society in the midst of the War for American Independence. To begin this assessment, we must bring Washington's Continentals to the center of the historical arena.

During the past twenty years, historians have learned that there were at least two Continental armies. The army of 1775–76 might be characterized as a republican constabulary, consisting of citizens who had respectable amounts of property and who were defending hearth and home. They came out for what they believed would be a rather short contest in which their assumed virtue and moral commitment would easily carry the day over seasoned British regulars not necessarily wedded to anything of greater concern than filling their own pocketbooks as mercenaries.

The first army had a militialike appearance. Even though phrases of commitment were high sounding, there was not much discipline or rigorous training. These early soldiers had responded to appeals from leaders who warned about "our wives and children, with everything that is dear to us, [being] subjected to the merciless rage of uncontrolled despotism." They were convinced that they were "engaged . . . in the cause of virtue, of liberty, of *God.*" Unfortunately, the crushing blows endured in the massive British offensive of 1776 against New York undercut such high-sounding phrases about self-sacrifice. The message at the end of 1775 had been "Persevere, ye guardians of liberty." They did not.

The second Continental establishment took form out of the remains of the first. Even before Washington executed his magnificent turnabout at Trenton and Princeton, he had called for a "respectable army," one built on long-term enlistments, thorough training, and high standards of discipline. The army's command, as well as many delegates in Congress, now wanted soldiers who could stand up against the enemy with more than notions of exalted virtue and moral superiority to upgird them. They called for able-bodied men who could and would endure for the long-term fight in a contest that all leaders now knew could not be sustained by feelings of moral superiority and righteousness alone.

To assist in overcoming manpower shortages, Congress and the states enhanced financial promises made to potential enlistees. Besides guarantees about decent food and clothing, recruiters handed out bounty moneys and promises of free land at war's end (normally only for long-term service). Despite these financial incentives, there was no great rush to the Continental banner. For the remainder of the war, the army's command, Congress, and the states struggled to maintain minimal numbers of Continental soldiers in the ranks.

In fact, all began to search diligently for new recruits. Instead of relying on propertied freeholders and tradesmen of the ideal citizen-soldier type, they broadened the definition of what constituted an "able-bodied and effective" recruit. For example, New Jersey in early 1777 started granting exemptions to all those who hired substitutes for long-term Continental service—and to masters who would enroll indentured servants and slaves. The following year Maryland permitted the virtual impressment of vagrants for nine months of regular service. Massachusetts set another kind of precedent in 1777 by declaring blacks (both slave and free) eligible for the state draft. Shortly thereafter, Rhode Islanders set about the business of raising two black battalions. Ultimately, Maryland and Virginia permitted slaves to substitute for whites. The lower South, however, refused to do so, even in the face of a successful British invasion later in the war.

The vast majority of Continentals who fought with Washington after 1776 were representative of the very poorest and most repressed persons in Revolutionary society. A number of recent studies have verified that a large proportion of the Continentals in the second establishment represented ne'er-do-wells, drifters, unemployed laborers, captured British soldiers and Hessians, indentured servants, and slaves. Some of these new regulars were in such desperate economic straits that states had to pass laws prohibiting creditors from pulling them from the ranks and having them thrown in jail for petty debts. (Obviously, this was not a problem with the unfree.)

The most important point to be derived from this dramatic shift in the social composition of the Continental army is that few of these new common soldiers had enjoyed anything close to economic prosperity or full political (or legal) liberty before the war. As a group, they had something to gain from service. If they could survive the rigors of camp life, the killing diseases that so often ravaged the armies of their times, and the carnage of skirmishes and full-scale battles, they could look forward to a better life for themselves at the end of the war. Not only were they to have decent food and clothing and regular pay until the British had been irrevocably beaten, they had also been promised free land (and personal freedom in the cases of indentured servants, black slaves, and criminals). Recruiters thus conveyed a message of personal upward mobility through service. In exchange for personal sacrifice in the short run, there was the prospect of something far better in the long run, paralleling and epitomizing the collective rebel quest for a freer political life in the New World. . . .

Respectably established citizens after 1775 and 1776 preferred to let others perform the dirty work of regular, long-term service on their behalf, essentially on a contractual basis. Their legislators gave bounties and *promised* many other incentives. Increasingly, as the war lengthened, the civilian population and its leaders did a less effective job in keeping their part of the agreement. One significant outcome of this obvious civilian ingratitude, if not utter disregard for contractual promises, was protest and defiance coming from Washington's beleaguered soldiers and officers.

That relations between Washington's post-1776 army and Revolutionary society deteriorated dramatically hardly comes as a surprise to those historians who have investigated surviving records. Widespread anger among the rank and file became most demonstrable in 1779 and 1780, at the very nadir of the war effort. . . . The army had come to believe that Revolutionary civilians had taken advantage of them—and had broken their part of the contract for military services.

There were real dangers hidden behind these words. With each passing month beginning in 1777, Washington's regulars, especially that small cadre that was signing on for the long-term fight, became more professional in military demeanor. Among other things, including their enhanced potential effectiveness in combat, this meant that soldiers felt the enveloping (and reassuring) bonds of "unit cohesion." The immediate thoughts of individual soldiers, whether recruited, dragooned, or pressed into service, became attached to their respective primary units in the army, such as the particular companies or regiments in which they served. The phenomenon was nothing more than a developing comradeship in arms. Any threat or insult thus became an assault on the group, especially if that threat or insult were directed at all members of the group. The bonding effect of unit cohesion suggests that collective protest and defiance would become more of a danger to a generally unsupportive society with each passing month, unless civilians who had made grand promises started to meet their contractual obligations more effectively.

Indeed, the most readily observable pattern in Continental army protest and defiance was that it took on more and more of a collective (and menacing) character through time. At the outset, especially beginning in 1776, most protest had an individual character. Frequently it was the raw recruit, quite often anxious for martial glory but quickly disillusioned with the realities of military service once in camp, who struck back against undesirable circumstances. Protest could come through such diverse expressions as swearing, excessive drinking, assaulting officers, deserting, or bounty jumping. One source of such behavior was the dehumanizing, even brutal nature of camp life. Another had to do with broken promises about pay, food, and clothing. A third was a dawning sense that too many civilians held the soldiery in disregard, if not utter contempt.

It must be remembered that middle- and upper-class civilians considered Washington's new regulars to be representative of the "vulgar herd" in a society that still clung to deferential values. The assumption was that the most fit in terms of wealth and community social standing were to lead while the least fit were to follow, even when that meant becoming little more than human cannon fodder. . . .

Thus it may be an error to dismiss heavy swearing around civilians or repeated drunkenness in camp as nothing more than manifestations of "time-honored military vices" . . .

At least in some instances, individual soldiers could have been making statements about their sense of personal entrapment. Furthermore, protest through such methods as drunkenness (this was a drinking society but not one that condoned inebriety) was a defensive weapon. One of Washington's generals, for instance, bitterly complained in 1777 that too many soldiers consistently made it "a practice of getting drunk . . . once a Day and thereby render themselves unfit for duty." To render themselves unfit for duty was to give what they had received—broken promises. Defiance that came in the form of "barrel fever" for some soldiers thus translated into statements about how society looked upon and treated them.

Only over time did individual acts of protest take on a more collective character. That transition may be better comprehended by considering the phenomenon of desertion. While it is true that a great many soldiers did not think of desertion as a specific form of protest, they fled the ranks with greater frequency when food and clothing were in very short supply or nonexistent, as at Valley Forge. However, primary unit cohesion worked to militate against unusually high desertion levels. Sustained involvement with a company or regiment reduced the likelihood of desertion. Hence as soldiers came to know, trust, and depend upon one another, and as they gained confidence in comrades and felt personally vital to the long-term welfare of their primary group, they were much less likely to lodge a statement of individual protest through such individualized forms as desertion. . . .

Then there were those individuals who neither deserted nor became hard-core regulars. By and large, this group defied civil and military authority through the practice of bounty jumping. The procedure . . . involved enlisting, getting a bounty, and deserting, then repeating the same process with another recruiting agent in another location. Some of the most resourceful bounty jumpers got away with this maneuver seven, eight, or even nine times, if not more. Most jumpers appear to have been very poor young men without family roots. The most careful of them went through the war unscathed. Bounties thus provided a form of economic aggrandizement (and survival) in a society that generally treated its struggling classes with studied neglect. To accept a bounty payment, perhaps even to serve for a short period, and then to run off, was a strongly worded statement of personal defiance.

Bounty jumping was invariably the act of protesting individuals; looting and plundering (like desertion) combined individual with collective protest. Certainly there were numerous occasions when hungry soldiers looted by themselves. Just as often, groups of starving men "borrowed" goods from civilians. Even before the second establishment took form, looting had become a serious problem. Indeed, it probably abetted unit cohesion. . . .

When army looting of civilian property continued its unabated course in 1777, General Washington threatened severe penalties. . . . Incident after incident kept the commander in chief and his staff buried in a landslide of civilian complaints. Threats of courts martial, actual trials, and severe punishments did not deter angry, starving, protesting soldiers. In 1780 and 1781 Washington was still issuing pleas and threats, but to little avail. Not even occasional hangings contained an increasingly defiant and cohesive soldiery . . . To strike back at hoarding, unsupportive citizens, as they had come to perceive the populace whom they were defending, seemed only logical, especially when emboldened by the camaraderie of closely knit fellow soldiers.

Above all else, two patterns stand out with respect to common soldier protest. First, as the war effort lengthened, defiance became more of a collective phenomenon. Second, such protest had a controlled quality. While there was unremitting resentment toward civilians who were invariably perceived as insensitive and unsupportive, protest rarely metamorphosed into wanton violence and mindless destruction. Soldiers may have looted and pillaged, they may have grabbed up bounties, and they may have deserted. But they rarely maimed, raped, or murdered civilians. . . .

The specter of collective defiance in the form of line mutinies had come close to reality with the near insubordination of the New Jersey officers in 1779. They had not demonstrated in the field, but they had made it clear that conditions in the army were all but intolerable—and that civil society, when desperate to maintain a regular force in arms, could be persuaded to concede on basic demands. Washington had used the phrase "extorted"; he had also pointed out that, "notwithstanding the expedient adopted for saving appearances," this confrontation "cannot fail to operate as a bad precedent." The commander in chief was certainly right about the setting of precedents.

Among long-term veterans, anger was beginning to overwhelm discipline. There had been small-scale mutinies before, such as the rising of newly recruited Continentals at Halifax, North Carolina, in February 1776. In 1779 Rhode Island and Connecticut regiments threatened mutinies, but nothing came of these incidents. Then in 1780 another near uprising of the Connecticut Line occurred. Invariably, the issues had the same familiar ring: lack of adequate civilian support as demonstrated by rotten food, inadequate clothing, and worthless pay (when pay was available). On occasion, too, the heavy hand of company- and field-grade officers played its part. The near mutiny of the Connecticut Line in 1780 had been avoided by a fortuitous shipment of cattle and by promises from trusted officers of better treatment. In the end, the Connecticut Line calmed itself down, according to [Private Joseph Plumb] Martin, because the soldiery was "unwilling to desert the cause of our country, when in distress.". . .

By the end of 1780, there were some veterans who would have disputed Martin's reasoning. They had all but given up, let come what might for the glorious cause. On January 1, 1781, the Pennsylvania Line proved that point. Suffering through yet another harsh winter near Morristown, New Jersey, the Pennsylvanians mutinied. Some one thousand determined comrades in arms (about 15 percent of the manpower available to Washington) ostensibly wanted nothing more to do with fighting the war. On a prearranged signal, the Pennsylvanians paraded under arms, seized their artillery, and marched south toward Princeton, their ultimate target being Philadelphia. These veterans had had their fill of broken promises, of the unfulfilled contract. They maintained that they had signed on for three years, not for the duration. If they were to stay in the ranks, then they wanted the same benefits (additional bounty payments, more free land, and some pay in specie) that newer enlistees had obtained.

Formal military discipline collapsed as the officers trying to contain the mutineers were brushed aside. The soldiers killed one and wounded two other officers, yet their popular commander, Anthony Wayne, trailed along, attempting to appeal to their sense of patriotism. Speaking through a committee of sergeants, the soldiers assured Wayne and the other officers that they were still loyal to the cause, and they proved it by handing over two spies that Sir Henry Clinton had sent out from New York to monitor the situation. Moreover, the mutineers, despite their anger and bitterness, behaved themselves along their route and did not unnecessarily intimidate civilians who got in their way.

Later checking demonstrated that many of the mutineers were duration enlistees, yet that was a moot point. When the soldiers reached Trenton, representatives of Congress and the Pennsylvania government negotiated with them and agreed to discharge any veteran claiming three years in rank. Also, they offered back pay and new clothing along with immunity from prosecution for having defied their officers in leaving their posts. Once formally discharged, the bulk of the mutineers reenlisted for a new bounty. By late January 1781 the Pennsylvania Line was once more a functioning part of the Continental army.

These mutineers won because Washington was in desperate need of manpower and because

they had resorted to collective defiance, not because their society wanted to address what had been grievances based on the contract for service. Unlike their officers, who had just won a major victory in driving for half-pay pensions, they were not in a position to lobby before Congress. Hence they employed one of the most threatening weapons in their arsenal, collective protest against civil authority, but only after less extreme measures had failed to satisfy their claims for financial justice. They were certainly not planning to overthrow any government or to foment an internal social revolution against better-placed members of their society. They had staked their hopes on a better life in the postwar period and had already risked their lives many times for the proposed republican polity. All told, the extreme nature of this mutiny demonstrated, paradoxically, both that Washington's long-term Continentals were the most loyal and dedicated republican citizens in the new nation, and that they were dangerously close to repudiating a dream that far too often had been a personal nightmare because of the realities of societal support and of service in the Continental army.

More worrisome in January 1781 than the matter of appropriate appreciation of the soldiers' actions was whether this mutiny, and its stillborn predecessors, would trigger further turbulence in the ranks. Also camped near Morristown during the winter of 1780–81 were veteran soldiers of the New Jersey Line. Their officers were aware that the Jersey regulars sympathized with the Pennsylvanians and had been in constant communication with them. Then, on January 20, 1781, the New Jersey Line, having witnessed the success of its comrades, also mutinied. The soldiers had each recently received $5 in specie as a token toward long overdue pay, but they were bothered by the better bounties and terms of enlistment offered newer recruits. Their leaders urged them on by shouting: "Let us go to Congress who have money and rum enough but won't give it to us!"

Within a few days, the Jersey Line had won acceptable concessions and was back under control. Washington, however, had decided that enough was enough. "Unless this dangerous spirit can be suppressed by force," he wrote to

Congress, "there is an end to all subordination in the Army, and indeed to the Army itself." To back up his strong words, the commander ordered Gen. Robert Howe and about five hundred New England troops near West Point to march to the Jersey camp at Pompton to make sure that the mutineers were back in line and summarily to execute the most notorious leaders. Howe did as instructed. He reached Pompton on January 27, three days after grievances had been redressed. Deploying his men around the campsite just before dawn, Howe caught the Jersey soldiers off guard. He ordered them to fall in without arms, then singled out three ringleaders and ordered their summary execution, to be shot to death by nine of their comrades. A Jersey officer intervened in one case, but the other two were put to death by firing squad.

It was a brutal ending for men who had dreamed of a better future despite all of society's violations of the contract. Perhaps because of the calculated coldheartedness of Washington's orders, or perhaps because the war picture began to brighten in 1781, there were no major uprisings among Washington's regulars after the mutiny of the New Jersey Line. Then again, the soldiery may have been too worn down physically and mentally to continue their protest and defiance in the name of financial justice, humane treatment, and psychological support. They may have passed beyond the point of despair to that of quiet acceptance of whatever came their way, whether just or unjust.

An important question that must be raised in conclusion has to do with political perceptions and fears: given real concerns in Revolutionary society that a regular army could obtain too much power, could corrupt the political system, and could threaten the civilian sector with some form of tyranny, such as a military dictatorship, why did officers and soldiers never unite effectively and put maximum pressure on the frail Revolutionary political structure by protesting in unison? They could have easily played on fears of a coup. But about the closest such union was the Jersey officers' defiance of 1779. Thus, while common soldiers got drunk, deserted, looted, or mutinied, officers pursued their own (and largely separate) avenues of protest. This is curious, especially since the officers too worried about the personal financial cost of service; they too came to resent civilian indifference, ineptitude, and greed; and they too were dismayed over society's inability to treat them with respect. They feared that their virtuous behavior and self-sacrifice would go unappreciated if not completely unrecognized and unrewarded. Having so much in common with their brethren in the rank and file, then, it is worth considering why the officers almost never aligned with them. For if they had, the alliance might have been powerful enough to have fomented something truly menacing to the vitals of Revolutionary society.

The officer corps developed its own forms of protest, and the pattern paralleled that of the common soldiers. The movement was from a dominant expression of individual defiance (resignations in 1776 and 1777) to collective protest (the drive for half-pay pensions which began in earnest during the fall of 1777 and climaxed with the Newburgh Conspiracy, 1782–83). Like common soldiers, the officers had collectivized their protest. In that sense, unit cohesion among comrades had come into play, but such cohesion never broke through the vertical hierarchy of military rank.

Part of the reason lay in the social gulf separating the two groups. . . .

Washington's veteran officers, even though they complained and protested with vehemence, also willingly accepted their responsibilities as the army's leadership cadre: The officers administered harsh discipline to deserters, looters, bounty jumpers, and mutineers whenever it seemed necessary—and sometimes when it was not. . . .

Many officers thus used their authority with impunity and rarely expressed sympathy for the plight of common soldiers in the ranks. They were much more concerned with societal stability and the protection of property, as well as with military decorum and hierarchy, all of which precluded the officer corps from working in harmony with the soldiery when protesting common grievances against the civilian sector.

Washington's officers, in reality, were caught between the rank and file, for which they had little sympathy, and the larger society, which had little sympathy for them. They pursued their half-pay pension demands, resorting to such defiant acts as threatening to resign en masse during the late summer of 1780. Later they became even more extreme as some toyed with the idea of a full mutiny, if not the possibility of a coup, during the Newburgh crisis. In the end, they failed in their short-term quest for pensions or commutation, as the soldiery fell short in its drive for minimal levels of respectable support. . . .

That [enlisted men and officers] did not [unite and mutiny] is more than a mere testament to class, hierarchy, and rank. It is also a statement about the evolving feelings among both hard-core officers and regulars, regardless of the multifold reasons that brought them to the service in the first place, that they were fighting for something worthwhile, something of consequence for their particular lives. If they protested, they still maintained residual faith in their personal dreams. They also came to comprehend that, for all of the pain and suffering that was their lot, they could make a lasting contribution. . . . That

is the way that these protesting, defying, long-term Continentals should be remembered, not as a "most undisciplined, profligate Crew," but as individuals who, for all of their defiance, made the necessary personal sacrifice to insure that the Revolution and its ideals would succeed when so many about them in their society did not.

After reading this selection, consider these questions:

1. To what extent could the individual advantage for which many soldiers fought be encompassed within the larger patriot cause?

2. How do the changes in the Continental army Martin describes relate to the notions of republicanism discussed by Gordon S. Wood in the first essay in this chapter?

3. How might one use the information provided by Martin to support Wood's contention that republicanism "helped to create the nineteenth-century acquisitive society of scrambling self-made men"?

SELECTION 3:

Benjamin Franklin Speaks in Favor of the Constitution

From May 25 to September 17, 1787, delegates met to recommend ways to amend the Articles of Confederation. During those weeks of debate, argument, and compromise, they forged a new constitution for the United States. The following is Benjamin Franklin's closing speech to the convention. The meetings of the Constitutional Convention were not open to the public, and no formal record of the proceedings was kept. This version of the speech is excerpted from notes taken by James Madison.

Monday, September 17, 1787: In Convention
The engrossed Constitution being read,

Doctor Franklin rose with a speech in his hand, which he had reduced to writing for his own conveniency, and which Mr. [James] Wilson [the Pennsylvania delegate] read in the words following.

Mr. President

I confess that there are several parts of this constitution which I do not at present approve, but I am not sure I shall never approve them: For having lived long, I have experienced many instances of being obliged by better information, or fuller consideration, to change opinions even on important subjects, which I once thought right, but found to be otherwise. It is therefore that the older I grow, the more apt I am to doubt my own judgment, and to pay more respect to the judgment of others. Most men indeed as well as most sects in Religion, think themselves in possession of all truth, and that wherever others differ from them it is so far error. Steele a Protestant in a Dedication tells the Pope, that the only difference between our Churches in their opinions of the certainty of their doctrines is, the Church of Rome is infallible and the Church of England is never in the wrong. But though many private persons think almost as highly of their own infallibility as of that of their sect, few express it so naturally as a certain french lady, who in a dispute with her sister, said "I don't know how it happens, Sister but I meet with no body but myself, that's always in the right—*Il n'y a que moi qui a toujours raison.*"

In these sentiments, Sir, I agree to this Constitution with all its faults, if they are such; because I think a general Government necessary for us, and there is no form of Government but what may be a blessing to the people if well administered, and believe farther that this is likely to be well administered for a course of years, and can only end in Despotism, as other forms have done before it,

when the people shall became so corrupted as to need despotic Government, being incapable of any other. I doubt too whether any other Convention we can obtain, may be able to make a better Constitution. For when you assemble a number of men to have the advantage of their joint wisdom, you inevitably assemble with those men, all their prejudices, their passions, their errors of opinion, their local interests, and their selfish views. From such an assembly can a perfect production be expected? It therefore astonishes me, Sir, to find this system approaching so near to perfection as it does; and I think it will astonish our enemies, who are waiting with confidence to hear that our councils are confounded like those of the Builders of Babel; and that our States are on the point of separation, only to meet hereafter for the purpose of cutting one another's throats. Thus I consent, Sir, to this Constitution because I expect no better, and because I am not sure, that it is not the best. The opinions I have had of its errors, I sacrifice to the public good. I have never whispered a syllable of them abroad. Within these walls they were born, and here they shall die. If every one of us in returning to our Constituents were to report the objections he has had to it, and endeavor to gain partizans in support of them, we might prevent its being generally received, and thereby lose all the salutary effects & great advantages resulting naturally in our favor among foreign Nations as well as among ourselves, from our real or apparent unanimity. Much of the strength & efficiency of any Government in procuring and securing happiness to the people, depends, on opinion, on the general opinion of the goodness of the Government, as well as of the wisdom and integrity of its Governors. I hope therefore that for our own sakes as a part of the people, and for the sake of posterity, we shall act heartily and unanimously in recommending this Constitution (if approved by Congress & confirmed by the Conventions) wherever our influence may extend, and turn our future thoughts & endeavors to the means of having it well administered.

On the whole, Sir, I can not help expressing a wish that every member of the Convention who may still have objections to it, would with me, on this occasion doubt a little of his own infalli-

Excerpted from *Writings,* edited by Galliard Hunt (New York: G.P. Putnam's Sons, 1903).

bility, and to make manifest our unanimity, put his name to this instrument. . . .

Whilst the last members were signing it Doctor FRANKLIN looking towards the President's Chair, at the back of which a rising sun happened to be painted, observed to a few members near him, that Painters had found it difficult to distinguish in their art a rising from a setting sun. I have, said he, . . . often in the course of the Session, and the vicisitudes of my hopes and fears as to its issue, looked at that behind the President without being able to tell whether it was rising or setting: But now at length I have the happiness to know that it is a rising and not a setting Sun.

The Constitution being signed by all the members except Mr. [Edmund] Randolph [of Virginia], Mr. Mason, and Mr. Gerry who declined giving it the sanction of their names, the Convention dissolved itself by an Adjournment sine die [final adjournment].

After reading this selection, consider these questions:

1. Franklin writes, "The opinions I have had of its errors, I sacrifice to the public good." Analyze Franklin's statement in the context of Gordon S. Wood's discussion of interest and disinterestedness.

2. Franklin praises the compromises that produced the Constitution. To what compromises does he refer?

SELECTION 4:

Thomas Jefferson Considers the New Constitution

Thomas Jefferson wrote the following letter to James Madison on December 27, 1787, three months after the Constitutional Convention completed its work.

The season admitting only of operations in the Cabinet, and these being in a great measure secret, I have little to fill a letter. I will therefore make up the deficiency by adding a few words on the Constitution proposed by our Convention. I like much the general idea of framing a government which should go on of itself peaceably, without needing continual recurrence to the state

legislatures. I like the organization of the government into Legislative, Judiciary and Executive. I like the power given the Legislature to levy taxes; and for that reason solely approve of the greater house being chosen by the people directly. For tho' I think a house chosen by them will be very illy qualified to legislate for the Union, for foreign nations &c. yet this evil does not weigh against the good of preserving inviolate the fundamental principle that the people are not to be taxed but by representatives chosen immediately by themselves. I am captivated by

Excerpted from *The Portable Thomas Jefferson,* edited by Merrill D. Peterson (New York: Penguin Press, 1975).

the compromise of the opposite claims of the great and little states, of the latter to equal, and the former to proportional influence. I am much pleased too with the substitution of the method of voting by persons, instead of that of voting by states: and I like the negative given to the Executive with a third of either house, though I should have liked it better had the Judiciary been associated for that purpose, or invested with a similar and separate power. There are other good things of less moment. I will now add what I do not like. First the omission of a bill of rights providing clearly and without the aid of sophisms for freedom of religion, freedom of the press, protection against standing armies, restriction against monopolies, the eternal and unremitting force of the habeas corpus laws, and trials by jury in all matters of fact triable by the laws of the land and not by the law of Nations. . . . Let me add that a bill of rights is what the people are entitled to against every government on earth, general or particular, and what no just government should refuse, or rest on inference. The second feature I dislike, and greatly dislike, is the abandonment in every instance of the necessity of rotation in office, and most particularly in the case of the President. Experience concurs with reason in concluding that the first magistrate will always be re-elected if the constitution permits it. He is then an officer for life. This once observed it becomes of so much consequence to certain nations to have a friend or a foe at the head of our affairs that they will interfere with money and with arms. A Galloman or an Angloman will be supported by the nation he befriends. If once elected, and at a second or third election outvoted by one or two votes, he will pretend false votes, foul play, hold possession of the reins of government, be supported by the states voting for him, especially if they are the central ones lying in a compact body themselves and separating their opponents: and they will be aided by one nation of Europe, while the majority are aided by another. The election of a President of America some years hence will be much more interesting to certain nations of Europe than ever the election of a king of Poland was. Reflect on all the instances in history ancient and modern, of elective monarchies, and

say if they do not give foundation for my fears, the Roman emperors, the popes, while they were of any importance, the German emperors till they became hereditary in practice, the kings of Poland, the Deys of the Ottoman dependancies. It may be said that if elections are to be attended with these disorders, the seldomer they are renewed the better. But experience shews that the only way to prevent disorder is to render them uninteresting by frequent changes. An incapacity to be elected a second time would have been the only effectual preventative. The power of removing him every fourth year by the vote of the people is a power which will not be exercised. The king of Poland is removeable every day by the Diet, yet he is never removed.—Smaller objections are the Appeal in fact as well as law, and the binding all persons Legislative, Executive and Judiciary by oath to maintain that constitution. I do not pretend to decide what would be the best method of procuring the establishment of the manifold good things in this constitution, and of getting rid of the bad. Whether by adopting it in hopes of future amendment, or, after it has been duly weighed and canvassed by the people, after seeing the parts they generally dislike, and those they generally approve, to say to them "We see now what you wish. Send together your deputies again, let them frame a constitution for you omitting what you have condemned, and establishing the powers you approve. Even these will be a great addition to the energy of your government." —At all events I hope you will not be discouraged from other trials, if the present one should fail of it's full effect.—I have thus told you freely what I like and dislike: merely as a matter of curiosity for I know your own judgment has been formed on all these points after having heard every thing which could be urged on them. I own I am not a friend to a very energetic government. It is always oppressive. The late rebellion in Massachusetts has given more alarm than I think it should have done. Calculate that one rebellion in 13 states in the course of 11 years, is but one for each state in a century and a half. No country should be so long without one. Nor will any degree of power in the hands of government prevent insurrections. France with all it's despotism, and two or three hundred thousand men always in arms has had three insurrections in the three years I have been here in every one of which greater numbers were engaged than in Massachusetts and a great deal more blood was spilt. In Turkey, . . . insurrections are the events of every day. In England, where the hand of power is lighter than here, but heavier than with us they happen every half dozen years. Compare again the ferocious depredations of their insurgents with the order, the moderation and the almost self extinguishment of ours.—After all, it is my principle that the will of the Majority should always prevail. If they approve the proposed Convention in all it's parts, I shall concur in it chearfully, in hopes that they will amend it whenever they shall find it work wrong. I think our governments will remain virtuous for many centuries; as long as they are chiefly agricultural; and this will be as long as there shall be vacant lands in any part of America. When they get piled upon one another in large cities, as in Europe, they will become corrupt as in Europe. Above all things I hope the education of the common people will be attended to; convinced that on their good sense we may rely with the most security for the preservation of a due degree of liberty. I have tired you by this time with my disquisitions and will therefore only add assurances of the sincerity of those sentiments of esteem and attachment with which I am Dear Sir your affectionate friend & servant.

After reading this selection, consider these questions:

1. Jefferson approves of the House of Representatives being chosen directly by the people, yet he believes that the representatives chosen "will be very illy qualified." Is this a contradiction? What does this say about Jefferson's views on democracy?

2. Which of Jefferson's objections were met before the Constitution was ratified? Which were not?

3. On what does Jefferson base his hope for the republic?

SELECTION 5:

The Federalist, No. 10

The Federalist papers consist of eighty-five letters to the public that appeared in New York newspapers beginning on October 27, 1787. Written by James Madison, Alexander Hamilton, and John Jay, and published under the pseudonym "Publius," the letters were intended to help win ratification of the Constitution in New York, an important state, but one in which ratification faced an uphill struggle. The letters were reprinted in other states and were later collected into a book entitled The Federalist.

Given their origin, it is not surprising that The Federalist *papers do not constitute a systematic treatise. They were composed as polemics, produced under the pressure of newspaper deadlines and in the heat of political battle. Nevertheless, they provide insight into the ideas of the framers of the Constitution and a defense of the federal form of government. Indeed,* The Federalist *represents the most comprehensive exposition of political thought produced by the founders. Of all the essays, perhaps the most influential one has been Madison's* Federalist *No. 10, in which he analyzes the problem of factions in a popular government.*

Among the numerous advantages promised by a well-constructed Union, none deserves to be more accurately developed than its tendency to break and control the violence of faction. The friend of popular governments never finds himself so much alarmed for their character and fate as when he contemplates their propensity to this dangerous vice. He will not fail, therefore, to set a due value on any plan which, without violating the principles to which he is attached, provides a proper cure for it. The instability, injustice, and confusion introduced into the public councils have, in truth, been the mortal diseases under which popular governments have everywhere perished, as they continue to be the favorite and fruitful topics from which the adversaries to liberty derive their most specious declamations. The valuable improvements made by the American constitutions on the popular models, both ancient and modern, cannot certainly be too much admired; but it would be an unwarrantable partiality to contend that they have as effectually obviated the danger on this side, as was wished and expected. Complaints are everywhere heard from our most considerate and virtuous citizens, equally the friends of public and private faith and of public and personal liberty, that our governments are too unstable, that the public good is disregarded in the conflicts of rival parties, and that measures are too often decided, not according to the rules of justice and the rights of the minor party, but by the superior force of an interested and overbearing majority. However anxiously we may wish that these complaints had no foundation, the evidence of known facts will not permit us to deny that they are in some degree true. . . .

By a faction I understand a number of citizens, whether amounting to a majority or minority of the whole, who are united and actuated by some common impulse of passion, or of interest, adverse to the rights of other citizens, or to the permanent and aggregate interests of the community.

There are two methods of curing the mischiefs of faction: the one, by removing its causes; the other, by controlling its effects.

There are again two methods of removing the causes of faction: the one, by destroying the liberty which is essential to its existence; the other, by giving to every citizen the same opinions, the same passions, and the same interests.

It could never be more truly said than of the first remedy that it was worse than the disease. Liberty is to faction what air is to fire, an aliment without which it instantly expires. But it could not be a less folly to abolish liberty, which is essential to political life, because it nourishes faction than it would be to wish the annihilation of air, which is essential to animal life, because it imparts to fire its destructive agency.

The second expedient is as impracticable as the first would be unwise. As long as the reason of man continues fallible, and he is at liberty to exercise it, different opinions will be formed. . . .

The latent causes of faction are thus sown in the nature of man; and we see them everywhere brought into different degrees of activity, according to the different circumstances of civil society. . . . So strong is this propensity of mankind to fall into mutual animosities that where no substantial occasion presents itself the most frivolous and fanciful distinctions have been sufficient to kindle their unfriendly passions and excite their most violent conflicts. But the most common and durable source of factions has been the various and unequal distribution of property. Those who hold and those who are without property have ever formed distinct interests in society. Those who are creditors, and those who are debtors, fall under a like discrimination. A landed interest, a manufacturing interest, a mercantile interest, a moneyed interest, with many lesser interests, grow up of necessity in civilized nations, and divide them into different classes, ac-

Excerpted from *The Federalist Papers,* by Alexander Hamilton, James Madison, and John Jay (New York: The New American Library, 1961).

tuated by different sentiments and views. The regulation of these various and interfering interests forms the principal task of modern legislation and involves the spirit of party and faction in the necessary and ordinary operations of government.

No man is allowed to be a judge in his own cause, because his interest would certainly bias his judgment, and, not improbably, corrupt his integrity. With equal, nay with greater reason, a body of men are unfit to be both judges and parties at the same time; yet what are many of the most important acts of legislation but so many judicial determinations, not indeed concerning the rights of single persons, but concerning the rights of large bodies of citizens? And what are the different classes of legislators but advocates and parties to the causes which they determine? . . .

It is in vain to say that enlightened statesmen will be able to adjust these clashing interests and render them all subservient to the public good. Enlightened statesmen will not always be at the helm. Nor, in many cases, can such an adjustment be made at all without taking into view indirect and remote considerations, which will rarely prevail over the immediate interest which one party may find in disregarding the rights of another or the good of the whole.

The inference to which we are brought is that the *causes* of faction cannot be removed and that relief is only to be sought in the means of controlling its *effects*.

If a faction consists of less than a majority, relief is supplied by the republican principle, which enables the majority to defeat its sinister views by regular vote. It may clog the administration, it may convulse the society; but it will be unable to execute and mask its violence under the forms of the Constitution. When a majority is included in a faction, the form of popular government, on the other hand, enables it to sacrifice to its ruling passion or interest both the public good and the rights of other citizens. To secure the public good and private rights against the danger of such a faction, and at the same time to preserve the spirit and the form of popular government, is then the great object to which our inquiries are directed. . . .

By what means is this object attainable? Evidently by one of two only. Either the existence of the same passion or interest in a majority at the same time must be prevented, or the majority, having such coexistent passion or interest, must be rendered, by their number and local situation, unable to concert and carry into effect schemes of oppression. If the impulse and the opportunity be suffered to coincide, we well know that neither moral nor religious motives can be relied on as an adequate control. . . .

From this view of the subject it may be concluded that a pure democracy, by which I mean a society consisting of a small number of citizens, who assemble and administer the government in person, can admit of no cure for the mischiefs of faction. A common passion or interest will, in almost every case, be felt by a majority of the whole; a communication and concert results from the form of government itself; and there is nothing to check the inducements to sacrifice the weaker party or an obnoxious individual. Hence it is that such democracies have ever been spectacles of turbulence and contention; have ever been found incompatible with personal security or the rights of property; and have in general been as short in their lives as they have been violent in their deaths. Theoretic politicians, who have patronized this species of government, have erroneously supposed that by reducing mankind to a perfect equality in their political rights, they would at the same time be perfectly equalized and assimilated in their possessions, their opinions, and their passions.

A republic, by which I mean a government in which the scheme of representation takes place, opens a different prospect and promises the cure for which we are seeking. . . .

The two great points of difference between a democracy and a republic are: first, the delegation of the government, in the latter, to a small number of citizens elected by the rest; secondly, the greater number of citizens and greater sphere of country over which the latter may be extended.

The effect of the first difference is, on the one hand, to refine and enlarge the public views by passing them through the medium of a chosen body of citizens, whose wisdom may best discern the true interest of their country and whose patriotism and love of justice will be least likely to sacrifice it to temporary or partial considerations. . . .

The question resulting is, whether small or extensive republics are most favorable to the election of proper guardians of the public weal; and it is clearly decided in favor of the latter by two obvious considerations.

In the first place it is to be remarked that however small the republic may be the representatives must be raised to a certain number in order to guard against the cabals of a few; and that however large it may be they must be limited to a certain number in order to guard against the confusion of a multitude. Hence, the number of representatives in the two cases not being in proportion to that of the constituents, and being proportionally greatest in the small republic, it follows that if the proportion of fit characters be not less in the large than in the small republic, the former will present a greater option, and consequently a greater probability of a fit choice.

In the next place, as each representative will be chosen by a greater number of citizens in the large than in the small republic, it will be more difficult for unworthy candidates to practise with success the vicious arts by which elections are too often carried; and the suffrages of the people being more free, will be more likely to center on men who possess the most attractive merit and the most diffusive and established characters.

It must be confessed that in this, as in most other cases, there is a mean, on both sides of which inconveniencies will be found to lie. By enlarging too much the number of electors, you render the representative too little acquainted with all their local circumstances and lesser interests; as by reducing it too much, you render him unduly attached to these, and too little fit to comprehend and pursue great and national objects. The federal Constitution forms a happy combination in this respect; the great and aggregate interests being referred to the national, the local and particular to the State legislatures.

The other point of difference is the greater number of citizens and extent of territory which may be brought within the compass of republican than of democratic government; and it is this circumstance principally which renders factious combinations less to be dreaded in the former than in the latter. The smaller the society, the fewer probably will be the distinct parties and interests composing it; the fewer the distinct parties and interests, the more frequently will a majority be found of the same party; and the smaller the number of individuals composing a majority, and the smaller the compass within which they are placed, the more easily will they concert and execute their plans of oppression. Extend the sphere and you take in a greater variety of parties and interests; you make it less probable that a majority of the whole will have a common motive to invade the rights of other citizens; or if such a common motive exists, it will be more difficult for all who feel it to discover their own strength and to act in unison with each other. . . .

Hence, it clearly appears that the same advantage which a republic has over a democracy in controlling the effects of faction is enjoyed by a large over a small republic—is enjoyed by the Union over the States composing it. . . .

The influence of factious leaders may kindle a flame within their particular States but will be unable to spread a general conflagration through the other States. . . .

In the extent and proper structure of the Union, therefore, we behold a republican remedy for the diseases most incident to republican government. And according to the degree of pleasure and pride we feel in being republicans ought to be our zeal in cherishing the spirit and supporting the character of federalists.

After reading this selection, consider these questions:

1. What does Madison believe causes the creation of factions?

2. Madison stood two millennia of accepted wisdom on its head when he argued that small republics were inherently unstable because of their inability to control factions. How did he support this position? What would serve to counter the evil of factions in a larger and more diverse republic such as the United States?

3. How, according to Madison, would the Constitution resolve the problem of factions?

UNIT 3

Antebellum America

CONTENTS

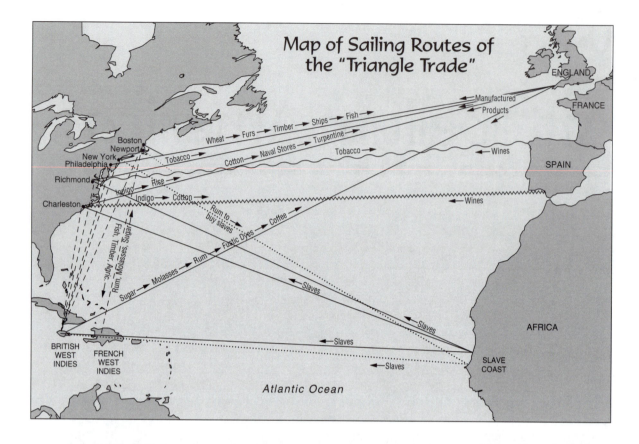

Map of Sailing Routes of the "Triangle Trade"

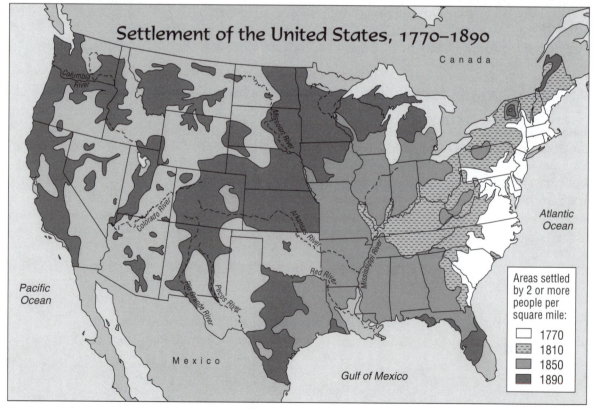

Settlement of the United States, 1770–1890

UNIT 3

Antebellum America

Growth and development characterized the early years of the new American republic. The young nation experienced rapid economic and geographic growth. Politics became increasingly democratic, and modern political parties emerged. A wave of religious revivals led to a wide variety of reform movements. Americans sought to perfect their society and bring on the millennium through Sabbatarianism (laws requiring businesses to close and banning public amusements on Sunday), crusades for temperance, feminism, abolitionism, and dietary reform. Some people sought to hurry the process by establishing utopian communities intended to lead to the ultimate perfection of human beings and human society. In the first half of the nineteenth century, America was a sprawling, sometimes chaotic, and profoundly optimistic country.

Lurking behind all of this, however, was the expansion of the institution of slavery. Cotton cultivation, with its heavy demand for labor, played an important role in the development of slavery in the South. Long staple cotton, a luxurious fiber, came from a delicate plant that grew well only on the Sea Islands off Georgia and South Carolina. Short staple cotton, a hardier plant, grew in a far wider variety of conditions, but its sticky seeds could be removed only by hand, a time-consuming process that made short staple cotton an uneconomical crop. The invention of the cotton gin, which efficiently removed the seeds from short staple cotton, led to the expansion of slavery and the plantation system into new areas. Even as the Southern economy became more and more tied to cotton production and slavery, industrial development transformed the North. Thus, the two regions embarked on separate paths of development.

The development of manufacturing and cotton cultivation contributed to the nation's prosperity. So, too, did geographic expansion. The story of hardy pioneers braving the difficulties of the trail and establishing farms and settlements has a strong basis in fact. Nevertheless, American expansionism had its victims. Native American tribes were displaced, and some were exterminated. Hispanic descendants of settlers who had occupied lands of the Southwest and West for centuries were also displaced and marginalized.

Moreover, the West was not only the story of white Anglo-Saxon settlers taming the wilderness. From its earliest days, the West was a polyglot place. African Americans, Hispanics, Asians, Jews, and women all made up part of the West's population. Brawling mining towns and wagon trains may be the stuff of Hollywood movies, but the West was settled by families, merchants, and all manner of less glamorous people. Taken as a whole, the westward movement was neither the unblemished triumph of older textbooks and movies nor the tale of unmitigated cruelty and savagery often told in modern texts. It was, in fact, a complicated, confusing combination of both.

After reading this unit, consider these questions:

1. What was the relationship between economic change and politics?

2. What was the effect of social and economic change on gender roles?

3. What caused the religious revivals known as the Second Great Awakening? How did that wave of revivals spark a powerful drive for social reform?

4. What role did women and minorities play in the American settlement of the West?

CHAPTER 11

Economic Development and Social Change

The development of factories dramatically changed the quantity and nature of goods available to Americans. It also substantially altered the nature of work for those who labored in the new factories. Traditionally, skilled craftsmen known as artisans produced goods by hand, most of which were custom made (called bespoke work because the customer spoke for it). Artisans usually marketed only to a limited geographical area.

The artisan system of labor was more than work; it was a pattern of life. Young boys became apprentices, which meant that they worked for a master craftsman for a period of time in exchange for food, lodging, and training in the trade. Once an apprentice had served his time, he became a journeyman, a free laborer who earned wages from a master craftsman, who owned the tools, shop, and raw materials, and sold the finished goods for a profit. Journeymen hoped one day to become masters themselves.

With the American Revolution and the end of British mercantilism, American merchants suddenly found nothing to stop them from forging their own markets along the Atlantic seaboard and the developing old Northwest. The expansion of the cotton-producing South provided another potentially lucrative market.

The rise of merchant capitalism, in turn, ushered in the factory age. Entrepreneurs, particularly in New York and Philadelphia, moved to gain control of supplies of raw materials and to extend their shipping and marketing contacts beyond their own cities. In outlying areas near large cities, particularly in New England, merchant capitalists began to erect large central shops and the first factories. Merchants and some wealthy masters began to divide work into its various components. They employed less-skilled workers, in some cases women and children, at lower wages and trained them to do one stage of the fabrication process. Instead of a skilled artisan performing every step of production, several less skilled workers contributed their efforts to an inferior, but less expensive, final product. Owners of these new shops sold substantial quantities of goods to slave owners, who purchased them for their slaves; to transient sailors; and to others. In the process, they squeezed out many smaller craftsmen.

Skilled artisans continued to serve a shrinking elite clientele through the bespoke trade, but masters moved more and more into the production of inferior goods by less-skilled hands for the market trade (or slop trade, as the artisans resentfully called it). This was especially true in shoemaking, tailoring, printing, and furniture making.

Competition between entrepreneurs led to downward pressure on wages. The fact that workers in factories needed fewer skills made them more easily replaceable. The new method of production had a devastating impact on the artisan system of labor. Masters also had to face new realities; many faced the choice of producing for the market trade or becoming wage workers themselves. Some survived as contractors; others left for areas yet untouched by the flood of goods for the market trade. Many, however, faced bankruptcy and a return to journeywork. Journeymen confronted declining wages and, because of the increased level of capital necessary to start up a shop, a diminishing likelihood of ever becoming a master.

These new factories were initially simply gatherings of workers and materials in the same place. Eventually, some factories changed from production by hand to production by machines powered by water and steam. This enabled the factories to produce goods more quickly and at a lower cost per unit. It also increased the downward pressure on wages and undercut the bargaining position of workers as it required less and less skilled labor to produce a finished product.

With industrialization, daily life changed radically for American workers. No longer did the rising and setting of the sun, the weather, or the cycle of the seasons regulate work patterns. Increasing numbers of workers worked at machines, and their labor was paced by the machines at which they worked. Factory production required that laborers work during the same hours. It is important to remember, however, that the change from agricultural labor or small shop labor to industrial labor did not come about at once. Nevertheless, over time that change altered the nature of work and the very definition of success for American workers.

After reading this chapter, consider theses questions:

1. How did artisan patterns of labor contrast with factory labor?

2. What drew workers to the new factories?

3. How did workers respond to the changing work environment?

4. What was the impact of manufacturing and industry on consumers?

SELECTION 1:

The Lifestyles of Philadelphia Artisans

Bruce Laurie, a professor of history at the University of Massachusetts at Amherst, demonstrates in the following article that the change to factory labor did not occur at once; rather, it came about unevenly and over a period of time. Indeed, the majority of workers in Philadelphia worked at home or in small shops without power-driven machinery as late as 1850. This style of labor gave rise not only to a culture of work but also to a larger workers' culture. By examining the leisure activities, political culture, and religious beliefs of Philadelphia's workers, Laurie reminds readers that the lives of these people consisted of more than their labor. They were not simply pliant tools in the hands of industrial capitalists.

Labor historians are only beginning to appreciate the cultural dimensions of working-class life. . . . This paper attempts to go beyond the narrow constraints of institutional history in order to explore preindustrial working-class culture and to examine how and why that culture changed between 1820 and 1850 in the city of Philadelphia.

Philadelphians saw their world dramatically altered by wholesale changes in transportation between 1820 and 1850. Private promoters and the State legislature invested heavily in transportation, developing in the process a network of canals and railroads which linked Philadelphia with New York and Baltimore, the coal region of northeastern Pennsylvania, and interior towns and cities in the west. Seagoing transportation developed and boomed as Philadelphians, following their more innovative rivals in New York, introduced packets in the coastal and transat-

lantic trade in the 1820s. More reliable than regular traders or transients, packets made scheduled runs and merchants quickly took advantage of them. By 1827 they carried more than half of the city's coastal trade, delivering agricultural products and manufactured goods to southern and Caribbean ports in return for cotton, hides, and other vital raw materials.

Improvements in transportation paved the way for mass production by reducing shipping costs and penetrating new markets. Manufacturers of textiles, shoes, clothing, and other commodities gained access to the rich markets in Pennsylvania's back country as well as in the Ohio Valley and also strengthened traditional ties with the South. The textile industry, in turn, spurred the city's small but innovative machine tool industry, which was the envy of many foreign observers. By the Civil War, Philadelphia was surpassed only by New York as a manufacturing center.

Rapid population increases and ethnic diversification went hand in hand with economic change. The population of Philadelphia County tripled between 1820 and 1850, increasing from about 136,000 to just over 408,000. The factors which

Excerpted from "'Nothing on Compulsion': Life Styles of Philadelphia Artisans, 1820–1850," by Bruce Laurie, *Labor History*, Summer 1974. Copyright © 1974 by *Labor History*. Reprinted with permission.

contributed to such impressive growth are not yet known, but it is probable that natural increase and in-migration from nearby farm areas gave way to immigration from western Europe. Ireland and Germany sent the bulk of the immigrants, and the greatest inflows probably occurred in the late 1820s–early 1830s and the mid 1840s. . . .

Most working people resided in the county's industrial suburbs, which formed a semi-circular ring around the old port city. They clustered according to occupation, ethnicity, or both, and lived in close proximity to their place of employment. Indeed, dwelling and shop were one for hand-loom weavers as well as for many tailors and shoemakers who worked at home under the putting-out system. For the great majority of the labor force, the shop was not the mill or factory which we commonly associate with the "take-off stage" of economic growth. The average shop size in 1850 hovered around ten workers; the median was slightly less than four. Most of these workers, moreover, did not operate power-driven machinery. Three-quarters of them were handicraftsmen employed by bosses whose sole source of power was the journeyman himself.

Even without the aid of mechanization this emerging capitalist order bore down heavily on the wage earner. Merchant capitalists captured mass markets by contracting with buyers in distant markets and with producers in Philadelphia. Most of these producers were small employers who increased productivity by closely supervising teams of highly specialized workers and by slashing piece rates at every opportunity. . . .

The response of these wage earners to such exploitation in the 1830s has been well charted. It is now common knowledge that between 1834 and 1839 all manner of wage earners—skilled and unskilled, native-born and foreign-born—formed trade unions and joined together under the aegis of the General Trades' Union of the City and County of Philadelphia in protest against low wages and excessive toil. . . .

The devastating depression of 1837 depleted the ranks of many trade unions and destroyed others, leaving workers defenseless against employers determined to restore the long work day. Millowners imposed longer hours when prosper-

ity resumed, and those who did not do so accomplished the same result by cutting piece rates. . . .

Yet these same wage earners complained about unemployment as bitterly as they complained about overwork. They repeatedly lamented the days, weeks, and even months spent jobless or in search of work. . . .

A number of factors contributed to sporadic employment, one of which was the nature of the transportation system. The very system which made mass production and its consequences possible also contributed to slack times. The "Transportation Revolution" may have penetrated new markets, but it did not reduce irregularities and discontinuities in supply and demand. Delays, spoilage, and loss of goods plagued Pennsylvania's canals. . . .

Railroads conquered the weather but little else. Lines that employed steam engines were so beset by breakdowns that they kept teams of horses in reserve. Service improved with advances in steam engines, but many problems remained. . . .

Coastal packets offered the most dependable mode of shipment, but they had their own drawbacks. They made scheduled sailings only during the "season," which stretched from early fall to late spring. Shippers cut back in summer, transferring some craft to the transatlantic run and sending others northward or southward only when guaranteed adequate cargo. Coastal packets therefore resembled ordinary traders in the warm months when they were governed by profits rather than schedules. Merchants and manufacturers sometimes waited months for an arrival.

The capriciousness of these transportation facilities may well have aggravated the nagging problem of erratic deliveries of goods. Such unpredictable deliveries inevitably made work itself unpredictable and helped shape the work habits of artisans. Wage earners could expect fairly steady employment when markets were good and raw materials available, but faced frequent lay offs when raw materials failed to arrive on time, if at all. . . . In slack times hatters and other journeymen either left the city to search for work elsewhere or took whatever employment they could find. Many shoemakers and tailors found temporary employment in repair work or day labor; some hand-loom weavers were so accustomed to shifting into casual labor during periodic downturns that they considered themselves weavers/laborers.

Winter months were unusually trying. Frozen waterways curtailed trade and brought on the slack season, throwing journeymen out of work for long periods and forcing them to seek relief from Philadelphia philanthropists who distributed soup, bread, and fuel. Seasonal fluctuations in trade also determined wage rates. Journeymen, aware that the warm months normally ushered in brisk business, negotiated differential wage scales, demanding higher rates in spring and summer. . . .

The shape of Philadelphia's industrial plant also determined the quantity and quality of employment. The dominant form of business organization, the small shop, was extremely fragile. Owners operated on hopelessly thin profit margins and were so anxious to reduce fixed costs that they slashed employment rolls at the "slightest hint" of a downturn in trade. They kept the best workers, leaving slower, less experienced hands to forage for work or wait until business improved.

Incessant toil, in a word, was not the bane of Philadelphia's antebellum artisan. What really gnawed at him was the combination of plummeting wage rates and the fitful pace of work, the syncopated rhythm of the economy with its alternating periods of feverish activity broken by slack spells. In slow months, the dull season, or periods with "broken days," he was on his own, without work or the ability to meet day-to-day costs of running the household. Such times could be extremely demoralizing. . . .

Fluctuations in trade were not the only determinants of employment. Popular attitudes towards work also figured prominently in the equation, for many artisans who lived in the transitional period between the preindustrial and industrial age adhered to values, customs, and traditions that went against the grain of early industrial discipline. Prizing leisure as well as work, they engaged in a wide spectrum of leisure-time activities, ranging from competitive sport to lounging on street corners. Many of them also belonged to volunteer organizations, which successfully competed with their places of employment for their attention and devotion.

Traditions die hard, and perhaps none died harder than preindustrial drinking habits. Advances in science and medicine, early industrial change and, as we shall see, the advent of revivalism, eroded customary drinking habits among some sectors of the medical profession, the clergy, and the emerging industrial elite. But the old commercial classes and most artisans still clung tenaciously to older ways. They valued alcohol for its own sake and used it as a stimulant or as medicine to combat fatigue, to cool the body in summer or warm it in winter, and to treat common illness.

Numerous contemporaries report that artisans were not particular about where they imbibed. Presbyterian minister Sylvester Graham found them drinking in workshops as well as at home in the early 1830s and, he lamented, they especially enjoyed a drink in the late afternoon when "treating" time arrived and journeymen took turns sipping from a jug. Graham's observations are supported by Benjamin T. Sewell, a tanner and vice president of the Trades' Union in 1834 and 1836 who became a Methodist minister in the 1850s. Looking back on his days as a journeyman, Sewell recalled that young apprentices learned to drink while they learned a trade. Journeymen arrived at work with flasks and appointed an apprentice to make periodic trips to the local pub in order to have them filled, "for which service" he "robs the mail . . . takes a drink before he gets back. . . ." This training ground turned many young wage earners into hardened drinkers, inclined to go on an occasional binge. . . .

Employers winced at such behavior, but one ought not assume that all of them were martinets who enforced regulations against drink. Owners of textile mills could afford to do so because they relied upon a semi-skilled labor force which could be replaced with relative ease. The concentration required by operators of power-driven machinery, moreover, caused some to relinquish drink without much prompting from employers. . . . Smaller employers, on the other hand, were more tolerant of workers who drank. . . . Many, if not most, small employers were former journeymen themselves steeped in preindustrial culture, and those who did custom work anticipated fluctuations in trade and therefore tolerated irregular work habits. These employers "expected" journeymen to shun the shop on holidays—official as well as self-proclaimed—and they endured drinking, as long as their journeymen worked "tolerably regularly" and managed to avoid getting "absolutely drunk."

Most artisans did their drinking in pubs, and pubs probably assumed greater importance in their life after some employers began to prohibit drinking in the shop. Working-class pubs had a style all their own. Signs with piquant inscriptions hung above entranceways and stood in bold contrast to the sedate placards which graced the vestibules of middle-class establishments. . . . Immigrant taverns sometimes advertised popular political causes. . . .

These taverns offered a wide variety of entertainment, illicit and otherwise. Cockfighting, a popular spectator sport in colonial times but eschewed by people of social standing thereafter, prospered in the working-class pubs of antebellum Philadelphia. . . .

Working-class gamblers not excited by cockfights could try their hand at games in the gambling halls or the taverns. Policy houses, which operated lotteries, dotted Philadelphia and concentrated in the suburbs. Furtively located on side streets and in back alleys, they lured workers who wagered from "3¢ to 50¢ with the sanguine hope of having this money returned fourfold. . . ." Taverns sponsored games that probably resembled "menagerie," in which participants sat around a circular board divided into pie-shaped units, each of which bore the picture of an animal. Each player placed a coin on his choice and waited breathlessly while a pinwheel whirled and designated the winner upon coming to a stop.

Despite these attractions most workers, we may believe, visited pubs for the sake of camaraderie. At the end of the workday, homebound artisans made detours to their favorite taverns, where they exchanged stories or discussed politics over drams or mugs of a variety of malt liquor. Outworkers broke the boredom of toiling alone by visiting the local pub during the day, and shopworkers probably went there to celebrate the completion of a task or an order. Most observers agree that tavern traffic increased dra-

matically on Sunday night and in winter when trade slowed.

Circuses and road shows also captured the fancy of workingmen. Heavily publicized in newspapers and in broadsides posted on fences, such entertainments rarely respected the industrial time clock. Occurring on weekdays as well as on weekends, they dazzled throngs of onlookers with bizarre acts and feats. . . . Less elaborate but equally exciting fare took place in the streets when daredevils or athletes visited Philadelphia. Sizable crowds gathered to watch balloonists ascend or to witness competition staged by tramping athletes. . . .

Though fascinated by these events, artisans especially enjoyed pastimes in which they could participate. They simply loved shooting matches and hunting small game, according to an observer who bemoaned that "every fair day" yielded a "temptation to forsake the shop for the field." The most avid hunters, he contended, were artisans who toiled indoors, for they found a jaunt in the fields especially relaxing. Artisans who resided in the same neighborhood sometimes set aside time for exercise by declaring holidays and staging competitive games. . . .

Sport, merrymaking, and drinking were also staples at ethnic gatherings. English, German, and Irish immigrants honored Old World customs and traditions, celebrated weddings and holidays, or gathered simply in order to socialize regardless of the time of day or day of the week. Germans, for instance, set aside Monday as their "principal day for pleasure," and festivities could spill into the middle of the week. . . . The Irish were also known to set aside Monday for outings in the suburbs. Their national games, the Donneybrook Fair, traditionally attracted hundreds of enthusiasts and no self-respecting Irish Protestant missed the annual July 12 parade commemorating the glorious victory on the banks of the Boyne in 1690. . . .

Membership in voluntary fire companies also interrupted the daily work routines of Philadelphia artisans. Indeed, the city fire department enjoyed its greatest growth between 1826 and 1852, when sixty-eight new companies appeared. . . . Firemen were fierce competitors. . . . Firemen loved racing their gaudy tenders and hose carriages through the city streets and went to extraordinary lengths to preserve their pride, shoving wrenches into the spokes of a rival rig, cutting its tow ropes, or assaulting its towers. Races usually ended in brief scuffles, but competition reached fever pitch in the 1840s when ethnic tensions polarized Philadelphians and artisans formed fire companies along ethnic lines. . . .

These pursuits and activities—drinking and gaming, participating in popular sports and in fire companies—characterized a vibrant, preindustrial style of life. A number of factors underpinned this style, the most significant of which were demographic and material. First, . . . it was repeatedly replenished by waves of immigrants and rural-urban migrants, who came from widely divergent sub-cultures but whose values and behavior collided with the imperatives of early industrial discipline. Second, and perhaps more important, at mid-century many wage earners worked in traditional (as against modern) settings which, together with the boom-bust quality of the economy, supported sporadic work habits. Those who know this environment best were outworkers—especially hand-loom weavers, shoemakers, and tailors—who toiled at home without direct supervision of employers and custom workers, who fashioned consumer goods to the taste of individuals and who thereby evaded the more vigorous regimen of workers producing for the mass market.

Outworkers and custom workers displayed traditional forms of behavior in that they made no sharp distinction between work and leisure. Blending leisure with work, they punctuated workdays with the activities sketched above. Nor did they respect the specialization of role and function which normally accompanies modernization. Instead they persisted in assuming the dual role of artisans and firemen in the face of strong opposition from urban reformers who wished to relegate firefighting to paid professionals. It is probable, moreover, that the values, activities, and organizations of this style of life filled the basic needs of its adherents by sanctioning and supplying vehicles for recreation, neighborhood cohesion, ethnic identity, and camaraderie.

After reading this selection, consider these questions:

1. What developments led to mass production, according to Laurie?

2. According to Laurie, in what ways might one account for the persistence of preindustrial behavior and attitudes among Philadelphia's workers?

3. What connections does Laurie draw between the nature of preindustrial work and the various amusements of Philadelphia's workers?

SELECTION 2:

Women Workers in Lowell, Massachusetts

Between 1820 and 1860, industrialism began to change both the economic and social structure of the United States. Textile manufacturers were among the first to employ machines in production. Many young women left their rural homes to work in textile factories. The first fully integrated textile factory began operating in Waltham, Massachusetts, in 1813. A group of businessmen from Boston established the Merrimack Manufacturing Company at the confluence of the Merrimack and Concord rivers in 1821. The town that developed around the enterprise incorporated as Lowell in 1826. The Lowell mills had a profound impact on the young women who worked there and presaged changes in gender roles throughout American society. The following is an excerpt taken from Thomas Dublin's book, Women at Work: The Transformation of Work and Community in Lowell, Massachusetts, 1826–1860. *Dublin, a professor of history at the State University of New York at Binghampton, discusses the reasons young women went to work in the mills and their backgrounds.*

According to the conventional view, women in the early Lowell mills were young, single women attracted from the surrounding New England countryside. They entered and left the mills frequently, working for repeated short stretches in the years before marriage. While in Lowell they resided in company boardinghouses, erected by the textile corporations and managed by boardinghouse keepers. These are time-honored generalizations, enunciated initially by contemporary observers and corroborated by the research of subsequent historians.

This description is basically correct and uncontroversial, but it does not take the analysis of the early work force in the Lowell mills far enough. . . .

It is possible to extend this framework beyond the confines of Lowell by tracing workers back to the rural families and communities from which they came. Such tracing illuminates the social origins, and also the motivations, of women workers in the early mills, besides placing the mill experience within the broader life cycle of rural women. . . .

Excluding Lowell itself, twelve of the fourteen towns that sent the largest numbers of workers to [the] Hamilton [Manufacturing Company] were found in New Hampshire, five of these in central Merrimack County. From the communities in Merrimack County that supplied so many work-

ers to Hamilton, I selected three towns with particularly complete published vital records—Boscawen, Canterbury, and Sutton—for detailed examination.

These towns were long-settled agricultural communities by the second third of the nineteenth century. The initial land grants for all three towns had been made by 1750; first settlement and incorporation of the towns were complete by 1784. They moved rapidly beyond the frontier stage and reached relative population peaks before 1830. Their populations held steady between 1830 and 1850, ranging from about 1,400 for Sutton to a bit more than 2,000 for Boscawen. The steady growth of previous decades halted as the good lands were absorbed and the local economies stagnated. Unable to fulfill their ambitions at home, the young people departed to more fertile western lands or to the growing cities of New England. In this respect the three sample communities shared an experience common to a majority of the hill-country towns of central Vermont and New Hampshire in the period: rapid growth followed by decline and outmigration. . . .

Women from these three New Hampshire towns were a representative cross section of the female work force at Hamilton. . . . In terms of the rooms they worked in, their age and marital status, and the length of their careers, they did not deviate significantly from the work force as a whole.

The New Hampshire women were distributed throughout the major rooms of the Hamilton Company in proportions quite similar to those for the overall female work force. . . .

Excerpted from *Women at Work: The Transformation of Work and Community in Lowell, Massachusetts, 1826–1860,* by Thomas Dublin (New York: Columbia University Press, 1979). Copyright © 1979 by Columbia University Press. Reprinted with permission.

There were slightly more weavers and proportionately fewer carders and spinners among the New Hampshire sample members than in the female work force as a whole. This occupational distribution suggests that sample members were probably earning wages somewhat higher than those of the female work force as a whole. These differences were not great enough, however, to indicate that they were a privileged stratum within the mills.

The ages of the New Hampshire operatives are consistent with . . . residents of Hamilton Company boardinghouses. Few children or older women came to the mills from these three rural communities. The mean age for beginning work at the company was 19.8, and women on the average completed their careers at Hamilton when they were 22.4 years old.

As with the boardinghouse residents enumerated in the 1830 and 1840 censuses of Lowell, about 80 percent of the women were between the ages of 15 and 29 when they began work at Hamilton. The proportion under 15, 14.3 percent, seems on the high side, but this age distribution catches the group at first entrance into the mills. By the time of their departures, only 4.5 percent of the women were under 15 years of age.

The data on age suggest that mill work attracted young women seeking employment for a brief period before marriage, and the evidence on marital status confirms this supposition. Almost 97 percent —124 of the 128 with usable marriage linkage— were single, never married at the beginning of their careers at Hamilton. At the end of their employment, fully 93 percent remained single. . . .

The married women in the sample group present a special and interesting case, and although their absolute numbers are small, they deserve some additional consideration. Their careers reveal a number of striking elements. As a group they tended to have very brief stays in the mills. . . . [T]hese married women worked before the birth of children. The living situations of the married working women were also unusual. Two of the women, Mary Morrill Chase and Lydia Currier Bickford, lived with sisters in Lowell during their stints in the mill. Perhaps their husbands' work, or the search for work, had taken them out of the city for a period. Also, the married couples may have been separated, as in the case of Mary Morrill Chase whose earnings were "trusteed"— that is garnished—by a grocery firm. This practice was common in dealing with men who absconded leaving bad debts behind. All in all, the little that is known about married women workers at Hamilton suggests that such employment was infrequent, that the work periods were brief, that women with children did not work, and that unusual family circumstances were often associated with employment.

Mill employment represented a stage in a woman's life cycle before marriage. . . .

These women came to the mills, of course, as individuals, but they also brought along with them a social position and cultural outlook from their home towns. . . .

The vast majority of women came from farming families. . . . The remainder of the fathers of millhands filled a variety of skilled occupations —blacksmith, stonemason, and wheelwright among others. The occupations of the fathers suggest that the women came from rather typical rural families. . . .

The women were drawn from almost the entire range of families in these towns. . . . Even though female-headed families were somewhat more likely to have a daughter working in the mills, more than 90 percent of linked operatives came from typical male-headed households. The female millhand supporting her widowed mother is hardly as common in actuality as contemporary sources suggest.

Property valuations of the fathers of operatives place them in the broad middle ranges of wealth in their home towns. . . .

The fathers of millhands in 1830 did not comprise a depressed group within the towns; nor is there any evidence that over time their economic conditions were worsening. . . .

The evidence undermines any argument that sheer economic need drove large numbers of women into the Lowell mills in the period 1830–1850. At least the economic needs of the families of operatives could not have been a compelling force. Some women, perhaps the 8 percent whose fathers had died, may well have worked in the mills in order to contribute to the support of their families. The evidence strongly suggests that most young women themselves decided to work in the mills. They were generally not *sent* to the mills by their parents to supplement low family incomes but went of their own accord for other reasons. When we also consider the distance separating mill operatives from their families, the probability is strong that it was the women themselves who decided how to spend their earnings.

The correspondence of a number of operatives supports this view. . . .

There [seems to have been] no great conflict between familial and individual interests for most women workers. Parents gave their approval to daughters' plans to work in the mills and were glad to see them earning money for themselves. Times were often hard in rural northern New England after 1830, and even in prosperous years there were few opportunities for women to earn anything while living at home. Whether or not working women actually contributed to support their families back home, each departure did mean one less mouth to feed. And with the growth of factory textile production, the contributions of farmers' daughters to the family economy declined significantly. . . .

The view of women's motivations that emerges from analysis of their social origins and correspondence with their families stands in sharp contrast to contemporary writings, especially to the *Lowell Offering,* an operatives' literary magazine of the period. In the repeated "factory tales" published in the *Offering,* writers stressed the selfless motivations that sent women into the mills. Characters in the stories were invariably orphans supporting themselves and younger brothers and sisters, or young women helping to pay off the mortgage on a family homestead or to send a brother to college, or widows raising and supporting families. Never, in the fiction at least, did an operative work in the mills in order to buy "new clothes" or to get away from a domineering father, though in real life these motivations must have been common enough. The more idealistic themes of the *Offering* presented the best possible case against those who argued that women should not work in the mills at all. The data on the social origins of

workers, together with their letters, tell a rather different story.

Mill work should not be viewed as simply an extension of the traditional family economy as work for women moved outside the home. Work in the mills functioned for women rather like migration did for young men who could see that their chances of setting up on a farm in an established rural community were rather slim. The mills offered individual self-support, enabled women to enjoy urban amenities not available in their rural communities, and gave them a measure of economic and social independence from their families. These factors made Lowell attractive to rural women and led them to choose to work in the mills. . . .

An additional finding that emerges from the study of the families of operatives is evidence that women came to Lowell not as isolated individuals but as members of broader kin networks. . . .

Kinship ties among mill operatives played a number of important roles for women in early Lowell. The existence of these bonds must have eased the shock of adjustment both to work in the factories and to the novel urban setting. The fact that so many pairs of sisters at Hamilton resided together in company boardinghouses and often worked in the same rooms at the mills strongly suggests the importance of a familial support network for newcomers. Experienced operatives probably arranged for housing accommodations ahead of time and may have been able to speak to the overseer on their sisters' behalf. . . .

But the support system extended beyond blood ties and included unrelated friends from the home towns as well. . . .

These kinship networks helped operatives adjust to urban life, but they also made a more direct contribution to women's success in the mills. Women operatives whose kin were also employed at Hamilton were able, on the whole, to secure better jobs in the mill. . . .

One of the consequences of better job placement of newcomers with kin was that they remained longer at the company. Those with relatives worked at Hamilton an average of 3.66 years; those without kin remained only 2.21 years. Having other members of the family at

Hamilton clearly opened up opportunities for women and led them to stay longer in the mills. It also aided the companies. Because mill managers often complained that no sooner had they trained newcomers than they quit, encouraging family ties among workers made good business sense. Family networks reduced labor turnover and resulted in a more experienced and more productive labor force, which in turn contributed to greater profits. In the end, both workers and corporations benefited from the growth of kinship networks in the mill work force.

Clearly, then, the rural backgrounds as well as the kinship and friendship networks of these women were important factors in their entry into Lowell and their careers in the mills.

After reading this selection, consider these questions:

1. What were the complex influences that led women to decide to work in the mills?

2. How did kinship patterns affect young women who went to work in the mills?

SELECTION 3:

A Mill Girl Writes Home

The third of four children born to Bela and Mary Briggs Paul, Mary Paul, quoted here in letters she wrote to her family in 1845 and 1846, grew up in northern Vermont. Mary's mother died when she was eleven. At the age of fifteen she left her father's home in Barnard to go to work as a domestic helper for a farming family, the Angells, in Bridgewater, located a few miles from her hometown. Unhappy with her situation, she went to stay with her uncle and aunt, Nathaniel and Nancy Miller, in Woodstock, a town about eight miles from Bridgewater. From there she went to work in Lowell's textile mills where she labored on and off for four years. Upon leaving Lowell she made coats in Vermont, lived in a utopian agricultural community in New Jersey, and worked as a housekeeper in New Hampshire. After supporting herself for twelve years, Mary Paul married in 1857. She and her husband lived in Lynn, Massachusetts.

Bridgewater [Vt.] July 25th 1845
Dear Father
    Mr. Angell received your letter on the 22nd And I supposed would do something about my

staying, but he has not. And so I thought I would write to you & have you come over yourself. I did not leave uncle Millers until Sunday morning. Aunt Sarah was quite sick [and I] have not heard from her since. Mrs. A did not speak to me after I got home till after supper but she has done remarkably well since your letter came. I suppose Mr A wants I should stay but I do not want to. I did not see as anything was going to be done

---

Excerpted from *Farm to Factory: Women's Letters 1830–1860,* edited by Thomas Dublin (New York: Columbia University Press, 1981).

and for that reason I write. I suppose Aunt Nancy expects me every day but she will not see me till you come.

I want you to start as soon as you receive this.

Yours,

Mary

[Woodstock, Vt.] Saturday Sept. 13th 1845
Dear Father

I received your letter this afternoon by Wm Griffith. You wished me to write if I had seen Mr. Angell. I have neither written to him nor seen him nor has he written to me. I began to write but I could not write what I wanted to. I think if I could see him I could convince him of his error if he would let me talk. I am very glad you sent my shoes. They fit very well indeed they [are] large enough.

I want you to consent to let me go to Lowell if you can. I think it would be much better for me than to stay about here. I could earn more to begin with than I can any where about here. I am in need of clothes which I cannot get if I stay about here and for that reason I want to go to Lowell or some other place. We all think if I could go with some steady girl that I might do well. I want you to think of it and make up your mind. Mercy Jane Griffith is going to start in four or five weeks. Aunt Miller and Aunt Sarah think it would be a good chance for me to go if you would consent—which I want you to do if possible. I want to see you and talk with you about it.

Aunt Sarah gains slowly.

Mary

Woodstock Nov 8 1845
Dear Father

As you wanted me to let you know when I am going to start for Lowell, I improve this opportunity to write you. Next Thursday the 13th of this month is the day set or the Thursday afternoon. I should like to have you come down. If you come bring [my brother] Henry if you can for I should like to see him before I go. Julius [another brother] has got the money for me.

Yours Mary

Lowell Nov 20th 1845
Dear Father

An opportunity now presents itself which I improve in writing to you. I started for this place at the time I talked of which was Thursday. I left Whitneys at nine o'clock stopped at Windsor at 12 and staid till 3 and started again. Did not stop again for any length of time till we arrived at Lowell. Went to a boarding house and staid until Monday night. On Saturday after I got here Luthera Griffith went round with me to find a place but we were unsuccessful. On Monday we started again and were more successful. We found a place in a spinning room and the next morning I went to work. . . . I wish that you and Henry would come down here. I think that you might do well. I guess that Henry could get into the mill and I think that Julius might get in too. Tell all friends that I should like to hear from them.

excuse bad writing and mistakes

This from your own daughter

Mary

P.S. Be sure and direct to No. 15 Lawrence Corporation.

Lowell Dec 21st 1845
Dear Father

I received your letter on Thursday the 14th with much pleasure. I am well which is one comfort. My life and health are spared while others are cut off. Last Thursday one girl fell down and broke her neck which caused instant death. She was going in or coming out of the mill and slipped down it being very icy. The same day a man was killed by the cars [presumably railroad cars]. Another had nearly all of his ribs broken. Another was nearly killed by falling down and having a bale of cotton fall on him. Last Tuesday we were paid. In all I had six dollars and sixty cents paid $4.68 for board. With the rest I got me a pair of rubbers and a pair of 50. cts shoes. Next payment I am to have a dollar a week beside my board. We have not had much snow the deepest being not more than 4 inches. It has been very warm for winter. Perhaps you would like something about our regulations about going in and coming out of the mill. At 5 o'clock in the morning the bell rings for the folks to get up and get breakfast. At half past six it rings for the girls to get up and at seven they are called into the mill.

At half past 12 we have dinner are called back again at one and stay till half past seven. I get along very well with my work. I can doff [strip a spinning frame] as fast as any girl in our room. I think I shall have frames [spinning] before long. The usual time allowed for learning is six months but I think I shall have frames before I have been in three as I get along so fast. I think that the factory is the best place for me and if any girl wants employment I advise them to come to Lowell. Tell Harriet that though she does not hear from me she is not forgotten. I have little time to devote to writing that I cannot write all I want to. There are half a dozen letters which I ought to write to day but I have not time. Tell Harriet I send my love to her and all of the girls. Give my love to Mrs. Clement. Tell Henry this will answer for him and you too for this time.

This from

Mary S Paul

After reading this selection, consider these questions:

1. In what ways do Mary Paul's letters reveal both her economic independence and her strong ties to her family?
2. How might her economic independence have affected her relationship with her father? How might it have affected her relationship with her husband?
3. How does Paul's story compare to Thomas Dublin's analysis of the mill girls?

SELECTION 4:

A Strike at Harpers Ferry

*M*anufacturing, and particularly the use of machinery in manufacturing, required greater regulation of work and workers. In some cases, workers resisted the growing regimentation of labor. When the superintendent at the U.S. armory at Harpers Ferry, Virginia (later West Virginia), installed a clock and imposed a ten-hour day, the workers went on strike. They subsequently sent a delegation to present their grievances to President John Tyler. The president assured them that they could return to their jobs without retribution but declined to intervene on their behalf. The first two letters, written by the military superintendent, Major Henry K. Craig, report the developing situation to his superior, Colonel George Talcott, chief of the Army Ordnance Department. The third letter is Talcott's response to an inquiry by John C. Spencer, the secretary of war.

[**M**ar. 21, 1842]

Excerpted from *Records of the Office of the Chief of Ordnance*, by Ordnance Department, Record Group 156, National Archives, Washington DC.

Sir,

This morning most of the piece workers, and many of the day hands at the Musket Factory, marched in a body to the Rifle Works, and their numbers being increased by recruits from that establishment, they returned and assembled in the

Arsenal Yard where one or more addresses were made by individuals of the league, after which they quietly departed to meet at some other place for the purpose of deliberation etc.

I was greatly surprised at this outbreak, not having had the slightest intimation that such matters were in agitation, nor do I yet know precisely the grounds of their complaints, though I believe they ostensibly, grew out of the late regulation requiring all workmen to conform to the hours for labour indicated by the Bell.

This affair having taken place at a moment when piece work is on the eve of being diminished for a time affords an opportunity of culling our ranks.

I suppose reason will be restored to the deluded portion of those who participated in the disorderly movement in the course of a day or two—I will then receive back such as it will be for the interest of the Government to employ.— Taking care to make examples of such of the instigators, and fomenters of the outbreak as are within our reach.

There are some I am inclined to think who are beyond it.

H.K. Craig.

Sir,

Our workmen still hold off, and it is said intend to visit Washington in a body, having chartered a canal boat for the purpose; I am inclined to think they will not act so unwisely. There is no appearance of disorder, or tumult; and setting aside the impropriety of their conduct in quitting work, the behaviour of the workmen has been as correct as could be expected.

H.K. Craig.

Lt. Col. Talcott to Jno. C. Spencer, Ord. Office, May 17, 1842.

The Armory question may be explained by setting forth a few of the facts.

1st. There now is, and has been, a greater number of men employed than would be necessary to perform all the work, in case they labored with reasonable diligence ten hours a day.

2d. At all private manufactures the operatives are required to labor 12 hours & upwards per day,

while at the Armories, only ten hours and at heavy forging only 7 to 8 hours labor are demanded.

3d. If the number now employed should labor ten hours a day—the annual appropriations, after providing the necessary materials, & tools,— would be entirely insufficient to pay the workmen, at present prices.

4th. The Regulations governing the workmen are *not changed*, they are *merely enforced*, every man being required to commence work at a fixed hour and labor during working hours—unless he finds it necessary to lose specific parts of a day, not less than a quarter being noted. The old practice of coming & going to suit the pleasure of each and working or playing—*in* hours or *out* of hours was an abuse formerly tolerated, but never sanctioned by regulations, & the pretext that *because men work by the piece,* they should be allowed to run machinery when they please & be absent whenever it suits their whim, finds no favor at private workshops nor can it be allowed where the work of one man depends on that done by another, for carrying on and keeping up all branches to a proper standard. The Master Armorer cannot keep all branches in a suitable state of advancement, unless he can rely on the quantity of work to be done by each man.

5th. The *real ground of opposition* to the present mode of supervision is well known to be this—The men have been paid high prices & were in the habit of working from 4 to 6 hours per day—& being absent whole days, or a week. At the end of a month their pay was generally the same in amount as if no absence had occurred.

They are now required to work full time and during fixed hours (according to old regulations) and the master of the Shop keeps a time account showing the time *actually spent in labor.* Here is the *great oppression* complained of. At the end of a month of *quantity* of *labor performed* for *product,* and the *time* during which it is effected are seen by a simple inspection of the Shop books. The degree of diligence used by each man is also known and hence results a knowledge of what is the *fair price* to be paid for *piece work!!!* The Armorers may attempt to disguise or hide the truth under a thousand clamors—but this is the *real cause* of their objections to a Military Superintendent. He enforces the Regulations which lay bare their secret practices (fraud—for I can use no better term). They can control a civil Supt. & have often done it! They have occasionally ousted one, and they have shot one. . . .

We say to the Armorers—here are our Regulations, if you will not abide by them—go elsewhere—for we know that as many good or better workmen can be had at any moment. They answer—no, we will not leave the armory. We insist on working for the United States and will fix our own terms!!! This is practically the fact & all private manufacturers at the North complain of the high prices paid at the Armories for *mechanical* skill of no great pretensions. Indeed, since the introduction of so many new machinery—very little skill is required to use them—a young man from the plough who had never used a tool in a workshop entered the armory in Feby. 1841—He now earns at present prices sixty dollars a month!! The subject can be extended almost indefinitely but I will stop.

G. Talcott.

After reading this selection, consider these questions:

1. Consider the work patterns described by Bruce Laurie's article earlier in this chapter. In what ways had the work patterns at Harpers Ferry been similar? What impact did industrialization have on such patterns? How did these changes look from the perspective of the workers? How did they look from the perspective of the managers?

2. What developments described by Talcott swing the advantage to employers (in this case, the U.S. government)?

SELECTION 5:

Watchmaking in Europe and America

Watchmaking *became one of the first industries to produce a precision instrument for a large consumer market. The American Watch Company (later the Waltham Watch Company) began producing inexpensive machine-made watches in the early 1860s. Watchmaking was one of the few metalworking industries to employ significant numbers of women. The following excerpt from Virginia Penny's* The Employment of Women: An Encyclopedia of Women's Work *(1863) compares watchmaking in Europe with the new industry in America.*

A watch is said to consist of 992 pieces. . . . In Switzerland, families, for generation after generation, devote themselves to making particular parts of watches. Women have proved their ability to execute the most delicate parts. Twenty thousand Swiss women earn a comfortable livelihood by watch making. They make the movements, but men mostly put them together. . . .

Excerpted from *The Employments of Women: An Encyclopedia of Woman's Work*, by Virginia Penny (Boston: Walker & Wise, 1863).

A traveller states: "We see women at the head of some of the heaviest manufactories of Switzerland and France, particularly in the watch and jewelry line." In England, women have been until lately excluded from watch making by men, but some are now employed in one establishment in London and in several of the provincial towns. "There is a manufactory at Christchurch, England, where five hundred women are employed in making the interior chains for chronometers. They are preferred to men, on account of their being naturally more dexterous with their fingers, and therefore being found to require less training." From the November number of the *Knickerbocker* we quote: "All imported watches are made by hand, the American watches being the only ones made by machinery in a single establishment by connected and uniform processes. The Waltham watches have fewer parts and are more easily kept in order than any others; and are warranted for ten years by the manufacturers. They have over one hundred artisans employed, more than half of whom are women." The manufactory occupies a space more than half an acre in extent. Hand labor is cheaper in Europe than this country, but American watches are cheaper, because made by machinery. . . . A manufacturer of chronometers in Boston writes: ". . . The principal objection to employing women is that they are very apt to marry just as they become skilful enough to be reliable; therefore, what does not require long apprenticeship or a great expense to learn, is most desirable for them. A good degree of intelligence is indispensable. The more, of course, the better." We would add to the requisites for a watchmaker, patience and ingenuity. The secretary of the American Watch Company at Waltham writes: "Women are employed at our factory. The employment is entirely healthy. We pay from $4 to $7 per week for intelligent girls, and women's average pay is $5. About half are paid by the piece. Men earn about double the wages of women, because, first, they do more difficult work, are more ingenious, more thoughtful and contriving, more reliant on themselves in matters of mechanics, are stronger, and therefore worth more, though not perhaps double, as an average; second, because it is the custom to pay women less than men for the same labor. Women and girls are paid from $2.50 to $4 per week during the first four months, while they are learning the particular part of our business we set them at. The requisites are a good common-school education, general intelligence, and quickness; light, small hands are best. The business is new to the country. We work every working day in the year, without detriment to the health of women, who seem to endure their labor as well as men. We work ten hours a day. . . . We employ seventy-five women out of two hundred hands, and because there are many parts of our work they can do *equally* well with men; but it is generally light and simple work, for which no high degree of mechanical skill is requisite. Nine tenths are American born. Our hands are all made perfectly comfortable in their labor. We employ female labor, where we can, as being cheaper; but we find women do not reach the posts where a high degree of skill is needed, as of course they do not those for which their strength is insufficient. They have abundant facilities for mental culture in the evenings. About half live with parents or relatives; the rest board, and pay from $2 to $3 a week, according to quality.

After reading this selection, consider these questions:

1. Compare the description of the advantages of machine production in Penny's account with Colonel George Talcott's assessment of the advantages of machine production.

2. What was the impact of machine production on skilled labor according to Penny?

3. According to Penny, how did the assignment of tasks in the American Watch Company reflect traditional gender roles?

CHAPTER 12

Antebellum Slavery

In the early decades of the nineteenth century, the North and the South embarked on different paths of economic development. In the North, manufacturing and railroads became the engines of economic growth. The South was less affected by industrialization, urbanization, and immigration from Europe. Cotton remained the mainstay of the Southern economy as well as America's most important export. The introduction of short staple cotton (a hardier, if less luxurious, variety) and the cotton gin paved the way for a dramatic expansion of cotton cultivation. The increasing importance of cotton, in turn, strengthened the hold of slavery on Southern agriculture. The production of tobacco, another crop that depended heavily on slave labor, was spurred by the introduction of new varieties of tobacco and the increased use of fertilizer.

As labor-intensive cotton and tobacco production spread to the West and the South and other regions turned more toward diversified agriculture, slave trading became an increasingly profitable business. Once considered an occupation of very low social standing, slave trading became an avenue of social advancement for people of humble origin, and it began to draw some people of somewhat higher social standing. The growth of slave trading had a devastating impact on some slave families and communities.

It is difficult to generalize about slavery. Some slaves lived and worked on plantations (operations with twenty or more slaves). Even on plantations, striking differences existed between those with twenty or so slaves and those with hundreds of slaves. In addition, many slaves lived and worked with white families who owned as few as one or two slaves. Aside from the size of the operation, much depended on the individual owner. Some masters were cruel to the point of sadism; others treated their slaves well. Most owners provided their slaves with adequate food, clothing, and shelter; slaves were expensive, and only a fool or a monster would fail to take care of such valuable property.

The system depended on the ability to extract labor from enslaved people. However inherently exploitive and cruel the system may have been, human interaction modified it. Bonds of affection and loyalty influenced the behavior of both masters and slaves. As the selection from Eugene D. Genovese, included in this chapter, points out, slavery was not only dictated from above; slaves also had some input into the arrangements between slave and master. Further, human emotions, including anger, lust, and jealousy, shaped the nature of the existence of slaves.

After reading this chapter, consider these questions:

1. How did human relationships shape an essentially inhuman institution? How did human interaction make the lives of slaves better? How might the same sorts of human interaction have made the lives of slaves more miserable and more bitter?

2. How did slaves influence the way they were treated? How did they influence the institution of slavery itself?

3. In what ways did slavery affect the lives of whites who held slaves?

SELECTION 1:

Paternalism and Slavery

Eugene D. Genovese broke new ground in the 1960s and 1970s with his studies of antebellum slave society. The Political Economy of Slavery *(1961) and* The World the Slaveholders Made *(1969) established him as a leading historian and paved the way for his masterpiece,* Roll, Jordan, Roll: The World the Slaves Made *(1974). Genovese maintains that, for all of its exploitation and reliance on force, slavery was not imposed exclusively from above; it was also shaped from below. Within the confines of the institution, slaves managed to mitigate their working conditions and carve out identities and lives separate from their status as slaves. In the following excerpt, Genovese describes the efforts of whites to gain the assent and cooperation of slaves through paternalism. Genovese has taught at a number of universities, including Rutgers University, Sir George Williams University (in Canada), the University of Rochester, the College of William and Mary, and the University of Georgia system.*

Excerpted from *Roll, Jordan, Roll: The World the Slaves Made,* by Eugene D. Genovese (New York: Pantheon Books, 1974). Copyright © 1974 by Pantheon Books. Reprinted with permission.

The Old South, black and white, created a historically unique kind of paternalist society. To insist upon the centrality of class relations as manifested in paternalism is not to slight the inherent racism or to deny the intolerable contradictions at the heart of paternalism itself. Imamu Amiri Baraka captures the tragic irony of paternalist social relations when he writes that slavery "was, most of all, a paternal institution" and yet refers to "the filthy paternalism and cruelty of slavery." Southern paternalism, like every other paternalism, had little to do with Ole Massa's ostensible benevolence, kindness, and good cheer. It grew out of the necessity to discipline and morally justify a system of exploitation. It did encourage kindness and affection, but it simultaneously encouraged cruelty and hatred. The racial distinction between master and slave heightened the tension inherent in an unjust social order.

Southern slave society grew out of the same general historical conditions that produced the other slave regimes of the modern world. The rise of a world market—the development of new tastes and of manufactures dependent upon non-European sources of raw materials—encouraged the rationalization of colonial agriculture under the ferocious domination of a few Europeans. African labor provided the human power to fuel the new system of production in all the New World slave societies, which, however, had roots in different European experiences and emerged in different geographical, economic, and cultural conditions. They had much in common, but each was unique.

Theoretically, modern slavery rested, as had ancient slavery, on the idea of a slave as *instrumentum vocale*—a chattel, a possession, a thing, a mere extension of his master's will. But the vacuousness of such pretensions had been exposed long before the growth of New World slave societies. The closing of the ancient slave trade, the political crisis of ancient civilization, and the subtle moral pressure of an ascendant Christianity had converged in the early centuries of the new era to shape a seigneurial world in which lords and serfs (not slaves) faced each other with reciprocal demands and expectations. This land-oriented world of medieval Europe slowly forged the traditional paternalist ideology to which the southern slaveholders fell heir.

The slaveholders of the South, unlike those of the Caribbean, increasingly resided on their plantations and by the end of the eighteenth century had become an entrenched regional ruling class. The paternalism encouraged by the close living of masters and slaves was enormously reinforced by the closing of the African slave trade, which compelled masters to pay greater attention to the reproduction of their labor force. Of all the slave societies in the New World, that of the Old South alone maintained a slave force that reproduced itself. Less than 400,000 imported Africans had, by 1860, become an American black population of more than 4,000,000.

A paternalism accepted by both masters and slaves—but with radically different interpretations—afforded a fragile bridge across the intolerable contradictions inherent in a society based on racism, slavery, and class exploitation that had to depend on the willing reproduction and productivity of its victims. For the slaveholders paternalism represented an attempt to overcome the fundamental contradiction in slavery: the impossibility of the slaves' ever becoming the things they were supposed to be. Paternalism defined the involuntary labor of the slaves as a legitimate return to their masters for protection and direction. But, the masters' need to see their slaves as acquiescent human beings constituted a moral victory for the slaves themselves. Paternalism's insistence upon mutual obligations—duties, responsibilities, and ultimately even rights—implicitly recognized the slaves' humanity.

Wherever paternalism exists, it undermines solidarity among the oppressed by linking them as individuals to their oppressors. A lord (master, *padrone, patron, padrón, patrão*) functions as a direct provider and protector to each individual or family, as well as to the community as a whole. The slaves of the Old South displayed impressive solidarity and collective resistance to their masters, but in a web of paternalistic relationships their action tended to become defensive and to aim at protecting the individuals against aggression and abuse; it could not readily pass into an effective weapon for liberation. Black leaders, especially the preachers, won loyalty and respect and fought heroically to defend their people. But despite their will and considerable ability, they could not lead their people over to the attack against the paternalist ideology itself.

In the Old South the tendencies inherent in all paternalistic class systems intersected with and acquired enormous reinforcement from the tendencies inherent in an analytically distinct system of racial subordination. The two appeared to be a single system. Paternalism created a tendency for the slaves to identify with a particular community through identification with its master; it reduced the possibilities for their identification with each other as a class. Racism undermined the slaves' sense of worth as black people and reinforced their dependence on white masters. But these were tendencies, not absolute laws, and the slaves forged weapons of defense, the most important of which was a religion that taught them to love and value each other, to take a critical view of their masters, and to reject the ideological rationales for their own enslavement.

The slaveholders had to establish a stable regime with which their slaves could live. Slaves remained slaves. They could be bought and sold like any other property and were subject to despotic personal power. And blacks remained rigidly subordinated to whites. But masters and slaves, whites and blacks, lived as well as worked together. The existence of the community required that all find some measure of self-interest and self-respect. Southern paternalism developed as a way of mediating irreconcilable class and racial conflicts; it was an anomaly even at the moment of its greatest apparent strength. But, for about a century, it protected both masters and slaves from the worst tendencies inherent in their respective conditions. It mediated, however unfairly and even cruelly, between masters and slaves, and it disguised, however imperfectly, the appropriation of one man's labor power by another. Paternalism in any his-

torical setting defines relations of superordination and subordination. Its strength as a prevailing ethos increases as the members of the community accept—or feel compelled to accept—these relations as legitimate. Brutality lies inherent in this acceptance of patronage and dependence, no matter how organic the paternalistic order. But southern paternalism necessarily recognized the slaves' humanity—not only their free will but the very talent and ability without which their acceptance of a doctrine of reciprocal obligations would have made no sense. Thus, the slaves found an opportunity to translate paternalism itself into a doctrine different from that understood by their masters and to forge it into a weapon of resistance to assertions that slavery was a natural condition for blacks, that blacks were racially inferior, and that black slaves had no rights or legitimate claims of their own.

Thus, the slaves, by accepting a paternalistic ethos and legitimizing class rule, developed their most powerful defense against the dehumanization implicit in slavery. Southern paternalism may have reinforced racism as well as class exploitation, but it also unwittingly invited its victims to fashion their own interpretation of the social order it was intended to justify. And the slaves, drawing on a religion that was supposed to assure their compliance and docility, rejected the essence of slavery by projecting their own rights and value as human beings.

After reading this selection, consider these questions:

1. Describe the operation of paternalism.

2. Genovese maintains that "slaves, by accepting a paternalistic ethos . . . developed their most powerful defense against the dehumanization implicit in slavery." Discuss.

SELECTION 2:

Slavery and Sexual Exploitation

Southern ideology in the antebellum era regarded interracial sex as an abomination. In practice, however, white slave owners had access to slave women, and interracial sex was not uncommon. In the following selection, Nell Irvin Painter, a professor of history at Princeton University, maintains that historians who have addressed this issue have argued either that slave women were at the bottom of a sexual hierarchy or that all Southern women were at the mercy of white men. Painter concludes that neither position adequately describes the complex dynamic of sexual exploitation of female slaves by male owners.

It has been no secret, then or now, that in the plantation South, owners and slaves lived on terms of physical closeness and often engaged in sexual intimacy. Yet historians have followed the lead of privileged nineteenth-century southerners who, though well aware that sex figured among the services masters demanded of slaves, briskly pushed the matter aside. . . . Virtually by default, the conclusion in southern history was that master-slave sex was a problem for the slaves, not the master; thus as a social phenomenon, interracial, interclass sexuality has been relegated to African-Americans alone. This is not the position I hold. Because intimate relations affected white as well as black families, I argue that such sexuality and its repercussions belong not to one race or the other, but must reside squarely in southern history. . . .

Lily is the title character of an 1855 novel by Sue Petigru King (Bowen) (1824–1875). King was a daughter of the very respectable Charlestonian Thomas Petigru. Having been educated in

Excerpted from "Race, Class, and Gender in the Slave South," by Nell Irvin Painter, *Georgia Historical Quarterly,* Summer 1992. Copyright © 1992 by *Georgia Historical Quarterly.* Reprinted with permission.

Charleston and New York, she had returned to South Carolina to pursue her career as a writer. Her Lily is the quintessential young plantation mistress: hyper-white, wealthy, and beautiful. Much better known today, thanks largely to the work of Jean Fagan Yellin and others, is "Linda Brent," who in contrast to Lily, was a slave. Brent is both the central character and the pseudonym under which the Edenton, North Carolina fugitive slave, Harriet Jacobs (1813–1897), used in her autobiography, *Incidents in the Life of a Slave Girl,* originally published with the help of Boston abolitionists in 1861.

If rich, white, and free Lily represents the top of the antebellum South's economic and racial hierarchies, then poor, yellow, and enslaved Linda Brent represents the near bottom. Linda, after all, has some free relations, and her grandmother, nominally enslaved, lives in her own house in town. Things could have been much worse for Linda Brent. Both Linda's and Lily's stories are about very young women and sex, and . . . they tell us a great deal about southern family dynamics in slaveholding households. . . .

Although historians have not begun to quantify its incidence, it is clear that sexual relations between male slavemasters and female slaves were exceedingly common in the antebellum South —as in any other slave society. . . . Nineteenth-century fugitive slave narratives, such as those of Frederick Douglass and Moses Roper, and the Fisk and WPA [Works Progress Administration] ex-slave narratives from the 1930s, are full of evidence that masters did not hesitate to sleep with their women slaves, despite the marital status of either. . . . On the other side of the class and racial continuums from the Frederick Douglass and Moses Ropers, white women—southerners and observers—penned and sometimes published criticisms of the institution of slavery based on what they perceived as the demoralization of white men who engaged in adultery and/or polygyny.

I began to draw my own conclusions as I concentrated on the journal of Ella Gertrude Clanton Thomas (1834–1907), published in 1990 as *The Secret Eye*. Thomas, wealthy, educated, and white, lived in and around Augusta, Georgia, for most of her life. She began keeping a journal in 1848, when she was fourteen years old, and stopped writing definitively in 1889, when she was fifty-five. Although she was born into an immensely wealthy, slave-owning family, Thomas married a man who was a poor manager. Her husband, Jefferson Thomas, succeeded financially as a planter before the Civil War, thanks to unpaid labor and continual financial help from Gertrude's father. But her father died in 1864 and their slaves were emancipated in 1865. After the war the Thomases entered a long cycle of debt that sent Gertrude into the paid labor force as a teacher. Her earnings kept the family afloat economically, but poverty imposed great strains on the family. This journal, therefore, chronicles a life of privilege before the Civil War, the trauma of supporting the losing side, the loss of the labor and prestige that slavery had assured her, and the chagrin of downward mobility. Thomas joined the Woman's Christian Temperance Union in the 1880s and became a suffragist in the 1890s. She died in Atlanta.

Initially I appreciated this journal for its value as a primary source for the study of the social history of the South, for which Thomas was an excellent witness. Extraordinary as her record is, however, it works on yet another level, which psychoanalysis is well equipped to explore. The journal contains a veiled text, characterized by the keeping of secrets, lack of candor, and self-deception. Whereas the surface of this text presents a southerner of a certain class at given historical junctures, a less straightforward message also emerges, though it is not so easy to glimpse. The veiled text, less bounded chronologically, is about families and gender, and it contains and reveals a great secret that is relatively timeless: adultery. I know from the "deception clues" and leakage in the journal that most certainly by the 1860s, probably by the 1850s, Thomas was painfully aware but unable to admit that her father had had children by at least one of his slaves. By the 1870s, possibly as early as the 1850s, Thomas also knew that her husband had fathered at least one child by a woman who was not white.

This should come as no surprise. Harriet Martineau in the 1830s spoke of the plantation mistress as "the chief slave of the harem." Fredrika Bremer in the 1850s coined a famous phrase that Thomas quotes in her journal, "these white children of slavery." And Mary Chestnut wrote of the mulatto children in every slaveholding household. Gertrude Thomas was far from alone.

Some of the most interesting evidence comes from fiction, which, considering the subject, should not be surprising. Most respectable nineteenth-century people retreated—or attempted to retreat—behind the veil of privacy, rather than reveal their actual patterns of sexuality. The very ability to conceal the rawer aspects of the human condition, an ability that we sum up in the term privacy, served as a crucial symbol of respectability when the poor had no good place to hide. Nonetheless the topic of interracial sexuality was of enough fascination to reappear in fiction under various disguises. Taking my cue from Gertrude Thomas, who was hypersensitive about sexual competition between women, I began to pursue sexuality through the theme of competition. Tracked in that guise, southern fiction reveals some interesting manifestations.

Sue Petigru King sounded themes that occur in the works of several white southern women writers, such as Caroline Lentz, Grace King, and Willa Cather. For example, Cather's final novel,

Sapphira and the Slave Girl (1940), is precisely and openly about a white woman's perception of sexual competition between herself and a Negro woman. In its racial candor, *Sapphira* is exceptional. More often the competition between women is not about individuals with different racial identities, but about two white characters who are color-coded in black and white. While I realize that European writers such as Sir Walter Scott and Honoré de Balzac used light (blonde) and dark (*la belle juive*) female characters symbolically, Anne Goodwyn Jones, Mary Kelley, and Jane Pease, scholars familiar with southern writing, corroborate my view that nineteenth- and early twentieth-century white southern women writers were singularly fascinated by competition between light and dark women. While most publications by these women followed the usual theme of a young women's quest for autonomy and her eventual marriage to a good man, they also very much echoed Gertrude Thomas' fixation on female rivalry.

Sue Petigru King is no longer very well known, but she loomed large in Gertrude Thomas' literary world and was known in Great Britain. William Thackeray, one of Britain's most celebrated authors, visited her on a trip to the United States. In the mid-nineteenth century King published several novels which repeatedly stressed themes of jealousy and competition between women, the best known of which is *Lily*.

Very briefly, *Lily* is the story of Elizabeth Vere, whom her father calls "Lily" because she is "as white as any lily that ever grew." Over the course of the novel's plot, Lily goes from age seven to seventeen. King described her heroine with words like "white," "pure," "innocent," "simple," and "lovely." The character with whom King paired Lily is her cousin, Angelica Purvis. Angelica is also a rich white woman, but King focused on the blackness of her dresses and the intense blackness of her hair. At one point, King contrasted Lily, who "seemed made up of light and purity," with Angelica, who "was dark, designing, distracting." Angelica is exotic; King described her as an "Eastern princess" and called her looks "Andalusian." Whereas Lily is pure, Angelica is passionate, evil, voluptuous. Angelica says of her attractiveness to men: "I am original sin. . . ." At the age of seventeen, Lily is engaged to her first great love, Clarence Tracy, a childhood friend who is a graduate of Princeton University. Despite all her goodness, however, Lily is not rewarded with love for Clarence is crazy in love with Angelica, who is married.

On the face of it, the most obvious theme in *Lily* is competition between two white women, which the less virtuous is winning. But race hovers in the very near background. First, these ostensibly white competitors are color-coded in black and white. Then, as though to make the point unambiguously, King abruptly introduces a new character, Lorenza, at the very end of the novel. Lorenza is Clarence's Negro mistress. On the night before Lily's wedding, Lorenza murders Lily out of jealousy over her impending marriage.

King left nothing to guesswork in this novel, and to hammer home her message she also addressed her readers directly. Her point was the same made by Mary Chestnut in her Civil War diary: that southern planter husbands repaid their wives' faithful virtue with base infidelity. Wealthy southern men married young, pure, rich, white girls like Lily, then left them for mistresses tinged with blackness, whether of descent or intimation. . . .

In *Lily*, the pure, young, rich, white daughter is the most dramatic loser in the southern sexual sweepstakes. In this interpretation of southern sexuality, the motif is competition between women and the victims are wealthy white women. Writers from the other side painted a disturbingly similar, yet differently shaded portrait.

While many ex-slave narratives discuss master-slave sexuality, the most extended commentary comes from Harriet Jacobs, who, writing under the pseudonym Linda Brent, told of being harassed by her master for sex from the time she was thirteen. Her character, Linda, becomes the most literal embodiment of the slave as sexual prey in the literature of slave narratives. . . .

White women, black women, and black men all resented deeply white men's access to black women. But the comments from the two sides of the color line are contradictory: where white women saw sexual competition—with connotations of equality—black men and women saw rank exploitation that stemmed from grossly disparate levels of power. Moses Roper, his master's child, relates the story of his near-murder, shortly after his birth, by his father's jealous wife. Frederick Douglass also noted that slave-owning women were distressed by the bodily proof of their husband's adulteries.

For Jacobs, as for other ex-slave narrators, the prime victim was the slave woman, not the slave-owning woman, no matter how the latter perceived the situation. Slave owners' sexual relations with their women slaves constituted one of several varieties of victimization by men whose power over them was absolute. Slaves of both sexes were oppressed by class and by race, but women suffered a third, additional form of oppression stemming from their gender. Extorted sex was part of a larger pattern of oppression embedded in the institution of slavery.

After reading this selection, consider these questions:

1. Analyze Nell Irvin Painter's statement that "where white women saw sexual competition —with connotations of equality—black men and women saw rank exploitation that stemmed from grossly disparate levels of power."

2. What kinds of evidence does Painter offer to support her assertion that "sexual relations between male slavemasters and female slaves were exceedingly common"? Is her evidence convincing?

SELECTION 3:

A Childhood in Slavery

Born to a slave mother and a white master in 1817 or 1818, Frederick Douglass escaped from slavery in 1838. He became active in the abolitionist movement and emerged as its most eloquent spokesperson. He published a newspaper from 1847–1860, urged President Abraham Lincoln to use black soldiers, and recruited for the Union army. After the Civil War, Douglass moved to Washington, D.C., and held government positions (marshall of the District of Columbia from 1877–1881 and recorder of deeds from 1881–1886). Later, he held several diplomatic posts, including minister and counsel general to the Republic of Haiti. The following document is an excerpt from his autobiography. Douglass's first master was known as Captain Anthony. When Douglass was seven or eight years old, his master sent him to Baltimore to live with Hugh Auld, the brother of Anthony's son-in-law. The new mistress about whom he writes is Auld's wife.

Excerpted from *First Person Past*, edited by Marian J. Morton and Russell Duncan (New York: Brandywine Press, 1994).

My mother was named Harriet Bailey. She was the daughter of Isaac and Betsey Bailey, both colored, and quite dark. My mother was of a darker complexion than either my grandmother or grandfather.

My father was a white man. He was admitted to be such by all I ever heard speak of my parentage. The opinion was also whispered that my master was my father; but of the correctness of this opinion, I know nothing; the means of knowing was withheld from me. My mother and I were separated when I was but an infant—before I knew her as my mother. It is a common custom, in the part of Maryland from which I ran away, to part children from their mothers at a very early age. Frequently, before the child has reached its twelfth month, its mother is taken from it, and hired out on some farm a considerable distance off, and the child is placed under the care of an old woman, too old for field labor. For what this separation is done, I do not know, unless it be to hinder the development of the child's affection toward its mother, and to blunt and destroy the natural affection of the mother for the child. This is the inevitable result.

I never saw my mother, to know her as such, more than four or five times in my life; and each of these times was very short in duration, and at night. She was hired by a Mr. Stewart, who lived about twelve miles from my home. She made her journeys to see me in the night, travelling the whole distance on foot, after the performance of her day's work. She was a field hand, and a whipping is the penalty of not being in the field at sunrise, unless a slave has special permission from his or her master to the contrary—a permission which they seldom get, and one that gives to him that gives it the proud name of being a kind master. I do not recollect of ever seeing my mother by the light of day. She was with me in the night. She would lie down with me, and get me to sleep, but long before I waked she was gone. Very little communication ever took place between us. Death soon ended what little we could have while she lived, and with it her hardships and suffering. She died when I was about seven years old, on one of my master's farms, near Lee's Mill. I was not allowed to be present during her illness, at her death, or burial. She was gone long before I knew any thing about it. Never having enjoyed, to any considerable extent, her soothing presence, her tender and watchful care, I received the tidings of her death with much the same emotions I should have probably felt at the death of a stranger.

Called thus suddenly away, she left me without the slightest intimation of who my father was. The whisper that my master was my father, may or may not be true; and, true or false, it is of but little consequence to my purpose whilst the fact remains, in all its glaring odiousness, that slaveholders have ordained, and by law established, that the children of slave women shall in all cases follow the condition of their mothers; and this is done too obviously to administer to their own lusts, and make a gratification of their wicked desires profitable as well as pleasurable; for by this cunning arrangement, the slaveholder, in cases not a few, sustains to his slaves the double relation of master and father.

I know of such cases; and it is worthy of remark that such slaves invariably suffer greater hardships, and have more to contend with, than others. They are, in the first place, a constant offence to their mistress. She is ever disposed to find fault with them; they can seldom do any thing to please her; she is never better pleased than when she sees them under the lash, especially when she suspects her husband of showing to his mulatto children favors which he withholds from his black slaves. The master is frequently compelled to sell this class of his slaves, out of deference to the feelings of his white wife . . .

Very soon after I went to live with Mr. and Mrs. Auld, she very kindly commenced to teach me the A, B, C. After I had learned this, she assisted me in learning to spell words of three or four letters. Just at this point of my progress, Mr. Auld found out what was going on, and at once forbade Mrs. Auld to instruct me further, telling her, among other things, that it was unlawful, as well as unsafe, to teach a slave to read. To use his own words, further, he said, "If you give a nigger an inch, he will take an ell. A nigger should know nothing but to obey his master—to do as he is told to do. Learning would *spoil* the best nigger in the world. Now," said he, "if you teach that nigger (speaking of myself) how to read, there would be no keeping him. It would forever unfit him to be a slave. He would at once become unmanageable, and of no value to his master. As to himself, it could do him no good, but a great deal of harm. It would make him discontented and unhappy." These words sank deep into my heart, stirred up sentiments within that lay slumbering, and called into existence an entirely new train of thought. It was a new and special revelation, explaining dark and mysterious things, with which my youthful understanding had struggled, but struggled in vain. I now understood what had been to me a most perplexing difficulty—to wit, the white man's power to enslave the black man. It was a grand achievement, and I prized it highly. From that moment, I understood the pathway from slavery to freedom. It was just what I wanted, and I got it at a time when I the least expected it. Whilst I was saddened by the thought of losing the aid of my kind mistress, I was gladdened by the invaluable instruction which, by the merest accident, I had gained from my master. Though conscious of the difficulty of learning without a teacher, I set out with high hope, and a fixed purpose, at whatever cost of trouble, to learn how to read. The very decided manner with which he spoke, and strove to impress his wife with the evil consequences of giving me instruction, served to convince me that he was deeply sensible of the truths he was uttering. It gave me the best assurance that I might rely with the utmost confidence on the results which, he said, would flow from teaching me to read. What he most dreaded, that I most desired. What he most loved, that I most hated. That which to him was a great evil, to be carefully shunned, was to me a great good, to be diligently sought; and the argument which he so warmly urged, against my learning to read, only served to inspire me with a desire and determination to learn. In learning to read, I owe almost as much to the bitter opposition of my master, as to the kindly aid of my mistress. I acknowledge the benefit of both.

After reading this selection, consider these questions:

1. Compare what Douglass writes about slave children fathered by the master of the plantation to Nell Irvin Painter's article in this chapter.

2. Teaching slaves to read was illegal in most Southern states. Why? What were Hugh Auld's objections to teaching slaves to read?

3. Why do you think that Mrs. Auld began to teach Douglass to read? What reasons might a slave owner have for wanting a slave to be able to read and perform basic calculations?

SELECTION 4:

Sexual Slavery

Louisa Picquet was born in about 1827. She worked as a slave in Georgia and Alabama until she was sold to John Williams, who kept her as a concubine in New Orleans. Upon Williams's death in 1848, she was freed and moved to Ohio with her children. Hiram Mattison, a white abolitionist clergyman, interviewed her in 1860 and published this account in 1861.

Q: How did you say you come to be sold?

A: Well, you see, Mr. Cook [my master] made great parties, and go off to watering-places, and get in debt, and had to break up, and then he took us to Mobile, and hired the most of us out, so the men he owe could not find us, and sell us for the debt. Then, after a while, the sheriff came from Georgia after Mr. Cook's debts, and found us all, and took us to auction, and sold us. My mother and brother was sold to Texas, and I was sold to New Orleans.

Q: How old were you, then?

A: Well, I don't know exactly, but the auctioneer said I wasn't quite fourteen. I didn't know myself.

Q: How old was your brother?

A: I suppose he was about two months old. He was little bit of baby.

Q: Where were you sold?

A: In the city of Mobile. . . . They put all the men in one room, and all the women in another; and then whoever want to buy come and examine, and ask you whole lot of questions. They began to take the clothes off me, and a gentleman said they needn't do that, and told them to take me out. He said he knew I was a virtuous girl, and he'd buy me,

anyhow. He didn't strip me, only just under my shoulders.

Q: Were there others there white [that is, light skinned] like you?

A: Oh yes, plenty of them. There was only Lucy of our lot, but others!

Q: Were others stripped and examined?

A: Well, not quite naked, but just [the] same.

Q: You say the gentleman told them to "take you out." What did he mean by that?

A: Why, take me out of the *room* where the women and girls were kept; where they examine them—out where the auctioneer sold us. . . . At the market, where the block is.

Q: What block?

A: My! Don't you know? The stand, where we have to get up.

Q: Did *you* get up on the stand?

A: Why, of course; we all have to get up to be seen.

Q: What else do you remember about it?

A: Well, they first begin at upward of six hundred for me, and then bid some fifty more, and some twenty-five more, and that way.

Q: Do you remember any thing the auctioneer said about you when he sold you?

A: Well, he said he could not recommend me for any thing else only that I was a good-lookin' girl, and a good nurse, and kind and affectionate to children; but I was never used to any hard work. He told them they could see that. My hair was quite short, and

Excerpted from *Louisa Picquet, the Octoroon: or Inside Views of Southern Domestic Life*, by Hiram Mattison (Boston: Hiram Mattison, 1861).

the auctioneer spoke about it, but said, "You see it good quality, and give it a little time, it will grow out again." You see Mr. Cook had my hair cut off. My hair grew fast, and look so much better than Mr. Cook's daughter, and he fancy I had better hair than his daughter, and so he had it cut off to make a difference.

Q: Well, how did they sell you and your mother? That is, which was sold first?

A: Mother was put up the first of our folks. She was sold for [a] splendid cook, and Mr. Horton, from Texas, bought her and the baby, my brother. Then Henry, the carriage-driver, was put up, and Mr. Horton bought him, and then two fieldhands, Jim and Mary. The women there tend mills and drive ox wagons, and plough, just like men. Then I was sold next. Mr. Horton run me up to fourteen hundred dollars. He wanted I should go with my mother. Then someone said "fifty." Then Mr. Williams allowed that he did not care what they bid, he was going to have me anyhow. Then he bid fifteen hundred. Mr. Horton said 'twas no use to bid anymore, and I was sold to Mr. Williams. I went right to New Orleans then.

Q: Who was Mr. Williams?

A: I didn't know then, only he lived in New Orleans. Him and his wife had parted, some way—he had three children, boys. When I was going away I heard someone cryin' and prayin' the Lord to go with her only daughter, and protect me. I felt pretty bad then, but hadn't no time only to say good-bye. . . . It seems fresh in my memory when I think of it—no longer than yesterday. Mother was right on her knees, with her hands up, prayin' to the Lord for me. She didn't care who saw her, the people all lookin' at her. I often thought her prayers followed me, for I never could forget her. Whenever I wanted any thing real bad after that, my mother was always sure to appear to me in a dream that night, and have plenty to give me, always.

Q: Have you never seen her since?

A: No, never since that time. I went to New Orleans, and she went to Texas. So I understood.

Q: Well, how was it with you after Mr. Williams bought you? . . .

A: Mr. Williams told me what he bought me for, soon as we started for New Orleans. He said he was getting old, and when he saw me he thought he'd buy me, and end his days with me. He said if I behave myself he'd treat me well; but, if not, he'd whip me almost to death.

Q: How old was he?

A: He was over forty; I guess pretty near fifty. He was grayheaded. That's the reason he was always so jealous. He never let me go out anywhere. . . .

Q: Had you any children while in New Orleans?

A: Yes, I had four.

Q: Who was their father?

A: Mr. Williams.

Q: Was it known that he was living with you?

A: Everybody knew I was housekeeper, but he never let on that he was the father of my children. I did all the work in his house—nobody there but me and the children.

Q: What children?

A: My children and his. You see he had three sons.

Q: How old were his children when you went there?

A: I guess the youngest was nine years old. When he had company, gentlemen folks, he took them to the hotel. He never have no gentlemen company home. Sometimes he would come and knock, if he stay out later than usual time; and if I did not let him in in a minute, when I would be asleep, he'd come in and take the light, and look under the bed, and in the wardrobe, and all over, and then ask me why I did not let him in sooner. I did not know what it meant till I learnt his ways.

Q: Were your children mulattoes?

A: No, sir! They were all white. They look just like him. The neighbors all see that. After a while he got so disagreeable that I told him, one day, I wished he would sell me, or "put me in his pocket"—that's the way we say—because I had no peace at all. I rather die than live that way.

After reading this selection, consider these questions:

1. Louisa Picquet had light skin "and was never used to any hard work." In addition, she believed that her master cut her hair short because it was "better" than his daughter's hair. What conclusions might one draw from this?

2. What does this account reveal about the complexities and ambiguities involving slave children of white masters?

3. Why do you think Hiram Mattison focused on the sexual exploitation of slaves?

4. What do you make of Louisa Picquet's response to Mattison's question about her children being mulattoes?

SELECTION 5:

A Southerner Attacks Slavery

Hinton Rowan Helper (1829–1909) published The Impending Crisis of the South, *an unbridled attack on slavery, in 1857. Helper's opposition to slavery did not derive from sympathy for blacks. Indeed, he considered them an "undesirable population" and supported colonization (returning the American black population to Africa). Rather, Helper's objections to slavery derived from his belief that slavery was detrimental to Southern whites. He compared economic progress in the South unfavorably to that of the North and blamed slavery. Moreover, Helper argued that slavery did the greatest harm to nonslaveholding Southern whites by concentrating wealth and power in the hands of the few and by degrading the work ethic.*

It is a fact well known to every intelligent Southerner that we are compelled to go to the North for almost every article of utility and adornment, from matches, shoepegs and paintings up to cotton-mills, steamships and statuary; that we have no foreign trade, no princely merchants, nor respectable artists; that, in comparison with the free states, we contribute nothing to the literature, polite arts and inventions of the age . . . that almost everything produced at the North meets with ready sale, while, at the same time, there is no demand, even among our own citizens, for the productions of Southern industry; that, owing to the absence of a proper system of business amongst us, the North becomes, in one way or another, the proprietor and dispenser of all our floating wealth, and that we are dependent on Northern capitalists for the means necessary to build our railroads, canals and other public improvements . . . and that nearly all the profits arising from the exchange of commodities, from insurance and shipping offices, and from the thousand and one industrial pursuits of the country, accrue to the North, and are there invested in the erection of

Excerpted from "The Impending Crisis of the South," by Hinton Rowan Helper (New York: Brundick Brothers, 1857).

those magnificent cities and stupendous works of art which dazzle the eyes of the South, and attest the superiority of free institutions! . . .

In our opinion, an opinion which has been formed from data obtained by assiduous researches, and comparisons, from laborious investigation, logical reasoning, and earnest reflection, the causes which have impeded the progress and prosperity of the South, which have dwindled our commerce, and other similar pursuits, into the most contemptible insignificance; sunk a large majority of our people in galling poverty and ignorance, rendered a small minority conceited and tyrannical, and driven the rest away from their homes; entailed upon us a humiliating dependence on the Free States; disgraced us in the recesses of our own souls, and brought us under reproach in the eyes of all civilized and enlightened nations—may all be traced to one common source, and there find solution in the most hateful and horrible word, that was ever incorporated into the vocabulary of human economy—*Slavery!*

Reared amidst the institution of slavery, believing it to be wrong both in principle and in practice, and having seen and felt its evil influences upon individuals, communities and states, we deem it a duty, no less than a privilege, to enter our protest against it, and to use our most strenuous efforts to overturn and abolish it! Then we are an abolitionist? Yes! not merely a freesoiler, but an abolitionist, in the fullest sense of the term. We are not only in favor of keeping slavery out of the territories, but, carrying our opposition to the institution a step further, we here unhesitatingly declare ourself in favor of its immediate and unconditional abolition, in every state in this confederacy, where it now exists! Patriotism makes us a freesoiler; state pride makes us an emancipationist; a profound sense of duty to the South makes us an abolitionist; a reasonable degree of fellow feeling for the negro, makes us a colonizationist. . . .

In the South, unfortunately, no kind of labor is either free or respectable. Every white man who is under the necessity of earning his bread, by the sweat of his brow, or by manual labor, in any capacity, no matter how unassuming in deportment, or exemplary in morals, is treated as if he was a loathsome beast, and shunned with the utmost disdain. His soul may be the very seat of honor and integrity, yet without slaves—himself a slave—he is accounted as nobody, and would be deemed intolerably presumptuous, if he dared to open his mouth, even so wide as to give faint utterance to a three-lettered monosyllable, like yea or nay, in the presence of an august knight of the whip and the lash. . . .

Notwithstanding the fact that the white non-slaveholders of the South, are in the majority, as five to one, they have never yet had any part or lot in framing the laws under which they live. There is no legislation except for the benefit of slavery, and slaveholders. As a general rule, poor white persons are regarded with less esteem and attention than negroes, and though the condition of the latter is wretched beyond description, vast numbers of the former are infinitely worse off. A cunningly devised mockery of freedom is guarantied to them, and that is all. To all intents and purposes they are disfranchised, and outlawed, and the only privilege extended to them, is a shallow and circumscribed participation in the political movements that usher slaveholders into office. . . .

Non-slaveholders of the South! farmers, mechanics and workingmen, we take this occasion to assure you that the slaveholders, the arrogant demagogues whom you have elected to offices of honor and profit, have hoodwinked you, trifled with you, and used you as mere tools for the consummation of their wicked designs. They have purposely kept you in ignorance, and have, by moulding your passions and prejudices to suit themselves, induced you to act in direct opposition to your dearest rights and interests. . . . Not at the persecution of a few thousand slaveholders, but at the restitution of natural rights and prerogatives to several millions of non-slaveholders, do we aim. . . .

Some few years ago, when certain ethnographical oligarchs proved to their own satisfaction that the negro was an inferior "type of mankind," they chuckled wonderfully, and avowed, in substance, that it was right for the stronger race to kidnap and enslave the weaker—that because Nature had been pleased to do a trifle more for the Caucasian race than for the African, the former, by virtue of its superiority, was perfectly justifiable in holding the latter in absolute and perpetual bondage! No system of logic could be more antagonistic to the spirit of true democracy. It is probable that the world does not contain two persons who are exactly alike in all respects; yet "*all* men are endowed by their Creator with certain *inalienable* rights, among which are life, *liberty,* and the pursuit of happiness." All mankind may or may not be the descendants of Adam and Eve. In our own humble way of thinking, we are frank to confess, we do not believe in the unity of the races. This is a matter, however, which has little or nothing to do with the great question at issue. Aside from any theory concerning the original parentage of the different races of men, facts, material and immaterial, palpable and impalpable— facts of the eyes and facts of the conscience —crowd around us on every hand, heaping proof upon proof, that slavery is a shame, a crime, and a curse—a great moral, social, civil, and political evil—an oppressive burden to the blacks, and an incalculable injury to the whites—a stumbling-block to the nation, an impediment to progress, a damper on all the nobler instincts, principles, aspirations and enterprises of man, and a dire enemy to every true interest.

After reading this selection, consider these questions:

1. In what ways does Helper argue that slavery has weakened the South?

2. How is it possible to reconcile Helper's moral critique of slavery with his belief in the inferiority of blacks?

CHAPTER 13

Politics in the Age of Jackson

After Andrew Jackson's inauguration, a boisterous crowd followed its hero down Pennsylvania Avenue to the White House. The throng of supporters crashed the official reception, smashing glassware, overturning furniture, soiling valuable rugs, and ruining upholstered sofas and chairs. Supreme Court justice Joseph Story disgustedly observed that "the reign of King 'Mob' seemed triumphant." For all their egalitarian language and talk of eliminating privilege, however, the Jacksonians were hardly egalitarian. They did not oppose slavery, they saw nothing wrong with displacing American Indians, and they accepted as inevitable a considerable disparity of wealth and social standing. Jackson himself was a wealthy planter and slave owner, and most of his leading supporters were gentlemen of property and standing. In most cases, however, they were not born to wealth and social prominence. From their perspective, they had attained success through their own efforts, and they intended to guarantee similar opportunities to others. The democratization of government that Jackson and his followers advocated excited workers and farmers, but in reality it represented a challenge to the power of Eastern elites by the entrepreneurs of the West and the South.

If it did not mean economic equality, or even intend it, the age of Jackson did transform American politics. Once the province of a relatively small group of property holders, politics became open to participation by virtually all white male citizens. Jacksonian ideology celebrated the dignity and virtue of common people. Above all, it attributed to them the capacity for self-government. At least in politics, the period deserved the title "the Era of the Common Man."

During the Jacksonian era, Americans debated, sometimes furiously, issues that would shape the rest of the nineteenth century: What role should the federal government play in the economy? What was the proper relationship between the federal government and the states? Should slavery continue? How should the federal government deal with American Indians?

After reading this chapter, consider these questions:

1. What role did the federal government play in economic development? Was it ever simply one of laissez-faire?

2. What issues separated Jackson's supporters from his opponents?

3. How did Jackson change the American presidency?

SELECTION 1:

Ethnic and Cultural Issues

In the 1940s Arthur Schlesinger Jr. wrote The Age of Jackson *in which he cast the politics of the Jacksonian era in terms of the people against the interests. According to Schlesinger, Jackson led farmers and workers in their struggle against wealth and special interests. That analysis came under attack from historians who argued that neither wealth nor class distinguished Jackson's supporters from his opponents. Some maintained that Jackson's populist rhetoric constituted nothing more than political opportunism. The debate took a different turn when some historians, using sophisticated quantitative techniques, analyzed voting behavior. They maintained that the real divisions in the age of Jackson were neither economic nor regional but ethnic and cultural. Beginning in the 1820s and 1830s, the majority of Whigs (and, in the 1850s, Republicans) and Democrats adhered to different religious faiths. In the following essay, Richard Jensen, formerly a professor of history at the University of Illinois at Chicago and now the editor of an online history journal, presents the ethno-cultural analysis.*

The most revolutionary change in nineteenth-century America was the conversion of the nation from a largely dechristianized land in 1789 to a stronghold of Protestantism by midcentury. The revivals did it. From the 1780s to the early twentieth century uncounted thousands of itinerant preachers—Methodists, Baptists, Presbyterians, Congregationalists, Disciples, and others—went to the people, warning of damnation and holding out the promise of salvation. Their success was remarkable everywhere. By 1890 more than 70 percent of the midwestern population was church-affiliated; of these, five out of nine belonged to the revivalistic camp. . . .

The revivals induced a theological confrontation that raged throughout the century. Led by Charles Grandison Finney of Oberlin, Nathaniel Taylor of Yale, Edward Park of Andover, and S.S. Schmucker of Gettysburg, the revivalist theologians abandoned the predestination doctrines of orthodox Calvinism and rejected the conservative, established Anglican, Catholic, and Lutheran dogmatism. The opponents of revivalism, led by John Nevin at Mercersberg (Reformed), Charles Hodge at Princeton Seminary (Presbyterian), Carl Walther at Concordia (German Lutheran), Augustus Strong at Rochester (Baptist), Charles Porterfield Krauth at Philadelphia (Lutheran), and John Hobart at General (Episcopalian) recognized the threat posed by the revivalists to the historical and ritualistic foundations of their faith and fought back brilliantly, sparking a theological and liturgical renaissance in their denominations.

Disputes over revivals broke out in every denomination, aligning the faithful into prorevival, or "pietistic," and antirevival, or "liturgical," camps. While this conflict was not the only divisive force in American religion, it was the most intense and long standing until the very end of the century, when the revivals declined sharply in importance and moderates sought to clear the air of the old bitterness. Until the mid-1890s the conflict between pietists and liturgicals was not only the noisiest product of American religion, it was also the force which channeled religious enthusiasm and religious conflict into the political arena.

The liturgical, or "high church," outlook consisted of much more than simple opposition to revivalism. It stressed the positive values of the institutionalized formalities and historic doctrines of the old orthodoxies, whether Calvinist, Anglican, Lutheran, Catholic, or Jewish. Salvation, the focus of all Christianity, required faithful adherence to the creeds, rituals, sacraments, and hierarchy of the church. The quintessence of the liturgical style appeared in Catholicism's lavish use of ornamentation, vestments, stylized prayers, ritualized sacraments, devotions to relics and saints, all supervised by an authoritarian hierarchy led by the pope, whose infallibility was pro-

claimed in 1870. Comparable ritualism developed rapidly among Episcopalians in the middle and late nineteenth century, while German Lutherans, orthodox Calvinists ("Old School" Presbyterians and many Baptists) increasingly stressed theological scholasticism and fundamentalism.

One key element in the liturgical outlook was particularism, the belief that the denomination was the one true church of God and that most outsiders were probably damned. The attitude was strong among Catholics, German Lutherans, Landmarkean Baptists (a movement inside the Baptist denomination), high-church Episcopalians, and predestinarian Presbyterians. The church itself would attend to all matters of morality and salvation, the particularists believed, hence the state had no right to assert a role in delineating public morality. . . .

Heresy, pride, and insubordination (matters totally outside the concern of the state) were the cardinal sins for the liturgicals. Consequently they devoted their intellectual resources to neoscholastic theology and their financial resources to building seminaries and parochial schools that would insulate their adherents from the follies of the aggressive pietistic denominations. The success of the Catholics and German Lutherans in building strong networks of parochial schools in the last third of the century seemed to pietists to be a threat to the public school system they controlled, and touched off an unusually bitter political controversy that climaxed in the elections of 1890 in Wisconsin and Illinois. The hostility of the pietists only encouraged the liturgical forces to redouble their efforts. The courageous pursuit of duty was the highest virtue for the liturgicals. . . .

The pietistic outlook flatly rejected ritualism. It showed little regard for elaborate ceremonies, vestments, saints, devotions, or even organ music. Theologically the key to pietism was Arminianism, the idea that all men can be saved by a direct confrontation with Christ (*not* with the church) through the conversion experience. The revival was the basis of growth—the preaching of hellfire, damnation, and Christ's love, the "anxious bench" for remorseful sinners, the moment of light wherein a man joyously gained faith and was saved forever. . . .

The pietists not only demanded a conversion experience as a condition of membership (a requirement softened as the century grew old), but also insisted on continuous proof of genuine conversion in the form of pure behavior. The Methodists did not hesitate to expel members whose conduct was unbecoming a true Christian; the liturgical churches only expelled heretics. Creeds and formal theology declined in importance for the pietists; heresy was never a major concern. Denominational boundaries softened, and pietists frequently switched church membership, a process that would have excited great alarm had it become common among liturgicals. The pietists cooperated generously in numerous voluntary societies; they banded together to distribute Bibles, Christianize the world, abolish slavery, and enforce total abstinence.

Pietists struggled with liturgicals in every denomination. In most cases one group or the other secured the upper hand, driving the minority to silence, schism, or transfer to a more congenial denomination. . . .

Round after round of withdrawals and schisms, mostly reflecting pietistic-liturgical conflict, produced a remarkable proliferation of smaller denominations in America; by 1890 the Census Bureau counted no fewer than 143 bodies. These smaller groups (like the Holiness and Pentecostal sects) played no great role in midwestern politics, but their continual formation indicated that pietistic-liturgical tensions persisted well into the twentieth century.

The bridge linking theology and politics was the demand by pietists that the government remove the major obstacle to the purification of society through revivalistic Christianity, institutionalized immorality. Specifically, the midwestern pietists demanded Sunday blue laws, the abolition of saloons, and, in the prewar era, a check to the growth of slavery, or even its abolition. Many pietists, identifying the heavy influx of Catholic immigrants (especially the Irish) as the chief source of the corruption of politics and the decay of the cities, and ultimately as a barrier to the success of the revival movement, also supported nativist movements. The liturgicals, as a rule, opposed Sunday laws and prohibition, denounced abolitionists, and avoided nativist movements.

The church, they insisted, should attend to morality, not the government. Although they were no more pleased with the evils of drunkenness and saloons than the pietists, the liturgicals rarely supported total prohibition and never demanded total abstinence as many pietists did. Furthermore they never denounced slaveholders as sinners, though many agreed that slavery was an evil thing. The liturgicals saved their strong condemnations for the pietists—"fanatics" they always called them—and grew fearful that the pietists would capture control of the government to impose different standards of morality.

The liturgicals' fears were well grounded. Beginning in the 1820s and 1830s the pietists established a grass-roots network of reform societies that demanded governmental action against slavery and saloons. In the late 1830s the pietists renounced the concept that moderation in drinking was an acceptable social standard; they demanded total abstinence and total legal prohibition of the manufacture and sale of all alcoholic beverages, including wine and beer. (The condemnation of fermented wines, including communion wines, struck the liturgicals as unscriptural, antisacramental and anti-Christian.) The pietistic congregations fell into line, and in 1851 secured their first great triumph, total prohibition in the state of Maine. Immediately the tempo of reform quickened. Prohibition laws or constitutional amendments were enacted in Illinois and Ohio in 1851, Michigan in 1853, Iowa and Indiana in 1855; steadfast German opposition in Wisconsin in 1853 was all that prevented a complete sweep of the Midwest. In 1853, 1854, and 1855 the primary forces reshuffling party allegiances in the Midwest were the pietistic antiliquor, antislavery and anti-Catholic crusades. The Democratic party everywhere adopted the liturgical position, usually with some success, while a new Republican party emerged as the chief vehicle of pietistic reform. After 1855 the pietists largely abandoned temperance movements to concentrate on antislavery, while the Republican party backed away from nativist and dry platforms to permit a broadening of support among voters who were repulsed by pietistic crusaders.

After reading this selection, consider these questions:

1. Explain how specific issues, such as abolitionism and temperance, formed a bridge between religious convictions and political affiliation.

2. How does Jensen's ethno-cultural interpretation explain the intense party loyalty and high voter turnout characteristic of nineteenth-century politics?

3. Is the ethno-cultural interpretation adequate to explain party affiliation? Keep in mind that the Civil War was fought between the North and the South, not, for example, Protestants and Catholics.

SELECTION 2:

Andrew Jackson and the Nullification Crisis

Few politicians so dominate an era that they seem to personify the age. Andrew Jackson did. He led a tumultuous life and presided over a time of profound change. During his presidency, large numbers of Americans moved to the West, factories and mills grew up in the East, and elite rule gave way to popular democracy (limited, of course, to white males). As president, Jackson expanded the powers of the executive branch and asserted the dominance of the national government.

Robert V. Remini, who taught history for many years at the University of Illinois at Chicago, stands as perhaps the preeminent scholar of Jackson's life and presidency. In the following selection, Remini describes Jackson's response to one of the great crises of his presidency. When Congress passed a tariff in 1828 that protected Northern and Western interests, Southern states denounced it. South Carolina took the lead in opposing the so-called Tariff of Abominations. John C. Calhoun, a South Carolinian and the newly elected vice president, provided an intellectual basis for opposition. He argued that states had the right to nullify federal laws that violated the U.S. Constitution. Jackson, the new president, favored states' rights, but only within a strong and perpetual Union. This set the stage for a confrontation over the tariff and Calhoun's theory of nullification.

Excerpted from *Andrew Jackson,* by Robert V. Remini (New York: Perennial Library, 1969). Copyright © 1969 by Perennial Library. Reprinted with permission.

During the first years of his presidency, Jackson's own thinking about issues and policies tended to be neo-Jeffersonian and conservative, leaning toward States' rights and the economics of laissez faire, but fundamentally pragmatic in concept, and suffused with a strong sense of popular need. Later in his administration he edged closer to the notion of a strong central government, but as he moved he was invariably motivated by sheer political necessity. Consequently whenever there was disagreement between sections on practically any political issue, Jackson tended to equivocate and, where possible, to seek a compromise. . . .

There was [however,] no possible confusion over his intentions with respect to South Carolina and the problem of the tariff.

Trouble had been brewing for a long time. Southerners resented the tariff protection accorded northern industries because, among other things, it meant they had to buy their manufactured goods on a closed market, while they sold their cotton abroad on an open one. . . . Northerners, on the other hand, argued that they had to have government protection if they were to sustain themselves against competition from Europe, particularly Great Britain. Unfortunately the last tariff, which jacked up the rates as high as their manipulators could get them, was conceived solely as a vehicle for Jackson's election, but now that he was safely ensconced in the White House, Southerners expected him to haul the rates down again. Indeed, if he did not, some of them were ready to do it for him, using the nullification device suggested by John C. Calhoun. Acting on the request of James Hamilton, Jr., Calhoun further explained his doctrine of nullification in a statement dated July 26, 1831, which became known as the "Fort Hill Address." According to his view, the Union was a compact of states, in which each state retained the right to examine the acts of Congress, and when necessary nullify within its borders any it felt was a violation of its sovereignty and rights. . . . To his credit, he did not favor secession. Nothing so blunt and sudden. What he proposed was the slow but inevitable dissolution of the Union through long legal and constitutional procedures. However, Southerners never really cared for the slow process. They preferred the quick bang. They never lost their affection for secession even when they trifled with nullification.

The testing of these various attitudes and doctrines came with the introduction of a new tariff in Congress by Henry Clay on January 9, 1832. . . .

The President promptly snatched leadership of the tariff question away from Henry Clay—whose bill he mistrusted—by substituting another more to his liking. The southern "nullies" naturally prepared to resist any tariff, unless it completely capitulated to their terms, and just as naturally the President rejected their excessive terms. Instead, he tried to shape a bill which was satisfactory to the North and West without inflicting severe penalties on the South. What resulted was the Tariff [of] 1832. . . . Generally, the rates of the bill hovered near those imposed by the Tariff of 1824; and although it was not a low tariff, it did include several new items on the free list. Even so, high duties were again imposed on such political essentials as wool, woolens, iron, and hemp. Jackson signed the tariff on July 14, 1832, under the genuine conviction that it represented a compromise, one that would win approval in the North and quell the discontent in the South. Indeed, many Democrats and National Republicans applauded it as a reasonable and judicious "middle course," perhaps not wholly satisfactory to all, but one with which all sections and classes of the country could live.

This tariff reform, approaching sectional balance and accommodation, was totally unacceptable to the South Carolina Nullifiers. . . . [T]he governor of the state, James Hamilton, Jr., summoned a special session of the South Carolina legislature, which in turn called for the election of a convention to meet at Columbia on November 19, 1832, to take appropriate action.

As South Carolina sped toward nullification, possible disunion and civil war, the President countered with several effective actions. First he examined and prepared his military strength. . . . Yet none of these measures seemed sufficient to cool the hotheads gathered at Columbia, and on November 24, 1832, the convention, by a vote of 136 to 26, adopted an Ordinance of Nullification declaring the tariffs of 1828 and 1832 null and void and forbidding the collection of duties required by these laws within the state of South Carolina. Also it warned the federal government that if force were used to coerce the state, South Carolina would secede from the Union.

Jackson's reaction to this threat was masterful. He did not, as many contend, respond in a wild outburst of promises to scourge the state with violence unless it immediately capitulated and obeyed the tariff laws. He proceeded cautiously, trying to be conciliatory. Nevertheless, he would not be bullied, nor would he tolerate the humiliation of the country. What he did was alternate between the gesture of conciliation and the menace of retaliation. At one moment, he professed his willingness to forgive and grant concessions; at the next, he let it be known that he was preparing an army to put down treason. And it was this change of pace that threw the "nullies" completely off balance, weakening their resolve to experiment with the most extreme form of protest.

In implementing his approach, Jackson did several things at once. He encouraged Unionists within South Carolina . . . And, good to his word, he transported arms and ammunition a short distance away in North Carolina. Also, he sent George Breathitt, the brother of the governor of Kentucky, to South Carolina, ostensibly as a postal inspector but actually to serve as a liaison with the Unionists and to keep the President informed of developments lest they suddenly deteriorate to the point of secession and require vigorous action. Then, shifting his approach, Jackson delivered to Congress his annual message in which he urged a policy of conciliation. ". . . In justice," he wrote, ". . . the protection afforded by existing laws to any branches of the national industry should not exceed what may be necessary to counteract the regulations of foreign nations and to secure a supply of those articles of manufacture essential to the national independence and safety in time of war. If upon investigation it shall be found, as it is believed it will be, that the legislative protection granted to any particular interest is greater than is indispensably requisite for these objects, I recommend that it be gradually diminished, and that . . . the whole scheme of duties be reduced. . . ." Jackson ended by noticing the danger in South Carolina but ventured that the laws were sufficient to handle any

eventuality. Privately, he admitted something more was necessary. "The union . . . will now be tested by the support I get by the people," he wisely said. "I will die with the union."

Then, in a Proclamation dated December 10, President Jackson spoke directly to the people of South Carolina. In his message, he blended words of warning with entreaty, demand with understanding, threat with conciliation. He appealed to their fears, their pride, their interests; at the same time he categorically rejected nullification and secession. The nation was supreme, he said; not the states. "The laws of the United States must be executed. I have no discretionary power on the subject; my duty is emphatically pronounced in the Constitution. Those who told you that you might peaceably prevent their execution deceived you. . . . Their object is disunion. But be not deceived by names. Disunion by armed force is *treason*. Are you really ready to incur its guilt?". . .

The publication of the Proclamation produced a chorus of patriotic shouts around the country. Meetings were organized to express support of the President; parades and bonfires demonstrated the ardor of Americans to stand behind Jackson. Thus, the Proclamation not only rallied the people to the President's side, prompting state legislatures (including those in the South) to denounce nullification and assure the General of their loyalty, but it also warned the nullifiers that if they rejected a peaceful settlement he was quite prepared to summon an armed force to execute the laws. In this respect, Jackson quietly let it be known that he could have fifty thousand men inside South Carolina within forty days and another fifty thousand forty days after that. Then, in a public display of his intention, he asked Congress for the necessary legislation to permit him to insure obedience of the tariff laws in South Carolina and the collection of the custom duties. When introduced into Congress the Force Bill (or Bloody Bill as it was called by some) received widespread support on a nonpartisan and intersectional basis.

Precisely within a week after Jackson's annual message, South Carolina indicated a willingness to respond to reason. Indeed, even when the ordinance of Nullification was first adopted, it was apparent that a negotiated settlement was possible by the very fact that the date for the Ordinance to go into effect was advanced to February 1, 1833, giving the national government enough time to suggest an agreeable compromise. On December 10, the South Carolina legislature went further and elected as governor, Robert Y. Hayne, who was much more moderate on the nullification issue than his predecessor. Two days later, it elected John C. Calhoun U.S. Senator, thereby stationing the state's strongest bargainer inside the Congress to work out a settlement. Calhoun resigned the vice-presidency on December 28, 1832, to take his new office and begin the task of finding a consensus that would spare his state the humiliation of military defeat. . . .

Gratified by South Carolina's seeming efforts at moderation, Jackson quickly responded to show the state that any favorable move to avoid violence would be met with similar forbearance. . . . Meanwhile, the administration threw its full weight behind a new tariff bill, introduced by Gulian C. Verplanck of New York and written with the assistance of the Secretary of the Treasury, which would lower protection by 50 per cent within two years. The bill elicited strong support from many northerners worried about the possibility of secession and civil war. Unfortunately, protectionists howled their fears over such a sharp reduction of duties proposed by the Verplanck Bill. To make matters worse, Henry Clay tried to steer a land bill through Congress that would distribute revenue from the sale of land to the states, thus reducing the government's revenue and forcing it to raise the tariff. It was "mischievous" business, . . . completely unworthy of its author, but Clay had just been dealt a decisive defeat by Jackson in the presidential election of 1832, and he was bitter, angry, and resentful over his loss of prestige. Despite his nationalistic sentiments, he refused to assist the President in his efforts at compromise. Instead, he plotted to scuttle any legitimate accommodation of the tariff question. He seemed more worried by Jackson's triumphs and popularity than South Carolina's defiance of law. To strengthen his tactical position in Congress, therefore, he concluded an alliance with Senator Calhoun on the assumption that such a coalition would operate to their mutual benefit and the President's discomfort. Working together, Clay and Calhoun would kill the Verplanck Bill and emasculate the Force Bill.

On February 12, 1833, Clay introduced into the Senate what was euphemistically called a "compromise" tariff. The bill provided for the reduction of rates over a ten-year period, at the end of which time, no duty would be higher than 20 per cent. But there was a joker buried in it: only the tiniest reductions would occur during the first years of the bill's operation, the major changes coming nine years later at the tail end of the period. And, as it turned out, they would prove so sharp a drop as to threaten the economy of the country. It was a bad law, written without regard to compromise, and done for political advantage and the caressing of Clay's *amour propre*. However, if it could extinguish the fires of nullification and disunion the administration would go along with it, however apparent the bill's defects. The measure passed the Senate on March 1 by a vote of 29 to 16, and the House on February 26 by a vote of 119 to 85. Almost all the South voted to accept it—the Congressmen literally falling over themselves to agree to any solution that would end the dispute and the possibility of civil war. New England and some of the Middle Atlantic states tended to vote against the bill, while the Northwest was split. That the passage of the Compromise Tariff of 1833 should be due almost entirely to the massive support it received from the South proved to some men how ridiculous politics could be.

While the tariff hared its way through Congress, the Force Bill was brought up for debate. Calhoun denounced the measure, finding it a suitable occasion to reargue his interpretation of the nature of the Union. He made a final effort to kill the bill by forcing an adjournment, but the Congress, conscious of the meaning of compromise, vetoed this maneuver. When the vote on the Force Bill was taken in the Senate, Calhoun and his followers strode out of the chamber. Only John Tyler of Virginia remained in his seat to cast the single vote against the bill. Reluctantly, Clay voiced approval of the measure during the debate, but on the day of the final vote he failed to appear, claiming poor health and the need to stay home and rest. The bill passed the House on March 1 by a vote of 149 to 48.

With great pride, Jackson signed both the Compromise Tariff and the Force Bill on March 2, 1833, just as his first term in office ended. South Carolina reassembled its convention on March 11 and repealed its nullification of the tariff laws but then proceeded to nullify the Force Bill. It was a pathetic gesture to save face, and the President chose not to quarrel with that.

Jackson's victory was an extraordinary display of tact and rare wisdom. He did not gain a total victory over South Carolina, nor did he want one. In politics total victory usually means eventual defeat. What he did was spare the Union the agony of civil conflict. He accomplished it not by waging war but by initiating compromise. . . . Through the careful use of presidential powers, rallying the people to his side, alerting the military, offering compromise while preparing for

treason, he preserved the Union and upheld the supremacy of federal law.

After reading this selection, consider these questions:

1. Thomas Jefferson believed in states' rights and a strict construction of the Constitution. Nevertheless, as president he purchased Louisiana in spite of a lack of clear constitutional authority to do so. Although less committed to the principle than Jefferson, Andrew Jackson also believed in states' rights. As president he asserted federal supremacy during the nullification crisis. How might one account for Jackson's position?

2. Particularly for his role in forging the Compromise of 1820 and the Compromise of 1850, Henry Clay was known as "the Great Compromiser." Discuss Robert Remini's account of the role Clay played during the nullification crisis in that context.

SELECTION 3:

Veto of the Maysville Road Bill

The role of the national government in the economy has always been a source of disagreement. The question of whether the federal government should support internal improvements (the building of roads, canals, bridges, and so on) provoked bitter disagreement in Jacksonian America. The National Republicans and later the Whigs, led by Henry Clay and Daniel Webster, generally favored federally supported internal improvements. Democrats, as a rule, opposed them. Jackson took a deliberately ambiguous position on the issue. However, he vetoed a bill providing for construction of a stretch of highway in Kentucky between Maysville and Lexington. Supporters of the road maintained that it would form an extension of the National Road and was therefore not local in character. In his veto message, excerpted below, Jackson took the position that the proposed road ran entirely within one state and was therefore unconstitutional. Beyond that, however, he rejected in general terms the constitu-

tionality of federal support for internal improvements. In spite of that, Jackson later approved several bills providing for federal assistance to internal improvements. The fact that the Maysville Road ran through the home state of a political enemy, Henry Clay, did not escape Jackson's notice. Thus, Jackson's actions did not always match his great statements of political principle.

T*o the House of Representatives.*

Gentlemen: I have maturely considered the bill proposing to authorize "a subscription of stock in the Maysville, Washington, Paris, and Lexington Turnpike Road Company," and now return the same to the House of Representatives, in which it originated, with my objections to its passage. . . .

The bill before me does not call for a more definite opinion upon the particular circumstances which will warrant appropriations of money by Congress to aid works of internal improvement, for although the extension of the power to apply money beyond that of carrying into effect the object for which it is appropriated has, as we have seen, been long claimed and exercised by the Federal Government, yet such grants have always been professedly under the control of the general principle that the works which might be thus aided should be "of a general, not local, national, not State," character. A disregard of this distinction would of necessity lead to the subversion of the federal system. That even this is an unsafe one, arbitrary in its nature, and liable, consequently, to great abuses, is too obvious to require the confirmation of experience. It is, however, sufficiently definite and imperative to my mind to forbid my approbation of any bill having the character of the one under consideration. I have given to its provisions all the reflection demanded by a just regard for the interests of those of our fellow-citizens who have desired its passage, and by the respect which is due to a coördinate branch of the Government, but I am not able to view it in any other light than as a measure of purely local character; or, if it can

be considered national, that no further distinction between the appropriate duties of the General and State Governments need be attempted, for there can be no local interest that may not with equal propriety be denominated national. It has no connection with any established system of improvements; is exclusively within the limits of a State, starting at a point on the Ohio River and running out 60 miles to an interior town and even as far as the State is interested conferring partial instead of general advantages. . . .

In the other view of the subject, and the only remaining one which it is my intention to present at this time, is involved the expediency of embarking on a system of internal improvement without a previous amendment of the Constitution explaining and defining the precise powers of the Federal Government over it. Assuming the right to appropriate money to aid in the construction of national works to be warranted by the contemporaneous and continued exposition of the Constitution, its insufficiency for the successful prosecution of them must be admitted by all candid minds. If we look to usage to define the extent of the right, that will be found so variant and embracing so much that has been overruled as to involve the whole subject in great uncertainty and to render the execution of our respective duties in relation to it replete with difficulty and embarrassment. It is in regard to such works and the acquisition of additional territory that the practice obtained its first footing. In most, if not all, other disputed questions of appropriation the construction of the Constitution may be regarded as unsettled if the right to apply money in the enumerated cases is placed on the ground of usage. . . .

If it be the wish of the people that the construction of roads and canals should be conducted by the Federal Government, it is not only highly expedient, but indispensably necessary, that a previous

Excerpted from *A Compilation of the Messages and Papers of the Presidents, 1789–1908,* by James D. Richardson (New York: Bureau of National Literature, 1897).

amendment of the Constitution, delegating the necessary power and defining and restricting its exercise with reference to the sovereignty of the States, should be made. Without it nothing extensively useful can be effected. The right to exercise as much jurisdiction as is necessary to preserve the works and to raise funds by the collection of tolls to keep them in repair can not be dispensed with.

After reading this selection, consider these questions:

1. In what ways would federal assistance to internal improvements have impinged on states' rights?

2. Other than his stated objections to the bill, what considerations seem to have influenced Jackson's decision to veto the measure?

SELECTION 4:

In Defense of the American System

After the War of 1812, in an attempt to reconcile competing sectional interests, Henry Clay proposed his American System, an ambitious plan for national development undertaken at the expense of the federal government. The American System included a national bank, public works, and protective tariffs. Designed to protect infant industries, tariffs formed a central feature of Clay's system. Clay defended protective tariffs in the name of the benefits manufacturing offered to society as a whole. Moreover, he maintained that if the United States remained an agricultural country, it would inevitably become a commercial colony of Great Britain.

Clay was one of the most important public figures of the first half of the nineteenth century and one of its great orators. In addition to serving for many years in the House and the Senate, he ran for the presidency three times and came close twice. Although Clay never won the White House, Congress enacted many of his proposals in the dozen years before 1828. As Robert V. Remini's article in this chapter notes, the Tariff of 1828 generated considerable opposition in the South. Responding to Southern criticism, Clay proposed a new tariff in 1832. In the following excerpt, Clay defends the achievements of his American System and protective tariffs.

Excerpted from *The Power of Words: Documents in American History,* edited by T.H. Breen (New York: HarperCollins College Publishers, 1996).

I have now to perform the more pleasing task of exhibiting an imperfect sketch of the existing state of the unparalleled prosperity of the country. On a general survey, we behold cultivation extended, the arts flourishing, the face of the country improved; our people fully and profitably employed, and the public countenance exhibiting tranquility, contentment and happiness. And if we descend into particulars, we have the agreeable contemplation of a people out of debt, land rising slowly in value, but in a secure and salutary degree; a ready though not extravagant market for all the surplus productions of our industry; innumerable flocks and herds browsing and gamboling on ten thousand hills and plains, covered with rich and verdant grasses; our cities expanded, and whole villages springing up, as it were, by enchantment; our exports and imports increased and increasing; our tonnage, foreign and coastwise, swelling and fully occupied; the rivers of our interior animated by the perpetual thunder and lightning of countless steam-boats; the currency sound and abundant; the public debt of two wars nearly redeemed; and, to crown all, the public treasury overflowing, embarrassing Congress, not to find subjects of taxation, but to select the objects which shall be liberated from the impost. If the term of seven years were to be selected, of the greatest prosperity which this people have enjoyed since the establishment of their present constitution, it would be exactly that period of seven years which immediately followed the passage of the tariff of 1824.

This transformation of the condition of the country from gloom and distress to brightness and prosperity, has been mainly the work of American legislation, fostering American industry, instead of allowing it to be controlled by foreign legislation, cherishing foreign industry. . . .

If the system of protection be founded on principles erroneous in theory, pernicious in practice—above all if it be unconstitutional, as is alledged, it ought to be forthwith abolished, and not a vestage of it suffered to remain. But, before we sanction this sweeping denunciation, let us look a little at this system, its magnitude, its ramifications, its duration, and the high authorities which have sustained it. We shall see that its foes will have accomplished comparatively nothing, after having achieved their present aim of breaking down our iron-founderies, our woollen, cotton, and hemp manufactories, and our sugar plantations. The destruction of these would, undoubtedly, lead to the sacrifice of immense capital, the ruin of many thousands of our fellow citizens, and incalculable loss to the whole community. But their prostration would not disfigure, nor produce greater effect upon the *whole* system of protection, in all its branches, than the destruction of the beautiful domes upon the capitol would occasion to the magnificent edifice which they surmount. Why, sir, there is scarcely an interest, scarcely a vocation in society, which is not embraced by the beneficence of this system.

It comprehends our coasting tonnage and trade, from which all foreign tonnage is absolutely excluded.

It includes all our foreign tonnage, with the inconsiderable exception made by the treaties of reciprocity with a few foreign powers.

It embraces our fisheries, and all our hardy and enterprising fishermen.

It extends to almost every mechanic and: to tanners, cordwainers, tailors, cabinet-makers, hatters, tinners, brass-workers, clock-makers, coach-makers, tallow-chandlers, trace-makers, rope-makers, cork-cutters, tobacconists, whip-makers, paper-makers, umbrella-makers, glass-blowers, stocking-weavers, butter-makers, saddle and harness-makers, cutlers, brush-makers, book-binders, dairy-men, milk-farmers, black-smiths, type-founders, musical instrument-makers, basket-makers, milliners, potters, chocolate-makers, floor- cloth-makers, bonnet-makers, hair-cloth-makers, copper-smiths, pencil-makers, bellows-makers, pocket book-makers, card-makers, glue-makers, mustard-makers, lumber-sawyers, saw-makers, scale-beam-makers, scythe-makers, wood-saw-makers, and many others. The mechanics enumerated, enjoy a measure of protection adapted to their several conditions, varying from twenty to fifty per cent. . . .

It extends to all lower Louisiana, the Delta of which might as well be submerged again in the Gulf of Mexico, from which it has been a gradual conquest, as now to be deprived of the protecting duty upon is great staple.

It effects the cotton planter himself, and the tobacco planter, both of whom enjoy protection.

The total amount of the capital vested in sheep, the land to sustain them, wool, woollen manufacturers, and woollen fabrics, and the subsistence of the various persons directly or indirectly employed in the growth and manufacture of the article of wool, is estimated at one hundred and sixty-seven millions of dollars, and the number of persons at one hundred and fifty thousand.

The value of iron, considered as a raw material, and of its manufacturers, is estimated at twenty-six millions of dollars per annum. Cotton goods, exclusive of the capital vested in the manufacture, and of the cost of the raw material, are believed to amount annually, to about twenty millions of dollars. . . .

When gentlemen have succeeded in their design of an immediate or gradual destruction of the American System, what is their substitute? Free trade? Free trade! The call for free trade is as unavailing as the cry of a spoiled child, in its nurse's arms, for the moon, or the stars that glitter in the firmament of heaven. It never has existed, it never will exist. Trade implies, at least two parties. To be free, it should be fair, equal and reciprocal. But if we throw our ports wide open to the admission of foreign productions, free of all duty, what ports of any other foreign nation shall we find open to the free admission of our surplus produce? We may break down all barriers to free trade on our part, but the work will not be complete until foreign powers shall have removed theirs. There would be freedom on one side, and restrictions, prohibitions and exclusions on the other. The bolts, and the bars, and the chains of all other nations will remain undisturbed. . . .

Gentlemen deceive themselves. It is not free trade that they are recommending to our acceptance. It is in effect, the British colonial system that we are invited to adopt, and, if their policy prevail, it will lead substantially to the recolonization of these States, under the commercial dominion of Great Britain.

After reading this selection, consider these questions:

1. How does Clay make the case that all sections have benefited from the American System?

2. What is Clay's objection to free trade?

3. Why does Clay assert that free trade would lead to "the commercial dominion of Great Britain"?

SELECTION 5:

Charles River Bridge v. Warren Bridge

When Chief Justice John Marshall died in 1835, Andrew Jackson appointed Roger Taney of Maryland to replace him. A loyal member of Jackson's cabinet, Taney took his seat on the nation's highest court in 1836. The new chief justice wrote the opinion for the Court in an important and highly contentious case, Charles River Bridge v. Warren Bridge (1837).

The Massachusetts legislature granted a charter to the Charles River Bridge Company in 1785 to build a bridge over the Charles River con-

necting Boston and Cambridge. The legislature also granted the company the right to collect tolls for forty years and later extended the right to collect tolls to seventy years. As Boston grew, the bridge became increasingly congested.

In 1828 the legislature gave a charter to the Warren Bridge Company to build a bridge close to the Charles River Bridge and authorized it to charge tolls for six years (long enough to pay for construction and a fixed profit). After that, the bridge would revert to the state and would be toll free.

The Charles River Bridge Company argued that the wording of the original charter implicitly conferred a monopoly that the new bridge would encroach on, thereby violating the contract clause of the U.S. Constitution. The Warren Bridge Company maintained that the legislature was responding to a public need and that the old bridge had paid for itself several times over. Further, if every aging turnpike or canal company could assert claims of an implied monopoly, they could effectively block new means of transportation, like the railroad.

In rejecting the arguments of the Charles River Bridge Company, Taney established the rule that no right or privilege held by the public could be deemed to be granted away by implication. The legislature granted a charter to build a bridge and collect tolls. It did not expressly grant a monopoly. Thus, even though construction of the Warren Bridge would destroy the income of the first bridge, granting a charter for the Warren Bridge did not violate the state's contract with the Charles River Bridge.

The case raised some of the most central political and economic issues of the age of Jackson. The following document is an excerpt from Taney's opinion.

The plaintiffs in error insist . . . the legislature of Massachusetts, of 1785 and 1792, by their true construction, necessarily implied, that the legislature would not authorize another bridge, and especially, a free one, by the side of this, and placed in the same line of travel, whereby the franchise granted to the "Proprietors of the Charles River Bridge" should be rendered of no value; and the plaintiffs in error contend; that the grant of . . . the charter to the proprietors of the bridge, [is a] contract on the part of the state; and that the law authorizing the erection of the Warren bridge in 1828, impairs the obligation of . . . [this] contract. . . .

This brings us to the act of the legislature of Massachusetts, of 1785, by which the plaintiffs were incorporated by the name of "The Proprietors of the Charles River Bridge;" and it is here, and in the law of 1792, prolonging their charter, that we must look for the extent and nature of the franchise conferred upon the plaintiffs. Much has been said in the argument of the principles of construction by which this law is to be expounded, and what undertakings, on the part of the state, may be implied. The court think there can be no serious difficulty on that head. It is the grant of certain franchises, by the public, to a private corporation, and in a matter where the public interest is concerned. The rule of construction in such cases is well settled, both in England, and by the decisions of our own tribunals. . . . The rule of construction in all such cases, is now fully established to be this—that any ambiguity in the terms of the contract, must operate against the adventurers, and in favor of the public, and the plaintiffs can claim nothing that is not clearly given them by the act. . . .

Excerpted from *Reports of Cases Argued and Adjudged in the Supreme Court of the United States, January Term 1837,* edited by Frederick C. Brightly (New York: Banks & Brothers, 1884).

The object and end of all government is to promote the happiness and prosperity of the community by which it is established; and it can never be assumed, that the government intended to diminish its power of accomplishing the end for which it was created. And in a country like ours, free, active and enterprising, continually advancing in numbers and wealth, new channels of communication are daily found necessary, both for travel and trade, and are essential to the comfort, convenience and prosperity of the people. A state ought never to be presumed to surrender this power, because, like the taxing power, the whole community have an interest in preserving it undiminished. And when a corporation alleges, that a state has surrendered, for seventy years, its power of improvement and public accommodation, in a great and important line of travel, along which a vast number of its citizens must daily pass, the community have a right to insist . . . "that its abandonment ought not to be presumed, in a case, in which the deliberate purpose of the state to abandon it does not appear." The continued existence of a government would be of no great value, if, by implications and presumptions, it was disarmed of the powers necessary to accomplish the ends of its creation, and the functions it was designed to perform, transferred to the hands of privileged corporations. . . . No one will question, that the interests of the great body of the people of the state, would, in this instance, be affected by the surrender of this great line of travel to a single corporation, with the right to exact toll, and exclude competition, for seventy years. While the rights of private property are sacredly guarded, we must not forget, that the community also have rights, and that the happiness and well-being of every citizen depends on their faithful preservation. . . .

The judgment of the supreme judicial court of the commonwealth of Massachusetts, dismissing the plaintiffs' bill, must, therefore, be affirmed, with costs.

After reading this selection, consider these questions:

1. What public policy was Taney trying to further?

2. How did Taney balance public interest and private property?

3. Historians have characterized Jacksonian Democracy as an era of men on the make. In what ways does Taney's opinion reflect that?

CHAPTER 14

Antebellum Reform

Few events had as much influence on the nineteenth century as the wave of religious revivals known as the Second Great Awakening. The revivals affected every section of the country and virtually every area of American life. The Second Great Awakening began in the 1790s in the Congregational churches of New England. It had its greatest impact, however, on the frontier, where churches had traditionally been weak. The camp meeting became a fixture of western life. Religious revivals also exerted a profound influence in the South. The religion preached at these revivals stressed salvation through personal faith. Calvinist emphasis on original sin and the essentially sinful nature of human beings gave way to a belief that a willingness to be saved could assure salvation.

The social upheaval caused by the market revolution increased the appeal of revivalism. Rapid economic development and the rise of cities brought in their wake crime, drunkenness, and prostitution. People, particularly the middle class, were horrified by these social consequences of the changing economy.

This social unrest combined with revivalism and the belief in the perfectibility of human beings (and therefore human society) to generate a powerful drive for social reform. The impulse toward perfectionism took many forms, including millenarian churches, utopian communities, abolitionism, Sabbatarianism, temperance, feminism, penal reform, crusades against vice, and the establishment of institutions for dealing with social problems (asylums, orphanages, etc.). The reform impulse pervaded all aspects of American life, as Americans sought to perfect their society and bring on the millennium.

After reading this chapter, consider these questions:

1. What were the links between social change and religious conversion?

2. How did commitment to evangelical religion lead to reform?

3. What was the nature of antebellum reform?

SELECTION 1:

Religious Revival and Reform

The rise of the factory system, settlement of the Ohio Valley, the expansion of cotton production and the plantation system into Alabama and Mississippi, and the construction of roads and canals combined to produce rapid economic growth by the 1830s. Prosperity, however, came with a cost. The profound social changes that drove the economic boom undermined social order and traditional institutions. Respectable Americans viewed with alarm an increasing incidence of drunkenness, prostitution, violations of the Sabbath, crime, and pauperism. They observed with equal alarm the decline of paternal authority and traditional family structures. The religious revivals of the early nineteenth century, known as the Second Great Awakening, represented a response to the social upheaval that came with booming prosperity. The revivals, in turn, spawned a series of social reforms, including temperance, abolitionism, Sabbatarianism, feminism, and penal reform, to name a few.

Nowhere was the force of social change felt more powerfully than Rochester, New York, and nowhere did the flames of religious revival burn with more heat. Charles Grandison Finney, a lawyer from Utica, New York, experienced a conversion in 1821. He held a series of revival meetings in towns along the Erie Canal beginning in 1825. The canal had recently brought the market revolution and its accompanying social dislocations to these towns. By 1830, Finney was famous, and the leaders of Rochester, New York, invited him to preach in their town. Rochester was a new city created by the commercialization of agriculture and the building of the Erie Canal. To many people in Rochester of 1830, men seemed more concerned with making money than with salvation; alcohol threatened family life, economic advancement, and the hope of social progress; politics had descended into a morass of corruption. Finney preached daily for six months and dominated the activities and conversation of the town.

In the following selection, Susan H. Armitage, a professor of history at Washington State University, describes the relationship between revivalism and reform.

The problems of America's urban centers, though slow to be solved, were not ignored. The passion for "improvement" that was such an important part of the new middle-class thinking was focused on the nation's cities. Indeed it seemed that most middle-class Americans shared a belief in progress and in the perfectibility of individuals as well as society, and that a great number of them were active members of associations devoted to social reform. The widespread movements engendered by these organizations made the period 1825–45 one of the most vibrant in . . . American history. . . .

The first response to the dislocations caused by the Market Revolution was local and voluntary. Associations of people who believed in individual reform tried to deal with the major social changes of the day. The reform message, begun by word of mouth, was vastly amplified by inventions such as the steam printing press, which made mass publication possible. Soon there were national networks of reform groups.

Alexis de Tocqueville remarked upon the vast extent of voluntary associations and their many purposes: "In no country in the world," he noted, "has the principle of association been more successfully used, or more unsparingly applied to a multitude of different objects, than in America." The widespread reform movements of the era depended on the energy and hope of communities of like-minded people.

Evangelical religion was fundamental to social reform. The Second Great Awakening, which began in the 1790s, spread to the North in the 1820s in a wave of urban revivals. Men and women who had been converted to the enthusiastic new faith assumed personal responsibility for making changes in their own lives. It was only a short step from reforming their own behavior to reforming society as a whole. These converts were encouraged in their social activism by such leading revivalists as Charles Finney. Finney preached a doctrine of "perfectionism," claiming it was possible for all Christians to personally understand and live by God's will and thereby become "as perfect as God." Furthermore, Finney predicted, "the complete reformation of the whole world" could be achieved if only enough converts put their efforts into moral reform. This new religious feeling was intensely hopeful: Members of evangelistic religions really did expect to convert the world and create the perfect moral and religious community on earth.

Much of America was swept by the fervor of moralistic reform, whether through appeals to individual conscience in revivals such as Finney's or by aggressive charity work. The agenda for reform was set by the new middle class, which applied new notions of morality to the movement.

The reforms all shared certain characteristics that were related to the social changes of the time. First of all, they arose from the recognition that the traditional methods of small-scale local relief were no longer adequate. In colonial times, families (sometimes at the request of local government) had housed and cared for the ill or incapacitated. Small local almshouses and prisons had housed the poor and the criminal. Reformers now realized that large cities had to make large-scale provisions for social misfits, and that institutional rather than private efforts were needed. This thinking was especially true of the institutional reform movements that began in the 1830s, such as the push for insane asylums.

A second aspect of reform efforts was a belief in the basic goodness of human nature. All reformers believed that the unfortunate—the poor, the insane, the criminal—would be reformed, or at least improved, in a good environment. Thus insane asylums were built in rural areas, away from the noise and stress of the cities, and orphanages had strict rules that were meant to encourage discipline and self-reliance. Prison reform carried this sentiment to the extreme. On the theory that bad social influences were largely responsible for crime, some "model" prisons completely isolated prisoners from one another, making them eat, sleep, work, and do their required Bible reading in their own cells. The failure of these prisons to achieve dramatic changes in their inmates (a number of isolated prisoners went mad, and some committed suicide) or to reduce the incidence of crime was one of the first indications that perhaps reform was not so simple after all!

A third characteristic of the reform movements was their moralistic dogmatism. Reformers knew what was right, and were determined to see their improvements enacted. As one historian has recently remarked, it is a very short step from individual self-discipline to imposing control on others. These reforms, then, were measures of *social control*. Lazy, sinful, intemperate, or unfit members of society were to be reformed for their own good, whether they wanted to be or not. This attitude was bound to cause controversy; by no means were all Americans members of reform groups, nor did many take kindly to being objects of reform.

Indeed, some aspects of the social reform movements were harmful. The intense religious feeling of the revival movement helped to foster the hostility experienced by Catholic immigrants from Ireland and Germany beginning in the 1830s. The temperance movement targeted immigrants whose drinking habits were freer than those of most older inhabitants. In these and other examples, reformers wished to enforce uniformity of behavior rather than tolerance. Thus social reform helped to foster the virulent nativism of American politics in the period 1840–60.

The extent of reform efforts was unprecedented. Regional and national organizations quickly grew from local efforts to deal with social problems such as drinking, prostitution, mental illness, and crime. As one example, in 1828 Congregationalist minister Lyman Beecher joined other ministers in forming a General Union for Promoting the Observance of the Christian Sabbath; the aim was to prevent business on Sundays. To achieve its goals, the General Union adopted the same methods used by political parties: lobbying, petition drives, fundraising, and special publications. This and other efforts, Beecher said, were all for the purpose of establishing "the moral government of God."

In effect, the sabbath reformers engaged in political action but remained aloof from direct electoral politics, stressing their religious mission. In any case, their goal was controversial. Workingmen (who usually worked six days a week) were angered when the General Union forced the Sunday closure of their favorite taverns, and were quick to vote against the Whigs, the party most sympathetic to reform thinking. Other reforms likewise muddied the distinction between political and social activity. It is not surprising that women, who were barred from electoral politics but not from moral and social activism, were major supporters of reform.

After reading this selection, consider these questions:

1. What connections can be drawn between Finney's doctrine of "perfectionism" and social reform?

2. What virtues do the reforms that grew out of the revivals advocate? How do these virtues relate to the social changes under way?

SELECTION 2:

Sylvester Graham and Dietary Reform

As noted in the introduction to this chapter, the impulse toward perfectionism took a variety of forms. Among the most interesting manifestations was the movement to reform the American diet. Food reformers attacked the American propensity to eat too much and to consume too much alcohol. Some sounded positively modern in their assault on fried food and on the bulging waistlines of their countrymen. Others focused on Americans' taste for "condiments." These critics argued that mustard, the hot red *peppers native to America, and imported black pepper excited the appetite to an unnatural degree and inhibited the effects of chewing and digestion. One of the most colorful of the food reformers was Sylvester Graham, father of the graham cracker. In the following excerpt, Harvey Green, deputy director for interpretation at the Strong Museum in Rochester, New York, describes the connection between dietary reform and social improvement.*

Reformers connected bad eating habits and social disorder precisely because they viewed the world, the human body, and any efforts at reforming or reshaping them as part of one organic whole. Morality and health as well as physical strength and mental stability were all linked, in the end, to both the nation's future and the fate of each Americans' soul at Judgment. The fear that the "passions" would become uncontrollable and find their expression in crime, in overt sexuality, or even in revolt against the government was ever present in America in the antebellum era. Clerical and lay writers warned that cities could become "volcanoes," ready to erupt in violence. The "passions" of unregenerate men and women and, for conservative ministers, even of those whose religious conversion was borne of the emotional embrace of grace, were an obstruction to the establishment of the good society. . . .

Sylvester Graham was Jacksonian America's most famous and unrelenting advocate of a vegetarian diet. Vegetarianism had been analyzed and discussed for decades before 1830. . . .

The debate about vegetarianism intensified in the broader context of reform and criticism that swept the nation during the thirty years before the Civil War. In 1829 the *Journal of Health* defended a primarily vegetarian diet, characteristically comparing American eating habits with those of apparently healthier (and poorer) cultures. Asian and Irish nationals were cited as examples of healthy peoples, and "the Lazzaroni of Naples, with forms so active and finely proportioned, [eat] coarse bread and potatoes . . . [and] a glass of iced water slightly acidilated." Throughout the

period, popular magazines and books contrasted the allegedly superior health and strength of nearly vegetarian peasant cultures (none of which had yet emigrated to the United States) with the less healthy meat and fat eaters of the far North (Eskimos and Laplanders) and with the mixed diets of northern Europeans. In 1856, [Catharine] Beecher continued this trend, suggesting a connection between working with one's hands, poverty, a vegetarian diet, and good health.

> The working people in Ireland live on potatoes. The peasantry of Lancashire and Cheshire, who are the handsomest race in England, live chiefly on potatoes and buttermilk. The bright and hardy Arabs live almost entirely on vegetable food. The brave and vigorous Spartans never ate meat. Most of the hardiest soldiers in Northern Europe seldom taste of meat. . . . Except in America, it is rare that the strongest laborers eat any meat.

The romantic celebration of the peasantry—with their strong backs, long lives, and (assumedly) happy lot—is a variant of the Edenic myth, a "state of nature" in which men and women lived innocently, peacefully, and healthily with one another and among the flora and fauna. This implicit critique of urbanized middle-class and wealthy living remains on safe ground: The working classes are portrayed as beneficiaries of their lot, which was not a vale of tears but an insurance of health. For the wealthy this myth implied that they need only adopt a proper diet to maintain their health and need not worry about the material well-being of the working class. . . .

Unlike Graham, Beecher did not argue for a strictly vegetarian diet. She allowed that when people "from any cause, need to be not only nourished but *stimulated* by food, then animal food is the best." For most Americans, however,

Excerpted from *Fit for America: Health, Fitness, Sport, and American Society,* by Harvey Green (New York: Pantheon Books, 1986). Copyright © 1986 by Pantheon Books. Reprinted with permission.

stimulation was unnecessary and potentially dangerous. Physicians were for the most part opposed to vegetarianism in the early nineteenth century because they were convinced that vegetable foods were more difficult to digest than meats, fowl, or fish, and that meats were essential to strength and vitality because they were most like human flesh. Even vegetarianism's most strident opponents warned against eating too much meat, however, since it might lead to "plethora" and excess of blood. The radical vegetarians—[Russell Thatcher] Trall, fellow water-curist Joel Shew, and others—argued that "internal putrefaction" resulted whenever meat was consumed. . . . Trall posited a link between blood that had been rendered impure by decayed meats or stimulants. In this sense he was repeating an idea expressed in the 1830s by Graham, who was convinced that disease originated in the disruption of the "vital spirit" caused by stomach disorders, which in turn affected the nervous system.

While vegetarianism was hardly common before (or after) 1830, it was widely discussed in the context of the debates about temperance, criminal reform, abolitionism, and the rights of women. Sylvester Graham stood at the center of the debate, at least in the 1830s and 1840s. Born in 1794, Graham was the seventeenth child of a family that lost its father within two years of his birth. His mother soon afterward became "deranged," and Graham himself was afflicted with tuberculosis in 1810. He recovered, only to suffer a nervous breakdown in 1823, the year he enrolled at Amherst College. In 1828 he entered the ministry, leaving the cloth two years later to participate in the temperance crusade as a general agent for the Pennsylvania Temperance Society in Philadelphia. There he read about anatomy, physiology, and dietetics, research he synthesized into an overall "Science of Human Life." He lectured at Philadelphia's Franklin Institute, and although he was a popular speaker, he remained a minor public figure until 1832, when the cholera epidemic catapulted him to prominence. Cholera attacked the gastrointestinal tract, and Graham posited that overstimulation of the digestive tract by the liquor, spices, and fats that Americans loved to consume had weakened them. When several patients survived after adopting Graham's dietary regimen, he became an important national presence. . . .

While in New York, Graham founded a boarding house to be run strictly on the principles set forth in his works. The daily routine indicated both Graham's strict Protestant upbringing and his bent for protomilitary arrangements. "The morning bell," he wrote in 1837, "is rung precisely at five o'clock as one hour at least is necessary for bathing and exercise before breakfast." In winter, he generously allowed his boarders to rise at six. The lights were extinguished and the doors closed at ten P.M. A second Grahamite boarding house, established in Boston in 1837, attracted many of the area's political and social radicals, including abolitionists William Lloyd Garrison and Arthur Tappan. The Boston institution was run by David Cambell, a Garrisonian delegate to the New York Anti-Slavery Convention of 1833, which was instrumental in the formation of the American Anti-Slavery Society.

Graham's Boston activities provoked criticism from a broad popular base, including newspapermen, physicians, and bakers (whom he attacked for using chemical additives, superfine and even adulterated flour, and other shortcuts to enhance their "pecuniary interest" at the expense of public health). In 1838, the *Boston Courier* asked "what can surpass that which finds long life in starvation, sees 'moral reform' in bran and cabbage . . . and promises to revolutionize the world with johnny-cake and boiled beans . . . ? Reader, if you wish to preserve your health . . . *eat your victuals and go about your business."* The *Boston Medical and Surgical Journal* asserted that "a greater humbug or a more disgusting writer never lived."

Professional medical journals also engaged in the debate; the 1836 volume of the *Boston Medical and Surgical Journal* is full of charges and countercharges about the validity and safety of Graham's brand of vegetarianism. Accusations that Grahamism led to insanity provoked equally vehement denials and counterattacks from Graham, who linked dyspepsia and overstimulation to a meat-laden diet.

In the conglomeration of reform movements active in Boston in the 1830s, the rancor about Graham's views stemmed in part from his extremist position and his stern conviction that diet, debility, and sexuality were inextricably linked. Graham was convinced that masturbation was a great evil. This belief did not separate him from other critics and advisors of this time. (Henry Ward Beecher, William Alcott, and Timothy Shay Arthur—all prolific authors of advice for the young, old, and in-between—cautioned against the "solitary vice.") But Graham was almost obsessive about the "problem," and his continual connection of diet to morality, and specifically to masturbation, led to his rapid isolation even in liberal Boston circles.

Graham moved from the hot controversies of Boston to the small-town atmosphere of Northampton, Massachusetts, in late 1837. His fame was such that even his adversaries in the *Boston Medical and Surgical Journal* had paid him a grudging compliment in 1836. "No man can travel by stage or steamboat, or go into any part of our country," the magazine asserted, "and begin to advocate a vegetable diet . . . without being immediately asked—'What. Are you a Grahamite?'" But if he was a famous man, Graham was not necessarily an effective one. Once in Northampton, he bombarded the local papers with letters, which were usually so full of self-importance that he became a caricature. . . .

After reading this selection, consider these questions:

1. What social problems did the advocacy of vegetarianism by Sylvester Graham and Catharine Beecher address?

2. In what ways does Graham's boardinghouse reflect Susan Armitage's analysis of reform?

SELECTION 3:

Brook Farm

Established on a farm of two hundred acres less than ten miles from Boston, Brook Farm was one of a number of utopian communities that grew out of the Second Great Awakening. All of these communities shared a belief in the perfectibility of human beings and societies. Many were reactions to the competitive nature of the new market economy. A number sought to transform the relationship between men and women.

In 1825 Robert Owen, a Scottish industrialist, founded the socialist community known as New Harmony on a site he purchased in Indiana. Another group, the Shakers, was an offshoot of Quakerism. By the 1830s the Shakers had established approximately twenty communities, each of which functioned as a large family. Shakers adopted communal ownership of property and a simple way of life. The residents practiced celibacy because they believed the millennium was close at hand and therefore saw no reason to reproduce. The Amana Community prospered in New York and Iowa in the 1840s and 1850s by developing manufacturing skills. John Humphrey Noyes's Oneida Community in Vermont practiced "complex marriage," in which every man in the group was married to every woman.

Brook Farm was the most famous of all of these communities. Founded by George Ripley and located in West Roxbury, the Brook Farm was an attempt to apply the ideas of American transcendentalism to everyday life. The residents, who never numbered more than two hundred people, supported themselves through farming, the manufacture of clothing, and teaching. Brook Farm attracted so much attention because of the celebrity of some of its residents, even though many stayed there only a brief time. The best known of these was Nathaniel Hawthorne, who based his novel The Blithedale Romance *on his experiences at Brook Farm.*

Three years after its founding, the community changed some of its principles to follow the philosophy of Charles Fourier. A French socialist thinker, Fourier urged the establishment of cooperative communities called phalanxes, each of which was to be set up as a joint stock company. Profits would be divided according to several factors, including the amount of money members had initially invested, their skill, and their labor. A fire destroyed the community's main building in 1847. Not long after, the community, which was already heavily in debt, disbanded.

A teacher and lecturer as well as a confidante of several leading transcendentalist writers, Elizabeth Palmer Peabody opened a book shop in Boston that became a center for literary and reform activities. The Dial, *the leading transcendentalist journal, was published from there. In the following document, originally published in the* Dial, *Peabody explains the ideas behind Brook Farm.*

A few individuals, who, unknown to each other, under different disciplines of life, reacting from different social evils, but aiming at the same object,—of being wholly true to their natures as men and women; have been made acquainted with one another, and have determined to become the Faculty of the Embryo University.

In order to live a religious and moral life worthy the name, they feel it is necessary to come out in some degree from the world, and to form themselves into a community of property, so far as to exclude competition and the ordinary rules of trade;—while they reserve sufficient private property, or the means of obtaining it, for all purposes of independence, and isolation at will. They have bought a farm, in order to make agriculture the basis of their life, it being the most direct and simple in relation to nature.

A true life, although it aims beyond the highest star, is redolent of the healthy earth. The perfume of clover lingers about it. The lowing of cattle is the natural bass to the melody of human voices.

On the other hand, what absurdity can be imagined greater than the institution of cities? They originated not in love, but in war. It was war that drove men together in multitudes, and compelled them to stand so close, and build walls around them. This crowded condition produced wants of an unnatural character, which resulted in occupations that regenerated the evil, by creating artificial wants. . . .

The plan of the Community, as an Economy, is in brief this: for all who have property to take stock, and receive a fixed interest thereon; then to keep house or board in commons, as they shall severally desire, at the cost of provisions purchased at wholesale, or raised on the farm; and for all to labor in community, and be paid at a certain rate an hour, choosing their own number of hours, and their own kind of work. With the results of this labor, and their interest, they are to pay their board, and also purchase whatever

Excerpted from "Plan of Brook Farm," by Elizabeth Palmer Peabody, *Dial,* January 1842.

else they require at cost, at the warehouses of the Community, which are to be filled by the Community as such. To perfect this economy, in the course of time they must have all trades, and all modes of business carried on among themselves, from the lowest mechanical trade, which contributes to the health and comfort of life, to the finest art which adorns it with food or drapery for the mind.

All labor, whether bodily or intellectual, is to be paid at the same rate of wages; on the principle, that as the labor becomes merely bodily, it is a greater sacrifice to the individual laborer, to give his time to it; because time is desirable for the cultivation of the intellect, in exact proportion to ignorance. Besides, intellectual labor involves in itself higher pleasures, and is more its own reward, than bodily labor.

Another reason, for setting the same pecuniary value on every kind of labor, is, to give outward expression to the great truth, that all labor is sacred, when done for a common interest. . . .

Besides, after becoming members of this community, none will be engaged merely in bodily labor. . . . This community aims to be rich, not in the metallic representative of wealth, but in the wealth itself, which money should represent; namely, LEISURE TO LIVE IN ALL THE FACULTIES OF THE SOUL. As a community, it will traffic with the world at large, in the products of Agricultural labor; and it will sell education to as many young persons as can be domesticated in the families, and enter into the common life with their own children. In the end, it hopes to be enabled to provide—not only all the necessaries, but all the elegances desirable for bodily and for spiritual health; books, apparatus, collections for science, works of art, means of beautiful amusement. These things are to be common to all; and thus that object, which alone gilds and refines the passion for individual accumulation, will no longer exist for desire, and whenever the Sordid passion appears, it will be seen in its naked selfishness. In its ultimate success, the community will realize all the ends which selfishness seeks, but involved in spiritual blessings, which only greatness of soul can aspire after. . . .

This principle, with regard to labor, lies at the root of moral and religious life; for it is not more true that "money is the root of all evil," than that *labor is the germ of all good.*

All the work is to be offered for the free choice of the members of the community, at stated seasons, and such as is not chosen, will be hired. But it is not anticipated that any work will be set aside to be hired, for which there is actual ability in the community. It is so desirable that the hired labor should be avoided, that it is believed the work will all be done freely, even though at voluntary sacrifice. If there is some exception at first, it is because the material means are inadequate to the reception of all who desire to go. They cannot go, unless they have shelter; and in this climate, they cannot have shelter unless they can build houses; and they cannot build houses unless they have money. It is not here as in Robinson Crusoe's Island. . . .

There are some persons who have entered the community without money. It is believed that these will be able to support themselves and dependents, by less work, more completely, and with more ease than elsewhere; while their labor will be of advantage to the community. It is in no sense an eleemosynary establishment [that is, one supported by alms], but it is hoped that in the end it will be able to receive all who have the spiritual qualifications. . . .

It should be understood also, that after all the working and teaching, which individuals of the community may do, they will still have leisure, and in that leisure can employ themselves in connexion with the world around them. Some will not teach at all; and those especially can write books, pursue the Fine Arts, for private emolument if they will, and exercise various functions of men.—From this community might go forth preachers of the gospel of Christ, who would not have upon them the odium, or the burthen, that now diminishes the power of the clergy. And even if *pastors* were to go from this community, to reside among congregations as now, for a salary given, the fact that they would have something to retreat upon, at any moment, would save them from that virtual dependence on their congregations, which now corrupts the relation.

Now there can be only one way of selecting and winnowing their company. The power to do this must be inherent in their constitution; they must keep sternly true to their principles.

In the first place, they must not compromise their principle of labor, in receiving members. Every one, who has any personal power, whether bodily or mental, must bring the contribution of personal service, no matter how much money he brings besides. . . .

Another danger which should be largely treated is the spirit of coterie. The breadth of their platform, which admits all sects; and the generality of their plan, which demands all degrees of intellectual culture to begin with, is some security against this. . . .

After reading this selection, consider these questions:

1. Discuss the ways in which Brook Farm was a reaction to the emerging commercial society of the early nineteenth century.

2. What kind of people do you think were attracted to Brook Farm? Peabody explains that "all the work is to be offered for the free choice of the members" and that "such as is not chosen, will be hired." Given the people attracted to Brook Farm, what kind of work was likely not to be chosen?

3. In what ways did Brook Farm reflect the influence of the Second Great Awakening?

SELECTION 4:

A Protest of Marriage

The eighth of nine children born to a poor farming family in western Massachusetts, Lucy Stone managed to stay in school long enough to become a teacher. She then worked her way through Oberlin College. After graduation in 1847, she became a speaker for the Anti-Slavery Society and an advocate of women's rights. Eventually, her focus shifted more toward women's rights. She attended the Seneca Falls Convention in 1848. In spite of her opposition to the legal disabilities marriage imposed on women (detailed in the following document), she married Henry Blackwell (the brother of two female physicians, Elizabeth and Emily) in 1855. She kept her surname and entered into a well-publicized marriage contract in which Blackwell renounced the superior legal status granted to husbands. Stone continued her activities on behalf of women's rights throughout her life. The document that follows is the marriage contract between Blackwell and Stone.

While acknowledging our mutual affection by publicly assuming the relationship of husband and wife, yet in justice to ourselves and a great principle, we deem it a duty to declare that this act on our part implies no sanction of, nor promise of voluntary obedience to such of the present laws of marriage, as refuse to recognize the wife as an

Excerpted from *History of Woman Suffrage*, edited by Elizabeth Cady Stanton, Susan B. Anthony, and Matilda Joslyn Gage (New York: Fowler & Well, 1881).

independent, rational being, while they confer upon the husband an injurious and unnatural superiority, investing him with legal powers which no honorable man would exercise, and which no man should possess. We protest especially against the laws which give to the husband:

1. The custody of the wife's person.
2. The exclusive control and guardianship of their children.
3. The sole ownership of her personal, and use of her real estate, unless previously settled upon her, or placed in the hands of trustees, as in the case of minors, lunatics, and idiots.
4. The absolute right to the product of her industry.
5. Also against laws which give to the widower so much larger and more permanent an interest in the property of his deceased wife, than they give to the widow in that of the deceased husband.
6. Finally, against the whole system by which "the legal existence of the wife is suspended during marriage," so that in most States, she neither has a legal part in the choice of her residence, nor can she make a will, nor sue or be sued in her own name, nor inherit property.

We believe that personal independence and equal human rights can never be forfeited, except for crime; that marriage should be an equal and permanent partnership, and so recognized by law; that until it is so recognized, married partners should provide against the radical injustice of present laws, by every means in their power.

We believe that where domestic difficulties arise, no appeal should be made to legal tribunals under existing laws, but that all difficulties should be submitted to the equitable adjustment of arbitrators mutually chosen.

Thus reverencing law, we enter our protest against rules and customs which are unworthy of the name, since they violate justice, the essence of law.

After reading this selection, consider these questions:

1. What legal rights did a woman lose upon marriage?

2. How did the law of marriage grant superior status to the husband?

3. How did Blackwell and Stone attempt to create a more equitable marriage by signing a binding contract?

SELECTION 5:

The Declaration of Sentiments

A *number of women became active in the various reform movements that sprang from the Second Great Awakening, including temperance, abolitionism, and Sabbatarianism. Within those movements they encountered discrimination that made them acutely aware of the subordinate position of women in American society. Abolitionists and temperance advocates, for example, would not permit women to address audiences of both men and women. When the World Anti-Slavery Convention met in London in 1840, male delegates refused to seat female delegates. Two of the would-be delegates, Elizabeth Cady Stanton and Lucretia Mott, began to consider a convention for women's rights. That convention took place in 1848 at Seneca Falls, New York. Two hundred delegates, including thirty-two men, attended.*

The purpose of this convention was to establish a platform for women's rights. Stanton drafted this platform, calling it the Declaration of Sentiments and modeling it on the Declaration of Independence. With some changes in wording, the convention adopted her declaration as well as a series of resolutions Stanton also drafted. All of the resolutions passed unanimously except the one demanding suffrage. That passed by a narrow majority.

Born in Johnstown, New York, in 1815, Stanton studied law in her father's law office. She married Henry B. Stanton, an abolitionist lawyer, in 1840. At her insistence, the word obey *was dropped from their marriage ceremony.*

The following document is the declaration passed by the Seneca Falls Convention.

When, in the course of human events, it becomes necessary for one portion of the family of man to assume among the people of the earth a position different from that which they have hitherto occupied, but one to which the laws of nature and of nature's God entitle them, a decent respect to the opinions of mankind requires that they should declare the causes that impel them to such a course.

We hold these truths to be self-evident: that all men and women are created equal; that they are endowed by their Creator with certain inalienable rights; that among these are life, liberty, and the pursuit of happiness; that to secure these rights governments are instituted, deriving their just powers from the consent of the governed. Whenever any form of government becomes destructive of these ends, it is the right of those who suffer from it to refuse allegiance to it, and to insist upon the institution of a new government, laying its foundation on such principles, and organizing its powers in such form, as to them shall seem most likely to effect their safety and happiness. Prudence, indeed, will dictate that governments long established should not be changed for light and transient

causes; and accordingly all experience hath shown that mankind are more disposed to suffer, while evils are sufferable, than to right themselves by abolishing the forms to which they were accustomed. But when a long train of abuses and usurpations, pursuing invariably the same object evinces a design to reduce them under absolute despotism, it is their duty to throw off such government, and to provide new guards for their future security. Such has been the patient sufferance of the women under this government, and such is now the necessity which constrains them to demand the equal situation to which they are entitled.

The history of mankind is a history of repeated injuries and usurpations on the part of man toward woman, having in direct object the establishment of an absolute tyranny over her. To prove this, let facts be submitted to a candid world.

He has never permitted her to exercise her inalienable right to the elective franchise.

He has compelled her to submit to laws, in the formation of which she had no voice.

He has withheld from her rights which are given to the most ignorant and degraded men—both natives and foreigners.

Having deprived her of this first right of a citizen, the elective franchise, thereby leaving her without representation in the halls of legislation, he has oppressed her on all sides.

Excerpted from *History of Woman Suffrage,* edited by Elizabeth Cady Stanton, Susan B. Anthony, and Matilda Joslyn Gage (New York: Fowler & Well, 1881).

He has made her, if married, in the eye of the law, civilly dead.

He has taken from her all right in property, even to the wages she earns.

He has made her, morally, an irresponsible being, as she can commit many crimes with impunity, provided they be done in the presence of her husband. In the covenant of marriage, she is compelled to promise obedience to her husband, he becoming, to all intents and purposes, her master—the law giving him power to deprive her of her liberty, and to administer chastisement.

He has so framed the laws of divorce, as to what shall be the proper causes, and in case of separation, to whom the guardianship of the children shall be given, as to be wholly regardless of the happiness of women—the law, in all cases, going upon a false supposition of the supremacy of man, and giving all power into his hands.

After depriving her of all rights as a married woman, if single, and the owner of property, he has taxed her to support a government which recognizes her only when her property can be made profitable to it.

He has monopolized nearly all the profitable employments, and from those she is permitted to follow, she receives but a scanty remuneration. He closes against her all the avenues to wealth and distinction which he considers most honorable to himself. As a teacher of theology, medicine, or law, she is not known.

He has denied her the facilities for obtaining a thorough education, all colleges being closed against her.

He allows her in Church, as well as State, but a subordinate position, claiming Apostolic authority for her exclusion from the ministry, and, with some exceptions, from any public participation in the affairs of the Church.

He has created a false public sentiment by giving to the world a different code of morals for men and women, by which moral delinquencies which exclude women from society, are not only tolerated, but deemed of little account in man.

He has usurped the prerogative of Jehovah himself, claiming it as his right to assign for her a sphere of action, when that belongs to her conscience and to her God.

He has endeavored, in every way that he could, to destroy her confidence in her own powers, to lessen her self-respect, and to make her willing to lead a dependent and abject life.

Now, in view of this entire disfranchisement of one-half the people of this country, their social and religious degradation—in view of the unjust laws above mentioned, and because women do feel themselves aggrieved, oppressed, and fradulently deprived of their most sacred rights, we insist that they have immediate admission to all the rights and privileges which belong to them as citizens of the United States.

In entering upon the great work before us, we anticipate no small amount of misconception, misrepresentation, and ridicule; but we shall use every instrumentality within our power to effect our object. We shall employ agents, circulate tracts, petition the State and National legislatures, and endeavor to enlist the pulpit and the press in our behalf. We hope this Convention will be followed by a series of Conventions embracing every part of the country.

After reading this selection, consider these questions:

1. Why did Stanton model her declaration on Thomas Jefferson's?

2. Stanton wrote that men withheld from women "rights which are given to the most ignorant and degraded men—both natives and foreigners." To what kind of men do you think she was referring? What does this say about Stanton and the other delegates to the Seneca Falls Convention?

CHAPTER 15

Expansion

Americans' desire to expand westward was one of the sources of friction with Great Britain that led to the American Revolution. Freed from British restraint, the new nation rapidly set about expanding across the Appalachian Mountains. In 1803 the Louisiana Purchase doubled the nation's territory. That same year Thomas Jefferson dispatched Meriwether Lewis and William Clark to explore as far as the Pacific Ocean. Fur traders and trappers exploited the abundant wildlife and marked trails that would later lead settlers to the West.

As early as the 1830s, American settlers began migrating overland to the far West. The lands into which Americans ventured were not uninhabited. Native Americans had occupied them for thousands of years, and Mexicans had lived in some areas for centuries. Native Americans resisted the encroachment on their lands, and the federal government established army posts and launched punitive expeditions. American settlement in Mexican-held Texas led to a revolution and the establishment of an independent state that was eventually annexed by the United States. A dispute over the border between Texas and Mexico touched off a war between the United States and its southern neighbor. As a result of that war, the United States gained California, Utah, Nevada, New Mexico, and parts of Arizona, Colorado, Kansas, and Wyoming.

In California on January 25, 1848, a handyman building a sawmill for John A. Sutter discovered gold. The first published account of the strike came in March. By the fall, word had reached the East Coast. News of the find led to gold fever. Men in California and all over the country, as well as in other countries, headed for California's gold country hoping to get rich. The following year eighty thousand men arrived in California (men outnumbered women by more than ten to one during the Gold Rush). Roughly half came overland and half came by sea (either around Cape Horn or by ship to the isthmus of Panama, overland to the Pacific, and then by ship to California). A substantial majority were Americans; others came from Europe, Latin America, or Asia. San Francisco's population quickly grew from under five hundred in 1847 to twenty thousand in a matter of months. By 1850 it had expanded to thirty-five thousand.

The society created by this diverse group of gold hunters was unruly and violent. San Francisco had over five hundred bars and one thousand gambling houses. Perhaps a thousand murders took place in San Francisco alone in the early 1850s; there was only one conviction. In the absence of effective government or law enforcement, merchants formed vigilance committees that used popular courts and lynchings to establish order. The entire city burned six times within an eighteen-month span.

Only a small percentage of miners ever struck it rich. Easily reached deposits played out early, and it required machinery (and therefore capital) to reach the deeper veins. Increasingly, miners in California worked as laborers for large companies. By the mid-1850s, the wild mining camps no longer set the tone for California. The state had a thriving economy based on agriculture and corporate mining. San Francisco emerged as a prosperous and culturally sophisticated city. However, none of this came without costs. Mining left scars on the landscape. Some Indian tribes were virtually exterminated. Original Hispanic residents were dispossessed, and a new ethnic minority, the Chinese, faced animosity and discrimination.

American institutions followed American settlement, but not all institutions arrived with the first American pioneers. Moreover, some institutions did not transplant without undergoing profound changes. New social and cultural forms sprung up to fill temporary voids. All in all, the West did not simply replicate society and the culture of the East any more than the original American colonists replicated the social and cultural structures of Great Britain.

American westward expansion was a story of courage, perseverance, determination, and achievement. It was also a story of failure, conquest, and exploitation.

After reading this chapter, consider these questions:

1. How did frontier life affect the development of civic institutions?

2. How did westward expansion and settlement affect various ethnic and racial groups differently?

3. What were the achievements of American expansion across the continent? At what cost did these achievements come?

SELECTION 1:

The Multifunctional Frontier Saloon

Most people associate frontier saloons with drinking, gun fights, and saloon girls. That image presents only one side of saloons, which also served as social centers, political gathering places, banks, music halls, libraries, and even places for religious worship. Often the first building constructed in a new town, saloons were centers of urban society in the West. In the following excerpt, Thomas J. Noel, a professor of history at the University of Colorado at Denver, describes the various social functions saloons performed in early Denver.

"A most forlorn and desolate-looking metropolis," is how the Boston journalist Albert D. Richardson described Denver upon his arrival by stagecoach in 1859. After crawling out of the stage, Richardson and his fellow journalist, Horace Greeley of the *New York Tribune,* found themselves surrounded by a crowd wearing slouch hats, tattered woolen shirts, and trousers sagging with knives and revolvers. Saloons emptied and the crowd thickened as word spread that "Go West" Greeley had come to town.

Stiff and sore from the bone-shaking stage trip, Greeley and Richardson rented rooms in the Denver House. In that dirt-floored resort, Greeley found that a guest was "allowed as good a bed as his blankets will make." The charges, he added, were "no higher than at the Astor and other first-class hotels, except for liquor—twenty-five cents a drink for dubious whisky, colored and nicknamed to suit the taste of the customers."

In the morning, Greeley sent to New York a dispatch in which he complained of the incessant clamor of all-night gamblers and of the inconvenience of dodging bullets fired by drunks. . . .

Horace Greeley's complaint about the saloon-infested town was a common one. His traveling companion, Richardson, was also repulsed by the "many rude shanties for the sale of whiskey and tobacco" and wrote that "gambling and dissipation were . . . universal." William Hepworth Dixon, a British visitor to Denver in 1866, likewise complained that "as you wander about these hot and dirty streets, you seem to be walking in a city of demons. Every fifth house appears to be a bar, a whisky-shop, a lager-beer saloon; every tenth house appears to be either a brothel or a gaming house; very often both in one." Libeus Barney, a pioneer Denver taverner, claimed that every third building in the raw mining capital was a groggery.

These critics exaggerated the number of saloons and also overlooked the town's reliance on saloons not only for social life but also for political, economic, and even religious activities. Saloons offered patrons far more than a nickel beer. They provided the cultural and social life of the French *salon,* the civic and political benefits of the Teutonic *saal* or public hall, the elegance of the Spanish *sala,* or parlor, and the sedate, private man's world of the British pub. Until government, churches, schools, banks, libraries, hospitals, the-

Excerpted from *The City and the Saloon: Denver, 1858–1916,* by Thomas J. Noel (Lincoln: University of Nebraska Press, 1982). Copyright © 1982 by University of Nebraska Press. Reprinted with permission.

aters, museums, and other institutions became well established, the saloon served as a multifunctional institution.

In Denver's early years, saloons served as community centers where the provisional and permanent governments for Denver City and Jefferson Territory (the extralegal predecessor of Colorado Territory) were conceived, chartered, constituted, and housed during their early years. Taverns also doubled as clubs, hotels, restaurants, bakeries, hospitals, museums, banks, information centers, and gathering places. Denver's first church services and first theater performances were held in drinking halls. Behind tavern doors, men marketed town lots, traded mining claims, and grubstaked miners. . . .

Saloonkeepers endeavored to meet as many of the needs and desires of their patrons as possible. "I flatter myself that I can please anyone," advertised Edward Jumps of the Criterion. David Hoyt's Pioneer promised to dispense choice wines, liquors, cigars, and other goods "in a scientific manner." Operating both over and under the counter, tavernkeepers could tell a fellow where to find a girl, a bed, a job, or the latest gold strike.

Of course, the functions of any given saloon might change frequently. Apollo Hall, a saloon and billiards hall housed in a two-story frame building erected in June 1859, provides a good example. Two months after its opening the Apollo made its debut as a hotel. The next month, on September 15, this Larimer Street establishment staged a grand opening ball offering five-dollar dinners and dancing to the "best music available." This drinking, billiards, sleeping, dining, music, and dance hall became Denver's first theater in October of 1859, when miners' candles were stuck into the walls and crude benches set up in the upstairs hall. Apollo Hall also accommodated churchless Presbyterians who met there in 1860 despite rattling billiard balls, drunken commotion, and occasional gunfire from the bar below. . . . The zenith of the Apollo's life came in September of 1860 when townsfolk gathered there to draft a municipal constitution establishing the "People's Government of the City of Denver."

Saloons housed many early religious services, since no churches were built until 1860, when a small Southern Methodist church and a Catholic chapel were completed. Years, even decades, passed before other denominations could afford their own buildings. Meanwhile, the Criterion Saloon served as a church for both Reverend John M. Chivington's Methodists and Reverend John H. Kehler's Episcopal flock, although one of Father Kehler's parishoners recalled that it was an ungodly place:

> On the first Sunday the gambling was carried on on the first floor while preaching was proceeding on the second. The flooring was of rough boards with wide cracks between them, and every word uttered by the occupants of the saloon, including those at the gaming tables, was as plainly heard by the congregation as the sermon. On the next Sunday the gambling was suspended for an hour while the preaching proceeded, which was considered quite a concession for that time.

The records of Father Kehler's parish suggest the difficulties of churches in frontier towns. Of the first twelve burial services that he conducted, five of the departed had been shot, two were executed for murder, one shot himself, and one died of alcoholism. Murders at the Criterion, Cibola Hall, Mountain Boys, Louisiana, St. Charles, Adler's, and Club House saloons accounted for almost half of Denver's homicides in 1859 and 1860. . . .

Many congregations borrowed saloon halls as their meeting places and sometimes used the bar as an altar and the bar's pianist as a choir director. Yet most churches found little use for groggeries once they had their own buildings. . . .

Commercial banks were even slower than churches to establish themselves on the frontier. Two banks opening in 1860 proved to be short-lived. The Kountze Brothers Bank (later Colorado National Bank), established in 1862, and the First National Bank of Denver, organized in 1865, survived, but no others opened between 1865 and 1870. Easterners with capital were reluctant to finance banks in the new West, where inflation, a society of transient borrowers, lack of law and order, and a dearth of investors made banking risky. The banks that did exist in pioneer Denver were primarily gold buyers, not moneylenders.

In this capital-short frontier town, many miners and small businessmen turned to the saloonkeeper for cash. "Uncle Dick" Wootton claimed that about nine-tenths of the arrivals during the winter of 1858–59 were cash-hungry. Many of them sought to borrow money from Wootton, who accepted ox teams as collateral and charged interest as high as 20 percent a day. "This was a matter of such frequent occurrence," Wootton recalled, "that lending money in this way became a part of my business." . . .

In the saloonkeeper's safe, regulars might keep their savings and other valuables. Some liquor houses maintained letter boxes for regulars and posted notices, business cards, and want ads. Inside saloon doors (Denver's climate precluded extensive use of the swinging batwings), a tippler might find almost anything. Liquor houses tried to provide all of the comforts of home, from washboards to bathtubs.

Among those who came to Colorado to gamble with pick and pan rather than cards and dice, capital was also in great demand. And since alcohol was generally sold for cash on the frontier, miners looking for grubstakes often approached saloonkeepers. Not only were tavernkeepers lenders, but they also often held onto gold dust or cash for their customers after deducting bar bills from the deposited account. As a banker, the mixologist offered warmer hospitality, longer business hours, and liquid fringe benefits that conventional bankers could not match. . . .

At least one saloonkeeper doubled as an insurance agent. Edward Van Endert, coproprietor of Mozart Hall, advertised in the 1871 *Rocky Mountain Directory and Colorado Gazetteer* as the Denver salesman for Germania Life Insurance. . . .

If one saloonkeeper insured early Denverites, others served as physicians. Before the arrival of the patent-medicine salesman with his wagonload of cure-alls and the physician with his black bag, saloonkeepers dispensed whiskey for everything from snake bites to impotency, from bullet holes to mountain fever. Richard Townshend, an Englishman, reported the use of Dowd's Twenty Mile House on Cherry Creek as a hospital. A gunshot victim was laid on the bar counter under a smoky petroleum lamp and surgery was performed with a razor. Whiskey served as the anesthetic for both patient and surgeon.

Alcohol was a widely used health aid. It was the key ingredient of many nineteenth-century patent medicines. However, if brewery advertisements could be believed, drinkers had no need for other elixirs. . . . Alcohol may have been safer than Denver's early drinking water, which came from the waste-filled Platte and Cherry Creek, from wells often adjacent to outhouses, and from the irrigation ditches that guttered city streets. The idea of alcohol as medicine became institutionalized in drugstore liquor licenses, sanctioned by both Denver's early ordinances and the first session of the state legislature. . . .

Shelter as well as dubious health care was furnished by early-day Denver saloonkeepers who liked to call their places houses. Inside, men might pay a quarter to sleep on sawdust floors or a dollar for the privilege of sleeping in a chair. These houses devoted most of their interior to bar space, but surrendered some back and upstairs rooms for sleeping. Some proprietors chalked off floor space at closing time and by dawn each of these spaces might house several snoring strangers. The less fortunate slept outside under wooden sidewalks, in empty barrels and boxes, in barns, stables, and outhouses.

Federal manuscript censuses reveal that quite a few saloonkeepers housed boarders. Many of Denver's early taverners were married men whose wives and children helped to make a home for the predominantly male, young, unmarried, transient miners. The saloonkeeper, his wife, and his children were very important in providing financial and occupational advice, health care, and company for the lonely young bachelors who had left their parents and sweethearts back in the states. . . .

The ebb and flow of frontier populations washed many of the sick, indigent, handicapped, homeless, unemployed, and shiftless into Denver. The promise of gold, silver, and a salubrious climate made high, dry Denver particularly attractive to the poor and the sickly. The boom-and-bust mining cycles and the national depressions of the nineteenth-century economy also dumped many unfortunates into the Mile-High City, including worn-out miners from the hills who retreated to Denver to recover or to die.

From the beginning, many of the indigent approached tavernkeepers for handouts. . . .

In frontier communities providing little or no charity and welfare, the men in the white aprons often contributed not only food and lodging but also cash to unfortunates. When yellow fever, caused by bad water, ravaged Denver in the 1870s, for instance, saloonkeepers John Kinneavy and Frank Parker donated bar receipts to fever victims.

If saloons provided frontier housing and welfare, they also offered cultural benefits, including reading material, art, music, theater, dancing, gardens, zoos, parks, and museums. Twenty years before Denver opened a permanent, free public library, the Rialto Billiard Saloon advertised, "Latest papers always on hand to while away a leisure hour." Andy Stanbury's Tambien offered beer sippers "files of daily, sporting, and illustrated papers." Along with imported and domestic cigars, meerschaum pipes, tobacco, and California wines, M.W. Levy kept "eastern, Colorado and California papers always on file." Literary-minded pioneers might also seek out Colonel Cheney's, which boasted elegant desks and reading tables where customers could read or write letters home amid all the appurtenances of a first-class bar, including "chaste, costly pictures."

Cheney's was not the only saloon to offer Denverites public art decades before an art museum existed. Henry Fuerstein's beer hall exhibited paintings on its walls, including the oil "Yosemite Valley." Art-minded patrons who liked the California landscape were invited to purchase two-dollar raffle tickets on it. Charles Stobie rented one of the upstairs rooms at Stanbury's Tambien, where some of his Colorado landscapes and Indian portraits were first exhibited and purchased for as much as one hundred dollars. . . .

If Denver's finer saloons touted their "chaste, costly art," lesser taverns prized their less chaste barroom nudes and portraits of presidents, pugilists, and military heroes.

Drama as well as art found an early home in Denver saloon halls. When the Apollo Hall gave the city its first theater performance in 1859, the proprietor reported that an audience of four hundred squeezed into the hall, demonstrating "the appreciation of art in this semibarbarous region.". . .

Theater, burlesque, minstrel shows, girly shows, and other stage performances were attractions at various bars. Of the sixty-odd theaters in Denver between 1859 and 1876, nearly all were in saloons. . . .

Like theater, music was performed in saloons, although the life of a beer-hall musician might be a short one. To protect themselves from gun-toting critics, the musicians of the Denver House built a sheet-iron cage; when the shooting began they would dive under this battlement. After the smoke cleared, they would pop up playing again. . . .

Tavern amusements ranged from Eureka Hall's freak museum to an exclusive dance club sponsored by the Broadwell House. The Diana Saloon featured Signor Franco, a stone swallower, and his more voracious companion, a sword eater. The Blake Street Bowling Alley billed itself as the "*ne plus ultra* of popular resorts." It boasted four bowling alleys, good music, free lunches, and a bar "with everything." Above and beyond all this was a nightly trapeze performance by "Professor" Wilson.

Bowling games and shooting galleries could be found in a few bars, but the crack and crashing of billiard balls was standard music in many public drinking halls. . . .

Perhaps the crowning contribution to culture in early Denver was a spectacle sponsored by the Criterion Saloon. The Criterion employed a petite acrobat known as Mademoiselle Carolista. Sometimes blindfolded, sometimes with a wheelbarrow, Mlle Carolista walked a tightrope suspended from the stage of the Criterion to a rear balcony. But her tightrope walk from the roof of the Criterion to a store across Larimer Street was a highlight in popular entertainment during Denver's first decade. As she tottered on the rope, townsfolk stood petrified below with mouths open and arms outstretched.

Beer gardens served as public parks and gardens during Denver's first two decades. . . . Denver had no city park system until the mayoralty of

Richard Sopris in the 1880s, no municipal zoo until 1896, when Mayor Thomas S. McMurray was given a black bear cub and asked the foreman of City Park to care for it, and no Museum of Natural History until 1900.

Nineteenth-century thirst parlors, like twentieth-century fern bars and taxidermy taverns, surrounded customers with potted plants and mounted animals. Liquor and cigar cases were filled with arrowheads and fossils, geodes and stamp albums. Customers could sip drinks and study collections of cowboy hats and Indian scalps, of butterflies and seashells, of weapons and pornography. Tipplers in their cups found company not only in tavern dogs and cats, but in caged birds and wide-eyed fish. . . .

The saloon's multifunctionalism was due to both the lack of other institutions and to the keen competition among the 270 taverns known to have existed in Denver during the territorial era. To attract customers saloons attempted to outdo each other in offering novel goods, useful services, and unique entertainment.

After reading this selection, consider these questions:

1. How and why did saloons emerge as financial institutions in Denver and other western towns?

2. Describe how saloons came to fill social welfare functions.

3. What civic functions did saloons perform? Might this have retarded the development of such services on the part of local government?

SELECTION 2:

The Trail of Tears

White settlement in North America proved disastrous for Native Americans from the earliest contact. One of the darkest episodes in this long history was the forcible removal of the Cherokee from their ancestral homelands in Georgia, North Carolina, and Tennessee. Ironically, the Cherokee had gone further than other tribes in accommodating their lifestyle to European and American ways. In the following selection, Dee Brown, formerly a librarian at the University of Illinois and a prolific writer on the American West and Native Americans, describes the tragedy of the Cherokee removal.

In the spring of 1838, Brigadier General Winfield Scott with a regiment of artillery, a regiment of infantry, and six companies of dragoons marched unopposed into the Cherokee country of northern

Georgia. On May 10 at New Echota, the capital of what had been one of the greatest Indian nations in eastern America, Scott issued a proclamation:

The President of the United States sent me with a powerful army to cause you, in obedience to the treaty of 1835, to join that part of your people who are already established in prosperity on the other side of the Missis-

Excerpted from *American History Illustrated,* by Dee Brown (Harrisburg, PA: National Historical Society, 1972). Copyright © 1972 by Dee Brown. Reprinted with permission.

sippi. . . . The emigration must be commenced in haste. . . . The full moon of May is already on the wane, and before another shall have passed away every Cherokee man, woman and child . . . must be in motion to join their brethren in the west. . . . My troops already occupy many positions . . . and thousands and thousands are approaching from every quarter to render resistance and escape alike hopeless. . . . Will you then by resistance compel us to resort to arms? Or will you by flight seek to hide yourselves in mountains and forests and thus oblige us to hunt you down? Remember that in pursuit it may be impossible to avoid conflicts. The blood of the white man or the blood of the red man may be spilt, and if spilt, however accidentally, it may be impossible for the discreet and humane among you, or among us, to prevent a general war and carnage.

For more than a century the Cherokees had been ceding their land, thousands of acres by thousands of acres. They had lost all of Kentucky and much of Tennessee, but after the last treaty of 1819 they still had remaining about 35,000 square miles of forested mountains, clean, swift-running rivers, and fine meadows. In this country which lay across parts of Georgia, North Carolina and Tennessee they cultivated fields, planted orchards, fenced pastures, and built roads, houses, and towns. Sequoya had invented a syllabary for the Cherokee language so that thousands of his tribesmen quickly learned to read and write. The Cherokees had adopted the white man's ways—his clothing, his constitutional form of government, even his religion. But it had all been for nothing. Now these men who had come across the great ocean many years ago wanted all of the Cherokees' land. In exchange for their 35,000 square miles the tribe was to receive five million dollars and another tract of land somewhere in the wilderness beyond the Mississippi River.

This was a crushing blow to a proud people. . . . Ever since the signing of the treaties of 1819, Major General Andrew Jackson, a man they once believed to be their friend, had been urging Cherokees to move beyond the Mississippi. Indians and white settlers, Jackson told them, could never get along together. Even if the government wanted to protect the Cherokees from harassment, he added, it would be unable to do so. "If you cannot protect us in Georgia," a chief retorted, "how can you protect us from similar evils in the West?"

During that period of polite urging, a few hundred Cherokee families did move west, but the tribe remained united and refused to give up any more territory. In fact, the council leaders passed a law forbidding any chief to sell or trade a single acre of Cherokee land on penalty of death.

In 1828, when Andrew Jackson was running for President, he knew that in order to win he must sweep the frontier states. Free land for the land-hungry settlers became Jackson's major policy. He hammered away at this theme especially hard in Georgia, where waves of settlers from the coastal lowlands were pushing into the highly desirable Cherokee country. He promised the Georgians that if they would help elect him President, he would lend his support to opening up the Cherokee lands for settlement. The Cherokees, of course, were not citizens and could not vote in opposition. To the Cherokees and their friends who protested this promise, Jackson justified his position by saying that the Cherokees had fought on the side of the British during the Revolutionary War. He conveniently forgot that the Cherokees had been his allies during the desperate War of 1812, and had saved the day for him in his decisive victory over the British-backed Creeks at Horseshoe Bend. . . .

Three weeks after Jackson was elected President, the Georgia legislature passed a law annexing all the Cherokee country within that state's borders. As most of the Cherokee land was in Georgia and three-fourths of the tribe lived there, this meant an end to their independence as a nation. The Georgia legislature also abolished all Cherokee laws and customs and sent surveyors to map out land lots of 160 acres each. The 160-acre lots were to be distributed to white citizens of Georgia through public lotteries.

To add to the pressures on the Cherokees, gold was discovered near Dahlonega in the heart of their country, . . . and a rabble of gold-hungry prospectors descended upon them.

John Ross, the Cherokees' leader, hurried to Washington to protest the Georgia legislature's actions and to plead for justice. In that year Ross was 38 years old; he was well-educated and had been active in Cherokee government matters since he was 19. He was adjutant of the Cherokee regiment that served with Jackson at Horseshoe Bend. His father had been one of a group of Scottish emigrants who settled near the Cherokees and married into the tribe.

In Washington, Ross found sympathizers in Congress, but most of them were anti-Jackson men and the Cherokee case was thus drawn into the whirlpool of politics. When Ross called upon Andrew Jackson to request his aid, the President bluntly told him that "no protection could be afforded the Cherokees" unless they were willing to move west of the Mississippi.

While Ross was vainly seeking help in Washington, alarming messages reached him from Georgia. White citizens of that state were claiming the homes of Cherokees through the land lottery, seizing some of them by force. . . .

During all this turmoil, President Jackson and the governor of Georgia pressed the Cherokee leaders hard in attempts to persuade them to cede all their territory and move to the West. But the chiefs stood firm. Somehow they managed to hold the tribe together, and helped dispossessed families find new homes back in the wilderness areas. . . .

In 1834, the chiefs appealed to Congress with a memorial in which they stated that they would never voluntarily abandon their homeland, but proposed a compromise in which they agreed to cede the state of Georgia a part of their territory provided that they would be protected from invasion in the remainder. Furthermore, at the end of a definite period of years to be fixed by the United States they would be willing to become citizens of the various states in which they resided. . . .

This new petition to Congress was no more effectual than their appeals to President Jackson. Again they were told that their difficulties could be remedied only by their removal to the west of the Mississippi.

For the first time now, a serious split occurred among the Cherokees. A small group of subchiefs decided that further resistance to the demands of the Georgia and United States governments was futile.

It would be better, they believed, to exchange their land and go west rather than risk bloodshed and the possible loss of everything. Leaders of this group were Major Ridge and Elias Boudinot. Ridge had adopted his first name after Andrew Jackson gave him that rank during the War of 1812. Boudinot was Ridge's nephew. Originally known as Buck Watie, he had taken the name of a New England philanthropist who sent him through a mission school in Connecticut. . . . Upon Boudinot's return from school to Georgia he founded the first tribal newspaper, the *Cherokee Phoenix,* in 1827 . . .

And so in February 1835 when John Ross journeyed to Washington to resume his campaign to save the Cherokee nation, a rival delegation headed by Ridge and Boudinot arrived there to seek terms for removal to the West. The pro-removal forces in the government leaped at this opportunity to bypass Ross's authority, and within a few days drafted a preliminary treaty for the Ridge delegation. It was then announced that a council would be held later in the year at New Echota, Georgia, for the purpose of negotiating and agreeing upon final terms.

During the months that followed, bitterness increased between the two Cherokee factions. Ridge's group was a very small minority, but they had the full weight of the United States Government behind them, and threats and inducements were used to force a full attendance at the council which was set for December 22, 1835. Handbills were printed in Cherokee and distributed throughout the nation, informing the Indians that those who did not attend would be counted as assenting to any treaty that might be made.

During the seven days which followed the opening of the treaty council, fewer than five hundred Cherokees, or about 2 percent of the tribe, came to New Echota to participate in the discussions. Most of the other Cherokees were busy endorsing a petition to be sent to Congress stating their opposition to the treaty. But on December 29, Ridge, Boudinot and their followers signed away all the lands of the great Cherokee nation. . . .

Charges of bribery by the Ross forces were denied by government officials, but some years afterward it was discovered that the Secretary of War had sent secret agents into the Cherokee country with authority to expend money to bribe chiefs to support the treaty of cession and removal. And certainly the treaty signers were handsomely rewarded. In an era when a dollar would buy many times its worth today, Major Ridge was paid $30,000 and his followers received several thousand dollars each. Ostensibly they were being paid for their improved farmlands, but the amounts were far in excess of contemporary land values.

John Ross meanwhile completed gathering signature of Cherokees who were opposed to the treaty. Early in the following spring, 1836, he took the petition to Washington. More than three-fourths of the tribe, 15,964, had signed in protest against the treaty. . . .

[Further,] the Cherokees . . . did have friends in Congress. Representative Davy Crockett of Tennessee denounced the treatment of the Cherokees as unjust, dishonest, and cruel. He admitted that he represented a body of frontier constituents who would like to have the Cherokee lands opened for settlement, and he doubted if a single one of them would second what he was saying. Even though his support of the Cherokees might remove him from public life, he added, he could not do otherwise except at the expense of his honor and conscience. Daniel Webster, Henry Clay, Edward Everett, and other great orators of the Congress also spoke for the Cherokees.

When the treaty came to a final decision in the Senate, it passed by only one vote. On May 23, 1836, President Jackson signed the document. According to its terms, the Cherokees were allowed two years from that day in which to leave their homeland forever.

The few Cherokees who had favored the treaty now began making their final preparations for departure. About three hundred left during that year and then early in 1837 Major Ridge and 465 followers departed by boats for the new land in the West. About 17,000 others, ignoring the treaty, remained steadfast in their homeland with John Ross.

For a while it seemed that Ross might win his long fight, that perhaps the treaty might be declared void. . . .

The inexorable machinery of government was already in motion, however, and when the expiration date of the waiting period, May 23, 1838, came near, Winfield Scott was ordered in with his army to force compliance. As already stated, Scott issued his proclamation on May 10. His soldiers were already building thirteen stockaded forts—six in North Carolina, five in Georgia, one in Tennessee, and one in Alabama. At these points the Cherokees would be concentrated to await transportation to the West. Scott then ordered the roundup started, instructing his officers not to fire on the Cherokees except in case of resistance. . . .

James Mooney, an ethnologist who afterwards talked with Cherokees who endured this ordeal, said that squads of troops moved into the forested mountains to search out every small cabin and make prisoners of all the occupants however or wherever they might be found. . . .

Knowing that resistance was futile, most of the Cherokees surrendered quietly. Within a month, thousands were enclosed in the stockades. On June 6 at Ross's Landing near the site of present-day Chattanooga, the first of many departures began. Eight hundred Cherokees were forcibly crowded into a flotilla of six flatboats lashed to the side of a steamboat. After surviving a passage over rough rapids which smashed the sides of the flatboats, they landed at Decatur, Alabama, boarded a railroad train (which was a new and terrifying experience for most of them), and after reaching Tuscumbia were crowded upon a Tennessee River steamboat again.

Throughout June and July similar shipments of several hundred Cherokees were transported by this long water route—north on the Tennessee River to the Ohio and then down the Mississippi and up the Arkansas to their new homeland. A few managed to escape and make their way back to the Cherokee country, but most of them were eventually recaptured. Along the route of travel of this forced migration, the summer was hot and dry. Drinking water and food were often contaminated. First the young children would die, then the older people, and sometimes as many as half the adults were stricken with dysentery and other ailments. On each boat deaths ran as high as five per day. On one of the first boats to reach Little Rock, Arkansas, at least a hundred had died. . . .

When John Ross and other Cherokee leaders back in the concentration camps learned of the high mortality among those who had gone ahead, they petitioned General Scott to postpone further departures until autumn. Although only three thousand Cherokees had been removed, Scott agreed to wait until the summer drought was broken, or no later than October. The Cherokees in turn agreed to organize and manage the migration themselves. After a lengthy council, they asked and received permission to travel overland in wagons, hoping that by camping along the way they would not suffer as many deaths as occurred among those who had gone on the river boats. . . .

With the ending of the drought of 1838, John Ross and the 13,000 stockaded Cherokees began preparing for their long journey to the West. . . . The first party of 1,103 started on October 1. . . .

Throughout October, eleven wagon trains departed and then on November 4, the last Cherokee exiles moved out for the West. . . .

Autumn rains softened the roads, and the hundreds of wagons and horses cut them into morasses, slowing movement to a crawl. To add to their difficulties, tollgate operators overcharged them for passage. Their horses were stolen or seized on pretext of unpaid debts, and they had no recourse to the law. With the coming of cold damp weather, measles and whooping cough became epidemic. Supplies had to be dumped to make room for the sick in the jolting wagons.

By the time the last detachments reached the Mississippi at Cape Girardeau it was January, with the river running full of ice so that several thousand had to wait on the east bank almost a month before the channel cleared. . . .

Meanwhile the parties that left early in October were beginning to reach Indian Territory. (The first arrived on January 4, 1839.) Each group had lost from thirty to forty members by death. The later detachments suffered much heavier losses, especially toward the end of their journey. Among the victims was the wife of John Ross.

Not until March 1839 did the last of the Cherokees reach their new home in the West. Counts were made of the survivors and balanced against the counts made at the beginning of the removal. As well as could be estimated, the Cherokees had lost about four thousand by deaths—or one out of every four members of the tribe—most of the deaths brought about as the direct result of the enforced removal. From that day to this the Cherokees remember it as "the trail where they cried," or the Trail of Tears.

After reading this selection, consider these questions:

1. Unlike many other tribes facing removal, the Cherokee found considerable support in Congress and the press. Drawing on Dee Brown's article and the information on Jacksonian politics in chapter 13, analyze why the Cherokee received such support.

2. Given the degree of support enjoyed by the Cherokee, why did the removal take place?

3. The Cherokee did not agree on how to react to the removal. What were the strengths and weaknesses of the arguments on either side?

SELECTION 3:

A Russian Jew in San Francisco

The discovery of gold in California's Sacramento Valley in 1848 led to a gold rush. Many went to California to seek gold, but others went to sell goods to the miners. Although a few miners struck it rich, the real money to be made was not gold but in supplying the miners. The sudden flood of miners created a scarcity of goods, which caused runaway inflation. Basic commodities sold for ridiculously inflated prices; pork brought as much as five dollars a pound and eggs as much as four dollars a dozen. A German Jewish immigrant named Levi Strauss, for example, established a thriving business selling tough work pants to the miners. However, merchants who sought to get rich by selling to miners faced great risks. Crime and violence were rampant; San Francisco burned to the ground six times in eighteen months. It was just as easy to go bust in San Francisco as it was in the gold fields. The following excerpt is from the memoirs of Morris Shloss, a Russian Jewish immigrant who migrated first to England, then to New York, and finally to San Francisco. In many respects, Shloss's story is the story of early San Francisco.

I was born in Russian Poland, in the year 1828. . . . I left my home in June, 1842, for Birmingham, England, lived there five years, left England in the year 1848, and arrived in New York in August, 1848. From New York I took passage, February 16th, 1849, on the ship "Elizabeth Ellen," [in command of] Captain Truman, stopped one week in Rio de Jane[i]ro, ten days in Valparaiso.

After rounding Cape Horn, . . . [I] arrived in San Francisco, September 25, 1849, landing at the foot of Broadway Street with my baggage.

I brought with me a wagon packed in a large box and, at the landing, a man asked me what was in the box. I told him, a wagon, and he asked the price of it. I answered $125, and he offered me $100, which rather surprised me, as the man had not seen the contents of the box. I accepted his offer, and he paid me in gold dust. I had only paid $15 for this wagon in New York, so I thought this was rather a good beginning for me.

The man was very careful in opening the box not to break the lid. And then, taking out the wagon, he said to me: "Stranger, you may keep the wagon, for I only want the box" (for which I had paid $3). "That case is what I want," he said. "I am a cobbler, and in the daytime it will be my shop, and at night, my residence." That box measured seven feet by four feet.

I then removed my baggage to Jackson Street, invested $100 in stationary which I exhibited in Portsmouth Square, then called the Plaza. I sold my stationary at a profit of 500 percent and made money very fast.

Excerpted from *Looking for America*, by Stanley I. Kutler (New York: W.W. Norton & Company, 1979). Copyright © 1979 by W.W. Norton & Company. Reprinted with permission.

I was then introduced by a friend to the proprietor of the El Dorado gambling house, a big tent on the southeast corner of Washington and Kearny Streets, to play music every evening, from seven to ten o'clock, for one ounce ($16), and from ten to eleven, extra pay of a *grab,* which meant a handful of silver from the monte table. About the middle of October, I rented a store on Washington Street, next to the El Dorado, four and one-half feet by twenty-five feet, for $400 per month. [I] speculated in buying trunks from passengers who were wild to go to the mines, and I made money faster than I ever expected to. In short, I made, in seven or eight weeks, between $5,000 and $6,000.

Then a fire, the first in the city, broke out in the Parker House, back of my store, and, as I had scattered [gun] powder all over my store, I had to run for my life, and lost all I had made since my arrival in the city. That fire spread over the block from Washington to Clay and from Kearny to Montgomery Sts.

I then engaged passage on the ship "Galinda" for Trinidad Bay [California]. There was great excitement and a rush in that direction, caused by the reports that nuggets of gold had been found scattered, all along the bay shore. When I landed, I found Dig[g]er Indians, but no signs of gold and no ship to return on; so I had to remain there four months, living on beans, crackers, and clams, the latter being very plentiful on the beach and easily found. Finally, a schooner brought me back to San Francisco, and I started in business again, and made money. . . .

I kept a store in Shasta, and express charges were very high on account of . . . [the bandit] Jaquin [Murrieta's] band raiding the Sacramento Valley. . . .

While I rested in Shasta, two men were hung by a Vigilant Committee, and one was tarred and feathered for insulting a married woman. We organized a secret order here, called Iclapsus Vitus, which consisted of judges, lawyers, doctors, merchants, and in fact the best eliment in the county.

After a year or so, we gave a grand ball in a large stable, illuminated with many tallow candles. The attendance was about 100 men to one lady. The music consisted of a fiddle and a banjo. To engage a partner for a dance was out of the question. I ventured to ask a Spanish girl for a dance, telling her my name was on her program. She cooly told me that I was a liar. That was the etiquette of those bygone days.

In 1851, my brother Solomon Shloss arrived in San Francisco, and I sent him up to Oregon with a stock of merchandise on the steamer "General Warren." The steamer was wrecked on the Columbia River bar, and forty-two lives were lost, my brother being one of them. I then opened a store at the southeast corner of Sansome and Commercial Streets.

In 1852, after being in business for three months, the greatest fire that ever occurred in San Francisco swept everything clean from California Street to Telegraph Hill, and from Dupont Street to Battery Street. I lost everything by this fourth fire, and I had not a cent of insurance, as there was not an insurance company in San Francisco at that time.

I then went to Humboldt Bay, hired a tent in Union Town (now the city of Eureka). I found five ships wrecked there on the beach. I remained there three months and then returned to San Francisco.

In 1853, I opened a store in Redding, Shasta County, and did very well. [I] made plenty of money in the ensuing two years, when a big fire broke out and the whole town was laid in ashes. I lost over $16,000, but managed to bring stock up again from San Francisco, although it took me six weeks to do so, for the Sacramento Valley was under water.

On my arrival with my goods, I was waited upon by a committee and told not to sell more than one pair of boots and one pair of blankets to each man, as there was no hope for any more goods to come in for the winter.

I again made a raise [stake], sold out, and left for San Francisco. [I] sent for my girl, got married, and settled down at last.

I then joined the Vigilance Committee [and] held a gun in my hand when [James P.] Casey and [Charles] Cora were hung. Was on guard in Fort Gunnybags at the time that Judge [David Smith] Terry was a prisoner [for knifing a Vigilante agent] and [Terry] came very near being hung. And [I was on guard] at the time that Yankee Sullivan [a ballot box stuffer] committed suicide by cutting his arm. And when, late in 1856, over 5,000 Vigilant Committeemen had a grand march and demonstration, we dispersed the thieves. Then we elected honest judges, banished all ballot box stuffers, and San Francisco was saved.

After reading this selection, consider these questions:

1. What was the medium of exchange in San Francisco? How did this contribute to inflated prices for goods? What else led to high prices?

2. What kinds of risks did businessmen face in early San Francisco?

3. Why do you think Shloss joined the Vigilance Committee?

SELECTION 4:

A Black Forty-Niner's Tale

Alvin Coffey came to California as a slave. His master brought him west during the Gold Rush. Once in California, Coffey earned five thousand dollars for his master while working in the mines. He also earned seven hundred for himself by working nights. His master confiscated the money Coffey earned for himself and then sold the slave to a new master. Coffey convinced his new owner to let him work to buy his freedom and that of his wife and children. This master kept to the agreement, and Coffey earned his freedom, brought his family to California, and established himself in Tehama County. Coffey became the only nonwhite member of the Society of California Pioneers. The following document, excerpted from his unpublished memoirs, describes his trip westward and his first days in California.

I started from St. Louis, Missouri, on the 2nd of April in 1849. There was quite a crowd of neighbors who drove through the mud and rain to St. Joe to see us off. About the first of May we organized the train. There were twenty wagons in number and from three to five men to each wagon.

We crossed the Missouri River at Savanna Landing on or about the 6th, no the 1st week in May. . . . At six in the morning, there were three more went to relieve those on guard. One of the three that came in had cholera so bad that he was in lots of misery. Dr. Bassett, the captain of the train, did all he could for him, but he died at 10 o'clock and we buried him. We got ready and started at 11 the same day and the moon was new just then.

We got news every day that people were dying by the hundreds in St. Joe and St. Louis. It was alarming. When we hitched up and got ready to move, [the] Dr. said, "Boys, we will have to drive day and night." . . . We drove night and day and got out of reach of the cholera. . . .

Excerpted from *Eyewitness: The Negro in American History,* edited by William Loren Katz (New York: Pitman Publishing Corporation, 1967).

We got across the plains to Fort Larimie, the 16th of June and the ignorant driver broke down a good many oxen on the trains. There were a good many ahead of us, who had doubled up their trains and left tons upon tons of bacon and other provisions. . . .

Starting to cross the desert to Black Rock at 4 o'clock in the evening, we traveled all night. The next day it was hot and sandy. . . .

A great number of cattle perished before we got to Black Rock. . . . I drove our oxen all the time and I knew about how much an ox could stand. Between nine and ten o'clock a breeze came up and the oxen threw up their heads and seemed to have new life. At noon, we drove into Black Rock. . . .

We crossed the South Pass on the Fourth of July. The ice next morning was as thick as a dinner-plate.

[The wagon train went on through Honey Lake to Deer Creek in Sacramento Valley and then to Redding Springs on October 13, 1849.] On the morning of the 15th we went to dry-digging mining. We dug and dug to the first of November, at night it commenced raining, and rained and snowed pretty much all the winter. We had a tent but it barely kept us all dry. There were from eight to twelve in one camp. We cut down pine trees for stakes to make a cabin. It was a whole week before we had a cabin to keep us dry.

The first week in January, 1850, we bought a hundred pounds of bear meat at one dollar per pound.

After reading this selection, consider these questions:

1. What dangers did Coffey and others in his train face?

2. In what ways were Coffey's experiences similar to those of Morris Shloss?

SELECTION 5:

A Woman's View of the Gold Rush

The scarcity of women in gold rush camps provided a wide range of economic opportunities for women. Not only were domestic skills such as cooking, sewing, washing laundry, and nursing in high demand, but some women also found occasion to engage in men's work, such as panning for gold. Mary B. Ballou went to California with her husband during the gold rush. There she ran a boardinghouse and found a number of other ways to make money. Boardinghouses were good business in the mining camps. In their frantic search for gold, most miners did not take time to build decent living quarters or to cook decent meals. Those who could afford it turned instead to boardinghouses. In the following letter dated October 30, 1852, and written to one of her sons, Ballou provides insight into her life in the mining camp at Negrobar, California.

My Dear Selden:

We are about as usual in health. Well I suppose you would like to know what I am doing in this gold region. Well I will try to tell you what my work is here in this muddy Place. All the kitchen that I have is four posts stuck down into the ground and covered over the top with factory cloth no floor but the ground. This is a Boarding House kitchen. There is a floor in the dining room and my sleeping room covered with nothing but cloth. We are at work in a Boarding House.

Oct. 27: This morning I awoke and it rained in torrents. Well I got up and I thought of my House. I went and looket into my kitchen. The mud and water was over my Shoes I could not go into the kitchen to do any work to day but kept perfectly dry in the Dining [room] so I got along verry well. Your Father put on his Boots and done the work in the kitchen. I felt badly to think that I was detined [destined] to be in such a place. . . .

Now I will try to tell you what my work is in this Boarding House. Well somtimes I am washing and Ironing somtimes I am making mince pie and Apple pie and squash pies. Somtimes frying mince turnovers and Donuts. I make Buiscuit and now and then Indian jonny cake and then again I am making minute puding filled with rasons and Indian Bake pudings and then again a nice Plum Puding and then again I am Stuffing a Ham of pork that cost forty cents a pound. Somtimes I am . . . making gruel for the sick now and then cooking oisters sometimes making coffee for the French people strong enough for any man to walk on that has Faith as Peter had. Three times a day I set my Table which is about thirty feet in length and do all the little fixings about it such as filling pepper boxes and vinegar cruits and mustard pots and Butter cups. Somtimes I am feeding my chickens and then again I am scareing the Hogs out of my kitchen and Driving the mules out of my Dining room. You can see by the description of that I have given you of my

kitchen that anything can walk into the kitchen that chooses to walk in and there being no door to shut from the kitchen into the Dining room so you see the Hogs and mules can walk in any time day or night if they choose to do so. Somtimes I am up all times a night scaring the Hogs and mules out of the House. Last night there a large rat came down pounce down onto our bed in the night. Sometimes I take my fan and try to fan myself but I work so hard that my Arms pain me so severely that I kneed some one to fan me so I do not find much comfort anywhere. I made a Bluberry puding to day for Dinner. Somtimes I am making soups and cramberry tarts and Baking chicken that cost four Dollars a head and cooking Eggs at three Dollars a Dozen. Somtimes boiling cabbage and Turnips and frying fritters and Broiling stake and cooking codfish and potatoes. I often cook nice Salmon trout that weigh from ten to twenty pound apiece. Somtimes I am taking care of Babies and nursing at the rate of Fifty Dollars a week but I would not advise any Lady to come out here and suffer the toil and fatigue that I have suffered for the sake of a little gold neither do I advise any one to come. Clarks Simmon wife says if she was safe in the States she would not care if she had not one cent. She came in here last night and said, "Oh dear I am so homesick that I must die," and then again my other associate came in with tears in her eyes and said that she had cried all day. She said if she had as good a home as I had got she would not stay twenty five minutes in California. I told her that she could not pick up her duds in that time. She said she would not stop for duds nor anything else but my own heart was two sad to cheer them much.

Now I will tell you a little more about my cooking. Somtimes I am cooking rabbits and Birds that are called quails here and I cook squrrels. Occasionly I run in and have a chat with Jane and Mrs. Durphy and I often have a hearty cry. No one but my maker knows my feelings. And then I run into my little cellar which is about four feet square as I have no other place to run that is cool.

October 21: Well I have been to church to hear a methodist sermon. His Text was let us lay aside every weight and the sin that doth so easely beset us. I was the only Lady that was present and about forty gentleman. So you see that I go to church when I can.

November 2: . . . The wind Blows verry hard here to day. I have three lights Burning and the wind blows so hard that it almost puts my lights out while I am trying to write. If you could but step in and see the inconvience that I have for writing you would not wonder that I cannot write any better you would wonder that I could write at all. Notwithstanding all the dificuty in writing I improve every leishure moment. It is quite cool here my fingers are so cold that I can hardly hold my pen. . . . There has been a little fighting here to day and one chalenge given but the chalenge given was not accepted they got together and settled their trouble. . . .

I washed out about a Dollars worth of gold dust the fourth of July in the cradle so you see that I am doing a little mining in this gold region but I think it harder to rock the cradle to wash out gold than it is to rock the cradle for the Babies in the States.

October 11: I washed in the forenoon and made a Democrat Flag in the afternoon, sewed twenty yards of splendid worsted fringe around it, and I made [a] Whig Flag. They are both swinging acrost the road but the Whig Flag is the richest. I had twelve Dollars for making them so you see that I am making Flags with all [the] rest of the various kinds of work that I am doing and then again I am scouring candle sticks and washing the floor and making soft soap. The People tell me that it is the first Soft Soap they knew made in California. Somtimes I am making mattresses and sheets. I have no windows in my room. All the light that I have shines through canvas that covers the House and my eyes are so dim that I can hardly see to make a mark so I think you will excuse me for not writing any better. I have three Lights burning now but I am so tired and Blind that I can scearcely see and here I am among the French and Duch and Scoth and Jews and Italions and Sweeds and Chineese and Indians and all manner of tongu[e]s and nations but I am treated with due respect by them all.

On the night of Election the second day of November was Burnt down and some lives lost. Adams['s] express office was Broken open by a band of robbers [and] a large quantity of money was taken. They took one man out of bed with his wife took him into the office and Bound him laid him on the floor and told him to give them the key to the safe or they would kill him. One of the robbers staid in the room [with] his wife; his face was muffled and Pistols by his side and [he] told her that if she made any noise for so long a time he would kill her. Only immagine what her feelings must be. I lived close by the office. I went in to see her the next morning [and] she told me that she nearly lost her sences she was so frigtned.

I immagine you will say what a long yarn this is from California. If you can read it at all. I must close soon for I am so tired and almost sick. Oh my Dear Selden I am so Home sick. I will say to you once more to see that Augustus has every thing that he kneeds to make him comfortable and by all means have him Dressed warm this cold winter. I worry a great deal about my Dear children. It seems as though my heart would break when I realise how far I am from my Dear Loved ones. This from your affectionate mother,

Mary B. Ballou

After reading this selection, consider these questions:

1. Describe the ethnic diversity of the mining camp, according to Ballou.

2. Compare the prices Ballou describes with those mentioned by Morris Shloss.

3. Discuss the ways in which the scarcity of women provided economic opportunity for women in mining camps.

UNIT 4

The Age of the Civil War

CONTENTS

The U.S. at the Beginning of the Civil War

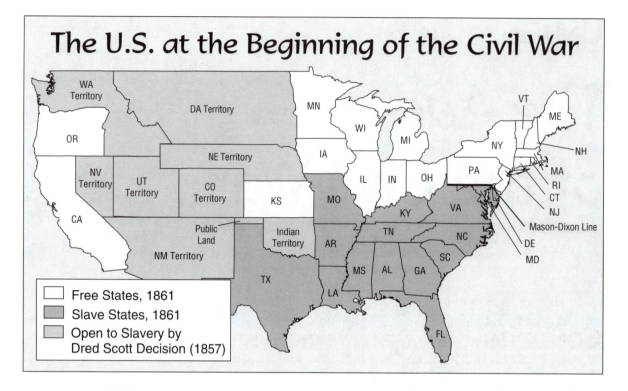

Free States, 1861

Slave States, 1861

Open to Slavery by
Dred Scott Decision (1857)

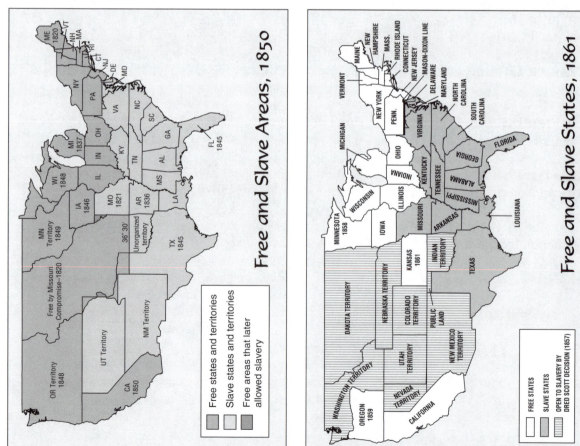

Free and Slave Areas, 1850

Free states and territories

Slave states and territories

Free areas that later
allowed slavery

Free and Slave States, 1861

FREE STATES

SLAVE STATES

OPEN TO SLAVERY BY
DRED SCOTT DECISION (1857)

UNIT 4

The Age of the Civil War

War often upsets the social order. Wars and the stresses they impose on society frequently develop a momentum that pushes participants beyond their original purposes. Emancipation provided an example of just such a process. Emancipation was not a Northern war aim at the beginning of the conflict; yet the exigencies of war led Abraham Lincoln to take that momentous step. Even the Confederacy debated the use of black soldiers and emancipation.

The Civil War was a war fought by highly literate soldiers on both sides and highly politicized ones. Indeed, ideology played an important role in the coming of the Civil War. A sectional crisis that evolved over decades led to the development of two coherent ideologies, and the differences between them had been debated and agitated for decades. In his book, *What They Fought For* (1994), James M. McPherson concludes that "a large number of those men in blue and gray were intensely aware of the issues at stake and passionately concerned about them." The selections by Eric Foner and George M. Fredrickson in chapter 17 provide insights into the ideologies of the North and the South.

The Civil War was a bloody struggle. The North enjoyed many material advantages; the South had many strategic advantages. In chapter 18, an essay by McPherson assesses the relative advantages of the North and the South; one by T. Harry Williams assesses the military leadership of the two sides.

The war upset the arrangement of the races in both the Union and the Confederacy. Lincoln's Emancipation Proclamation marked an important point in the evolution of Northern war aims. Eventually, the eradication of slavery became an inevitable consequence of Northern victory. At the same time, the Union had to struggle with the decision to use blacks as soldiers—a decision that derived more from the necessities of war than any commitment to racial equality. Aside from any changes in perception, the progress of the war itself had a profound impact on the lives of slaves and Southern blacks. Slaves freed by Union armies began new lives. Some served in the armed forces (as did a number of blacks from the

North). Others, including black women, served the Union army in noncombatant roles.

If the war challenged the racial status quo, it also challenged traditional gender roles. Women on both sides replaced men in factories, on farms, in expanding government bureaucracies, and in front of classrooms. Even women who never made a deliberate decision to participate in the war effort or to take on new economic roles did not escape the impact of the war. On both sides, the war left thousands of widows, spinsters, and wives of disabled veterans.

The victory of the North meant not only a victory for the Union and the abolition of slavery but also the ultimate triumph of Northern industrial capitalism. American society would never be the same.

After reading this unit, consider these questions:

1. What role did ideology play in the coming of the Civil War?

2. What events contributed to the coming of the war?

3. In what ways did the Civil War change American society?

4. What unexpected consequences emerged from the experience of the war?

5. How did the war affect African Americans?

6. How did the war affect women?

CHAPTER 16

Sectional Crisis

The United States grew rapidly in the first half of the nineteenth century. Spurred by immigration as well as natural increase, its population increased more than fourfold. The Union, which had consisted of sixteen states in 1800, had thirty-four states by 1850, and its territory expanded across a continent. The real per capita income of Americans doubled over the same time span. America's cities experienced dramatic growth.

Over all of the signs of success, however, loomed a darkening cloud. The North and the South had embarked on different paths of development and had evolved into two distinct societies with radically different worldviews. The North was increasingly urban, commercial, and industrial; the South remained committed to plantation agriculture and slave labor. From a Northern perspective, the South appeared an economically undeveloped region dominated by a small slave-owning aristocracy. Slavery, believed many Northerners, was not only immoral but also hindered economic development and the spirit of enterprise. Southerners, on the other hand, regarded their production and export of cotton as the main source of national economic growth, from which Northerners benefited enormously. In addition, Southerners did not regard slavery as a brutal and immoral institution; rather, they saw it as a benevolent institution offering great advantages to an inferior race. Slave owners contrasted their paternalistic treatment of their slaves with the harsh lives of "wage slaves" in the North and accused antislavery northerners of gross hypocrisy.

The struggle over slavery in the territories acquired from Mexico brought the differences between the sections to the fore. Sectionalism had been a cause for concern from the earliest days of the American republic. Nevertheless, most people never doubted the ability of the Union to overcome sectional discord. Events of the 1850s led many to question that assumption.

After reading this chapter, consider these questions:

1. What led to separate economic development in the North and the South?

2. How did separate economic development lead to the emergence of separate societies?

3. What specific political issues arose from separate economic development?

4. What brought the disagreements between the North and the South to a head?

SELECTION 1:

The Nullification Crisis and the Slavery Issue

The nullification crisis, described by Robert Remini in chapter 13, was ostensibly a disagreement about the protective tariff. In his classic book, Prelude to Civil War: The Nullification Controversy in South Carolina, 1816–1836 *(1965), William W. Freehling, a professor of history at the University of Kentucky, argues that underlying the debate over the tariff was Southern insecurity over slavery. South Carolina's position in the tariff controversy, argues Freehling, was in actuality an "indirect defense of slavery." In the following essay, Freehling summarizes that argument.*

They did not look like an oppressed minority.

The fastidiously dressed squires, fresh from bouts at the feasting table, swaggered up to embattled Charleston Bay. Retinues of black slaves trailed respectfully at a distance. Peering across the water, white knights scoffed at plebeians in federal forts. It seemed hardly worth a gentleman's time to blast the rabble out.

To hear John C. Calhoun tell it, these South Carolina slaveholders were themselves enslaved. The scruffy soldiers training federal guns on Charleston were agents of majority despotism.

The polished patricians pushing to give President [Andrew] Jackson his comeuppance were verging on extinction. Jackson's notion that he was but preserving the majority's right to make law was nonsense. Unless oppressed minorities could nullify illegitimate majoritarian law, democracy would become but "might makes right." In that case, the rich and mighty would fall. America could become the land of the scummy herd.

The South Carolina nullifiers' notion that the rich need protection from the poor was nothing new under the American sun. It had informed much Federalist rhetoric and some Jeffersonian. It was endemic to the conservative outcry of ultra-Whigs like [New York City mayor] Phillip Hone no less than to the extremist measures of [U.S. vice president] John C. Calhoun. Men of property will ever tremble that the democratic beast could get out of hand.

But what thrust nullifiers into shivering isolation was the way they defined minority interest. Their exalted minority was not an embattled upper class. It was not even the planter segment of the American upper class. It was a fragment of a fragment of a fragment. Theirs was the notion that tiny and isolated extremes should give law to massive majorities. They lost. They won in the losing. Their victory commenced a trail of victories which threw the very meaning of majority rule in doubt.

The grand crisis in ideology started as a provincial battle over taxes. In 1828 and again in 1832, national congressional majorities passed high protective tariffs. South Carolina planters, aware that discouraging imports would discourage cotton and rice exports, believed that southern exporters would slide towards bankruptcy. High tariffs, they urged, violated the Constitution. Moreover, if a northern high tariff majority could trample on the Constitution, southern minorities had no constitutional protection against antislavery laws.

South Carolina's peculiar social structure led to an early and acute sensitivity to such problems. The more ocean-bound, lower half of the state was a dense, malaria-infested swamp kept from relapsing into jungle by a veritable army of slaves. A ten-to-one ratio of blacks to whites typified most low-country areas. Improved land costs of $100 per acre were common. Allow emancipation, everyone believed, and the white slaveholder's most fabulous kingdom would become a genuine African jungle.

The upper half of the state, in contrast, was the Cotton South's most degenerating empire. Upcountry Carolina, as the first Deep South recipient of the Eli Whitney cotton-gin bonanza, was also the first to gut its soil. Whereas every other Deep South state was clearing land, buying slaves, and flexing muscles like an audacious adolescent, up-country Carolinians were abandoning plantations, hemorrhaging away population, and wailing about ebbing vitality.

The two halves of South Carolina, taken together, were the oldest of Deep South states, the most unified, the most proud, the most aristo-cratic, the most declining, the most frightened, and the most convulsively committed. Such characteristics goaded Carolinians to spy monopolists and abolitionists where other southerners saw but the thin air. Some lethal weapon, Carolina nabobs believed, had to be found to rouse the South and rout the North.

The best weapon available was John C. Calhoun's doctrine of nullification. Vice President Calhoun, in a secret report to the South Carolina legislature in 1828, had argued that no arm of the federal government had final power to interpret the Constitution. Otherwise, minorities would be powerless. Majorities elected the Congress and the President; and a majoritarian President could conspire with a majoritarian Congress to place majoritarian judges on the Supreme Court. The final judge of constitutional issues, Calhoun affirmed, must be the state conventions which had originally adopted the Constitution. Every significant minority could control at least one state. If any one state could declare unconstitutional laws null and void, King Law would replace King Numbers. Majorities would rule without trampling on minorities.

In November of 1832, a South Carolina convention gave Calhoun's theories practical expression. The convention declared the federal tariff laws of 1828 and 1832 null and void in South Carolina. Attempts to collect duties by force would be resisted by force. The minority had spoken. The majority must halt.

President Andrew Jackson, recently swept into office for a second term by a heady majority, had no intention of halting. He ordered reinforcements into Charleston Harbor. He secured a Force Bill from Congress. The majority, he said, must rule. The Union, he proclaimed, must be preserved.

Some South Carolina hotheads were in fact aching to bust up the Union. Calhoun was not of their number. The Vice President, now resigning to become Senator from South Carolina, considered his brainchild the only way to preserve the Union. If fire-eaters like his brethren had no protection against majoritarian slavery and tariff outrages, the Union would eventually be smashed. Fanatical minorities would unceremoniously walk out of uncontrolled democracies. At issue was more than the legitimacy of majorities. At stake was the very survival of working democracy. . . .

The very rhetoric of slaveholders calling themselves enslaved called attention to Calhoun's incongruous position as minority spokesman. To slaveholders, no incongruity existed. Only blacks were slaves. Only whites were citizens. Only citizens had rights. . . .

The anti-nullification minority in South Carolina no less mocked nullification as minority salvation. Non-slaveholding yeomen in up-country mountains and non-slaveholding merchants in Charleston eagerly volunteered for Jackson's army. They had no other protection against being jailed as traitors for minority protests against Calhoun's majoritarian dictatorship at home. . . .

While protests in South Carolina undermined Calhoun's position as minority spokesman, protests from other southern states exploded his position as representative of a planter minority. Most southern planters thought nullification extreme. They had not yet lost hope that the majority would lower the tariff. They were not yet sure slavery was in danger. They disliked the notion that majority will becomes law only when every minority of a minority agrees. Calhoun had called nullification viable because every interest controlled one state. In fact, the plantation minority controlled many states and hoped nullification would be repudiated.

Calhoun's theories thus seemed to unravel wherever messy reality intruded. The supposedly enslaved minority was itself one of the world's greatest slaveholders. The allegedly helpless national minority was a tyrannical state majority. The supposed representative of planter interest was wildly unrepresentative. What with opposition in Carolina and outrage elsewhere, the arch nullifier seemed destined for a noose as he headed into Jackson's Washington. Instead, he all but dictated terms of a settlement. He thus gave the coup de grace to his own notion of powerless minorities.

Calhoun's victory was obscured, not least to Calhoun himself, by Jackson's demolition of nullification. Congress, in the Force Bill, gave the President all necessary power to make South Carolina obey the law. The Force Bill was a perpetual national monument warning that state veto would never be tolerated.

But Congress also lowered the tariff Carolina had called intolerable. The majority gave in and passed the Compromise Tariff of 1833 partly because most Americans wanted lower tariffs anyway. The high tariff laws of earlier Congress were overdue for overhauling. In a nation of exporting farmers, free trade easily became sacred text.

In one sense, the successful blackmail vindicated Calhoun's exploded theory. He had urged that democracy would collapse if potentially secessionist extremes were left dangerously disgruntled. President Jackson and the American majority had indirectly accepted that logic. Revolutionary extremes must be appeased if the democratic consensus is to endure. The majority's own desire for tariff reform had made the appeasement of 1833 easy. But how would the system work when the blackmailer demanded that majority give noxious appeasement? And how could democracy survive if the blackmailer was not appeased?

The ensuing thirty years of American history would provide answers to those questions. . . .

In the years after nullification, the Carolina position that the world was closing in on slavery became slowly more plausible to others in the Cotton South. The South was ever more clearly in a permanent minority. Abolition was ever more surely sweeping bondage from Latin America. Abolitionists were ever more stridently demanding action from the North. Yankees, although with massive misgivings, showed signs of someday listening. Some southern areas, particularly in the more northern South, showed signs of someday surrendering. If Deep South slaveholders were to avoid becoming the last of a vanishing breed, proslavery perpetualists saw need to blast the tendencies of history aside. . . .

Such hidebound reactionaries are beyond soothing. Their antennas register the softest hint of danger, and American antislavery hints were not the softest. No matter how often the northern majority indicated willingness to let well enough alone, southern extremists could not forget what the northern minority wanted—and where an age of romantic democracy was drifting.

Again and again, plantation ultras sought to nullify their age. They did not call it nullification. Jackson's Force Bill had made state veto disreputable. But nullification as a power play had little to do with state veto. The iron behind Calhoun's velvet was the threat of secession, and that threat, emanating especially from South Carolina, became a great staple of American antebellum politics.

In prewar years, as in the nullification confrontation, southern ultras gained power by taking normal southern fears to an extreme. Everywhere in southern plantation black belts, men worried about "holier-than-thou" northerners and about secretly disloyal southerners. Throughout the slaveholding South, bondage was considered the bulwark keeping black men this side of barbarism. Accordingly, whenever southern extremists sought to bring off confrontation, southern moderates used the occasion to demand concessions. Northern Democrats continued to consider appeasing the demand patriotism to party and country. The plantation South thus had the leverage of the nation's majority party. The ultimatums of a few helped turn democracy into minority rule.

The first post-nullification ultimatum came three years after nullification had supposedly been nullified. In 1835, southerners demanded that Congress gag discussion of slavery. If a Gag Rule was not passed, warned a minority of the southern minority, the South would smash the Union. Southern Democrats demanded concessions. Northern Democrats obliged. A Gag Rule was passed.

In 1850, southerners demanded that Congress force northerners to return alleged fugitive slaves without a prior jury trial. Even if a Fugitive Slave Law was passed, warned a minority of the southern minority, South Carolina and a couple of other states would try to smash the Union. Northern Democrats and more moderate southerners wished to isolate so ferocious an extreme. A Fugitive Slave Law was passed.

In 1854, southerners demanded that Congress repeal the sanctified Missouri Compromise and open the plains of Kansas to the possibility of enslavement. Again, the minority threatened. Again, southern Democrats demanded. Again, northern Democrats acquiesced.

But the northern Democrats' cave-in came with escalating outrage. Northerners, watching a system supposedly based on majority rule continually yield minority triumphs, came to believe a conspiracy was sabotaging democracy. A slave-power conspiracy, so the Yankee argument went, was demolishing the system and had to be stopped. The way to stop the conspiracy was to replace the Democratic party.

After 1854, a Republican party opposition grew like a hurricane in the North. Northern Democrats, trapped between southern demands and constituents' disgust, found their numbers drastically dwindling in Congress. They came to believe, along with their Republican opponents, that it was high time to call the blackmailers' bluff.

The bluff was first called in 1860. At the national Democratic party convention in Charleston, southern extremists demanded that the party endorse slave protection in national territories. Otherwise, said [representative] William L. Yancey and fellow spirits, they would walk out. Northern Democrats said nay. Yancey walked. Only a minority of southern delegates followed. They were enough to set in motion a stream of party combat that savaged the last major, national, pre–Civil War party.

During the ensuing national presidential canvass, many Deep South planters urged secession if Abraham Lincoln won. Lincoln won. The southern majority then wished to wait and see if Lincoln tried overt antislavery acts. The minority of the southern minority, particularly in South Carolina, had waited too long. South Carolina's secession was enough to set in motion a stream of national disintegration which could only end in trial by war.

After reading this selection, consider these questions:

1. Why did South Carolina planters consider themselves a minority?

2. How does Freehling connect nullification with secession?

3. In the nullification crisis, both sides pulled back from the brink. What had changed by 1860–1861?

SELECTION 2:

Bleeding Kansas

The Compromise of 1850 admitted California to the Union as a free state. However, it made no mention of slavery in the Utah and New Mexico territories. Southerners retained the right to bring slaves there, but most people believed that natural conditions were such that none would do so. Other elements of the compromise included banning the slave trade in Washington, D.C., and passing a new fugitive slave law.

Four years later, Senator Stephen A. Douglas, in an effort to expedite westward expansion, introduced a bill organizing the area west and northwest of Missouri as the Nebraska Territory. Since the area lay north of latitude thirty-six degrees, thirty minutes (under the Missouri Compromise, territory acquired in the Louisiana Purchase north of that line was closed to slavery), most presumed that any states admitted from that area would be free states.

Responding to pressure from Southern senators, Douglas amended his bill so that it divided the area into two territories (Kansas and Nebraska) and left the decision on slavery to the settlers of the territory under the doctrine of popular sovereignty. This effectively repealed the provision of the Missouri Compromise banning slavery north of latitude thirty-six degrees, thirty minutes. Many saw this as a means of admitting Nebraska as a free state and Kansas as a slave state. Douglas skillfully guided the bill through Congress, but it led to a bloody guerrilla war in Kansas.

James M. McPherson is a professor of history at Princeton University and the author of what many consider to be the best book ever written on the Civil War, Battle Cry of Freedom *(1988). In the following excerpt from another of his books, McPherson describes the brutal conflict in Kansas.*

The Republicans took over the Free Soil commitment to the principle of the Wilmot Proviso as their central tenet: no slavery in the territories, no more slave states. When the antislavery forces lost the congressional battle for a free Kansas, they vowed to carry the struggle to the territory itself. "Since there is no escaping your challenge," Senator [William H.] Seward told his Southern colleagues, "I accept it in behalf of the cause of freedom. We will engage in competition for the virgin soil of Kansas, and God give the victory to the side which is stronger in numbers as it is in right." On the other side, Senator [David] Atchison of Missouri wrote: "We are playing for a mighty stake; if we win we carry slavery to the Pacific Ocean, if we fail we lose Missouri, Arkansas, and Texas and all the territories; the game must be played boldly."

And boldly did he play. Although the Free Soil forces organized first, forming the New England Emigrant Aid Company in the summer of 1854

Excerpted from *Ordeal by Fire: The Civil War and Reconstruction,* by James M. McPherson (New York: Alfred A. Knopf, 1982). Copyright © 1982 by Alfred A. Knopf, Inc. Reprinted with permission.

to finance settlements in Kansas, it was Atchison's people who did the first settling. Most of the early settlers in Kansas came from Missouri. Some brought their slaves with them. Most of the free soil settlers came from Midwestern states. Only a sprinkling of New Englanders migrated to Kansas, but the publicity surrounding the New England Emigrant Aid Company provoked proslavery partisans to portray a Yankee conspiracy to abolitionize the West. Much of the subsequent conflict between free soil and proslavery settlers was of the sort typical in frontier communities: clashes over land claims or town sites or water rights, and the inevitable violence of settlements without established institutions of law and order. But because Kansas was the national cockpit of the slavery question, all conflicts became polarized around this issue.

In the fall of 1854, Andrew Reeder, a Pennsylvania Democrat, arrived in Kansas to begin his duties as territorial governor. His first task was to supervise an election for the territory's delegate to Congress. The proslavery men were determined to make this initial test of popular sovereignty come out in their favor. On election day, 1,700 armed Missourians crossed the border to vote in Kansas. These "border ruffians," as the antislavery press dubbed them, swelled the overwhelming majority that sent a proslavery delegate to Washington.

The border ruffians repeated their tactics in the election of a territorial legislature in March 1855. This time, four or five thousand of them swarmed across the border. Atchison returned home from the Senate to lead the invasion. "There are eleven hundred coming over from Platte County to vote," he told his followers, "and if that ain't enough we can send five thousand—enough to kill every Goddamned abolitionist in the Territory." Although by this time bona fide settlers from free states were in the majority, the proslavery voters cast 5,247 ballots, the free soilers 791. A congressional investigation later concluded that 4,968 of the proslavery votes were fraudulent. But Governor Reeder, intimidated by the Missourians, refused to order a new election. Although urged to take corrective action, President [Franklin] Pierce did nothing. The Southern press applauded. "Missourians have nobly defended

our rights," declared an Alabama newspaper. The legislature (or "bogus legislature," as antislavery men called it) passed a draconian slave code. It restricted officeholding to avowed proslavery men. Anyone who questioned the legality of slavery in Kansas could be imprisoned, and anyone who advocated a slave rebellion or aided the escape of fugitive slaves could be put to death.

Outraged free-state settlers began to organize in self-defense. They turned the town of Lawrence into an antislavery stronghold and began arming themselves with "Beecher's Bibles" (so called because antislavery clergyman Henry Ward Beecher had said that Sharps rifles would do more than Bibles just then to enforce morality in Kansas). They organized a free-state party, held an election for a constitutional convention (boycotted by the proslavery voters), met in Topeka to draw up a constitution prohibiting slavery, and established their own legislature in the winter of 1855–1856. To prove that they were not the "abolitionist fanatics" portrayed by the proslavery press, the free-staters adopted an ordinance banning the entry of free blacks as well as of slaves.

Kansas now had two territorial governments —one legal but fraudulent, the other illegal but representing a majority of settlers. In Washington, the President and the Democratic-controlled Senate recognized the former, while the Republican-organized House favored the latter. When Governor Reeder declared his sympathy with the free-staters, Pierce replaced him with a solid proslavery man, Wilson Shannon. The Republican party benefited from Northern anger at the border ruffians, whose buccaneering practices the antislavery press played up for all they were worth.

Meanwhile in Kansas the sporadic violence took more organized form. In November 1855, each side mobilized several hundred armed men along the Wakarusa River. The Missourians prepared to attack Lawrence, but at the last minute Governor Shannon persuaded them to desist. This "Wakarusa War" amounted to nothing more than a few skirmishes. The harsh winter that followed kept everyone indoors for several months. But with the coming of spring, violence burst forth once again. On May 21 an army of seven hundred proslavery men rode into Lawrence, destroyed the offices of two newspapers and threw their presses into the river, burned down the hotel and the house of the free-state "governor," and pillaged the stores. . . .

Thus far, Southerners had committed most of the violence in the Kansas controversy. But out in Kansas was a man who believed in an eye for an eye. John Brown looked and acted like an Old Testament prophet. A Connecticut-born abolitionist who had failed in most of his business and farming enterprises, Brown had drifted west and in 1855 settled in Kansas with several of his sons. He raised a free-state military company that participated in the Wakarusa War. In May 1856, this company was on its way to defend Lawrence when word reached it that the town had already been sacked. When he heard this news Brown was seized with "frenzy." It was time to "fight fire with fire," he said, to "strike terror in the hearts of the proslavery people." When the company learned the next day about the caning of [Charles] Sumner [who had been attacked on the floor of the Senate by Preston Brooks, a congressman from South Carolina], Brown "went crazy—*crazy,*" according to witnesses. "It seemed to be the finishing, decisive touch." Brown led a party containing four of his sons and two other men on a nighttime raid along Pottawatomie Creek. They seized five proslavery settlers from their cabins and murdered them in cold blood by splitting their skulls with broadswords.

This butchery launched full-scale guerrilla war in Kansas. Although shocked antislavery people in the East denied—or chose not to believe —the truth about these killings, most Kansans knew who had done them. For the next four months, hit-and-run attacks by both sides raged in Kansas and were exaggerated by the national press into full-scale battles. Several newspapers had a standing headline for news from Kansas: "Progress of the Civil War." John Brown participated in these skirmishes, and one of his sons was killed. About two hundred other men died in the Kansas fighting during 1856. In September, President Pierce finally replaced the ineffective Governor Shannon with John Geary, a tough but fairminded Pennsylvanian who had won his spurs as a captain in the Mexican War and as San Francisco's first mayor. Combining persuasion with a skillful deployment of federal troops, Geary imposed a truce on the two sides and brought an uneasy peace to Kansas in the fall of 1856. By this time the larger question of which Kansas was a part—slavery in the territories— was the focus of the presidential election.

After reading this selection, consider these questions:

1. Look up the Missouri Compromise in your textbook and examine a map of the United States. Why were proslavery forces better able to send settlers into Kansas?

2. Stephen Douglas guided Henry Clay's Compromise of 1850 through Congress. To understand why he was willing to undo his own work just four years later, one must consider that he was a director of the Illinois Central Railroad and a land speculator. Look at a map of the United States and consider why Douglas was so anxious to see the Nebraska Territory organized.

SELECTION 3:

Senator Calhoun Threatens Secession

The question of extending slavery and potentially shifting the balance between free and slave states divided the nation from the earliest days of the new republic. Discord over the issue flared in 1820, but the Missouri Compromise quieted the matter for a few years. However, the annexation of Texas, the war with Mexico, and the subsequent acquisition of territory in the Southwest combined to bring the contentious issue to the fore once again.

By this time, moreover, the two sections had embarked on separate paths of development, and each had come to view the other with deep suspicion. A crisis arose when the sudden increase in California's population after the gold rush raised the question of statehood for California. Inextricably connected to statehood for California was the organization of the other territories acquired from Mexico. Would these territories be open to slavery?

In an attempt to defuse a controversy that threatened the Union, Senator Henry Clay proposed the Compromise of 1850. The debate over Clay's compromise produced one of the most extraordinary episodes in the history of the Senate. Clay, John C. Calhoun, and Daniel Webster, who had dominated legislative politics for a generation, took center stage for the last time. The nation tottered on the edge of disunion, but both sides stared into the abyss and pulled back.

The following document is an excerpt from Calhoun's passionate defense of the Southern cause and the need for accommodation to the Southern position if the South were to remain in the Union. Dying of tuberculosis and too ill to read the lengthy speech himself, the senator from South Carolina sat and listened while Senator James Mason of Virginia read it for him.

I have, Senators, believed from the first that the agitation of the subject of slavery would, if not prevented by some timely and effective measure, end in disunion. . . . The agitation has been per-

Excerpted from *Sources of the American Republic: Documentary History of Politics, Society, and Thought,* edited by Marvin Meyers, Alexander Kern, and John G. Cawelti (Chicago: Scott, Foresman and Company, 1960).

mitted to proceed, with almost no attempt to resist it, until it has reached a period when it can no longer be disguised or denied that the Union is in danger. You have thus had forced upon you the greatest and the gravest question that can ever come under your consideration: How can the Union be preserved? . . .

The first question, then, presented for consideration, in the investigation I propose to make, in order to obtain such knowledge, is: What is it that has endangered the Union?

To this question there can be but one answer: that the immediate cause is the almost universal discontent which pervades all the States composing the southern section of the Union. . . . It commenced with the agitation of the slavery question, and has been increasing ever since. . . .

It is a great mistake to suppose, as is by some, that it originated with demagogues, who excited the discontent with the intention of aiding their personal advancement, or with the disappointed ambition of certain politicians, who resorted to it as the means of retrieving their fortunes. On the contrary, all the great political influences of the section were arrayed against excitement, and exerted to the utmost to keep the people quiet. . . . Some cause, far deeper and more powerful than the one supposed, must exist, to account for discontent so wide and deep. The question, then, recurs: What is the cause of this discontent? It will be found in the belief of the people of the southern States, as prevalent as the discontent itself, that they cannot remain, as things now are, consistently with honor and safety, in the Union. The next question to be considered is: What has caused this belief?

One of the causes is, undoubtedly, to be traced to the long-continued agitation of the slave question on the part of the North, and the many aggressions which they have made on the rights of the South during the time. . . .

There is another, lying back of it, with which this is intimately connected, that may be regarded as the great and primary cause. That is to be found in the fact that the equilibrium between the two sections in the Government, as it stood when the constitution was ratified and the Government put in action, has been destroyed. At that time there was nearly a perfect equilibrium between the two, which afforded ample means to each to protect itself against the aggression of the other; but, as it now stands, one section has the exclusive power of controlling the Government, which leaves the other without any adequate means of protecting itself against its encroachment and oppression. . . .

The census is to be taken this year, which must add greatly to the decided preponderance of the North in the House of Representatives and in the electoral college. The prospect is, also, that a great increase will be added to its present preponderance in the Senate during the period of the decade, by the addition of new States. Two Territories, Oregon and Minnesota, are already in progress, and strenuous efforts are making to bring in three additional States from the territory recently conquered from Mexico; which, if successful, will add three other States in a short time to the northern section, making five States; and increasing the present number of its States from fifteen to twenty, and of its Senators from thirty to forty. On the contrary, there is not a single territory in progress in the southern section, and no certainty that any additional State will be added to it during the decade. . . . This great increase of Senators, added to the great increase of members of the House of Representatives and the electoral college on the part of the North, which must take place under the next decade, will effectually and irretrievably destroy the equilibrium which existed when the Government commenced. . . .

What was once a constitutional Federal Republic is now converted, in reality, into one as absolute as that of the Autocrat of Russia, and as despotic in its tendency as any absolute Government that ever existed.

As, then, the North has the absolute control over the Government, it is manifest that on all questions between it and the South, where there is a diversity of interests, the interests of the latter will be sacrificed to the former, however oppressive the effects may be, as the South possesses no means by which it can resist through the action of the Government. But if there was no question of vital importance to the South, in reference to which there was a diversity of views between the two sections, this state of things might be endured without the hazard of destruction to the South. But such is not the fact. There is a question of vital importance to the southern section, in reference to which the views and feelings of the two sections are as opposite and hostile as they can possibly be.

I refer to the relation between the two races in the southern section, which constitutes a vital portion of her social organization. Every portion of the North entertains views and feelings more or less hostile to it. . . .

[A] small fanatical party began to acquire strength; and with that to become an object of courtship to both the great parties. The necessary consequence was a further increase of power, and a gradual tainting of the opinions of both of the other parties with their doctrines until the infection has extended over both; and the great mass of the population of the North who, whatever may be their opinion of the original abolition party, which still preserves its distinctive organization, hardly ever fail, when it comes to acting, to cooperate in carrying out their measures. . . .

Instead of being weaker, all the elements in favor of agitation are stronger now than they were in 1835, when it first commenced, while all the elements of influence on the part of the South are weaker. Unless something decisive is done, I again ask what is to stop this agitation, before the great and final object at which it aims—the abolition of slavery in the States—is consummated? Is it, then, not certain that if something decisive is not now done to arrest it, the South will be forced to choose between abolition and secession? Indeed, as events are now moving, it will not require the South to secede to dissolve the Union. . . .

If the agitation goes on, the same force, acting with increased intensity, as has been shown, will finally snap every cord, when nothing will be left to hold the States together except force. . . .

Having now, Senators, explained what it is that endangers the Union, and traced it to its cause, and explained its nature and character, the question again recurs, How can the Union be saved? To this I answer, there is but one way by which it can be, and that is, by adopting such measures as will satisfy the States belonging to the southern section that they can remain in the Union consistently with their honor and their safety.

After reading this selection, consider these questions:

1. Why does Calhoun believe that the position of the South is growing weaker?

2. What does Calhoun say has endangered the Union?

3. What does he recommend to save the Union?

4. How does Calhoun's speech support William W. Freehling's analysis (excerpted in this chapter) of South Carolina's position?

SELECTION 4:

Senator Webster Speaks for the Union

The increase of sectional tensions after the Mexican war strained the unity of the Whig Party. Ultimately, the Whigs would not survive, and the antislavery wing would join the new Republican party in 1856. Daniel Webster, a senator from Massachusetts, was a longtime rival of Henry Clay for the leadership of the Whig Party and for the presidency. Three

*days after Calhoun gave the speech from which the previous document
was excerpted, Webster, who had been a nationalist Whig throughout his
career, rose in defense of Clay's compromise and the Union. Clay's compromise proposed the admission of California as a free state and the organization of the rest of the Mexican cession without any restriction against
slavery. Webster argued that, "beyond all terms of human enactment . . .
slavery cannot exist in California or New Mexico" and that both were thus
"destined to be free." He therefore opposed a ban on slavery in those territories on the grounds that it was a useless exercise and constituted an
unnecessary insult to the South. Antislavery Whigs, also known as conscience Whigs, regarded Webster's position as a betrayal. He had, after
all, voted for the Wilmot Proviso (which would have banned slavery from
the territory gained from Mexico). In the following excerpt from Webster's
speech, he pleaded passionately for the preservation of the Union and further infuriated antislavery Whigs by defending the fugitive slave law that
was part of Clay's compromise.*

Mr. President, I wish to speak to-day, not as a Massachusetts man, nor as a northern man, but as an American, and a member of the Senate of the United States. . . . It is not to be denied that we live in the midst of strong agitations, and sur-rounded by very considerable dangers to our institutions of government. . . . I speak to-day for the preservation of the Union. "Hear me, for my cause.". . .

We may reflect for a moment upon the entire coincidence and concurrence of sentiment between the North and the South upon this question, at the period of the adoption of the Constitution. . . .

There was unanimity of sentiment, if not a general concurrence of sentiment, running through the whole community, and especially entertained by the eminent men of all portions of the coun-try, in regard to this subject. But soon a change began at the North and the South, and a sever-ance of opinion soon showed itself—the North growing much more warm and strong against slavery, and the South growing much more warm and strong in its support. . . .

The honorable member from Carolina [John C. Calhoun] observed, that there has been a ma-jority all along in favor of the North. If that be

true, sir, the North acted either very liberally and kindly, or very weakly; for they never exercised that majority five times in the history of the Gov-ernment. Never. Whether they were out-generalled, or whether it was owing to other causes, I shall not stop to consider, but no man acquainted with the history of the country can deny, that the gen-eral lead in the politics of the country, for three-fourths of the period that has elapsed since the adoption of the Constitution, has been a southern lead. . . .

Mr. President, in the excited times in which we live, there is found to exist a state of crimma-tion and recrimination between the North and the South. There are lists of grievances produced by each; and those grievances, real or supposed, alienate the minds of one portion of the country from the other, exasperate the feelings, subdue the sense of fraternal connection, and patriotic love, and mutual regard. I shall bestow a little at-tention, sir, upon these various grievances, pro-duced on the one side and on the other. I begin with the complaints of the South: I will not an-swer, farther than I have, the general statements of the honorable Senator from South Carolina, that the North has grown upon the South in con-sequence of the manner of administering this Government, in the collecting of its revenues, and so forth. These are disputed topics, and I have no inclination to enter into them. But I will state

Excerpted from *The Congressional Globe,* edited by John C. Rives (Washington, DC: Office of John C. Rives, 1850).

these complaints, especially one complaint of the South, which has in my opinion just foundation; and that is, that there has been found at the North, among individuals and among the Legislatures of the North, a disinclination to perform, fully, their constitutional duties, in regard to the return of persons bound to service, who have escaped into the free States. In that respect, it is my judgment that the South is right, and the North is wrong. Every member of every northern Legislature is bound, by oath, like every other officer in the country, to support the Constitution of the United States; and this article of the Constitution, which says to these States, they shall deliver up fugitives from service, is as binding in honor and conscience as any other article. . . .

Mr. President, I should much prefer to have heard, from every member on this floor, declarations of opinion that this Union should never be dissolved, than the declaration of opinion that in any case, under the pressure of any circumstances, such a dissolution was possible. I hear with pain, and anguish, and distress, the word secession, especially when it falls from the lips of those who are eminently patriotic, and known to the country, and known all over the world, for their political services. Secession! Peaceable secession! Sir, your eyes and mine are never destined to see that miracle. . . .

Peaceable secession! peaceable secession! The concurrent agreement of all the members of this great Republic to separate! A voluntary separation, with alimony on one side and on the other. Why, what would be the result? Where is the line to be drawn? What States are to secede? What is to remain American? What am I to be?—an American no longer? Where is the flag of the Republic to remain? Where is the eagle still to tower? or is he to cower, and shrink, and fall to the ground? Why, sir, our ancestors—our fathers, and our grandfathers, those of them that are yet living among us with prolonged lives—would rebuke and reproach us; and our children, and our grandchildren, would cry out, Shame upon us! . . . I know, although the idea has not been stated distinctly, there is to be a southern Confederacy. I do not mean, when I allude to this statement, that any one seriously contemplates such a state of things. I do not mean to say that it is true, but I have heard it suggested elsewhere, that that idea has originated in a design to separate. I am sorry, sir, that it has ever been thought of, talked of, or dreamed of, in the wildest flights of human imagination. But the idea must be of a separation, including the slave States upon one side, and the free States on the other. Sir, there is not—I may express myself too strongly perhaps—but some things, some moral things, are almost as impossible, as other natural or physical things; and I hold the idea of a separation of these States—those that are free to form one government, and those that are slaveholding to form another—as a moral impossibility. We could not separate the States by any such line, if we were to draw it. We could not sit down here to-day, and draw a line of separation, that would satisfy any five men in the country. There are natural causes that would keep and tie us together, and there are social and domestic relations which we could not break, if we would, and which we should not, if we could. . . .

And now, Mr. President, instead of speaking of the possibility or utility of secession, . . . let our comprehension be as broad as the country for which we act, our aspirations as high as its certain destiny; let us not be pigmies in a case that calls for men. Never did there devolve, on any generation of men, higher trusts than now devolve upon us for the preservation of this Constitution, and the harmony and peace of all who are destined to live under it. Let us make our generation one of the strongest, and the brightest link, in that golden chain which is destined, I fully believe, to grapple the people of all the States to this Constitution, for ages to come.

After reading this selection, consider these questions:

1. What argument does Webster make in defense of the fugitive slave law?

2. On what specific issues does Webster disagree with John C. Calhoun?

SELECTION 5:

Senator Seward Invokes a Higher Law

Not only did the debates over the Compromise of 1850 represent the last time such giants as Henry Clay, James C. Calhoun, and Daniel Webster would play so prominent a role, it also provided a stage for a new generation of congressional leaders. Rising politicians such as Stephen A. Douglas and William Henry Seward, who would shape the politics of the next decade, emerged as important leaders. In the following excerpt, Seward, an emerging Whig leader who would later become a prominent figure in the new Republican Party, argues against the compromise.

I am opposed to any such compromise, in any and all the forms in which it has been proposed, because, while admitting the purity and the patriotism of all from whom it is my misfortune to differ, I think all legislative compromises radically wrong and essentially vicious. . . .

What am I to receive in this compromise? freedom in California. It is well; it is a noble acquisition; it is worth a sacrifice. But what am I to give as an equivalent? a recognition of a claim to perpetuate slavery in the District of Columbia; forbearance towards more stringent laws concerning the arrest of persons suspected of being slaves found in the free States; forbearance from the *proviso* of freedom in the charters of new territories. None of the plans of compromise offered, demand less than two, and most of them insist on all of these conditions. The equivalent then is, some portion of liberty—some portion of human rights in one region, for liberty in another region. But California brings gold and commerce as well as freedom. I am, then, to surrender some

Excerpted from *The Congressional Globe,* edited by John C. Rives (Washington, DC: Office of John C. Rives, 1850).

portion of human freedom in the District of Columbia, and in East California and New Mexico, for the mixed consideration of liberty, gold, and power on the Pacific coast. . . .

But, sir, if I could overcome my repugnance to compromises in general, I should object to this one, on the ground of the *inequality* and *incongruity* of the interests to be compromised. Why, sir, according to the views I have submitted, California ought to come in, and must come in, whether slavery stands or falls in the District of Columbia, whether slavery stands or falls in New Mexico and Eastern California, and even whether slavery stands or falls in the slave States. California ought to come in, being a free State, and under the circumstances of her conquest, her compact, her abandonment, her justifiable and necessary establishment of a constitution, and the inevitable dismemberment of the empire consequent upon her rejection. I should have voted for her admission, even if she had come as a slave State. California ought to come in, and must come in, at all events. It is, then, an independent —a paramount question. What, then, are these questions arising out of slavery, thus interposed, but collateral questions? They are unnecessary and incongruous, and therefore false issues, not introduced designedly, indeed, to defeat that great policy, yet unavoidably tending to that end. . . .

Another objection arises out of the principle on which the demand for compromise rests. That principle assumes a classification of the States as northern and southern States, as it is expressed by the honorable Senator from South Carolina, [Mr. Calhoun] but into slave States and free States, as more directly expressed by the honorable Senator from Georgia, [Mr. Berrien]. The argument is, that the States are severally equal, and that these two classes were equal at the first, and that the Constitution was founded on that equilibrium. . . .

How is the original equality of the States proved? It rests on a syllogism of [Emmeric de] Vattel [a Swiss theorist of natural law], as follows: All men are equal by the law of nature and of nations. But States are only lawful aggregations of individual men, who severally are equal; therefore States are equal in natural rights. All this is just and sound; but assuming the same premises, to wit: that all men are equal by the law of nature and of nations, the right of property in slaves falls to the ground; for one who is equal to the other, cannot be the owner or property of that other. But you answer that the Constitution recognizes property in slaves. It would be sufficient, then, to reply, that this constitutional recognition must be void, because it is repugnant to the law of nature and of nations. But I deny that the Constitution recognizes property in man. I submit, on the other hand, most respectfully, that the Constitution not merely does not affirm that principle, but, on the contrary, altogether excludes it.

The Constitution does not *expressly* affirm anything on the subject; all that it contains are two incidental allusions to slaves. These are— first, in the provision establishing a ratio of representation and taxation; and secondly, in the provision relating to fugitives from labor. In both cases the Constitution designedly mentions slaves, not as slaves, much less as chattels, but as *persons.* . . .

I deem it established, then, that the Constitution does not recognize property in man, but leaves that question, as between the States, to the law of nature and of nations. . . .

The Constitution regulates our stewardship; the Constitution devotes the domain to union, to justice, to defence, to welfare, and to liberty.

But there is a higher law than the Constitution, which regulates our authority over the domain, and devotes it to the same noble purposes. The territory is a part—no inconsiderable part—of the common heritage of mankind, bestowed upon them by the Creator of the universe. We are his stewards, and must so discharge our trust as to secure, in the highest attainable degree, their happiness.

After reading this selection, consider these questions:

1. On what grounds does Seward reject compromise?

2. Henry Clay called Seward's speech "wild, reckless, and abominable." What in Seward's words so alarmed Clay?

CHAPTER 17

Ideology

As the North and the South embarked on separate paths of development, they engendered separate, and competing, ideologies. Those ideologies served to widen the gap between the two sides. Each side came to view the other with growing suspicion.

Northerners believed that individuals should be free to learn any trade or craft they chose and to enter any profession. In short, individuals had the right to seek economic advancement. Abraham Lincoln expressed the free labor ideology as well as anyone. "The prudent, penniless beginner in the world," he explained, "labors for wages awhile, saves a surplus with which to buy tools or land for himself, then labors on his own account another while, and at length hires another new beginner to help him."

Moreover, this system was the best for society. People contributed most to society in seeking to improve their own condition and that of their family. The republic was best served by independent individuals, people who owned their own farms, shops, and so forth. If an individual failed to achieve economic independence, it was because he or she had a dependent nature or lacked wisdom or ability to strike out on his or her own. Even though more and more Americans worked as employees and an increasing number would remain wage earners throughout their lives, the system provided enough mobility to sustain the ideology.

By the 1850s, a growing number in the North concluded that slavery threatened this system and the values associated with it.

Southerners, on the other hand, developed an imposing critique of northern industrial capitalism and a defense of the system of slavery. What Northerners called "free society," argued Southern polemicists such as George Fitzhugh, made cannibals of everyone (see the excerpt from his book in this chapter). Northern industrial workers, so the Southern argument went, were "wage slaves," no more free and less well fed, housed, and cared for than Southern slaves.

Aside from their criticism of Northern society, Southerners emphasized the positive virtues of their own social system. They stressed order and function in society. Fitzhugh once wrote that "to secure progress we must unfetter genius and chain down medioc-rity. Liberty for the few—Slavery, in every form, for the mass."

Pointing to the importance of cotton production in American eco-nomic development, Southern apologists argued that the realities of world trade supported slavery. Moreover, just as Northerners were convinced that a Southern slave power wanted to spread slavery to every part of the nation, Southerners were convinced that the North wanted to destroy their "peculiar institution."

These ideologies became the rallying points around which men would go to war.

After reading this chapter, consider these questions:

1. How did the North view itself?

2. How did Northerners regard the South?

3. How did Southerners see themselves?

4. How did Southerners regard the North?

5. What role did ideology play in the coming of the Civil War?

SELECTION 1:

Politics, Ideology, and the Origins of the Civil War

*E*ric Foner, *a professor of history at Columbia University, is one of the most influential historians writing about the mid–nineteenth century. His book* Free Soil, Free Labor, Free Men *(1970) remains the best analysis of the ideology of the Republican Party. In the following essay, Foner de-scribes how ideology served to break down the cohesion of the two na-tional parties (Whig and Democrat) and to form a basis for a new, more ideological party, the Republicans. For Foner, the breakdown of the two national parties played a central role in the coming of the Civil War.*

Excerpted from *A Nation Divided: Problems and Issues of the Civil War and Reconstruction,* edited by George M. Fredrickson (Min-neapolis, MN: Burgess Publishing Company, 1975). Copyright © 1975 by Burgess Publishing Company. Reprinted with permission.

For much of the seventy years preceding the Civil War, the American political system functioned as a mechanism for relieving social tensions, ordering group conflict, and integrating the society. The existence of national political parties, increasingly focused on the contest for the Presidency, necessitated alliances between political elites in various sections of the country. A recent study of early American politics notes that "political nationalization was far ahead of economic, cultural, and social nationalization"—that is, that the national political system was itself a major bond of union in a diverse, growing society. But as North and South increasingly took different paths of economic and social development and as, from the 1830's onwards, antagonistic value systems and ideologies grounded in the question of slavery emerged in these sections, the political system inevitably came under severe disruptive pressures. Because they brought into play basic values and moral judgments, the competing sectional ideologies could not be defused by the normal processes of political compromise, nor could they be contained within the existing inter-sectional political system. Once parties began to reorient themselves on sectional lines, a fundamental necessity of democratic politics—that each party look upon the other as a legitimate alternative government—was destroyed.

When we consider the causes of the sectional conflict, we must ask ourselves not only why civil war came when it did, but why it did not come sooner. How did a divided nation manage to hold itself together for as long as it did? In part, the answer lies in the unifying effects of inter-sectional political parties. On the level of politics, the coming of the Civil War is the story of the intrusion of sectional ideology into the political system, despite the efforts of political leaders of both parties to keep it out. Once this happened, political competition worked to exacerbate, rather than to solve, social and sectional conflicts. . . .

It is no accident that the break up of the last major inter-sectional party preceded by less than a year the break up of the Union or that the final crisis was precipitated not by any "overt act," but by a presidential election.

From the beginning of national government, of course, differences of opinion over slavery constituted an important obstacle to the formation of a national community. . . .

Although the slavery question was never completely excluded from political debate in the 1790's, and there was considerable Federalist grumbling about the three-fifths clause of the Constitution after 1800, the first full demonstration of the political possibilities inherent in a sectional attack on slavery occurred in the Missouri controversy of 1819–21. These debates established a number of precedents which forecast the future course of the slavery extension issue in Congress. Most important was the fact that the issue was able for a time to completely obliterate party lines. In the first votes on slavery in Missouri, virtually every northerner, regardless of party, voted against expansion. . . .

The 1830's witnessed a vast expansion of political loyalties and awareness and the creation of party mechanisms to channel voter participation in politics. But the new mass sense of identification with politics had ominous implications for the sectional antagonisms which the party system sought to suppress. . . . The mass, non-ideological politics of the [Andrew] Jackson era created the desperately needed link between governors and governed. But this very link made possible the emergence of two kinds of sectional agitators: the abolitionists, who stood outside of politics and hoped to force public opinion—and through it, politicians—to confront the slavery issue, and political agitators, who used politics as a way of heightening sectional self-consciousness and antagonism in the populace at large.

Because of the rise of mass politics and the emergence of these sectional agitators, the 1830's was the decade in which long-standing, latent sectional divisions were suddenly activated, and previously unrelated patterns of derogatory sectional imagery began to emerge into full-blown sectional ideology. Many of the antislavery arguments which gained wide currency in the 1830's had roots stretching back into the eighteenth century. The idea that slavery degraded white labor and retarded economic development, for example, had been voiced by Benjamin Franklin. After 1800, the Federalists, increasingly localized in New England, had developed a fairly coherent critique, not only of the social and economic effects of slavery, but of what Harrison Gray Otis called the divergence of "manners, habits, customs, principles, and ways of thinking" which separated northerners and southerners. And, during the Missouri debates, almost every economic, political, and moral argument against slavery that would be used in the later sectional debate was voiced. . . .

It was the abolitionist assault which brought into being the coherent defense of slavery. The opening years of the 1830's, of course, were ones of crisis for the South. The emergence of militant abolitionism, Nat Turner's rebellion, the Virginia debates on slavery, and the nullification crisis suddenly presented assaults to the institution of slavery from within and outside the South. The reaction was the closing of southern society in defense of slavery, "the most thorough-going repression of free thought, free speech, and a free press ever witnessed in an American community." At the same time, southerners increasingly abandoned their previous, highly qualified defenses of slavery and embarked on the formulation of the proslavery argument. . . .

The South, of course, was hardly as united as [Senator John C.] Calhoun asserted. But the progressive rejection of the Jeffersonian tradition, the suppression of civil liberties, and the increasing stridency of the defense of slavery all pushed the South further and further out of the inter-sectional mainstream, setting it increasingly apart from the rest of the country. Coupled with the Gag Rule and the mobs which broke up abolitionist presses and meetings, the growth of proslavery thought was vital to a new antislavery formulation which emerged in the late 1830's and which had been absent from both the Federalist attacks on slavery and the Missouri debates—the idea of the slave power. . . . Abolitionists could now argue that slavery was not only morally repugnant, it was incompatible with the basic democratic values and liberties of white Americans. . . . In other words, a process of ideological expansion had begun, fed in large measure by the sequence of response and counter-response between the competing sectional outlooks. Once this process had begun, it had an internal dynamic which made it extremely difficult to stop. This was especially true because of the emergence of agitators whose avowed purpose was to sharpen sectional conflict, polarize

public opinion, and develop sectional ideologies to their logical extremes.

As the 1840's opened, most political leaders still clung to the traditional basis of politics, but the sectional, ideological political agitators formed growing minorities in each section. In the South, there was a small group of outright secessionists and a larger group, led by Calhoun, who were firmly committed to the Union but who viewed sectional organization and self-defense, not the traditional reliance on inter-sectional political parties, as the surest means of protecting southern interests within the Union. In the North, a small radical group gathered in Congress around John Quincy Adams and Congressmen like Joshua Giddings, William Slade, and Seth Gates—men who represented areas of the most intense abolitionist agitation and . . . [who] were determined to force slavery into every Congressional debate. They were continually frustrated but never suppressed. . . .

The northern political agitators, both Congressmen and Liberty party leaders, also performed the function of developing and popularizing a political rhetoric, especially focused on fear of the slave power, which could be seized upon by traditional politicians and large masses of voters if slavery ever entered the center of political conflict.

In the 1840's, this is precisely what happened. . . . Once introduced into politics, slavery was there to stay. The Wilmot Proviso, introduced in 1846, had precisely the same effect as the proposal two decades earlier to restrict slavery in Missouri—it completely fractured the major parties along sectional lines. As in 1820, opposition to the expansion of slavery became the way in which a diverse group of northerners expressed their various resentments against a southern-dominated administration. And, as in 1821, a small group of northern Democrats eventually broke with their section, reaffirmed their primary loyalty to the party, and joined with the South to kill the Proviso in 1847. . . .

But the slavery extension debates of the 1840's had far greater effects on the political system than the Missouri controversy had had. Within each party, they created a significant group of sectional politicians—men whose careers were linked to the slavery question and who would therefore resist its exclusion from future politics. And in the North, the 1840's witnessed the expansion of sectional political rhetoric—as more and more northerners became familiar with the "aggressions" of the slave power and the need to resist them. At the same time, as antislavery ideas expanded, unpopular and divisive elements were weeded out, especially the old alliance of antislavery with demands for the rights of free blacks. Opposition to slavery was already coming to focus on its lowest common denominators—free soil, opposition to the slave power, and union.

The political system reacted to the intrusion of the slavery question in the traditional ways. At first, it tried to suppress it. . . .

Both parties also attempted to devise formulas for compromising the divisive issue. For the Whigs, it was "no territory"—an end to expansion would end the question of the spread of slavery. The Democratic answer, first announced by Vice President [George] Dallas in 1847 and picked up by [Senator] Lewis Cass [who was the Democratic party's presidential candidate in 1848], was popular sovereignty or nonintervention: giving to the people of each territory the right to decide on slavery. . . . Popular sovereignty formed one basis of the compromise of 1850, the last attempt of the political system to expel the disease of sectional ideology by finally settling all the points at which slavery and national politics intersected.

That compromise was possible in 1850 was testimony to the resiliency of the political system and the continuing ability of party loyalty to compete with sectional commitments. But the very method of passage revealed how deeply sectional divisions were embedded in party politics. Because only a small group of Congressmen—mostly northwestern Democrats and southern Whigs—were committed to compromise on every issue, the "omnibus" compromise measure could not pass. The compromise had to be enacted serially with the small compromise bloc, led by Stephen A. Douglas of Illinois, aligned with first one sectional bloc, then the other, to pass the individual measures. . . .

It is, of course, highly ironic that it was Douglas' attempt to extend the principle of popular sov-ereignty to territory already guaranteed to free labor by the Missouri Compromise which finally shattered the second-party system. We can date almost exactly the final collapse of that system—February 15, 1854—the day a caucus of southern Whig Congressmen and Senators decided to support Douglas' Nebraska bill, despite the fact that they could have united with northern Whigs in opposition both to the repeal of the Missouri Compromise and the revival of sectional agitation. But in spite of the sectionalization of politics which occurred after 1854, Douglas continued his attempt to maintain a national basis of party competition. In fact, from one angle of vision, whether politics was to be national or sectional was the basic issue of the Lincoln-Douglas debates of 1858. The Little Giant presented local autonomy—popular sovereignty for states and territories—as the only "national" solution to the slavery question, while Lincoln attempted to destroy this middle ground and force a single, sectional solution on the entire Union. There is a common critique of Douglas' politics, expressed perhaps most persuasively by [historian] Allan Nevins, which argues that, as a man with no moral feelings about slavery, Douglas was incapable of recognizing that this moral issue affected millions of northern voters. This, in my opinion, is a serious misunderstanding of Douglas' politics. What he insisted was not that there was no moral question involved in slavery but that it was not the function of the politician to deal in moral judgments. To Lincoln's prediction that the nation could not exist half slave and half free, Douglas replied that it had so existed for seventy years and could continue to do so if northerners stopped trying to impose their own brand of morality upon the South. . . .

To this, Lincoln's only possible reply was the one formulated in the debates—the will of the majority must be tempered by considerations of morality. . . .

By 1860, Douglas' local majoritarianism was no more acceptable to southern political leaders than Lincoln's national and moral majoritarianism. The principle of state rights and minority self-determination had always been the first line of defense of slavery from northern interference, but southerners now coupled it with the demand that Congress intervene to establish and guarantee slavery in the territories. The Lecompton fight [Proslavery leaders in Kansas convened a constitutional convention in Lecompton. When free soilers refused to participate, the rump convention drafted a proslavery constitution, which they refused to submit to a vote of all settlers.] had clearly demonstrated that southerners would no longer be satisfied with what Douglas hoped the territories would become—free, Democratic states. And the refusal of the Douglas Democrats to accede to southern demands was the culmination of a long history of resentment on the part of northern Democrats, stretching back into the 1840's, at the impossible political dilemma of being caught between increasingly anti-southern constituency pressure and loyalty to an increasingly pro-southern national party. For their part, southern Democrats viewed their northern allies as too weak at home and too tainted with antisouthernism after the Lecompton battle to be relied on to protect southern interests any longer.

As for the Republicans, by the late 1850's they had succeeded in developing a coherent ideology which, despite internal ambiguities and contradictions, incorporated the fundamental values, hopes, and fears of a majority of northerners. As I have argued elsewhere, it rested on a commitment to the northern social order, founded on the dignity and opportunities of free labor, and to social mobility, enterprise, and "progress.". . . And it defined the South as a backward, stagnant, aristocratic society, totally alien in values and social order to the middle-class capitalism of the North. . . .

The slave power idea gave the Republicans the anti-aristocratic appeal with which men like [Senator William H.] Seward had long wished to be associated politically. By fusing older antislavery arguments with the idea that slavery posed a threat to northern free labor and democratic values, it enabled the Republicans to tap the egalitarian outlook which lay at the heart of northern society. At the same time, it enabled Republicans to present antislavery as an essentially conservative reform, an attempt to reestablish the antislavery principles of the founding fathers and rescue the federal government from southern usurpation. And, of course, the slave power idea had a far greater appeal to northern self-interest than arguments based on the plight of black slaves in the South. . . . In summary, the slave power idea was the ideological glue of the Republican party—it enabled them to elect in 1860 a man conservative enough to sweep to victory in every northern state, yet radical enough to trigger the secession crisis.

After reading this selection, consider these questions:

1. What efforts did party leaders make to keep slavery out of national politics?

2. Discuss the ways in which the emergence of national parties, which had an interest in keeping sectional disputes out of the national political discourse, provided the vehicle for the entrance of sectional ideology into national politics.

SELECTION 2:

The Southern Defense of Slavery

While the North developed an ideology based on free labor and grew increasingly suspicious of the "slave-power conspiracy," southern attitudes evolved as well. At the time of the Constitution, Southerners defended slavery as a necessary evil. Under attack from abolitionists, the Southern argument developed into defenses of slavery as a positive good. That argument became the basis for a Southern ideology that included a critique of Northern industrial society and drew on traditional notions of order and function in society. In the following excerpt, George M. Fredrickson, a professor of history at Stanford University, describes the evolution of Southern ideology.

Prior to the 1830s, black subordination was the practice of white Americans, and the inferiority of the Negro was undoubtedly a common assumption, but open assertions of *permanent* inferiority were exceedingly rare. It took the assault of the abolitionists to unmask the cant about a theoretical human equality that coexisted with Negro slavery and racial discrimination and to force the practitioners of racial oppression to develop a theory that accorded with their behavior. Well before the rise of radical abolitionism, however, spokesmen for the lower South gave notice that they were prepared to defend slavery as an institution against any kind of attack that might develop. In the 1820s the leadership of the major cotton-producing states made it clear that a national colonization effort was unacceptable because in their view slavery was an essential and Constitutionally protected local institution which was no concern of the Federal government or the

nonslaveholding states. These apologists for black servitude characteristically answered the colonizationists by agreeing with them that emancipation on the soil was unthinkable and then proceeding to point out not only that colonization was impractical as a program of Negro removal but also that its very agitation was a danger to the security of a slave society because the expectations it raised among blacks threatened to undermine the discipline of the plantation. A permanent and rigid slave system, it was argued, was both economically necessary in the rice- and cotton-growing areas and vital as a system of control for a potentially dangerous black population. Such a viewpoint soon triumphed in all the slaveholding states. In 1831 and 1832, the Virginia legislature debated a colonization proposal that might have opened the way to gradual emancipation, but its defeat marked the end of a serious search, even in the upper South, for some way to set slavery on the path to extinction.

After the Virginia debate, Professor Thomas R. Dew of William and Mary College, speaking for the victorious proslavery faction, set forth the most thorough and comprehensive justification of

Excerpted from *The Black Image in the White Mind,* by George M. Fredrickson (New York: Harper & Row, 1971). Copyright © 1971 by George M. Fredrickson. Reprinted by permission of the publisher.

the institution that the South had yet produced. Dew's effort should properly be seen as reflecting a transitional stage in the proslavery argument. Since he was refuting the proponents of gradual emancipation and colonization who still thrived in western Virginia and not the new and radical abolitionists of the North, his arguments stressed practicality and expediency and, in a sense, did little more than help bring Virginia in line with the kind of proslavery sentiment already triumphant farther South. Much of his lengthy essay was devoted to showing that colonization was an impossible scheme because the natural increase of the black population would outrun any number that could possibly be colonized. His justification of slavery rested first of all on the contention that servitude had been a necessary stage of human progress and hence could not be regarded as evil in itself. He then went on to argue that the concrete circumstances of Southern life required the institution and that no set of abstract principles should be invoked to obscure the basic fact that the Negro was not prepared for freedom. Although this was fundamentally an extension of the kind of argument that had previously been the basis of the defense of slavery as "a necessary evil," Dew implied that such a practical adjustment to reality had no evil in it, and he raised expediency to the level of conservative principle when he cited [British statesman] Edmund Burke's dictum that "circumstances give in reality to every political principle its distinguishing color and discriminating effect."

In his discussion of Negro character and prospects, Dew did not deviate forthrightly and insistently from traditional quasi-environmentalist assumptions about the nature of most racial differences. Although at the beginning of his essay he described Negroes as "differing from us in color and habits and vastly inferior in the scale of civilization," he did not deal consistently with the question whether this inferiority resulted from innate character or from the "habits" engendered by a long exposure to inhibiting circumstances. In his discussion of "obstacles to emancipation," Dew at one point provided an analysis not incompatible with the conservative environmentalism of the colonizationists. "The blacks," he

wrote, "have now all the habits and feelings of slaves, the whites have those of masters; the prejudices are formed, and mere legislation cannot improve them. . . . Declare the Negroes of the South free tomorrow, and vain will be your decree until you have prepared them for it. . . . The law would make them freemen, and custom or prejudice, we care not which you call it, would degrade them to the condition of slaves." Such a prediction, he indicated, was merely an application of the rule that "each one should remain in society in the condition in which he has been born and trained, and not [try] to mount too fast without preparation."

This ultraconservative principle could presumably have been applied to slaves or serfs of any race; and, as if to substantiate this inference, Dew went on to give as an example of premature emancipation the attempt to liberate the Polish peasants in the 1790s. But Dew could also describe black behavior as if it were predetermined by innate racial traits; for he contradicted his suggestion that Negro characteristics were simply acquired habits of servility by arguing, somewhat obscurely, that the supposed indolence of free blacks resulted from "an inherent and intrinsic cause." And when he asserted that "the free black will work *nowhere* except by compulsion," he decisively parted company with the colonizationists. If Dew was a transitional figure in the general defense of slavery because he combined arguments from expediency with hints of a conservative, proslavery theory of society, he was equally transitional as a racial theorist, because of his vacillation between arguments for black inferiority drawn from a perception of the force of "habits," "customs," and "prejudices" and those suggesting that a permanency of racial type justified enslavement.

By the middle of the 1830s the full impact of the abolitionist argument had been felt in the South, and Dew's ambiguous treatment of the racial factor and his contention that slavery was sometimes justified by circumstances no longer provided Southern apologists with what they regarded as a fully adequate defense of the institution. The abolitionists' charge that slavery was inherently sinful was now met increasingly by the unequivocal claim that slavery was "a positive good." Furthermore their practical assertion of racial equality as something to be achieved in the United States and not through colonization inspired proslavery spokesmen to clarify their racial views and to assert, as a major part of their case, the unambiguous concept of inherent Negro inferiority.

South Carolinians led the way. In 1835 Governor George McDuffie told the South Carolina General Assembly that the Negroes were "destined by providence" for slavery and that this was made evident not only by the color of their skin but also by "the intellectual inferiority and natural improvidence of this race." They were, he indicated, "unfit for self-government of any kind," and "in all respects, physical, moral, and political, inferior to millions of the human race." McDuffie professed astonishment that anyone should "suppose it possible to reclaim the African race from their destiny" as slaves or subjects of some other form of absolute despotism. The Charleston lawyer William Drayton said much the same thing the following year in a pamphlet attacking the abolitionists: "Personal observation must convince every candid man, that the negro is constitutionally indolent, voluptuous, and prone to vice; that his mind is heavy, dull, and unambitious; and that the doom that has made the African in all ages and countries, a slave—is the natural consequence of the inferiority of his character." In 1837 John C. Calhoun made his famous defense of slavery before the Senate of the United States and showed how important racial doctrines really were in the new and militant defense of servitude which developed in the 1830s.

"I hold that in the present state of civilization, where two races of different origin, and distinguished by color, and other physical differences, as well as intellectual, are brought together, the relation now existing in the slaveholding states between the two, is, instead of an evil, a good—a positive good."

It was thus in tandem with the concept of slavery as "a positive good" that the doctrine of permanent black inferiority began its career as a rationale, first for slavery itself and later for post-emancipation forms of racial oppression. The attitudes that underlay the belief that the Negro was doomed by nature itself to perpetual slavishness and subordination to the whites were not new, nor was the doctrine itself if considered as a popular belief that lacked intellectual respectability; but when asserted dogmatically and with an aura of philosophical authority by leading Southern spokesmen and their Northern supporters in the 1830s, it became, for the first time, the basis of a world view, an explicit ideology around which the beneficiaries of white supremacy could organize themselves and their thoughts.

After reading this selection, consider these questions:

1. What arguments did Southerners use to support their contention that slavery was a positive good?

2. How did arguments that slavery was a positive good play into Northern fears of a slave-power conspiracy bent on the expansion of slavery?

SELECTION 3:

George Fitzhugh Defends Slavery

As George M. Fredrickson notes in his article earlier in this chapter, Southerners developed a spirited defense of slavery beginning in the 1820s and 1830s. That argument was in full cry by the 1850s. Although not the most influential of the proslavery intellectuals, George Fitzhugh may have carried the argument the furthest.

A product of aristocratic society in Alexandria, Virginia, he spent his adult life in Port Royal, Virginia, something of a rural backwater. Fitzhugh practiced law there and was the master of a modest plantation. Although he held an appointment as clerk to the attorney general during the administration of James Buchanan, most of his income after 1850 came from his books and articles.

Fitzhugh rejected the idea of a free society. According equal rights to unequal men, he argued, would result in the exploitation of the weak by the strong. Given the childlike nature of blacks, he maintained, slavery was not only necessary but a great benefit to the enslaved. At the same time, Fitzhugh rejected race as the basis for slavery. He held that, irrespective of race, humans were born with unequal inheritances of money and talent. Therefore, for the vast majority, liberty meant only the right to be exploited by those more rich, powerful, or intelligent. Fitzhugh put forward these ideas in two books, Sociology for the South; or the Failure of a Free Society *(1854) and* Cannibals All! or, Slaves Without Masters *(1857). The following excerpt is from* Cannibals All!

We are all, North and South, engaged in the White Slave Trade, and he who succeeds best is esteemed most respectable. It is far more cruel than the Black Slave Trade, because it exacts more of its slaves, and neither protects nor governs them. We boast that it exacts more when we say, "that the *profits* made from employing free labor are greater than those from slave labor." The

profits, made from free labor are the amount of the products of such labor, which the employer, by means of the command which capital or skill gives him, takes away, exacts, or "exploitates" from the free laborer. The profits of slave labor are that portion of the products of such labor which the power of the master enables him to appropriate. These profits are less, because the master allows the slave to retain a larger share of the results of his own labor than do the employers of free labor. But we not only boast that the White Slave Trade is more exacting and fraudulent (in fact, though not in intention) than Black Slavery;

Excerpted from *Constructing the American Past,* edited by Elliott J. Gorn, Randy Roberts, and Terry D. Bilhartz (New York: Harper-Collins College Publishers, 1995).

but we also boast that it is more cruel, in leaving the laborer to take care of himself and family out of the pittance which skill or capital have allowed him to retain. When the day's labor is ended, he is free, but is overburdened with the cares of family and household, which make his freedom an empty and delusive mockery. But his employer is really free, and may enjoy the profits made by others' labor, without a care, or a trouble, as to their well-being. The negro slave is free, too, when the labors of the day are over, and free in mind as well as body; for the master provides food, raiment, house, fuel, and everything else necessary to the physical well-being of himself and family. The master's labors commence just when the slave's end. No wonder men should prefer white slavery to capital, to negro slavery, since it is more profitable, and is free from all the cares and labors of black slave-holding. . . .

The negro slaves of the South are the happiest, and, in some sense, the freest people in the world. The children and the aged and infirm work not at all, and yet have all the comforts and necessaries of life provided for them. They enjoy liberty, because they are oppressed neither by care nor labor. The women do little hard work, and are protected from the despotism of their husbands by their masters. The negro men and stout boys work, on the average, in good weather, not more than nine hours a day. The balance of their time is spent in perfect abandon. Besides, they have their Sabbaths and holidays. White men, with so much of license and liberty, would die of ennui; but negroes luxuriate in corporeal and mental repose. With their faces upturned to the sun, they can sleep at any hour; and quiet sleep is the greatest of human enjoyments. "Blessed be the man who invented sleep." 'Tis happiness in itself—and results from contentment with the present, and confident assurance of the future. We do not know whether free laborers ever sleep. They are fools to do so; for,

whilst they sleep, the wily and watchful capitalist is devising means to ensnare and exploitate them. The free laborer must work or starve. He is more of a slave than the negro, because he works longer and harder for less allowance than the slave, and has no holiday, because the cares of life with him begin when its labors end. He has no liberty, and not a single right. . . .

We agree with Mr. [Thomas] Jefferson that all men have natural and inalienable rights. To violate or disregard such rights, is to oppose the designs and plans of Providence, and cannot "come to good." The order and subordination observable in the physical, animal, and human world show that some are formed for higher, others for lower stations—the few to command, the many to obey. We conclude that about nineteen out of every twenty individuals have "a natural and inalienable right" to be taken care of and protected, to have guardians, trustees, husbands, or masters; in other words, they have a natural and inalienable right to be slaves. The one in twenty are as clearly born or educated or some way fitted for command and liberty. Not to make them rulers or masters is as great a violation of natural right as not to make slaves of the mass. A very little individuality is useful and necessary to society—much of it begets discord, chaos and anarchy.

After reading this selection, consider these questions:

1. Hinton Rowan Helper's attack on slavery, *The Impending Crisis of the South* (see chapter 12), was published the same year as *Cannibals All!* and was written by another Southerner. Compare Helper's views on African Americans with those of Fitzhugh.

2. What would Northerners, fearful of the slave-power conspiracy, think about Fitzhugh's recommendation that slavery should not be limited to African Americans?

SELECTION 4:

Abraham Lincoln Ponders Slavery and the Union

In the wake of the Kansas-Nebraska Act of 1854, the Whig Party began to disintegrate. Various groups opposed to the expansion of slavery began to coalesce in the new Republican Party. A Whig politician named Abraham Lincoln did not abandon his party; he ran for Congress unsuccessfully as an anti-Nebraska Whig in 1854. When he wrote the following letter to Judge George Robertson in 1855, Lincoln had not yet joined the Republicans. In this letter, Lincoln expressed doubt that the nation could continue half slave and half free. Three years later, in his famous "House Divided" speech, Lincoln would assert positively, "I believe this government cannot endure, permanently half slave and half free." Robertson, who had served in Congress from 1817 through 1821, visited Springfield, Illinois, in July 1855 but found Lincoln away. He left a copy of his collected speeches and papers inscribed to Lincoln, which was the occasion for Lincoln to write this letter.

My dear Sir: The volume you left for me has been received. I am really grateful for the honor of your kind remembrance, as well as for the book. The partial reading I have already given it, has afforded me much of both pleasure and instruction. It was new to me that the exact question which led to the Missouri compromise, had arisen before it arose in regard to Missouri, [Northern members of Congress unsuccessfully attempted to ban slavery from the Arkansas Territory in 1819.] and that you had taken so prominent a part in it. Your short, but able and patriotic speech upon that occasion, has not been improved upon since, by those holding the same views; and, with all the lights you then had, the views you took appear to me as very reasonable.

You are not a friend of slavery in the abstract. In that speech you spoke of *"the peaceful extinction of slavery"* and used other expressions indicating your belief that the thing was, at some time, to have an end[.] Since then we have had thirty six years of experience; and this experience has demonstrated, I think, that there is no peaceful extinction of slavery in prospect for us. The signal failure of Henry Clay, and other good and great men, in 1849, to effect any thing in favor of gradual emancipation in Kentucky, together with a thousand other signs, extinguishes that hope utterly. On the question of liberty, as a principle, we are not what we have been. When we were the political slaves of King George, and wanted to be free, we called the maxim that "all men are created equal" a self-evident truth; but now when we have grown fat, and have lost all dread of being slaves ourselves, we have become so greedy to be *masters* that we call the same maxim "a self-evident lie." The fourth of July has not quite

Excerpted from *The Collected Works of Abraham Lincoln,* edited by Roy P. Basler (New Brunswick, NJ: Rutgers University Press, 1953).

dwindled away; it is still a great day—*for burning fire-crackers!!!*

That spirit which desired the peaceful extinction of slavery, has itself become extinct, with the *occasion,* and the *men* of the Revolution. Under the impulse of that occasion, nearly half the states adopted systems of emancipation at once; and it is a significant fact, that not a single state has done the like since. So far as peaceful, voluntary emancipation is concerned, the condition of the negro slave in America, scarcely less terrible to the contemplation of a free mind, is now as fixed, and hopeless of change for the better, as that of the lost souls of the finally impenitent. The Autocrat of all the Russias will resign his crown, and proclaim his subjects free republicans sooner than will our American masters voluntarily give up their slaves.

Our political problem now is "Can we, as a nation, continue together *permanently—forever—* half slave, and half free?" The problem is too mighty for me. May God, in his mercy, superintend the solution.

After reading this selection, consider these questions:

1. In what ways does Lincoln's letter exemplify the Northern ideology described in Eric Foner's article earlier in this chapter?

2. In this letter (1855), Lincoln questioned whether the nation could continue together half slave and half free. In his "House Divided" speech (1858), Lincoln asserted that he did not believe the government could "endure permanently half *slave* and half *free.*" Consult your textbook for events that took place between the letter and the speech. What might account for the change in Lincoln's ideas?

3. What would Lincoln have thought about George Fitzhugh's *Cannibals All!*?

SELECTION 5:

Senator Sumner Assails the Slavocracy

The Kansas-Nebraska Act touched off a struggle over the fate of Kansas, as described in the excerpt by James M. McPherson in chapter 16. Outraged by the events in Kansas, Senator Charles Sumner of Massachusetts rose to deliver an attack on supporters of slavery and of the expansion of slavery. His two-day verbal assault, entitled "The Crime Against Kansas," inveighed against the violence in that territory. With an irritating air of moral superiority, Sumner extended his attack to include slavery, the South, and the slave power. He singled out for particular abuse Senator Andrew Pickens Butler of South Carolina and Butler's home state. The vituperation directed at Butler was intensely personal and offensive. As Sumner put it, the senator from South Carolina had taken "the harlot, Slavery," as his "mistress." Moreover, Butler suffered from a slight paralysis of his mouth, and Sumner mocked the physical affliction with a reference to "the loose expectoration of his speech." Compounding matters, Sumner directed his attack at a generally popular senator who was not even present to defend himself.

Sumner's speech outraged Preston S. Brooks, a relative of Butler then serving in the House of Representatives. Two days after Sumner's tirade, Brooks entered the Senate chamber, walked to Sumner's seat, explained that he had come to punish Sumner for insulting an aged and absent relative, and then beat Sumner repeatedly with a cane. Suffering from shock as well as physical injury, Sumner did not return to the Senate for three years, during which time the Massachusetts legislature reelected him and left his seat vacant as a silent rebuke to Southern violence. Although Southern members of the House banded together to block a motion of censure brought against Brooks, he resigned his seat; however, voters in his district unanimously reelected him. The attack on Sumner enraged many Northerners and became a potent weapon for Republicans. Although some Southern moderates deplored the incident, most Southerners applauded what they regarded as a demonstration of Southern chivalry and patriotism.

The wickedness, which I now begin to expose is immeasurably aggravated by the motive which prompted it. Not in any common lust for power did this uncommon tragedy have its origin. It is the rape of a virgin Territory, compelling it to the hateful embrace of Slavery; and it may be clearly traced to a depraved longing for a new slave State, the hideous offspring of such a crime, in the hope of adding to the power of Slavery in the National Government. . . .

The Senator from South Carolina [Andrew Pickens Butler] has read many books of chivalry, and believes himself a chivalrous knight, with sentiments of honor and courage. Of course he has chosen a mistress to whom he has made his vows, and who, though ugly to others, is always lovely to him; though polluted in the sight of the world, is chaste in his sight—I mean the harlot, Slavery. For her, his tongue is always profuse in words. Let her be impeached in character, or any proposition made to shut her out from the extension of her wantonness, and no extravagance of manner or hardihood of assertion is then too great for this Senator. . . . If the slave States can-

not enjoy what, in mockery of the great fathers of the Republic, he misnames equality under the Constitution—in other words, the full power in the National Territories to compel fellow-men to unpaid toil, to separate husband and wife, and to sell little children at the auction block—then, sir, the chivalric Senator will conduct the State of South Carolina out of the Union! Heroic knight! Exalted Senator! A second Moses come for a second exodus!

But not content with this poor menace, which we have been twice told was "measured," the Senator, in the unrestrained chivalry of his nature, has undertaken to apply opprobrious words to those who differ from him on this floor. He calls them "sectional and fanatical;" and opposition to the usurpation in Kansas he denounces as "an uncalculating fanaticism." To be sure, these charges lack all grace of originality, and all sentiment of truth; but the adventurous Senator does not hesitate. He is the uncompromising, unblushing representative on this floor of a flagrant *sectionalism,* which now domineers over the Republic, and yet with a ludicrous ignorance of his own position—unable to see himself as others see him—or with an effrontery which even his white head ought not to protect from rebuke, he applies to those here who resist his *sectionalism*

Excerpted from *The Congressional Globe,* edited by John C. Rives (Washington, DC: Office of John C. Rives, 1856).

the very epithet which designates himself. The men who strive to bring back the Government to its original policy, when Freedom and not Slavery was national, while Slavery and not Freedom was sectional, he arraigns as *sectional*. This will not do. . . .

To the charge of fanaticism I also reply. Sir, fanaticism is found in an enthusiasm or exaggeration of opinions, particularly on religious subjects; but there may be a fanaticism for evil as well as for good. Now, I will not deny, that these scenes, with these precise objections, have been renewed in the American Senate.

With regret, I come again upon the Senator from South Carolina, who, omnipresent in this debate, overflowed with rage at the simple suggestion that Kansas had applied for admission as a State; and, with incoherent phrases, discharged the loose expectoration of his speech, now upon her representative, and then upon her people. There was no extravagance of the ancient Parliamentary debate which he did not repeat, nor was there any possible deviation from truth which he did not make, with so much of passion, I am glad to add, as to save him from the suspicion of intentional aberration. But the Senator touches nothing which he does not disfigure—with error, sometimes of principle, sometimes of fact. He shows an incapacity of accuracy, whether in stating the Constitution or in stating the law, whether in the details of statistics or the diversions of scholarship. He cannot [open] his mouth, but out there flies a blunder. . . .

But it is against the people of Kansas that the sensibilities of the Senator are particularly aroused. Coming, as he announces, "from a State"—ay, sir, from South Carolina—he turns with lordly disgust from this newly-formed community, which he will not recognize even as "a body-politic." Pray, sir, by what title does he indulge in this egotism? Has he read the history of "the State" which he represents? He cannot surely have forgotten its shameful imbecility from Slavery, confessed throughout the Revolution, followed by its more shameful assumptions for Slavery since. He cannot have forgotten its wretched persistence in the slave trade as the very apple of its eye, and the condition of its participation in the Union. . . . And yet the Senator, to whom that "State" has in part committed the guardianship of its good name, instead of moving, with backward treading steps, to cover its nakedness, rushes forward, in the very ecstasy of madness, to expose it by provoking a comparison with Kansas. South Carolina is old; Kansas is young. South Carolina counts by centuries; where Kansas counts by years. But a beneficent example may be born in a day; and I venture to say, that against the two centuries of the older "State," may be already set the two years of trial, evolving corresponding virtue, in the younger community. In the one, is the long wail of Slavery; in the other, the hymns of Freedom.

After reading this selection, consider these questions:

1. What was Sumner's point in comparing Butler's embrace of slavery with the embrace of a mistress?

2. What in this speech would a Southern gentleman have found particularly offensive?

3. In your opinion, how did Brooks's attack on Sumner support Northern perceptions of the slave South?

CHAPTER 18

The Civil War

The Civil War transformed the United States from a union of states into a nation. Before the Civil War, politicians typically referred to "these united states." After the war, the usage became less common; it was restricted largely to politicians trying to signal solemn import. No one could have foreseen this consequence.

Indeed, even more immediate consequences of this momentous struggle were not at all obvious to people as events moved toward war. Few who voted for Abraham Lincoln believed that the Southern states would secede, and most Southern secessionists did not believe that the North would resort to arms to save the Union. Certainly, no one could have predicted the horrendous loss of life. The North lost almost 365,000 lives; the South lost roughly 260,000, almost a fifth of its population of adult white males. Many more on both sides were wounded, and a good number of these wounded would carry the physical damage of the war to their graves in the form of missing limbs, disfigured faces, and constant pain. The war left thousands of widows and orphans on both sides.

The economic consequences of the war were equally significant and unforeseeable. The war devastated the Southern economy. In contrast, it accelerated important changes already underway in the North, including the nationalization of markets, the dominance of larger manufacturing firms, and the concentration of wealth.

Historians often refer to the Civil War as the first modern war. The importance of industrial capacity to the war effort, the use of railroads and telegraphs for military purposes, and the use of rifled firearms and rifled artillery helped define the war as the world's first modern military conflict.

Rifling is a groove cut into the barrel of a rifle or cannon that imparts a spin to the projectile as it emerges from the barrel. The effect is like the spiral of a football pass. The projectile cuts the air more cleanly and therefore travels more accurately over a longer distance. As a result, rifled muskets and artillery killed effectively at considerably longer ranges. Repeating rifles added to the killing capacity. All of this contributed to the war's staggering toll in human lives.

The Civil War was modern in another sense: It was a war of ideas. The South fought to defend states' rights, their interpretation of the Constitution, and slavery. The North fought to defeat the slave-power conspiracy and to defend the Union. As the war progressed, Northern objectives changed. The North fought not only to preserve the Union but to end slavery, to ensure what Abraham Lincoln described as "a new birth of freedom."

The essays and documents in this chapter deal with the military balance between the North and the South, the quality of generals on both sides and their ability to adapt to the changing realities of war, and the nature of Northern objectives in the conflict.

After reading this chapter, consider these questions:

1. Why do historians consider the Civil War to be the first modern war?

2. How did the military objectives of the two sides correspond to the political objectives?

3. What material advantages did each side enjoy, and how did these advantages relate to larger objectives?

4. How did military and political commanders deal with the changing realities of warfare?

5. What was the role of ideology in the conflict?

SELECTION 1:

The Balance Between the North and the South

Conventional wisdom maintains that the North won the Civil War because of its advantage in manpower and industrial capacity. In the following excerpt, James M. McPherson, a professor of history at Princeton University, assesses the balance of forces and concludes that the story is considerably more complicated.

Excerpted from *Ordeal by Fire: The Civil War and Reconstruction,* by James M. McPherson (New York: Alfred A. Knopf, 1982). Copyright © 1982 by Alfred A. Knopf, Inc. Reprinted with permission.

In 1861 the Union states had nearly three and a half times as many white men of military age as had the Confederacy. Of course the slaves were a military asset to the South, for they could do the home-front tasks done by free men in the North and thus release an equivalent number of whites for army service. On the other hand, the North also drew on former slaves for military labor and eventually enlisted more than 150,000 of them in its armed forces. Altogether an estimated 2,100,000 men fought for the Union and 800,000 for the Confederacy (the exact number is not known because the Union records enumerate the number of enlistments, which must be adjusted to avoid the double counting of men who reenlisted, and many Confederate records were destroyed). Just over half the men of military age in the North served in the army or navy; close to four-fifths of the white men in the South did so, a *levée en masse* [mass mobilization] made possible only by the existence of slavery.

Ironically the South, which went to war to protect individual and states' rights against centralized government, was compelled to enact military conscription a year earlier than the North. By the fall of 1861 the romantic enthusiasm that had stimulated volunteering in the early months was wearing off. . . . More than half the Confederate soldiers on the rolls were one-year volunteers who had enlisted in the spring of 1861 (the rest were three-year men). Faced with the prospect of a large part of their armies melting away just as the Yankees launched their spring offensives in 1862, the Confederate Congress in December passed an act offering to all one-year men who would reenlist a $50 bounty, one month's furlough, and the opportunity to join new regiments with new elected officers if the reenlistees did not like their old ones. But this failed to produce enough reenlistments. In March 1862 Robert E. Lee, then serving as Jefferson Davis's military adviser, urged passage of a national conscription law as the only way to avert disaster.

The Confederate Congress complied in April with legislation making able-bodied white males (including those whose enlistments were expiring) aged eighteen to thirty-five liable to conscription for three years' service. The law exempted persons in several war-production occupations plus militia officers, civil servants,

clergymen, and teachers. . . . A supplemental conscription law passed in October 1862 exempted one white man on any plantation with twenty or more slaves. The Confederacy also allowed drafted men to hire substitutes to serve in their stead. . . . By 1863 the going price for substitutes had risen to $6,000 in Confederate currency (about $300 in gold). Along with the "20-Negro law," substitution produced the bitter saying that it was "a rich man's war but a poor man's fight."

As Confederate manpower needs became more desperate, the conscription law was strengthened. Congress raised the upper age limit to forty-five in September 1862 and fifty (with the lower limit reduced from eighteen to seventeen) in February 1864. The substitute clause was repealed in December 1863, and men who had previously furnished substitutes became eligible for the draft. . . . The new conscription act of February 1864 required all men then in the army to stay in, thus making sure that the three-year men of 1861 would not go home when their enlistments expired.

So unpopular was conscription that it was impossible to enforce in some parts of the South, especially in the upcountry and mountain regions. In nonslaveholding areas the "rich man's war" theme was particularly strong. . . .

Several of the South's leading politicians also denounced the draft as being contrary to the goals the Confederacy was fighting for. . . . [Georgia's governor, Joseph E.] Brown did everything he could to frustrate the draft. . . . Other governors, particularly Zebulon Vance of North Carolina, also resisted the draft on libertarian and states' rights grounds. . . .

But despite opposition, despite inefficiency and fraud in its enforcement, conscription did produce men for the Confederate armies. Without the draft the South could scarcely have carried the war past 1862. . . . Perhaps 20 percent of the Confederate soldiers were draftees and substitutes, compared with 8 percent of the Union army. The compulsory reenlistment of volunteers in the South meant that every Confederate soldier served for the duration unless killed or discharged because of wounds or disease. In the Union, by contrast, men whose terms expired could not be drafted or compelled to reenlist. Thus while the total number of men who fought for the Union was two and a half times greater than those who fought for the Confederacy, the difference in the number of veterans in the ranks at any given time was much smaller. Since one veteran was believed to be worth at least two recruits, the Confederacy's inferiority in manpower was less than it appeared to be.

In resources necessary to wage war, however, the South was at an even greater disadvantage than in manpower. The North possessed close to 90 percent of the nation's industrial capacity. In certain industries vital to military production, Union superiority was even more decisive. According to the 1860 census, the North had eleven times as many ships and boats as the South, produced fifteen times as much iron, seventeen times as many textile goods, twenty-four times as many locomotives, and thirty-two times as many firearms (though an important market for the last had always been the South). In food production, the Northern superiority was little better than two to one (or about the same per capita as the South). But the Union had more than twice the density of railroad mileage per square mile and several times the amount of rolling stock. The South's inferiority in railroads, intensified by a lack of replacement capacity, produced transportationbottlenecks that created frequent shortages of food and supplies at the front. The North's advantage in horses and mules was less than two to one, but many of the Confederacy's animals were in portions of the upper South soon overrun by Union armies.

With all these disadvantages, how could Southerners expect to win? "Something more than numbers make armies," wrote a Confederate journalist. "Against the vast superiority of the North in material resources," he insisted, the South had "a set-off in certain advantages."

The most important advantage stemmed from the contrasting war aims of the two sides. To "win," the Confederates did not need to invade the North or to destroy its armies; they needed only to stand on the defensive and to prevent the North from destroying Southern armies. Southerners looked for inspiration to the American Revolution,

when Britain's relative material superiority was even greater than the North's in 1861.

To win the war, the North had to invade, conquer, and destroy the South's capacity and will to resist. Invasion and conquest are logistically far more difficult than defense of one's territory. . . . [T]he London *Times* [observed] early in the war . . . [that] "no war of independence ever terminated unsuccessfully except where the disparity of force was far greater than it is in this case.". . .

The intangible but vital factor of morale favored an army fighting in defense of its homeland. . . . When the Confederates became the invaders, this morale advantage went over to the Yankees. On the first day of the battle of Gettysburg a Union officer wrote: "Our men are three times as Enthusiastic as they have been in Virginia. The idea that Pennsylvania is invaded and that we are fighting on our own soil proper, influences them strongly.". . .

One of the South's important military advantages was geography. The Confederacy covered a large territory—750,000 square miles—twice as large as the thirteen colonies in 1776. The topography in the eastern part of the Confederacy favored the defense against invasion. The Appalachian chain was a formidable barrier that resisted penetration until [General William T.] Sherman's invasion of Georgia in 1864. The Shenandoah Valley of Virginia formed a natural route of invasion, but this favored the Confederacy rather than the Union because it ran southwest, away from Richmond and the main battle theater in Virginia. Indeed, the Confederacy used the valley three times for invasions or threats against the North ([Stonewall] Jackson in 1862, [Robert E.] Lee in his Gettysburg campaign in 1863, and Jubal Early in 1864), for in that direction the valley pointed toward important Northern cities, including Washington itself. Much of the South was heavily wooded, providing cover for armies operating on the defensive. Between Washington and Richmond, six rivers and numerous streams ran from west to east, each of them a line of defense. In the western portion of the Confederacy, by contrast, the river system favored an invading force. The Cumberland and Tennessee rivers were highways of invasion into

Tennessee, northern Mississippi, and northern Alabama, while the Mississippi River was an arrow thrust into the heart of the lower South.

But away from the rivers an invading force was dependent on railroads or roads, and railroads were especially vulnerable to guerrillas and cavalry, who developed the destruction of trackage, bridges, and rolling stock into a fine art. The Union engineer corps became equally adept at repairing the damage, . . . but Northern military movements were repeatedly delayed or stopped by the destruction of supply lines in their rear. In this way, a few hundred guerrillas or cavalry could neutralize an entire army and force it to detach thousands of men to guard its communications.

Once an army moved away from its railhead or river-landing supply base, its marching men, artillery, and supply wagons had to move by road. Union armies campaigning in the South averaged one wagon for every forty men and one horse or mule for every two or three men. An invading army of 100,000 men would thus be encumbered with 2,500 wagons and at least 35,000 animals and would consume 600 tons or more of supplies each day. The South's wretched roads became an important Confederate military asset. Most of them were dirt tracks without ditches or anything else to prevent them from becoming impassable in wet weather. Wagons and artillery often sank to the axles, especially in Virginia, where the red clay soil formed a mud with the character almost of quicksand. . . .

Of course the roads were as bad for the Rebels as for the Yankees. But an army operating in its own territory is closer to its base and needs fewer wagons because it can gather much of its food and forage from the friendly countryside. Then, too, Johnny Reb traveled lighter than Billy Yank. Carrying his few necessities in a blanket roll rather than a knapsack, getting along without a shelter tent, subsisting on less food, the Confederate infantryman usually marched with thirty to forty pounds of equipment including rifle and ammunition. The fully equipped Union soldier carried about fifty pounds. The very abundance of Northern war production encouraged some Union generals to requisition so lavishly that their troops became bogged down in their own supplies. . . .

The deeper the Union army penetrated into enemy territory, the longer became its supply lines and the greater became the necessity to detach troops to guard these lines. By the time Sherman reached Atlanta in 1864 only half of his total forces were at the front; the rest were strung out along his 470-mile rail lifeline back through Chattanooga and Nashville to Louisville. As an invading power, the Union army also had to assign large numbers of troops to occupation duties.

For these reasons, scarcely half of the 611,000 men present for duty in the Union armies at the beginning of 1864 were available for front-line combat service, while probably three-fourths of the Confederate total of 278,000 were so available. Thus the usual Southern explanation for defeat ("They never whipped us, Sir, unless they were four to one. If we had anything like a fair chance, or less disparity of numbers, we should have won our cause and established our independence".) requires some modification. Indeed, one writer has maintained that in the war's fifty main battles, the number of Union combat soldiers averaged only 2 percent more than the enemy. This probably understates Union numerical superiority. A calculation based on the sixty battles listed in the best statistical study of the subject shows that the Union armies averaged 37 percent more men than the Confederates. But even this was a far cry from the "overwhelming numbers" portrayed in much Civil War historiography.

Other advantages accruing to the Confederacy from fighting on the defensive were interior lines of communication, better knowledge of topography and roads, and a superior intelligence network. The term "interior lines" means simply that armies fighting within a defensive arc can shift troops from one point to another over shorter distances than invading armies operating outside the perimeter of the arc. Several instances of this occurred in the Virginia theater. . . .

The South was laced with obscure country roads not marked on any map. Only local knowledge could guide troops along these roads, many of which ran through thick woods that could shield the movement from the enemy but where a wrong turn could get a division hopelessly lost. Here the Confederates had a significant advantage. Rebel units used such roads to launch surprise attacks on the enemy. . . . Numerous examples could also be cited of Union troops getting lost on similar roads because of inaccurate or nonexistent maps. . . .

Operating amid a hostile population, the Union army was at a distinct disadvantage in the matter of military intelligence. Even the women and children, reported a Northern officer, "vied with each other in schemes and ruses by which to discover and convey to the enemy facts which we strove to conceal." Confederate officers often treated information obtained in this way with a grain of salt and relied mainly on their excellent cavalry for intelligence. But the cavalry, of course, functioned more effectively among a friendly than a hostile population. And many examples of important information conveyed by civilian spies could be cited.

After reading this selection, consider these questions:

1. What Southern advantages offset Northern superiority in manpower?

2. What mitigated the Northern superiority in industrial capacity?

3. Looking at the balance of forces at the beginning of the war as McPherson describes it, which side would you think more likely to win?

SELECTION 2:

Military Leadership of the North and the South

Whereas conventional wisdom grants material superiority to the North, it attributes superior generalship to the South. In the following excerpt, T. Harry Williams, the author of several books on the Civil War and a professor of history at Louisiana State University from 1941 until his death in 1979, challenges that conventional wisdom, particularly with respect to the abilities of Robert E. Lee and Ulysses S. Grant.

Early in the essay, in a part not included here, Williams discusses the influence on military tactics of Antoine Henri Jomini, a brilliant Swiss officer who served with Napoléon. The majority of both Northern and Southern generals received their military training at West Point, where they were imbued by Jominian tactics. Jomini placed high value on swift, offensive strikes. In addition, he regarded war as an exercise conducted by professionals with little relationship to larger political or social matters.

Williams argues that Southern generals, and especially Lee, were superior in their use of Jominian tactics. However, the Civil War was the first modern war; it was the first war to see the extensive military use of the railroad and telegraph, combat between iron-plated warships, the wider use of rifled artillery and rifled small arms, the use of repeating rifles,

*trench warfare, and even the experimental development of machine guns.
This new kind of war called for different tactics, and Northern generals
such as Grant and William Tecumseh Sherman pioneered the development
of strategy and tactics that would win modern wars.*

Let us concede that many of the tributes to Lee are deserved. He was not all that his admirers have said of him, but he was a large part of it. But let us also note that even his most fervent admirers, when they come to evaluate him as a strategist, have to admit that his abilities were never demonstrated on a larger scale than a theater. . . . Lee was pre-eminently a field or a theater strategist, and a great one, but it remains unproven that he was anything more or wanted to be anything more. . . . For his preoccupation with the war in Virginia, Lee is not to be criticized. He was a product of his culture, and that culture, permeated in its every part by the spirit of localism, dictated that his outlook on war should be local. Nevertheless, it must be recognized that his restricted view constituted a tragic command limitation in a modern war. The same limitation applied to Southern generalship as a whole. The Confederates, brilliant and bold in executing Jominian strategy on the battlefield, never succeeded in lifting their gifts above the theater level.

In many respects Lee was not a modern-minded general. He probably did not understand the real function of a staff and certainly failed to put together an adequate staff for his army. Although he had an excellent eye for terrain, his use of maps was almost primitive. He does not seem to have appreciated the impact of railroads on warfare or to have realized that railroads made Jomini's principle of interior lines largely obsolete. His mastery of logistics did not extend beyond departmental limits. In February, 1865, he said that he could not believe Sherman would be able to move into North Carolina. The evidence of Sherman's great march was before him, and yet he was not quite sure it had really happened.

The most striking lack of modernity in Lee was his failure to grasp the vital relationship between war and statecraft. Here the great Virginian was truly a Jominian. Almost as much as [Union general George B.] McClellan, he thought of war as a professional exercise. One of his officers said admiringly that Lee was too thorough a soldier to attempt to advise the government on such matters as the defense of Richmond. When late in the war a cabinet member asked Lee for his opinion on the advisability of moving the capital farther south, the general replied: "That is a political question . . . and you politicians must determine it. I shall endeavor to take care of the army, and you must make the laws and control the Government." And yet what could be a more strategic question than the safety of the capital? Lee attained a position in the Confederacy held by no other man, either in civil or military life. There was little exaggeration in the statement General William Mahone made to him: "You are the State." But Lee could not accept the role that his eminence demanded. . . . It has been suggested that Lee did not try to impose his will on the government because of his humility of character, and this may well be true. But it would also seem to be true that he did not know that a commander had any political responsibility.

Lincoln's first generals did not understand that war and statecraft were parts of the same piece. But none of the Confederate generals, first or last, ever grasped this fact about modern war. The most distinguishing feature of Southern generalship is that it did not grow. Lee and the other Confederate commanders were pretty much the same men in 1865 that they had been in 1861. They were good, within certain limits, at the beginning, and they were good at the end but still within the original limits. They never freed themselves from the influence of traditional doctrine. The probable explanation . . . is that the Confederates won their first battles with Jominian strategy and saw no

Excerpted from *Why the North Won the Civil War,* edited by David Donald (Baton Rouge: Louisiana State University Press, 1960). Copyright © 1960 by Louisiana State University Press. Reprinted with permission.

reason to change and that the Southern mind, civil and military, was unreceptive to new ideas. The North, on the other hand, finally brought forward generals who were able to grow and who could employ new ways of war. Even so doctrinaire a Jominian as [General in Chief Henry W.] Halleck reached the point where he could approve techniques of total war that would have horrified the master. But the most outstanding examples of growth and originality among the Northern generals are Grant and Sherman.

The qualities of Grant's generalship deserve more analysis than those of Lee, partly because they have not been sufficiently emphasized but largely because Grant was a more modern soldier than his rival. First, we note that Grant had that quality of character or will exhibited by all the great captains. (Lee had it, too.) Perhaps the first military writer to emphasize this trait in Grant was C.F. Atkinson in 1908. Grant's distinguishing feature as a general, said Atkinson, was his character, which was controlled by a tremendous will; with Grant action was translated from thought to deed by all the force of a tremendous personality. . . .

Common sense Grant had, and it enabled him to deal with such un-Jominian phenomena as army correspondents and political generals. Unlike Sherman, Grant accepted the reporters—but he rendered them harmless. "General Grant informs us correspondents that he will willingly facilitate us in obtaining all proper information," Junius Browne wrote S.H. Gay, then added significantly that Grant was "not very communicative." Unlike McClellan, who would not accept General Hamilton for political considerations urged by [President Abraham] Lincoln, Grant took John A. McClernand at the President's request. He could not imagine why Lincoln wanted a command for McClernand but assumed that there must be some reason important to his civil superior. He put up with McClernand until he found a way to strike him down to which Lincoln could not object. In this whole affair Grant showed that he realized the vital relation between politics and modern war.

It was Grant's common sense that enabled him to rise above the dogmas of traditional warfare. On one occasion a young officer, thinking to flat-ter Grant, asked his opinion of Jomini. Grant replied that he had never read the master. He then expressed his own theory of strategy: "The art of war is simple enough. Find out where your enemy is. Get at him as soon as you can. Strike at him as hard as you can and as often as you can, and keep moving on." After the war Grant discussed more fully his opinion of the value of doctrine. He conceded that military knowledge was highly desirable in a commander. But he added: "If men make war in slavish observance of rules, they will fail. No rules will apply to conditions of war as different as those which exist in Europe and America. . . . War is progressive, because all the instruments and elements of war are progressive." He then referred to the movement that had been his most striking departure from the rules, the Vicksburg campaign. To take Vicksburg by rules would have required a withdrawal to Memphis, the opening of a new line of operations, in fact, a whole new strategic design. But Grant believed that the discouraged condition of Northern opinion would not permit such a conformity to Jominian practice: "In a popular war we had to consider political exigencies." It was this ability of Grant's to grasp the political nature of modern war that marks him as the first of the great modern generals.

The question of where to rank Sherman among Civil War generals has always troubled military writers. He is obviously not a Jominian, and just as obviously he is not a great battle captain like Grant or Lee. . . . Sherman had the most complete grasp of the truth that the resisting power of a modern democracy depends heavily on the popular will and that this will depends in turn on a secure economic and social basis. Sherman, a typical Jominian at the beginning of the war, became its greatest exponent of economic and psychological warfare. Nobody realized more clearly than Sherman the significance of the techniques he introduced. Describing to Grant what he meant to do on his destructive march, he said, "This may not be war, but rather statesmanship." At the same time we must recognize that Sherman's strategy by itself would not have brought the Confederacy down. That end called for a Grant who at the decisive moment would attack the enemy's armed forces. . . . The North was fortunate in finding two generals who between them executed [Prussian army officer Carl von] Clausewitz's three objectives of war: to conquer and destroy the enemy's armed forces, to get possession of the material elements of aggression and other sources of existence of the enemy, and to gain public opinion by winning victories that depress the enemy's morale.

After reading this selection, consider these questions:

1. What limitations does Williams ascribe to Lee?

2. In what ways did Grant accommodate the new realities of modern war?

3. Using information in your textbook as well as Williams's article, discuss the purposes of Sherman's march to the sea. What did Sherman mean when he wrote that "this may not be war, but rather statesmanship"?

SELECTION 3:

General Sherman's Special Field Orders

*I*n the eastern theater of the war, Robert E. Lee's masterful tactics produced a series of victories until 1863. In the western theater, however, Northern armies under Ulysses S. Grant gained the upper hand from the outset. Grant moved East to assume command of all Union forces in March 1864. In addition to attacking Lee's army in Virginia, Grant placed William T. Sherman in command of the army in northern Georgia with orders to destroy the Confederate army commanded by Joseph Johnston and to capture Atlanta. When Johnston proved unable to stop Sherman's advance, Jefferson Davis replaced him with John Bell Hood in July 1864. Hood also failed to stop Sherman, and Sherman's forces marched into Atlanta in September 1864. From there, Sherman advanced three hundred miles to the sea, took Savannah, and then turned his army northward. On the march from Atlanta to the sea, Sherman's army abandoned its supply lines and lived off the land, taking what they needed and destroying much of what was left. The following document is an excerpt from Sherman's special field orders, issued on November 9, 1864, as his army prepared to depart from Atlanta.*

Excerpted from *Sources of the American Republic: A Documentary History of Politics, Society, and Thought,* by Marvin Meyers, Alexander Kern, and John G. Cawelti (Chicago: Scott, Foresman and Company, 1960). Copyright © 1960 by Scott, Foresman and Company. Reprinted with permission.

3. There will be no general train of supplies, but each corps will have its ammunition-train and provision-train, distributed habitually as follows: Behind each regiment should follow one wagon and one ambulance; behind each brigade should follow a due proportion of ammunition-wagons, provision-wagons, and ambulances. In case of danger, each corps commander should change this order of march, by having his advance and rear brigades unencumbered by wheels. The separate columns will start habitually at 7 A.M., and make about fifteen miles per day, unless otherwise fixed in orders.

4. The army will forage liberally on the country during the march. To this end, each brigade commander will organize a good and sufficient foraging party, under the command of one or more discreet officers, who will gather, near the route traveled, corn or forage of any kind, meat of any kind, vegetables, corn-meal, or whatever is needed by the command, aiming at all times to keep in the wagons at least ten days' provisions for his command, and three days' forage. Soldiers must not enter the dwellings of the inhabitants, or commit any trespass; but, during a halt or camp, they may be permitted to gather turnips, potatoes, and other vegetables, and to drive in stock in sight of their camp. To regular foraging-parties must be intrusted the gathering of provisions and forage, at any distance from the road traveled.

5. To corps commanders alone is intrusted the power to destroy mills, houses, cotton-gins, etc.; and for them this general principle is laid down: In districts and neighborhoods where the army is unmolested, no destruction of such property should be permitted; but should guerrillas or bushwhackers molest our march, or should the inhabitants burn bridges, obstruct roads, or otherwise manifest local hostility, then army commanders should order and enforce a devastation more or less relentless, according to the measure of such hostility.

6. As for horses, mules, wagons, etc., belonging to the inhabitants, the cavalry and artillery may appropriate freely and without limit; discriminating, however, between the rich, who are usually hostile, and the poor and industrious, usually neutral or friendly. Foraging-parties may also take mules or horses, to replace the jaded animals of their trains, or to serve as pack-mules for the regiments or brigades. In all foraging, of whatever kind, the parties engaged will refrain from abusive or threatening language, and may, where the officer in command thinks proper, give written certificates of facts, but no receipts; and they will endeavor to leave with each family a reasonable portion for their maintenance.

7. Negroes who are able-bodied and can be of service to the several columns may be taken along; but each army commander will bear in mind that the question of supplies is a very important one, and that his first duty is to see to those who bear arms.

8. The organization, at once, of a good pioneer battalion for each army corps, composed if possible of negroes, should be attended to. This battalion should follow the advance-guard, repair roads and double them if possible, so that the columns will not be delayed after reaching bad places. Also, the army commanders should practise the habit of giving the artillery and wagons the road, marching their troops on one side, and instruct their troops to assist wagons at steep hills or bad crossings of streams.

After reading this selection, consider these questions:

1. Many historians have described Sherman's march as a form of psychological warfare. What in his special field orders supports that view?

2. Sherman's march is often portrayed as the beginning of the savagery that is modern war, and Sherman is often portrayed as cold and cruel. What in his special field orders supports these images? What contradicts them?

SELECTION 4:

Ulysses S. Grant Recalls the Confederate Surrender at Appomattox

When the Civil War broke out, Ulysses S. Grant was thirty-eight years old and was working as a clerk in his father's leather goods store in Galena, Illinois. A graduate of West Point, where he finished in the middle of his class, Grant fought in the Mexican War. After serving at posts in California and Oregon, he resigned from the army in 1854. He tried farming and real estate speculation in Missouri but failed at both and went to work for his father. With the coming of the Civil War, Grant's military education and experience helped him get a commission as a colonel, and he was promoted to brigadier general before seeing any action. His capture of Forts Henry and Donelson constituted the first major Union victories of the war. The siege of Vicksburg firmly established Grant as a winning general. After the war, he won election to two terms as president. In retirement, he put his money into his son's investment firm, which failed in 1884. Dying of cancer and nearly destitute, he worried about providing for his wife. His friend Mark Twain encouraged him to write his memoirs. Grant finished the two-volume work just days before he died. Grant's autobiography is the best written by any American president and is one of the best military memoirs ever penned. The following is his description of Lee's surrender at Appomattox.

I had known General [Robert E.] Lee in the old army, and had served with him in the Mexican War; but did not suppose, owing to the difference in our age and rank, that he would remember me; while I would more naturally remember him distinctly, because he was the chief of staff of General [Winfield] Scott in the Mexican War.

When I had left camp that morning I had not expected so soon the result that was then taking place, and consequently was in rough garb. I was without a sword, as I usually was when on horseback on the field, and wore a soldier's blouse for a coat, with the shoulder straps of my rank to indicate to the army who I was. When I went into the house I found General Lee. We greeted each other, and after shaking hands took our seats. I had my staff with me, a good portion of whom were in the room during the whole of the interview.

What General Lee's feelings were I do not know. As he was a man of much dignity, with an impassible face, it was impossible to say whether he felt inwardly glad that the end had finally

Excerpted from *Personal Memoirs*, by Ulysses S. Grant, edited by Caleb Carr (New York: The Modern Library, 1999).

come, or felt sad over the result, and was too manly to show it. Whatever his feelings, they were entirely concealed from my observation; but my own feelings, which had been quite jubilant on the receipt of his letter, were sad and depressed. I felt like anything rather than rejoicing at the downfall of a foe who had fought so long and valiantly, and had suffered so much for a cause, though that cause was, I believe, one of the worst for which a people ever fought, and one for which there was the least excuse. I do not question, however, the sincerity of the great mass of those who were opposed to us.

General Lee was dressed in a full uniform which was entirely new, and was wearing a sword of considerable value, very likely the sword which had been presented by the State of Virginia; at all events, it was an entirely different sword from the one that would ordinarily be worn in the field. In my rough traveling suit, the uniform of a private with the straps of a lieutenant general, I must have contrasted very strangely with a man so handsomely dressed, six feet high and of faultless form. But this was not a matter that I thought of until afterwards.

We soon fell into a conversation about old army times. He remarked that he remembered me very well in the old army; and I told him that as a matter of course I remembered him perfectly, but from the difference in our rank and years (there being about sixteen years' difference in our ages), I had thought it very likely that I had not attracted his attention sufficiently to be remembered by him after such a long interval. Our conversation grew so pleasant that I almost forgot the object of our meeting. After the conversation had run on in this style for some time, General Lee called my attention to the object of our meeting, and said that he had asked for this interview for the purpose of getting from me the terms I proposed to give his army. I said that I meant merely that his army should lay down their arms, not to take them up again during the continuance of the war unless duly and properly exchanged. He said that he had so understood my letter.

Then we gradually fell off again into conversation about matters foreign to the subject which had brought us together. This continued for some little time, when General Lee again interrupted the course of the conversation by suggesting that the terms I proposed to give his army ought to be written out. I called to General Parker, secretary on my staff, for writing materials, and commenced writing out the following terms:

> APPOMATTOX C.H., VA.,
> Apl. 9th, 1865.

GEN. R.E. LEE,
Comd'g C.S.A.

GEN: In accordance with the substance of my letter to you of the 8th inst., I propose to receive the surrender of the Army of N. Va. on the following terms, to wit: Rolls of all the officers and men to be made in duplicate. One copy to be given to an officer designated by me, the other to be retained by such officer or officers as you may designate. The officers to give their individual paroles not to take up arms against the Government of the United States until properly exchanged, and each company or regimental commander sign a like parole for the men of their commands. The arms, artillery and public property to be parked and stacked, and turned over to the officer appointed by me to receive them. This will not embrace the side arms of the officers, nor their private horses or baggage. This done, each officer and man will be allowed to return to their homes, not to be disturbed by United States authority so long as they observe their paroles and the laws in force where they may reside.

> Very respectfully,
> U.S. GRANT,
> Lt. Gen.

When I put my pen to the paper I did not know the first word that I should make use of in writing the terms. I only knew what was in my mind, and I wished to express it clearly, so that there could be no mistaking it. As I wrote on, the thought occurred to me that the officers had their own private horses and effects, which were important to them, but of no value to us; also that it would be an unnecessary humiliation to call upon them to deliver their side arms.

No conversation, not one word, passed between General Lee and myself, either about private property, side arms, or kindred subjects. He appeared to have no objections to the terms first proposed; or if he had a point to make against them he wished to wait until they were in writing to make it. When he read over that part of the terms about side arms, horses and private property of the officers, he remarked, with some feeling, I thought, that this would have a happy effect upon his army.

Then, after a little further conversation, General Lee remarked to me again that their army was organized a little differently from the army of the United States (still maintaining by implication that we were two countries); that in their army the cavalrymen and artillerists owned their own horses; and he asked if he was to understand that the men who so owned their horses were to be permitted to retain them. I told him that as the terms were written they would not; that only the officers were permitted to take their private property. He then, after reading over the terms a second time, remarked that that was clear.

I then said to him that I thought this would be about the last battle of the war—I sincerely hoped so; and I said further I took it that most of the men in the ranks were small farmers. The whole country had been so raided by the two armies that it was doubtful whether they would be able to put in a crop to carry themselves and their families through the next winter without the aid of the horses they were then riding. The United States did not want them and I would, therefore, instruct the officers I left behind to receive the paroles of his troops to let every man of the Confederate army who claimed to own a horse or mule take the animal to his home. Lee remarked again that this would have a happy effect.

He then sat down and wrote out the following letter:

HEADQUARTERS ARMY OF
NORTHERN VIRGINIA,
April 9, 1865

GENERAL:—I received your letter of this date containing the terms of the surrender of the Army of Northern Virginia as proposed by you. As they are substantially the same as those expressed in your letter of the 8th inst., they are accepted. I will proceed to designate the proper officers to carry the stipulations into effect.

R.E. LEE, General.
LIEUT.-GENERAL U.S. GRANT.

While duplicates of the two letters were being made, the Union generals present were severally presented to General Lee.

The much talked of surrendering of Lee's sword and my handing it back, this and much more that has been said about it is the purest romance. The word sword or side arms was not mentioned by either of us until I wrote it in the terms. There was no premeditation, and it did not occur to me until the moment I wrote it down. If I had happened to omit it, and General Lee had called my attention to it, I should have put it in the terms precisely as I acceded to the provision about the soldiers retaining their horses.

General Lee, after all was completed and before taking his leave, remarked that his army was in a very bad condition for want of food, and that they were without forage; that his men had been living for some days on parched corn exclusively, and that he would have to ask me for rations and forage. I told him "certainly," and asked for how many men he wanted rations. His answer was "about twenty-five thousand": and I authorized him to send his own commissary and quartermaster to Appomattox Station, two or three miles away, where he could have, out of the trains we had stopped, all the provisions wanted. As for forage, we had ourselves depended almost entirely upon the country for that.

Generals Gibbon, Griffin and Merritt were designated by me to carry into effect the paroling of Lee's troops before they should start for their homes—General Lee leaving Generals Longstreet, Gordon and Pendleton for them to confer with in order to facilitate this work. Lee and I then separated as cordially as we had met, he returning to his own lines, and all went into bivouac for the night at Appomattox.

After reading this selection, consider these questions:

1. Grant was sometimes criticized during the war for the number of casualties suffered by his army. How does he portray himself in his memoirs? Do you think he was deliberately answering his critics on this count? If so, how?

2. When news of Lee's surrender reached Grant's soldiers, they began firing their guns in celebration. Grant wrote, "I at once sent word, however, to have it stopped. The Confederates were now our prisoners, and we did not want to exult over their downfall." What other gestures did Grant make to the defeated Confederates? Why, after four years of bitter conflict, do you think he behaved in such a generous fashion?

SELECTION 5:

Lincoln's Gettysburg Address

The Civil War was a war of ideas. In the ideological conflict, the North had a tremendous asset in Abraham Lincoln, a president who could powerfully express the ideas and ideals for which his side fought. By any measure, Lincoln was an extraordinary figure. He had almost no formal education. Unlike some self-taught people, he did not read voraciously; rather, he read the same two books—the works of Shakespeare and the Bible—over and over. Yet, among American political leaders, only Thomas Jefferson rivaled him for eloquence. Lincoln's Gettysburg Address was a masterpiece, perhaps the finest ten sentences of political expression in the English language. Delivered at the commemoration of the National Soldiers' Cemetery on the Gettysburg battlefield on November 19, 1863, Lincoln's brief speech changed the meaning of the Civil War. It was not, according to Lincoln, merely a war to suppress a rebellion; it was not a war over states' rights, sectionalism, or property. Rather, it was a war to give the nation "a new birth of freedom." He traced the first birth of freedom to the Declaration of Independence, which declared that "all men are created equal," rather than to the Constitution, which tolerated slavery. In short, Lincoln aimed to define the ideological meaning of the war, and he succeeded. As the noted historian Gary Wills has observed, "The Civil War is, to most Americans, what Lincoln wanted it to mean."

Four score and seven years ago our fathers

Excerpted from *The Collected Works of Abraham Lincoln,* edited by Roy P. Basler (New Brunswick, NJ: Rutgers University Press, 1953).

brought forth on this continent, a new nation, conceived in Liberty, and dedicated to the proposition that all men are created equal.

Now we are engaged in a great civil war, testing whether that nation, or any nation so conceived and so dedicated, can long endure. We are met on a great battle-field of that war. We have come to dedicate a portion of that field, as a final resting place for those who here gave their lives that that nation might live. It is altogether fitting and proper that we should do this.

But, in a larger sense, we can not dedicate—we can not consecrate—we can not hallow—this ground. The brave men, living and dead, who struggled here, have consecrated it, far above our poor power to add or detract. The world will little note, nor long remember what we say here, but it can never forget what they did here. It is for us the living, rather, to be dedicated here to the unfinished work which they who fought here have thus far so nobly advanced. It is rather for us to be here dedicated to the great task remaining before us—that from these honored dead we take increased devotion to that cause for which they gave the last full measure of devotion—that we here highly resolve that these dead shall not have died in vain—that this nation, under God, shall have a new birth of freedom—and that government of the people, by the people, for the people, shall not perish from the earth.

After reading this selection, consider these questions:

1. Why did Lincoln seek to redefine the Northern cause? Would people have thought that states' rights or property rights justified the carnage of the battle of Gettysburg?

2. At the beginning of the war, Lincoln maintained that the North fought to preserve the Union. The Emancipation Proclamation seemingly changed that. Can one argue that the Gettysburg Address changed Northern war aims even more fundamentally?

CHAPTER 19

African Americans in the Civil War

The Civil War marked a watershed for African Americans. Although the abolition of slavery was not a Northern war aim at the beginning of the war, it became one. A major step in that process came in 1862; Abraham Lincoln's Emancipation Proclamation freed slaves in any state still in rebellion on January 1, 1863. Another important step came with the decision to use African Americans in the Union army. That decision came in spite of the racist objections of the Northern public and doubts on the part of Lincoln. By the war's end, 186,000 African Americans, including free blacks from the North and escaped slaves from the South, fought for the Union cause.

The war inevitably affected race relations in the Confederacy as well. Late in the war, facing a desperate need for manpower to counter the advances of Ulysses S. Grant and William T. Sherman, the Confederacy contemplated the use of slaves as soldiers and, in the process, came to debate emancipation as well.

Aside from any policy considered by the Confederacy, the war itself had an impact on the lives of many slaves. Advancing Union armies presented opportunities for slaves to escape to freedom, and many did. A significant number of these slaves served in the Union army. Women as well as men served the Union; escaped female slaves worked as cooks, laundresses, nurses, and in many other capacities.

The war presented new opportunities, but it did not eradicate all old barriers. While profoundly changing the status of African Americans, the war left the future of race relations a question to be settled in the future.

After reading this chapter, consider these questions:

1. What impact did events of the war have on African Americans?

2. To what extent did the war change white attitudes in the North?

3. How did the war upset the racial order in the South?

4. Was independence or the preservation of slavery the main Southern objective?

SELECTION 1:

The Union Decides to Use Black Soldiers

Early in the war, African Americans tried to join the Union army but were rejected. Democrats charged that proposals to recruit black soldiers were part of a Republican plot to establish equality of the races. In fact, abolitionists and black leaders, if not mainstream Republicans, intended just that. They believed that if African Americans fought for the Union, it would advance their claim to equal rights. Events, however, rather than concern for black equality, pushed the North toward the use of black troops. Some Union commanders organized black regiments in 1862. The Emancipation Proclamation gave legitimacy to this policy. Further, white enlistments slowed by 1863, and the North had to resort to a draft. All of this argued in favor of using African Americans as soldiers. In the following excerpt from his book The Negro's Civil War *(1965), James M. McPherson, a professor of history at Princeton University, describes the evolution of the decision to use black soldiers.*

In the first year of the war many Northern Negroes offered their services to the Union government as soldiers. But the government and the Northern people considered it a "white man's war" and refused to accept the offers. Nevertheless, Negro leaders continued to urge the necessity of enrolling colored troops. They knew that if the black man proved his patriotism and courage on the field of battle, the nation would be morally obligated to grant him first-class citizenship. . . .

Excerpted from *The Negro's Civil War,* by James M. McPherson (New York: Pantheon Books, 1965). Copyright © 1965 by James M. McPherson. Reprinted with permission.

[Frederick] Douglass was one of the most persistent and eloquent advocates of arming the Negro. In August 1861, when the war was more than four months old and the North had yet to win a major victory, Douglass chided the government in an editorial entitled "Fighting Rebels with Only One Hand":

What upon earth is the matter with the American Government and people? Do they really covet the world's ridicule as well as their own social and political ruin? What are they thinking about, or don't they condescend to think at all? So, indeed, it would seem from their blindness in dealing with the tremendous issue now upon them. Was there ever anything like it before? They are sorely pressed on every hand by a vast army of slaveholding rebels, flushed with success, and infuriated by the darkest inspirations of a deadly hate, bound to rule or ruin. . . .

Our Presidents, Governors, Generals and Secretaries are calling, with almost frantic vehemence, for men.—"Men! men! send us men!" they scream, or the cause of the Union is gone; . . . and yet these very officers, representing the people and Government, steadily and persistently refuse to receive the very class of men which have a deeper interest in the defeat and humiliation of the rebels, than all others. . . . What a spectacle of blind, unreasoning prejudice and pusillanimity is this! The national edifice is on fire. Every man who can carry a bucket of water, or remove a brick, is wanted; but those who have the care of the building, having a profound respect for the feeling of the national burglars who set the building on fire, are determined that the flames shall only be extinguished by Indo-Caucasian hands, and to have the building burnt rather than save it by means of any other. Such is the pride, the stupid prejudice and folly that rules the hour.

Why does the Government reject the negro? Is he not a man? Can he not wield a sword, fire a gun, march and countermarch, and obey orders like any other? . . . If persons so humble as we can be allowed to speak to the President of the United States, we should ask him if this dark and terrible hour of the nation's extremity is a time for consulting a mere vulgar and unnatural prejudice? . . . We would tell him that this is no time to fight with one hand, when both are needed; that this is no time to fight only with your white hand, and allow your black hand to remain tied. . . . While the Government continues to refuse the aid of colored men, thus alienating them from the national cause, and giving

the rebels the advantage of them, it will not deserve better fortunes that it has thus far experienced. . . .

Negroes and abolitionists pointed out that black men had fought for America in the Revolution and the War of 1812. In February 1862, Douglass said sarcastically: "Colored men were good enough to fight under Washington. They are not good enough to fight under McClellan. . . . They were good enough to help win American independence, but they are not good enough to help preserve that independence against treason and rebellion. . . .

There were two main objections to the enlistment of Negro troops. The first was the deep-seated racial prejudice of most Northerners. "We don't want to fight side and side with the nigger," wrote Corporal Felix Brannigan of the Seventy-fourth New York Regiment. "We think we are a too superior race for that.". . .

Secondly, most people in the North believed that colored men, especially the ex-slaves, were too servile and cowardly to make good soldiers. When General David Hunter proposed to raise a regiment of freedmen on the South Carolina Sea Islands in May 1862, many of the missionaries and teachers there were skeptical. One of them wrote: "I don't believe you could make soldiers of these men at all,—they are afraid, and they know it.". . . Lincoln summed up both types of opposition to Negro enlistment in two public statements. On August 4, 1862, an Indiana delegation offered the government two regiments of colored men from their state, but the President declined the offer. "To arm the negroes," he said, "would turn 50,000 bayonets from the loyal Border States against us that were for us." And six weeks later Lincoln told another delegation that "if we were to arm [the Negroes], I fear that in a few weeks the arms would be in the hands of the rebels."

Despite the government's official opposition to Negro soldiers, several Union generals tried to enlist black men in 1862. General Hunter proceeded with his organization of a regiment on the Sea Islands, although he had to resort to a draft to fill up his ranks. The War Department refused to sanction the regiment, however, and Hunter disbanded all but one company in August. Out in Kansas General James H. Lane raised two regiments of colored men composed of fugitive slaves from Missouri and free Negroes from the North. Lane's black troopers were not officially recognized by the War Department until early in 1863, but in the meantime they had participated in several fights against rebel bushwhackers in Kansas and Missouri. Down in New Orleans the free Negroes, who had formed a Confederate regiment in 1861, offered their services to Union General [Benjamin] Butler after the fall of the Crescent City in the spring of 1862. Butler refused the offer at first, but when he was threatened by a Confederate attack in August, the Massachusetts general hurriedly recruited three regiments of Negroes from southern Louisiana. These regiments took the field in November 1862, despite the fact that they had not yet been mustered in by the War Department.

Meanwhile Northern public opinion was being gradually converted by the pressure of events to the idea of arming the Negroes. In the summer of 1862 the Union forces suffered a series of military defeats, which struck a sharp blow at Northern morale. War-weariness was beginning to sap the willingness of white men to join the army, and the administration began to consider more seriously the possibility of recruiting colored men to supplement declining white manpower. On July 17, 1862, Congress passed two acts providing for the enlistment of Negroes as soldiers. The first was the Confiscation Act, which empowered the President "to employ as many persons of African descent as he may deem necessary and proper for the suppression of this rebellion." The second was a militia act repealing the provisions of the 1792 law barring colored men, and authorizing the employment of free Negroes and freedmen as soldiers.

There was still a considerable amount of opposition in the North to the enlistment of Negro soldiers, but on August 25 the War Department nevertheless authorized General Rufus Saxton, military governor of the South Carolina Sea Islands, to raise five regiments of black troops on the islands, with white men as officers. . . . Volunteers came forward slowly at first, but by November 7 the regiment was filling up rapidly and was mustered in as the First South Carolina Volunteers.

The Massachusetts abolitionist Thomas Wentworth Higginson was appointed colonel of the regiment in November. A few days after his arrival at Beaufort, Higginson wrote in his journal:

> It needs but a few days to show the absurdity of doubting the equal military availability of these people, as compared with whites. There is quite as much average comprehension of the need of the thing, as much courage, I doubt not, as much previous knowledge of the gun, & there is a readiness of ear & of imitation which for purposes of drill counterbalances any defect of mental training.

In January 1863, Higginson took part of his regiment on a raid along the St. Mary's River, which forms the boundary between Florida and Georgia. Upon his return, the Colonel submitted the following official report:

> . . . The men have been repeatedly under fire; have had infantry, cavalry, and even artillery arrayed against them, and have in every instance come off not only with unblemished honor, but with undisputed triumph. . . .

> Nobody knows anything about these men who has not seen them in battle. I find that I myself knew nothing. There is a fiery energy about them beyond anything of which I have ever read, except it be the French Zouaves. . . . [T]he black gunners, admirably trained by Lieutenants Stockdale and O'Neil, both being accomplished artillerists, and Mr. Heron, of the gunboat, did their duty without the slightest protection and with great coolness amid a storm of shot. . . .

> No officer in this regiment now doubts that the key to the successful prosecution of this war lies in the unlimited employment of black troops. Their superiority lies simply in the fact that they know the country, while white troops do not, and, moreover, that they have peculiarities of temperament, position, and motive which belong to them alone. Instead of leaving their homes and families to

fight they are fighting for their homes and families, and they show the resolution and the sagacity which a personal purpose gives. It would have been madness to attempt, with the bravest white troops, what I have successfully accomplished with black ones. Everything, even to the piloting of the vessels and the selection of the proper points for cannonading, was done by my own soldiers.

A second Negro regiment was organized on the islands, with James Montgomery as its colonel. Higginson and Montgomery led their men on several successful raids into the interior of Georgia and Florida, and in March 1863 they captured and occupied Jacksonville.

On April 30, General David Hunter, Commander of the Department of the South, reported to Secretary [of War Edwin] Stanton:

I am happy to be able to announce to you my complete and eminent satisfaction with the results of the organization of negro regiments in this department. . . . In the field these regiments, so far as tried, have proved brave, active, docile, and energetic, frequently outrunning by their zeal and familiarity with the Southern country the restrictions deemed prudent by certain of their officers and . . . so conducting themselves, upon the whole, that even our enemies, though more anxious to find fault with these than with any other portion of our troops, have not yet been able to allege against them a single violation of any of the rules of civilized warfare.

. . . They are imbued with a burning faith that now is the time appointed by God, in His All-wise Providence, for the deliverance of their race; and under the heroic incitement of this faith I believe them capable of courage and persistence of purpose which must in the end extort both victory and admiration. . . .

I am also happy to announce to you that the prejudices of certain of our white soldiers against these indispensable allies are rapidly softening or fading out.

These enthusiastic official dispatches were written for the eyes of the Northern public as well as the Secretary of War, and most of the reports found their way into the newspapers. But the private reactions of those who watched the development of Higginson's regiment were almost as favorable as the public statements. . . .

The reports from South Carolina were beginning to convince the Republican press and the Lincoln administration of the wisdom and necessity of recruiting a large Negro army. On March 28, 1863, the New York *Tribune* stated editorially:

Facts are beginning to dispel prejudices. Enemies of the negro race, who have persistently denied the capacity and doubted the courage of the Blacks, are unanswerably confuted by the good conduct and gallant deeds of the men whom they persecute and slander. From many quarters comes evidence of the swiftly approaching success which is to crown what is still by some persons deemed to be the experiment of arming whom the Proclamation of Freedom liberates.

Two days earlier Lincoln had written to Andrew Johnson, War Governor of Tennessee:

I am told you have at least *thought* of raising a negro military force. In my opinion the country now needs no specific thing so much as some man of your ability and position to go to this work. . . . The colored population is the great *available* and yet *unavailed of* force for restoring the Union. The bare sight of 50,000 armed and drilled black soldiers upon the banks of the Mississippi would end the rebellion at once. And who doubts that we can present that sight if we but take hold in earnest?

On April 1 Lincoln informed General Hunter that "I am glad to see the accounts of your colored force at Jacksonville, Florida. . . . It is important to the enemy that such a force shall *not* take shape, and grow, and thrive, in the South; and in precisely the same proportion, it is important to us that it *shall*." The President had experienced a complete change of mind since the previous September when he had feared that arms placed in the hands of Negroes would soon find their way into the hands of rebels.

In the spring of 1863 General Nathaniel P. Banks began to recruit a "Corps d'Afrique" from the Negro population of Louisiana. . . . By the end of August Banks had recruited nearly fifteen thousand black soldiers in Louisiana.

In March 1863 Secretary of War Stanton had sent Adjutant General Lorenzo Thomas to the lower Mississippi Valley to recruit and organize as many Negro regiments as possible from among the freedmen in that area. On May 22 the Bureau of Colored Troops was established in the War Department to coordinate and administer the raising of Negro regiments in every part of the country. . . .

By the first week of August 1863, there were fourteen Negro regiments in the field or ready for service, and twenty-four additional regiments were in the process of organization. Five of the fourteen battle-ready regiments had been recruited in the North.

After reading this selection, consider these questions:

1. What arguments does Frederick Douglass use to support the use of black soldiers?

2. Discuss Abraham Lincoln's evolving position.

3. How did the Emancipation Proclamation provide support for the use of black soldiers?

SELECTION 2:

The Confederacy Debates the Use of Black Soldiers

As James M. McPherson describes in the preceding essay, the changing conditions of the war moved the North to use black soldiers. More surprising, perhaps, is that a similar, although even more agonizing, debate took place within the Confederacy. Some Southerners argued that if the Confederacy did not arm Southern blacks, the North would. Indeed, some went so far as to argue that the Confederate government should emancipate slaves and use them as soldiers. According to this reasoning, if the South lost the war, Northerners would destroy the social order of the South. On the other hand, if the use of black soldiers helped fend off Northern armies, Southern whites would at least maintain control of the land, the economy, and the political system of the South.

This debate revealed much about the importance of slavery to the South. Slavery was central to the Confederacy, and the reluctance of many Southerners even to consider emancipation indicated the primacy of slavery over independence as a war aim. The debate also revealed that many Southerners knew or suspected what they would not admit, perhaps even to themselves: Their slaves wanted freedom and were willing to fight for it.

Eventually, exigencies of war led President Jefferson Davis and the Confederate Congress to move toward arming slaves and emancipating them. Although some slaves began training, the war ended before they could be used in combat.

One of the finest historians of the South, Robert F. Durden, professor emeritus of history at Duke University, provides a detailed account of the Southern debate over arming slaves and emancipation in his book The Gray and the Black *(1972). The following excerpt, from a never-before-published paper, summarizes his argument.*

That the Confederacy in its waning days frantically turned to the idea of arming the slaves has long been known by students of the Civil War. What has not been properly emphasized is that the central issue before the Southern people and leaders in this last great crisis of the Confederacy was not really the arming of the slaves but whether or not the South should itself voluntarily initiate a program of emancipation.

A proposal for Confederate emancipation was made by none other than Jefferson Davis himself. Many of the history books have strangely missed a key element of the paradoxical drama that unfolded when the President of the Confederacy called for the freeing of a significant portion of the slaves. Historians may have largely missed Davis's point, but his contemporaries certainly did not. From October, 1864, until the end of the war in the following April, the Confederacy exploded in an intensely passionate debate that cut to the heart of what the Civil War was all about as far as the South was concerned. Davis and a few other leaders attempted to force the South to face the desperate alternative of sacrificing one of its war aims—the preservation of slavery—in order to make a last-ditch effort to achieve the other—an independent Southern nation. Most articulate Southerners, despite certain fascinating exceptions, made it tragically clear that they yet lacked, even in this ultimate crisis, the intelligence, moral courage, and imagination to begin voluntarily to abandon the peculiar institution. The South had

spent forty or so years convincing itself that slavery was ordained by God as the best, indeed the only, solution to the massive presence of the Negro. The debate in the winter of 1864–1865 demonstrated anew and with a sad finality that most Southerners were unwilling or unable to consider voluntary alterations to the racial status quo, even as that status quo was crumbling about them in the closing phases of the Civil War.

After the war ended, a cardinal element of the Southern apologia, and an idea cherished by some Southerners well into the twentieth century, was the emphatic denial that the South had fought to preserve slavery as a primary aim in the Civil War. Liberty, independence, and especially states' rights were advanced by countless Southern spokesmen as the hallowed ingredients of the Lost Cause. Even during the war, some Southerners minimized the defense of slavery, and thus anticipated the postwar apologia. But by and large the Confederates themselves were not as elusive and confused on the subject as their descendants would be.

In the first place, the Confederate constitution, unlike the original model of 1787, avoided euphemisms such as "other persons" and "persons held to service or labor" and referred to slavery by name in several places. . . .

Underscoring the central significance of these provisions for slavery in the Confederate constitution, the newly elected Confederate vice-president, Alexander Stephens, in a famous speech delivered at Savannah, Georgia, on March 21, 1861, declared that . . . Jefferson and other founding fathers, holding ideas that were "fundamentally wrong" concerning the equality of races, had built the old government on a "sandy foundation."

"Our new government," Stephens boasted, "is founded upon exactly the opposite idea; its foundations are laid, its corner-stone rests upon the great truth, that the negro is not equal to the white man; that slavery—subordination to the superior race—is his natural and normal condition." . . .

Perhaps the earliest indications to Southern leaders that the vaunted cornerstone might also pose something of a problem came from the Confederacy's first diplomatic envoys to Britain and France. . . . Once in Europe and out of the parochial, ultra-defensive atmosphere that surrounded the question of slavery in the South, other Confederate emissaries repeatedly tackled the task of telling the Richmond government unwelcome truths about European antislavery sentiment. That sentiment was by no means the only obstacle to the Anglo-French recognition that was so crucial to the Confederacy; but it was clearly an important complicating factor. And it became even more of one when [President Abraham] Lincoln announced in September, 1862, that as of the first day of 1863 he would, as commander-in-chief, take the step of declaring free the slaves of rebels. . . .

Diplomatically, England and France no longer faced the choice between a proslavery South and a North that was neutral or silent concerning slavery in the states. Lincoln had, in short, made it more difficult for the European nations to consider the recognition of the Confederacy.

Politically, the Lincolnian move struck a sensitive nerve in the South, for it spotlighted the difference in "interests" between the majority of the Southern whites (and the larger part of the Confederate army) who owned no slave property and of the powerful minority who did. . . .

Most importantly of all, Lincoln's simultaneous programs of emancipation and recruiting Negro soldiers threatened militarily to weaken the South as they also opened a significant new reservoir of manpower for the Union army. . . .

[Blacks] were enlisted in the Union army, and their gradually increasing military significance by no means went unnoticed in the South.

Numerous scattered suggestions that the Confederacy should make greater military use of adult male slaves were made by various South-erners in the newspapers and in communications to officials in Richmond in 1863 and even earlier. But the first significant proposal came early in 1864 from a brilliant major-general in the Confederate army, Patrick R. Cleburne. . . .

Cleburne was fresh from the humiliating Confederate defeat at Chattanooga in late 1863 and in winter quarters in north Georgia. He brooded about the extensive preparations that General W.T. Sherman was making and the large army that he was gathering for a spring campaign. At the same time, the ranks of the Army of Tennessee, now commanded by General Joseph E. Johnston, steadily dwindled because of death, disability, and desertion. Realizing the critical need to recruit men for the exhausted Confederate ranks and ignoring the cautionary warnings of his friends, Cleburne boldly cut to the core of the Southern dilemma. . . .

Apart from "the assistance that home and foreign prejudice against slavery" gave to the North, he insisted that slavery had become a "source of great strength to the enemy in a purely military point of view": it supplied him with a vast army drawn from Southern fields, and wherever it was disturbed by the actual or threatened presence of Federal troops, slavery had become a "vulnerable point, a continued embarrassment, and in some respects an insidious weakness." As Federal armies approached, according to Cleburne, whites grew apprehensive about their property and proportionately cooler toward the Confederate side because they hoped that Lincoln would ultimately not disturb the slave property of "loyal" citizens. Along the battle lines, slavery had become "comparatively valueless" for labor, yet it was "of great and increasing worth to the enemy for information;" it was, in fact, "an omnipresent spy system."

What, then, could be done? Grasping the nettle firmly, Cleburne urged . . . "that we immediately commence training a large reserve of the most courageous of our slaves, and further that we guarantee freedom within a reasonable time to every slave in the South who shall remain true to the Confederacy in this war." "As between the loss of independence and the loss of slavery," he postulated, "we assume that every patriot will freely give up the latter—give up the negro slave rather than be a slave himself."

In orthodox Southern eyes at the time, perhaps Cleburne's most heretical idea, and one that Jefferson Davis would himself eventually advance, was the candid recognition that the Negro wished to be free. . . .

Cleburne asserted that the Confederacy could enlist the sympathies of the slave more effectually than could the North because the South could "give the negro not only his own freedom, but that of his wife and child and . . . secure it to him in his old home." "If, then, we touch the institution at all," he reiterated, "we would do best to make the most of it, and by emancipating the whole race upon reasonable terms, and within such reasonable time as will prepare both races for the change, secure to ourselves all the advantages, and to our enemies all the disadvantages that can arise, both at home and abroad, from such a sacrifice."

Would the slaves fight? Cleburne pointed to the Negro victors in Saint Domingo and the Jamaican Maroons who so long and successfully resisted their masters. His most telling evidence, however, came from the Civil War itself, where experience proved, according to Cleburne, that "half-trained negroes have fought as bravely as many other half-trained Yankees." "If, contrary to the training of a lifetime, they can be made to face and fight bravely against their former masters," he argued, "how much more probable is it that with the allurement of a higher reward, and led by those masters, they would submit to discipline and face dangers." . . .

Although some dozen or so of his fellow officers, including three brigadier generals, endorsed the proposal, General Johnston refused to forward it to Richmond on the grounds that "it was more political than military in tenor."

If another of Cleburne's associates had not been so indignant that he took it upon himself to inform Jefferson Davis directly, Richmond might never have even heard of the proposal. Major General W.H.T. Walker asserted that, "The gravity of the subject, the magnitude of the issues involved, my strong convictions that the further agitation of such sentiments . . . would ruin the efficacy of our Army and involve our cause in ruin and disgrace constitute my reasons for bringing the document before the executive."

Davis immediately replied that he deemed it "injurious to the public service that such a subject should be mooted, or even known to be entertained by persons possessed of the confidence and respect of the people. . . ." He believed that the "best policy" was to "avoid all publicity," for if it "be kept out of the public journals its ill effect will be much lessened." The secretary of war accordingly issued a directive to Johnston, who in turn informed Cleburne and the other high officers involved. All copies of the proposal were destroyed—save one that fortuitously survived to turn up towards the end of the century.

Given the realities of the Confederate constitution, and more importantly, the dominant Southern thought-patterns about slavery, Jefferson Davis probably did the only thing he could possibly have done in suppressing Cleburne's proposal. . . .

[However,] events in 1864 . . . seemed to push the Confederacy closer to the precipice. In January, 1864, when Davis suppressed the Cleburne document, General Grant had not yet begun his relentless, bloody hammering at Lee's army. By November, that onslaught had been raging intermittently for some six months, and General Lee had been forced to make this candid assessment to President Davis: "Unless we can obtain a reasonable approximation to Grant's force I fear a great calamity will befall us. . . . The inequality is too great." If Lee's plight was grim, that of the other great Confederate force, the Army of Tennessee, was worse. Atlanta fell to Sherman in early September.

This was the tightening noose that inspired Davis finally to attempt a drastic change of policy, to make a last desperate effort to gain both manpower for the army and recognition of the Confederacy by England and France. . . . In his message to the Confederate congress on November 7, 1864, Jefferson Davis emerged in a role that is not generally associated with him, that of would-be Confederate emancipator.

Before Davis made his own bid for such a drastic change, various lesser voices clamored in the early fall of 1864 for greater military use of the blacks by the Confederacy. Described by one historian as "perhaps the finest daily newspaper in the South," the Richmond *Enquirer* in October, 1864, floated a trial balloon that commanded widespread attention, not only throughout the South but in the North and even in England. "We should be glad to see the Confederate Congress provide for the purchase of two hundred and fifty thousand negroes," the *Enquirer* boldly announced, "present them with their freedom and the privilege of remaining in the States, and arm, equip, drill and fight them." The Richmond paper expressed its belief that "the negroes, identified with us by interest, and fighting for their freedom here, would be faithful and reliable soldiers. . . ."

The *Enquirer*'s proposal inspired a quickening controversy throughout much of the South, for the five daily newspapers of Richmond, described by one Northern journalist as being "in many respects the ablest on the continent," were closely watched and widely quoted by Southern as well as Northern newspapers. From the deep South the Mobile *Register,* which had earlier advocated a greater Confederate use of the blacks, urged favorable consideration of the *Enquirer*'s scheme. . . .

Much of the journalistic opposition to any Confederate tampering with the "cornerstone" lay low as the controversy first began. One exception was the Lynchburg *Republican,* which declared that if the South were "to be abolitionized in the end, it would have been far better for us to have been abolitionized in the beginning, and that, if such a terrible calamity is to befall us at all, we infinitely prefer that Lincoln shall be the instrument of our disaster and degradation, than that we ourselves should strike the cowardly and suicidal blow. . . . If our people are not capable of vindicating their title to property in negroes, then they ought to quietly surrender the question, stop the war, abolish slavery and confess themselves eternally disgraced."

Also emerging early as a vehement foe of any Confederate move against slavery was the Charleston *Mercury,* edited by Robert Barnwell Rhett, Jr., and long since made famous as the vehicle for the views of his fire-eating, secessionist father. . . .

Wracked though the Southerners were with the agony of a war that they were losing, most Confederates, contrary to those people who read history backwards, did not know in November, 1864, that they were beaten. Indeed, the very duration and magnitude of the war made defeat seem all the more unimaginable and unacceptable to them. Of none was this apparently truer than of Jefferson Davis. By November 7, 1864, when he sent his presidential message to the Confederate congress, Davis had clearly decided, as far as slavery was concerned, that the time had come to cross the Rubicon. He had, probably in conjunction with his close associate, Secretary of State [Judah P.] Benjamin, hit upon a scheme that was both modest in its immediate impact and far reaching in its implications; one that might hold diplomatic as well as military hope for the South; and, above all, one that he believed could be reconciled with a constitution that so elaborately left slavery in the sole hands of the states.

Naturally, Jefferson Davis, whom many Southerners were now making the scapegoat for their miseries, broached the subject gingerly and in the most cautious language. After reviewing the military, foreign, and financial situations, he turned to the matter of several proposals for adding "to the number and efficiency of the Army." In February, 1864, Congress had passed, upon his urging, a law authorizing the Confederate government to hire or impress the labor of up to 20,000 free Negroes or slaves to serve with the army as teamsters, cooks, nurses, and manual workers. Davis now frankly admitted that the law had "produced less result than was anticipated, and further provision is required to render it efficacious." But, the President continued—and here he verbally waved a red flag that called for attention—his present purpose was to invite the consideration of congress to "the propriety of a radical modification in the theory of the law."

A basic feature of Jefferson Davis's proposal was the distinction, long established in law even if often blurred in practice, between the slave as property and the slave as person. . . . "Viewed merely as property, and therefore the subject of impressment," the President explained, "the service or labor of the slave has been frequently claimed for short periods in the construction of defensive works." Furthermore, the government had accepted the liability to pay the owner for any pecuniary loss that might result from the slave's services.

"The slave, however, bears another relation to the state," Davis continued, "—that of a person." Even for the non-combatant duties enumerated in the act of February, 1864, careful instruction was needed and length of service added greatly to the value of the slave's labor. Many hazards were involved, and "the duties required of them demand loyalty and zeal." "In this respect," the President suggested, "the relation of person predominates so far as to render it doubtful whether the private right of property can consistently and beneficially be continued, and it would seem proper to acquire for the public service the entire property in the labor of the slave, and to pay therefore due compensation rather than to impress his labor for short terms. . . ."

Next came the real dynamite, for up to this point the President had merely proposed that the Confederate government itself should become the largest slaveowner in a society of slaveholders. Now he broached the subject of emancipation. "Whenever the entire property in the service of a slave is thus acquired by the Government," Davis postulated, "the question is presented by what tenure he should be held. Should he be retained in servitude, or should his emancipation be held out to him as a reward for faithful service; and if emancipated, what action should be taken to secure for the freedman the permission of the State from which was drawn to reside within its limits after the close of his public service?"

President Davis expressed his belief that the states would more readily grant permission for the emancipated Negroes to reside therein as "a reward for past faithful service." And, no doubt thinking of Lincoln's well known colonization proposals, the Southern leader urged that those Negroes employed by the Confederacy would have a "double motive for a zealous discharge of duty," that is, they would have the promise of "their freedom and the gratification of the local attachment which is so marked a characteristic of the negro,

and forms so powerful an incentive to his action." . . . "If this policy should recommend itself to the judgment of Congress," Davis concluded, " . . . the number should be augmented to 40,000." . . .

Jefferson Davis undoubtedly knew all too well that his proposal would face rough sledding in the Confederate congress, particularly in the senate. . . .

What may have surprised the Confederate President was the vehemence and extent of the influential journalistic opposition to his plan. In Richmond, the brilliantly edited *Examiner,* one of the most powerful of the critics of the Davis administration, broke its silence upon what it declared to be a provocative, impractical subject. In urging a promise of freedom for the 40,000, Davis had, according to the *Examiner,* advanced "an idea which, if admitted by the Southern people as a truth, renders their position on the matter of slavery utterly untenable." The *Examiner* explained that the South believed that the Negro as a slave was in the "condition which is the best for him; . . . that while living with the white man in the relation of slave he is in a state superiour and better for him than that of freedom." But the President would give him freedom as a reward for services to the country, as a "boon" and a "natural good of which our laws deprive him and keep him from." Precisely that, the *Examiner* sourly concluded, was "the whole theory of the abolitionist, and we have the sorrow to think that if one portion of this Presidential message means anything it means that."

The Richmond *Whig* insisted that if the slave had to fight, "he should fight for the blessings he enjoys as a slave, and not for the miseries that would attend him if freed." . . .

With three of the five Richmond newspapers expressing such views, no one could have been surprised that there were cries of outrage and shock from various newspapers in the states to the south of Virginia. . . .

Given the angry reception that the President's proposal met, no wonder that the Richmond *Sentinel,* one of the more consistent but by no means sycophantic supporters of the Davis administration, had earlier suggested that to enter into a discussion of freeing and arming slaves would be "premature and hurtful" and that it would be "injudicious" to debate the "delicate question."

When the question, delicate or not, obviously was not fading away but growing hotter by the day, the *Sentinel* finally flailed into those who loudly professed a desire to prosecute the war for independence with any and all resources, but who then attacked the President's proposal as one that gave up the cause. "What cause?" demanded the *Sentinel*. "We thought that *independence* was, just now, the great question. Is it giving up *that?* No; but it is giving up the *slavery* question. To this an obvious answer is, that if it be *necessary* to give up slavery in order to secure independence, we *ought* to give it up."

The *Sentinel* asserted that Southerners could not "too vividly realize that subjugation meant the loss" of their "liberties *and emancipation too.*". . .

Reaffirming its orthodoxy in the matter of slavery's Divine sanction, the *Sentinel* concluded by reiterating the "obvious impropriety" of too much public discussion of the matter and expressing its wish that General Robert E. Lee, who "knows better what the necessity is than we," would speak.

The *Sentinel* was not alone, of course, in looking longingly toward Lee for guidance. The gallant, enigmatic Virginian had captured the imagination and admiration of a war-weary people as had no one else, yet he carefully stayed in what he regarded as his proper military sphere. . . .

Lee did frequently "speak," of course, to Davis as well as many other officials and citizens, high and low, civil and military. But his numerous conferences and many letters were private, rather than the great public and dramatic acts of leadership for which a growing number of Southerners desperately looked to him. Lee's views became increasingly crucial in the controversy, but the public at large could only hear about them secondhand, that is through various officials who claimed to know his opinions. Breaking a long, strict policy of silence on political questions, Lee would eventually speak out directly and publicly in favor of freeing and arming the slaves, as will be discussed subsequently; but he did not do so until February, 1865, after hope

was gone for the plan advanced by President Davis in November.

Lee's support for the "radical modification" proposed by Jefferson Davis might or might not have made a difference. At any rate, the support never came and, given the proud and always correct punctiliousness of both Lee and Davis, it was probably never sought. With only a few newspapers scattered around the South left to protest, the majority of Confederate congressmen hastened to bury and try to forget the heretical notions that had been put forth by the President. Jefferson Davis had, of course, some loyal supporters in both houses of congress, but on his proposal relating to emancipation they were clearly a hopeless minority. . . .

Perhaps the best ray of hope for Davis appeared on December 7, 1864, when Governor [William] Smith of Virginia in his message to the state legislature carefully reviewed the pros and the cons of the agonizing question and then emphatically declared: "For my part, standing before God and my country, I do not hesitate to say that I would arm such portion of our able-bodied slave population as may be necessary, and put them in the field, so as to have them ready for the spring campaign, even if it resulted in the freedom of those thus organized."

Perhaps it was the hope of joint action by Virginia and the Confederate government that inspired Jefferson Davis and Secretary of State Benjamin to make their last great effort to secure recognition and assistance from Britain and France. The Confederate leaders were obviously taking a desperate gamble of dubious constitutionality, and they proceeded with cautious secrecy and with a minimum of written documentation. Nevertheless, the mission of Duncan F. Kenner as secret envoy empowered to discuss Confederate emancipation, among other things, in exchange for Anglo-French recognition has long been known. . . .

Although the Kenner mission was doomed to end in failure, Davis and his allies could not, of course, know that, and they tried to rouse public pressure that might prod the Confederate congress, as well as the Virginia legislature, into some action other than unending debate, much of it in secret session, and parliamentary maneuvering. . . . In December, 1864, the Army of Tennessee suffered a crushing defeat, and Savannah fell to Sherman. In mid-January, 1865, the Federals captured Fort Fisher, which protected the last important Confederate seaport, Wilmington, North Carolina, and Sherman headed into the Carolinas. Confederate despondency and war-weariness, as well as wishful thinking about the terms of peace that Lincoln might agree to, had reached such proportions that Jefferson Davis in January, 1865, reluctantly participated in the train of developments that culminated in the famed peace conference at Hampton Roads, Virginia, on February 3. . . .

The outcome of the Hampton Roads conference had an electrifying impact on the South. Lincoln had made it emphatically clear, even to those who much wanted to believe otherwise, . . . there would be peace when there was a restored union without slavery. . . .

"There are no peace men among us now!" the Richmond *Sentinel* proclaimed. . . . The same sentiment was echoed by countless other papers, and a series of great public meetings—really Confederate revival services—began in Richmond and then in other places throughout the unconquered portions of the South. . . .

At the second of these mass meetings in Richmond at noon on February 9, 1865, . . . Judah Benjamin . . . seized the occasion to make a dramatic appeal for the freeing and arming of the slaves through joint action of the Confederate government and Virginia. . . .

After reminding his excited hearers of the crucial use that Lincoln was making of the 200,000 blacks in the Federal army, Benjamin declared: "Let us say to every negro who wishes to go into the ranks on condition of being made free—'Go and fight; you are free.' If we press them, they will go against us." . . . Changing now from the earlier plan that President Davis and he had vainly pushed, Benjamin explained: "It can only be done by the states separately. What State will lead off in this thing? [A Voice—'Virginia.']" Seizing upon the cue from his audience, he quickly recalled the Southwide jubilation when Virginia threw in with the other Confederate states after

Fort Sumter. "Let your legislature pass the necessary laws, and we will soon have twenty thousand men down in those trenches fighting for the country," Benjamin promised. "You must make up your minds to try that, or see your army withdrawn from before your town. I came here to say disagreeable things. I tell you, you are in danger unless some radical measure be taken."

Although "radical" measures were, at long last, indeed introduced in the Confederate congress, none of them were passed. The measure that ultimately was enacted, introduced by Representative Ethelbert Barksdale of Mississippi on February 10, 1865, the day after Benjamin's speech, made no provision for emancipating slaves. It merely authorized the President to accept from the owners of slaves "the services of such number of able-bodied negro men as he may deem expedient . . . to perform military service in whatever capacity he may direct." Or if the President were unable to obtain sufficient troops through the voluntary action of owners, he was authorized to call on each state for its quota of 300,000 (black) troops, provided that not more than twenty-five per centum of the male slaves between the ages of eighteen and forty-five should be called from any one state. The crucial last section of the law stated: "That nothing in this act shall be construed to authorize a change in the relation which the said slaves shall bear toward their owners, except by consent of the owners and of the States in which they may reside, and in pursuance of the laws thereof."

Even this cautious measure required extraordinary efforts by Barksdale and his allies in the government before it could be passed by the House. Benjamin on February 11 successfully sought Lee's help in obtaining from the army "an expression of its desire to be reinforced by such negroes as for the boon of freedom will volunteer to go to the front. . . ."

General Lee's letter of February 18, 1865, to Congressman Barksdale turned the tide. Undoubtedly with the general's permission, the letter quickly appeared in the Richmond papers and then gradually in other Southern journals. Views that Lee had expressed earlier in private or semi-private circumstances now became incredibly influential public knowledge. The general avowed that he thought "the employment of negroes as soldiers" was "not only expedient but necessery." . . . Those "who are employed should be freed," Lee declared, for it "would be neither just nor wise . . . to require them to serve as slaves." The best course would be to "call for such as are willing to come with the consent of their owners," since coercion "would make the measure distasteful" both to the Negroes and to their owners. . . .

As magic as Lee's name had already become, not even his opinion was convincing for many powerful Southerners. True, certain newspapers which had earlier stoutly opposed the idea now capitulated. The Richmond *Examiner,* for example, held out until February 25 when it concluded a long editorial with the comment that if Lee said the measure was necessary to avoid "submission to the enemy" then "no good Southern man will hesitate." . . .

Not the Charleston *Mercury.* Even as Sherman's army approached, the Rhetts clung to their dogmas and declared that neither the Confederate congress nor "certain make-shift men in Virginia" could force upon South Carolina "their mad schemes of weakness and surrender." *"We want no Confederate Government without our institutions,"* the *Mercury* flatly avowed. . . .

Certain Confederate senators proved to be almost as obdurate as the *Mercury,* for the majority of the senate, after killing the relevant bills that had been introduced in the upper house, insisted on a restrictive and time-consuming amendment (the limit of twenty-five per centum on the designated male slaves in any one state) to the Barksdale measure. . . .

The Virginia legislature helped to save the bill allowing the Confederate government to arm black soldiers; but not even Robert E. Lee's counsel could persuade the legislature to embrace emancipation. Only slightly less dilatory than the Confederate congress, the Virginia legislature on March 4 and 6, 1865, enacted measures that were vital complements to the Barksdale bill. With no mention whatsoever of emancipation, the first of these measures . . . authorized the Confederate government to call upon Virginia through her governor for her able-bodied male free Negroes between the ages of eighteen and forty-five and if necessary for up to twenty-five per centum of her able-bodied male slaves in the same age bracket, with the call for slaves to be properly apportioned among the different counties and corporations and with no more than one slave in every four between the ages indicated to be taken from any one owner. The second measure merely made it lawful for free Negroes and slaves who became Confederate soldiers to bear arms "as other soldiers in the Army."

Although both the Confederate congress and the Virginia legislature had steered clear of emancipation, President Davis and the Confederate army in promulgating the new policy bootlegged freedom into the picture. They did this by including among the army's own regulations, printed beneath the new Confederate law, this order: "No slave will be accepted as a recruit unless with his own consent and with the approbation of his master by a written instrument conferring, as far as he may, the rights of a freedman, and which will be filed with the superintendent."

Clearly it was this promise of freedom, more or less smuggled in though it had been, that accounted for the fact that there were Negroes ready to fight for the Confederacy. . . .

The question ceased to be theoretical by mid-March, 1865, and the Richmond newspapers reported a flurry of recruiting activity among the Negroes. A reporter from the *Examiner* found some three dozen uniformed and equipped blacks at a specially designated "rendezvous for negro troops, corner of Cary and Twenty-first streets." About a dozen of the recruits were said to be free Negroes who had volunteered. . . .

Davis and Lee, though disappointed by the legislation that had been enacted, continued to pin their hopes on the blacks, even though both leaders ruefully admitted that time was running out. . . .

For his part, Robert E. Lee obviously had less and less time even to think of the matter, as Grant's forces began to advance. Yet the last letter that Lee wrote to Davis from Petersburg, on April 2, discussed the recruiting of Negro troops and Lee's pleasure in the news that the President was appealing to the governors. On the same day, Lee sent the telegrams informing Davis that

Richmond would have to be evacuated. Lee and the Army of Northern Virginia were on the road to Appomattox.

After reading this selection, consider these questions:

1. What arguments might be made, from a Confederate perspective, in favor of the use of slaves as soldiers? What arguments might be mustered to oppose the plan?

2. Consider Durden's assertion (in *The Gray and the Black*) that "differences between North and South in fundamental matters concerning the Negro and the relations of the races have always been a matter of differences in degree, not in kind." Taking into account the essay by James M. McPherson earlier in this chapter, does the debate over the use of black soldiers by the Union and by the Confederacy support Durden's position?

SELECTION 3:

A Slave Escapes to Union Lines

Wherever the Union army or navy advanced in the South, slaves in proximity to the advance fled to Union lines. Escaped slaves could be regarded as enemy property or as people who had made themselves free by escaping from slavery. Some Union commanders returned escaped slaves to their masters; most, and an increasing number, did not. In May 1861 General Benjamin Butler refused to return slaves who had escaped to his lines in Virginia on the ground that they were "contraband of war." From that point on, slaves making their way to Union lines were known as contrabands. The matter came to the fore when Union forces captured the Sea Islands of South Carolina at the end of 1861. The largest of these islands was Port Royal, which contained the town of Beaufort. The few whites who lived there fled, leaving some ten thousand slaves behind. Abolitionists and others formed societies in Boston, New York, and Philadelphia that sent teachers and labor superintendents to demonstrate that blacks would work for wages.

William Summerson, a slave in his early twenties from South Carolina, fled to the Union naval blockade in 1862. Summerson had worked on a steamer before the war and was working as a clerk in his master's store in Charleston. Faced with the prospect of separation from his wife, Summerson plotted an elaborate and successful escape to Union lines. Eventually, Union officers sent Summerson and his wife to Port Royal.

*The following document is from Summerson's account of his escape,
published in the December 27, 1862, issue of the* National Anti-Slavery
Standard.

Ever since I knew enough to know right from wrong, I have wanted to get my freedom, but there was no way of escape. Slavery walled me in. While I was in Charleston, in March 1862, I was married. The May following, my wife was to be carried back into the country, and I might never see her again; so I hid her from the last of April until we escaped together. She was hidden with some of my friends, and as the slaves escaped so constantly to the blockade, no one searched for her. At 12 o'clock on Friday, June 13, my mistress sent down to the store for me, and told me to go down to lawyer Porter, in Broad Street. He was brother to my mistress. He said to me, "William, would you rather go into the country with your mistress or be sold?" A great agony came over me, for I should have to leave my wife, and might never see her face again. I told him I would rather go with my mistress, and he said, "No, you cannot go with your mistress; you must be sold."

Then he took me to the Court-House to have some traders estimate my value. One said I was worth $1,000, another $1,100. He then told me he would give me till the next day to find a man to buy me. I could not find anyone to buy me, and he knew I could not. This was only a form, to make me submit. While I was in the Court-House, and the traders were examining me, I lifted my heart to the Almighty, and besought him to make a way for me to escape. After I left the Court-House, I went back to the store, and that night, the last that was left me, as I prayed and groaned before the Almighty, He put a plan into my head which carried me safely to freedom.

The plan was this: I had a friend, also a slave, who came from the country three times a week with vegetables. The place was called Sanandros [St. Andrew's] Parish; it was about seven miles from Charleston. I thought after he had disposed of his load, I would get him to put me in a rice barrel and take me back in his wagon. This was the only way I could get out of the city. The days on which he came in were Monday, Thursday, and Saturday. He had a pass for the wagon. I saw him on Saturday morning. I was to be sold that afternoon, and we made the agreement. I left the store at 12 o'clock that day, and went to the place where I had agreed to meet him, and hid under a piazza. He drove up to the piazza, and I got into the barrel, and he headed me up, and I was put into the wagon, and he drove away.

After we drove through the city we came to the new bridge over the Ashley River. There were fifty pickets stationed by this bridge. One read the pass at the bridge, and we passed on. Every half mile for seven miles we met a rebel picket, who stopped the wagon, read the pass, and had the right to search the wagon. I took my clothes, and a picture of [abolitionist] John Brown, which I had kept with my few treasures, in the barrel with me. We left Charleston at 6 P.M., and reached the plantation at 10 P.M. I got out at 10:30 P.M.; so I was in the barrel four hours and a half. This driver went back to the city, and was to bring my wife in the same way. She was taken to a stable, and put in a barrel and headed up. He took her through the city as he did me, but the mule had worked all the day before, and would not draw well, so they had to stop and rest, which made it at midnight when she got there. She got into the barrel at 4 P.M., so she was eight hours and a half therein.

On the road one of the rebels got into the wagon and sat on the barrel she was in, and rode half a mile in that way, and only the power of the Almighty kept the barrel from breaking and bringing her to light. After she got there, she could not move, and was drenched with perspiration. We fanned her, and finally managed to restore her. We staid there till Wednesday, 12:30 midnight. We walked three miles through a swamp, with the water up to our knees. After we

Excerpted from *Sources of the African-American Past,* edited by Roy E. Finkenbine (New York: Longman Press, 1997).

got to this point, we had to cross a railroad bridge about fifty feet high. We walked across on the sleepers. It was about half a mile long, and was on the Charleston and Savannah railroad. About a quarter of a mile beyond was a boat that my friend, the driver of the vegetable wagon, had brought for me. I found a man there who wanted to escape, but did not dare venture; but I persuaded him to go with us. We then started.

We had fifteen miles to go before we could get to the Federal blockade, and on the way we had to pass a rebel gunboat and a fort. I meant to wait till the tide fell, so that the gunboat would go back into the Cut where she lay at low water, but I did not see her till I got close upon her, and heard the men talking, and looked up and saw them on the deck. I kept close to the marsh, so they might not see me, and managed to get round the point. About a mile and a half above this point was the fort which I had to pass. I passed the fort in the same way as I passed the boat. After I got a little beyond, I crossed on to the same shore that she was, and after I got a little way along the shore, day broke as clear as could

be. I looked back and could not see the fort, and I knew I was out of their reach.

About two hours and a half later we reached the Federal gunboats in the Stono River. When I got in sight of the Union boats, I raised a white flag, and when I came near, they cheered me, and pointed to the flagship Pawnee. There I had the pleasure of a breakfast of hot coffee, ham, nice butter, and all under the American flag—all strange things in Charleston. There I gave the Almighty praise and glory for delivering me so far. On board the Pawnee I told the Captain about Charleston harbor and how the vessels run the blockade, and the next day but one they took two vessels from the information I gave them.

After reading this selection, consider these questions:

1. In what ways was Summerson an unusual slave? How did his particular experience help with his escape?

2. What attitudes did Summerson have toward the Confederacy?

SELECTION 4:

A Former Slave Recalls Her Life with the Union Army

L ike William Summerson and thousands of other male slaves, thousands of female slaves fled to Union lines and freedom. One such slave was a young woman (she was born in 1848) named Susie King (later known as Susie King Taylor). After her escape from slavery, King traveled with a regiment of former slaves known as the First South Carolina Volunteers (the regiment would later be renamed the Thirty-third United States Colored Troops). She remained with the regiment from 1862 until *the end of the war. Years later, in 1902, she published an account of her experiences titled,* Reminiscences of My Life in Camp with the Thirty-Third United States Colored Troops. *The following is an excerpt from that account.*

I was enrolled as company laundress, but I did very little of it, because I was always busy doing other things through camp, and was employed all the time doing something for the officers and comrades. . . . I learned to handle a musket very well while in the regiment and could shoot straight and often hit the target. I assisted in cleaning the guns and used to fire them off, to see if the cartridges were dry, before cleaning and reloading, each day. I thought this was great fun. I was also able to take a gun apart and put it together again. . . . I often got my own meals and would fix some dishes for the noncommissioned officers also. . . .

About the first of June 1864, the regiment was ordered to Folly Island, staying there until the latter part of the month, when it was ordered to Morris Island. We landed on Morris Island between June and July 1864. This island was a narrow strip of sandy soil, nothing growing on it but a few bushes and shrubs. The camp was one mile from the boat landing, called Pawnell Landing. . . .

The regiment under Colonel Trowbridge did garrison duty, but they had troublesome times from Fort Gregg, on James Island, for the rebels would throw a shell over on our island every now and then. Finally orders were received for the boys to prepare to take Fort Gregg, each man to take 150 rounds of cartridges, canteens of water, hardtack, and salt beef. This order was sent three days prior to starting, to allow them to be in readiness. I helped as many as I could to pack haversacks and cartridge boxes.

The fourth day, about five o'clock in the afternoon, the call was sounded, and I heard the first sergeant say, "Fall in, boys, fall in," and they were not long obeying the command. Each company marched out of its street, in front of their colonel's headquarters, where they rested for half an hour, as it was not dark enough, and they did not want the enemy to have a chance to spy their movements. At the end of this time the line was formed with the 103rd New York (white) in the rear, and off they started, eager to get to work. It was quite dark by the time they reached Pawnell Landing. I have never forgotten the goodbyes of that day, as they left camp. Colonel Trowbridge said to me as he left, "Good-by, Mrs. King, take care of yourself if you don't see us again." I went with them as far as the landing, and watched them until they got out of sight, and then I returned to the camp. There was no one at camp but those left on picket and a few disabled soldiers, and one woman, a friend of mine, Mary Shaw, and it was lonesome and sad, now that the boys were gone, some never to return. . . .

About four o'clock, July 2, the charge was made. The firing could be plainly heard in camp. I hastened down to the landing and remained there until eight o'clock that morning. When the wounded arrived, or rather began to arrive, the first one brought in was Samuel Anderson of our company. He was badly wounded. Then others of our boys, some with their legs off, arm gone, foot off, and wounds of all kinds imaginable. They had to wade through creeks and marshes, as they were discovered by the enemy and shelled very badly. A number of the men were lost, some got fastened in the mud and had to cut the legs of their pants, to free themselves. The 103rd New York suffered the most, as their men were very badly wounded.

My work now began. I gave assistance to try to alleviate their sufferings, I asked the doctor at the hospital what I could get for them to eat. They wanted soup, but that I could not get; but I had a few cans of condensed milk and some turtle eggs, so I thought I would try to make some custard. I had doubts as to my success, for cooking with turtle eggs was something new to me, but the

Excerpted from *Sources of the African-American Past,* edited by Roy E. Finkenbine (New York: Longman Press, 1997).

adage has it, "Nothing ventured, nothing done," so I made a venture and the result was a very delicious custard. This I carried to the men, who enjoyed it very much. My services were given at all times for the comfort of these men. I was on hand to assist whenever needed.

After reading this selection, consider these questions:

1. What kind of services did Susie King Taylor perform for the soldiers? Which services fell within traditional gender roles? Which did not?

2. The officers of the First South Carolina Volunteers were white, something that Taylor does not mention. What might one conclude from that omission?

SELECTION 5:

A Black Soldier Demands Equal Pay

*T*he North began recruiting black soldiers in earnest in 1863. The Enlistment Act of July 17, 1862, provided that whites holding the rank of private receive $13 a month (and $3.50 for clothing). Blacks holding the rank of private received only $7 a month and $3 for clothing. A number of black units protested the inequality. The Fifty-fourth Massachusetts Regiment refused to accept pay for over a year rather than accept the lower wages. In July 1864, Attorney General Edward Bates ruled that blacks who had been free at the outset of the war and volunteered for military service should receive the same pay as whites. Not until March 1865, however, did Congress decree that freed slaves should receive the same pay as whites.

The Fifty-fourth Massachusetts, the regiment that refused to accept inferior pay, was the war's most famous black regiment. In 1863 the governor of Massachusetts gained permission from the War Department to raise a black regiment. Enough men enlisted to form two regiments, the Fifty-fourth and Fifty-fifth Massachusetts. Commanded by Colonel Robert Gould Shaw, the son of a prominent abolitionist family, the Fifty-fourth Massachusetts spearheaded the assault against Fort Wagner, a Confederate earthwork on Morris Island that commanded the entrance to Charleston Harbor. The Fifty-fourth lost nearly half of its men in the attack, including Colonel Shaw; but the black soldiers actually took Fort Wagner's parapet and held it for an hour before being driven back.

Corporal James Henry Gooding of the Fifty-fourth Massachusetts wrote the following letter on September 28, 1863, to protest the lower pay for black soldiers. Gooding never lived long enough to collect full pay as a Union soldier.

Your Excelency Abraham Lincoln:

Your Excelency will pardon the presumtion of an humble individual like myself, in addressing you, but the earnest Solicitation of my Comrades in Arms, besides the genuine interest felt by myself in the matter is my excuse, for placing before the Executive head of the Nation our Common Grievance: On the 6th of the last Month, the Paymaster of the department informed us, that if we would decide to receive the sum of $10 (ten dollars) per month, he would come and pay us that sum [white soldiers were paid $13]. . . . Now the main question is, Are we *Soldiers* or are we LABOURERS. We are fully armed, and equipped, have done all the various Duties, pertaining to a Soldiers life, have conducted ourselves, to the complete satisfaction of General Officers, who were, if any, prejediced *against* us, but who now accord us all the encouragement, and honour due us: have shared the perils, and Labour, of Reducing the first stronghold, that flaunted a Traitor Flag: and more, Mr. President, Today, the Anglo Saxon Mother, Wife, or Sister, are not alone, in tears for departed Sons, Husbands, and Brothers. The patient Trusting Decendants of Africs Clime, have dyed the ground with blood, in defense of the Union, and Democracy. Men too your Excellency, who know in a measure, the cruelties of the Iron heel of oppression, which in years gone by, the very Power, their blood is now being spilled to Maintain, ever ground them in the dust. But When the war trumpet sounded o'er the land, when men knew not the Friend from the Traitor, the Black man laid his life at the Altar of the Nation,—and he was refused. When the Arms of the Union, were beaten, in the first year of the War, And the Executive called [for] more food, for its ravaging maws, again the black man begged, the privelege of Aiding his Country in her need, to be again refused. And now, he is in the War: and how has he conducted himself? Let their dusky forms, rise up, out of the mires of James Island, and give the answer. Let the rich mould around Wagners parapets be upturned, and there will be found an Eloquent answer. Obedient and patient, and Solid as a wall are they, all we lack, is a paler hue, and a better aquaintance with the Alphabet. Now your Excellency We have done a Soldiers Duty. Why cant we have a Soldiers pay? . . .

We appeal to You, Sir: as the Executive of the Nation, to have us Justly Dealt with. The Regt, do pray, that they be assured their service will be fairly appreciated, by paying them as american Soldiers, not as menial hierlings. Black men You may well know, are poor, three dollars per month, for a year, will supply their needy Wives, and little ones, with fuel. If you, as Chief Magistrate of the Nation, will assure us, of our whole pay, we are content, our Patriotism, our enthusiasm will have a new impetus, to exert our energy more and more to Aid Our Country. Not that our hearts ever flagged, in Devotion, spite the evident apathy displayed in our behalf, but We feel as though, our Country spurned us, now we are sworn to serve her.

Please give this a moments attention.

After reading this selection, consider these questions:

1. What arguments does Gooding offer in behalf of equal pay for black soldiers?

2. What does Gooding mean when he writes, "Let the rich mould around Wagners parapets be upturned, and there will be found an Eloquent answer"?

3. The attack on Fort Gregg, described by Susie King Taylor in the previous document, took place very near to the assault on Fort Wagner, to which Gooding refers. What conclusion can one draw about the significance of black troops in the campaigns along the coast of South Carolina?

Excerpted from *Letter of Corporal James Henry Gooding to President Abraham Lincoln,* by James Henry Gooding (Washington, DC: National Archives, 1863).

CHAPTER 20

Women in the Civil War

The Civil War brought significant transformations in the role of women. In both the North and the South, on farms and in factories, women took the places of men who had gone to war. Similarly, the war accelerated the entry of women into teaching. The expansion of government bureaucracies along with the departure of male clerks, many of whom had left to join the army, created vacancies, and women filled a significant number of them.

The outbreak of hostilities led to the formation of soldiers' aid societies, hospital societies, and other voluntary associations. Women often played important roles in these organizations, the most important of which was the U.S. Sanitary Commission. The commission emerged as an essential adjunct of the Union army's medical bureau. Women made up most of the U.S. Sanitary Commission's volunteers as well as the bulk of the nurses it provided to army hospitals. Along similar lines, women also took the lead in pressing the medical branches of both sides to provide more humane care for sick and wounded soldiers.

Like the soldiers who fought the Civil War, the women they left behind were largely literate. A considerable number of women kept diaries that preserved the experience of women during the war. In the South, many women suffered from privation as well as grief. The three primary documents in this chapter come from diaries kept by Southern women—one from Virginia and two from Louisiana. These firsthand accounts provide powerful insights into life in the Confederacy during the war.

After reading this chapter, consider these questions:

1. In what ways did the war change women's lives?

2. Did the war impact women differently in the North and the South?

3. What experiences were uniquely Southern?

SELECTION 1:

The Civil War and Women's Work

The Civil War not only disrupted the lives of soldiers but those of women as well. Some women worked as nurses; others worked as government clerks or for the U.S. Sanitary Commission. However, the war also changed the lives of many women who never made a decision to participate in the war effort. Women managed farms and plantations; they went to work in jobs left vacant by men. Even those who neither contributed directly to the war effort nor took over the duties of absent men still found their lives altered. The war created a generation of widows, spinsters, and wives of disabled husbands whose lives would be forever affected. In the following excerpt, Nancy Woloch, a professor of history at Barnard College, provides a brief overview of the impact of the Civil War on women's work.

The Civil War affected women's work, in the long run, by spurring productivity and business incorporation, which would later expand the labor market. It had immediate effects as well, though these were different North and South. Among Union women, the war opened up new jobs and new routes to civic involvement, which stimulated the next generation of middle-class reformers and professionals. It also provided models of the large-scale corporate-style associations that women would form in the postwar decades. During the war, under the aegis of male-run organizations—such as the U.S. Sanitary Commission, religious commissions, and freedmen's aid societies—a galaxy of women agents, volunteers, and nurses contributed to the Union effort. Exhilarated by their new roles, women celebrated their contributions for the rest of the century. "At the war's end," nurse Clara Barton claimed in 1888,

"woman was at least fifty years in advance of the normal position which continued peace would have assigned her."

Though Barton's claim was a vast overstatement, other contributors to the Union effort shared her sentiments. Through work with refugees, freedmen, and the wounded, women war workers, paid and unpaid, found a gratifying entry into public service and saw themselves as vital participants in national affairs. Ministering to the "boys" in the wards, serving as "schoolmarms" for former slaves, rolling bandages or visiting camps, they integrated their public service with domestic ideals. The Sanitary Commission, which involved thousands of women at the local level, abetted this fusion by a singular rhetoric of affection and instruction, quickly adopted by its supply collectors and ward inspectors. Commission women liked to view the Union, and especially its army, as an extended family. But their maternal spirit often cloaked new aggression.

Western Commission agents—such as Annie Wittenmyer of Iowa, Laura Haviland of Michigan,

Excerpted from *Women and the American Experience,* by Nancy Woloch (New York: Alfred A. Knopf, 1984). Copyright © 1984 by Alfred A. Knopf, Inc. Reprinted with permission.

Mary Livermore of Illinois, and "Mother" Bickerdyke of Ohio—were good examples. Consistently exceeding their authority, they excelled at manipulating officers and denouncing incompetents. Resigned to these "prima donnas of benevolence," Commission officials conceded that women were more effective than men as fund raisers and supply collectors. To women, however, war work was a source of inspiration. The woman in the war, concluded Mary Livermore, her most energetic publicist, "had developed potencies and possibilities of which she had been unaware and which surprised her, as it did those who witnessed her marvelous achievement."

While providing a need for service, paid and volunteer, the war era also provided Union women with other opportunities. They were able to take over men's jobs in teaching, a field women had already entered, and to assume for the first time positions as clerks in government offices and stores. Such opportunities were born of necessity. Women needed work, and in this instance, employers needed women workers. Nursing, however, was the major occupational battlefront of the war. Like other types of "progress" for women, this too depended on need: Male nurses were in short supply. Nursing was also a model of the back-door approach to a field monopolized by men. To gain acceptance, nursing pioneers created a highly domesticated vocation, one that combined menial services with medical ones. The main prerequisite for Civil War nursing, moreover, was a capacity for self-sacrifice and solicitude, rather than training or expertise. The highest nursing post of the war, in fact the only major federal appointment won by a woman, went to Dorothea Dix, a leading spirit of benevolence, which was deemed a more important qualification than experience in medicine. Many women war workers tended to refer to themselves as "nurses," whatever their functions or responsibilities.

Some 3,000 women on both sides of the war served as nurses, most without training or skills, many without pay, and all inspired by the British example set by Florence Nightingale in the Crimean War, a helpful precedent. Union nurses were more organized and visible than their Confederate counterparts. Originally part of a relief program started by New York women in 1861, the preparation of nurses was soon taken over by the quasi-official Sanitary Commission, which coordinated relief efforts and staffed hospitals, and by the surgeon general, to whom Dix was responsible. Only a minority of women nurses served under Dix as paid appointees. Most were self-appointed volunteers, who stationed themselves in hospitals. But all were to find that wartime nursing was a fusion of medical care and domestic service. New York nurse Sophronia Bucklin, a former schoolteacher and a Dix appointee, wrote an inspired account of her war work, full of mangled limbs and medical emergencies. The bulk of her time, however, like that of other nurses, was spent as housekeeper, since she was also expected to cook, clean, and do laundry for her patients.

Despite the fusion of menial and medical, Civil War nursing met with great resistance, especially from army doctors and officers who disliked the influence of women in the wards and tried to curtail, disparage, or demean it. Women were unfit as nurses, it was argued, because they were variously too weak, annoying, refined, or imprudent, and in any event incapable of dealing with the bodies of strange men. In response, women stressed their traditional roles as caretakers of the sick and feeble at home. "The right of woman to her sphere, which includes housekeeping, cooking, and nursing, has never been disputed," Sanitary Commission agent Jane Hoge argued. The most effective argument in favor of nursing, ultimately, was that women had already done it. After the war, determined nursing veterans administered hospitals, wrote textbooks, and founded training programs. . . .

The nursing vocation, as well as other job opportunities provided by the war in offices and classrooms, were primarily for middle-class women with some skills. But the war affected the work of a great many more women by another factor, its casualties. Over a million men were killed or wounded, more than in any other American war before or since. These casualties affected women's role in the labor force by reducing the number of able men, by creating a generation of widows, spinsters, and wives with disabled husbands, and by enlarging the pool of women in dire need of employment. The war's demographic impact on women was perhaps the most far-reaching and long-lasting. For many of the war's women victims, including those living off meager widow's pensions and those who would never marry at all, the problem was self-support. This was a problem with which many women were ill-equipped to cope. Most had few skills to market outside the home beyond that of sewing. So many seamstresses sought work during and immediately after the war that wages fell for all forms of needlework. But the problem of self-support, though national in scope, had its most dire impact on the postwar South.

The southern states after the war were a world in which women were in excess by the thousands, as historian Anne Firor Scott has pointed out. In 1870, for instance, women outnumbered men by 36,000 in Georgia and 25,000 in North Carolina. Widows remained a standard feature of southern society until the end of the century, and many had to support themselves. Indeed, the middle-class woman of the late-nineteenth-century South often had to earn income of necessity rather than by personal choice. Much of the income-producing work done by women, such as managing farms and plantations, was unrecorded by the census, although Scott assumes it was widespread. More noticeable was the rise in paid employment of white, middle-class women who needed income. Postwar expansion of public education made teaching jobs available to some, since prerequisites were minimal. Others found work in local factories—binderies, box factories, cigarette factories, and textile mills. In 1890, more than two out of every five southern textile workers were women (and almost one out of four was a child).

By the end of the century, single women in southern towns and cities, like their urban counterparts in the north, were taking jobs in stores and offices —as stenographers, typists, bookkeepers, cashiers, and saleswomen. One woman commentator in the 1890s concluded that more "well-bred" women were at work in the South than anywhere else in the world.

Such liberation from domesticity, as women workers stressed, was both involuntary and unanticipated. Eliza Frances Andrews, author of a famous war memoir and subsequently a newspaper editor and educator, explained that she found it necessary to earn a living in the 1870s "though wholly unprepared either by nature or training for a life of self-dependence." Widows and spinsters seeking work during Reconstruction, another southern woman wrote, had "come to the front, forced there by other movements which they neither anticipated nor are responsible for nor fully comprehend." Postwar employment of southern white women was less a sign of "progress" than an index of need. An irony of defeat was that southern black women were entering the paid labor force at the same time. The war had freed 1.9 million slave women, and as many as half their number soon became wage earners.

After reading this selection, consider these questions:

1. In what ways did the Civil War open opportunities for women?

2. How did women defend their participation as nurses in terms of traditional gender roles?

3. How did the war and its aftermath affect women who did not serve as nurses or government workers during the war?

SELECTION 2:

Southern Women and the Civil War

As Nancy Woloch suggests in the previous selection, Northern and Southern women shared many common experiences during the Civil War. In some respects, however, the experience of Southern women was profoundly different from their Northern sisters. Anne Firor Scott, a professor emeritus at Duke University, was one of the pioneers of women's history and particularly the history of Southern women. The following excerpt from her classic study The Southern Lady *(1970) sketches the impact of the Civil War on Southern women.*

The Civil War passed over the South like a giant tidal wave, cracking many structures so fatally that it was only a matter of time before they fell to pieces. Some parts of the old order were fitted into the new, which began to emerge even before the war was over; others disappeared entirely.

The breaking up and remaking of institutions affected the whole society and had profound consequences for the lives of southern women. Individuals as well as institutions were altered by the war experience and, like the institutions, some never recovered, while others adapted themselves to the new patterns of the postwar years as best they could.

The visible and immediate consequences of the outbreak of war upon women's lives have been described again and again. The challenge of war called women almost at once into new kinds and new degrees of activity. "They became planters, millers, merchants, manufacturers, managers," wrote one woman. Soldiers' aid societies sprang into being as if southern women

had all their lives been used to community organization. The number of these societies approached a thousand, and though some bowed to convention and asked a male clergyman to preside over their meetings, the groups were the result of women's initiative and ran on women's energies.

The North's advantage in manpower was clear from the beginning. In the South the women, left at home without their men, assumed responsibility for maintaining and if possible increasing the food supply, for producing cotton and wool and making clothing, flags, tents, bandages, and other things soldiers needed. This was not purely an administrative effort: women whose closest association with a needle had been to supervise slave seamstresses were soon pricking their fingers along with their poorer neighbors who were not so new to the task. The experience of years of providing food and clothing for slaves was now applied to feeding and clothing an army.

Husbands hurrying off to the army or to the Confederate Congress sent back all kinds of instructions about the planting, harvesting, and marketing of crops, the management of slaves, the education of children, the budgeting of money,

Excerpted from *The Southern Lady,* by Anne Firor Scott (Chicago: The University of Chicago Press, 1970). Copyright © 1970 by the University of Chicago. Reprinted with permission.

the collecting of old debts, and every other aspect of their business, apparently in perfect confidence that their wives would somehow cope. The women, in their turn, were polite about asking advice and begged for guidance, while carrying on as if they had always been planters, business managers, overseers of slaves, and decision makers. Many would later be confronted with invading soldiers and would hastily improvise ways to meet that crisis.

The demands of the war cut across class lines. While a yeoman farmer's wife shouldered burdens of plowing, planting, fence-repairing, and so on, beyond anything expected of her in peacetime, an aristocratic lady was proud that she had learned to calculate lumber measurements well enough to run a sawmill on the Congaree River. War widows and women whose sources of income had been cut off by the war became clerks in government offices. Mills, especially those created to produce supplies for the war, hired women operators. Schoolteaching was taken over by women, as native schoolmasters answered the call to arms and those from the North went home. And, *in extremis,* almost any woman could sew for money.

A return to handweaving and spinning was noted all over the South. . . .

With the first battle, the care of sick and wounded men became a central focus of women's concern. The least demanding form of service was that of sending supplies, and for this purpose hospital aid societies were organized in many communities. Women with a greater urge to make sacrifices could nurse, as many did, and the sturdiest souls became hospital matrons or superintendents, often to the dismay of male surgeons. . . .

Phoebe Yates Pember, member of a large and distinguished Savannah family, became head matron of a hospital in Richmond. Her arrival did not delight the chief surgeon, who shared the suspicion of many of his brethren that the advent of women was bound to lead to an unpleasant form of "petticoat government." His fears were gradually allayed by experience, and for four years Mrs. Pember carried on every imaginable sort of labor while organizing and administering the hospital in the interests of better care for the wounded and more efficiency in the use of medical resources. She even took charge of the whiskey barrel, one aspect of the hospital the misuse of which was causing her great trouble. And, when a group of drunken soldiers entered her apartment in search of the precious supply of whiskey, she held them at bay with a pistol. Her diary, a running account of her experiences in the hospital, reveals a tough, hardworking administrator who preserved her sanity with a fine sense of humor. She had nothing but scorn for the notion that no southern lady would be found in such a rude circumstance as an army hospital. . . .

Kate Cumming of Mobile was born in Scotland, but grew up a southern lady. She responded to a minister's appeal for ladies to go to the front and nurse the wounded, though her family disapproved and she herself admitted, "I had never been inside of a hospital and was wholly ignorant of what I should be called upon to do, but I knew that what one woman [Florence Nightingale] had done another could." Most of her fellow volunteers from Mobile (including the novelist Augusta Evans) changed their minds, but she persisted, was put in charge of a hospital, and by 1862 was regularly enlisted in the Confederate medical department. Like Mrs. Pember, Kate Cumming was a strong woman with a considerable capacity for administration, and though she lacked Mrs. Pember's sense of humor she shared her fortitude in facing the endless arrival of sick and wounded soldiers for whom so little could be done. She shared, also, an astonishing capacity to endure physical hardship, evidence for which appears on almost every page of her diary. Perhaps her own patient courage lay behind her scorn for those less tough than herself. "A young lady, . . . one of the handsomest women in Mobile, sat near me at table, and when I told her how I had been employed since the war, she said she had often wished to do the same. I wondered what hindered her."

Sally Louisa Tompkins, a twenty-eight-year-old spinster in Richmond, commandeered a friend's house and made it into a hospital whose life-saving record was so impressive that in order to assure the continuation of her work, the Confederate government made her a captain in the army.

She was said to have treated, during the whole war, more than 1,300 soldiers and to have lost only 73. Ella King Newsome, a wealthy Arkansas widow, used her own money as well as her time and energy in a series of hospitals which moved ahead of the Yankees; she came, inevitably, to be called "the Florence Nightingale of the South." Mrs. Newsome's skill was apparently equaled by her charm and tact, so that her example considerably diminished the social disapprobation visited upon women who worked in hospitals.

For many women life after 1862 was a series of traumas. As they worked to keep plantations, farms, and homes going, the fate of husbands and sons in the army was a constant source of anxiety. One old soldier, reminiscing in the eighties, thought it had been harder for the women than for the soldiers themselves: the soldier at least knew if he was still alive, while his wife worried constantly. Many families had several sons in uniform; one was recorded with twelve sons in combat, nine of whom were killed. Josephine Habersham's boys survived one battle after another only to die together very near the end of the war. Hetty Cary, said to be the most beautiful girl in Richmond, married her soldier sweetheart and returned to the same church two weeks later for his funeral. A South Carolina woman lost five brothers and a fiancé before the carnage ended. Toward the end of the war an Atlanta woman wrote:

> Were these the same people—these haggard, wrinkled women, bowed with care and trouble, sorrow and unusual toil? These tame, pale, tearless girls, from whose soft flesh the witching dimples had long since departed, or were drawn down into furrows—were they the same school girls of 1861? These women who, with coarse, lean and brown hands . . . these women with scant, faded cotton gowns and coarse leather shoes—these women who silently and apathetically packed the boxes, looking into them with the intense and sorrowful gaze that one casts into the tomb.

Then there were the invasions of northern armies, especially Sherman's. Not only was it Sherman's fixed policy to destroy so much that the people in his path would lose their taste for war entirely but many units of his army were simply out of control, running wild in their urge to harass and destroy. The widow and daughter of a wealthy minister-planter of Liberty County, Georgia, were visited by successive groups of soldiers from Sherman's army late in 1864, each group repeating the search and seizure of its predecessor. Neither the white hairs of the mother nor the pregnancy of the daughter protected them against the soldiers' wanton cruelty, such as the theft of the only remaining well chain, so that the women could no longer draw water.

The experiences, and reactions, of southern women were similar in broad outline but varied enormously in detail.

The broadest division was simply between those who faced up to the demands of the times and those who evaded them or ran away. In some parts of the South, where the invader never came, it was possible for the first two years to go on living a fairly normal life. This was especially true for young women who were not yet betrothed and who had no father or brother in the service. By the end of the war the number who fitted this description must have been small. Other women, with men in the army and challenges all around them, tried to continue a gay social life, and though some succeeded for a time this response, too, became more difficult to maintain as the years passed. A few actually ran away, to Canada or to Europe, to evade entirely . . . the action and passion of their times.

After reading this selection, consider these questions:

1. Nancy Woloch's essay (selection 1 in this chapter) maintains that "Union nurses were more organized and visible than their Confederate counterparts." In what ways does Anne Firor Scott's account contradict or support that assertion?

2. In what respects did the experience of Southern women differ from that of women in the North?

SELECTION 3:

Diary of Lucy Breckinridge

Lucy Gilmer Breckinridge was the daughter of an old Virginia family whose seat was the Grove Hill plantation in Botetourt County. Only eighteen when the war began, Breckinridge started keeping a diary in August 1862. By the end of the war, five of her brothers had joined the Confederate army. The fighting of the valley campaign took place to the north and east of Grove Hill, so the plantation and the family living there were spared the devastation of battle. Nevertheless, the war was part of daily life. Women at Grove Hill sewed clothing, made bandages, cared for the sick and wounded, read about the war, and prayed for their loved ones in the military.

In the following excerpt from her diary, dated August 24, 1862, Breckinridge recalls receiving news of the death of her brother John, who died in the Battle of Seven Pines. He was seventeen years old. Breckinridge also refers to her youngest brother, George, who was fifteen years old, and two of her sisters, Eliza and Emma.

It rained so steadily today that we could not go to church. I sat all the morning in the library with George talking about "reds" and marraiges. He said very earnestly, "Well, Luce, take my advice and do not get married until the war is over. There are many reasons why you should not; for instance, you might be a widow in a short time." Then, after thinking a few minutes, it seemed to strike him that it would not be such a bad thing to be a pretty young widow. He has an idea that I am engaged, and seems to take a great deal more interest in me; treats me with marked respect and unwonted tenderness. He is a funny boy and a very sweet one. I never loved him so much before, because all my special love was given to John. He and I were so nearly the same age, and never were separated in any way until the last two or three years. I loved him better than anyone on earth. Though we were playmates from our baby-

hood, I do not remember ever having been angry with John. I was more intimate with him and stayed with him more than I did with Eliza. We never formed a plan for the future in which we were not connected. Everything seems changed to me since he died. He was the noblest and best of us all, and all his life had been the favorite with his brothers and sisters. "God takes our dearest even so; the reason why we cannot know; helpless he leaves us crushed with woe."

Eliza and Emma went over to the graveyard and put up a white cross with John's name on it and the date of the Battle of Seven Pines [1862] with the inscription, "He hath entered into peace," and put garlands of ivy on it. It is only a temporary mark for the grave. All of his brothers and sisters wish to raise a monument to his memory, the first of our band who has been taken from us. What a sad summer this has been. John came home on Saturday, the 17th of May, and we were so happy the ten days he stayed at home. We tried to vanish all sadness from our minds and make him happy, but it is singular that we all felt that it

Excerpted from *Lucy Breckinridge of Grove Hill: The Journal of a Virginia Girl, 1862–1864,* edited by Mary D. Robertson (Kent, OH: The Kent State University Press, 1979).

was his last visit. On the 27th of May, he left. He was not strong and well, and we begged him to stay, but he said he thought there would be a battle in a few days and it was his duty to be there. And when he saw how sad Ma looked, he said he would come home again after the battle, and stay longer. Five days after he left he was mortally wounded. Late on Monday night as Eliza and I lay awake talking, we heard a strange footstep in the passage, and then a scream of agony, and in a few minutes Ma came upstairs almost fainting, and handed us a dispatch from Mr. Gwathmey. Ma intended starting to Richmond the next day, but fortunately was too ill to travel. But on Wednesday, she went to Bonsacks and was detained there by a slide on the railroad, and the next day George told her she must come home, and handed her the dispatch, dated Tuesday, 3rd of June, telling us that our noble boy was dead. On Sunday the 8th, he was buried.

After reading this selection, consider these questions:

1. Breckinridge's sadness is personal. To what extent might that reflect, at least in part, the stage of the war and her age?

2. What conclusions might one draw from the conversation between George and Lucy about her prospects for marriage?

SELECTION 4:

Diary of Sarah Morgan

Unlike Lucy Gilmer Breckinridge, who lived on a large plantation in a rural environment, Sarah Morgan lived in Baton Rouge, Louisiana. She was nineteen when she began her diary in January 1862; at the end of February, she would turn twenty. Her first entries dealt with two tragedies that had befallen her family the year before. In April 1861, just as he was about to embark on a medical practice, her brother, Harry, was killed in a duel in New Orleans. Her father, Thomas Gibbes Morgan, died in November 1861. He had been a prominent attorney and had also served as district judge and district attorney. During Louisiana's debate over secession, Judge Morgan supported the preservation of the Union, a position his daughter shared. When the war came, however, both father and daughter became loyal Confederates. Nevertheless, the war divided the Morgan family. Richard C. Drum, a son-in-law of Judge Morgan, served as a Union officer in California; and Philip Hicky Morgan, the judge's son from his first marriage, remained a Unionist and sat out the war in Union-occupied New Orleans.

From May 1862, Baton Rouge was occupied by the Union army. Confederates repeatedly attempted to retake the city, and the fighting forced the Morgans to flee their home several times. At one point, they stayed for several months with friends on a plantation north of the city, but the course of battle chased them from that location as well. Eventually, Sarah and her mother went to New Orleans, where they found refuge with Philip Hicky Morgan, Sarah's Unionist half brother.

Sarah lost two brothers in January 1864. Both died of illness while serving the Confederate cause—one in a Union prisoner-of-war camp, the other while serving with his unit.

The first two excerpts are taken from entries made in May 1862, not long after the Union army occupied Baton Rouge. The third entry is from January 1863, after an unsuccessful Confederate attempt to retake Baton Rouge, during which the Morgan home was damaged. The State House burned on the night of December 28, but it was not, as Sarah Morgan believed, an act of war or arson.

M ay 9th [1862] . . .

Last evening came the demand: the town must [be] surrendered immediately; the federal flag Must be raised, they would grant us the same terms they granted to New Orleans. Jolly terms those were! . . . Glorious! What a pity they did not shell the town! But they are taking us at our word, and this morning they are landing at the Garrison, and presently the Bloody banner will be floating over our heads. "Better days are coming, we'll all go right."

"All devices, signs, and flags of the confederacy shall be suppressed." So says Picayune Butler [General Benjamin F. Butler, the Union commander. A *picayune* was a coin of little value (five cents)]. Good. I devote all my red, white, and blue silk to the manufacture of Confederate flags. As soon as one is confiscated, I make another, until my ribbon is exhausted, when I will sport a duster emblazoned in high colors, "Hurra! for the Bonny blue flag!" Henceforth, I wear one pinned to my bosom—not a duster, but a little flag—the man who says take it off, will have to pull it off for himself; the man who dares attempt it—well! a pistol in my pocket will fill up the gap. I am capable, too.

This is a dreadful war to make even the hearts of women so bitter! I hardly know myself these last few weeks. I, who have such a horror of bloodshed, consider even killing in self defense murder, who cannot wish them the slightest evil, whose only prayer is to have them sent back in peace to their own country, *I* talk of killing them! for what else do I wear a pistol and carving knife? I am afraid I *will* try them on the first one who says an insolent word to me. Yes, and repent for ever after in sack cloth and ashes! O if I was only a man! Then I could don the breeches, and slay them with a will! . . .

May 14th, [1862]

. . . I have a brother-in-law in the Federal army that I love and respect as much as anyone in the world, and shall not readily agree that his being a Northerner would give him an irresistible desire to pick my pockets, and take from him all power of telling the truth. No! There are few men I admire more than Major Drum, and I honor him for his independence in doing what he believes Right. Let us have liberty of speech, and action in our land, I say, but not gross abuse and calumny. Shall I acknowledge that the people we so recently called our brothers are unworthy of consideration, and are liars, cowards, dogs? Not I! *If* they conquer us, I acknowledge them as a superior race; I will not say we were conquered by cowards, for where would that place us? It will take a brave people to gain us, and that the Northerners undoubtedly are. I would scorn to have an inferior foe; I fight only my equals. These women may acknowledge that *cowards* have won battles in which their brothers were engaged, but I, I will ever say *mine* fought against brave men, and won the day. Which is most honorable? To the glory of our nation be it said, that it is only the women who talk that way. The men are all fighting, and

Excerpted from *Sarah Morgan: The Civil War Diary of a Southern Woman*, edited by Charles East (New York: Simon and Schuster, 1991).

these poor weak females sit over their knitting and pour out a weak, spiteful, pitiful stream of deluted [*sic*] rage against Cowards (?) their husbands and brothers think it worth while to fight against!

I hate to hear women on political subjects; they invariably make fools of themselves, and it sickens me to see half a dozen talking at once of what *they* would do, and what ought to be done; it gives me the greatest disgust, so I generally contrive to absent myself from such gatherings, as I seldom participate. But in this cause, it is necessary for me to express my opinion, sometimes, so I give it here, that I may not believe in after years I am quite a weathercock. I was never a secessionist, for I quietly adopted father's views on political subjects, with out meddling with them; but even father went over with his state, and when so many outrages were committed by the fanatical leaders of the North, though he regretted the Union, said "Fight to the death for our liberty." I say so too. I would want to fight until we win the cause so many have died for. I don't believe in Secession, but I do in Liberty. I want the South to conquer, dictate its own terms, and go back to the Union for I believe that apart, inevitable ruin awaits both. . . .

January 1st. Thursday. 1863. . . .

I learn, to my unspeakable grief, that the State House is burned down. Those blessed Yankees have been in the town some three weeks, and this is the result, confound them! Adieu, Home and Happiness! Yankees inhabit my first, and have almost succeeded in destroying my second. Let the whole town burn, now; without our State House, it is nothing. Without its chief ornament, what does our poor little town look like? Do wretched Yankees, standing in the little room at home, look through the single window without seeing the white towers against the blue sky? How can Baton Rouge exist without our pride? I can hardly fancy it. Though desecrated, mutilated, pillaged, almost destroyed within by the Yankees in their previous visit, still we had the outside left untouched, at least, until this crowning act of barbarism. Our beautiful gardens! Our evening walks! Oh Yankees! If you were only in glory! You'd have fire enough there, to induce you to dispense with the burning of our beautiful State House!

I can never realize it until I see it myself. Would it not be awful to come before it unexpectedly, and, opening your eyes, look at the white walls and glittering windows, meet instead that awful void, that blue nothing that hangs between our beautiful gardens and heaven? Baton Rouge is ruined forever now; let it burn; I would hardly cry. O my home! Our "city of bowers"! I wish you had been laid low before you were desecrated by the touch of Yankee heathens! Nothing but fire can purify you now. Burn, then, and may the Yankees burn with you!

After reading this selection, consider these questions:

1. Compare Sarah Morgan's attitude toward Yankees in her entries of May 1862 with that of her entry from January 1863. What might account for the change?

2. How might one reconcile Morgan's Unionist sentiments with her intense loyalty to the Confederacy?

SELECTION 5:

Diary of Clara Solomon

Clara Solomon was even younger than Lucy Breckinridge and Sarah Morgan. Only sixteen when she made the first entry in a diary she kept from June 1861 until July 1862, Solomon's experience differed in important respects from those of Breckinridge and Morgan. A native and resident of New Orleans, the largest urban center in the South, she was also Jewish. Like Morgan, Solomon saw her city occupied by Union troops; the Union navy captured the city in April 1862. The Solomon family lived comfortably; they employed an Irish servant and owned a household slave. Clara and her entire family were staunch Confederates. Her father, a merchant, was forty-six years old when the war began. He served the Confederacy as a sutler (someone who supplied clothing and equipment to the troops). Early entries in Clara's diary express optimism, but even in the brief period she kept her diary, that optimism faded in the face of mounting death tolls, shortages of food and merchandise, and the occupation of her city by Union forces.

Clara's mention of the "immortal Ellsworth" (in the entry of July 5, 1861) refers to Ephraim Ellsworth, a colonel serving with the Union force that occupied Alexandria, Virginia. Ellsworth saw a Confederate flag flying over a hotel, whereupon he dismounted and, accompanied by two of his men, climbed to the roof to take down the flag. On the rooftop, the hotel owner shot and killed Ellsworth and was, in turn, killed by one of Ellsworth's men.

Saturday, July 6th, 1861

. . . I had just arisen from the bed, when Alice came tripping up the stairs. She had in her hand a paper, containing the picture of the *"immortal Ellsworth"*.

He is quite a fine looking young man, of about 23! Although not in favor of the manner in which he lost his life, I can but admire his heroism. He though *he* was acting right when he transplanted the "Confederate flag". Do we not admire [Ellsworth's killer, hotel owner James] Jackson?

'Tis true, the Northerners are raging an unholy and unrighteous war against us, but do they not think that they have Justice on their side. We know they haven't. Does that cure them of their fanaticism—We laud the *truly* heroic Jackson, they, Ellsworth. It is natural. . . .

Sunday, July 7th, 1861

. . . We were somewhat startled at Pa's voice & when he called us, I was still more so when he called us. He said "Charley Dreux is dead; he was shot in the head in a skirmish"!!! I was horrified. He was so fine, intelligent and well-liked, man. I immediately thought of his young wife and child, whom he left. How she grieved and mourned at his departure—and what horrible news would she

Excerpted from *The Civil War Diary of Clara Solomon,* edited by Elliot Ashkenazi (Baton Rouge: Louisiana State University Press, 1995).

soon be made aware of. He held a position as Colonel, which is an exalted one for so young a man—

I thought that it probably some error, but to-day's paper sadly affirms it—He is the first of the Louisianian Officers who has paid the penalty of his life. He is very brave. The skirmish occurred at Newport News. The loss on the Confederate side was three killed; that of the enemy is yet un-known. It will indeed be to his wife, a terrible af-fliction. And think how many more, valuable lives will be terminated before the cruel war is at an end.

In the agony of her grief will she exclaim, "Why was *he* not spared"! Will this be selfish-ness? It does seem hard, that he, so worthy, should be singled out from many as unworthy— And tis said that officers stand the least chance of being killed. But stop, we are quarrelling with Divine Providence. "*He* doeth all things well."

How many heart-rending tales like this, have we yet to hear. When first he received his wound, and felt that it must be fatal, instantaneously, thoughts of his dear wife and child must have crossed his mind, and with their names last on his lips, he was ushered into eternity—How painful will be the duty of the one who will unfold to her a tale, which will blight her young life, crush her dearest hopes, and perhaps, forever cast a gloom over her future. . . .

Tuesday, September 17th, 1861
8 1/4 P.M. . . . We have just repaired from the din-ing room, where we have been indulging in bread and molasses, and wishing for one of those nice fish suppers, of which nothing but the memory of them, now remains. . . .

Thursday, April 24th, 1862 . . .
The paper states that there was continual & vig-orous firing at the forts, but no damage done, & they are confident of ultimate success & pro-pound the question "why is the city so despon-dent"? Already they have consumed $400,000 worth of powder, & what have they effected? The killing of a few men. My heart aches as I daily read the long lists of death. "Died from wounds received at the battle of Shiloh". . . .

Sunday, May 4th, 1862 . . .
A gloom has settled o'er my spirit, a gloom en-velopes our dearly-beloved city. My breaking heart but aches the more, when I am prepared to record events, which can never fade from my memory, & did I not consider it a duty, I should spare myself the unpleasant task. Nevertheless I promise to go into no minutiae, but to record merely *facts,* devoid of their accompanying inci-dents or circumstances of the past week im-pressed upon that most lasting page, the mind. . . . The Yankees had passed our forts & were on their way to our city, it having been decided to be the most daring naval exploit ever attempted, as they passed under our fires, our brave men, fighting to the last. . . . Oh! *never* shall I forget the 25th of Apr. 1862. Such expressions of woe as were on the faces of every one, & such sad-ness as reigned in every heart. Oh! that that day should ever come! . . . Oh! to think we are in a captured city. But how disappointed are they! Not a bale of cotton fell into their hands for $2,000,000 worth was consigned to the flames. . . . The supply of this large population with the necessaries of life is a question of the greatest moment to our people. The land forces of U.S. have occupied Opelousas R.R. & forbid commu-nication by that, our principal means of trans-portation of fresh supplies. We have since learned that they have made arrangements for us to receive provisions, so ideas of starvation are now abandoned. They are camping in Lafayette Square! . . .

When I am in the street I do not seem to breathe a free atmosphere. It is not free. Laden with the breath of those invaders. I am sick at heart. What a victory. The taking of N.O. [New Orleans]. The Fed. [Union] flag over our Custom House. They have the valley of the Mississippi at their command. I am alarmed to walk the street & would not be out after dark. In fact, all citizens are requested to be in doors by 9. . . . Beef is 40 cts. a pound. Everything in proportion. No bread at all. There is no flour. . . .

Thursday, May 8th, 1862 . . .
The Square is still occupied by some & there are a few remaining tents there. But the St. Charles

[Hotel]! My heart sank within me when I beheld it. *Never* in connection with the Yankees have I experienced such sensations. It looks to be a perfect wreck. They are loitering around it, lying down, playing cards, & their clothes hanging around. Oh! it was a loathsome sight, & I wondered how men could submit to it. I *couldn't*. Saw stragglers on my way to Canal St. & there saw more, who are strutting along with such an air of defiance as I never saw, so scornful, so unassuming. Their looks being, "We have conquered you". They were sporting uniforms with any quantity of brass buttons. Oh! that our streets should be ever disgraced. But few stores are opened & in some that we went Con. money was *refused*.

After reading this selection, consider these questions:

1. Compare Clara Solomon's observations about Ephraim Ellsworth and James Jackson to Sarah Morgan's early reflections on her brother-in-law's service in the Union army. What might this indicate about Confederate attitudes?

2. Compare Solomon's perception of Charley Dreux's death with her entry of April 24, 1862. What changes have taken place over the year?

3. How do Solomon's attitudes toward the Union occupiers compare with Morgan's?

Index